THE ENCYCLOPEDIA
OF POLITICS AND RELIGION

THE
ENCYCLOPEDIA
OF POLITICS
AND RELIGION

Robert Wuthnow, *Editor in Chief*

VOLUME I

Congressional Quarterly Inc.
Washington, D.C.

Published in the United Kingdom by Routledge
11 New Fetter Lane, London EC4P 4EE

Book design and production by Kachergis Book Design,
Pittsboro, North Carolina

Printed and bound in the United States of America

The paper used in this publication meets the minimum requirements of the American National Standard for Information Sciences—Permanence of Paper for Printed Library Materials, ANSI Z39.48-1984.

LIBRARY OF CONGRESS CATALOGING-IN-PUBLICATION DATA
Encyclopedia of politics and religion / Robert Wuthnow,
    editor in chief.
        p.   cm.
        Includes bibliographical references (p.   ) and indexes.
        ISBN 1-56802-164-X (set : alk. paper).
        ISBN 1-56802-162-3 (v. 1 : alk. paper).
        ISBN 1-56802-163-1 (v. 2 : alk. paper)
        1. Religion and politics—Encyclopedias.   I. Wuthnow, Robert.
    BL65.P7E53 1998
    322'.1'03—dc21   98-29879

About the Editors

Contents

Preface

The Encyclopedia of Politics and Religion examines the interconnections of politics and religion, considering how these two elemental institutions of society have combined to shape public discourse, affect social attitudes, spark and sustain collective action, and influence policy, especially over the past two centuries.

The principle of the separation of church and state, and the related idea that politics and religion are and ought to be distinct, has been one of the most crucial factors in the rise of national secular states. But even though it is the bedrock of modern political institutions and international relations, this principle has been challenged in recent years until it has become the fault line in societies and religious movements around the world. Religion has played an important secular role in much of the political turmoil of our era. Any effective analysis of or long-lasting solution to such turmoil requires attention to religion in its political matrix. The encyclopedia's aim is to describe the historical roots of the relations between politics and religion in the modern world and to explain the web of their global interconnections. This work, the first of its kind to be published, is intended to serve as a sorely needed guide to understanding, scholarship, and communication.

The encyclopedia includes 256 signed articles by prominent scholars from many nations. As well as essays on broad themes, such as millennialism and pluralism, it includes articles on specific religions, individuals, geographical regions, institutions, and events. In preparing this work, the editors and contributors have aimed to represent the vast diversity of ways in which religions and political systems are influencing each other throughout the contemporary world.

The articles, ranging from a few hundred to eight thousand words, are written to be accessible to students and interested adults as well as to scholars. Most articles include references to related articles and brief bibliographies to assist in further reading. Each volume of the work contains a detailed index.

In addition to the articles, the encyclopedia includes an introduction by Robert Wuthnow of Princeton University, who served as editor in chief. An appendix contains the excerpts from or the complete texts of twenty-one source documents that relate to articles in the volume. The appendix also includes excerpts from twenty-seven world constitutions with provisions on religion, a glossary of terms, and a compilation of Internet sites, as of mid-1998, that may be of use to readers who wish to explore certain subjects through that medium.

Acknowledgments

The encyclopedia is the work of hundreds of authors, editors, and researchers who began the project in 1995. It has been under the general direction of Professor Wuthnow, who was assisted throughout the project by an editorial board of seven scholars, each expert in their own fields, and in the early planning stages by an advisory board. Members of the editorial board, all of whom participated actively throughout the preparation of the work, are James A. Beckford, University of Warwick (England); L. Carl Brown, Princeton University; Karen E. Fields, University of Rochester; Charles F. Keyes, University of Washington; Daniel H. Levine, University of Michigan; Lamin Sanneh, Yale University; and Kenneth D. Wald, University of Florida. Members of the editorial board read all of the material to ensure its quality and consistency. In the end the work is the product of the 203 authors who gave generously of their time to share their knowledge of the many subjects covered in the work.

The publisher has enjoyed the benefit of an excellent group of editors and assistants who have been responsible for bringing all the parts together for publication. Ann Davies, managing editor of textbooks and reference, who suggested the concept for the book, and Christopher M. Karlsten, project editor, have been principally responsible for editing the manuscript and overseeing production. They were assisted throughout by freelance editors Joanne S. Ainsworth, Sabra Bissette Ledent, and Jane Sevier Sánchez. Assistant Editor Gwenda Larsen ably and often magically kept track of the hundreds of articles and authors involved in the encyclopedia. The numerous illustrations that enhance many articles were selected and located by Megan Q. Campion. Joe Fortier and Leslie Rigby proofread the typeset volumes, and Patricia R. Ruggiero prepared the index. The book was designed and composed by Kachergis Book Design. As CQ sponsoring editors, Jeanne Ferris and David Tarr were responsible for planning with the editorial board and seeing through the acquisition of the encyclopedia's contents. Nancy A. Lammers, director of operations, was actively involved in the production from the beginning.

A Note on Transliteration

In transliterating names of people and places from languages not originally written in Latin characters, such as Chinese and Arabic, the editors have used diacritics sparingly. In general, transliterated words appear in a form that will be familiar to English-speaking readers.

Congressional Quarterly Editors

Alphabetical List of Articles

Contributors

A

ADAMEC, LUDWIG W.
University of Arizona
Afghanistan

AHO, JAMES
Idaho State University
Violence

AKHAVI, SHAHROUGH
University of South Carolina
Khomeini, Ruholla Musavi

ALLEN, DOUGLAS
University of Maine
Enlightenment

APPLEBY, R. SCOTT
University of Notre Dame
Catholicism, Roman
Fundamentalism
Papacy
Vatican Council, Second

ARJOMAND, SAID AMIR
*State University of New York
    at Stony Brook*
Bahai
Iran
Revolutions

AULT, JAMES M., JR.
Secular humanism

AVRUCH, KEVIN
George Mason University
Israel
Zionism

B

BAHRY, LOUAY
University of Tennessee
Iraq
Nasser, Gamal Abdel

BARBOUR, HUGH
Earlham School of Religion
Friends, Society of (Quakers)

BARKER, EILEEN
London School of Economics
Unification Church

BAUBÉROT, JEAN
*Ecole Pratique des Hautes Etudes
    (Vème section)—Sorbonne*
Anticlericalism

BECKFORD, JAMES A.
University of Warwick
Cults
Great Britain
Religious organization

BERNDT, UWE
*Arnold Bergstraesser Institute
    (Germany)*
Germany

BERRYMAN, PHILLIP
Temple University
Central America
Romero, Oscar A.

BEYER, PETER
University of Ottawa
Globalization

BLOCKER, JACK S., JR.
Huron College
Temperance movements

BLUMHOFER, EDITH
*Public Religion Project, University
    of Chicago*
Pentecostalism

BOLI, JOHN
Emory University
Education

BOURDEAUX, MICHAEL
Keston Institute (England)
Communism
Russia

BOYER, PAUL S.
University of Wisconsin
Millennialism

BRADY, BERNARD V.
*University of St. Thomas
    (Minnesota)*
Communitarianism

BRAND, LAURIE A.
University of Southern California
Jordan

BROWN, L. CARL
Princeton University
Ibn Taimiyya

BUTLER, JON
Yale University
Revivalism

C

CALLAHAN, WILLIAM J.
University of Toronto
Spain

CASPER, GRETCHEN G.
Pennsylvania State University
Philippines

CEADEL, MARTIN E.
New College, Oxford University
Pacifism

CHRISTELOW, ALLAN
Idaho State University
Algeria

CHRISTIANSEN, DREW
Woodstock Theological Center
Vatican

CLART, PHILIP
University of British Columbia
China

CLEARY, EDWARD L.
Providence College
CELAM
Latin America
Mexico

COMSTOCK, GARY DAVID
Wesleyan University
Sexuality

COOK, MICHAEL
Princeton University
Muhammad

COSER, LEWIS A.
Boston University
Durkheim, Emile

COVELL, RALPH
Denver Seminary
Christianity in Asia

CRAGG, KENNETH
Muslim encounters with the West

CRAHAN, MARGARET E.
*Hunter College of the City University
    of New York*
Cuba

CREEVEY, LUCY E.
University of Connecticut
Senegal

CROWLEY, PAUL G.
Santa Clara University
Atheism

D

DANEEL, MARTHINIUS
Boston University
African independent churches

DAVIE, GRACE
University of Exeter
Europe, Western

DAVIES, TONY
Teresa, Mother

DAVIS, DEREK
Baylor University
Constitution, U.S.

DENNIS, MATTHEW
University of Oregon
Native Americans

DOBBELAERE, KAREL
Katholieke Universiteit
Low Countries

E

EICKELMAN, DALE F.
Dartmouth College
Morocco

ELAZAR, DANIEL J.
Jerusalem Center for Public Affairs
Covenant
Judaism

ELLER, CYNTHIA
Princeton University
Feminism
Witchcraft (with Elizabeth Reis)

ERNST, CARL W.
*University of North Carolina
    at Chapel Hill*
Iqbal, Muhammad
Sufism

F

FENN, RICHARD K.
Princeton Theological Seminary
Liturgy

FIELDS, KAREN E.
University of Rochester
Jehovah's Witnesses
Weber, Max

FILATOV, SERGEY BORISOVICH
*Sociological Center of the Russian
    Scientific Fund (Moscow)*
Orthodoxy, Russian

FLEET, MICHAEL H.
Marquette University
Christian democracy

FOREST, JIM
Merton, Thomas

FORMICOLA, JO RENEE
Seton Hall University
Human rights

FOX, RICHARD WIGHTMAN
Boston University
Niebuhr, Reinhold

FRANCE, JOHN
University of Wales Swansea
Crusades

FRIEDMAN, ISAIAH
Ben-Gurion University
Herzl, Theodor

FULTON, JOHN
St. Mary's University College
Ireland

G

GAMWELL, FRANKLIN I.
University of Chicago
Pluralism

GARDINER, STEVEN L.
Coalition for Human Dignity
Survivalism

GHAREEB, EDMUND
Druze
Kurds
Libya

GIGGIE, JOHN
Princeton University
Abolitionism

GILBERT, JAMES B.
University of Maryland at College Park
Science and technology

GINSBERG, BENJAMIN
Johns Hopkins University
Anti-Semitism

GLAUDE, EDDIE S.
Bowdoin College
Douglass, Frederick
King, Martin Luther, Jr.

GOLDEN, RENNY
Northeastern Illinois University
Sanctuary

GORSUCH, RICHARD
Fuller Theological Seminary
Prejudice

GRASMICK, HAROLD G.
University of Oklahoma
Crime and criminal justice

GREEN, JOHN C.
University of Akron
Evangelicalism (with James L. Guth,
    Lyman A. Kellstedt, and Corwin E.
    Smidt)

GRIFFIN, ROGER
Oxford Brookes University
Fascism

GUTH, JAMES L.
Furman University
Evangelicalism (with John C. Green, Lyman A. Kellstedt, and Corwin E. Smidt)

GUTMANN, EMANUEL
Hebrew University of Jerusalem
Gush Emunim
Jerusalem

H

HACKETT, DAVID G.
University of Florida
Freemasonry

HAEBERLE, STEVEN H.
University of Alabama at Birmingham
Homosexuality

HALL, DAVID
University of Texas at El Paso
Confucianism
Confucius

HALL, PETER DOBKIN
Yale University
Humanitarianism

HARDACRE, HELEN
Harvard University
Japan
Shinto

HARDY, DANIEL W.
University of Cambridge
Bonhoeffer, Dietrich

HARRISON, TIMOTHY P.
Northwestern University
African American experience

HASHMI, SOHAIL
Mt. Holyoke College
Jihad

HASTINGS, ADRIAN
University of Leeds
Christianity
Jesus

HEFNER, ROBERT W.
Boston University
Conversion
Indonesia
Islam, Southeast Asian
Sukarno, Achmad

HENDERSON, LAWRENCE W.
Angola

HENDRICKS, OBERY M., JR.
Payne Theological Seminary
Heresy

HERVIEU-LEGER, DANIÈLE
École des Hautes Études en Sciences Sociales (Paris)
France

HIMMELSTEIN, JEROME L.
Amherst College
Conservatism

HOFRENNING, DANIEL J. B.
St. Olaf College
Lobbying, Religious

HOMAN, ROGER E.
University of Brighton
Traditionalism

HUISKAMP, GERARD
Haverford College
Marxism (with Christian Smith)

I

ILESANMI, SIMEON O.
Wake Forest University
African traditional religions

IRELAND, ROWAN
La Trobe University
Brazil

J

JANSEN, JAN
Leiden University
Africa, West: The Mande world

JELEN, TED G.
University of Nevada at Las Vegas
Morality

JOYCE, KATHLEEN M.
Duke University
Medicine

JUERGENSMEYER, MARK
University of California at Santa Barbara
Nationalism

K

KAMEN, HENRY
Higher Council for Scientific Research (Barcelona)
Inquisition

KAPLAN, EDWARD K.
Brandeis University
Heschel, Abraham Joshua

KEDDIE, NIKKI
University of California at Los Angeles
al-Afghani, Jamal al-Din

KELLSTEDT, LYMAN A.
Wheaton College
Communication (with Paul Kellstedt)
Evangelicalism (with John C. Green, James L. Guth, and Corwin E. Smidt)

KELLSTEDT, PAUL M.
Brown University
Communication (with Lyman A. Kellstedt)

KENDALL, LAUREL
American Museum of Natural History
Korea

KERŠEVAN, MARKO
University of Ljubljana
Yugoslavia

KEYES, CHARLES F.
University of Washington
Buddha
Buddhism, Theravada
Ethnicity
Nhat Hanh, Thich
Vietnam

KIERNAN, BENEDICT F.
Yale University
Genocide and "ethnic cleansing"

KLAUSNER, SAMUEL Z.
University of Pennsylvania
Martyrdom

KLEINBERG, AVIAD M.
Tel Aviv University
Saints

KNISS, FRED
Loyola University Chicago
Anabaptists

KOKOSALAKIS, NIKOS
Panteion University
Balkan states
Orthodoxy, Greek

KSELMAN, THOMAS
University of Notre Dame
Miracles

KUMAR, KRISHAN
University of Virginia
Utopianism

KURTZ, LESTER R.
University of Texas at Austin
War

L

LAL, DEEPAK K.
University of California at Los Angeles
Economic development

LANDIS, JOSHUA M.
Princeton University
Sadat, Anwar
Syria

LAUNAY, ROBERT G.
Northwestern University
Ivory Coast

LAWSON, RONALD L.
*Queens College, City University
    of New York*
Seventh-day Adventism

LEVINE, DANIEL H.
University of Michigan
Base communities
Liberation theology

LONSDALE, JOHN
Trinity College, University of Cambridge
Kenya

M

MADAN, T. N.
Institute of Economic Growth (India)
Gandhi, Mohandas Karamchand
Hinduism
India

MADURO, OTTO
Drew University
Maryknoll

MALIK, HAFEEZ
Villanova University
Ahmad Khan, Sir Sayyid
Jinnah, Muhammad

MAMIYA, LAWRENCE H.
Vassar College
Nation of Islam

MANNING, CHRISTEL J.
Sacred Heart University
Paganism

MARDIN, ŞERIF
American University
Atatürk, Kemal
Turkey

MARTIN, WILLIAM
Rice University
Graham, Billy

MARTY, MARTIN E.
*Public Religion Project,
    University of Chicago*
Lutheranism
United States of America

MARTY, WILLIAM R.
University of Memphis
Civil disobedience

MCADAM, DOUG
University of Arizona
Civil rights movement

MCCLAY, WILFRED M.
Tulane University
Tocqueville, Alexis de

MCDONOUGH, PETER
Arizona State University
Jesuits

MCHUGH, FRANCIS P.
*St. Edmund's College, University
    of Cambridge*
Natural law

MELLONI, ALBERTO
Instituto per le Scienze Religiose (Italy)
Italy

MEWS, STUART
*Cheltenham and Gloucester College
    of Higher Education*
Methodism

MICHEL, PATRICK
*Centre National de la Recherche
    Scientifique, Paris*
Europe, Eastern

MILLER, JON P.
University of Southern California
Missionaries

MONROE, KRISTEN RENWICK
University of California at Irvine
Holocaust

MOORHEAD, JAMES H.
Princeton Theological Seminary
Presbyterians

MORAN, PETER K.
University of Washington
Buddhism, Tibetan
Dalai Lama

MORTON, BARRY
University of Natal
Botswana

MOYSER, GEORGE H.
University of Vermont
World Council of Churches

N

NADELMAN, HEATHER
Educational Testing Service
James, William

NASR, SEYYED VALI REZA
University of San Diego
Mawdudi, Sayyid Abu al-Ala
Pakistan

NOLL, MARK A.
Wheaton College
Canada

NORTHCOTT, MICHAEL S.
University of Edinburgh
Environmentalism

NORTON, AUGUSTUS RICHARD
Boston University
Lebanon

NOVAK, MICHAEL
American Enterprise Institute
Maritain, Jacques

O

OCHSENWALD, WILLIAM
Virginia Tech
Saudi Arabia

P

PADEN, JOHN N.
George Mason University
Nigeria

PAREKH, BHIKHU
University of Hull
Censorship

PERKINS, KENNETH J.
University of South Carolina
Bourguiba, Habib
Tunisia

PETERS, FRANCIS E.
New York University
Mecca
Sacred places

PRESLER, TITUS LEONARD
*St. Peter's Episcopal Church,
    Cambridge, Massachusetts*
Zimbabwe

R

REEVE, ANDREW
University of Warwick
Liberalism

REID, DONALD MALCOLM
Georgia State University
Banna, Hasan al-
Egypt
Muhammad Abduh
Qutb, Sayyid

REIS, ELIZABETH
University of Oregon
Witchcraft (with Cynthia Eller)

RICHARDSON, JAMES T.
University of Nevada at Reno
Christian Science

RIEMER, NEAL
Drew University
Madison, James

RIIS, OLE
Aarhus Universitet
Scandinavia
State churches

ROBERTS, RICHARD H.
Lancaster University
Barth, Karl
Capitalism
Havel, Václav

ROGERS, WILLIAM B.
Drew University
Jefferson, Thomas

ROOF, WADE CLARK
University of California at Santa Barbara
Protestantism

RYAN, PATRICK J.
Fordham University
Ghana

S

SACK, DANIEL EDWARD
*Material History of American
    Religion Project*
Social Gospel

SANNEH, LAMIN
Yale University
Ibn Khaldun
Separation of church and state: a
    principle advancing the struggle for
    human rights

SANTINO, JACK
Bowling Green State University
Holidays

SCHACHT, RICHARD
University of Illinois
Nietzsche, Friedrich Wilhelm

SCHERVISH, PAUL G.
Boston College
Philanthropy

SCHÜSSLER FIORENZA, ELISABETH
Harvard University
Gender

SEGERS, MARY C.
Rutgers University
Day, Dorothy

SELIGMAN, ADAM B.
Boston University
Citizenship
Civil society

SHAIN, BARRY ALAN
Colgate University
Individualism

SHAMSUL A. B.
Universiti Kebangsaan
Malaysia

SHUPE, ANSON
*Indiana University and Purdue University
    at Fort Wayne*
Latter-day Saints, Church of
    Jesus Christ of

SMIDT, CORWIN E.
Calvin College
Evangelicalism (with John C.
    Green, James L. Guth, and Lyman A.
    Kellstedt)

SMIT, DIRK J.
*University of the Western Cape, Bellville,
    South Africa*
South Africa

SMITH, BRIAN H.
Ripon College
Nongovernmental organizations

SMITH, CHRISTIAN
*University of North Carolina
    at Chapel Hill*
Marxism (with Gerard Huiskamp)

SMITH, GARY SCOTT
Grove City College
Calvinism

SMITH, ORAN P.
Foundation for American Education
Baptists

SMITH, RUTH
Worcester Polytechnic Institute
Justice, Social

SOMMERVILLE, C. JOHN
University of Florida
Secularization

STURM, DOUGLAS
Bucknell University
Burke, Edmund
Hobbes, Thomas

SWATOS, WILLIAM H.
*Association for the Sociology of Religion
    and the Religious Research Association,
    Holiday, Florida*
Reformation

T

TINKER, HUGH
Lancaster University
Colonialism

TIPTON, STEVEN M.
Emory University
Public theology

TOMKA, MIKLÓS
*Hungarian Religious Research
    Centre (Hungary)*
Hungary

V

VERTER, BRADFORD
Princeton University
Nativism

VOLENSKI, LEONARD
Seton Hall University
Poland

VOLL, JOHN O.
Georgetown University
Islam
Mahdi
Sudan

W

WALD, KENNETH D.
University of Florida
Presidents, American
Voting

WALLS, ANDREW F.
*University of Edinburgh and
    Princeton Theological Seminary*
Africa, Christian

WEBER, PAUL J.
University of Louisville
Freedom of religion
Separation of church and state:
    a potent, dynamic idea in
    political theory
Taxation
Theocracy

WETTERAU, BRUCE
Solzhenitsyn, Aleksandr I.

WILCOX, CLYDE
Georgetown University
Abortion

WILLIAMS, RHYS H.
Southern Illinois University
Unitarians
Voluntarism

WILSON, JOHN
Duke University
Denominationalism

WOLFFE, JOHN
The Open University
Anglicanism

WOOD, RICHARD L.
University of New Mexico
Community organizing

WUTHNOW, ROBERT
Princeton University
Civil religion

Z

ZAKI, MAMOON A.
LeMoyne-Owen College
Qaddafi, Muammar al–

ZARET, DAVID
Indiana University
English Revolution

List of Appendix Materials

Documents on Politics and Religion

Selected Readings

Reference Materials

Introduction

The complex relationships between politics and religion have emerged as some of the most pressing social issues of our time. Examples include questions about the reemerging role of fundamentalist movements in shaping political discussion, conflicts among ethnoreligious groups seeking to maximize political and territorial advantage, and religious leaders' efforts to promote human rights or improve cooperation among nations. These relationships have a profound effect on the world in which we live, influencing international relations, the stability of governments, and the rights of people to worship freely and express their religious views.

The continuing interaction between religion and politics was not anticipated by social scientists as recently as a generation ago. Many scholars believed the secular worldviews of science and Enlightenment philosophy were rapidly pushing religion to the margins of advanced democratic societies, while others noted the suppression of religious loyalties under totalitarian regimes. Theories of social change, emphasizing the differentiation of institutions in modern societies around specialized social functions, suggested that citizens would resolve collective concerns about public values through politics, whereas religion would be relevant only to private concerns such as rearing children or responding to grief and fears of death. Academic treatises on secularization and political development left little room for predictions that people would continue to hold firmly to their religious communities and mobilize these communities to achieve political aims.

But recent scholarship has recognized the importance of examining religion in efforts to understand the character of politics, just as it has seen the necessity of attending to politics in the study of religion. Studies have examined the changing relationship of politics and religion in virtually every country and region of the world. This research has influenced understandings of changes within religious traditions and necessitated new interpretations of historical connections between religion and politics. Although many questions remain to be explored, resources have been available in the past several decades to train and employ large numbers of social scientists who have gained access to archives and contemporary information in many parts of the world.

The Encyclopedia of Politics and Religion was initiated to bring together the results of this impressive body of research and to consolidate it for students, scholars, religious leaders, policy makers, and general readers. It consists of 256 original articles by prominent scholars in their respective fields. The articles range from several hundred words to eight thousand words in length. They focus mainly on the nineteenth and twentieth centuries, although some deal with earlier topics that continue to be of importance for understanding contemporary discussions. Collectively, they represent the vast diversity of ways in which religions and political systems influence each other in the contemporary world.

Articles in the encyclopedia examine these influences by focusing on particular countries or regions (such as Afghanistan, Italy, and Syria or Latin America and Western Europe), major world religions and traditions or movements within these religions (such as Theravada Buddhism, Confucianism, and Roman Catholicism), thematic topics that provide comparative perspectives and generalizations (base communities, civil society, millennialism, and secularization), events (the Crusades, the Holocaust, and revolutions), and individual religious and political leaders (Muammar al-Qaddafi, Frederick Douglass, and Dorothy Day).

The authors and editors do not take a particular position on the relationships between politics and religion, nor do they agree on the significance of these relationships or indicate that certain patterns are preferable to others. Their perspective is not that religion and politics should influence each other but that the two inevitably do interact in complex ways. To examine this complexity, the editorial board commissioned articles that focus on all major regions of the world and in many cases on particular countries where the relationships between politics and religion have been problematic or where these relationships have had an impact on the wider world; it was not our intention to include articles on all countries. The same is true of articles on leaders, events, religions, and themes. Although it was not possible to include every topic on which something important might be written, we have tried to be diverse in our coverage. What distinguishes these essays from those that might appear in more general sources about religion or politics is that we have focused as much as possible in each case on those aspects of religion that relate to politics and those aspects of politics that relate to religion.

This introduction offers an overview of common issues and highlights some of the recurrent themes in the articles. The first section discusses major social changes that have influenced the relationships between politics and religion. The second section examines the variety of ways in which politics and religion interact. The final section considers contemporary challenges that are likely to remain important for religious and political leaders in coming decades.

Social Change Affecting Politics and Religion

Contemporary relationships between politics and religion are the product of social forces, movements, and conditions that have accumulated over many centuries. These influences are inevitably local, varying with geography and tradition as much as from particular events, such as wars, ethnic rivalries, and the rise and fall of political and religious leaders. Social developments, too, particularly during the past two centuries, have influenced many parts of the world and often have consisted of international connections or nation-building processes that stemmed from common sources.

The fifteenth to eighteenth centuries laid the groundwork for modern relationships between politics and religion. Territorial rulers consolidated power by raising standing armies and supported them from the profits of trade, agriculture, and taxation. In many cases, these regimes gained legitimacy from religious functionaries whose military protection and financial support in turn depended on maintaining satisfactory relationships with secular authorities. Military conquests, rivalries among dynastic factions, and disputes over theological interpretations often resulted in religious wars.

By the end of the eighteenth century, efforts were being made to create systems of government that depended less on religious legitimation and more on ideas of practicality, tolerance, and democratic assent. The premises of religious leaders were sometimes challenged by scientists and literary figures whose work and ideas were supported by political leaders eager to extricate themselves from religious claims. Although these developments were most clearly evident in western Europe, they were experienced in other parts of the world as a result of long-distance trade, exploration, and colonization as well as from indigenous reforms and intellectual movements. By the early nineteenth century, methods of governing as well as precedents for the violent overthrow of established regimes by revolutionary movements—most notably in the French Revolution—had spread to Latin America and eastern Europe. These generated both successful efforts to establish regimes free of religious legitimation and reassertions of traditional rule elsewhere.

The industrial revolution dramatically altered the relationships between politics and religion during the nineteenth century. Industrialization drew people away from livelihoods rooted in agriculture, where local economic self-sufficiency was often a strong basis for maintaining loyalty to communal religions and folk religious practices. Large-scale displacement from rural areas to urban areas opened possibilities for new religious movements to develop among urban workers. Some of these movements reproduced the customs of rural life, while others emphasized individual autonomy to a greater extent than communal loyalties. Political movements built on the strength of labor unions or aimed at establishing socialist or communist parties often competed with religious movements for the time and energy of working people.

Industrialization created great disparities of wealth, strengthening the political power of a new class of elites whose fortunes were linked to the ownership of factories and commercial enterprises. Some of the religious conflict during this period can be understood in relation to the struggles between these rising industrial elites and those whose power was based on land holdings and birth. The industrial elites, along with members of the rising middle classes, also became instrumental in many of the religious reform movements of the nineteenth century, including temperance movements and efforts to launch charitable and philanthropic associations. Industrialization also altered the power relationships between men and women. As the franchise expanded, men typically were included in the electorate whereas women were not. Women in turn were either drawn away from the household to gainful employment in factory production or, among the middle classes, were expected to play more elaborate domestic roles. They were regarded as safeguards of domestic values and often were expected to play a greater role in the daily activities of religious organizations.

Colonization, which spread rapidly at the end of the nineteenth century, reaching far into Africa, East Asia, Southeast Asia, and the Middle East, also affected the relationships between politics and religion. Much of this intensity was fueled by rivalries among the western European powers, especially Britain, Germany, France, and Belgium. Each of these powers established distinctive relationships with the peoples they colonized. The effects on colonized peoples were generally significant. Economic development was encouraged by new opportunities for trade, which disrupted locally autonomous commercial and agricultural systems. Some elites prospered from the new relationships, while many became economically dependent on foreign markets over which they exercised no control. Internal population shifts occurred, as well as some migration to the colonizing countries. And, finally, foreign missionaries often accompanied colonization, spreading not only their religious teachings but also new ideas about schooling, medical care, and gender roles.

Although the effects of colonization continue to be debated, they should not be regarded as entirely negative or positive; nor should it be assumed that they pertained only to the underdeveloped world. Colonization brought many important changes to western Europe and the United States as well, including a heightened sense of religious mission, greater awareness of other world religions, and the periodic colonial conflicts that culminated in the world wars of the twentieth century. Recent scholarship on colonization also shows more clearly that its effects on developing countries were greatly influenced by long-standing struggles and instabilities in some of these countries as well. Exposure to Western religion sometimes generated reforms in indigenous religions, and these reforms often set in motion conflicts between religious traditionalists and religious reformers that continued well after colonialism ended.

The wars and rivalries among industrialized nations that dominated most of the nineteenth century and continued during the twentieth century influenced religion and politics on an unprecedented scale. The territorial or "state" churches that came into being in western Europe during the sixteenth and seventeenth centuries were typically drawn into their nations' war efforts, sometimes as a result of violence perpetrated against missionaries in colonized regions but more often through official endorsements of government military policy. Some of the so-called secularization of western Europe can be traced to reactions against the established churches, especially among members of the working classes, because of the churches' support for costly and unpopular wars. Other effects of these wars include the establishment of communism in eastern Europe and its attempts to suppress traditional religion, totalitarianism and the rise of fascism, heightened rivalry between religiously based political parties and socialist or labor parties, persecution in some areas of minority religions, and the emergence of new religious organizations and denominations that defined themselves in opposition to the state and state-related religions.

The expansion of science and higher education, from modest beginnings in the seventeenth century to the establishment of research universities and government-sponsored laboratories at the end of the nineteenth century, was another decisive influence on the relationship between politics and religion. Political leaders looked to science and higher education for legitimation, rather than to religious leaders, and scientific discoveries encouraged rethinking of some theological suppositions about the natural world. Rather than simply retreating in the face of science, however, religious organizations responded by expanding their own programs of higher education, including church-related colleges, divinity schools and theological seminaries, mission schools, and publishing ventures. In many countries, the nineteenth century and early twentieth century witnessed the growth of a professional clergy or religious elite who were interested in reconciling science and theology, combating science on its own terms, or bringing moral reflection to bear on scientific and technological developments. In the developing world, new elites often emerged who combined higher education with interests in religious reform and modernization.

The integration of regional and national cultures to form a single global culture has been one of the dominant developments of the twentieth century. Although this integration is rooted in the exploration, migration, and colonization of earlier periods, it was significantly advanced in the twentieth century by faster and more reliable forms of oceanic and rail transportation, by the spread of telegraph and telephone technology, by the emergence of air transportation, and most recently by high-speed computing technology. Religions have had to find new ways of maintaining the plausibility of particular teachings and practices in the face of greater awareness of alternatives from around the world. On the one hand, the new technologies have been used by religious groups to spread their message; on the other hand, religious teachings have often registered concern about the messages of the secular media and have encouraged adherents to focus more on the gratifications of belonging to communities of believers than on exclusive religious claims about absolute truth. Governments have played an important role in promoting and regulating transportation and communication; religious leaders' concerns about these developments have resulted in efforts to address questions about who has the right to impose regulations and whether those regulations should champion certain assumptions about morality and decency.

The twentieth century has witnessed some of the most devastating violence associated with totalitarianism and war in human history, and this devastation has evoked strong responses from religious communities. Peace movements and humanitarian efforts have been mobilized by religious leaders, as have campaigns to protect human rights and guarantee freedom of religious expression. Rivalries among superpowers have at the same time suppressed religious freedom in the name of national security. Few religions have been able to avoid being drawn into debates about the merits of democracy, capitalism, communism, and socialism.

One unforeseen consequence of the two world wars was a new opportunity for anticolonialism and neocolonialism. Movements in developing countries for independence and national autonomy were able to emerge in part because of the developed world's preoccupation with waging these wars, and in their aftermath the costs of maintaining colonial empires were sometimes too great for these countries to sustain. As colonial governments pulled back, indigenous national movements often drew on traditional religious sentiments to spark patriotism. At the same time, minority ethnoreligious groups were often suppressed. The collapse of the Soviet bloc in the late 1980s led to a similar wave of ethnic and religious factionalism, along with new freedom for religious expression, in the 1990s.

Although many of these larger and long-term social developments appear to be outside the influence of religion, affecting it by bringing about economic, technological, demographic, and political change, it should not be assumed that religion played no part in initiating these developments. Social scientists recognize that religious teachings often promote standards of moral discipline that condition how people respond to new economic and political challenges and that some religions encourage their followers to work for social change in the name of divine mandate, whereas other

religions focus attention more on the inner life of the individual or on otherworldly rewards. Such teachings are sufficiently malleable to have different effects in different situations; yet the capacity of religious teachings to motivate people and to mobilize them to take extreme action in unusual situations cannot be understood simply in terms of economic or political opportunities.

Scholars also debate the effects of cultural developments that are difficult to measure or define, such as the influences of "modernity" or "individualism." Some of these developments are associated with such profound changes in the functioning of institutions that their effects on religion and politics can hardly be doubted. For example, modernity is evident in the complex, rational planning procedures in which most governments engage and in the bureaucratic structures by which these procedures are carried out. For religious organizations to interact effectively with governments, it has been necessary for them to adopt some of these same procedures and structures. National offices with oversight of local religious congregations, religious lobbying organizations, and lawyers capable of interpreting tax laws affecting religious bodies are examples. Individualism is a set of cultural assumptions about the inherent rights, dignity, and freedom of the individual, as well as patterns of behavior that correspond with these assumptions, such as breaking marital or ethnic ties that constrain individual opportunity or levying trade sanctions against countries that violate modern understandings of individual rights. Religious teachings that emphasize believers' capacity to receive direct revelations from God, or that give precedence to individual responsibilities to God, have reinforced individualism in other spheres.

Whether secularity itself is a cultural development affecting religion and politics is an important consideration. Secularity is generally defined as a set of social norms that encourage activities to be performed by specialists in particular fields rather than by religious practitioners. Heightened levels of secularity in the twentieth century are evident in the fact that medicine is practiced largely by physicians, instead of by shamans or priests, and in similar developments with respect to therapy, social work, law, and engineering. In politics, it is generally assumed that special training and expertise are needed and that complex political decisions should be made by specialists, rather than by clergy. The fact that these decisions must meet the approval of an electorate in democratic societies or of other institutional leaders in nondemocratic societies nevertheless means that religious convictions can be a means of influencing them.

Interaction between Politics and Religion

As the foregoing discussion suggests, politics and religion interact at different levels and in ways that vary from context to context. Indeed, what counts as politics and as religion is itself subject to varying definitions. In the most general sense, politics refers to any social relationship in which power is involved, making it possible to speak of, say, office politics or the politics of gender roles. In the narrower sense in which it is used here, however, politics refers to the institution through which collective goals are determined and authority is maintained within a society.

Central governing bodies, such as monarchies, dictatorships, parliaments, presidencies, and legislatures are the most obvious components of political institutions, and their structure and organization has varied significantly over the past two centuries and among societies. In addition, politics includes organizations that serve the purposes of central governing bodies, such as armies and courts, and subsidiary levels of government, such as local, state, or regional jurisdictions. Politics also includes the varying mechanisms by which members of a society mobilize to gain representation on governing bodies or to influence them, such as parties, political movements, interest groups, and individual activities such as voting or signing petitions.

In turn, religion also varies from society to society, but it generally refers to institutionalized social arrangements and activities concerned with the supernatural or some other expression of transcendence. In broadest terms, definitions of religion sometimes include any activities that serve these functions, whether they are called religion (such as prayer) or not (such as art or a spectator sport). For present purposes, the focus is on organizations and activities that for the most part are formally identified as religion, such as churches, synagogues, temples, and mosques. It also includes forms of religious organization that may be less clearly demarcated from politics, such as religious movements that seek political power or religious leaders who hold public office.

The range of interactions between politics and religion is suggested by the variety of organizations and activities that constitute each institution. Some of these relationships are arm's-length, formal transactions, such as diplomatic negotiations between heads of state and heads of religious bodies, while others are informal and thus harder to characterize. In fact, one of the important aspects of relationships between politics and religion are the symbols and rituals that distinguish the two. For example, religious leaders may attempt to identify an issue as moral or religious, thereby giving themselves a right to speak on the subject, whereas political leaders may contend that the issue is technical or scientific or a matter only of public policy.

During the past two centuries, conflict and violence have been the forms of interaction between religion and politics that have generated the most interest and concern. Political leaders have been responsible for violence committed against religious adherents, as in the case of persecution of religious minorities, and religious leaders have sparked conflict and violence, especially in cases of one religious group waging war against another. These acts range from full-scale efforts to suppress or annihilate another group to more localized or individual events, such as hate crimes against a religious group or desecration of holy places or sacred objects.

The likelihood of conflict and violence is heightened by the fact that people in homogeneous religious communities increasingly interact with people in other communities as a result of trade, migration, and mass communication. Political boundaries have been drawn and redrawn in ways that create religiously pluralistic populations whose subgroups may compete for scarce resources. When central governing bodies are strong, as in the case of totalitarian regimes, this conflict may be suppressed, whereas weaker states may be less capable of restraining it. Democratic systems of representation provide means by which competing religious groups can express their wishes, as do concordats, legal agreements, and negotiated settlements among religious bodies. Ecumenical councils and interreligious organizations have grown as ways to coordinate the relationships of religious groups to prevent more severe conflict or violence from erupting. Whereas power was once more readily controlled by religious groups, who were thus able to use it to engage in violence against other groups, it is currently more likely to be in the hands of secular authorities. Although there are exceptions, it has become more likely for political entities to commit violence against religious groups than the reverse.

Whether or not conflict and violence are involved, religion often interacts with politics in an adversarial role, particularly by helping to mobilize protest movements or opposition to established leaders and policies. Religion plays a prominent role in such protests and opposition because it provides higher beliefs and principles in relation to which political leaders and policies can be judged. A particular political program can be criticized not simply as ineffective or costly but as morally wrong or evil. Movements may be organized by a charismatic leader whose charisma depends on having special access to divine wisdom, such as being able to interpret sacred texts or having received divine revelation. The appeal of charismatic leaders sometimes extends well beyond followers who believe devoutly in the same revelation because these leaders provide opportunities for other grievances to be expressed. But religion's capacity to mobilize dissent also depends on its own organizational strength. Protests are sometimes rooted in the fact that local religious organizations provide places for people to meet and link them with others in their own community or in other communities through clergy councils, pilgrimages, or religious assemblies. Apart from direct involvement in protest movements, religion is also a source of nongovernmental social interaction that can be perceived as a threat to social stability. For instance, a reform movement aiming to change the beliefs and practices of an established religion can threaten a political regime whose power rests on support from the leaders and followers of that religion.

The social conditions under which religious protests and movements arise are variable, but they often are characterized by uncertainty produced by changing social, economic, and political arrangements. This uncertainty may be the result of rapid economic development that gives some groups new opportunities and erodes the life chances of other groups, or it may stem from war, military coups, or political instability in neighboring countries. The likelihood of movements emerging is greater if this uncertainty disrupts the communities on which people rely for social and emotional support or the channels through which they ordinarily express political grievances.

Some studies suggest that religious movements function largely to comfort the psychological anxieties associated with unsettled social conditions. But studies also suggest that psychological explanations of this kind are insufficient. Unsettled conditions create opportunities for entrepreneurial religious leaders to formulate new ideas. Such conditions usually generate many alternative movements and ideas, which then compete to attract followers. In time, those that survive are often the ones that have secured a distinctive niche for themselves and have found ways to protect the resources available within that niche. For instance, a religious movement that appeals to an economically disadvantaged

ethnic minority is more likely to survive if it can maintain in-group loyalty by emphasizing the importance of ethnic boundaries and the dangers posed by assimilation.

Although religion is sometimes regarded as the guardian of traditional values, especially in relation to political regimes that may wish to implement innovative policies, it is important to recognize the dynamic character of religion as evidenced in the frequency with which new religious movements appear. In recent decades, this frequency has surprised many observers because they thought people would express their collective interests through secular movements or would regard religion as a private matter with few implications for broader social issues. But religious movements have emerged repeatedly in response to new social policies that were perceived by religious adherents to threaten their communities, as well as in response to new opportunities to expand or improve their social position. Religious leaders generally recognize that religious organizations can fall away from the truth, and thus need reform, or that traditional understandings need to be applied in new ways to contemporary situations.

Although religious movements that take adversarial positions in relation to politics often gain the most attention, religion and politics just as commonly interact by accommodating one another. Accommodation ranges from situations in which religious and political leaders passively agree not to cause trouble for one another to situations in which leaders actively support one another and share power. In many instances, accommodation is less a conscious decision than the result of mutual exposure and living within similar social conditions. For example, religious teachings in advanced capitalist societies may emphasize individual freedom, the necessity of personal choice, ethical relativism, and the possibility of divine favor being evident in material goods. All of these teachings reduce the likelihood that religious leaders will oppose government programs aimed at expanding markets, even if expansion is gained at the expense of families and local communities.

Examples of political arrangements accommodating tacitly to religious teachings are harder to find but might include maintaining tax exemptions for religious bodies or incorporating religious language into civil ceremonies. More overt forms of accommodation are illustrated by religious leaders endorsing political candidates or favoring particular parties or platforms and, on the other hand, by political leaders courting religious leaders who promise to rally their adherents or working out legal arrangements that protect the rights of religious bodies to operate schools, colleges, or social welfare programs. Accommodation of this kind has often come as a result of religious wars or protest movements that threatened the stability of regimes unless some formal arrangements were made. Although majority religions can more likely gain suitable accommodations from political regimes than can minority religions, the rights of minority religions are often protected constitutionally in democratic societies, and these minorities may be able to maintain their political voice by offering to support coalitions that would tip the balance of power in one direction or another.

Whereas accommodation may consist of tacit or behind-the-scenes agreements, cooperation is a form of interaction between religion and politics that openly acknowledges their complementary roles. Traditionally, cooperation usually involved some acknowledgment of political regimes' coercive capacities, such as their ability to impose taxes or field armies and navies. Religion's recognized role included conducting funerals, providing solace in times of illness and bereavement, training clergy, creating opportunities for worship, and assisting families in passing religious values to the next generation. For these reasons, political regimes often cooperated with religious organizations in raising money to build houses of worship, seminaries, and schools, while religious leaders depended on political leaders to protect them against external enemies or subversives who might be intent on destroying religious organizations.

In contemporary societies, these forms of cooperation often continue, but they are supplemented by more complex social arrangements. Governments sometimes continue to channel financial resources to religious organizations, such as schools, orphanages, and nursing facilities, because these organizations have experience that new ones lack. Moreover, religious organizations can rely on volunteers to help reduce the costs of delivering social services, or they can provide these services more reliably than newcomers because they have knowledge of local needs and customs. Governments often find it politically expedient to establish overall policy goals and then let religious organizations participate along with secular agencies in implementing these goals. Religious organizations may be enlisted for tasks that cannot easily be evaluated in terms of efficiency, such as providing opportunities to worship, whereas political organizations may retain tighter control over tasks where accountability to the wider public is desired.

Apart from cooperative or adversarial relationships, separatism is one of the distinctive strategies religions sometimes adopt in relating to politics. Separatist orientations have been prominent especially in Christianity and Buddhism where teachings may encourage adherents to maintain a pure life that would be sullied by participation in politics. Separatism may be practiced by individuals who simply refrain from taking an interest in politics or by religious communities whose activities may range from discouraging individual members from engaging in politics to collectively refusing to pay taxes, serve in military units, or abide by safety and health regulations.

In the past, utopian communities with beliefs that required them to live pure lives or wait for the coming of a messiah were often able to separate themselves politically from the rest of society by establishing themselves in remote geographic regions. With mass communication and greater population densities, most societies are less able to provide isolated locations for such groups than they once were. Some writers also argue that separatism has become more difficult because governments exercise greater control over their populations than in the past. Thus religious groups that refuse public schooling may find themselves having to interact with public officials charged with maintaining the quality of alternative educational programs, and parents who believe their children should not receive medical care are likely to find themselves in violation of child abuse laws.

The relationships between politics and religion are sufficiently complex that numerous mediating or brokering mechanisms have emerged. Religion does not interact with politics only through the activities of individuals or local congregations but through an array of specialized organizations. Hierarchical organizations that include local congregations aggregated into regional, provincial, national, or international bodies are one such mechanism. These organizations often parallel similar divisions within politics, making it possible for negotiations to take place, say, at the state level or at the national level. They provide ways for policy positions to be developed internally to religious organizations that can then be presented on behalf of the clergy or membership of those organizations. They also permit internal disputes to be resolved so that measures (such as lawsuits or violence) can be avoided that might result in power being yielded to secular authorities.

In addition to representing individual members and clergy, these organizations also permit resources to be channeled toward special functions that may be needed in negotiating with political leaders. Examples include religious lobbyists, constitutional lawyers, tax lawyers, media specialists, international diplomats, community organizers, and investors. While many of these specialties are provided by large-scale, formal religious organizations that represent local congregations, others are organized separately and work on a consulting basis; still others are supplied by special interest groups. These groups have arisen especially in advanced industrial societies to mobilize religious constituencies around particular issues, for example, the rights and interests of the elderly, women, men, homosexuals, nationality groups, and racial and ethnic minorities. By focusing their attention on one issue or a limited set of issues, these groups are able to achieve political aims that larger, multipurpose organizations are unable to attain. Whereas they typically aim to influence public policy, other specialized organizations have come into being to fulfill cooperative ventures involving religion and politics. So-called faith-based or parachurch organizations that combine funds from government and religion to serve needs such as food distribution or disaster relief are examples.

Political organizations are less likely than religious organizations to invent special mechanisms to broker the relationships between religion and politics because such organizations may be deemed beyond the purview of public functions. It is nevertheless evident that the political sphere broadly speaking has many ways of dealing with religion other than such obvious methods as incorporating members of religious groups into the electorate as individual citizens or entertaining high-level meetings between heads of religious organizations and heads of state. The courts have become one of the most important mechanisms for dealing with religious issues. Disputes settled in the courts range from ones in which religious parties themselves are the primary disputants, to cases brought by religious bodies against the state (for example, concerning laws regulating religious practices), to those of general social importance to which religious bodies join as interested participants (such as cases about abortion or capital punishment).

In countries with traditions of established religion, offices at all levels of government may exist to deal with such issues as parochial schools or the maintenance of religious buildings. In other countries, similar offices have sometimes been established to oversee public relations with religious groups, as in the case of a liaison between a governor's office or a

president's office and religious groups. Government agencies concerned with regulating or administering social programs have also become an important location for relationships with religion. Examples include departments of education that set standards to which religiously affiliated colleges must comply, health officials that monitor potential abuses of children's well-being by religious groups, and departments of state to which religious groups may turn for help in promoting the rights of religious counterparts in other societies.

As these examples suggest, interaction between religion and politics generally has implications for other institutions and for this reason often occurs through the participation of third parties. Economic organizations are one of these third parties. Businesses attempt to influence government policy through lobbying, campaign contributions, bribes, or well-placed staff members, but typically they try to exclude religious groups from these forms of influence by arguing that moral and ethical concerns are strictly matters of individual conscience. Yet on occasion religious bodies aim to affect businesses by initiating boycotts of their products or organizing shareholder resolutions. Business leaders may also court the support of religious organizations by making personal statements favoring religion or by encouraging philanthropic giving to religion. Labor organizations vary from excluding religion on grounds that it is likely to divert their resources, to cooperating with religious organizations to mobilize workers around particular issues or candidates, to working jointly on community efforts and social programs.

Secular nonprofit organizations have increasingly become another interested party to the relationships between religion and government, sometimes finding themselves competing with religious organizations to provide similar charitable services and at other times needing the cooperation of religious organizations to solicit favorable legislation on such issues as tax exemption or subsidies for social programs. Increasingly, the mass media also have taken on the characteristics of an interested third party, often looking to government for protection against religious claims that would seem to limit their freedom, but also working with religious organizations to publicize particular points of view on moral and ethical issues.

The Prospects for Politics and Religion

In coming decades, the relationships between politics and religion are likely to remain complex, vibrant, mutually reinforcing, and occasionally fraught with conflict and violence, just as they have been in the past. Indeed, past relationships easily serve as models for the strategies that religious and political leaders are likely to take toward one another. Yet there are developments in recent years that point to several areas in which particular attention needs to be devoted to forging better understanding and cooperation between religion and politics.

Questions about civil society have surfaced in recent years because of concerns in advanced industrial democracies about the limitations of government and because of opportunities to revitalize civil society in the aftermath of the disintegration of the Soviet Union and in developing countries. Although civil society has varying connotations in different traditions of political theory, it is generally understood to include the voluntary associations and public aspects of family and community relations through which citizens mobilize, express their political opinions, and serve their own needs.

Civil society is in this understanding the larger public context in which politics exists, although it differs from formal mechanisms of government and is public in a way that the personal or intimate relationships within families are not. It is concerned with the common good in ways that go beyond the activities of businesses and other economic organizations. Religion is one of the most important components of civil society in most countries, both because of the beliefs and values it upholds and because of the local organizations and networks of which it consists.

Although it was sometimes assumed that civil society could flourish strictly in terms of secular voluntary associations, the continuing role of religion is increasingly recognized. But the nature of this role is problematic. Religious groups in pluralistic societies often argue about differences concerning fundamental values and thus raise worries about their ability to contribute to social cohesion. Religious groups may encourage their own members to interact with and support one another but discourage efforts to bridge and harmonize with other groups. Religious groups may orient their efforts so fully toward the transcendent that they pay little attention to social needs. And religious groups may be weakened by government programs or the efforts of secular voluntary organizations to supply social services that have traditionally been the domain of religion. Some observers argue that religion is so important to civil society that

public officials should do all they can to preserve and strengthen religion. Other observers point to the problems inherent in religious groups and suggest caution.

Recognizing the importance of civil society at least casts the relationship between religion and politics in a wider context. It suggests that religion and politics do not operate strictly in adversarial or cooperative ways but that the two come together as contributors to many of the activities on which the strength of the larger society depends. For instance, religious organizations may nurture the development of social skills, such as leading a meeting or soliciting help from volunteers, which become useful when citizens participate in politics. Religious organizations may encourage discussions of parental responsibilities and marital obligations that strengthen the family and thus reduce the need for government programs for juvenile delinquency or child care. Questions about civil society nevertheless suggest a paradox as well: religion may be encouraged because it promotes broader social networks, skills, and values, but it may do so most effectively through activities that are potentially divisive and self-interested.

A significant aspect of the debate about civil society is the issue of political participation. Participation includes voting and engagement in electoral politics, but it also includes activities that may pertain in less democratic societies, such as keeping aware of political developments or working on behalf of advocacy and resistance movements. Religion has been an important stimulus to political participation in the past because people who take part in religious organizations are more likely to hear about issues than are their nonreligious counterparts, or they are tied to networks that spark their interest in politics. As levels of political participation have declined in many societies, the prospect of religion being able to revitalize this interest has become increasingly important. Yet it is unclear if political participation is as closely related to religious involvement as in the past, or if it depends more on work-related networks or the role of media in generating interest in elections.

Some observers also suggest that political parties have become sufficiently ingrown or susceptible to manipulation by wealthy business interests that grassroots religious participation can make little difference. If participation is ambiguously related to religious involvement, the direction of support for particular candidates and issues is even more ambiguous. In some countries, religiously based political parties still command the loyalties of their respective religious traditions, while in other societies special interest groups have mobilized support for policies and candidates by appealing to people of particular religious backgrounds. Yet religious identities and social issues are sufficiently complex that strong relationships between the two may be less likely in coming years.

Closely related to questions about civil society is the issue of volunteerism. As the naturally occurring sources of support that exist in extended families or local communities erode, more of the work of caring for the needy and disadvantaged has had to be arranged through larger and more formal organizations. Over the past century and a half, government has played a prominent role in this work, and its role is likely to continue, especially by virtue of its capacity to raise public funds and exercise standards of fairness. But the increasing integration of international markets has imposed competitive pressures in even the most affluent societies to limit government expenditures for social services. Expenditures raise taxes and therefore increase the price of domestically produced goods or decrease the purchasing power of consumers in domestic markets. Mobilizing volunteer assistance has become a popular alternative or supplement to government programs, and in some societies religious organizations have proved to be a good place in which to recruit volunteers. These organizations generally promote altruistic values and facilitate social interaction through which volunteers can be solicited.

Much of this religious-based volunteering takes place with little relationship to politics. Yet, because it is viewed as an alternative to public expenditures, it is inevitability colored with political implications. Politicians look to religious organizations for help in the face of government cutbacks; religious organizations may eagerly try to take up the slack in hopes of finding a larger place for themselves, although they may also argue for continuing government involvement.

These issues vary from society to society, depending on how much government has been involved in social services, but they appear to be common to advanced industrial societies, despite different religious traditions. In developing countries, volunteering is becoming increasingly regarded as an important form of social service as well. Volunteering is likely to be one of the important issues at the intersection of religion and politics in the immediate future as religious organizations debate how much of a role they can play in mobilizing volunteer efforts, as they compete with other volunteer organizations, and as governments formulate policies affecting the roles of volunteer agencies. These policies include taxation, questions about volunteer agencies engaging in advocacy, and competition between these agencies and businesses.

Both civil society and volunteering are issues that have surfaced as part of larger questions about the future of democracy. The latter half of the twentieth century witnessed the emergence of dozens of new democracies in the developing world and as a result of the collapse of the Soviet Union. Yet it remains unclear how viable many of these democracies will be. Many have emerged in societies with few traditions that favor democratic rule, and many are plagued with economic problems that could be exploited by totalitarian leaders. Whether religion is a force in favor of democracy or in opposition to it is an open question. On the one hand, religious groups often promote grassroots political self-determination, as they have done especially through base communities in Latin America, and these groups may be opposed to authoritarian regimes. On the other hand, established religious organizations have sometimes been co-opted by totalitarian leaders or subjected to persecution that effectively silences voices of opposition.

Another development in recent decades is the resurgence of debates about the effects of politics and religion on the family. Although it has often been assumed that religion and traditional family roles are mutually supportive, new questions have been opened by evidence suggesting that the family is weakening and by changes in the meanings of family roles. Governments often took the view that families should be left alone, except for cases of extreme poverty or in emergencies, but this view has shifted as governments have become more interested in regulating population growth, curbing domestic violence, or encouraging women to participate in the paid labor force. Questions about "family policy" (itself a revealing term) revolve around complex issues including individual rights, gender equality, reproduction and fertility, economic costs, the economic viability of households, religious values, and auxiliary concerns pertaining to schooling, job training, and crime.

Religious organizations have been unable to escape these issues. Even when refraining from addressing questions about family policy, they have been profoundly involved in discussions about the changing social roles of women and men, paternalistic teachings within their own traditions, marital responsibilities, birth control, and the training of children. Policy makers have looked to religious organizations to provide guidance on bioethical questions of relevance to families as well as to counsel marriage partners and administer day care facilities and retirement homes. It seems likely that family policy will continue to be an issue that brings religion and politics together in controversial ways.

Bioethical questions are but one set of many issues that new developments in technology and medicine are raising that will bring religion and politics together in complementary or adversarial roles. Human genetic engineering has been supported through government funding, and to the extent that it has been regulated these regulations have largely been created and enforced by governments. Religious leaders have raised fundamental moral and ethical questions about the propriety of certain kinds of research, yet their ability to influence government policy has varied. Even in countries with strong popular involvement in religion, the terms of debate have often focused more on expedience than on fundamental principles. Environmental risk management, biological warfare, nuclear safety, and space exploration are other issues that necessarily bring religious and political issues together. One of the major challenges these issues raise for religious leaders is the fact that highly specialized expertise is generally required to address them, yet the resources available to religious organizations for training and employing such specialists is small compared with those available to political organizations.

For political and religious leaders alike, one of the greatest challenges of coming decades is the globalization of markets, societies, and cultures. Globalization, though facilitated by electronic communication and air transportation, is driven especially by firms seeking new markets and cheaper pools of labor. For political regimes, it is both a stabilizing and destabilizing force. Regimes that can sell natural resources or inexpensive labor in wider markets earn revenue that can be used to stabilize their control, while other regimes are increasingly at the mercy of international flows of capital over which they have little influence. Religions are affected by the stability or instability of host regimes and by the shifting economic opportunities available to their members.

Ideologically, the major world religions have often espoused exclusivist orientations toward one another that make it difficult to accept other traditions to which they are exposed as coequals. Yet these religions also embrace universalistic values, such as love or respect for human dignity, that make possible greater cooperation.

At a practical level, religions have responded to globalization by curtailing the missionary activities of the nineteenth and early twentieth centuries that were aimed at proselytizing members of other religions. These activities have been replaced in part by humanitarian efforts, especially through support from international nongovernmental organizations concerned with emergency relief, agricultural development, and human rights. As these international efforts have responded to the greater awareness of global human needs made possible by satellite television, a countertendency toward more interest in local affairs has also taken place. Some religious organizations in effect respond to the overwhelming realities of world needs by focusing on needy families within their local congregations or suggesting that personal problems of members must be dealt with before any attempts can be made to address global issues.

If globalization presents abstract or remote issues for some religious leaders, it nevertheless brings greater religious diversity that cannot be easily escaped even at the local level. Societies that formed around single religious traditions or that gradually overcame religious conflict are now faced with many more religious traditions than in the past or with more sizable religious minorities. Migration has been a major source of this diversity, fueled in turn by countries seeking new sources of labor or giving asylum to political refugees. Countries previously populated exclusively by Christians and Jews, for example, are becoming increasingly populated by Muslims, Hindus, or Buddhists.

Pluralism has also brought greater levels of complexity because of conversions and interreligious marriage. Government policy has often been strained in coming to terms with these heightened levels of pluralism. Observances of religious holidays, for example, have had to be rethought, as have constitutional guarantees for certain religious practices. More than the sheer presence of religiously diverse groups, however, the cultural implications of pluralism remain to be fully examined and understood. Growing numbers of Christians, for example, may be deeply influenced by Buddhist practices, even if they do not recognize the origins of these practices, and large numbers of Muslims and Hindus may have substantial exposure to both traditions.

One implication of pluralism is that individuals' commitments to particular religious organizations may be lessened, and for this reason they may be less influenced than they were formerly by the political leanings or interests of a specific religious group. This implication suggests that religious beliefs may indeed become more private, personal, and variable, leaving political issues to be determined by other factors. Another implication, however, is that religious beliefs will continue to be important but will be defended on grounds other than their claim to be expressions of ultimate truth. Some observers worry that a shift of this kind undermines the ethical basis for political action, while others regard it as a move toward greater tolerance and acceptance.

Robert Wuthnow

THE ENCYCLOPEDIA
OF POLITICS AND RELIGION

A

Abolitionism

Abolitionism is the political and religious conviction that the practice of human bondage is morally wrong. It is impossible to study the political and social history of the Americas without studying the history of slavery. The modern development of the countries that compose the Americas proceeded hand in hand with the modern development of slavery. Questions of slavery's economic value, political viability, and morality deeply influenced the character of these countries from the moment of initial contact between the indigenous peoples and the European settlers until abolitionism took firm root and led eventually to the end of the practice of human bondage.

The United States was home to slavery from its birth as a nation until the end of its Civil War in 1865. And as long as slavery existed, groups of men and women condemned it as a moral and political evil. Historically, slaves themselves practiced their own forms of abolitionism, seeking to increase their liberty and control over their lives through sabotage and slow-downs at work, flight, and, occasionally, revolt. Yet the political fires of abolitionism burned brightest from 1830 to 1860, the thirty-year period preceding the Civil War. Before then, only a few Anglo-Americans saw slavery as a moral or ethical evil. To be sure, there were notable exceptions. Some of the most prominent of the founders, including George Washington and Thomas Jefferson, questioned the morality and political wisdom of holding slaves and wondered, at least in private, if a nation conceived in liberty could sustain itself when slavery was a common practice.

Religious groups historically censured slavery. In 1758 the Quakers condemned slavery at their annual conference and remained resolute in their conviction from that point onward. The Baptists and Methodists did the same at the turn of the nineteenth century, arguing that no man could serve as master over his brother because all were equal in the eyes of the Lord. Yet these two groups ultimately softened their opposition. By the early 1800s they had traded an antislavery stance for a measure of social respectability because they were convinced that few politicians or slaveholders would sanction emancipation under any circumstance.

Early Abolitionists and U.S. Politics

The most famous organized and sustained resistance to slavery before 1831 was the American Colonization Society, begun in 1816 by a coterie of affluent Northerners dedicated to the gradual and voluntary emancipation of enslaved Americans. Officials proposed that masters be financially compensated for freeing their slaves and that freed people be repatriated to Africa. The society actually transported several thousand blacks to Africa in the early 1800s, particularly to Liberia. Its activities, however, ignited a firestorm of protest from pro-slavery groups, and particularly northern free blacks, who countered that no one should be forced to emigrate against his or her will. Richard Allen, founder of the country's first all-black denomination, the African Methodist Episcopal Church (in Philadelphia in 1816), and other prominent spokespersons for the free black community, such as David Walker and Frederick Douglass, stood steadfastly against slavery. Unlike most white politicians, these abolitionists unflaggingly portrayed human bondage as a wicked act against God and called for immediate emancipation.

Notwithstanding these acts and words of protest, most white Americans until the early 1800s generally viewed black slaves as naturally inferior and consigned by God to bondage.

Abolitionism emerged as a dominant debate within national politics in the 1830s because of major changes in the environment. First, innovations in technology made it easier to build large, national political movements. Canals and railroads expanded at an unprecedented rate. Improvements in printing dramatically lowered the cost and increased the speed of producing newspapers and pamphlets. These transformations allowed people from distant corners of the country to share ideas and organize support for issues like abolitionism.

At the same time, a powerful series of religious revivals swept through the West and the East, popularizing new ideas about sin and salvation and nurturing a reform-minded culture in which abolitionism flourished. Beginning in the late 1700s, revivals burst forth in Kentucky and Tennessee and gradually spread eastward, touching residents of the hinterlands and the cities alike. Charles Finney was the best known of the new evangelists, and this one-time Presbyterian conducted revivals in western New York State in the late 1820s and in New York City in the early 1830s. Finney taught that man was not predestined for heaven or hell but instead was able to affect his eternal future by his behavior. Man could strive to perfect his sins and those of his society, instructed Finney, and thus prepare the way for the imminent return of Jesus and the subsequent start of the millennium. In this world of evangelical Protestantism, there was no compromise with the devil, no backing down from sin. And in this world, few sins were more heinous than slavery.

Evangelical Protestantism and Free Labor

For some, the opposition to slavery was a natural extension of evangelical Protestantism. Evangelists taught that modern society was a battleground between humans' moral free agency and duty to follow God and their unregulated passions. No one should tolerate individuals or institutions that corrupted humans' ability to act on their own; all must labor to liberate their spirits from social influences that imprisoned them, be it alcohol, prostitution, work on Sundays, or especially slavery. Slavery was the worst of these sins because, for hundreds of years, it had disfigured not only the slave's capacity to act freely but also the master's, binding both to an economy in which bodies were trafficked, beaten, abused, and sold. Indeed, for many evangelical Protes-

tants, slavery was part of a world that they hoped to change forever.

Perhaps no one embodied the intersection of evangelical Protestantism and abolitionism better than William Lloyd Garrison, who founded his antislavery newspaper, the *Liberator,* on the first day of 1831. He spoke to the hearts of many evangelists when he called for an utter and instant end to slavery. Unlike many earlier opponents of human bondage, and in particular members of the American Colonization Society, Garrison condemned slavery as a national sin that divided Americans from God and required expiation in the form of immediate emancipation. He founded the American Anti-Slavery Society in Philadelphia, in 1833, and articulated the antislavery leanings of many Northerners, especially residents of New England, western New York, and southern Ohio—places where changes in technology and Protestantism were greatest.

Significantly, abolitionism as a single-issue political movement never attracted widespread support. Its most radical spokespersons, like Garrison, drew relatively few disciples. Rather, many evangelists, including Finney, argued that emancipation, though a lofty goal, must be accomplished slowly and proceed only as slave owners experienced conversion. Talk of immediate action, they feared—prophetically—risked alienating slaveholders and driving the nation to the brink of civil war. Still, the issue of abolitionism stoked the flames of a new political consciousness in the antebellum era, forcing people into two categories—those who opposed slavery and those who did not—and providing a critical plank in the platform of a new and rising electoral political party in the 1850s, the Republicans.

Republican politicians, most notably Abraham Lincoln of Illinois, rose to prominence by fusing the issue of antislavery to new economic and political philosophies and creating the ideology of free labor. As its name suggests, free labor posited that the health of a civilization depended directly on the ability of its laborers to work freely. All men desire to improve themselves and thus would practice those habits that promised the greatest chances of success, namely thrift, discipline, diligence, and temperance.

A man, regardless of what station in life he was born into, could work his way up the ladder of success. Work done by hand and for hire was honorable because it was temporary, only a starting point from which free men of drive and ambition could advance to become their own bosses. But the presence of social mobility in a free-labor ideology rested on the absence of slavery. Slavery denied its workers a chance to lift themselves out of their status, and thus the system of bonded workers, without hope for social advancement, worked inefficiently. Slavery also degraded the dignity of manual labor by equating it with fixed servitude.

Human Rights

Besides opposing slavery for economic reasons, most Republicans shared with evangelical Protestants a belief in the immorality of human bondage. African Americans, they claimed, were by nature inferior to whites, but they still deserved an opportunity to earn bread by the sweat of their own brows and receive a modicum of civil liberties. Yet Republicans in the 1850s stopped far short of demanding immediate emancipation. Instead, they called for the containment of slavery within its borders, arguing that emancipation was inevitable because slavery was unprofitable and doomed to fail.

The Republican cry for the containment of slavery was self-serving. Free-labor ideology relied on free soil or the fresh acquisition of lands free of slavery. Indeed, to advance people must have access to free soil. The issue was made critical by the North's rapid change in the first half of the 1800s from a largely agrarian economy to an industrial one in which men worked factory jobs that promised little opportunity for advancement. The basic solution to dead-end manufacturing jobs was the chance to move up and out, to start a farm or a business in a place of limited competition and cheap land. Thus, as territories like Kansas and Nebraska petitioned for statehood in the 1850s, free-labor ideologues insisted that they enter as states free of slavery, but pro-slavery spokespersons asserted the opposite. Tensions flared in Congress and in the future states, leading to bloody skirmishes in the midwestern territories and prefacing the battles over slavery fought in the Civil War.

When the North and the South took up arms in 1861, the issue of abolitionism in the United States received its final hearing. When President Lincoln issued the Emancipation Proclamation on January 1, 1863, he officially freed all slaves in the Confederate states and explicitly made the war into a struggle about the fate of slavery. In his second inaugural address on March 4, 1865, Lincoln directly linked the cause and ultimate meaning of the war to slavery, arguing that the widespread loss of life occasioned by the fighting was a type of national atonement for the sin of human bondage.

Slavery's demise in North America came at the point of a bayonet. Any charting of the political career of abolitionism, however, cannot fully capture the steady trajectory of resistance by slaves themselves to their earthly fate. Slaves challenged their condition from the start. Whether at the original point of enslavement on the western coast of Africa, during the middle passage across the Atlantic, on the sugar or cotton plantation, or in the domestic household, they worked the system of human bondage to its minimum disadvantage through flight, rebellion, malingering, sabotage, theft, and deception. Changes in the North's economy, the spread of evangelical Protestantism, and the rise of the Republican Party made it possible for abolitionism to occupy center stage in national and sectional politics, but antislavery had always been at the center of politics for African Americans, free or enslaved.

Abolitionism in the Americas

The Union states' victory in the U.S. Civil War invigorated the cause of abolition throughout the Americas. Slaves in other countries and colonies historically had challenged their fate through various sorts of resistance. As early as 1522, for example, slaves in southeastern Hispaniola staged the first significant slave revolt; it was on a sugar plantation owned by a son of Christopher Columbus.

The modern age of emancipation in the Caribbean and Central and South America perhaps began in 1791, when slaves in the French colony of Saint-Domingue rebelled against their oppressors and fought for independence. Thirteen years later, when the smoke finally cleared and victory was declared, these insurgents renamed the country Haiti. The rebellion reflected diverse influences, including the fiery ideology of the French Revolution, a history of slave resistance, a widely shared popular religion called Vodun, a common language of Creole, and the superb generalship of Toussaint L'Ouverture.

The Haitian revolution, as a rebellion that led directly and speedily to emancipation, was distinctive. But it served as a symbol and source of energy for the cause of antislavery throughout the region, making the issue of emancipation critical to changing ideas of citizenship and economy. In 1792 Denmark became the first European colonial power to abolish the slave trade, reflecting a growing popular sentiment throughout Europe to end slavery in the early 1800s as the philosophy and demands of international commerce changed. The British Parliament, bowing to public support for abolitionism that grew also from the popularization of evangelical Christianity at the turn of the nineteenth century, in 1834 abolished slavery throughout its Caribbean colonies. By 1848 France, Holland, and Denmark had followed suit.

In the Americas, the Haitian revolution led to official acts of abolition in several newly independent states of the region—in Chile in 1823, in the countries of Central America in 1824, and in Mexico in 1829. Other countries, often those with large concentrations of slaves, were slower to initiate emancipation. Slaveholding elites fought to keep privileges of power, limit the rights and freedoms of former slaves, and ease the transition from a slave-based economy to a wages for hire one. Abolition was declared in Uruguay in 1846, Colombia in 1850, the Argentine Republic in 1853, Venezuela and Peru in 1854, and, finally, Paraguay in 1870.

Two exceptions to the path of gradual emancipation in Latin America were Cuba and Brazil, where elites successfully circumvented the end of the slave trade. Whether they operated sugar plantations in the Spanish colony of Cuba or coffee plantations in imperial Brazil, rulers bought new slaves directly from Africa, developed new lands in their own countries, and nurtured new overseas markets. Yet these strategies were ultimately insufficient to keep plantation slavery profitable. Not only was there an insatiable need to buy more slave bodies but also a growing problem of domestic insurgency. Cuban rebels forced Spain to enact cautious laws of gradual emancipation in 1870. Within sixteen years, a persistent rebellion in eastern Cuba and widespread resistance by slaves forced Spain to declare an end to bondage in 1886. In Brazil laws of gradual emancipation went into effect in the early 1870s, as many urban professionals believed that the future of the economy lay not in slavery but in immigrant labor. But slave resistance, particularly in the form of flight and theft, accelerated the process and forced reluctant plantation owners to move quickly toward emancipation. In 1888 abolition became the rule of the land in Brazil and, finally, throughout all the Americas.

See also *Evangelicalism; Human rights.*

John M. Giggie

BIBLIOGRAPHY
Klein, Herbert S. *African Slavery in Latin America and the Caribbean.* New York: Oxford University Press, 1986.
Sewell, Richard H. *Ballots for Freedom: Antislavery Politics in the United States, 1837–1860.* New York: Oxford University Press, 1976.
Stewart, James B. *Holy Warriors: The Abolitionists and American Slavery.* New York: Hill and Wang, 1976.
Tomich, Dale W. "The 'Second Slavery': Bonded Labor and the Transformation of the Nineteenth Century World Economy." In *Rethinking the Nineteenth Century: Movements and Contradictions,* edited by Francisco O. Ramirez. New York: Greenwood Press, 1988.
Wade, Peter. *Blackness and Race Mixture: The Dynamics of Racial Identity in Colombia.* Baltimore: Johns Hopkins University Press, 1993.
Walters, Ronald G. *American Reformers, 1815–1860.* New York: Hill and Wang, 1978.

Abortion

Governments worldwide are struggling with the issue of whether and in what conditions women should be allowed to terminate pregnancies, a procedure known as abortion. At stake are conflicting values and worldviews, often embodied in a clash between religious conservatives, on the one hand, and religious progressives and secular citizens, on the other.

Many religious conservatives argue that life begins at conception and that the termination of a pregnancy amounts to the killing of an unborn child. Most feminists and civil libertarians argue that there is no consensus on when or if a fetus is an unborn child, a potential child, or merely tissue growing in a woman's body and that a pregnant woman should be allowed to make the complex moral decision to terminate a pregnancy without interference from the state. Many liberal religious groups have adopted positions that are generally supportive of women's right to choose an abortion.

Although abortion has been used to control reproduction for most of recorded human history, it has been a source of moral and religious controversy. Greek philosophers in the fifth century B.C. disagreed on the moral justification for abortion; and abortion and infanticide were widespread in ancient Rome, where they were a subject of at least some debate. During this period, however, infanticide was more common than abortion since most abortion procedures posed grave risks to the life and health of the mother. In the nineteenth and twentieth centuries, as medical procedures for both abortion and childbirth became safer, religious groups began to confront the moral issue. Today most religious bodies have officially considered a position on abortion, although many lack an explicit policy.

In the United States the abortion debate rose to a new level of controversy after the U.S. Supreme Court ruled, in 1973, in *Roe v. Wade* that women's rights to privacy entailed a

Demonstrators on both sides of the abortion debate gather in front of the U.S. Supreme Court to await the Court's decision in Planned Parenthood of Southeastern Pennsylvania v. Casey *(1992). In that case the Court upheld the right to an abortion while permitting some state restrictions.*

right to an abortion during the first two trimesters (the first six months) of pregnancy. The Court's ruling overturned state laws regulating or banning abortion in most states and invalidated many national laws as well. After the Court ruling, anti-abortion forces organized a "right to life," or "pro-life," movement to seek to reverse the decision, while supporters of abortion rights reorganized existing abortion-reform organizations into "pro-choice" groups.

In the 1990s the debate over abortion turned violent in the United States, as radicals on the fringe of the pro-life movement shot abortion providers and bombed abortion clinics. The pro-life movement generally condemned this violence, although some ideological leaders publicly sympathized with the frustration of those who resorted to violence, perhaps thereby signaling acceptance.

The Roman Catholic Position

The Roman Catholic Church is the largest organized religious opponent of legal abortion. The Catholic Church holds that abortion is murder because the fetus is a child from the moment of conception. The church opposes abortion in all circumstances, including cases in which the mother's life would be put in danger by completion of the pregnancy. Catholic opposition to abortion is grounded in the teachings of religious leaders, especially popes, who based their arguments on natural law.

Although Catholic theologians have grappled with abortion for centuries, the position of opposition to all abortions was solidified during the nineteenth and twentieth centuries. Many but not all early Catholic thinkers distinguished between abortions performed before the fetus was active in the mother's womb, a time when the soul was thought to enter the fetus, and those performed afterward. By the end of the nineteenth century, however, the church officially opposed abortions in almost all circumstances. In the twentieth century Pope Pius XII declared that the right to life from God was immediate, and Pope Paul VI in his 1968 encyclical *Humanae Vitae* opposed abortion and contraception as interfering with the procreative nature of sexual union and thereby perverting the purpose of the divine gift of human sexuality.

Although the Catholic position on abortion has been clearly enunciated, *Humanae Vitae* is a teaching document, not an *ex cathedra* papal pronouncement that is considered infallible. Nonetheless, the Catholic bishops in the United States have focused more on abortion than on any other political issue, and at times Catholic leaders have threatened to excommunicate Catholic lawmakers who support abortion rights. Many Catholic bishops have subsumed the abortion issue into a larger doctrine of the "seamless garment of life," which includes a series of "life-affirming" stances on issues such as opposition to abortion, the death penalty, and nuclear weapons and support for programs that provide nutrition assistance for poor pregnant women.

The Catholic Church has lent its considerable organizational resources to the pro-life movement. Most Catholic priests deliver at least one homily on abortion each year, and many dioceses have organized pro-life groups that are supported in large part by the church. The Catholic bishops organized the National Committee for a Human Life Amendment in 1973, to attempt to push a constitutional amendment to ban abortions, and the group received considerable grassroots support from Catholic parishes.

There is considerable dissent among the Catholic laity and some Catholic religious elites in the United States and in other countries to the official church position on abortion. Despite the clear teaching of a hierarchical religious institution, there is also little evidence that Catholics have fewer abortions than other Americans. In the United States and other countries, Catholics are generally more conservative on abortion than are other citizens, but only a small minority support a ban on all abortions, even among those who attend Mass regularly.

Evangelical Opposition

A second religious source of opposition to legal abortion in the United States comes from the evangelical Protestant community. Evangelical Protestant churches in the United States are generally critical of abortion, and most denominations' official position allow abortions only in very limited circumstances, such as to save the life and health of the mother. A number of evangelical denominations, especially fundamentalist Baptists and pentecostal Assemblies of God, have served as the organizational backbone of the pro-life movement in the South and Midwest and have lent their considerable resources to opposing legal abortion. Moreover, evangelical organizations of the Christian right, such as the Christian Coalition and Concerned Women for America, have lobbied for restrictive policies on abortion in national and state legislatures.

Evangelical churches base their opposition to abortion on biblical Scripture, especially Exodus 21:22–23: "If men strive, and hurt a woman with child, so that her fruit depart from her, and yet no mischief follow: he shall be surely punished, according as the woman's husband will lay on him; and he shall pay as the judges determine. And if any mischief follow, then thou shalt give life for life." Pro-life evangelicals argue that this verse prescribes penalties for abortion providers; a few even suggest that this verse dictates the death penalty. Evangelical pastors also point to verses that suggest activity by John the Baptist and Jesus in their mothers' wombs and to the commandment against killing. Pro-choice evangelicals offer alternative readings and argue that the verse from Exodus seems to describe a miscarriage brought on by violence, not an abortion.

The congregants in evangelical churches are generally slightly more conservative than American Catholics in their views on abortion, and members of the Assemblies of God exhibit the highest level of opposition to legal abortion of any U.S. denomination. Yet even among evangelicals, there are more pro-choice than pro-life congregants, even among those who attend church regularly.

Other Views

Mainline Protestant churches in the United States and much of Europe, while generally criticizing "frivolous" abortions, have usually supported a woman's legal right to choose. Their reasoning is that the fetus is not a fully developed human with a soul. For example, the American Episcopal Church in its 1968 general convention held that the church "emphatically oppose[d] abortion as a means of birth control, family planning, sex selection or any reason of mere convenience." Members considering abortion were encouraged to seek counsel from the Christian community and to pray. Most mainline Protestant churches have similar official positions. Many mainline Protestant denominations are members of the Religious Coalition for Reproductive Choice, which seeks to ensure that abortion remains legal in the United States.

In Europe, mainline Protestants and Catholics have occasionally disagreed quite visibly on abortion politics, especially in countries such as Germany with large numbers of adherents to both faiths. Members of mainline Protestant churches in the United States and Europe are more liberal than other citizens on abortion, but those who attend church regularly are more conservative than those who attend infrequently.

Orthodox Jews hold that abortion is mandatory if necessary to save the life of the mother but that it should generally be avoided; the decision is usually left to the family. Many Orthodox rabbis support pro-life politics. Reform, Conservative, and Reconstructionist Jews take a pro-choice position by viewing threats to the mother's health in the broadest possible way. American Jews are overwhelmingly pro-choice. Muslims generally have supported abortion as a medical procedure when the health of the mother is in question but otherwise have discouraged it. Islamic doctrine concerning the role of women in society and within their families, and the Islamic condemnation of extramarital sex, all combine to make many Muslim theologians take conservative positions. Yet by no means is this a unanimous view.

The denominational differences in attitudes toward abortion are echoed to a lesser extent in the attitudes of elites. Studies have shown that votes on abortion in the U.S. Congress and in state legislatures are at least somewhat predictable by taking into consideration the religious affiliation of individual members. A significant number of Catholic legislators, however, support pro-choice policies.

Conservatives and Secularists

Religion has been a source of the political debate on abortion in the United States and in other countries in several ways. First, religious denominations have provided support in the form of money, infrastructure, and official doctrine for both sides of the conflict. Second, religious activists have been visible on both sides of the debate. Third, religious rhetoric and values have been used in framing the debate. Pro-life forces, however, have received significantly greater support from organized religion than has the pro-choice side. Churches have provided the resources to form pro-life groups and lent their facilities for meetings, endorsed the cause from the pulpit, and instructed their lobbyists to work to restrict access to abortion.

Indeed, the activist struggle over abortion is often portrayed as a struggle between religious conservatives and secularists. Kristin Luker's classic study of abortion activists in California, for example, found that pro-life activists were intensely religious and disproportionately Catholic converts, while many pro-choice activists lacked formal ties to organized religion. The intense religiosity of the pro-life activists led them to view unplanned pregnancies as a gift from God and never an obstacle to career or family goals.

Among nonactivist citizens, this split between secular and religious citizens is smaller, but within every religious tradition (including those that take an official pro-choice position), frequent attenders at religious services are more likely to oppose abortion than are those who attend less often. Thus, for all groups, strong commitment to religious values appears to be associated with greater opposition to abortion. Some researchers suggest that this connection between strong commitment and opposition to abortion is because frequent attenders are likely to encounter pro-life activists in church services. Others argue, however, that those who frequently attend church are likely to be traditional in their views of sexual morality and to believe that events (such as unexpected pregnancies) are God's will.

Within every religious group there is at least some debate about the official doctrine on abortion. As new technologies continue to transform the possibilities of childbirth and abortion, it seems likely that the religious debate on abortion will continue.

See also *Feminism; Lobbying, Religious; Medicine; Morality; Natural law; Sexuality.*

Clyde Wilcox

BIBLIOGRAPHY

Bowen, Donna Lee. "Abortion, Islam, and the 1994 Cairo Population Conference." *International Journal of Middle East Studies* 29 (1997): 161–184.
Connery, John. *Abortion: The Development of the Roman Catholic Perspective.* Chicago: Loyola University Press, 1977.
Cook, Elizabeth Adell, Ted G. Jelen, and Clyde Wilcox. *Between Two Absolutes: Public Opinion and the Politics of Abortion.* Boulder, Colo.: Westview Press, 1992.
Ellington, Mark. *The Cutting Edge: How Churches Speak on Social Issues.* Grand Rapids, Mich.: Eerdmans, 1993.
Luker, Kristin. *Abortion and the Politics of Motherhood.* Berkeley: University of California Press, 1984.
Noonan, John T., Jr. "An Almost Absolute Value in History." In *The Morality of Abortion: Legal and Historical Perspectives,* edited by John T. Noonan Jr. Cambridge: Harvard University Press, 1970.

Adventism

See *Seventh-day Adventism*

al-Afghani, Jamal al-Din

Muslim reformer and anticolonialist. Jamal al-Din al-Afghani (1838 or 1839–1897) was one of the first to restate the Muslim tradition in response to Western encroachments. He reinterpreted Islam, stressing such modern values as activism, human reason, and the need for political and military strength and unity. Seeking these values in Islamic traditions, he could influence believers more than could those who simply appropriated Western ideas. He is a parent of later trends that reject both pure tradition and pure Westernism. Best known as a pan-Islamist, Afghani is also identified with Islamic modernism, Islamic revivalism, and even pan-Arabism and other nationalisms. Although his influence is often exaggerated, he remains one of the world's best-remembered Islamic activists and thinkers, and his style of interpreting the Islamic past in modern or nationalist terms has been increasingly popular throughout the Muslim world.

Although Afghani usually claimed that he was born and brought up in Afghanistan, evidence is overwhelming that he was born and raised in Iran and had a Shi'i, not a Sunni, education. His followers, who are mostly Sunnis, often discount the evidence of his Iranian origin and Shi'i education. Iranians call him Asadabadi, after the town of his birth.

From his first appearance in the political record in Afghanistan, in 1864, Afghani expressed strongly anti-British views. He encouraged the Afghan emir to join Russia to fight the British. This anti-British feeling was probably aroused during his first trip to India during the time of the Indian mutiny of 1857. Anti-British agitation continued to be a leitmotif during most of his life, and he used language later identified with anti-imperialism, though he was rarely severe in his criticisms against French or Russian imperialism.

Afghani came into public view in Istanbul in 1869–1870, where he was appointed to the Council on Education. In a public lecture he showed his debt to the great Islamic philosophers like the controversial theologian and physician Abu Ali Husayn Ibn Sina (980–1037), known to the West as Avicenna, who were still taught in religious schools in Iran but were seen as heretical by Sunni clerics. Afghani's talk was taken as an excuse to expel him and dismiss the head of the new, secular university. He went to Egypt, where he helped to educate a generation of Egyptian reformist and nationalist intellectuals, including Muhammad Abduh, a prominent religious reformer.

After being expelled from Egypt by the new khedive, Taufiq, in 1879, Afghani went to Hyderabad, India, where he wrote several important articles and his only treatise, *The Refutation of the Materialists*. In 1883 he went to London and then Paris, where he entered into debate with Ernest Renan on Islam and science. Writing for a Western audience, Afghani abandoned the religious tone he used in the Muslim world and criticized religion as limiting and intolerant, although he regarded it as needed by the nonintellectual masses. In 1884 he made his first major appearance as a pan-Islamist in an Arabic newspaper co-edited with Muhammad Abduh. The newspaper, *al-'Urwa al Wuthqa* ("The Strongest Link"), was distributed throughout the Muslim world.

After involvement in London with the schemes of a pro-Arab Englishman, Wilfrid Blunt, to settle with the Sudanese Mahdi, Afghani spent two years in Russia trying to get Russian leaders to start a war with Britain. In late 1889 he returned to Iran, where he helped to inspire agitation against a series of economic concessions to the British. Blaming a fiery anticoncession leaflet on Afghani, the shah expelled him to Iraq in early 1891. There he contacted the leader of the Shi'i *ulama* (Muslim scholars), who became a central figure in a successful uprising against a British tobacco concession in 1891–1892.

Afghani accepted an invitation from the Ottoman sultan Abdulhamid to go to Istanbul, where he spent the last five years of his life. Although he was not allowed to write or speak publicly, the sultan did encourage him to try to persuade Shi'i clergy through Iranians in Istanbul to support the sultan as the head of all Islam. Resentful against the shah for expelling him, Afghani encouraged a disciple to assassinate Naser al-Din Shah in Iran, in 1896. He himself died of cancer in 1897.

Although many of Afghani's ideas were borrowed, and his activism fluctuated between appeals to the powerful and appeals to the masses against the powerful, his example, his writings, and his myth have inspired a wide variety of figures and movements in the Muslim world.

See also *Islam; Muhammad Abduh; Muslim encounters with the West.*

Nikki R. Keddie

BIBLIOGRAPHY

Keddie, Nikki R. *An Islamic Response to Imperialism: Political and Religious Writings of Sayyid Jamal ad-Din "al-Afghani."* Berkeley: University of California Press, 1968.

———. *Sayyid Jamal ad-Din "al-Afghani": A Political Biography.* Berkeley: University of California Press, 1972.

Kedourie, Elie. *Afghani and Abduh: An Essay on Religious Unbelief and Political Activism in Modern Islam.* Portland, Ore.: Frank Cass, 1997.

Afghanistan

Located in Central Asia at the crossroads between Europe, East Asia, and the Indian subcontinent, Afghanistan has been a gateway of invasions from the days of Alexander the Great in the fourth century B.C.E. to the Soviet intervention in the 1980s *(see map, p. 588)*. The country owes its existence to the martial character of its people and, since the eighteenth century, to the fact that it formed a buffer between Russia and the British Empire in India. The country was ruled both by the sword and by Islamic law.

Since Ahmad Shah founded the State of Afghanistan in 1747, religion has limited the powers of tribal rulers, kings, and presidents. Islamic law *(shari'a),* administered by religious functionaries *(ulama),* is the law of the state, which even the rulers of a short-lived Marxist regime (1978–1992) had to respect. But there always existed a dichotomy between customary law (the "king's law") and the *shari'a* ("God's law"), with the latter increasingly relegated to the sphere of family law.

Ahmad Shah, who ruled until 1773, had absolute power. The courts were in the hands of the *ulama,* but the death penalty had to be approved by the king or a governor. Ahmad Shah forbade the mutilation of limbs, a traditional form of punishment, and drafted a legal code, though it was not enacted. Little was changed until the time of Amir Abd al-Rahman (1888–1901), who centralized all power in his hands. The "Iron Amir" claimed temporal and spiritual powers, and the only restraint on his arbitrary rule was the obligation to conform to the rules of Islamic law. Tribal revolts, often instigated by the *ulama,* were severely suppressed.

A process of secularization began with King Amanullah (1919–1929), who proclaimed a constitution in 1924 that enumerated the prerogatives of the ruler and the rights of the ruled. It formed the basis for democratization under Zahir Shah (1933–1973), whose reforms culminated in the promulgation of the 1964 constitution. But Zahir Shah's efforts were impeded by the country's poverty and illiteracy. Universal education, envisioned by the constitution, was an aim rather than a reality, and Afghanistan remained largely illiterate. The introduction of secular schools, in addition to the traditional mosque system, produced two essentially hostile elites: eventually the modernist side assumed political power.

Muhammad Daud, a cousin of the king, staged a coup in 1973 and proclaimed a republic; Daud set up a one-party government, a "democracy based on social justice." His con-

stitution, promulgated on February 14, 1977, was intended to give power to the majority—farmers, workers, and youth. Land reforms were to be carried out and cooperatives were to be encouraged. Women were to enjoy equal rights and obligations, and every Afghan citizen eighteen years or older was to have the right to vote. When some of his Marxist followers overthrew Daud in 1978, reformist policies were continued. But a reaction of *mujahedin* ("holy warriors") defeated the Afghan Marxists in April 1992, after a futile intervention by the Soviet Union (1980–1989).

Then followed a civil war between the victorious forces in which the Taliban (students of Islamic schools) became the dominant force. Since their emergence in November 1994, the Taliban have captured about two-thirds of the country and established a theocratic regime. Mulla Muhammad Omar was proclaimed "Commander of the Faithful," and a government was established in which the leaders were members of the *ulama*. Women, who had been active in the professions, were no longer permitted to carry out their duties; they were forced to wear a veil covering the entire body. Schools for girls were closed; radio and television were permitted only to broadcast religious programs. Music, photography, and various games were forbidden, and men were enjoined to grow full beards and wear traditional dress. Attendance at prayers became obligatory. Islamic punishments, long discontinued, were reinstated: adultery was punished with stoning, and the penalty exacted for theft was mutilation. The Taliban, however, were selective in their persecutions. They failed to stop the lucrative production of drugs, making Afghanistan one of the world's biggest opium suppliers.

The Taliban's harsh interpretation of Islam and their totalitarian policies make it unlikely that Western states will recognize the new regime in the near future. For the first time in its history, much of Afghanistan is ruled as a theocracy, and the Taliban's success has encouraged Islamist radicals throughout the world to carry on the revolution to establish an Islamic state.

See also *Banna, Hasan al-, Fundamentalism; Islam; Mawdudi; Qutb, Sayyid; Theocracy.*

Ludwig W. Adamec

BIBLIOGRAPHY

Adamec, Ludwig W. *Historical Dictionary of Afghanistan.* Lanham, Md., and London: Scarecrow Press, 1997.
Dupree, Louis. *Afghanistan.* Princeton: Princeton University Press, 1973.

Esposito, John L., ed. *Voices of Resurgent Islam.* New York and Oxford: Oxford University Press, 1983.

Roy, Olivier. *Afghanistan: From Holy War to Civil War.* Princeton: Darwin Press, 1995.

Rubin, Barnett R. *The Fragmentation of Afghanistan: State Formation and Collapse in the International System.* New Haven and London: Yale University Press, 1995.

Africa, Christian

Christian Africa has a continuous history from the second century C.E., antedating the expansion brought by Roman Catholic missionaries since the fifteenth century and Protestant missionaries since the eighteenth century. Christianity in Africa has since its early manifestations in Ethiopia tended to develop distinctively African features. The missionary period (which was coming to an end in the late twentieth century) provided the basis for much of Africa's educational and health services. The dissemination of Christian ideas has had a profound effect on the political systems of the African states, just as the states have influenced the development of the Christian churches.

Within the Roman Empire

In the parts of Africa that lay within the Roman Empire (the Mediterranean coastlands and their hinterlands up to the Atlas Mountains and the desert, and Lower and Upper Egypt), Christianity spread rapidly as a popular movement, challenging the official cult. After the Roman Empire granted favored status to Christianity early in the fourth century, Africa produced expressions of the faith reflecting local political and social priorities, often at variance with the official forms. The form of Christianity called "Donatist" became the majority religion in Roman Africa (modern Tunisia) and in the less Romanized areas westward; it eventually declined through its failure to take hold outside Africa. From the fifth century Egypt largely defied imperial pressure for confessional unity in favor of its own confession, often called "monophysite." This confession, influenced by Egyptian thought and religious practice, described the union of the human and divine natures in Christ in a way that to Western Christians appeared to undermine his humanity.

Outside the Roman Empire

Several African states outside the Roman Empire also adopted Christianity. Most important was Aksum in the Horn of Africa, whose king converted in the fourth century. The Upper Nile states of Nobatia, Makkurah, and Alwah united in a single Nubian Christian state in 710. Here too the conversion of the monarchs led to the official adoption of Christianity. All these states maintained ecclesiastical relationships (usually monophysite) with Christians in the Roman Empire.

The North African Christian communities dwindled away over several chaotic centuries, the Muslim Arabs being the last of many invaders. In Egypt, where alienation from the Roman Empire led monophysite Christians at first to see Arab rule as liberation, Christians gradually passed from majority to hereditary minority with *dhimmi* status. Dhimmis were Jewish, Christian, or other religious communities under Islamic sovereignty. Although accorded political security, dhimmis were subject to restrictions on religious practice and sometimes to civil disabilities. Nubia, flowering in the tenth century, retained its Christian status until around 1450. Aksum became the kernel of an inland Ethiopian state.

Ethiopian Christianity

Ethiopian Christianity, developed in the highlands, was a unique blend of Judeo-Semitic and African elements and a vital constituent of Ethiopian identity. Ethiopian territorial expansion took with it Ethiopian Christianity, Amharic language and culture, and a distinctive Ethiopic tradition of literature and learning. Despite frequent isolation Ethiopia maintained a link with Christians elsewhere by bringing its *abuna* (bishop) from the (monophysite) church of Alexandria, in Egypt. Down to the last emperor, Haile Selassie II (reigned 1928–1974), the monarchy (claiming descent from the biblical Solomon) was a periodic source of reform of the church. Equally, the church was a periodic brake on the power of the monarchy, which it has outlived. In the nineteenth and twentieth centuries Ethiopia, as representing an Africa primordially Christian, became a powerful symbol elsewhere in Africa and in the Caribbean. Many African religious movements, especially those asserting a Christianity independent of Western domination, have adopted the name Ethiopian.

Afro-Portuguese Christianity

The Portuguese arrival in Africa in the late fifteenth century initiated an ongoing relationship with Europe and, through the Atlantic slave trade, with the Americas. In a pan-Christian alliance Portuguese troops helped Ethiopia to survive a fierce Muslim *jihad* in the 1540s; Ethiopia shook off a subsequent attempt to bring its church into Latin Christianity. In Angola and Mozambique Christian communities arose from Portuguese settlement, occupation, and intermarriage. In other areas the Portuguese tried to negotiate agreements with African rulers that included the adoption of Christianity. There was at least one notable success: the elective monarchy of Mbanza Kongo at the Congo mouth, whose king accepted baptism in 1491, developed as an African Christian state, uncomfortable with its relations with Portugal and seeking direct links with Rome.

The slave trade, adopted into the economies of African coastal states, produced a vast permanent transatlantic African population. In Brazil an Afro-Catholic leadership emerged with some influence in the Portuguese capital of Lisbon. The diplomacy of one such leader, Lourenço da Silva de Mendonça, "procurator-general of the congregation of Blacks and Mulattos of Our Lady," reached beyond the Portuguese court to the Vatican and secured an explicit, if ultimately ineffectual, papal condemnation of African slavery in 1686.

Early Protestant Christianity

As Portugal's power faded, North European powers succeeded to much of her commercial interest in Africa. In the seventeenth century the Dutch established a colony at the Cape of Good Hope; by the eighteenth, Britain had become the chief carrier for the Atlantic slave trade. These Protestant nations showed little official enthusiasm for the Portuguese policy of extending Christendom. Thus the early Protestant missions to the Khoi, the aboriginal people of the Cape, were by 1742 effectively squeezed out by European settlers.

The Protestant missionary movement combined evangelicalism and humanitarianism in strong opposition to slavery. The establishment of the colony of Sierra Leone (founded 1787; refounded 1792; crown colony of Great Britain, 1808) was intended both to demonstrate the viability of an African economy without slavery and to provide a base for missions in the interior. Its first stable population consisted of Christian Afro-Americans, former slaves. It was later strengthened, after British abolition of its slave trade in 1807, with recaptives from the slave ships, brought to Christianity by missionary effort. Sierra Leone helped to inspire a parallel settlement of Christian Africans from America in Liberia.

The settlements in Sierra Leone and Liberia strengthened the concept of an African Christian civilization—free of

slavery, African-led, but in all essentials resembling the Protestant West. The most influential statement of this vision was Thomas Fowell Buxton's *African Slave Trade and Its Remedy* (1840), which argued for British policy in Africa to stimulate agriculture, stifle the slave trade, and develop an independent economy. Suffering Africa could be redeemed by drawing out her own resources, economic and human, and could share in the interrelated blessings of Christianity, commerce, and civilization. The Niger Expedition of 1841, which was intended to give this policy expression, led to the loss of so many lives that the government quickly abandoned the project, but Buxton's ideals continued to influence missions and, even more, the Christian populations in West Africa and the Caribbean, producing the seed of a Christian pan-Africanism. In the Cape similar humanitarian ideals brought the chief spokesman of missions, John Philip (1777–1851), into sharp conflict with the settlers, both Dutch and English speaking, who saw those ideals as a threat to their interests.

Outside the small European colonies early nineteenth century missions entered into relationships with traditional African states. Frequently they worked with multiple agendas, providing a service desired by the state, such as Western education, while seeking to gather a Christian community within it and to influence social customs in such matters as slave trading, war, or ritual killing. African states, which often found missionaries useful intermediaries with whites, reacted variously. Calabar accepted a gradual modification of religious and social institutions; Abeokuta opened the way to a Buxtonian economic policy and other aspects of modernization. King Moshoeshoe (c. 1786–1870), while slow to identify personally with Christianity, built the Sotho nation by mission-guided religious and social reform; Chief Khama III enthusiastically embraced Christianity as a powerful integrative force in his Tswana state. In Buganda the party identifying with Protestantism emerged victorious in a power struggle with Catholic and Muslim rivals.

Other African states resisted all attempts by Christian missionaries to implement change; traditional rulers often found the Christian community, living in open breach of many established African customs, threatening to their authority.

Colonial Influences

The rapid European occupation of Africa after 1880 was generally welcomed by the missions as providing conditions in which Christianity could spread freely. Missionary endeavor expanded under colonial rule. Protestant missions flourished most in British territory, Catholic missions in French territory, and both in the Belgian Congo. Colonial conditions created higher demand for Western education, a regular feature of mission activity. The colonial state, always on restrictive budgets, found it economical to use missions to provide the infrastructure for education and health services. With the articulation in the 1920s of a British government policy of subsidizing (and inspecting) mission schools, missions increasingly saw education as a means of influencing Africans in a time of social change, a view reflected in the Le Zoute conference of the International Missionary Council (1926), which urged missions to greater investment in education.

Elsewhere, missionary and colonial interests often collided. Administrative considerations restricted mission entry in areas under Muslim rulers; a substantial Islamic advance followed in Nigeria and Sudan, and missions tended to complain that colonial governments favored Islam. Nevertheless, in spite of these obstacles to missionary work, the International Missionary Council helped to mitigate the conditions of forced labor in East Africa and to secure from Britain a declaration of the importance of African interests in Kenya, which also had white and Indian populations.

Colonial rulers tended to marginalize the educated African leadership that had emerged in the earlier "emancipation phase" of missions and had little sympathy with their pan-African ideals. Moreover, missions in the colonial period were less ready than their predecessors to put Africans in full charge. Some Africans, frustrated, established independent African-led institutions. Nevertheless, church structures gave Africans leadership opportunities not open to them in most other spheres, and social and political networks wider than the locality or ethnic group. Mission education exposed people to ideas—some of biblical origin, some of secular—that strengthened desires for self-determination. During and after the First World War, a series of movements led by African prophets aroused hostility in colonial governments and ambivalence in missions. In inspiration and intent, these movements represented African appropriations of Christian doctrine and principles and their application to contemporary life.

Emergence of African Nation-States

The dissemination of Christian ideas, mission education, and experience of church life contributed to the movement for decolonization and the emergence of the new African states, which came into being after World War II. However, few mission churches (as distinct from their individual members) were active in the independence movement. The new states followed colonial, not traditional or ethnic, boundaries; most were religiously plural and, outside the Islamic north, adopted secular institutions. (Botswana, an exception, had an established church.) Early national leaders, frequently from mission schools, articulated themes from Christian teaching. The churches acknowledged responsibilities in "nation building" through education, health and social services, and moral and spiritual influence. Western Christian missions, rapidly declining in significance locally, were prominent in the movement for Western economic and humanitarian aid to Africa.

The mission situation under colonial rule did not encourage a steady church critique of government, and this critique developed slowly. It emerged first in Ghana, the first new state, originally on specifically religious issues (for example, President Kwame Nkrumah's use of libation to the ancestors at state ceremonies). It intensified when governments tried to take over education and broadened as issues of injustice, corruption, and abuse of power multiplied. The vehicles of criticism included the national Councils of Churches (representing the older Protestant churches) and the Catholic Bishops' Conferences. In Uganda even churchmen who were identified with the traditionally otherworldly revival movement became politically conscious under the regime of Idi Amin in the 1970s. Social and political concern was equally reflected at the regional and national levels in the conferences and publications of the All Africa Conference of Churches and its Association of Member Episcopal Conferences of East Africa. Autocratic rulers responded with favors to African independent, evangelized, and pentecostal churches outside the Protestant mainstream represented by the councils.

The late 1980s and early 1990s saw movements for democratization overthrowing many dictatorial or oppressive regimes. In Madagascar and Malawi the churches were direct agents in effecting political change. In Ghana, Kenya, and even in Muslim Mali they highlighted governmental abuses. In Benin, Congo-Brazzaville, Gabon, Togo, Zaire (now the Democratic Republic of the Congo), and Zambia, church leaders provided the machinery for the transition to democracy. In many countries the churches were the main, or even only, form of civil society still functioning vigorously.

South Africa offers a special case of the democratization process. Here a highly localized thread of Calvinistic theory within the Dutch Reformed Church, one centered on race and the hierarchy of power, was used by a white government to legitimize permanent white rule of the other races. Reformed churches outside South Africa denounced this theory as heretical, as did most black Reformed Christians. Many members of English-speaking churches in South Africa, while not espousing the theory, contentedly accepted the practice. A Christian alternative to the apartheid doctrine was pressed by dissident Reformed ministers, notably Beyers Naude, and affirmed by the South African Council of Churches. For several years the churches, despite many of their white members, formed the most effective legal opposition to the white South African government. Among black Christians several streams of "Black Theology" developed. Some of these simply stood apartheid theology on its head; others affirmed continuity with the established Reformed tradition. All stressed the God-given value and dignity of black identity. In Rhodesia (later Zimbabwe), which entrenched white rule without the ideological underpinning of apartheid, some, but not all, the leaders of the black nationalist movements identified with the Christian churches.

Two African nations reflect particularly complex relations of religion and identity. Nigeria has perhaps a quarter of the continent's population and roughly equal numbers of Muslims and Christians. Christianity was part of the self-identity of the southeastern territory of Biafra in its secession and the subsequent civil war (1966–1970). Heavy Islamic dominance in the north has encouraged several attempts to make Nigeria an Islamic state; the contiguity of Muslim and Christian populations in the middle belt makes that area a frequent center of religious tension and political struggle. In Sudan power has always lain with the Arabized north, which sees itself as part of the Islamic world. The quite different identities of many of the African peoples in the south of the country have been sharpened by the widespread adoption of Christianity. The area has known decades of bitter warfare.

The rapid spread of Christianity in sub-Saharan Africa, which has taken place since the mid-nineteenth century under precolonial, colonial, and postcolonial conditions alike, and Christianity's increasing adaptation to African society, are likely to remain significant factors in political developments in the continent.

See also *Africa, West: The Mande world; African independent churches; Colonialism; Egypt; Ghana; Kenya; Missionaries; Nigeria; Sudan; Tunisia; Zimbabwe.*

Andrew Walls

BIBLIOGRAPHY

Bayart, Jean-Francois. *The State in Africa: The Politics of the Belly.* London and New York: Longman, 1993.

Elphick, Richard, and Rodney Davenport, eds. *Christianity in South Africa: A Political, Social, and Cultural History.* Berkeley and Los Angeles: University of California Press, 1997.

Fyfe, Christopher, and Andrew Walls, eds. *Christianity in Africa in the 1990s.* Edinburgh: Centre of Asian Studies, 1996.

Gifford, Paul, ed. *The Christian Churches and the Democratisation of Africa.* Leiden: Brill, 1995.

Gray, Richard. *Black Christians and White Missionaries.* New Haven: Yale University Press, 1990.

Hastings, Adrian. *The Church in Africa: 1450–1950.* Oxford: Clarendon Press; New York: Oxford University Press, 1994.

———. *A History of African Christianity, 1950–1975.* Cambridge and New York: Cambridge University Press, 1979.

Sanneh, Lamin. *Piety and Power: Muslims and Christians in West Africa.* Maryknoll, N.Y.: Orbis Books, 1996.

Taddesse Tamrat. *Church and State in Ethiopia.* Oxford: Clarendon Press, 1972).

Africa, West: The Mande world

The Mande world is an area in sub-Saharan West Africa that covers large parts of Mali, Guinea, Guinea-Bissau, The Gambia, Senegal, Côte d'Ivoire, and Sierra Leone. It is inhabited by linguistically and culturally related ethnic groups who share the memory of a common heritage and political unity.

The ethnic groups living in the Mande world—among them the Bamana (Bambara), Maninka (Malinke), Mandingo, Soninke, and Jula (Dioula)—trace their descent to ancient or medieval empires such as Ghana, Wagadu, and Mali-Mande, which are celebrated in epic oral traditions. Scholars generally associate the founding of the medieval Mali empire with some of the Mande peoples and note its central place in the political history of West Africa, based on reports from medieval Muslim writers. Probably through expansion and trade, state policies, and internal dynamics, Mande cultural traits have spread over large parts of West Africa and provide the basis for national and ethnic identities.

Cosmology and Social Organization

Traditional religion in the Mande world was characterized by a great variety in ritual practices. Trees, wells, bushes,

and stones could be sacred sites devoted to sacrifices. These communal rituals expressed concern for the fertility of the land and the veneration of ancestors. Nowadays, many expressions of traditional religion have become marginal and have even disappeared in large parts of the Mande world; socioreligious rituals are practiced more extensively in communities to the south.

Ceremonies involving carved masks and vibrant dances, for example, were commonly performed to celebrate the harvest, rites of passage, or merely social well-being. Komo societies, in which blacksmiths perform a central role, also observe a well-known set of ceremonies related to initiation into esoteric knowledge. They, however, face opposition because of the growing influence of Islam and changes in wider society. Most notable are changing labor relations

within extended families and other transformations associated with the shift from self-sufficiency to a cash-crop economy. Nonetheless, hunters' societies, another widespread socioreligious form of organization, flourish and attract people from both urban and rural areas in spite of the fact that game has almost disappeared in large parts of the Mande world because of environmental deterioration and growing population.

The Mande world is characterized by an ideology based on social division in three status categories—noble freemen, slaves, and artisans *(nyamakalaw)*. To this last group belong blacksmiths, female potters, bards, and leather workers. Membership in a social category is ascriptive. Since the formal abolition of slavery under colonial rule, the tripartite division has gradually transformed itself into an opposition between freemen-agriculturists and nyamakalaw, although national charters that stress the equality of all people deny this distinction.

A central concept in Mande culture is *nyama,* which might best be translated as "transformative power" (some would even suggest "occult power"). Nyama is released by certain actions, such as offerings of food, the killing of animals, and nyamakalaw activities. Only specialists, the Mande people believe, can cope with nyama. The concept of nyama is explicitly incorporated into the social identity of the nyamakalaw. Nyamakalaw groups clearly identified with these powers are blacksmiths, potters, and leather workers, who transform raw material into usable products, and bards, who achieve a similar end by attributing historically rooted identities to individuals, thus structuring society. Hunters also release nyama in their activities but are not considered nyamakalaw in large measure because the killing of game occurs outside the borders of villages. Despite their invaluable contributions to society, nyamakalaw have an ambivalent status in the Mande world because they release nyama within the borders of the village.

Political Organization and National Identities

Although the Mande people may be historically connected to great empires, their political organization in the nineteenth century did not resemble that of a centralized state. Society was segmented, petty kings and war leaders were numerous, and rule was not direct over a territory but indirect and over people. Elaborate royal rituals, such as existed in the Benin and Ashante kingdoms of the West African coast, were not practiced. At every level of society, people forged alliances relying on kinship relations as the basis for collaboration.

Descent from Sunjata, founder of the Mali empire, was used most often in creating political alliances. In the republic of Mali, where Mande groups have dominated politically, they expressed this solidarity by renaming their independent nation Mali in 1960 (it was formerly the French colony of Sudan). Other nation-states where Mande ethnic groups form a large part of the population also trace their nations' history to Sunjata; Mande cultural concepts and images have become dominant in national politics in Guinea and The Gambia, as well as in Mali, as a means of building feelings of national unity. Radio programs, records, films, dance performances, and theater plays were used to link the people to the heritage of Sunjata and the Mali empire.

Mande solidarities also operate below the level of national politics. The most obvious means of appeal to a shared history is the patronymic. There are relatively few patronymics in West Africa—within the limits of one region, large parts of the population may bear patronymics such as Keita, Traore, Camara, Diawara, or Toure or patronymics related to these according to oral tradition. Each of them traces its origin from Sunjata himself or from a legendary male hero who helped him. In this way, the past lives in the present.

Such stories about the ancestors are sometimes wrongly portrayed as a part of traditional religion. Indeed, families used to have cults celebrating famous male ancestors within their own patrilineage, but such expressions of traditional religion must not be confused with the status and glory expressed by and represented by the patronymic. The great deeds remembered and evoked by the patronymic are prerequisites for establishing and maintaining social relationships with non-kin in all levels of society.

Mande patronymics offer the postcolonial governments vehicles for constructing historical national identities that appeal to every single person as a member of a specific social group. In this way nation-states seek the legitimacy that would befall the successor regimes to the great medieval empires, the Mali empire in particular. Governments in these countries of West Africa employ bards to instill feelings of national unity.

The Kamabolon ceremony in Kangaba in southern Mali is one example of this complex relationship between heritage and politics. In this traditional septennial restoration of the Kamabolon sanctuary, the authorized version of the Sunjata epic is performed in the Kamabolon. Outsiders are not allowed in this performance, and the ultimate truth thus remains a secret. The Kamabolon ceremony was once a regional event in which the deceased kings were celebrated and a new age group was inaugurated, but now the Malian government financially supports the ceremony. Thus the sanctuary has acquired the status of a national emblem, expressing, among other things, Sunjata's role as the founder of the nation.

Islam

Postindependence regimes, dictatorial or not, have apparently not been eager to promote traditional religion. Islam increasingly is becoming a feature of society. West African ruling classes had already practiced Islam at least since the eighteenth and nineteenth century *jihads,* or holy wars, which, originating from different areas and reflecting the charisma of their leaders, successively spread over West Africa. After El Haji Oumar Tall's mid-nineteenth century jihad, Samori Toure—a Malinke of humble origin—organized a jihad that greatly influenced the Mande world. In the second half of the nineteenth century he conquered large parts of today's Guinea, Mali, and Côte d'Ivoire before he was captured by the French colonial forces in 1898. Samori's war made the Mande people more open to conversion to Islam, although traditional religious rituals were abandoned on a grand scale only after the 1950s, when Islam became the hegemonic religion in the Mande world.

Islam is not the official state religion in any of the Mande nation-states, but Islam's symbolism is present in every level of civil society. Fundamentalism is a growing political factor in some urban areas. Islamic organizations and practices have affected society politically in very different ways. For instance, in Senegal Islamic brotherhoods such as the Mourides help mold national politics, and in Mali some Muslim spiritual leaders are considered to be a powerful force in national politics. These *marabouts* are religious specialists trained in knowledge of the Qur'an, as well as in traditional medicine, the making of amulets, and occult science. They embody the complex relationship between state, Islam, and traditional religion in West Africa. Sometimes maraboutic knowledge gives way even to a kind of counterculture. This is, for instance, the case with the Guinean marabout Suleyman Kante, who invented a writing system for his own Maninka language, called Nko, and set up a literacy program that is gaining ground far beyond Guinea. This literacy program produces texts on religion, history, and medicine, thus clearly representing the complexities of the present-day Mande world.

See also *African traditional religions; Islam; Jihad; Senegal.*

Jan Jansen

BIBLIOGRAPHY

Austen, R. A., ed. *In Search of Sunjata: The Mande Epic as History, Literature, and Performance.* Bloomington: Indiana University Press, 1998.

Conrad, D. C., and B. E. Frank, eds. *Status and Identity in West Africa: Nyamakalaw of Mande.* Bloomington: Indiana University Press, 1995.

Dieterlen, G. *Essai sur la religion Bambara.* Brussels: Institute of Sociology and Social Anthropology, Brussels University, 1988.

Hanson, J. H. *Migration, Jihad, and Muslim Authority in West Africa.* Bloomington: Indiana University Press, 1996.

Launay, R. *Beyond the Stream: Islam and Society in a West African Town.* Berkeley: University of California Press, 1992.

Levtzion, N. *Ancient Ghana and Mali.* London: Methuen, 1973.

African American experience

The civil rights movement, a social and political movement in the United States to desegregate public institutions and transportation and to provide civil protections to African Americans in voting and employment, was one of the most significant events of the African American experience.

From labor organizations to women's clubs to citizens' groups, social and political activism in the United States during the twentieth century has had many bearers. One of the most significant has been the awakened political religiosity of African American religious communities. As a source of indigenous strength for the civil rights movements of the 1950s and 1960s, this political religiosity was at the center of effective civil resistance. At difficult yet pivotal moments of America's social and political history, it also provided a platform for cultivating new leaders, essential for radical new movements—in racial liberation, interracial cooperation, and feminism.

Indigenous Strength: Black Women and the Church

Among the key organizational strengths of the civil rights movement, three indigenous collectives were critical to the origins of its social activism: the southern branches of the National Association for the Advancement of Colored People (NAACP), especially the Legal Defense and Education Fund within it; the southern black colleges and the many determined and hopeful students; and southern black Baptist churches and the thousands of church women who made up the majority of the parishioners. Front and center of what is commonly known as the origins of the civil rights movement and the heart and soul of the political activism of the 1950s and 1960s is this meeting of the black church and black women. In launching an effective political mobilization, each of these three original collectives occupied an important niche. The NAACP chapters and its legal unit focused on desegregating public schools; the black colleges worked on integrating lunch counters. The black church fought simultaneously for the desegregation of public institutions and public transportation.

As the center of most black communities, the black church was a likely place to foment political activism. It had financial resources, well-respected community leaders, a stable physical structure to hold meetings, and, most important, thousands of members who would be drawn into action. It was the ideal location to educate the community, open lines

Future U.S. Supreme Court justice Thurgood Marshall, fourth from right, and other NAACP Legal Defense and Education Fund attorneys for the plaintiffs in the landmark school desegregation decision, Brown v. Board of Education *(1954), congratulate each other on their monumental victory.*

of communication, and build networks. The black church was a logical center for political action because it represented a common space where similar people with similar grievances and like experiences could come together and push for needed societal and political reforms. It is the importance of the black church within black communities that made it an essential and critical factor in the civil rights movement.

Similarly, the presence of the thousands of black women in churches across the South provided the civil rights movement with the necessary numbers of people to hold effective boycotts and marches. Many of these church women like their male counterparts were frustrated and angry with the treatment they received in public spaces. They found energy by sharing their grievances and becoming politically active. This activism engendered the demonstrations during the early days of the movement. The lives of southern black women in the 1950s were filled with hard work, low pay,

long days, and little respect. The racial indignities they endured for years could no longer be tolerated. The church, although often a needed haven and escape for blacks, had not always or even typically been the source of political activism. However, the decades during which political engagement had been shunned gradually gave way to a new age of political involvement.

A now well-documented and well-known bus incident in Montgomery, Alabama, provided the necessary spark that transformed ordinary church women into activists. One day in 1955 Rosa Parks, a black woman, was arrested for refusing to vacate her seat aboard a Montgomery city bus, as was law and custom if one was needed by a white patron. In response, the black church and its women sponsored a very effective boycott movement that eventually led not only to the integration of the city buses but also spawned movements in other cities. The church of the Reverend Ralph Abernathy, a Baptist minister, became the center of the boycott movement. It is there that parishioners were educated on the issues and organized for the boycott. And it is there that a young Reverend Martin Luther King Jr. began his ascent to the leadership of the civil rights movement.

Political Action

The use of civil disobedience in the Birmingham, Alabama, campaign in 1963 and in the march from Selma, Alabama, to Montgomery in 1965 highlights one of the most effective tactics employed by the civil rights movement. This tactic required demonstrators to place themselves in cities where they knew they would elicit immediate and often brutal reaction from hostile whites. The tactic enabled parishioners to actualize Jesus' teaching to "turn the other cheek," thus building a political religiosity out of religious religiosity. The sit-ins, marches, and demonstrations provoked the most vicious of responses. The likes of Bull Conner, the police chief in Birmingham, and his counterpart Jim Clark in Selma were ruthless in their attempt to retain the status quo of segregation. An increasingly receptive media, however, etched into the public memory the assaults on the marchers. Vivid images were shown of fire hoses and police dogs attacking peaceful demonstrators, including children. The spectacle of these events put pressure on President Lyndon B. Johnson and Congress to pass the Civil Rights Act of 1964 and the Voting Rights Act of 1965, both considered the high points of the civil rights movement.

As was the case with the Montgomery bus boycott, the march from Selma to Montgomery and the Birmingham campaign for justice and to end racial segregation were sponsored and led by the black religious community. With the Southern Christian Leadership Conference and its members spearheading these demonstrations and the thousands of church women and men sacrificing their safety in the campaigns, the civil rights movement took an important turn in the early 1960s. Church leaders held invitational periods at mass meetings to ask for volunteers for these campaigns. They were generously rewarded with thousands of soldiers for the movement, thus making a parallel with and linkage between this and the classic Baptist "invitation" to give oneself over to Christ. The devout followers who regularly attended church saw the mass meetings for political action as part and parcel of their religious duty and obligation. Those who attended church infrequently were also drawn into the church to listen and volunteer. The campaigns echoed with the African American spirituals of freedom, love, redemption, and nonviolence. By being met with hate and brutal violence in the South, the campaigns exposed the immorality, inhumanity, and contradictions among the opposition, most of whom claimed Christianity as their faith.

Cultivating Leadership

While self-admittedly not born civil rights leaders, Martin Luther King Jr. and Ralph Abernathy among others were groomed by their church and the exigencies of their time to assume leadership roles that could have gone unfilled. As point men and women of the movement who were there for the worst of the opposition's response, the leaders were forced to grapple with the contradictions of their faith. Through their activities they became easy targets for criticism, assault, and assassination.

But the cultivation of leadership existed beyond those ordained. The often unsung leaders of the civil rights movement were the devoted lay persons thrust into a call for action. Both Ella Baker and Fannie Lou Hamer were grounded in the black church. As executive director of the Southern Christian Leadership Conference, Ella Baker helped to spearhead the development of the Student Nonviolent Coordinating Committee (SNCC), one of many contributions she would make. The political activist Fannie Lou Hamer led the Mississippi Freedom Democratic Party to fight for black inclusion during the 1964 Democratic Party Convention. The efforts of both Baker and Hamer in the pursuit of change were anchored by a commitment to justice and equality and facilitated by a religious zeal that sustained them when the opposition was brutal or when change was slow to come. In the end, both ordained and lay leaders were essential to the mix of forces in the civil rights movement.

Radical Religiosity

At the core of the civil rights movement, the activism of thousands of participants was at once religious—rooted in the theistic traditions of Christianity and Judaism—and secular—concerned with the dignity and deliverance from bondage of all persons. It was an existential Christianity shaped by a strong belief in the individual's worth, plight, possession of free will, and struggle with right and wrong. That philosophy led to principles of rights, equality, democracy, and self-worth. This amalgamation of the religious and the secular is perhaps what radicalized the social activism of the 1950s and 1960s and made it universally appealing to supporters of the civil rights movement worldwide.

The liberating elements of the civil rights movement, however, came from factions of American Christianity, Judaism, and the Democratic Party that were left of center. None of the factions should be confused, however, with extreme left ideologies or factions of religion and politics found in the United States and worldwide. While certainly transformative and consequential, the underlying ethos of the civil rights movement was not revolutionary. The leaders, activists, and ideas that predominantly shaped the civil rights movement were not looking to overturn the U.S. government or undo the basic governing fabric, laws, and traditions of the United States. The movement revolved around reformist social activism.

A reform movement like the civil rights activism of the 1950s and 1960s sought inclusion into the mainstream for the excluded black population. Such movements, including the women's movement and the gay and lesbian movement, among others, agitated for new antidiscrimination laws with enforcement power and prodded America to live up to the principles embedded in its democratic tradition, namely, liberty, equality, and justice. Taking guidance and moral legitimation from religion, the activists pushed for social and political reforms that ultimately challenged and tested the limits of a democratic society. In refashioning what it meant to be Christian, the thousands of activists not only exposed centuries of religious contradictions, but more specifically challenged the tacit acceptance by Christians of racial oppression. Moreover, they demonstrated that their faith must be employed to fight the injustices inflicted on others and on themselves.

The paradoxes of Christianity were evident in the 1950s and 1960s. On the one hand, black and white Christians created new forms of interracial cooperation and a burgeoning radical feminism. On the other, those same Christians were heirs to a tradition that promoted separation between the races and, besides, shaped sexist, even misogynist, conceptions of women and their "rightful" place in society. The thousands of black women, from college coeds to grandmothers, who joined black men in boycotting, marching, and leading demonstrations were joined by white women and men.

Traditional gender norms had a rebirth after World War II, and black communities did not escape it. At critical moments, therefore, women like Rosa Parks, Ella Baker, and Fannie Lou Hamer forthrightly challenged not only sexualized norms and expectations but also those ministers and

churches that were reluctant to take an active role in the movement. As leaders willing to speak out on injustice and lead resistance actions, they confronted community leaders who were accustomed to being the "race leaders" but unaccustomed to women's assuming prominent roles. As usual, they found the means to undo the status quo.

Similarly, the participation in the movement of many southern white women began in their churches. In challenging the contradictions of their faith, which housed racist and sexist norms, many southern white women found inspiration and guidance from the black women involved in the struggle for justice and equality. In crossing borders of race, sex, and class, especially in working with and developing political, social, and sexual relationships with black men, these women fought not only for the liberation of blacks but for their own liberation. The activism among these women was critical to providing some of the building blocks for and fomenting the modern women's movement of the 1960s and 1970s. Many of the early participants of the women's movement were active in the civil rights movement and had begun to question, rethink, and reshape putative gender norms and to reawaken a dormant political feminism. As was the case with black women, the church and societal custom that had long resisted the notion of any significant presence of women in the public sphere was ultimately used to fight for racial and gender justice. The antiegalitarian and antipolitical strains of Christianity and of Judaism that particularly worked to keep white women out of the public and political sphere were transformed into an idealism and passionate concern for social justice.

The involvement of white women and many white men of the Christian and Jewish faiths also speaks to the use of religion to sponsor interracial cooperation and coalitions. From white campus ministries and groups like the Methodist Student Movement, Young Women's Christian Association, and United Student Christian Council to interracial organizations such as the NAACP and SNCC in its early days, the civil rights movement showcased an experiment with interracial cooperation in the struggle for justice that had not been seen before except perhaps during the abolitionist movement.

Despite religious norms that harbored racist and sexist ideas and practices, black and white activists were able to cull elements of their faiths with which to build new movements for racial liberation, feminism, and interracial cooperation. The civil rights movement highlights the vibrancy of political religiosity during the 1950s and 1960s and stands as one of the most significant world movements of the twentieth century.

See also *Civil disobedience; Civil rights movement; Human rights; King, Martin Luther, Jr.*

Timothy P. Harrison

BIBLIOGRAPHY

Evans, Sara. *Personal Politics: The Roots of Women's Liberation in the Civil Rights Movement and the New Left.* New York: Vintage Books, 1979.

Giddings, Paula. *When and Where I Enter: The Impact of Black Women on Race and Sex in America.* New York: William Morrow, 1984.

King, Martin Luther, Jr. *Stride toward Freedom.* New York: Harper and Row, 1958.

McAdam, Doug. *Political Process and the Development of Black Insurgency, 1930–1970.* Chicago: University of Chicago Press, 1982.

Marable, Manning. *Race, Reform, and Rebellion: The Second Reconstruction in Black America, 1945–1990.* Jackson: University Press of Mississippi, 1991.

Payne, Charles M. *I've Got the Light of Freedom: The Organizing Tradition and the Mississippi Freedom Struggle.* Berkeley: University of California Press, 1995.

Piven, Francis Fox, and Richard A. Cloward. *Poor People's Movements: Why They Succeed, How They Fail.* New York: Vintage Books, 1977.

West, Cornel. *Prophesy Deliverance! An Afro-American Revolutionary Christianity.* Philadelphia: Westminster Press, 1982.

African independent churches

African independent churches (AICs), also called African initiated or instituted churches, are a new Christian phenomenon in sub-Saharan Africa. The movement comprises thousands of churches founded by black Africans for black Africans and is devoted to the well-being, salvation, and liberation of African people.

Origins and Growth

African independent churches date back to the early eighteenth century when a young woman, Kimpa Vita, resisted Portuguese rule in the Congo by proclaiming a black Christ and a utopian African kingdom. In 1706 the Portuguese rulers burned her at the stake as a heretic and forcibly subdued her followers.

By the beginning of the twentieth century, when African nationalism emerged as a significant force in southern Africa, AICs had established themselves as an enduring, fast-growing movement. After the first major schism in South Af-

rica in 1884, led by Nehemiah Tile, a Methodist minister, and the formation of the first "Ethiopian" church by Mangena Mokone in 1892, Ethiopian-type churches began to flourish. The Zionist movement, in turn, came into being after Daniel Bryant, an "overseer" of Dowie's Christian Catholic Apostolic Church in Zion, near Chicago, had baptized the first converts in South Africa, in 1904. African missionaries of both of these movements, independent of the Western-led mission churches, soon operated throughout South Africa, establishing new churches. When rapid AIC expansion triggered a process of ecclesial fragmentation, many new groups emerged. Through the conversion of labor migrants from neighboring countries the AIC movement spread from South Africa to Botswana, Namibia, Mozambique, Zimbabwe, Zambia, and Malawi. While many of the early movements in South Africa and the Congo were distinctly nativistic, millennialistic, and radically antiwhite in political disposition, the West African AICs developed more peacefully, with an emphasis on placing the Christian faith within the context of African culture and religion.

African independent churches vary in size from small, single-family churches, composed of only a few related adults and their children, to the more widely known churches with millions of adherents. Some of the most prominent of the latter are the *amaNazareta* of Isaiah Shembe and the Zion Christian Church of Engenas Lekganyane in South Africa; Samuel Mutendi's Zion Christian Church and Johane Maranke's African Apostolic Church (the *vaPostori* has some two million members with congregations as far north as Zaire) in Zimbabwe; Alice Lenshina's Lumpa Church in Zambia; Simon Kimbangu's Church of Jesus Christ in Zaire (the largest AIC, with an estimated membership of between ten and fifteen million); and the Cherubim and Seraphim Church and the Church of the Lord (Aladura), both in Nigeria.

Types and Distinctive Features

AICs originate in either the pre-Christian or Christian movements. The neo-pagan pre-Christian movement represents a reversion to traditional African religion in an attempt to achieve stability in the face of intrusive religious influence from the West. The vast majority of AICs are distinctly Christian; they believe in the triune Christian God as portrayed in the Old and New Testaments, consider the Scriptures part of their lives, develop congregations for joint worship and the use of the sacraments, and develop spiritualities that convincingly witness to the existential reality of Christ and the movement of the Holy Spirit in their existence. Some AICs suffer from a lack of theological training for their leadership, limited doctrinal development, fragmented Bible interpretation, and syncretistic trends of interreligious encounter. Yet, in terms of missionary activity, numerical strength, holistic Christian communities that cater to both the spiritual and physical needs of people, and Bible-oriented church life, AICs qualify as mainline Christianity rather than as peripheral or sectarian Christian movements.

Scholars tend to classify AICs originating in the Christian movement into three main types. The *Ethiopian-type churches,* or nonprophetic movements, adopt patterns of church leadership, organization, and worship that are fairly similar to those of the Methodist, Congregationalist, Anglican, Reformed, and other mission churches on which they are partly modeled. These churches originated largely as a reaction to white-led mission churches. Political development and the knowledge that a colonial power, such as the Italians in Abyssinia (now Ethiopia), had been successfully resisted in East Africa contributed to the development of an Ethiopian ideology, which tended to foster a sense of self-esteem and responsibility for the expansion of God's kingdom in Africa. This ideology took root mainly in East and South Africa between 1890 and 1920. Despite the decline of the ideology, "Ethiopian" continues to feature in the names of some AICs.

The *Spirit-type churches,* or prophetic movements, emphasize the work of the Holy Spirit, manifested in emotional forms of worship, speaking in tongues, prophetic activity, and faith healing. This category comprises all Zionists, such as the Zion Christian churches, and a wide range of Apostolic churches. Prophetic faith healing, based on the diagnostic and therapeutic powers of the Holy Spirit and manifested in a wide range of exorcistic and individual- or group-cleansing ceremonies, is at the center of the Spirit-type churches.

Finally, the so-called *Messianic churches* represent a development of leadership within the prophetic movements. Messianism occurs when the eminence of a movement's founder-leader—his or her mystical powers, healing miracles, image as resistance figure against colonial rule, or closeness to God as mediating representative of his or her followers—captures the attention of members to such an extent that Christ's salvific work is obscured, either wholly or in part. This classification is controversial because few AIC leaders actually claim to be black Christ figures and members of AICs generally consider the "gate-keeping function" at the

portals of heaven as an extension of the leaders' ecclesial duties on earth, without it necessarily circumventing the salvific mediation of Christ or the final judgment of God.

Religiocultural and Socioeconomic Liberation

AICs have served as sources of liberation—religiocultural, socioeconomic, and political—for their members. The spontaneous, celebratory life of the AICs—especially in song, dance, sermons, and healing—is largely the result of their emancipation from the paternalist structures and austere and dogmatically correct forms of worship that the Western mission churches maintained by means of funding and staffing. This liberative process, insofar as it includes a reevaluation of indigenous culture and religion, has led to numerous rites informed by African worldviews. In the Spirit-type churches trends of confrontation and Christianizing transformation are evident. As a result, the Gospel message is introduced at an existential level to cater to Africans' needs in a new way, just as the High-God cult, ancestor veneration, and magical rites had done in earlier times.

Faith-healing practices in the Spirit-type churches in Zimbabwe clearly reveal that religiocultural liberation is not just a reaction against Western control and medical science, accompanied by uncritical affirmation of indigenous custom. It also implies liberation from the besetting fear of spiritual powers and life-threatening sorcery inculcated by traditional religion. The Zionist and Apostolic prophets' healing rites represent pastoral, psychological liberation for people threatened by destructive forces. Prophetic diagnosis is still based on the ancient worldview in which the traditional causes of misfortune or danger are demonstrated and taken seriously. But in prophetic therapy, the healing and protective power of Christ and the Holy Spirit emerges in symbolic purificatory or exorcist rites. Thus the Christian God is convincingly and visibly presented as a God directly involved in the joys and sorrows of the community.

The socioeconomic liberation represented by AICs is evident in both the rural and urban areas of Africa. In rural areas the extensive leadership structures of the AICs enable people who have little political say or social standing to enjoy greater recognition and improve their social status. At the weekly gatherings church members, appearing in their dignified uniforms or robes bearing their leadership monograms, proudly assume a meaningful new identity as well as responsibility for the attainment of congregational goals. This helps to enliven their village life and give them a sense of control over the problems of peasant existence. Leadership structures have been adapted to the traditional kinship codes and codes of authority, making it possible to distribute group responsibilities in a way that makes sense to the people. All this liberates participants from the blight of social obscurity and drudgery.

In a subsistence peasant economy the AICs also represent economic progress. The good news they communicate is that of freedom from economic impotence and from fatalism in the face of poverty and inefficient farming methods. This message is conveyed through identification with the poor and concerted application of modern farming methods, resulting in improved cash crop yields. In Zimbabwe the Zionist bishops in particular were economically progressive, qualifying as master farmers and buying up farms in the erstwhile Native Purchase Areas. In recent years ecumenical AIC institutions, notably *Fambidzano* in Zimbabwe, have attempted to raise funds for member churches to engage in economic development projects.

Most rural Africans who migrate to the city encounter almost insurmountable problems. Lack of mobility often breaks up families. The stabilizing kinship codes and tribal mores no longer function in heterogeneous mass society, resulting in social isolation or degeneracy. New models and criteria are needed for a meaningful existence. In this complexity the independent churches are "reorientation centers"—communities offering security and a chance for reintegration, a new home providing stability in a harsh, competitive world.

Political Liberation

The political liberation offered by the AICs has been found in both rural/tribal politics and national politics. The history of many African churches contains an element of struggle against colonial domination in which a politically oriented liberation theology is implicit, even though the leaders of these churches did not necessarily use this terminology. In the colonial situation of southern Africa the traditional Supreme Being sometimes appeared indifferent to Western pressures on tribal politics. The sermons and catechesis of mission churches created an impression of a God concerned about individual morals and salvation rather than one directly involved in the lives of rural headmen, in the problems of divided loyalties in tribal politics, in the dispossession of territory, in boundary disputes, and in the inheritance of tribal leadership.

In this situation the prophetic church leaders in particular transformed the image of a remote God into one of direct divine involvement in tribal and national politics. Outstanding prophetic figures such as Shembe and Lekganyane Senior in South Africa, Mutendi and Maranke in Zimbabwe, and Kimbangu in Zaire were all leaders who, through their close contact with tribal heads, were aware of the problems of local administration and addressed their Gospel messages to these problems.

Like Shembe in South Africa, Bishop Samuel Mutendi of the Zimbabwean Zion Christian Church recruited a large number of chiefs and headmen for his church. Tribal leaders were attracted by his resistance to colonial rule in the educational and religious spheres, for which he was arrested by the Rhodesian administration on several occasions and spent short spells in detention. As a figure of resistance against the white regime and a representative of indigenous political and cultural values, Mutendi appeared to his followers as an emissary, a "man of God"—a title by which he always was respectfully addressed, not only in the religious sense but also in the political arena.

Bishop Mutendi introduced the Christian message into tribal politics by having his Zionist prophets appointed to the tribal courts of affiliated chiefs. In this way the guidance and revelations of the Holy Spirit, as experienced by Zionists, could directly influence the traditional judiciary and various facets of rural government. Thus he established a wide network of mutual allegiance between the "man of God" in Zion City and traditional leaders across large parts of the country, which also gave him considerable influence over tribal politics. Well aware that headmen were torn by the opposing claims of the administration, on the one hand, and the tribesmen, on the other—two worlds that, because of differing cultural and religious values, were in continual friction—the "man of God" set himself the aim of offering frustrated headmen spiritual anchorage and protection, which helped them to function optimally in a situation that constantly highlighted their impotence in the face of the white overlords.

It was in this kind of context that a message of liberation evolved. This message did not promise easy solutions or revolutionary changes in the political constellation that would bring sudden freedom from bondage. Yet it was through the involvement and continuous availability of Zionist prophets that God drew nigh in the affairs of tribal dignitaries. The once remote deity now enabled chiefs and headmen to cope with a complex and often critical political situation. They were being liberated from their fears and anxiety.

In the national politics of Zimbabwe the independent churches generally kept a low profile. Their sympathies with their people's struggle for political independence did not lead to unreserved participation in militant political activities, largely because they were reluctant to allow their organizations to be used as a platform for party politics. Their liberation theology was not confined to religiocultural freedom from the mission churches, socioeconomic advancement of their members, and overt opposition to the administration of the day such as Mutendi's. It also concerned maintaining a unique identity in the midst of political pressure. A classic example of the refusal of AICs to be manipulated politically occurred in the 1960s in Zambia, where members of Alice Lenshina's Lumpa Church were massacred because of the prophetess's refusal to order her followers to join the ruling United National Independence Party.

During the 1950s and 1960s some of the more prominent Zimbabwean independent churches openly defied the black nationalist parties ZANU (Zimbabwe African National Union) and ZAPU (Zimbabwe African People's Union) by rejecting violent resistance. Their motives were pragmatic ones of self-preservation. The church leaders were aware of the omnipresence of members of the Rhodesian intelligence service, and that they could not effectively oppose the colonial power with their own numbers. But aloofness from organized violence did not imply political apathy. Black nationalist sentiments were continually expressed in the sermons and activities of the AICs in the form of propagation of ideas of racial equality, the dignity of the black race, and blacks' competence to rule themselves. Thus the main contribution of the AICs to political liberation lay in providing religious justification for the liberation struggle, for which they could, moreover, adduce the necessary scriptural proofs. In this sense, the AICs were the religious vanguard of black nationalism.

Among the *vaPostori,* resistance to white rule was manifested in sermons and in charges that whites had killed Christ and deliberately withheld his message from blacks. The prophet Johane Maranke had brought an end to the age of white privilege and had restored the despised house of Ham (that is, black Africans) to glory in order that they, guided by the Holy Spirit, might fulfill Jesus Christ's task in the world under a new dispensation.

The role of the independent churches in the liberation history of Zimbabwe, as enacted in the bush war (the second *chimurenga,* or liberation struggle, 1965–1980), still has to be written. For members of both mission and independent churches it largely was a matter of survival between the Scylla of the Rhodesian forces and the Charybdis of the guerrilla freedom fighters. Notwithstanding the fact that some guerrilla groups, using the slogan "Down with Jesus, the white man's god," actively opposed the churches, burning their buildings and even Bibles, in the 1970s virtually all independent churches appeared to have actively supported the freedom fighters.

Clearly, then, the Zimbabwean independent churches contributed significantly to the second *chimurenga,* and many of them are justly proud of their share in the reconquest of their "lost territory" and the attainment of political independence. Given the Zimbabwean history of AIC political involvement, it would be difficult for South African exponents of black theology to criticize the allegedly apolitical attitude of AICs on the subcontinent. If one considers the combination of pragmatic and prophetic-ideological elements of Bishop Mutendi's resistance strategy, it is conceivable that the public statements of Zionist Christian Church bishop Lekganyane in South Africa, which during apartheid rule seemed to be supportive of the political status quo, did not preclude either individual involvement of Zionist Christian Church members in the liberation struggle or the provision of religious justification for and active support of black nationalist ideals. Comprehensive studies of the histories of AICs are bound to compel African theologians, who have tended to limit the merits of these churches to the indigenization of church praxis, to accord greater recognition to their sociopolitically liberative roles.

Although black theology is undeniably more militant and revolutionary than Zionist theology, this by no means implies that the former has a kind of monopoly on liberation and sociostructural change. Both in academic circles and in the communications media the exponents of black theology have conducted an impressive public campaign that is recognized internationally. But at the grass-roots level of church life the independent churches—through their marked identification with the struggle and aspirations of black Africans, expressed in a holistic, enacted theology—have made an existential contribution to liberation whose impact on African society has been insufficiently assessed and appreciated in academic circles.

See also *Africa, Christian; African traditional religions; Bots-*

wana; Colonialism; Liberation theology; Millennialism; Nativism; Nigeria; Pacifism; South Africa; Zimbabwe.

Marthinius L. Daneel

BIBLIOGRAPHY

Barrett, D. B. *Schism and Renewal in Africa: An Analysis of Six Thousand Contemporary Religious Movements.* Nairobi: Oxford University Press, 1968.

Daneel, M. L. *Old and New in Southern Shona Independent Churches.* Vol. 1, *Background and Rise of the Major Movements.* The Hague: Mouton, 1971.

———. *Old and New in Southern Shona Independent Churches.* Vol. 2, *Church Growth: Causative Factors and Recruitment Techniques.* The Hague: Mouton, 1974.

———. *Quest for Belonging: Introduction to a Study of African Independent Churches.* Gweru, Zimbabwe: Mambo Press, 1987.

Ndiokwere, Nathaniel I. *Prophecy and Revolution: The Role of Prophets in the Independent African Churches and in Biblical Tradition.* London: SPCK, 1981.

Sundkler, B. G. M. *Bantu Prophets of South Africa.* London: Oxford University Press, 1961.

Turner, H. W. "A Typology for African Religious Movements." *Journal of Religion in Africa* I, no. 1 (1967).

West, M. *Bishops and Prophets in a Black City: African Independent Churches in Soweto, Johannesburg.* Cape Town: Phillip, 1975.

African traditional religions

African traditional religions are the indigenous religious practices that were in existence before the advent of Christianity and Islam in Africa and that continue to exist today alongside these two major world religions and to play an important role in daily existence. Although no one can ascertain their origin or founders, their general characteristics are held to include a belief in the supreme being, in divinities and spirits, in life after death, and in some mysterious powers. These special powers and beings constitute the objects of religious acts or rituals, which are usually performed in commonly recognized sacred places. Authorities at these rituals, such as diviners, prophets, priests, and sacred kings, serve to facilitate communication between the human world and the sacred world, and shrines and temples provide the dramatic setting for this divine-human encounter. The priest's job is to perform prayers and sacrifices that carry people's desires to the spiritual world; the priest, in turn, communicates the will of the spiritual beings to the people. Lacking the monotheism of the major world religions, the traditional religions continue to demonstrate their resiliency through

their ability to absorb outside influences while transforming them in their African transplantations.

The various expressions of religious practices in traditional precolonial Africa indicate an important connection between politics and religion. In Africa, religion penetrates all areas of human existence. Human affairs in the journey from birth to death and reincarnation are infused with religious meaning. Social and political arrangements are accordingly affected, with religion helping to shape and give expression to the people's worldview. The preservation of a religious moral order is the chief goal of political institutions, while religious rituals are used as instruments to preserve social and political order. The rituals of the religious life reinforce this close interconnection between the social and political order and the moral order.

Kingship and Priesthood

The political scheme in this sense is dependent on the primacy of the moral order by virtue of which it seeks and finds divine favor for success in political undertakings. The traditional kingship and priesthood exist side by side to give expression to this cohesive view of life. Thus the rituals of the religious life are enacted to maintain a favorable balance of cosmic forces on which depend personal, communal, and political well-being. Sometimes the religious and political are so closely connected that the king carries his scepter as a divine emblem and performs ritual functions as a consequence. Divine kingship expresses the successful fusing of the political and the religious, of the secular and the sacred. In proper balance, this overlap of the political and religious promotes harmony and moderation. When the balance is disrupted, however, it can produce an inflexible ideology of political absolutism in which religion no longer acts to check excesses in the political order.

Among the Yoruba of southwestern Nigeria, for example, the king's justice is unquestioned and unquestionable. He holds the power of life and death over his subjects who hail him as *ekeji Orisa,* the one whose power is like that of the gods, being coequal with death. Yet the Yoruba also believe that to whom much is given much is also required; so power is qualified by accountability. Although in theory the will of the king is the absolute law of the land, in practice the king's power is curtailed by obligations that demand the performance of rituals and by evidence of his people's well-being. Misfortunes in the kingdom imply inadequacies or even transgressions in the political order. If the king had been faithful to tradition and observation of the rituals, so the reasoning goes, misfortune would not have afflicted the realm. A king risks losing his throne with the occurrence of misfortune. Similarly, the advantages of security, peace, abundance, good health, and success are imputed to the king's benevolence. So we can say that the stability of the kingly throne is at the mercy of events in the social and natural order and that a breakdown in that order portends a corresponding breakdown in the political realm. Often political revolutions are predicated on such misfortunes.

This fusing of the political and religious is by no means universal in all of Africa. In some societies, there is a functional separation of the political order from the religious. The territorial sphere of the king's authority is recognized in exchange for the rights of priests to preside over the ritual acts of the state. Nevertheless, king and priest cooperate to ensure fertility, rain, and the general warding off of misfortune from land and people. The effectiveness of the king's authority requires the proper observance of rituals. In rituals of succession and coronation, the priest presides. The ruler is anointed not simply as a political figure but as the guardian and defender of sacred custom and as the symbol of continuity with ancient tradition. Once installed, the ruler becomes patron of the various religious customs in society. His palace becomes a center of pilgrimage, and he is the object of civil reverence.

Colonialism and Missionaries

One effect of European colonialism, which began in the fifteenth century in Africa, peaked in the nineteenth, and gave way to independence movements in the twentieth, was to loosen the close connection of politics and religion. Colonialism and Christian missionary work restructured indigenous cultural systems and in certain respects hindered their natural development. Where colonialism was able to combine with Islam, which was entrenched in much of northern Africa, further deleterious effects on African religious customs were felt. Muslims opposed traditional customs as incompatible with the teachings of the Qur'an, their holy Scripture. The effect of such combined pressure was to introduce much confusion into ideas of how politics and religion should be related. Only a strenuous effort at revitalizing African religions can remedy the damage.

There is evidence that such an indigenous revitalization is under way in several places. African religions have absorbed many common elements from Christianity and Islam, adapted some elements to make them conform to their own character, and rejected others that conflicts with their norms. So far, however, national states have been slow to recognize the role of religion in the political and social spheres, especially the role of religion in fostering a pluralist practice.

See also *Colonialism; Missionaries.*

Simeon O. Ilesanmi

BIBLIOGRAPHY

Bozeman, Adda B. *The Future of Law in a Multicultural World.* Princeton: Princeton University Press, 1971.

Fortes, M., and E.E. Evans-Pritchard, eds. *African Political Systems.* London and New York: Kegan Paul, 1987.

Idowu, E. Bolaji. *Olodumare: God in Yoruba Belief.* London: Longman, 1962.

Olupona, J. K. *Kingship, Religion, and Rituals in a Nigerian Community.* Stockholm: Almqvist and Wiksell, 1991.

Ray, Benjamin C. *African Religions: Symbol, Ritual, and Community.* Englewood Cliffs, N.J.: Prentice-Hall, 1976.

Ahmad Khan, Sir Sayyid

Indian modernist writer, educational and religious reformer, and political leader. Khan (1817–1898) claimed lineal descent from the prophet Muhammad, and his ancestors had migrated to Mughal India from Afghanistan in the seventeenth century. Despite having lived in India for nearly two hundred years, Khan's family remained conscious of their foreign origin. Khan's formal education was strictly traditional; he ceased formal schooling at eighteen. Conservative critics considered him unqualified to undertake the reforms he proposed for the modernization of Islam. Yet through personal study and independent investigation he laid the groundwork for a modern interpretation of Islam.

While working in the court system of the British Raj, Khan lived through the Indian Mutiny of 1857–1859. He emerged from this ordeal as both a loyal functionary of the British government and a staunch Muslim nationalist.

After the mutiny Khan worked to create understanding between Muslims and Christians, to establish scientific organizations that would help Muslims understand the secret of the West's success, and to analyze objectively the causes for the revolt. He was the only Muslim scholar ever to venture a commentary on the Old and New Testaments, in his *Mahomedan Commentary on the Holy Bible* (1862).

To refute the British view that the rebellion was led by

Muslims, he wrote *An Account of the Loyal Mahomdans of India* (1860–1861) to show that the majority of influential Muslims remained loyal to the British government and that they were by no means enemies of the British. This attempt enabled him to elicit British support for a fair Muslim share in the Indian political system.

In May 1869 Khan arrived in London and remained in Britain for fifteen months to study British culture, including modern scientific education and the capitalist economy characterized by social and political laissez-faire. In London he published *A Series of Essays on the Life of Mohammad* (1870). To study British educational institutions he visited the universities of Cambridge and Oxford, as well as private preparatory schools. These educational models enabled him to develop the blueprint for the Mohammedan Anglo-Oriental College, which he established in 1875 at Aligarh; in 1920 the college became Aligarh Muslim University.

Equipped with modern ideas and orientations, Khan returned to India in October 1870 and initiated his movement of religious and cultural modernism among Muslims. He resigned his position in the judicial service in 1876, and until his death devoted himself to modernizing the life of Muslims in the Indian subcontinent.

Most of his efforts went to promoting modern education among Muslims, especially through the All-India Mohammedan Educational Conference, which existed from 1886 to 1937. From 1886 to 1898 the Educational Conference was pitted against the All-India National Congress, which espoused secular Indian nationalism. Khan endorsed a form of Muslim nationalism that accentuated separatist Muslim politics in India and gave rise to the All-India Muslim League, which in the 1930s and 1940s spearheaded the movement for the creation of Pakistan.

Khan promoted an Islamic modernism that drew inspiration from the writings of Indian rationalist Islamic reformer Shah Waliy Allah (1703–1762) and emphasized a rational approach to Islam and social reforms in Muslim culture. What made Khan controversial was his emphasis on religious modernism, which rejected the traditional practices and orientations of the orthodox, and his advocacy of modern education, which lured young Muslims from orthodox religious seminaries into Western-style schools and colleges. In recognition of his accomplishments, the British government knighted him in 1888.

See also *India; Islam; Pakistan.*

Hafeez Malik

BIBLIOGRAPHY

Malik, Hafeez. *Sir Sayyid Ahmad Khan and Muslim Modernization in India and Pakistan.* New York: Columbia University Press, 1980.

———, ed. *Political Profile of Sir Sayyid Ahmad Khan: A Documentary Record.* Islamabad: National Institute of Historical and Cultural Research, 1982.

———, ed. *Sir Sayyid Ahmad Khan's Educational Philosophy: A Documentary Record.* Islamabad: National Institute of Historical and Cultural Research, 1989.

Troll, Christian W. *Sayyid Ahmad Khan: A Reinterpretation of Muslim Theology.* New Delhi: Vikas Publ. House, 1978.

Algeria

Algeria, a North African country whose population is almost entirely Muslim, borders the Mediterranean Sea in the north and reaches far into the Sahara to the south. The majority of the population is Arabic speaking, with minorities speaking Berber dialects. Previously made up of a number of smaller political formations, Algeria took shape in the early sixteenth century, when inhabitants of the region appealed to the Ottoman Empire to help in defense against Spanish incursions. Turkish-speaking Ottoman soldiers ruled the country until 1830, when the French began their conquest of Algeria, but the Ottomans remained a small minority of the population.

Traditionally, Islamic religious leadership in Algeria involved a combination of knowledge of the written sources of Islam with prestige inherited from a forebear renowned for piety. Families of religious leaders had an identity clearly distinct from military and political leaders. In both city and countryside, Sufi mystical orders played a major role in religious life; their rituals supplemented the core practices of Islam, creating bonds of community among initiates. In times of crisis, Sufi initiates lent their influence to political mobilization. Women also participated in Sufi activities with their own distinct organizations.

The Colonial Period

For four decades after 1830 the French occupiers faced widespread resistance in which Islamic leaders and Sufi orders were the moving forces. Amir Abd al-Qadir, the most prominent of these, fought the French from 1832 until his surrender in 1847. Algeria was declared French territory in 1848. The French feared the potential of Islamic leaders to inspire rebellion but also saw their ability to promote peace.

Thus French policy vacillated between repression and conciliation. The French restricted Islamic law to family matters and subordinated Muslim courts to the French Court of Appeal. Although the European settlers never exceeded 15 percent of Algeria's total population, they were a majority in major cities.

By the early 1900s a combination of socioeconomic change and the extension to Algeria of the French law of 1905 separating church and state stimulated the rise of a new form of voluntary organization that emphasized modern Islamic education. By 1931 local groups had coalesced into a nationwide organization, the Algerian Association of Ulama (Muslim scholars), led by Abd al-Hamid Ben Badis. As well as maintaining an educational role, this group, usually termed Islamic reformists, opposed what they viewed as the heterodox practices of Sufism.

After the death of Ben Badis in 1940, Bashir al-Ibrahimi assumed leadership of the Association of Ulama. The years immediately after World War II were marked by a rapid growth of the association and by the emergence of a strong nationalist movement. Ibrahimi campaigned for the return of Islamic endowment properties confiscated by the French in the previous century, hoping that these would ensure the autonomy of religious leaders and insulate them from the pressures of politics. Opposed by the French administration and by the Sufi orders, Ibrahimi's campaign failed. Frustrated, he went into exile in Cairo, Egypt, where he formed ties with the Muslim Brethren, a radical religious organization that sought the establishment of an Islamic state.

In November 1954 a revolution against colonial rule broke out in Algeria; it was led by the National Liberation Front (FLN), an outgrowth of secular nationalist political parties. The Association of Ulama supported the revolution, and many of its younger members joined the ranks of the FLN. Through nearly eight years of war (1954–1962), the FLN stressed the connection between Islam and the Algerian national identity. They used *fatwas,* or Islamic judicial rulings, to further the ends of the nationalist cause. A widely followed injunction against tobacco consumption, which cut into the revenues of the French tobacco monopoly, demonstrated the public support given the FLN.

During the war some members of the Roman Catholic clergy in Algeria, including the archbishop of Algiers, Léon-Étienne Duval, worked to support the cause of independence and denounced the human rights abuses carried out by the French military and the police. At the end of the war

Duval took the initiative to return the cathedral of Algiers, which had been a mosque seized by the French in 1832, to the Algerian government for reconsecration as a mosque. Nearly all the French settlers left Algeria at independence in 1962.

After Independence

The first independent Algerian regime, led by Ahmad Ben Bella from 1962 to 1965, had a mainly secular and socialist orientation. During the war the Association of Ulama had been dismantled, its assets confiscated by the French. Thus it was not in a position to act as an independent force in the early postrevolution period. Nonetheless, Ibrahimi spoke out against Ben Bella's secularism, and Ibrahimi's funeral in 1965 was an occasion for public protest against the regime.

Houari Boumedienne, a soldier who replaced Ben Bella as president in a 1965 coup, was the product of a religious education. He enlisted reformist religious leaders in the service of his regime, while opposing the Sufi orders that he saw as tied to conservative rural interests. But his main thrust was a program of rapid industrialization, along with the promotion of Arabic in place of French as the medium of instruction. He and his successor, Chadeli Benjedid, who came to power in 1979, promoted Islam as the "religion of the state." Their regimes constructed mosques, trained and employed religious personnel, and catered to conservative Islamic views in matters of family law. But the Islamic resurgence they helped to advance soon was beyond their control.

A new grassroots Islamic movement first expressed itself in the 1970s as urban neighborhood groups began building mosques without first requesting government authorization. As President Benjedid began his own version of Soviet leader Mikhail Gorbachev's policy of *glasnost,* or dismantling authoritarian control, Islamic groups established a political organization, the Islamic Salvation Front (FIS). Its leaders included Abbasi Madani, a man strongly influenced by the Algerian Islamic philosopher Malik Bennabi (died 1973). In the 1970s Madani pursued a doctorate in education at the University of London. There he came into contact with Islamic intellectuals from many countries and joined in their quest to create an Islamic political ideology viable in the modern world. Madani is widely seen as the leader of the FIS's moderate wing. The radical element finds its expression in Ali Ben Hajj, the youthful *imam,* or leader, of a mosque in a poor neighborhood near the center of Algiers, known for his fiery oratory.

The FIS drew its support from a variety of sources, including older, traditionally conservative Muslims; well-educated members of a younger generation, for whom Islam served as a symbol of personal identity and pride; and angry young people with few prospects, living on the margins of urban society, for whom the Islamic resurgence held out the hope of a better life.

The Islamic resurgence also took root in Algerian and other immigrant Muslim communities in France, where, by the 1970s, many immigrant workers had begun to see themselves as permanent residents. They voiced demands for prayer rooms and mosques in their factories and places of residence. Many French institutions, including corporations, labor unions, housing authorities, and the Catholic Church worked to accommodate these new demands. At the same time, right-wing French groups, such as Jean-Marie Le Pen's National Front, expressed increasing hostility to Muslim immigrants.

In the mid-1980s, with the decline of prices for oil and gas (Algeria's primary exports) and a rapidly growing population of youth, the Algerian government faced a severe challenge. Following violent riots by frustrated urban youth in October 1988, President Benjedid committed himself to a process of democratic opening. Some analysts argue that he sought to turn the Islamic movement to the advantage of his own reformist, free-market followers within the FLN. But the old guard within the governing elite, still tied to state-controlled economic policies, opposed his strategy.

In local elections in June 1990 the FIS scored major victories, especially in urban areas, while other opposition parties had only localized support. Many FIS activists were young, idealistic, and well educated; in running municipal governments they gained a reputation for honesty and competence. In some cases, such as in enforcing strict dress codes for women, they also proved dogmatic. Legislative elections were scheduled for January 1992, but the military moved to block them, ousted Benjedid, and outlawed the FIS, arresting its principal leaders. Some Islamic activists then took to guerrilla warfare, forming the Armed Islamic Group (GIA).

The result has been a stalemate, with both Islamic activists and the government torn between pragmatists and hard-liners who refuse compromise. The brutal tactics of the hard-liners make negotiation nearly impossible. In the mountainous region where GIA strength is concentrated, just south of Algiers, entire villages have been massacred. It is commonly thought that Islamist militants carry out these killings, though they never claim responsibility. Terrorist activities have occasionally spilled over into France, as Islamic radicals seek to pressure the French government into withdrawing its support from the government regime. Europeans working in Algeria have also been targets of violence. But the most frequent individual victims of violence have been independent-minded journalists and intellectuals, both secular and Islamic.

Outside Algeria some attempts have been made to promote a negotiated solution to the conflict, most notably a meeting of opposition groups, including the FIS and the FLN, held in Rome in January 1995. The Catholic Church helped facilitate this meeting, continuing an earlier commitment to peace and justice in Algeria. The Algerian government, now in the hands of former general Liamine Zeroual, rejected any dialogue, however. Soon after the meeting Islamic militants offered their own answer by planting a bomb in downtown Algiers that killed numerous civilians. In the summer of 1996 Islamic militants kidnapped and killed a group of Catholic monks and also killed the bishop of Oran by car bomb.

In 1997 Zeroual's regime pursued a course of tightly controlled political opening, dominated by a newly created government-sponsored party. Madani was released from detention, with the proviso that he abstain from politics. When he suggested to the press that he could negotiate an end to hostilities, he was placed under house arrest. The more radical Hajj remained in detention.

See also *Colonialism; France; Islam; Muslim encounters with the West; Sufism; Violence.*

Allan Christelow

BIBLIOGRAPHY

Burgat, François, and William McDowell. *The Islamic Movement in North Africa.* Austin: University of Texas Press, 1993.

Christelow, Allan. *Muslim Law Courts and the French Colonial State in Algeria.* Princeton: Princeton University Press, 1985.

Clancy Smith, Julia. *Rebel and Saint: Muslim Notables, Populist Protest, Colonial Encounters (Algeria and Tunisia, 1800–1904).* Berkeley: University of California Press, 1994.

Entelis, John. *Algeria: The Revolution Institutionalized.* Boulder, Colo.: Westview Press, 1986.

Kepel, Gilles. *Les banlieues de l'Islam: Naissance d'une religion en France.* Paris: Editions du Seuil, 1991.

Rouadjia, Ahmed. *Les frères et la mosquée: Enquête sur le mouvement islamique en Algerie.* Paris: Karthala, 1990.

Ruedy, John, ed. *Islamism and Secularism in North Africa.* New York: St. Martin's, 1994.

Amish

See *Anabaptists*

Anabaptists

Anabaptists emerged in mid-sixteenth century Europe as a radical wing of the Protestant Reformation. The term "Anabaptist," from the Greek for "rebaptizer," denotes their practice of rebaptizing adult converts. Anabaptism itself had multiple origins and took a variety of forms. The earliest groups developed in Switzerland, Austria, Moravia, Germany, and the Netherlands. There is ongoing scholarly debate about the breadth of Anabaptist origins and whether or not it is even correct to speak of Anabaptists as Protestants. Because they opposed infant baptism and religious establishment, they frequently experienced repression by both Catholic and Protestant religious and political authorities. In the face of opposition, most Anabaptist groups abstained from violent resistance. Thus their history has been marked by frequent migrations in pursuit of religious freedom or tolerance. Most of the migrations from the seventeenth century onward went either westward to North America or eastward to Prussia and Russia.

Anabaptist involvement in politics and the state was profoundly shaped by two core religious ideas. First, they held to a "two kingdom" theory that posited a sharp antinomy between the "kingdom of God" and the "kingdom of the world." Second, most Anabaptist groups adhered to the principle of "nonresistance," which called for the renunciation of warfare and other coercive means in pursuit of personal or social interests.

These core ideas interacted with varying social and political contexts to produce a range of political responses by Anabaptists. Where the two-kingdom notion combined with powerful apocalyptic impulses, some early Anabaptists attempted to establish the kingdom of God using political and military force. For example, Anabaptist followers of Melchior Hoffman in northern Germany took control of Münster, the major city of Westphalia, for sixteen months during 1534 and 1535. They established a sociopolitical regime marked by community of goods and polygamy. More commonly, the two-kingdom idea and the principle of nonresistance combined to produce a more passive sectarian withdrawal from the political world. By the late sixteenth century, sectarian nonresistance was established as the Anabaptist norm. Thereafter, Anabaptists usually responded to political opposition by either accommodating or migrating to more hospitable regions. The tension between the activist and sectarian impulses, however, has continued to shape Anabaptist politics into the modern period.

Anabaptists in North America

Mennonites and Amish are the largest North American religious groups descended from the European Anabaptist movement. (The Brethren in Christ denomination and the Hutterite communes in the western United States and Canada also have roots in the European Anabaptist movement.) Mennonites derive their name from Menno Simons, an early Dutch Anabaptist leader. There are records of some Dutch Mennonites in New York as early as 1644, but the first successful American settlement was established in Germantown, Pennsylvania, near Philadelphia, in 1683 by immigrants from the Lower Rhine in Germany. Later waves of migration arrived from South Germany, Switzerland, and Alsace-Lorraine until the mid-1800s. These groups settled first in eastern Pennsylvania and later went directly to Ohio and In-

Amish men build a barn near Zelionople, Pennsylvania. Such community "barn raisings," benefiting a single Amish family or individual, are a regular feature of Amish life.

diana. Within the United States migrations continued westward from Pennsylvania, north into Canada, and south into Virginia in pursuit of farmland and in flight from war. Still later, there were successive waves of Mennonite immigration from Russia, in flight from political upheaval and military conscription there. Mennonites arriving from Russia settled primarily in the plains regions of Canada and the United States.

Thanks to their commercial and tourist appeal, the Old Order Amish are probably the most well known American group of Anabaptist descent. Amish groups originated in a schism among Swiss Anabaptists in 1693 led by Jakob Ammann (c. 1644–c. 1730), an Anabaptist bishop. Ammann promoted stricter cultural restrictions, more frequent observance of communion, and stricter enforcement of shunning, the practice of social ostracism of members who transgressed church discipline. Amish immigrants began coming to the United States in the 1730s, and the first American Amish congregation was established in 1749.

Parallel communities of Mennonites and Amish emerged in most states and provinces where Mennonites settled. The key distinction between the two was the Amish community's greater emphasis on congregational polity. That is, among

the Amish groups, primary religious authority was located at the congregational level rather than in regional or denominational hierarchies. About 1865, the American Amish experienced a schism in which traditionalists withdrew to form what came to be known as the Old Order Amish. Most of the more progressive and culturally accommodative Amish groups merged with their Mennonite counterparts in the late 1800s and early 1900s.

North American Mennonite and Amish groups exhibit a broad range of religious forms and political stances. By 1996, in the United States alone, the broader Mennonite "family" of religious groups consisted of thirty-two organizationally independent multicongregational bodies. ("Denominations" is a problematic term for some of these groups.) At least twelve other distinct groups exist only in Canada. This variety results from a complicated history of immigration from various parts of Europe in various periods, and numerous schisms within U.S. and Canadian groups. The two largest groups in the United States (excluding the Old Order Amish, who have about 65,000 members) are the Mennonite Church General Assembly (90,139 members in 970 congregations) and the General Conference Mennonite Church (34,040 members in 226 congregations). The distinction between these two groups has its earliest roots in a schism in eastern Pennsylvania in 1847. In 1995 the two denominations voted to approve a process leading toward merger.

With such organizational variety, it is not surprising that Anabaptist groups can be found across the entire right-left political spectrum. Some groups have accommodated themselves to North American culture, while others have remained sectarian. Even within groups, the emphasis on religious voluntarism (in other words, membership by choice rather than by birth, and relatively easy congregational switching) and congregational polity has produced a wide variety of political stances. Some congregations embrace conservative politics and American patriotic values, while others are more leftist and activist in their politics, taking an oppositional approach to the state and mainstream political institutions and policies. Support for political positions on both the right and the left can be found in Anabaptist tradition. The Anabaptist emphasis on biblical and communal moral authority has affinities with many conservative positions in the North American context. On the other hand, Anabaptists' pacifism and their goals of building an alternative social order in the here and now have affinities with the left.

Amidst this variety, however, there are two general and interrelated trends that deserve more detailed discussion. The first is the ongoing negotiation of the relation between church and state, especially with respect to military conscription. The second is the move from sectarian nonresistance to active pacifism as the dominant political stance, especially among North American Mennonites.

Church-State Relations: From Sectarian Nonresistance to Active Pacifism

For Anabaptist groups, relations between church and state are complicated by a two-kingdom theory that views the church as the embodiment of the kingdom of God and sees the state as representing the kingdom of the world (to which the kingdom of God is essentially opposed). The constitutional separation of church and state in North America (and the small size of Anabaptist groups) permitted such an oppositional stance and made repression by external authorities less likely. Tension between Anabaptists and the state emerged most explicitly when the state made demands which would require Anabaptists to violate principles they believed essential to their citizenship in the kingdom of God. Such tension was sharpest during times of war and mil-

itary conscription. Over the past two centuries in North America, the relations between Anabaptist groups and the state have been hammered out in the crucible of war times.

During the American Revolution, Mennonites and Amish tried to maintain a neutral stance. Most of them refused to join militias, take oaths of allegiance, or provide direct material support to the revolutionary cause. State and local responses included special taxation of conscientious objectors, fines or forfeitures, withholding of political rights such as voting privileges, and, occasionally, imprisonment. Mennonites and Amish disagreed among themselves over whether it was legitimate for individuals to pay substitutes to join the military in their stead. They also differed over whether to refuse payment of taxes that were explicitly in lieu of military service. The consequence of this war was that the distinctions between Anabaptist groups and their neighbors was heightened. As their sectarian identity increased, their involvement in routine political activity such as voting decreased.

By the time of the U.S. Civil War (1861–1865), Mennonite and Amish enclaves had become relatively prosperous agricultural communities—on both sides of the North-South divide. Under the draft laws of Abraham Lincoln's administration, conscientious objectors to war could hire substitutes or pay a $300 exemption fee. Most Anabaptist groups willingly accepted these options, though a few Mennonites enlisted in the Union army. In Virginia, Mennonites were unlikely to be sympathetic to the Confederate cause. They were not slaveholders and they had ties of kinship and loyalty to Mennonite communities in the North. No Mennonites willingly joined the Confederate army, and when forced into service, they refused to shoot. To avoid forced conscription, some Mennonites hired substitutes, others hid, and a few were imprisoned. After 1862 Virginia passed a law allowing conscientious objectors to avoid military service by paying a $500 fee and a 2 percent tax on property, a provision most Mennonites accepted willingly. Since Mennonites were largely in sympathy with the Northern cause, the consequences of the Civil War were an increased tolerance by Anabaptists for the state and a willingness to accept its provisions for conscientious objection without opposing state militarism.

World War I brought renewed tensions with the state and caught Mennonites and Amish unprepared. Almost fifty years had passed since the Civil War, and the new generation of Mennonite and Amish leaders were unschooled and naive in their dealings with the government. Further, Anabaptists'

Germanic culture did not facilitate any easy accommodations between their church and the state's war effort. As a consequence, they failed to obtain meaningful concessions for conscientious objectors. Young men who were drafted were required to report to military camps. There, if they demonstrated the sincerity of their convictions by conscientiously refusing to follow orders, they were considered for agricultural furloughs. This led to a rather chaotic situation in the camps, where military officers varied in the extent to which they understood or cooperated with this policy. Many conscientious objectors were subjected to ill treatment and some were imprisoned following courts martial.

Those who were not conscripted faced other issues in their home communities. One divisive question concerned the purchase of Liberty Bonds to support the war effort. Official denominational policy opposed their purchase, but the policy's application was varied and at times confused. In some communities, there were creative compromises worked out with bankers so that Mennonites technically would not purchase war bonds but would deposit money in local banks, thus freeing other bank funds for investment in Liberty Bonds. During this period Mennonites and Amish learned much about dealing with the state. They benefited, as well, from occasional cooperation with the more politically savvy Quakers. They were active participants in postwar relief efforts and began to develop ideas and institutions that supported engagement in alternative service during times of war. This move toward alternative service for conscientious objectors was further developed during World War II.

Mennonites were not caught so unawares by World War II as they had been by World War I. Their leaders were more experienced in dealing with government officials, and their official position as conscientious objectors was institutionalized in various church programs and recognized by outsiders. Throughout 1940 there was a long series of complicated negotiations between representatives of the "historic peace churches" and officials of the legislative and executive branches of American government. The upshot, in 1941, was President Franklin D. Roosevelt's Executive Order 8675, establishing the Civilian Public Service (CPS). Initially the CPS plan assigned drafted objectors to conservation camps where they would work in soil conservation and forestry projects. Later in the war, as the number of conscientious objectors grew, groups of young men were assigned to a variety of other projects as well—including work in mental hospitals, hookworm eradication projects in the South, forest-fire

skydiving units in the West, and service as "guinea pigs" for various experiments at the National Institutes of Health. The consequences of World War II for Anabaptist groups were a strengthening of their identity as pacifists and the development of attitudes, skills, and institutions that supported greater social and political activism outside their sectarian communities.

By the time of the Vietnam War, the U.S. government had recognized conscientious objection as legitimate and had institutionalized alternative service provisions. As a consequence, Anabaptist groups were free to take a more aggressive oppositional stance to government military policies; and they were more likely to do so, thanks to their increasingly active social involvement during and following the World War II era. Throughout the 1960s various official denominational statements challenged the U.S. government's militarism, especially its involvement in Vietnam. By the late sixties and early seventies many Mennonites were active in the antiwar movement, both through institutionalized means such as lobbying Congress and sending letters to the president, and through noninstitutionalized means such as protest marches and draft resistance. Both of the largest Mennonite denominations issued official statements declaring both legal alternative service programs and illegal draft resistance as valid expressions of nonresistance.

Since the end of the Vietnam War, official Mennonite statements and program policies have moved beyond the pursuit of peace to a larger concern for "justice." Mennonite positions have tended to the left on a variety of social and economic issues, such as opposition to capital punishment, support for the rights of women and minorities, and solidarity with environmental concerns. The exception to this trend is the issue of abortion, on which Mennonites have tried to articulate a "consistent pro-life" position that envelops opposition to militarism, capital punishment, and abortion.

Qualifying the General Trend

There are several important qualifications regarding the general trend from passive nonresistance to active pacifism. The first is that Amish communities have not been part of the shift toward political activism. While they cooperated with Mennonites and other "peace churches" in the attempts to gain concessions for conscientious objectors during both world wars, they did not accompany Mennonites on their path to activism in the 1960s. Their stance toward political involvement has continued in a mainly passive non-resistant mode. Their interactions with the state, via the National Amish Steering Committee, have been primarily defensive attempts to gain concessions from regulations that would require them to violate their religious convictions. Court cases regarding education have been the most publicized, but the Amish have also clashed with the state in cases concerning traffic and occupational safety issues, health concerns, and land use issues. These cases have helped to define the boundaries of federal and state protection of the free exercise of religion. The most important court decision was the 1972 U.S. Supreme Court case, *Wisconsin v. Yoder,* in which the Court established a four-part test regarding religious liberty that significantly increased the state's burden of proof in such cases.

A second important caveat is that the experience of Anabaptist groups in Canada differs in significant respects from that of U.S. groups. Canadian Mennonites and Amish have found the Canadian government quite hospitable to their particular religious and cultural interests. Neither have Anabaptist groups in Canada been faced with issues of war and militarism as intensely as their U.S. counterparts. For this reason there has been less of an adversarial relationship between Anabaptists and the state, along with higher rates of participation in political institutions. Canadian Mennonites are significantly more likely to vote and hold public office than Mennonites in the United States.

Finally, it is important to stress that the left-leaning political activism that has characterized official Mennonite institutions and policies during the past few decades is not unambiguously reflected in the Mennonite populace. As noted earlier, local congregations, even within the same denomination or regional conference, exhibit a broad range of political views and activities. The same is true of Mennonite individuals. Good survey data are available from 1972 and 1989 only, but they indicate that, in the United States, a significant (and increasing) plurality of Mennonite individuals identify themselves as conservative Republicans. The number of Mennonites identifying themselves as liberal Democrats also increased from 1972 to 1989, but was still less than 10 percent. A similar pattern exists in Canada, with the largest number of Canadian Mennonites (47 percent) identifying themselves as Progressive Conservatives in 1989.

See also *Freedom of religion; Pacifism; Separation of church and state; Traditionalism; Violence; War.*

Fred Kniss

BIBLIOGRAPHY

Driedger, Leo, and Donald B. Kraybill. *Mennonite Peacemaking: From Quietism to Activism.* Scottdale, Pa.: Herald Press, 1994.

Epp, Frank H. *Mennonites in Canada, 1886–1920: The History of a Separate People.* Toronto: Macmillan, 1974.

———. *Mennonites in Canada, 1920–1940: A People's Struggle for Survival.* Toronto: Macmillan, 1982.

Graber Miller, Keith. *Wise as Serpents, Innocent as Doves: American Mennonites Engage Washington.* Knoxville: University of Tennessee Press, 1996.

Kauffman, J. Howard, and Leo Driedger. *The Mennonite Mosaic: Identity and Modernization.* Scottdale, Pa.: Herald Press, 1991.

Keim, Albert N., and Grant M. Stoltzfus. *The Politics of Conscience: The Historic Peace Churches and America at War, 1917–1955.* Scottdale, Pa.: Herald Press, 1988.

Kniss, Fred. *Disquiet in the Land: Cultural Conflict in American Mennonite Communities.* New Brunswick, N.J.: Rutgers University Press, 1997.

Kraybill, Donald B., ed. *The Amish and the State.* Baltimore: Johns Hopkins University Press, 1993.

Redekop, Calvin. *Mennonite Society.* Baltimore: Johns Hopkins University Press, 1989.

Schlabach, Theron, ed. *The Mennonite Experience in America.* 4 vols. Scottdale, Pa.: Herald Press, 1985–1996.

Anglicanism

The tradition of Christian belief and practice associated with the Church of England is known as Anglicanism, or the Anglican Communion. The Church of England became the established church in England after King Henry VIII renounced the authority of the pope in 1533. Since the late eighteenth century Anglicanism has spread to many other countries. A balanced appreciation of the political significance of contemporary Anglicanism requires both an understanding of the nature of the tradition's origins and historical development in early modern England and an awareness of the diversifications that have occurred during the past two centuries.

Origins

The initial chain of events leading to the formation of the Church of England was only indirectly connected to the wider pattern of religious reform and revolt in mid-sixteenth-century Europe. Henry VIII's motivation for setting himself up as "Supreme Head" of the Church of England and repudiating the authority of the pope in Rome was essentially political rather than religious. In particular, he desperately wanted a male heir and therefore sought legitimacy, which the pope had denied him, for his decision to divorce

Catherine of Aragon and remarry. More generally, his government sought to repudiate what it saw as papal interference in English internal affairs. Henry, however, had no desire otherwise to change the Catholic character of the Church of England, and during his lifetime (until 1547)—although the monasteries were dissolved in the late 1530s—pressure for reform in a Protestant direction was largely resisted. It was during the short reign of the boy-king Edward VI (1547–1553) that the Reformers gained the ascendancy, although under Mary I (1553–1558), an uncompromising supporter of Roman Catholicism and the pope, strenuous efforts were made to reassert the authority of Rome.

A lasting settlement was achieved only in 1559, at the beginning of the reign of Elizabeth I. The Act of Supremacy established the position of the queen and her successors as "Supreme Governor" (rather than head) of the church. The Act of Uniformity required the use of the Book of Common Prayer and made absence from church punishable by a fine, a measure directed against Roman Catholics and Protestant separatists (who rejected the Church of England as insufficiently reformed). Elizabeth's intention was that the Church of England should be as comprehensive as possible, thereby enabling it to serve as a focus for national unity and as a key support of the Crown. The Church of England retained the extensive property holdings of the medieval church and its episcopal organizational structure—that is, a hierarchical governing structure headed by the archbishops of Canterbury and York and twenty-four diocesan bishops. Its authority extended over Wales as well as England, and a parallel Church of Ireland was established. In Scotland, however, the Reformation followed a very different course: a Presbyterian state church developed, while episcopalians there were a small and often persecuted minority. Scottish episcopalianism nevertheless survived and developed as a tradition organizationally distinct from the Church of England.

Only after the Elizabethan settlement did the Church of England begin to define its theological and doctrinal position. The first step came with the issuing of the Thirty-nine Articles, a statement of the church's doctrine, in 1563. Richard Hooker was the church's leading apologist. In his *Laws of Ecclesiastical Polity* (1594–1597) he deferred to natural law (rather than biblical Scripture) as the ultimate source of authority, argued that the church still possessed valid continuity with the medieval English church, and defended the maintenance of the church's governance by bishops. The word *Anglican,* which was not used at all in the Elizabethan era, gained only a limited currency in the seventeenth century. Gradually, however, it came into use, denoting a middle way between Roman Catholicism and Calvinism. In summary, Anglicanism was characterized by a rejection of papal supremacy but the retention of bishops; a limited belief in the rites of the sacraments but advocacy of justification by faith; and acknowledgment of the authority of reason and tradition alongside that of Scripture.

Meanwhile, the church was closely bound up with the turbulent politics of the seventeenth century. In the 1630s attempts by the archbishop of Canterbury, William Laud, to restore aspects of pre-Reformation liturgical practice outraged the Puritans, who wanted to move the church closer to Calvinist reforms, and contributed to the tensions that erupted in the Civil War. After the victory of Parliament and the execution of Charles I in 1649, episcopacy was temporarily abolished and an attempt was made to extend a Scottish-style Presbyterian system of church governance to England. In 1655 Oliver Cromwell, the Lord Protector, prohibited the use of the prayer book. In 1660, however, the restored monarchy brought back the bishops, and the Act of Uniformity of 1662 reimposed a modified version of the Book of Common Prayer, which remains the official liturgy of the Church of England. Clergy who were unwilling to conform left the church, thereby beginning the history of other Protestant denominations in England, known as Dissenters and later as Nonconformists.

In subsequent decades both Parliament and the Church of England became divided between those who asserted that royal and ecclesiastical authority was divinely sanctioned (Tories and High Churchmen) and those who held to a more limited view of monarchy and episcopacy and a more fluid interpretation of doctrine (Whigs and latitudinarians). These struggles reached their climax in the Glorious Revolution of 1688, in which James II, who was believed to want to restore Catholicism to England, was removed from the throne and the crown was offered to William of Orange and his wife Mary (James's daughter). The Glorious Revolution gave political ascendancy to the Whigs and to Parliament and ensured the Protestant succession, while Tory and High Church attitudes continued to enjoy considerable ecclesiastical support. The Act of Settlement of 1701 required that future monarchs and their consorts be Protestants and "join in Communion" with the Church of England. It has remained in force.

Following the accession of George I, in 1714, tensions

subsided and the eighteenth century saw the Church of England in relatively stable and close alliance with the secular fabric of politics and society. The choice of bishops was likely to be made in the political interests of the government; the parish clergy often came to enjoy considerable local political power as magistrates and landlords. Meanwhile, the conflicts of earlier ages had left their mark in considerable internal doctrinal diversity.

Reform and Expansion

From the late eighteenth century onward England became increasingly industrialized and urbanized. These changes were associated with substantial increases in the strength of religious dissent—in part because of disruption of the Anglican-dominated social fabric of pre-industrial society, in part because of the development of new industrial settlements remote from existing Anglican churches. From Dissenters came irresistible pressure to reform the nature of the relationship between the Church of England and the state to reflect the more diverse nature of society. Nonconformists, Roman Catholics, and, eventually, Jews and atheists became eligible to take seats in Parliament, thus ending the illusion that the practice of politics was exclusively Anglican. An Ecclesiastical Commission, the ancestor of the modern Church Commissioners, was set up in 1835 to administer the church's wealth on behalf of Parliament. New dioceses and parishes were created in response to the enormous growth in population. Tithes and church rates (a local levy on property), which had obliged landowners and taxpayers to contribute to the support of the church, were gradually reformed and removed. The Church of Ireland was disestablished in 1871, and there was considerable pressure for a complete severance of ties between church and state in England. This radical step was successfully resisted, although the Church in Wales was to be disestablished in 1920. All these changes were a source of considerable political controversy and parliamentary debate.

Meanwhile, the religious identity of Anglicanism was intensely contested in struggles between Evangelicals, Anglo-Catholics, and Broad Churchmen. At stake was the question of whether Anglicanism was essentially Protestant (but not sectarian), essentially Catholic (but not Roman), or comprehensive in ethos and liberal—or at least nonprescriptive—in theology. By the end of the nineteenth century an uneasy stalemate had resulted, in which all parties had secured their position within the church but none had gained an incontestable ascendancy. The inclusiveness of the Church of England in the late nineteenth and twentieth centuries was both cause and consequence of its continued ties with the state insofar as its all-encompassing nature rendered the church a credible representation of the religious life of the nation as a whole.

During this period Anglicanism began to be exported outside England, Wales, and Ireland. After American independence Samuel Seabury sought consecration as the first bishop of what was to become the Protestant Episcopal Church in the United States. It was impossible for him to be consecrated in England because the order of service there required an oath of allegiance to the king. No such difficulty existed in Scotland (because the Episcopal Church was not established), and accordingly Seabury was consecrated in Aberdeen, in 1784. A process of gradual convergence between the Church of England and the Scottish Episcopal Church can be dated from this period. During the nineteenth century numerous bishoprics were established in countries where there was English colonization or missionary endeavor, notably in Africa, Australia, Canada, New Zealand, and the West Indies. These Anglican churches (including the Scottish Episcopal Church and the Church in Wales after its disestablishment) lacked the ties with the state existing in England; they came to operate as largely autonomous ecclesiastical provinces under the umbrella of the Anglican Communion in which the archbishop of Canterbury has a primacy of prestige, but not of authority.

The Modern Era

During the twentieth century the internal diversity of Anglicanism increased still further. The Evangelical and Anglo-Catholic wings adopted strongly contrasting liturgical practices as well as theologies, while some liberals moved toward radical rejection of traditional Christian dogma. Further sources of dissension since the 1960s have been the influence of the charismatic movement, which sought to exercise the gifts of the Holy Spirit in the worship and ministry of the contemporary church, and the debate over the ministry of women. (In 1992 the General Synod of the Church of England allowed the ordination of women to the priesthood. Decisions on the ordination of women varied within the Anglican Communion; in the Protestant Episcopal Church in the United States, for example, women were first ordained in 1974.) In some Anglican dioceses and provinces outside England it is possible to discern a certain

As leader of the worldwide Anglican Communion, the archbishop of Canterbury represents the communion in international debates. In a 1992 sermon at St. George's Cathedral, in Jerusalem, Archbishop of Canterbury George Carey called on both Israelis and Palestinians to recognize each other's rights to disputed lands.

uniformity of approach in the face of such diversity: for example, in the predominant evangelicalism of the archdiocese of Sydney in Australia and in the relative liturgical conservatism of the American Episcopal Church. The Church of England, however, has become something of a microcosm of the wider divergencies within the Anglican Communion.

Ties between the Church of England and the state also underwent significant change in the twentieth century. In 1919 the Enabling Act created the Church Assembly, to which Parliament delegated the discussion of legislation concerning the church, while itself retaining a right of veto. In 1970 this body was combined with the Convocations (historic assemblies of the clergy) to constitute the General Synod. Nevertheless, substantial links between church and state remain. The sovereign continues as supreme governor of the church and therefore must be an Anglican. Diocesan bishops and some other senior clergy are formally appointed by the Crown on the recommendation of the prime minister, although procedures introduced in the 1970s ensure that in practice the church exercises considerable influence on

the process. The archbishops and the twenty-four most senior bishops have seats in the House of Lords. Although no public money is given to support its religious functions, the church continues to benefit from the substantial endowments managed by the Church Commissioners; these funds, however, have been somewhat depleted in recent years, leading to a much greater dependence on the voluntary offerings of congregations. The Church of England, through its tenure of the cathedrals and numerous historic churches and other buildings, is the custodian of a major part of the British national heritage. It continues to be the religious point of reference for a substantial proportion of the population—though in 1989 only slightly more than 3 percent of the English population regularly attended Anglican Sunday worship. (A survey in 1974 had suggested that 41.6 percent of the population retained a nominal identification with Anglicanism.)

In a predominantly secular age the Church of England has moved toward the periphery of political life in Britain, but it retains the capacity sometimes to capture the limelight. Notable occasions were in 1927–1928, when a revised prayer book proposed by the Church Assembly was rejected by Parliament, and in the later phases of the Second World War, when George Bell, bishop of Chichester, strenuously opposed the saturation bombing of German cities. In the 1960s Archbishop Michael Ramsey took a strong stand against racism, while in the 1980s bishops were among the strongest critics of the economic and social policies of Margaret Thatcher's governments. Such occurrences show that the continuing state connection does not necessarily render the church subservient to the government of the day, although it does tend to contribute to an avoidance of political positions that could be construed as narrowly partisan. Outside England, Anglican leaders are under even less constraint, but they do not necessarily carry the same weight as leaders in Britain. Nevertheless, in South Africa the moral leadership of Archbishop Desmond Tutu, who played an important role in ending racial apartheid, is a striking example of the successful exercise of political influence by a prominent clergyman.

Anglicanism, having been originally shaped for political purposes, with a view to achieving as great a degree of comprehensiveness as possible, has a capacity to accommodate internal diversity of a kind that would almost inevitably lead to schism in more tightly defined traditions. The possibility of disestablishment continues periodically to resurface in England, but there seems to be no inherent reason why the state connection is more vulnerable now than it has been in the recent past. What is clear, however, is that, in view of the historic role of Anglicanism in the whole fabric of English national and constitutional identity, serious future debate over disestablishment would raise far-reaching questions.

See also *Burke, Edmund; Catholicism, Roman; English Revolution; Great Britain; Ireland; Protestantism; Reformation; Religious organization; State churches.*

John Wolffe

BIBLIOGRAPHY

Chadwick, Owen. *The Victorian Church.* 2 vols. London and New York: Oxford University Press, 1966, 1970.

Collinson, Patrick. *The Religion of Protestants: The Church in English Society, 1559–1642.* Oxford: Clarendon Press, 1982.

Habgood, John (Archbishop of York). *Church and Nation in a Secular Age.* London: Darton, Longman, and Todd, 1983.

Hastings, Adrian. *A History of English Christianity, 1920–1990.* 3d ed. London: SCM Press, 1991.

Parsons, Gerald, ed. *The Growth of Religious Diversity: Britain from 1944.* 2 vols. London and New York: Routledge, 1993, 1994.

Parsons, Gerald (with James Moore and John Wolffe), ed. *Religion in Victorian Britain.* 5 vols. Manchester: Manchester University Press, 1997.

Spurr, John. *The Restoration Church of England, 1646–1689.* New Haven and London: Yale University Press, 1991.

Sykes, Norman. *Church and State in England in the Eighteenth Century.* Cambridge: Cambridge University Press, 1934.

Walsh, John (with Colin Haydon and Stephen Taylor), ed. *The Church of England, c.1689–c.1837.* Cambridge: Cambridge University Press, 1993.

Angola

The long interaction between politics and religion in the Republic of Angola, located south of the Congo River on the west coast of Africa, has been motivated principally by colonialism: in the first period (the fifteenth to the nineteenth centuries) by the imposition of Portuguese rule and in the twentieth century by the defeat of colonialism. Reflecting the links between politics and religion in the very name by which it has been known since the beginning of colonial rule, Angola comes from the Kimbundu word *ngola,* a small piece of iron revered as a sacred relic, to which was attributed the power exercised by the headmen of kinship groups. The relic thus combined political and religious meanings: political, in its relation to the kinship structures, and religious, in that sacred power was ascribed to it.

Roman Catholicism

Along with colonial rule the Portuguese introduced Roman Catholicism into Angola. The king of the Congo, the northern region of Angola, was baptized on Easter 1491 and from that time communicated with the king of Portugal as "My Brother." This relationship between religion and politics was strengthened by the *Padroado* (Patronage), an agreement between the Catholic Church and the Portuguese government in which the church gave special rights and responsibilities to the Portuguese state for the spread of the faith within its territories. In the following three centuries hundreds of Catholic missionaries evangelized Angola, baptizing thousands. Because these missionaries came not only from Portugal but also from Spain, France, and Italy, there was tension among them and at times conflict as the European scramble for Africa intensified.

The influence of the Catholic Church declined dramatically in Angola in the nineteenth century, and by 1853 there

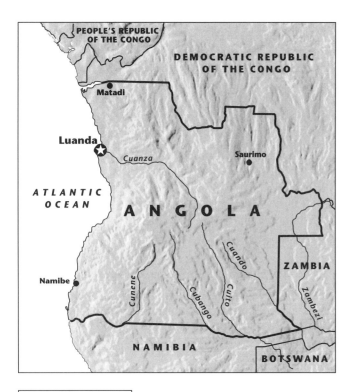

were only five priests in the country, all Africans. This decline in influence was not peculiar to Angola. The church in Italy, Spain, and Portugal, which had sent most of the Catholic missionaries in the fifteenth to eighteenth centuries, suffered reverses at the end of that period and into the nineteenth century. As a result, other mission fields similarly contracted.

The replanting of the Catholic Church in Angola was due primarily to the work of the Congregation of the Holy Ghost. This French missionary order sent its first missionaries to Angola in 1866, but because of illness they stayed only four years. The French missionaries were suspect by the Portuguese since the political and commercial interests of France and Portugal frequently clashed in the Congo basin. The Congregation of the Holy Ghost continued sending missionaries to Angola, and they revitalized the Catholic Church. Their success was also strengthened by the Patronage, which, although it was abolished by the Council of Trent in the sixteenth century for most of the world, allowed Portugal to continue creating dioceses and establishing convents and monasteries. The Patronage also imposed certain obligations on Portugal to construct and maintain church properties and to support the clergy.

Entry of Protestant Missions

In the last quarter of the nineteenth century three Protestant missions established stations in the center of Angola's three largest ethnolinguistic groups: the Kikongo, Kimbundu, and Umbundu. The first Protestant missionaries arrived in São Salvador, the capital of the Kingdom of the Congo, in 1878, having been sent by the Baptist Missionary Society of London. The king of the Congo, Dom Pedro V, received the Baptists cordially, attending their services and requesting personal instruction. At the same time, he wrote a letter to the governor general of Angola, and another to the director of the Cabinda Catholic mission, requesting that Catholic priests return to São Salvador. The Baptist mission found young people who were eager to learn to read and write. With the encouragement of the king, the Baptists established two more mission stations among the Bakongo.

The second Protestant mission to enter Angola was the American Board of Commissioners for Foreign Missions, the oldest Protestant mission society in North America, with headquarters in Boston. The first three missionaries sailed for Angola in 1880. They disembarked at the port of Benguela and trekked inland two hundred miles to Bailundo, capital of the largest of the thirteen Umbundu kingdoms. In the next four decades they founded five more mission stations, each near the capital of an Umbundu kingdom.

The third Protestant mission was that of the Methodists, arriving in 1885 at Luanda, the capital of Angola. Bishop William Taylor led a band of forty-five Americans (twenty-nine adults and sixteen children), who had been chosen because they had the skills to support themselves: businessmen, doctors, teachers, mechanics, artisans, farmers, as well as evangelists and pastors. In a whirlwind tour Taylor's pioneers established five mission stations in six months in the center of the Kimbundu people, from Luanda to Malange.

With the arrival of the Protestant missions a new dimension of religious and political interaction developed. From the fifteenth through most of the nineteenth century the interaction between religion and politics in Angola had been between traditional African religion and political structures, as illustrated by the *ngola,* or between the Catholic Church and Angolan kingdoms. The Portuguese colonial government was the patron of the Catholic Church, while the Protestant churches were only tolerated. The Protestants were endured only because international treaties required colonial powers to allow the free activity of foreign religious and scientific organizations.

Anticolonial Activity and Civil War

In the early twentieth century the Portuguese, attempting to achieve political control after three uprisings, established a colonial administration that used the traditional Angolan rulers as subordinates or as mere puppets. By the middle of the twentieth century Great Britain, France, and Belgium felt the pressure of anticolonial movements in Africa. Portugal, however, refused to admit that it had colonies, calling them provinces.

As Angolan liberation movements organized in the 1950s, the Portuguese believed that Protestants were the principal force behind their formation. The National Front for the Liberation of Angola (FNLA), with its roots among the Bakongo, was led by Holden Roberto, who had been educated in a Baptist mission. The president of the Popular Movement for the Liberation of Angola (MPLA), which was organized within the Kimbundu area, was Agostinho Neto, who had been the secretary of the Methodist bishop in Luanda. The National Union for the Total Independence of Angola (UNITA) was created by Jonas Savimbi, who was educated in the schools of the Congregational missions among the Ovimbundu. The backgrounds of these three men convinced the Portuguese that the Protestant missions had been promoting anticolonialism and training leaders to oppose Portuguese rule.

Each of the liberation movements had its roots in a community dominated by one Protestant denomination and one ethnolinguistic group. The ethnic groups and denominations were not solid blocs, but they were sufficiently cohesive to be identifiable. The Catholic Church, which was established throughout Angola, did not identify with any one of the liberation movements.

From 1961 until 1974 the liberation movements fought against the Portuguese military forces, at the same time fighting among themselves. The end of the colonial war was not brought about by a military victory of the three movements over the Portuguese. Rather, it was precipitated by a coup d'état in Portugal that overthrew the government on April 25, 1974. The coup was organized by the Movement of the Armed Forces, a coalition primarily of left-wing Portuguese military officers who had fought in the colonial wars in Angola, Mozambique, and Guinea.

The new Portuguese government was committed to decolonization and recognized the right of its African colonies to self-determination. Angola declared its independence on November 11, 1975. Although the three liberation movements had agreed to form a coalition government to rule the new nation, that agreement soon crumbled. The Soviet-backed MPLA, based in Luanda, formed the new government for independent Angola and attacked the anticommunist FNLA in the north and UNITA in the south. A twenty-year civil war (1975–1994) ensued in which hundreds of thousands would die.

The MPLA government, exercising its authority in Luanda, begin to reshape Angolan society according to a Marxist-Leninist model. In 1977 President Agostinho Neto declared that Christians could not be members of the party.

During the civil war the churches urged the warring parties to declare a cease-fire and agree to reconciliation and peace. The Catholic Conference of Bishops regularly circulated pastoral letters focusing on the need to structure the political community according to divine law. The Protestants, through the Council of Christian Churches and the Association of Evangelicals of Angola, called for peace and justice.

The civil war technically ended in 1994 when the MPLA government and UNITA signed a peace plan. All conditions of the peace plan were not fulfilled, however, and conflict has continued.

See also *Africa, Christian; African traditional religions; Colonialism; Missionaries.*

Lawrence W. Henderson

BIBLIOGRAPHY

Bozeman, Adda B. *Conflict in Africa: Concepts and Realities.* Princeton: Princeton University Press, 1976.

Childs, Gladwyn Murray. *Umbundu Kinship and Character.* London: Oxford University Press, 1949.

Henderson, Lawrence W. *Angola: Five Centuries of Conflict.* Ithaca, N.Y.: Cornell University Press, 1979.

————. *The Church in Angola.* Cleveland, Ohio: Pilgrim Press, 1992.

Idowu, E. Bolaji. *African Traditional Religion: A Definition.* Maryknoll, N.Y.: Orbis Books, 1973.

MacGaffey, Wyatt. *Religion and Society in Central Africa: The Bakongo of the Lower Zaire.* Chicago: University of Chicago Press, 1973.

Marcum, John. *The Angolan Revolution.* Vol. 2. Cambridge: MIT Press, 1978.

Miller, Joseph C. *Kings and Kinsmen: Early Mbundu States in Angola.* Oxford: Clarendon Press, 1976.

Anticlericalism

Anticlericalism is a social movement found in some societies that challenges the cultural and political domination of Roman Catholicism. Although criticism of the clergy can be found in many countries and at many times, the term *anticlericalism* usually refers to the hostility toward and struggle against the Catholic Church's position of power and influence on cultural and social policy in Europe, particularly in France.

Anticlericalism is linked to the ideas of the eighteenth-century Enlightenment, the French Revolution, and nineteenth-century liberalism. The Revolution in France took away the privileges of the clergy (the clerics) that dated from the Middle Ages and confiscated the church's large property holdings. Anticlerics—who accused the clergy of claiming special privileges and attempting to dominate the minds and morals of the people and the government—worked to emancipate civil and political society from the influence of the church, particularly in social matters relating to marriage, divorce, and education.

Anticlerical movements have also arisen in other countries where Catholicism predominates; among them are Belgium, Spain, Italy, Portugal, and Mexico. The *Kulturkampf* ("culture struggle") in Germany in the 1870s was closely akin to anticlericalism. Under Chancellor Otto von Bismarck the government of the newly united German state clashed with the Vatican over control of social institutions.

Three basic ideas are behind the Catholic Church's claim to precedence, and each of these must be present before an anticlerical movement will arise. First, the church makes a distinction between the clergy and the laity—a difference in essence, not just in function—with the clergy taking on the nature of the sacred. Second, the church claims doctrinal authority based on biblical revelation, ecclesiastical tradition, and natural ethics and makes universal judgments in these domains. And, third, the church proclaims itself to be a universal institution.

The church becomes a target of anticlericalist sentiment when these three elements are not conditioned by moderating forces (for example, the pressure for religious freedom that led to the reforms instituted by the Second Vatican Council in the 1960s) and when the doctrines of the church conflict with civil society. With the elimination of illiteracy, it becomes much more difficult for the church to justify its position that clerics are naturally superior to the laity. When culture and religion become independent, and when Catholicism is one doctrine among others, the church cannot maintain its claim to supremacy. And when the structure of nation-states is based on citizenship and nationality, political interference from a supranational church is regarded as abusive.

There is not necessarily a conflict between clericalism and anticlericalism in predominantly Catholic countries. Catholicism can represent national feeling (for example, in Ireland under British rule and in Poland under communism). Furthermore, there is a decline in anticlericalist feeling when the church agrees to a separation between civil law and religious law. Examples are Spain (1976–1980), when reform laws were instituted after the death of Francisco Franco, the dictator who had been supported by the church, and Italy after Vatican II.

Confrontation between clericalist and anticlericalist elements continued in France until 1905, when a law was passed separating church and state. The conflict in France involved two political and cultural forces, both convinced that they represented universal values: Catholic France (regarded as defender of the monarchy) and secular France (the promoter of human rights). But this conflict was transformed into the normal tension that occurs in any democratic society. Disagreements continue, however, especially concerning public funds for private Catholic schools and over questions of birth control.

Generally, although the process of secularization in the modern world prevents clericalism (and therefore anticlericalism), a new form of conflict that might be characterized as anticlericalism has arisen between fundamentalist religious groups and secularized societies. Examples are evident in Islamic countries (for example, Turkey and Iran), in Israel (ultra-Orthodox Jews), and in the United States (fundamentalist Christians).

See also *Catholicism, Roman; Christian democracy; France; Pluralism; Secularization; Vatican Council, Second.*

Jean Baubérot

BIBLIOGRAPHY

Baubérot, Jean. *Morale laïque ou ordre moral.* Paris: Le Seuil, 1997.
Bertocci, Pietro. *Republican Anticlericalism and Cultural Politics in France, 1848–1890.* Princeton: Princeton University Press, 1978.
Martin, David. *A General Theory of Secularization.* Oxford: Blackwell, 1978.
Remond, René. *L'Anticléricalisme en France depuis 1815 à nos jours.* Paris: Fayard, 1976; Brussels: Complexe, 1985.

Sanchez, J. M. *Anticlericalism: A Brief History.* Notre Dame: University of Notre Dame Press, 1972.

Schapiro, J. S. *Anticlericalism: Conflict between Church and State in France, Italy, and Spain.* Princeton: Princeton University Press, 1967.

Anti-Semitism

Anti-Semitism, or the hostility toward Jews that occasionally manifests itself in discriminatory legislation, hostile political movements, and even violence, has been a recurrent feature of political life in the modern world. Most theories endeavoring to explain anti-Semitism seek to identify its roots in ethnic hatred. Some theorists locate the source of such hatred in economic relations. Others emphasize the role of religious institutions. Still others look to cultural differences and misunderstandings.

No doubt, all of these explanations have some validity; however, it is not clear that there is any mystery to be explained. Whatever its psychological, social, economic, or even evolutionary basis, suspicion of strangers is the norm in all societies, while acceptance of outsiders is unusual and generally ephemeral. When times are good and foreigners play a recognized and useful role in the community, they may be tolerated. On the other hand, when times are hard and outsiders seem to compete with their hosts, any latent popular xenophobia is more likely to manifest itself and foreigners may become useful targets for rabble-rousing politicians. Attacks on immigrants in Western Europe in the 1990s are unambiguous examples of this phenomenon.

Certainly, everywhere that Jews have lived, their social or economic marginality—their position "outside society," as social theorist Hannah Arendt put it—sooner or later exposed them to suspicion, hostility, and discrimination. In the United States, Jews currently appear to be accepted by the larger community. Nevertheless, at least in part by their own choosing, American Jews continue to maintain a significant and visible measure of communal identity and distinctiveness in religious, cultural, and political matters. At the same time, many gentiles continue to perceive Jews to be a distinctive group. Although Jews have learned to look, talk, and dress like other Americans, they are not fully assimilated either in their own minds or in the eyes of their neighbors. Even in America the Jews' marginality makes them at least potentially vulnerable to attack. This potential has been realized during several periods in American history, most recently during the New Deal era of the 1930s, when anti-Semitic movements flourished.

Moreover, in the United States as elsewhere Jews are outsiders who often are more successful than their hosts. Because of their historic and, in part, religiously grounded emphasis on education and literacy, when given an opportunity Jews have tended to prosper. And, to make matters worse, Jews often secretly or not so secretly conceive of themselves as morally and intellectually superior to their neighbors. Jews by no means have a monopoly on group or national snobbery. In contemporary America every group is encouraged to take pride in its special heritage and achievements. The problem is that Jews are more successful than virtually all the others.

The roots of anti-Jewish sentiment are not as difficult to understand as the conditions under which such sentiment is likely to be politically mobilized. Where an anti-Semitic politics becomes important, usually more is involved than simple malice toward the Jews. In politics, principles—even as unprincipled a principle as anti-Semitism—are seldom completely divorced from some set of political interests. Major organized campaigns against the Jews reflect not only ethnic hatred, but they also represent efforts by the political opponents of regimes or movements with which Jews are allied to destroy or supplant them. Anti-Semitism has an instrumental as well as an emotive character. Thus, to understand the cycle of Jewish success and anti-Semitic attack, it is necessary to consider the place of Jews in politics, particularly, as Arendt noted, their relationship to the state.

Jews and the State

For nearly two thousand years, from the time of their exile from Palestine in 586 B.C.E., Jews lived as scattered minorities while preserving a considerable measure of communal identity and cultural distinctiveness from the societies that surrounded them. This distinctiveness was maintained by Jews' religious and communal institutions and was often reinforced by the hostility of their neighbors and the antipathy of Muslim and Christian religious institutions. Because Jewish religious practice required male participants to read prayers and other texts, Jewish men received a measure of education that made them considerably more literate and numerate than the people among whom they lived. Their geographic dispersion and literacy combined to help Jews become important traders in the medieval and early modern worlds. Jewish merchants, linked by ties of religion, culture, and often family, played an important role in international commerce.

At the same time, however, their literacy, commercial acumen, and even their social marginality often made Jews useful to kings, princes, and sultans. Into the eighteenth century rulers regularly relied upon Jews as a source of literate administrators and advisers. European monarchs, moreover, depended upon Jewish financiers to manage their fiscal affairs and relied heavily upon Jewish merchants and bankers for loans. In addition, because Jews remained outsiders to the societies in which they lived, sovereigns found them useful instruments for carrying out unpopular tasks, notably collecting taxes.

For their part, Jews, like Sikhs of northern India and other ethnic minorities provided with the state's protection in exchange for services, have usually considered it to be to their advantage to undertake these tasks. Indeed, Jews often saw this acquiescence as their only viable alternative. Social marginality made Jews the objects of popular hostility that at times shaded into violence, and kings could offer a Jewish community protection in exchange for its services. At the same time, the crown could provide Jews with financial opportunities and allow them to enter commercial fields that otherwise would have been closed to them. This exchange of protection and opportunity for service was the foundation for a centuries-long relationship between Jews and the state. Such alliances were responsible for the construction of some of the most powerful states of the Mediterranean and European worlds, including the Habsburg, Hohenzollern, and Ottoman Empires of Central Europe and modern-day Turkey.

These patterns persisted into the nineteenth and twentieth centuries. Jews have maintained a sense of distinctiveness from surrounding societies and have, as a result, continued to experience a measure of suspicion, hostility, and discrimination. Concern about their neighbors' attitudes toward them has continued to lead Jews to seek the protection of the state. At the same time, modern Jewish secular culture, like its religious antecedents, has emphasized education. This focus has enabled Jews to acquire professional and technical skills that can make them as valuable to presidents and prime ministers as they had been to monarchs.

Where Jews have been unable to obtain protection from existing states, they have often played active roles in movements seeking to reform or supplant these regimes with new ones more favorably disposed toward them. Thus, in the

nineteenth century, middle-class Jews were active in liberal movements that advocated the removal of religious restrictions. At the same time, working-class Jews were prominent in socialist and communist movements that sought the overthrow of existing regimes in the name of full social equality. In some cases, including Germany and Austria-Hungary, regimes provided access to a small number of very wealthy Jews while subjecting the remainder to various forms of exclusion. In those cases, Jews could be found both at the pinnacles of power and among the leaders of the opposition.

Over the past several centuries, then, Jews have played a major role both in strengthening existing states and in working to supplant established regimes with new ones. Their relationship to the state has often made it possible for Jews to attain great wealth and power. At the same time, however, relationships between Jews and states have also been the chief catalysts for organized anti-Semitism.

Even when they are closely linked to the state, Jews usually continue to be a separate and distinctive group in society and so to arouse the suspicions of their neighbors. Indeed, in the service of the state, Jews have often become visible and powerful outsiders and so awakened more suspicion and jealousy than ever before. As a result, the relationship between Jews and the state is always problematic. An identification with Jews can weaken the state by exposing it to attack as the servant of foreigners. Correlatively, Jews' identification with the state invites political forces that are seeking to take over or destroy the established order to make use of anti-Semitism as a political weapon.

In contemporary America, for example, radical populist fringe groups such as "The Order" and the "White Aryan Resistance" refer to the administration of the United States as the ZOG, or Zionist Occupation Government—a corrupt tool of the Jews who are so prominent in the American political elite. Not so differently, columnist and 1996 presidential candidate Patrick Buchanan has referred to the U.S. Congress as "Israeli occupied territory," thus defining a political institution controlled by his liberal Democratic foes as nothing more than a Jewish front. It is in these struggles between regimes and their enemies that popular suspicion of Jews is often mobilized by contending political forces and transformed into organized anti-Semitism.

The Politics of Anti-Semitism

Historically, alliances between Jews and states or state-building movements have been the chief catalysts for organized anti-Semitism. Anti-Semitic campaigns proceed from a mixture of motives. Pure hatred of Jews obviously is one important animus for the participants in anti-Semitic groups and movements. As was noted earlier, however, in societies where an anti-Semitic politics becomes important, usually more is involved than simple dislike of Jews. Anti-Semitism can have an important instrumental aspect.

There are three circumstances in which anti-Semitism is likely to become an important political force. First, political forces that oppose a state in which Jews are prominent may seek to undermine the regime and its supporters by attacking its Jewish backers and depicting the government as the puppet of an alien group. Typically, in this circumstance, anti-Semitic appeals are used to create what might be termed coalitions of the top and bottom. In the modern world these are associated with Nazism, but in early modern Europe they were sometimes associated with efforts by the church or aristocracy to rally popular support against the crown. They are used by forces that attempt to mobilize the masses while avoiding threats to the interests and property of the elite. Thus anti-Semitic ideologies are typically espoused either by radical populists who court elite support or by a segment of the upper class seeking to arouse and mobilize a mass base for an assault on the established order.

Elites normally are fearful of popular mobilization, especially when it develops to the level of excitement and, perhaps, violence associated with the overthrow of a regime. They are, moreover, fearful of the rabble-rousers with whom they may have to ally themselves in coalitions of the top and bottom. As a result, such coalitions are likely to emerge only when elites face the most severe economic crises or political threats. Anti-Semitism in the French Third Republic (1871–1940) and the many anti-Semitic movements manifesting themselves in Weimar Germany (1919–1933) are major cases in point. American anti-Semitic movements during the Great Depression of the 1930s also follow this pattern.

The destruction of a regime associated with Jews by a coalition of the top and bottom is sometimes followed by the continued use of anti-Semitic appeals to attack and discredit institutions and social classes affiliated with the old political regime. Attacks on the Jews can help the new regime clear away the vestiges of the old order and prepare the way for the construction of a new one. Early modern Spain (in the fifteenth century) and Nazi Germany (1930s and 1940s) are the most important cases. In both Spain and Germany regimes were able to institutionalize the anti-Semitic fervor

they had mobilized. In Spain this was accomplished through the Inquisition, an organ of the Roman Catholic Church that sought out Jews, and in Nazi Germany through the SS, the secret police, and the incorporation of anti-Semitic principles throughout the civil administration. Both these regimes were able simultaneously to discourage sporadic anti-Semitic agitation—a source of turmoil and instability—and to use anti-Semitism as a source of state power.

Second, anti-Semitic campaigns often emerge from the internal politics of a regime linked to Jews. Campaigns against the Jews may develop when Jews' erstwhile allies feel that they can consolidate and enhance their own power by casting off their former Jewish associates. Russia under Joseph Stalin from 1929 to 1953 is a case in point. Often, rival factions within a governing coalition endeavor to displace their nominal Jewish colleagues and so to aggrandize their own power. This strategy was typical of court politics in the medieval Middle East. Similarly, in contemporary America, the use of anti-Semitic rhetoric by some black politicians is designed to serve the purpose of expanding African American influence within the liberal Democratic coalition at the expense of the Jews who, since the New Deal, have been an important force within that alliance. Jesse Jackson is one prominent African American politician who has used this tactic.

In a related sense, when a regime linked to Jews comes under external attack, Jews' allies may feel compelled (or see an opportunity) to throw the Jews to the wolves to save themselves. For example, in twelfth-century England Jewish financiers provided the funds that supported the British Crown's efforts to expand its authority in relation to the aristocracy. As a result, when the barons moved to restrict the powers of the Crown during the thirteenth century, the Jews were among their chief targets. In the Magna Carta of 1215 the barons compelled King John to accept limits on the capacity of the Jews to recover debts from the landed gentry. The king was also forced to agree to accept limits on his own ability to acquire and recover debts that members of the gentry originally owed to the Jews. The acquisition of such debts had been a significant—and hated—mechanism through which the Crown extracted resources and enhanced its power over the nobility. Subsequently, the Crown distanced itself from the Jews, first imposing severe restrictions on them and later expelling them from England—though not before expropriating as much of their capital as could be found.

Hungary is a more recent example. In pre–World War I

Following their rise to power, the Nazis sought to shore up the new political regime by directing anti-Semitic attacks against the old. Scenes like this one, in which a Nazi soldier stands guard outside a Jewish-owned department store, were not uncommon in Germany in the 1930s. The sign reads, "Germans! Defend yourselves! Don't buy from Jews!"

Hungary, the Magyar governing class was closely allied with the Jews, who dominated business and the professions and extended Magyar influence in the provinces. As a result of this alliance, Hungarian Jews enjoyed complete political freedom and social acceptance. Indeed, Jews were sometimes given access to noble status. Between the two world wars, however, the Magyar elite's relationship with the Jews came under attack from radical populists within Hungary as well as from Hungary's German allies. To save itself, the aristocra-

cy agreed to restrict the political, economic, and civil rights of its former partners. Ultimately, large numbers of Hungarian Jews perished at the hands of the Germans.

Similarly, Jews in seventeenth-century Ukraine were aligned with the Polish nobility, whom they served as estate managers, tax collectors, administrators, and operators of such enterprises as mills and breweries. In 1648, however, the Ukrainian peasantry led by Bogdan Chmielnicki revolted against the Poles and their Jewish subordinates. The Poles sought to save themselves by handing the Jews over to the Ukrainians in exchange for their own lives. Thousands of Jews were killed when denied access to or evicted from the fortified Polish towns where they had sought refuge. In the United States nineteenth-century business elites who had been closely allied with Jewish financiers and bankers rid themselves of their Jewish colleagues when this alliance came under attack from the Populists and from groups that wanted to restrict immigration.

Finally, where Jews play a major role in efforts to supplant an existing regime, the state or social forces under attack may respond with an anti-Semitic campaign designed to protect the established order and discredit its antagonists. Generally, such a campaign involves inciting popular forces by claiming that the government's opponents are unpatriotic and linked to Jews and other foreign elements. Because most governments view rabble-rousing of this sort as destabilizing and potentially dangerous, they generally endeavor to keep the popular forces they mobilize on a short leash and to rein them in as soon as possible. Tsarist Russia is an important example.

Thus, over the past several centuries, Jews have played important roles in the construction of states as well as in movements seeking to reform or supplant regimes to which they were unable to obtain access. Jews have traditionally offered their services to the state in exchange for the regime's guarantee of security and opportunity. Ironically, however, precisely this relationship between Jews and the state has often sparked organized anti-Semitic attacks. To be sure, where Jews forge a close relationship with the state, they may well obtain protection and a considerable measure of power. In ancient Babylonia all citizens were required to bow before the leader of the Jewish community. During the eighteenth-century heyday of the European court Jew, Shakespeare's *Merchant of Venice* could be performed in Berlin only if preceded by an apology to Jewish members of the audience. In twentieth-century Russia, Jews helped to build and lead powerful instruments of terror and repression.

The power and protection offered Jews by the state, however, has tended to be evanescent. It lasts only as long as Jews' allies in governing coalitions continue to find them useful and "their" state continues to have the capacity to defend them from attack. In the meantime, by employing the state to hold off their enemies, the Jews add its foes to their own.

See also *Genocide; Holocaust; Inquisition; Judaism.*

Benjamin Ginsberg

BIBLIOGRAPHY

Arendt, Hannah. *The Origins of Totalitarianism.* Rev. ed. New York: Harcourt, 1967.

Birnbaum, Pierre, and Ira Katznelson, eds. *Paths of Emancipation: Jews, States, and Citizenship.* Princeton: Princeton University Press, 1995.

Dinnerstein, Leonard. *Anti-Semitism in America.* New York: Oxford University Press, 1994.

Ginsberg, Benjamin. *The Fatal Embrace.* Chicago: University of Chicago Press, 1993.

Hilberg, Raul. *The Destruction of the European Jews.* New York: Holmes and Meier, 1985.

Johnson, Paul. *A History of the Jews.* New York: Harper, 1987.

Langmuir, Gavin. *Toward a Definition of Anti-Semitism.* Berkeley: University of California Press, 1990.

Pulzer, Peter. *The Rise of Political Anti-Semitism in Germany and Austria.* Cambridge: Harvard University Press, 1988.

Rapoport, Louis. *Stalin's War against the Jews.* New York: Free Press, 1990.

Apocalyptic literature

See *Millennialism*

Assemblies of God

See *Pentecostalism*

Assimilation, Opposition to

See *Nativism*

Atatürk, Kemal

Turkish soldier, nationalist, and statesman. Mustafa Kemal Atatürk (1881–1938) was the founder of modern republican Turkey and its first president. The National Assembly bestowed the name Atatürk (Father Turk) on him in 1934 for his service to his country.

On November 30, 1918, the Ottoman government signed the armistice of Mudros, which recognized the defeat of the Ottoman Empire against the Allied forces in World War I. Atatürk's last position in the Ottoman military was in Syria

Kemal Atatürk

as commander of the Special Ottoman Army Corps. After the Greeks occupied Izmir, in May 1919, encouraged by British prime minister David Lloyd George, Atatürk joined the broad-based resistance to the occupation of Asia Minor, the rump left from the Ottoman Empire. Sent to the city of Samsum to disband the resistance, he instead organized a gathering of officials, the military, and notables in a congress at Erzurum, with himself as commander of the Turkish army. In the fall of 1922 this new government defeated the Greeks, who then evacuated Anatolia.

On October 29, 1923, the Turkish Republic was proclaimed, and Atatürk was elected president. A constitution was accepted on April 20, 1924. Determined to make Turkey a secular state, Atatürk declared that the truest brotherhood was that of civilization. By civilization, he meant the Western social, political, economic, and cultural systems that were a source of inspiration for his drive toward secularization. Under his guidance, Turkey adopted a civil code based on the Swiss civil code and a criminal code based on the Italian.

Other measures followed: the call to prayer was read in Turkish instead of Arabic; the Latin alphabet and the Western calendar were adopted, with A.D. denoting dates in the common era; Arabic and Persian were eliminated from the schools; and Islam was removed from the constitution as the state religion of Turkey. In 1934 women were granted the right to vote in national elections and to be elected to the Turkish parliament. In 1937 the constitution was changed to declare the Turkish state republican, nationalist, populist, secular, and reformist.

Atatürk distrusted the Muslim clerics, the *ulama,* and feared their influence on the population. He promoted instead Turkish nationalism and the secular foundation of the republic. Secularism was successful to the extent that it blended with Turkish nationalism and was most effective while Turkey was ruled by the single party that Atatürk had created. Later, with the transition to a multiparty system (1946), the antisecular demands of a large number of Turkish citizens who had not been part of the secular vanguard began to be reflected in the parliament. In the 1990s there has been a growing rift between the secular establishment that Atatürk promoted and conservative Islamic movements.

See also *Turkey.*

Şerif Mardin

BIBLIOGRAPHY

Kazancigil, Ali, and Ergun Özbudun, eds. *Atatürk, Founder of a State.* London: Hurst, 1981.

Kinross, Lord [John Patrick Balfour]. *Atatürk, the Rebirth of a Nation.* 2d ed. London: Weidenfeld and Nicolson, 1964.

Atheism

The denial of the existence of and belief in God is called atheism. The word derives from the Greek *a* (without; not) and *theos* (god). The term *atheism* has a range of inconsistent and seemingly contradictory meanings and a long history marked by controversy. Its meaning in any specific instance depends on how it is defined and on the persons to whom it refers. For example, when early Christians were accused by Roman state authorities of being atheists because of their refusal to participate in the state-sponsored cults, the word was a term of opprobrium. What the Christians denied was a particular *theism* enshrined in the state religion; they were called atheists by others who rejected the theistic beliefs of the Christians. By contrast, the followers of Madalyn Murray O'Hair, who founded American Atheists in 1965, actively have taken upon themselves the label *atheist.* They have flaunted the term as a quasi-theological position and have taken it to imply a strict separation of church and state and of religion from culture.

Atheism is to be distinguished from *agnosticism,* a term

coined by Thomas H. Huxley, an English biologist, in the nineteenth century. Agnosticism is the refusal to enter into judgment, either affirmative or negative, about the existence of God.

In general, when we speak of atheism we are referring to those serious philosophical positions, such as some forms of idealism and of materialism, that reject traditional theological arguments for the existence of God and, by implication, reject the notion of belief in God. These positions emerged from the period of the eighteenth-century Enlightenment, with its stress on emancipation from traditional religious authorities, including the authoritative interpretation of the Bible. Philosophical and even theological questions gradually focused on natural philosophy and the possibility of a universal mechanics that would make nature intelligible on its own terms. Arguments for the existence and attributes of God rested largely on the design, pattern, and order of nature. These arguments were gradually superseded by later extrapolations from Isaac Newton's physics to a self-sustaining and self-explanatory universe without a god. But the Enlightenment itself was in some ways the final flowering of an earlier Renaissance humanism. This humanism gave the world a new idea of science freed from theology, an interest in the agency of the human person in the political sphere, tremendous religious and theological change, and the rediscovery of academic skepticism. The Catholic theologian Henri de Lubac argued that these philosophic forms of atheism must be taken seriously on their own terms if one is to understand how profound their implications are for the social and political order and a recovery of authentic humanism.

These philosophic forms of atheism cannot be adequately understood apart from that which they reject, which is not only a belief in a god per se but often also the theologies and religious and cultural structures that have traditionally supported the transmission of belief in a god. As the Catholic theologian Michael Buckley has argued, atheism is "parasitic" in that it feeds on that which it rejects. The earliest forms of modern atheism depended in part on the repudiation of theologies that had unsuccessfully argued for the existence and attributes of a god, often on the basis of physical or natural principles rather than strictly theological ones. In this sense, Buckley argues, religion generated its own antithesis.

For some, ecclesiastical infighting and power intrigues and the scandals of religious wars created a context within which the rejection of religious belief in God was only made easier. Such was the case for many of the disaffected intelligentsia in postrevolutionary France. In the twentieth century the systematic atheism of Soviet communism was not only the ideological expression of Marxist atheism but a rejection of the religious and political culture that had helped sustain the Orthodox faith in Russia prior to the revolution in 1917.

In considering the relationship between atheism and politics, one must distinguish among the atheism of the Enlightenment and post-Enlightenment periods, the structured acceptance or adoption of atheism in political systems, and the newer forms of atheism that have emerged from "postmodern" cultures. Here one must also consider the newest forms of atheism that do not bear the name of atheism but which can be seen in the irrelevancy of God as a question, in the political and economic struggles of developing nations, and in the various forms of nihilism, both nonreligious and religious, that emerge from a lack of transcendence.

Enlightenment and Post-Enlightenment Atheism

The origins of modern atheism are often traced to the emergence of the rational ego in the philosophy of René Descartes, a seventeenth-century French mathematician and philosopher. For Descartes, ideas held by the rational ego displaced the philosophy of being (ontology) and the traditional foundations of metaphysics that had been handed down from Plato and Aristotle through Thomas Aquinas as the ultimate foundation of knowledge. The new autonomy of the rational ego allowed for the elaboration of a universal mathematics, which would explain the world and would be the source of any real affirmation of God. About the same time, the British mathematician Isaac Newton developed a universal mechanics in which the physical universe was understood as a vast and comprehensible system that had been set in motion and was kept in motion by God, the provident governor and designer of the universe. Newton's achievement was enthusiastically received by some theologies, such as that of Samuel Clarke, which had argued for the existence and attributes of a god on the basis of physical or natural principles. This helped give rise to a permutation of the traditional Christian theology of God, *deism,* in which God was perceived as the distant creator of a well-designed universe that otherwise ran according to its own internal laws of motion, with very rare instances of a provident divine intervention.

It was a short step from deism to conscious attempts to explain the universe on purely materialistic grounds without the benefit of God whatsoever. The first phase of this development of atheism is found in the eighteenth century in the writings of the *philosophes* of the French Enlightenment (especially Voltaire and Denis Diderot). These intellectuals railed vehemently at least as much against religion and its institutions as against belief in God per se. But their writings opened the door for more concerted philosophical efforts to deny the existence of God altogether. Atheism received its clearest philosophical expression in the *System of Nature* (1770) by Paul-Henri Dietrich d'Holbach. D'Holbach argued for a completely materialistic universe and deliberately set forth a scheme for a thoroughgoing philosophical denial of the existence of God as a transcendent being. Deism and the theology that supported it had become the natural ancestor of an atheism that held that the universe could be explained without any further need of the hypothesis of God.

A second phase in the development of modern atheism occurred during the post-Enlightenment period of early German idealism and, later, romanticism. In the work of the German philosopher G. W. F. Hegel (1770–1831), the rational ego of Descartes was transformed into a pure consciousness. Within that consciousness, according to Hegel, the knowledge of all of reality was collapsed in a dialectical relation between the world as object of knowledge and the knower's self-consciousness as subject. Immanuel Kant (1724–1804) shifted the entire field of philosophical inquiry from traditional metaphysics to epistemology, the study of the basis of knowledge. In Kant's philosophy, practical judgment and morality, rather than metaphysics or even traditional epistemology, were where one could establish the existence of God. In making moral judgments the human person requires an ultimate confirmation of the direction and rightness of those judgments. That ultimate confirmation is God. And to the German theologian Friedrich Schleiermacher (1768–1834) this God is known through an experience he called "feeling." The absence of metaphysics and such a strong turn to experience placed the metaphysical grounds for the affirmation of the existence of God in jeopardy.

Among the first to see this slippage in metaphysical foundations for belief in God was another German philosopher, Ludwig Feuerbach. In *The Essence of Christianity* (1841), Feuerbach held that belief in God is merely the projection onto the "sky" of the deepest aspirations and inner necessities of the self-conscious human subject, who is a member of a larger species sharing the same aspirations and needs. "Species consciousness" thus marks the human from other species. The gods themselves are a projection of this species consciousness. The existence of a god is therefore finally dependent on the transcendental subjectivity of human persons, that is, the capacity to transcend oneself in knowledge. But in fact no god exists apart from human subjectivity. The deepest reality about religion is that it is a veiled atheism. In its focus on gods and powers to whom humans must be subservient, religion results in an alienation of human persons from themselves and from others. Emancipation from this alienation comes from a critical understanding of the fundamental atheism underlying religion.

In his psychoanalytic theory, Sigmund Freud (1856–1939) built on Feuerbach's philosophical foundations and saw the nature of belief as the struggle of the id in relation to the ego and the superego. The model for this struggle for freedom was the individuation of the son from the mother and the ensuing rejection of the father. Religion thus became understood as a playing out of primitive psychological forces. Final emancipation came in the form of atheism. In an early work, *The Future of an Illusion,* Freud developed yet another thesis, that God is a human response to the fear of death and the terrors of nature. Religion itself can be explained as the social framework within which this fear is ritualized and tamed. But human beings, he believed, must finally free themselves from the tyranny of religion.

Friedrich Nietzsche stood in this tradition by arguing in *The Gay Science* (1882) that God was dead. His point was that God no longer served even as a projection of consciousness; the marketplace and its bourgeois social and political values had replaced God with a nihilism in which traditional metaphysics no longer functioned and the eternal truths were no longer certain. The issue was not whether God was a projection of consciousness but of acknowledging that the conditions for the possibility of such a projection no longer existed because the consciousness that had once given rise to God was dead. In Nietzsche's book, the "Madman" in the marketplace shouts that God has been murdered. Human beings are left with a will to power and the ultimate achievement of a new form of humanity (the *Übermensch,* or "superman").

Karl Marx stood in Feuerbach's lineage in his understanding of belief in God as an expression of the alienation of the subject (worker) from himself as well as from other human beings. This alienation was a remote expression of the fundamental alienation from self that religion had brought about.

It would be overcome only through actual historical events in the playing out of dialectical materialism. Marx argues in *The Economic and Philosophic Manuscripts of 1844* that until that final emancipation, religion would serve as the sigh of the oppressed creature, an opiate for the masses. Atheism was thus intrinsic to Marxist theory, both as a quasi-theological foundation and as an anticipated result of the dialectical forces of economic history.

In addition to these developments in Germany, there was a flowering of atheism during the nineteenth century in England and the United States. This could be attributed in part to the rising faith in economic progress, the emergence of Darwinism as an alternative to what was considered benighted religion, the appeal of social Darwinism to the educated classes, and a positivist view of science. In the United States the influence of the philosopher John Dewey (1859–1952) cannot be underestimated as a source of secularist and even atheistic ethics. Dewey's thought, which heavily influenced American thinkers such as Reinhold Niebuhr, was to go far toward building what would later be called "civil religion."

Political Implications of Modern Atheism

The political implications of the beliefs that gained currency in the Enlightenment and after were massive. As measured by the religion and piety of the American political founders, it was the deist god (not the god of the much earlier Puritans or of a later evangelical Christianity) who undergirded the great Enlightenment political project of the United States. While certainly not intended as a form of atheism, deism did allow for the possibility of toleration of a range of theological convictions and insisted on the freedom to pursue them. Deism was also fed by the streams of Unitarianism (an offshoot of Anglicanism that denied the traditional Christian theology of God) and Freemasonry (a quasi-religious movement that tolerated and even encouraged atheism). Out of these streams there emerged two principles dear to the American political project: freedom of religion and the separation of church and state, both enshrined in the First Amendment to the Constitution of the United States. These principles were fueled at least as much by Enlightenment rejection of religious authority and monarchy as by memories of past religious persecution. The First Amendment helped shelter within American political culture the development and toleration of various expressions of atheism. Nevertheless, the United States became a nation of ex-

traordinary religious vitality, and atheism has never been embraced by the masses.

France was another country whose new political structures were strongly shaped by Enlightenment thought. The development of atheism was inextricably intertwined with anticlericalism and the cultural skirmishes between the Catholic Church and the new French state. It also bore the marks of a rejection of religion, not only by intellectual elites but also by significant portions of the working classes.

Perhaps the most important development out of the American project was civil religion, that is, the notion of a society in which belief in God stands alongside political culture and in some ways supports it but does not officially buttress or undergird it except in formulaic ways (for example, "In God We Trust," the slogan on American currency). The emergence of this civil religion in the United States allowed for the development of a markedly secular society within which some religious values could nevertheless thrive. But as the sociologist Robert Bellah has demonstrated, civil religion encourages individualist religious philosophies and spiritual quests. It has contributed to the development of a society where belief in God is largely held as a matter of private pursuit and where questions about God as a public or common intellectual matter have never taken root, even in academic circles. There has thus emerged a society within which believers (Christian, Jewish, Muslim) coexist alongside atheists and agnostics, although differences have often been played out in the political and legal domains. This is in sharp contrast to those theocracies (Iran, for instance) where atheism, unimaginable except as a sin within a religious context, is also treated as a civil crime.

The second phase of the development of modern atheism, the post-Enlightenment thought following upon Feuerbach, led in subtle ways to the development of two of the major political phenomena of the twentieth century, Nazi fascism and Soviet communism. Political fascism, at least in its National Socialist (Nazi) form, depended on some religious (church) cooperation and actually made use of religious and quasi-religious imagery. As an ideology, however, it fundamentally rejected a society based on faith, substituting for belief in God submission to the führer and the fanatic ideology of racial purity as a transcendent ideal and concrete political goal. In this sense it was profoundly a-theistic. While Nietzsche's Madman had announced the "death of God" and while the *Übermensch* was the symbol of a will to power without the benefit of God, Nietzsche is too easily invoked as the philosophical forebear of the "atheism" of Nazi socialism. In fact, it could be argued that Nietzsche was calling for the discovery of a new sense of the transcendent, outside traditional theologies, despite his dark and pessimistic social outlook. This recovery of transcendence has been the aim of some "postmodern" thought.

Similarly, Soviet communism was an explicitly and aggressively atheistic system that attempted to institutionalize what Marx had limned in theory. The Soviet system, however, was based on a fundamental misreading of Marxist atheism that can be attributed to the totalitarian nature of the Soviet system. Whereas Marx believed that religion would eventually be overcome through the dialectic of economic forces, the Soviet system began with the brutal suppression of religion and the imposition of official state atheism. While atheism was an intrinsic philosophical foundation of Marxist theory, in Soviet communism it became an intrinsic part of the political process, as it did also under China under Mao Zedong. The demise of the Soviet system in 1989–1991 demonstrated that the roots of belief in God lay barely below the surface of official atheism. However, it has also been amply demonstrated that a totalitarian regime can, over a few short generations, succeed in seriously crippling that belief, both by retarding its development and by violently hacking at its roots.

Nazi fascism, Soviet communism, and even Maoism, emerged in an age when it was possible to imagine the total rejection of the theistic (or more broadly, religious) underpinnings of Western societies by political organizations. This could only have happened once atheism had been established as an alternative to faith in God. The atheism of fascism and of communism has also been echoed in various forms of totalitarianism that depend on strict control of religion and, implicitly, on denial of God as transcendent reality.

Postmodern Forms of Atheism

Alongside these more "traditional" forms of atheism that have emerged in the Western world and that depend on a well-conceived philosophical position, atheism has also assumed forms that do not correspond to the older models. These can be addressed here as unbelief, idolatry, and the lack of a sense of transcendence (a position expounded by the Czech president, Václav Havel).

Unbelief is to be distinguished from older "modern" atheism in that, in many respects, God as a possible reality is not explicitly in question in the first place. According to the Catholic theologian Karl Rahner (1904–1984), this stance is based not so much on rejection of the idea of God as on the tacit assumption that the question of the existence of God is irrelevant, at least as a matter of common intellectual concern. In its most severe forms, unbelief folds into nihilism, a loss of the values and common points of reference that have enabled cultures to cohere in the past.

The roots of unbelief are complex. Secularism, the forces of the market economy, the assurances of technology, and the dominance of a positivist view of science have all contributed to its pervasive influence. Secularism, the belief that a culture best functions in the absence of religious influence, is an axiom of Western political societies. As an ideology, it is to be distinguished from the principle of separation of church from state, from which it partly derives. The principle of separation of church and state allows for religious influence upon culture, as in civil religion; secularism seeks to cleanse culture of religion.

Secularism has paved the way for a market ideology within which the market economy assumes the absolute value that religion once held. This development, in which economies of variant cultures are radically dependent on one another, and in which these economies function according to wholly secular principles, has resulted in a pan-culture in which "unbelief" is a tacit assumption, even in non-Western societies. Various libertarian political and economic programs, originally propounded by such thinkers as Ayn Rand (1905–1982), have also promoted a radical secularism. Libertarianism stresses the absolute authority of reason, rugged individualism, government minimalism, and the "objective" power of market forces over any transcendent values, political or religious.

Linked with these developments is the universal influence of technology, which has given human beings the illusion of the ultimate comprehensibility of the universe and, on a more mundane level, a certain hubristic confidence in the manageability of problems without any reference to transcendence.

Finally, certain philosophically naive views of science, involving a nearly unquestioning confidence in the truth claims of science, have also contributed to the phenomenon of unbelief. In this arena, as in the universe of market ideology, unbelief characterizes certain sectors of the educated elites not only in the Western world but beyond it. In this sense, one could speak, for example, of a culture of unbelief in some of the countries of Asia, such as Japan.

Idolatry is a category of analysis employed by some followers of liberation theology. The theology of liberation was the outgrowth of the work of the Catholic theologian Gustavo Gutiérrez in the 1970s. It addressed the problems of poverty in developing countries and the socioeconomic and political structures that helped give rise to and sustain it. In most liberation theologies, atheism per se is not at issue. Atheism in the modern sense exists in these countries but primarily among the educated elites and in those sectors, such as labor unions, that have traditionally been influenced by anticlericalism in these cultures. Modern atheism is not generally found among the vast masses of the poor and middle classes. Theologies of liberation, therefore, invoke the tradition of the biblical prophets and inveigh against various forms of "idolatry" that characterize a "godless" society.

The Salvadoran theologian Jon Sobrino cites the idolatries of wealth, materialism, and political power wielded by the rich over the poor. The theological question thus becomes not whether one believes in God, but in which god one believes. The "idols" of wealth, materialism, and power demand that the human person offer himself or herself up to the mechanisms of an unjust political order. Later writings in the theology of liberation, especially those since the advent of neoliberalism in the 1990s, stress not so much the divide between rich and poor as they do a "communitarian" approach to the solving of social problems, balancing a social justice agenda with a prudent use of market economics.

The *lack of a sense of transcendence* has been noted especially in Western Europe, where the structures and traditions of the Christian faith—and, because of the Holocaust, of Judaism—suffered massive implosions in the last half of the twentieth century. As political leaders such as Havel have noted, this pervasive lack of the transcendent does not necessarily obviate the quest for transcendence on a personal level or, culturally, through politics. Indeed, the "postmodern" alienation from religion, ironically, is often tied to a quest for the spiritual or the transcendent but outside the traditional theologies of God. Havel's political and philosophical writings stress the importance of this postmodern search for transcendence in the face of the absence of God, not only as a personal quest but as a dimension of life that societies badly need to recover if they are to survive. But Havel's writings generally stress as well that the transcendence for which people are searching will not necessarily be found in traditional religions or theologies.

Theological Reactions to Atheism

Although it has been established that religion contributed to the rise of atheism, there have been notable theological reactions to atheism, which have had some political implications. These can be included generally under the headings of political theology and explicit ecclesiastical responses to atheism.

Political theology emerged in Europe, primarily in Germany, France, and Belgium, after the Second World War. The aim of political theology was to pursue the implications of faith at a time when it was clear that the Christendom of old Europe, including belief in God, no longer held sway. The question became what faith and politics together might look like in a post-Christian age. Theologians like the Catholic Johannes B. Metz reinterpreted the imagery of the Book of Revelation and searched its apocalyptic imagery for keys to recovering a sense of God in building a new society, while the Protestant Jürgen Moltmann produced a theology of hope that took into account the full force of the cross as a symbol of divine involvement in social and political suffering. In American Protestantism this political interest took the form of a "secular" theology, in which some theologians argued for finding God within the political and cultural world. These thinkers were following an older and well-established path of political theology in Protestantism going back to John Calvin, the sixteenth-century Protestant reformer. In the mid-twentieth century it was forcefully expressed as an American political theology by Reinhold Niebuhr and, in the categories of Christ and culture, elaborated by his brother H. Richard Niebuhr. In Europe, the theologians Karl Barth and Dietrich Bonhoeffer had elaborated these themes in the context of the experience of the Protestant churches during the Third Reich.

The ecclesiastical response of the Western churches to atheism has been most forcefully expressed by the Roman Catholic Church. In its "Pastoral Constitution on the Church in the Modern World" *(Gaudium et Spes),* the Second Vatican Council (1962–1965) moved beyond its traditional position of repudiating atheism as a sinful rejection of God to an expressed desire for dialogue with atheists. The theological reasons for this shift are complex and depend on developments in theological anthropology and in an understanding of God's self-communication (grace) as a divine offer made to all human beings, not only to Christians or believers. But the reasons are also conciliatory. The dialogue with atheists, therefore, is for the "political" goal of the common good.

Catholic theologians such as Karl Rahner engaged in active dialogue with Marxists and atheists in the years following the Second World War. A Vatican "Secretariat for Non-Believers" was established in 1965. In that same year Pope Paul VI commissioned the Society of Jesus (Jesuits) to undertake dialogue with atheists as a primary mission and to devote their intellectual attention to the problem of atheism in the modern world. These missions of the church toward engagement with atheism were intended not only to combat atheism, which continued to be viewed as incompatible with Christian faith, but to engage it positively with the goal of finding common horizons in the interest of the good of humanity.

As some indication of how the thinking of the Roman Catholic Church itself has changed in regard to the phenomenon of atheism, the name of the Secretariat for Non-Believers was changed in 1991 to the Pontifical Council for Dialogue with Non-Believers, and, in 1993, to the Pontifical Council on Culture. This reflects a tacit admission that the phenomenon of atheism is no longer an intellectual position alone, the "modern" rejection of the existence of and belief in God, but is a reality embedded in the secular culture that increasingly involves all social and political systems around the globe.

See also *Barth, Karl; Bonhoeffer, Dietrich; Civil religion; Communism; Communitarianism; Enlightenment; Fascism; Freedom of religion; Havel, Václav; Liberation theology; Marxism; Niebuhr, Reinhold; Nietzsche, Friedrich; Secular humanism; Separation of church and state.*

Paul G. Crowley

BIBLIOGRAPHY

Bellah, Robert. *Habits of the Heart: Individualism and Commitment in American Life.* New York: Harper and Row, 1986.

Buckley, Michael J. *At the Origins of Modern Atheism.* New Haven: Yale University Press, 1987.

De Lubac, Henri. *The Drama of Atheistic Humanism.* New York: New American Library, 1963.

Gallagher, Michael John. *What Are They Saying about Unbelief?* Mahwah, N.J.: Paulist Press, 1995.

Murray, John Courtney. *The Problem of God.* New Haven: Yale University Press, 1964.

Sobrino, Jon. *Jesus the Liberator: A Historical-Theological View.* Translated by Paul Burns and Francis McDonagh. Maryknoll, N.Y.: Orbis Books, 1993.

Ayatollah

See *Islam*

B

Bahai

The Bahai faith had its origin in a millenarian movement of the Shi'ite Muslims of mid-nineteenth century Iran, the Babi movement. Its founder, Sayyid Ali Muhammad of Shiraz (d. 1850), first proclaimed himself as the Gate *(bab)* to the Hidden Twelfth Imam, whom the Shi'ites believed to be the mahdi, the rightly guided leader of the end of time. At the close of 1844 the twenty-five-year-old Bab, as he became generally known, declared himself to be the Hidden Imam, returning after a thousand years of concealment.

His movement spread rapidly in his native land and culminated in a series of millenarian uprisings between 1848 and 1850 in which his followers abrogated Islamic law to mark the beginning of the new era. The Bab was imprisoned and condemned as a heretic by the Shi'ite clergy in 1848 and was executed in 1850. The movement was ferociously suppressed after a group of Babis unsuccessfully attempted to assassinate the monarch in 1852. Mirza Husayn Ali Nuri (1817–1892), a government official who had joined the Babi movement in 1844, was imprisoned. Cleared of the charge of complicity in the plot, he was nevertheless exiled to Ottoman Baghdad in 1853. Ten years later in a garden in Baghdad, he proclaimed himself to be "he whom God shall manifest," of whom the Bab had spoken. He assumed the title of Baha'ullah (the Glory of God), and his followers considered him the last prophet and manifestation of God.

The Bahai religion, which may be considered the youngest of the world religions and has about five million followers throughout the world, was thus founded in April 1863. The great majority of Babis accepted Baha'ullah's messianic claims and became Bahais. A small minority led by his brother, known as the Subh-i Azal (Dawn of Eternity), refused to do so, however, and remained Babis.

The Ottoman government exiled Baha'ullah to Palestine in 1868. From there, he sent epistles, tablets, and missionaries to Iran and the rest of the world until his death in 1892. In 1873 the Bahai community in Iran asked for a book of law to supersede the Bab's as well as Islamic law, and he sent them the Most Holy Book *(Kitab i-Aqdas)*. During Baha'ullah's lifetime the Bahai community in Iran grew to an estimated one hundred thousand, and the Bahai faith expanded mainly in the east: Iraq, Turkey, Syria, Egypt, the Caucasus, Turkistan, and India. From 1892 to 1921, under the leadership of his son and designated successor, Abbas, known as Abdul-Baha' (the Servant of the Glory), the Bahai religion expanded globally, spreading into East Asia, Europe, North America, South America, and South Africa.

The first Bahai mission in the United States was established in Chicago by Ibrahim George Kheialla in 1894. When Abdul-Baha' visited the United States in 1912 there were already several thousand American Bahais. These Americans had a considerable effect on the evolution of the Bahai religion.

The expansion of the Bahai faith continued under the vigorous leadership of the grandson of Abdul-Baha', Shoghi Effendi (1899–1957), from 1921 to 1957. Shoghi Effendi died childless, and, because he had excommunicated his eligible relatives, Bahai leadership devolved upon a Universal House of Justice that had been envisioned by Baha'ullah. Its trustees are elected every five years. The first Universal House of Justice trustees were elected by the International Bahai Council in 1963. Five of its nine trustees were American, two British, and two Iranian. Since 1957 mass conversions to Bahaism have been recorded in Bolivia, India, and Uganda. The historically important mother community in Iran now constitutes only 10 percent of the world's Bahais.

The development of the Bahai religion from Babi millenarianism illustrates the transition from revolutionary militancy to political pacifism, and from a theocratic fusion of religion and politics to their strict separation within the framework of participatory government. Two historical factors were decisive for this transition: the early exposure of Baha'ullah and Abdul-Baha' to the Ottoman reform movement and constitutionalism in the 1860s and 1870s, and the expansion of the Bahai religion in the United States.

From the very beginning, Baha'ullah distanced his "realized messianism" from the militant millenarianism of the Babis by declaring that his religion had abrogated holy warfare, "the rule of the sword." At the same time, he declared the separation of religion and politics in marked divergence from their fusion in Babism. These declarations paved the way for constitutionalist ideas concerning government, on the one hand, and the advocacy of universal peace, on the other. The influence of the Ottoman reforms and constitutionalist ideas are evident in Baha'ullah's writings in the late 1860s and 1870s. Baha'ullah advocated the rule of law and constitutional monarchy, hailing the advent of constitutionalism and parliamentary government as the final manifestation of reason among mankind. Baha'ullah adopted the idea of universal peace, which was popular among the Ottoman and Egyptian intellectuals of the period, as an extension of his abolition of holy war, and made it a cornerstone of the universalism of his religion.

The Ottoman administrative reforms, especially those of 1856 concerning the self-regulation of the religious minorities, also influenced Baha'ullah's institution of consultative forms of self-regulation for the Bahai communities. His *Most Holy Book* set up local councils called "houses of justice," consisting of at least nine members, as governing bodies of Bahai communities. These local councils became the basic units of Bahai administration that has grown considerably since. These elected councils administer both the religious and the civic affairs of Bahai communities, and their growth prevented the emergence of any Bahai clergy out of the nucleus of original missionaries.

During the constitutional decade (1870s) Baha'ullah had told his son not to leave the writing on political affairs to nonbelieving intellectuals, but to write a book on the science of politics. Both in the book on the subject he wrote in 1875 and in a prologue to his anonymous history of the Babi movement (1888) Abdul-Baha' presented equality, liberty, and universal human rights as the signs of the latest stage of civilization. During the Iranian constitutional revolution (1906–1911), however, Abdul-Baha'—now the leader of the Bahai religion in his own right—refused to support the Iranian constitutionalists. The main reason for this refusal was the prominent role of his more radical sectarian rivals, the Azali Babis. Abdul-Baha' did, however, stress the separation of religion and politics. This separation was reaffirmed by his grandson and successor Shoghi Effendi, who also confirmed that the machinery of the internal administration of the Bahai communities should not supersede the governments of their respective countries.

The increasing influence of the American Bahai community largely accounts for the ending of the separation of men and women during the leadership of Abdul-Baha', who was also prevailed upon to allow women to serve in the local house of justice. The American Bahais have since been influential in reinforcing the machinery of self-regulation in Bahai communities and in the development of national and international conventions.

The Bahais of Iran attracted international attention again after the Islamic revolution of 1979. Although they consistently confirmed the separation of religion and politics and reaffirmed the apolitical nature of their faith in the 1970s, they have been severely persecuted by the Islamic theocratic regime in Iran, which considers them, religiously, defectors from Shi'ism and, politically, agents of imperialism and Zionism. Bahai properties have been confiscated and all their local councils have been dissolved. Some two hundred Bahais have been killed, many more imprisoned, and thousands purged from the army and civil service or forced to recant.

See also *Iran; Iraq; Islam; Mahdi*.

Said Amir Arjomand

BIBLIOGRAPHY

"Bahai Faith or Bahaism." *Encyclopaedia Iranica*. Vol. 3. London: Routledge and Kegan Paul, 1989.
Cole, J. R. I. *Modernity and the Millennium*. New York: Columbia University Press, 1998.
Smith, Peter. *The Babi and Baha'i Religions: From Messianic Shi'is to a World Religion*. New York: Cambridge University Press, 1987.

Balkan states

The Balkan states, which include the former Yugoslavia, Bulgaria, Romania, Albania, and Greece, are predominantly Eastern Orthodox, but they also have significant Muslim and Roman Catholic populations. Politics and religion have interacted in the Balkans at least since the ninth century, when Byzantine missionaries led by Cyril and Methodius christianized the Slavs and the Bulgarians. From about the same time, three major religious cultures—Eastern Orthodoxy, Roman Catholicism, and Islam—have been involved in a complex religious-ideological and political struggle in the region. Over the second millennium, religion and politics in the Balkans have been shaped by empires and their legacies, especially the Orthodox Byzantine, which ended in the fifteenth century with the conquest of Constantinople (today Istanbul in Turkey) by Mehmet II (1453), and the Muslim Ottoman, which lasted from the fifteenth to the twentieth century. In the early twentieth century the largely Catholic Austro-Hungarian Empire (1867–1918) wielded considerable influence in the region, and from 1945 to 1990, religion endured communist rule.

The collapse of empires resulted in long-lasting social, political, and cultural consequences. Over the past two hundred years in particular, social change and the interaction of religion and politics in the Balkans have been deeply affected by the collapse of the Ottoman and the Austro-Hungarian Empires and the socialist bloc.

Independence and Modernization

In Western societies modernity, modernization, capitalism, industrialization, democratization, and secularization developed in unison. Not so in the Balkans, where modernity had little chance to take firm root within the ailing Ottoman Empire of the eighteenth and nineteenth centuries. Influenced in some measure by the ideas of the Enlightenment and above all by the spirit of nationalism then sweeping Europe, one after the other the people of the Balkans rose to claim their independence from the Turkish yoke during the nineteenth century. Orthodoxy, a central element of the ethnic identity of these people, played a crucial, legitimizing, ideological role in the independence of Greece (1830), Serbia (1830), Romania (1862), Bulgaria (1878), and Albania (1920). But "independent," in this case, must be carefully qualified. These new nation-states were not just economically dependent on loans from the Great Powers

(Britain, France, Prussia, Russia), but in large measure they were under their political tutelage also.

With the exception of Serbia, the first monarchs of the new Balkan states were Catholics called to rule over predominantly Orthodox populations. Political institutions in the region were largely superimposed from outside. Throughout this period national borders kept shifting as the Ottoman and the Austro-Hungarian Empires gradually disintegrated and wars became endemic in the region. The Crimean War (1854–1856), the Russo-Turkish War (1875–1878), the Greek-Turkish War (1897), the Balkan Wars (1912–1913), and the First World War (1914–1917) all involved extensive outside intervention and interest. Ethnoreligious factors were central to all these conflicts and crucial to the consolidation of the nation-state. The ethno-religio-political puzzle in the region, which still remains unresolved and unpredictable, must be understood as it relates to globalization.

Industrialization and capitalism, for example, came very late in the Balkans because most of the region consisted of peasant societies up to the 1960s. (In the 1950s, 78 percent of the working population in Yugoslavia was in agriculture—75.5 percent and 70 percent, respectively, in Bulgaria and Romania.) But although the Communist regimes that took over after 1945 emphasized fast industrialization, a real industrial infrastructure has never developed in these countries. Class structure, social organization, and division of labor never followed Western patterns either, so industrial working and middle classes similar to those of Western Europe never developed in the Balkans. Politics in the region developed along clientilistic and ethnic-nationalistic lines—votes were exchanged for personal or family favors arranged by local patrons representing politicians. So, given the mosaic of ethnoreligious groups and the historical divisions among the major religions in the region, socioeconomic and political issues have tended to express themselves as ethnoreligious conflicts.

In the aftermath of such ethno-religio-political strife in the former Yugoslavia after the collapse of the socialist regime in 1990, American political scientist Samuel Huntington has implied that Orthodoxy and Islam are religious cultures that, if not incompatible, certainly are not conducive to democracy and pluralism. That thesis must be rejected for Orthodoxy. Orthodox theology poses the person and personal freedom as the central social ideal of Christianity. Unlike Roman Catholicism, Orthodoxy does not accept the authority and infallibility of the pope. In principle Orthodoxy not only is not a hindrance to democracy, but, as a political culture, it is deeply democratic. This being the case, the reason democracies have not fared well in the Balkans cannot be sought in the culture of Orthodoxy, which is the major religion in the region. In the Balkans secularization is less advanced than in the West, but apart from the historical explanation for this, the fact that Orthodoxy is resistant to secularization but Protestantism seems compatible with it does not mean that Orthodoxy is undemocratic or antipluralist.

A better explanation for the historical politico-religious developments in the Balkans comes from the interaction of political and socioeconomic developments and the role of religion in the region. Moreover, these developments should be understood within the context of global social change.

Church and State Relations

Theologically, church and state relations in the Orthodox tradition are based on the Biblical principle "Give unto Caesar. . . ." In Byzantium, which was the seat of Eastern Christendom between 320 and 1453, religion and politics were diffused in a Christian, theocentric commonwealth, but there was no confusion in the exercise of sacred and political authority. Sacred authority belonged to the church in the person of the ecumenical patriarch of Constantinople, who had honorary primacy (*primus interpares*—first among equals) among other Orthodox patriarchs, and political authority to the emperor, who was also holy. This schema has been called *Caesaropapism,* meaning political subjugation of church to state. Some modern scholars reject this interpretation, however, because emperors sometimes lost not just their thrones but also their heads because of their religious policies.

During Ottoman rule (1453–1923) the Orthodox Church, led by the patriarch of Constantinople, became the social and civil administrator of the Orthodox people under the sultan. This strengthened the bonds of the Balkan peoples to Orthodoxy and gave the church a new political status. But this standing changed radically with the emergence of the nation-states in the nineteenth century. As they acquired their independence, one after the other also demanded a church independent (*autocephalous,* or with its own head bishop) from the ecumenical patriarchate, which in each case the patriarchate had to concede reluctantly as a fait accompli. From then on most national churches in the Balkans have been under the almost total control of the state and have been made to serve ethnic and even party and sectional political ends.

With the coming of Communist rule after 1945, church-state relations in the Balkans entered their worst phase in history. In socialist society the presence of the church was an anomaly in the eyes of the state. But since it could not be abolished altogether, despite the persecution, it had to be used and tolerated for propaganda purposes insofar as it was cooperating with the regime. If they wanted to survive, the churches had to play that game.

Former Yugoslavia

After the First World War, the kingdom of the Serbs, the Croats, and the Slovenians was established in 1918 and, after 1920, was called Yugoslavia. With a population in 1990 of about 24 million, 50 percent of the people were classified as Orthodox, 30 percent as Roman Catholic, 19 percent as Muslim, and 1 percent as other (Jews, evangelicals, and so on). The Orthodox live mainly in Serbia and Montenegro, the Catholics in Croatia and Slovenia, and the Muslims in Bosnia and Kosovo. But there have long been significant

Serbian Orthodox minorities within Bosnia and Croatia, where brutal war broke out (1991–1994) after these provinces declared their independence from Yugoslavia. Sarajevo, the center of the conflicts, was also the city that sparked the First World War after the 1914 assassination there of Archduke Franz Ferdinand, heir to the Habsburg throne, by a Serb nationalist.

The Serbian church was established in 1219 by Savas Nemania, its first archbishop, who gave it an ethnic character prevalent to the present day. It was always a patriarchate and in 1879 acquired formal autocephalous status from the ecumenical patriarchate. Since 1920 its coexistence with the Catholic Church of Croatia and Slovenia within a single state has been a source of conflict and tension, especially because the Vatican intervened to protect or promote the interests of the Catholics. During the Second World War, Serbs and Croats found themselves in opposing camps as Croatia remained independent under the pro-Fascist, Croat nationalist party, which under its leader, Ante Pavelić, attempted to exterminate its Serbian minority. With Nazis in power, the Serbs as a whole paid a heavy toll, with about one million slaughtered, including six Orthodox bishops, four hundred priests, and many monks. Because many Croatian civilians were cooperating with the Germans against the Serbs, traditional mistrust and tension between the two communities turned into deep hatred.

The Communist regime (1945–1990) of Josip Broz Tito's Yugoslavia could not eradicate such hatred. At first the regime opposed all religions. Then came a period of mutual toleration between church and state, followed by a period of mutual compromise. The Serbian church, however, was used as a tool of foreign policy to show the world that religious freedoms were not suppressed; this stance rather increased Croat fears of serbianization and the loss of their ethnic identity. In 1990 Croats welcomed the collapse of the Communist bloc, and they, along with their fellow Catholic Slovenians, were first to declare Croatia and Slovenia sovereign states (1991). But cutting the umbilical cord with Yugoslavia was not easy. Significant Serbian Orthodox minorities lived in Croatia and Slovenia, and with recent hatreds now revived, their extrication would lead to bloodshed and atrocities on both sides and hundreds of thousands of refugees.

The situation in Bosnia proved even worse. According to the 1981 census the republic consisted of Muslims (39.5 percent), Serbs (32 percent), and Croats (18.4 percent) mixed and scattered throughout Bosnia. The actual number of Muslims is estimated at 2.5 million. In 1990 a Muslim-led coalition elected Alija Izetbegović their leader and was in favor of a loose confederation of sovereign states within former Yugoslavia. This angered the Serbs of Bosnia, who declared that they would create their own autonomous regions. It also angered the Croats and the government of Slobodan Milošević in Belgrade. A savage war broke out in the province in 1992 that lasted more than three years, cost hundreds of thousands of lives, and caused incalculable human suffering.

In southern Yugoslavia a sovereign state called Macedonia was also declared in 1992. The United Nations has given the state the name Former Yugoslavian Republic of Macedonia, and it has a population of 2.2 million (Orthodox, 60 percent; Muslim, 40 percent). Ethnically, the Muslims are mostly of Albanian origin, and the Orthodox are mostly of Bulgarian origin. Greece refuses to recognize Macedonia as the state's name for historical and cultural reasons and because a major northern province of Greece is also called Macedonia.

International bodies such as the United Nations and the countries of the European Union and the United States have been actively working to resolve the crisis within the new states of the former Yugoslavia.

Bulgaria

In 1878 the Treaty of Berlin established the Bulgarian state, but the Bulgarian Orthodox Church had already declared its independence from the ecumenical patriarchate in 1870 as a prelude to its nationalist aspirations. The patriarchate did not endorse this act and declared the church schismatic. Like the Serbian and the Greek churches, the Bulgarian church acquired an intensely ethnic character that has been used to promote nationalist interests in the various conflicts in the region. As in Greece, the Bulgarian monarchy was initially Catholic but later became Orthodox; unlike Greece, the church has not been closely tied to the state. The ecumenical patriarchate granted the church autocephalous status in 1945, just as it fell under a hostile Communist regime. At first the party attempted to disrupt the church from within but later started using it as a tool for its nationalist policy and as a banner of the ethnic culture. Since the collapse of socialism in the country, the church has attempted to reorganize itself, and, without being involved in politics, it takes active part in the post-Communist reconstruction. Political and economic developments, however, tend to create tensions in the church.

Apart from the Orthodox, who make up the great majority in Bulgaria, there is also a significant Muslim minority, who consider themselves Turks. In 1989, at the height of the conflict of the Muslim community with the (still Communist) government, 350,000 Muslims left for Turkey, most of them to return later, still uncertain about their economic prospects in Bulgaria.

Romania

In the nineteenth century Romania was perhaps the richest and most cultured area in the Balkans, thanks to its Greek Phanariot (so called from the Greek quarter of Constantinople, from which many came) princes. But when the independent Romanian kingdom was established in 1862, King Charles Hohenzollern, a Catholic, expropriated most church property, closed down ecclesiastical presses, and declared the Romanian Orthodox Church independent. The ruling classes were secularized and kept the church low in status and despised. Formal recognition of its independence by the ecumenical patriarchate came in 1885. After the First World War the church was strengthened when Transylvania, with its substantial Orthodox population, was incorporated into the Romanian kingdom, making it the largest Orthodox Church after the Russian.

After the Second World War state policy toward the church, especially during Nicolae Ceausescu's regime, was rather contradictory. Religion was repudiated and the church was persecuted through expropriation of its lands and imprisonment of its clergy; yet religion and the church (which has its clergy paid by the state) were very much used to support the special brand of Romanian nationalism the regime promoted. Since 1990 the Orthodox Church has become again one of the major cultural institutions in Romania, and much of Romania's friendship and cooperation with Serbia grows out of the common religious tradition of the two countries. There is, however, tension with the Catholic Hungarian minority (about 17 percent).

Albania

The last of the Balkan states to be liberated from the Turks (1920), Albania has a population of 3.2 million, of which the majority (about 65 percent) are Muslims and the rest are Orthodox (22 percent) and Catholic (13 percent). Even before independence the nationalists promoted establishment of an independent Orthodox Church, which the patriarchate recognized in 1937. The Communist regime of Enver Hoxha (1945–1985) proved the most antireligious of all Marxist-Leninist states. After 1951 there was total suppression of religious freedom. A decree (4337 13.11.1967) formally declared Albania the first Marxist-atheist state. All ecclesiastical schools were closed, along with 2,169 religious establishments. Violation of religious and human rights continued in the 1980s, bringing severe protests from Greece and from many European states. After Hoxha's death the penal code was modified, and in 1991 the new democratic government in its constitution (Articles 7 and 45) restored religious and political freedoms.

The Orthodox Church was reestablished (1991) with Anastasios Gianoulatos, a professor from the Theological Faculty of Athens, appointed as archbishop by the ecumenical patriarchate. The majority of the Orthodox are ethnically Greek and live in Southern Albania (Northern Epirus), which was Greek territory for a while before 1921. Catholics also have reconstituted their religious organization with a papal nuncio and four bishops, and Muslims are opening mosques.

Greece

Greece differs from the rest of the Balkan states not only in its language, history, and culture but also in its relatively advanced economy and membership in the European Union. The great majority (96.5 percent) of the country's population (10 million) are Orthodox. The rest are Catholics, Muslims, Jews, Jehovah's Witnesses, and members of various Protestant denominations and sects.

After its war of independence in the 1820s, Greece was a small state. It was first a republic under President Ioánnis Kapodistrias (1827–1831) and then a monarchy from 1833 to 1862 under the young Bavarian prince Otto of Wittelsbach, who became King Otto I, a Catholic. The head of his Bavarian regency council—Otto was only seventeen years old at his accession—was a Protestant. The Bavarian administration attempted to modernize society without considering Orthodox religious culture. It declared the Greek church independent from the ecumenical patriarchate, made it subservient to the state, and closed more than four hundred monasteries, expropriating their lands. In 1852 the patriarchate recognized the church as autocephalous. By then Greek nationalism and Orthodoxy had combined to form the "great idea," a romantic vision of reestablishing modern Greece within its pre-Ottoman occupation boundaries. That dream ended on September 9, 1922, in what has come to be known in Greece as "the Asia Minor catastrophe." On that date—perhaps the most significant in twentieth-century

Greece—the Turkish troops of Mustafa Kemal (later known as Atatürk) routed Greek forces at Smyrna. More than one million Greeks fled to Greece from Asia Minor before the January 1923 refugee convention allowed the exchange of Christian and Muslim populations between Greece and Turkey.

Orthodoxy continued to be the dominant religion, and the Orthodox Church, always tied to the state, continued to exercise an indirect cultural hegemony over Greek society. Church and religion followed the patterns of the turbulent political history of the country. Throughout the twentieth century, not a single archbishop was elected according to normal canonical procedures, and several times the synod of the hierarchy—the highest governing body of the Church of Greece, which is presided over by the archbishop of Athens and all Greece and includes all diocesan bishops—was abolished and reinstated by the state.

After the Second World War and the civil war that followed in Greece, the church was involved even more in political developments. During a military dictatorship that lasted from 1967 to 1974, the ruling junta used the church and religion to support and legitimize its own special brand of Greek-Christian civilization. Since the return to civilian rule in 1975, there has been periodic tension between church and state. Although the constitutional subjugation of church to state has not changed, there has been a gradual disengagement of religion from politics, but Greek nationalism and Orthodoxy are still significantly linked.

See also *Globalization; Orthodoxy, Greek; Religious organization; State churches; Yugoslavia.*

Nikos Kokosalakis

BIBLIOGRAPHY

Critic, Christopher. *Remaking the Balkans.* London: Royal Institute of International Affairs, Pincer Publishers, 1991.

Huntington, Samuel P. "The Clash of Civilizations?" *Foreign Affairs* (September–October 1993).

Kouloumbis, Th., and Th. Veremis. "In Search of New Barbarians: Samuel P. Huntington and the Clash of Civilizations." *Mediterranean Quarterly* 5 (winter 1994): 36–44.

Jelavich, Charles. *The Establishment of the Balkan National States, 1804–1920.* Seattle and London: University of Washington Press, 1977.

Poulton, Hugh. *The Balkan Minorities States.* London: Minorities Rights Publications, 1991.

Ramet, Pedro, ed. *Eastern Christianity and Politics in the Twentieth Century.* Durham, N.C.: Duke University Press, 1988.

Wolf, Robert Lee. *The Balkans in Our Time.* Cambridge: Harvard University Press, 1956.

Bangladesh

See *Pakistan*

Banna, Hasan al-

Egyptian teacher, Islamic reformer, and founder of the Muslim Brethren. The father of al-Banna (1906–1949) was a teacher and *imam* (leader in prayer) at a mosque near Alexandria. Banna attended Qur'an school briefly and joined a mystical Sufi order, but he took his formal schooling in government primary and teacher training schools and at Dar al-Ulum, a college in Cairo. The mix of religious and modern subjects at Dar al-Ulum, from which he graduated in 1927, prepared him for teaching. A post as a primary teacher in Ismailiyya started him on a nineteen-year career with the Ministry of Education.

In 1928 Banna founded the Society of Muslim Brethren *(al-Ikhwan al-Muslimin),* to oppose secularization and promote a return to the ideals of early Islam as found in the Qur'an. Inspired by the teachings of Jamal al-Din al-Afghani, Muhammad Abduh, and Rashid Rida, Banna emphasized piety, education, and religious charity, while denouncing Christian missionaries, the moral bankruptcy of the West, Egyptians who aped decadent Western ways, and Egypt's British occupiers. (Britain had occupied Egypt since 1882 and still substantially controlled Egyptian affairs even after declaring the country nominally independent in 1922.) Ismailiyya was situated in the Suez Canal Zone, where resentment of the foreign-owned Suez Canal Company and British occupation troops facilitated recruiting for the Brethren.

When Banna obtained a teaching post in Cairo in 1932, he moved the Brethren's headquarters there. He set up branches throughout Egypt and, later, in neighboring countries. He insisted that the Muslim Brethren was not a political party, but the economic hardships of the Great Depression of the 1930s, the Zionist challenge of Jewish settlers in Palestine, and Britain's repression of Egyptian nationalists during World War II inexorably drew him into politics. By 1949 Banna had created a mass organization that challenged the status quo from outside the parliamentary and constitutional system. Despairing of peaceful, legal change, the Brethren's underground "secret apparatus" planned some of the assassinations and terrorist bombings that struck Egypt in the late 1940s. Banna approved of *jihad,* or struggle, against the British, but his writings did not preach terrorist violence. The degree of his responsibility for terrorist attacks remains elusive.

When the Egyptian government armed volunteers to fight against the new Jewish state in Palestine in 1948, the Muslim Brethren secretly stockpiled arms for future use at home. Egypt's defeat by Israel called the regime's legitimacy into question. When Cairo's chief of police was killed in a student riot in December 1948, Prime Minister Mahmud Fahmi Nuqrashi banned the Brethren on charges of conspiring against the government. He arrested most of its leaders but was assassinated by a student member of the Brethren. Banna denounced Nuqrashi's killing and denied any conspiracy, yet his slogans challenged the regime: "The Qur'an is our constitution" and "No other constitution but the Qur'an and Muhammad is our model." As Banna tried desperately to rein in the secret apparatus, he realized that the government's failure to arrest him meant that his life was in danger. On February 12, 1949, the political police shot him dead. His assassins were convicted in 1954, but the nearly certain culpability of higher officials went unproved.

After experiencing torture and the death of comrades in President Gamal Abdel Nasser's jails, surviving leaders of the Brethren renounced violence in pursuit of their cause. Alternately tolerated and repressed, and still not formally legalized, the Muslim Brethren today remain a mass movement that carries on Banna's work in Egypt and in other Arab countries. Extremist offshoots have embraced terrorist tactics and denounced the mainstream movement for selling out its principles.

See also *al-Afghani, Jamal al-Din; Fundamentalism; Islam; Jihad; Muhammad Abduh; Muslim encounters with the West; Nasser, Gamal Abdel; Qutb, Sayyid.*

Donald Malcolm Reid

BIBLIOGRAPHY

Abu-Rabi', Ibrahim M. *Intellectual Origins of Islamic Resurgence in the Modern Arab World.* Albany: State University of New York Press, 1996.
Carré, Olivier. "Banna, Hasan al-." In *The Oxford Encyclopedia of the Modern Islamic World.* Oxford: Oxford University Press, 1995, 1:195–199.
———, and Gérard Michaud. *Les Frères Musulmans, Egypt et Syrie, 1928–1982.* Paris: Gallimard, 1983.
Mitchell, Richard P. *The Society of the Muslim Brothers.* London: Oxford University Press, 1969.

Baptists

Baptists are Christians who trace their roots to England but enjoy their strongest following in the American South. Born in the seventeenth century as a result of differences with mainline Protestants on several theological issues, Baptists in the twentieth century have gained converts around the world through their missionary work. Traditionally, they have believed in a strict separation of church and state and emphasize a personal approach to religion based on biblical Scripture. Local Baptist congregations operate autonomously, rather than being bound to a strict hierarchical church governing body, though practice varies among the several denominations that call themselves Baptist. These denominations cover the spectrum of Protantism from left to middle to right, from mainline to evangelical to fundamentalist.

Baptists got their name from their belief that baptism is by immersion and for professing believers only. Only adults and children mature enough to make a public profession of faith in Christ are baptized. The usual method of Baptist baptism is a minister's plunging of a believer completely under water ("buried with Christ") and then returning that person to the standing position ("risen with Christ to walk in a newness of life"). These immersion-style baptisms are usually performed in indoor facilities built into Baptist churches for this purpose, but Baptists have been known to baptize in lakes, rivers, and even portable baptistries on the battlefield.

From the beginning of American history, Baptists and politics have been connected, and the connection has usually caused controversy. In the seventeenth century, with their fierce opposition to church entanglement with matters of state, Baptists helped to change the way religion and government would interact, and a "wall of separation" appeared. But in the last decades of the twentieth century, some argue that Baptists have led the effort to reunite the two. Much to the chagrin of strict separationist Baptists (who are some of the most fervent apologists for the faith), Baptists and politics were strongly linked in the 1980s and 1990s. This linkage applied to political figures as well as to political movements. In 1998, for example, a Baptist political roll call of American government included the four top-ranking national officers: President Bill Clinton, Vice President Al Gore, House Speaker Newt Gingrich, and Senate president pro tempore Strom Thurmond. If House minority leader Richard Gephardt,

Senate majority leader Trent Lott, and House majority whip Tom DeLay were included, we would find that the entire U.S. government in the late 1990s is Baptist, with the exception of Senate minority leader Tom Daschle and House majority leader Dick Armey. Baptist-backed political movements include efforts to restore prayer in public schools and to reverse the *Roe v. Wade* Supreme Court decision that loosened restrictions on abortion.

Reaching into history we find many Baptist politicians: Sens. Herman Talmadge of Georgia, Theodore Bilbo of Mississippi, and Claude Pepper of Florida; Rep. Wright Patman of Texas; Govs. Lester Maddox and Eugene Talmadge of Georgia; and the most self-conscious Baptist politician of our time, President Jimmy Carter. President Harry Truman was known to prefer the Baptist faith but quarreled with Baptist leaders.

Famous African American Baptists include the late Barbara Jordan, a representative from Texas (who was the daughter of a Baptist minister); Marian Wright Edelman, founder of the Children's Defense Fund; former NAACP director Benjamin Hooks; and Rep. J. C. Watts of Oklahoma.

European Heritage, American Growth

The Baptist faith traces its history to 1609, when an English Noncomformist minister, John Smyth (a different John Smith from Pocahontas's husband), rejected infant baptism most dramatically by rebaptizing himself and several adult followers. In Amsterdam at the time, Smyth had fled England when Anglican (Church of England) authorities found his ideas heretical and led a crackdown. By the time Thomas Helwys succeeded Smyth in 1611, the group felt safe to return to England, but Helwys was in prison within a year. Soon, however, the Act of Toleration of 1689 opened up new religious choices to the English people, and Baptists thrived. By the middle of the seventeenth century, Baptists enjoyed such strength that in true Baptist fashion rival Baptist denominations formed, each with its unique brand of faith.

Even given this history, some scholars of religion still call the Baptist faith the "American religion," a faith that is to religion what Coca-Cola is to beverages: a phenomenon created by and for Americans and exported to the world. There is some truth to this assertion. Baptists had their roots in the Old World, but it is in America that they have flourished. The name itself was at first controversial. When Roger Williams, a Cambridge-educated Nonconformist clergyman, immigrated to the Massachusetts Bay colony from

Roger Williams

England in 1631, he refused an invitation to pastor a Boston church because it had not broken its link to the Church of England. To Anglicans, Williams was a "dissenter." He believed in the concept of separation of church and state and resisted a state church, like the Anglican Church, funded by government tax collections. Williams was so controversial in Anglican-Puritan Massachusetts that he was banished from that colony in 1635. Fleeing to what later became Rhode Island, he had baptized several believers within a year and established, in Providence, what is considered the first Baptist church in America. Williams later left the church he established but remained in public life, becoming president of the Rhode Island Colony in 1654.

The Baptists in what Anglicans called "Rogues Island" were evangelical, however, and spread their faith throughout Britain's American colonies. More stable Baptist congregations were soon established in Newport, Rhode Island, and in Philadelphia, Pennsylvania. In 1707 the Philadelphia Association of Baptist Churches was organized, linking Baptists throughout the colonies. A southern association was founded in 1751, in Charleston, South Carolina, to establish a fellowship for the growing number of Baptists in the South. (The First Baptist Church of Charleston had been established in 1696.) In 1814 a national organization, the General Missionary Convention of the Baptist Denomination in the United States of America for Foreign Missions, was established. Because it met every three years, it was soon known unofficially by the shorter name Triennial Convention.

Missionary Work

Baptists in America began ambitious world missionary efforts even before they were well established at home. An Englishman, William Carey, went to India in 1792 as the first Baptist missionary, but he was soon followed, in 1812 in Burma, by three Americans: Ann Hasseltine Judson, Adoniram Judson, and Luther Rice. In 1846 American missions expanded to Africa with the appointment of black Baptists John Day and A. L. Jones, who began service in Sierra Leone and Liberia. Two years later Thomas J. Bowen, a white Baptist from Georgia, went to Nigeria with African Americans Robert F. Hill and Harvey Goodale. Already active in Baptist work, African Americans, by the end of the century, would have their own denomination and two mission boards, the National Baptist Convention and the Lott Carey Baptist Foreign Mission Convention. (The latter was named in honor of an African American Baptist from Richmond, Virginia, who founded the first African Baptist missions society in 1815.)

With the creation of the Baptist World Alliance, in 1905, Baptist missions became more coordinated. For example, Northern Baptists directed Baptist work in northern and central Europe, while Southern Baptists looked to southern and later to eastern Europe. Conferences in London, England, in 1920 and 1948 assisted with this coordination. After World War II, European Baptists affiliated with the alliance began to send missionaries as well as receive them; more than six hundred were serving at the end of the twentieth century.

North and South

When delegates south of the Mason-Dixon line (a line drawn between Pennsylvania and Maryland separating North and South) broke from the Triennial Convention in 1845 over the issue of slavery and other disputes, there were almost ten thousand Baptist churches nationwide, up from ten in 1700. Southerners called themselves the Southern Baptist Convention, and Northerners became the American Baptist Missionary Union. In 1907 the northern group became the Northern Baptist Convention before reverting to the American Baptist Convention in 1950, and finally, in 1972, the American Baptist Churches in the U.S.A.

For decades, the two denominations grew in their respective regions, with the northern group taking a looser, voluntary approach and the southerners becoming more and more denominational in their organization. After the Civil War (1861–1865), Southern Baptists struggled with the war's legacy of poverty, leaning on the border states and Texas to fund their work. (Southerners and Southern Baptists would not fully recover from the Civil War until after World War II ended in 1945.) But just as the founding of the new nation afforded the evangelical Baptists fertile ground for planting churches (it was the largest denomination in the country by 1800), the growth of the Sunbelt states in the twentieth century made the Southern Baptist Convention the country's largest Protestant denomination (at 14 million members by the 1990s). This phenomenal size led Martin Marty, a scholar of religion, to jest that "in the South, there are more Baptists than people."

"The American Religion"

For Baptists, rapid growth in America is no mere coincidence, however. Certain elements had to be in place for this faith to take root. The founding of the United States in the eighteenth century came from several notions about how government should be run. These included the belief that all men are created equal (Declaration of Independence, 1776), that there is a social contract in government that protects the liberty of the people (Declaration), that the church and the state must be kept separate (First Amendment to the Constitution, 1791), that the preponderance of power should be at the local level (Tenth Amendment to the Constitution, 1791), and that the economic system should be based on the idea of capitalist free enterprise.

These are Baptist ideas as well. The keystones to the Baptist faith as it touches politics are "the priesthood of all believers," which makes forgiveness of sin a personal matter; "soul liberty," which makes scriptural interpretation a matter between the individual soul and the Holy Spirit; and a localistic view, which makes Baptist congregations the most independent of any organized denomination. Local Baptist churches buy land, build buildings, call ministers, adopt budgets, and accept or reject members, all with little supervision from the national organization. That is why it is improper in most cases to refer to the national organization as "the Baptist Church" as one might the Roman Catholic Church or the Episcopal Church. A person may be a Baptist but not a member of "the Baptist Church," unless the reference is to a single, local congregation. As for capitalism, Baptists have few rivals in fund raising among their members and in attracting new "customers" through an aggressive entrepreneurial approach. Many congregations borrow marketing techniques from free enterprise to build "megachurches" the size of shopping malls.

The Baptists also grew because of their evangelical nature. Baptists have few rivals in their eagerness to spread the Gospel message and gain converts. In the individualistic, entrepreneurial American culture, Baptists found fertile ground in the marketplace of ideas. Free enterprise promoted an upfront, no-holds-barred willingness to "sell" like nowhere else on the globe. The Baptists seized on this with vigor, using the openness to new ideas to build the largest communion in the country. Like siblings in a family, the Baptist denomination grew along with the United States. Evangelicalism is so closely identified with Baptists that, unlike among the Lutherans or Methodists or Presbyterians, there is no Evangelical Baptist Church. It is understood that such a name would be redundant.

An old joke among Baptists is that "we multiply by division," and indeed it is difficult to name the many different "flavors" of Baptists in America. There are at least a couple of ways to group Baptists, however. The easier is by denomination. But there are certain characteristics that cut across denomination. In general, Baptists are either "regular" (or "Charleston tradition" after the South Carolina city where this tradition was best known) or "pietistic" (or "Sandy Creek tradition" after Sandy Creek, North Carolina, where it was popular). In general, the regular Baptists were of a city-oriented, Calvinistic, High Church tradition, and the pietistic Baptists were more rural, evangelistic, and Low Church in their worship. In their long history, Baptists have also been labeled General Baptist and Particular Baptist, following a demarcation similar to regular and pietistic. As for denominations, there are National Baptists, Southern Baptists, independent Baptists, Free Will Baptists, Primitive Baptists, American Baptists, Reformed Baptists, Conservative Baptists, North American Baptists, and even Pedo-Baptists.

Baptist Politics

The type of Baptist faith one chooses has political implications as well. Operation PUSH founder Jesse Jackson, Christian Coalition founder Pat Robertson, Moral Majority co-founder Jerry Falwell, and presidential spiritual adviser Billy Graham are all Baptists. Jackson and his organization infused the Democratic Party with a host of African American civil rights activists. Robertson and Falwell brought conservative Christians into the Republican Party. Graham has served as informal spiritual adviser to a half-dozen U.S. presidents of both parties.

African American Baptists have since the 1932 election, when Franklin D. Roosevelt was first elected president, been associated with the Democratic Party. But before that, the party of Abraham Lincoln, the Republican Party, enjoyed almost universal support from the black Baptist community. In all cases, however, the local Baptist church has been a central meeting ground for black political activism. Candidates often attend church to promote their candidacies, and civil rights leaders in need of support for their legal and political work tap into church fund-raising networks.

Civil rights leadership and black Baptist leadership have overlapped at times also. A number of African American political leaders have been Baptist leaders. Martin Luther King Jr. first attracted the attention of the nation as pastor of the Dexter Avenue Baptist Church in Montgomery, Alabama, in 1954. He later became co-pastor of his father's Atlanta church in 1960. King Jr. and King Sr. were leaders in the National Baptist Convention, as was Adam Clayton Powell Jr., a prominent black clergyman and politician, and Jesse Jackson. The National Baptist Convention, the largest African American Baptist group, was formed with the merger of three smaller denominations in 1895. It has roughly 8.5 million members and 33,000 churches. Other African American Baptist groups include the National Baptist Convention of America (1915) and the Progressive National Baptist Convention (1961). Black and white Democratic Party leaders are frequent speakers at African American Baptist meetings.

Independent Baptists are as Republican as African American Baptists are Democratic. Independent Baptists are fundamentalist Baptists who either seceded from major national Baptist groups or have chosen not to align themselves with major denominations whose practices and belief they consider too liberal. Most, however, associate themselves informally with other independents as part of a "fellowship." During the last decade of the twentieth century, the most well-known independent Baptist was Jerry Falwell. Falwell's Thomas Road Baptist Church in Lynchburg, Virginia, is a part of a loose association of independent Baptists called the Bible Baptist Fellowship. This group was founded in 1950 and by 1997 had more than 1.4 million members. Falwell mobilized the independent Baptists and other conservative Christians in the early 1980s as a part of the Moral Majority and has been intermittently politically active since. The Moral Majority represented the first professional attempt to organize conservative Christians politically, focusing on banning abortion, restoring school prayer, and electing Ronald Reagan as president.

The even more fundamentalist Bob Jones University, though Methodist in origin, is mostly independent Baptist as well. Many of the churches in the fifty-state network that supply Bob Jones with students belong to the Fundamental Baptist Fellowship, and most of the university's ministerial graduates become independent Baptist preachers and evangelists. Bob Jones University is very political. It has battled with the Internal Revenue Service over its tax-exempt status, all but controls local Republican politics in its hometown, and regularly hosts leading national conservative politicians. Many fundamentalists associated with Bob Jones have been active Republicans since Barry Goldwater's presidential campaign in 1964; others were energized by Reagan's social agenda in 1976 and 1980. Like the Moral Majority, Bob Jones University has a great deal of national political influence, though it is much less public than Falwell's organization.

Southern Baptists, the largest Baptist organization in the world, have been at the center of political controversy since conservatives took control of the denomination in 1979. Politics and political issues were the key to its shift from a moderate to a fundamentalist operation that year. At times, the line between theology and politics blurred as the Southern Baptist Convention became entangled in wars over the inerrancy of the Bible, prayer in the schools, abortion, separation of church and state, and women in ministry. After a decade or so of consolidating their power over the convention's various agencies, conservatives in the Southern Baptist Convention focused more and more on politics. The Convention has established an Ethics and Religious Liberty Commission office in Washington, forged alliances with conservative African Americans and Republican Catholics, and led a boycott of the Walt Disney Company. Religion and Republicanism, patriotism and piety have merged to such an

extent in the organization that sociologist Ellen Rosenburg has dubbed the Southern Baptists "hyper-Americans."

American Baptists, the old Northern Baptist Convention, which numbers 1.5 million people, tend to be less political than the Southern Baptists. From the beginning, the denomination was much less willing to create a denominational structure than were their brothers and sisters to the south. Many members of the Cooperative Baptist Fellowship and the Alliance of Baptists, both of which came out of the moderate wing of the Southern Baptists, have sought to forge ties with the American Baptist Churches.

Counting Baptists can be difficult. But to sort out the relative strength of Baptist groups, a good rule of thumb is to remember that about half of the nation's 26 million Baptists are Southern Baptist (14 million), and half of African American Christians are members of Baptist churches (13 million).

Harvesting New Fields

Worldwide, there are approximately 35 million Baptists. Much of this strength is accounted for in the relatively recent expansion of Baptists into Europe. One Baptist historian reported that at the time of the Battle of Waterloo (1815) there was no Baptist church on the Continent, but by the end of World War I (1918) there were between 1 million and 2 million European and Asian Baptists. Areas cited as particularly fruitful for the Baptist harvest during that period were Russia (which had "the largest Baptist community in Europe" at the time of the 1918 revolution) along with Germany, Sweden, Romania, Latvia, Estonia, Poland, and Hungary.

Eastern-bloc Baptists struggled under communism, the most notable Baptist dissident being Georgi Vins, general secretary of the Council of Evangelical Christian-Baptist Churches in the Soviet Union. Vins was a political prisoner in Siberia from 1974 until 1979, when U.S. president Jimmy Carter, himself a Baptist, negotiated Vins's release and with great drama attended a Baptist church with him in Washington several days later.

Communist regimes were unpredictable in their attitudes toward Baptists and acted inconsistently from country to country. Because Baptists were thought to undermine the hold of the Russian Orthodox Church, the Soviet Union was somewhat friendly to Baptists at its beginning, in 1918, but the regimes of Joseph Stalin and Nikita Khrushchev restricted religious exercise severely. With the collapse of the Soviet Union in 1991, Baptists expanded in Eastern Europe and Asia but struggled at the turn of the millennium with revived resistance from Orthodox Church authorities. The Orthodox Church helped persuade the Russian Duma (parliament) to pass legislation restricting the activities of foreign missionaries.

In its new frontiers, as in seventeenth-century England and America, Baptists are expanding their version of "simple democratic Christianity." With a worldwide missionary force supported by more than fifty Baptist mission agencies in the United States alone, Baptists face the twenty-first century with renewed hope, faith, and resources.

See also *African American experience; Calvinism; Civil rights movement; Evangelicalism; Fundamentalism; Graham, Billy; King, Martin Luther, Jr.; Russia.*

Oran P. Smith

BIBLIOGRAPHY

Ammerman, Nancy Tatom. *Baptist Battles: Social Change and Religious Conflict in the Southern Baptist Convention.* New Brunswick and London: Rutgers University Press, 1990.

Baker, Robert A. *The Southern Baptist Convention and Its People, 1607–1972.* Nashville, Tenn.: Broadman Press, 1974.

Estep, William R. *Whole Gospel, Whole World: The Southern Baptist Foreign Mission Board, 1845–1995.* Nashville, Tenn.: Broadman and Holman, 1994.

Lincoln, C. E., and L. Mayima. *The Black Church in the African-American Experience.* Durham, N.C.: Duke University Press, 1990.

Martin, Sandy D. *Black Baptists and African Missions: The Origin of a Movement, 1880–1915.* Macon, Ga.: Mercer University Press, 1989.

McBeth, H. Leon. *A Sourcebook for Baptist Heritage.* Nashville, Tenn.: Broadman, 1990.

Montgomery, William E. *Under Their Own Vine and Fig Tree: The African-American Church in the South.* Baton Rouge: Louisiana State University Press, 1994.

Rosenburg, Ellen M. *The Southern Baptists: A Subculture in Transition.* Knoxville: University of Tennessee Press, 1989.

Shurden, Walter B. *The Baptist Identity: Four Fragile Freedoms.* Macon, Ga.: Smyth and Helwys, 1993.

Smith, Oran P. *The Rise of Baptist Republicanism.* New York and London: New York University Press, 1997.

Barth, Karl

Swiss-German theologian in the Reformed Church tradition and one of the most significant Protestant thinkers of the twentieth century. Barth (1886–1968) studied at universities in Switzerland and Germany. After a period of ministry in neutral Switzerland during the First World War, he

Karl Barth

became professor of theology at Göttingen and Bonn, in Germany, where he was an early opponent of the Nazi regime. After refusing to take an oath of allegiance to Adolf Hitler, he was expelled from Germany in 1935. He spent most of the remainder of his career at Basel, in Switzerland. Barth's political thought was both theologically driven and contextually related to the time; it was also frequently controversial.

Early Work

In his student days in Marburg, Barth had followed the path of nineteenth-century liberal rationalism. This phase came to an abrupt end in 1914, with the outbreak of World War I, when ninety-three German intellectuals issued a manifesto endorsing the war policy of the German kaiser, Wilhelm II. For Barth, the presence of the names of his most respected theological teachers on this list was a catastrophic ethical failure. Their action ignited his theological creativity, and throughout the war he engaged in a quest for the basic meaning of Christianity and became a radical critic of liberal theology's accommodation to modern society. Becoming a Christian socialist, Barth regarded the European conflict as an imperialist struggle between the elites of rival capitalist nations that were contrary to the interests of the working classes. As a preacher and well-known local political activist, he rediscovered the theology of St. Paul, the early Christian interpreter of Jesus' life and work, exploring Paul's writings through preaching and testing his ideas in daily correspondence with his life-long friend, Eduard Thurneysen.

In 1919 Barth published the *Römerbrief,* a renowned theological commentary on Paul's Epistle to the Romans. Later that year at the Tambach conference of Christian socialists, he lectured on "The Christian in Society," arguing that the Gospel and Jesus' teachings should take precedence in society. In 1922 he rewrote the *Römerbrief* in more radical terms. The second *Römerbrief* is one of the most important theological texts of the twentieth century. The political consequences of his theology, known as dialectical theology, amounted to a paradox: insofar as it succeeded in focusing the rhetorical power and charismatic energy sufficient to launch a new theological movement within Protestant Christianity, to that extent it distanced Christian theory and practice from the mediation and compromise that attend politics understood as the "art of the possible." Barth later moved away from dialectical theology.

The major crisis of Barth's life occurred after the German general election of March 1933, when Hitler's National Socialists extended their control to the church and to the teaching of theology. As a professor in Bonn, Barth resisted this process, claiming the absolute autonomy of the God and Gospel of the Bible. In stiffening theological resistance to Nazism in the church, and above all through his role in formulating the Barmen Declaration of May 1934, Barth saw himself as acting politically. The Barmen Declaration was the foundation of the "Confessing Church," which declared itself to be the evangelical church in Germany in contrast to the established German church that accommodated the Nazi regime. Simply to undertake the task of theology under such conditions "as though nothing had happened" (as he maintained in June 1933) was simultaneously to enact a political act and to follow a theological vocation. Barth's contribution to the resistance of the Confessing Church to Hitler may nonetheless be regarded as the political high point of his life.

Later Work and Influence

With the end of the Second World War in 1945, Barth again applied his political theology, this time under the more ambiguous circumstances of the communist revolutions across Eastern Europe. Jan Hromadka, a Czech Reformed theologian, attempted with Barth's support to equate Christian and socialist commitments. For Hromadka, this advocacy was to have tragic personal consequences, for Marxism was to show as little mercy for free thinking as had Nazism. Barth's apparent ambivalence toward Marxist socialism, as contrasted with his outright opposition to National Socialism, attracted much criticism.

The interpretation of Barth's work has always been controversial. Ernst Bloch, a German Marxist philosopher, for example, maintained in 1923 that Barth propounded a bourgeois theology that had negative implications for emancipatory politics, whereas Friedrich-Wilhelm Marquardt has argued that Barth's theology explores and enacts a revolutionary revealed God. By contrast, R. W. Ward, an English historian of religious socialism, represented Barth as a man solely concerned with abstract theological issues and out of touch with real politics. He regarded Barth as a poseur whose interventions were little more than an inflated pseudo-political discourse that masked a relentless theological drive toward self-maximization and dominance.

Barth's politics were always subordinated to theological concerns. The relative success or failure of the former was more the product of contingent interaction with changing historical contexts than the conscious result of the discrimination and adjustments that might be characteristic of the genuinely politically minded.

See also *Communism; Fascism; Germany; Marxism.*

Richard H. Roberts

BIBLIOGRAPHY

Barth, Karl. *The Epistle to the Romans.* (English translation of *Der Römerbrief.*) Translated by Edwyn C. Hoskyns. Oxford: Oxford University Press, 1933.
———. *The Word of God and the Word of Man.* Translated by Douglas Horton. Boston: Pilgrim Press, 1928.
Busch, Eberhard. *Karl Barth: His Life from Letters and Autobiographical Texts.* Translated by John Bowden. London: SCM Press, 1976.
Hunsinger, George A. *Karl Barth and Radical Politics.* Philadelphia: Westminster, 1976.
Marquardt, Friedrich-Wilhelm. *Theologie und Sozialismus: Das Beispiel Karl Barths.* Munich: Kaiser Verlag, 1972.
Roberts, Richard H. *A Theology on Its Way? Essays on Karl Barth.* Edinburgh: T. and T. Clark, 1992.

Base communities

Base communities, a form of association that began emerging in Roman Catholicism in Latin America in the late 1960s, were originally intended as a response to shortages of clergy. The goal was to provide small-scale, familiar, and accessible environments in which people could meet for reflection and common action, without the presence of clergy. The creation of base communities is best understood in relation to the emergence and overall impact of liberation theology in Latin America during this period. The two are linked historically, related as theory is to practice. There was no single, first base community but rather a pattern of simultaneous creation as activists inspired by liberation theology began to "go to the people" in these years, identifying with their struggles for freedom and economic justice and creating new organizations, base communities among them.

The full name is "base ecclesial community" (in Spanish, *comunidad eclesial de base*). A common working definition takes off from the meaning of these three words: striving for *community* (small and homogeneous); stressing the *ecclesial* (links to the church); and constituting a *base* (either the faithful at the base of the church's hierarchy or the poor at the base of a class-and-power pyramid). Whatever else they may be, most base communities are small groups of ten to thirty people homogeneous in social composition, most commonly poor and female. Whatever else they may do, they gather regularly (once every week or two) to read and comment on the Bible, to discuss common concerns, and occasionally to act together toward some concrete end. Reading and commenting on the Bible in a community setting soon became the common foundation of group activities. Stress on participation and equal access to sacred knowledge, through the Bible, reinforces ideas of egalitarianism and action in common as the outgrowth of a transformed religious faith.

A New Autonomy

The newness of base communities is found above all in the model of governance created and the degree of autonomy claimed within the church. Governance was conceived in an egalitarian and participatory way. Breaking with traditional Catholic trickle-down models—in which the bishop knows more than the priest, the priest knows more than the sisters, the sisters know more than the laity, and so on down to the bottom—base communities and similar groups with different names underscored equal access to knowledge (through the Bible) and equal participation in managing group affairs. Relative autonomy left groups free, at least in principle, to seek alliances with others, rather than checking everything with clerical advisers.

The working model of community that was put into practice gave place of preference to ideals of active and informed participation, with religious practice structured around small, self-governing groups able to operate without clerical supervision. Learning from experience in familiar settings where all participate as equals lays the groundwork for new models of governance in everyday practice. The value placed on participation in the day-to-day routine of base communities spills over to a general insistence that participation is good in itself. More participatory groups are better: strategies and tactics that enhance and extend participation to the utmost are an ideal to be pursued.

There is much dispute over precisely what counts as a base community. Widely varying kinds of organizations are often lumped together and presented under this heading. What passes for a base community in El Salvador or Brazil often bears little relation to groups of the same name encountered in Colombia or Argentina. Conversely, a group that meets all of the normal definitions may not call itself a base community. There is also intense competition within countries between alternative models, as progressives and conservatives each try to advance their goals through groups with this name. Base communities are rarely spontaneous creations, springing unbidden and full blown "from the people." They are born linked to the churches, specifically to initiatives by bishops, religious orders, priests, nuns, or lay agents commissioned by the church. These ties are maintained through a regular routine of courses, visits by clergy and especially sisters, and through the distribution of mimeographed circulars, instructional material, and cassettes. Base communities may be popular in social composition, but they are not autonomous or isolated from the institutional church. Rather, they are constantly influenced by it and subject to its monitoring and control.

All base communities begin with pastoral agents reaching out to communities. Initial contact is most often made by nuns in conjunction with seminarians. Popular receptivity has not been unlimited; in many cases clerics tried but failed to create base communities. Failure has been more likely when pastoral agents attempted to encourage the formation of highly politicized groups from the outset.

Religion, Community, and Action

Success has been more common when religion and community were initial and continuing goals. The ordinary practice of most base communities is religious in quite conventional ways. Members pray a lot, both individually and as a group. They also value and practice a number of traditional prayers and rites (rosaries, nocturnal vigils, adorations, and celebrations like processions and pilgrimages) that have often been spurned by Catholic radicals anxious to move on to the "real work" of social and political transformation. The clash of popular desires for liturgy with activist stress on "useful" collective action is a permanent feature of much base community life.

Most base community meetings follow a standard pattern. The group gathers weekly or biweekly in a church facility or community center or on a rotating basis in the homes of members. The session opens with reading from the Bible, followed by commentary and discussion aimed at connecting the scriptural passage to personal and community issues. Although the Bible is central to group life, base communities should not be confused with fundamentalists. They do not view the Bible as an inerrant text, a source of formulas to be applied in some mechanical fashion, but rather as a set of values, ideals, and role model. Discussion is active and open, with members jumping in to point out how what is spoken of in the Bible is happening here and now, to people like them.

The links between base communities and explicitly political action have been varied, but all begin with a community decision to address some pressing local need. Health committees, cooperatives, schools, and local efforts to supplement subsistence (for example, by organizing community kitchens) are prominent. These short-term connections are amplified by the way participation in base communities legitimizes activism and autonomous organization. By diffusing skills of organization and providing spaces for the practical expression of democracy and self-governance, base communities contribute to a general democratization of culture. Efforts to translate these cultural and religious predispositions into directly political activism have rarely been successful.

Part of the difficulty in building political movements out of base communities arises from a palpable gap between the hopes and expectations of activists and intellectuals and the goals and dispositions of members. Contrary to what early commentators believed, members of base communities

rarely come from the very poorest of the poor. Members are more likely to be recruited from the stable poor: peasants with some land, city dwellers with steady jobs. Members are also overwhelmingly female. Because church organizations are culturally sanctioned vehicles for women, they draw hitherto silent voices into public spaces. But many women remain wary of specifically political activism and are constrained by family obligations, including pressure from male relatives, to stay out of politics, regarded as men's work.

Together these characteristics shape the kind of activism that most members are disposed to support. Commitment is more limited, local, and less confrontational than many activists have wanted to recognize. Goals are distinctly modest, nonpolitical, and nonrevolutionary. Members look for fellowship, moral support, and specific improvements like access to water, education, credit, or health services. No matter what the social or political agenda may be, from child care to sewing circles, from cooperatives to strikes or land invasions, in all instances there is great stress on prayer, Bible study, and liturgy. In any event, most of the social and political agenda at issue is quite conventional. Typical activities include sewing, visiting the sick, or social action, which usually means collecting money, clothing, or food for those in extreme need. There are also commonly attempts to found cooperatives, which for the most part remain limited to very small scale savings-and-loan operations, or at most to collective-marketing or common-purchase arrangements.

Repression and Grassroots Activism

Although the initial impetus behind the formation and spread of base communities was religious, not political, in practice communities have had subtle and far-reaching effects on politics. From the beginning, base communities developed in ways that responded to the needs of popular sectors for participatory experiences that could provide meaning, structure, and support as they faced a difficult and changing world. All this was appealing and would have had some impact in any event. But in those countries where the communities later became particularly visible in politics (for example, El Salvador, Nicaragua, Chile, Brazil), repression and authoritarian rule decisively magnified and extended their impact. By restricting political spaces and closing organizations such as unions or political parties, fearful governments drove activists into the churches. There was often nowhere else to go.

Ironically, it is precisely those regimes that complain most bitterly about the "political" impact of liberation theology and base communities, and about excessive "politicization" of the churches generally, that have been prime creators of what they deplore and condemn so strongly. Their own intense repression created a clientele and made the logic of resistance and activism all the more meaningful. In Latin America authoritarianism was a prime growth medium for popular religious movements. Instead of frightening activists into apathy, official threats and violence reinforced the dedication of many bishops and pastoral agents, who intensified efforts to create and defend base communities.

At issue here is a complex process of exchange and mutual influence among new commitments to the poor articulated through liberation theology, social changes, and repression. When the churches began to promote ideas about justice, rooting them in participatory, reinforcing group structures, they found a ready audience. The moral sanction of the churches, reinforced by solidarity and mutual support in the groups, helped sustain membership and uphold its commitments as possible and correct, even in the face of great danger. As the needs of members were echoed and reinforced by guiding ideas derived from liberation theology, originally limited religious agendas broadened. Together these changes undergirded a range of new commitments and activities.

Legacy

Beginning in the mid-1980s the resolution of Central America's civil wars and the return of civilian rule and democratic politics elsewhere in Latin America reduced the pressures that helped turn base communities to politics. More open conditions have led to a proliferation of organizational alternatives. Base communities now encounter vigorous competition from a wide range of groups, including political parties and trade unions, as well as evangelical and Pentecostal Protestants and Catholic charismatics, who stress gifts of the Holy Spirit such as healing or speaking in tongues. At the same time, many of the movements that had spun off from base communities in earlier years divided or simply failed. They fell victim to a combination of repressive violence (which took a particularly heavy toll in Central America) and, in some sense, to the impact of democracy itself. As the common enemy of military and authoritarian rule disappeared, members split among available alternatives and, in many instances, movements were left in the lurch as allies on the left splintered or pursued their own agendas.

The legacy of base communities is a heightened awareness of the possibilities for participation and democratic self-governance, not only within the church but also in society and politics as a whole. The appeal of Bible study is evidence of the powerful attraction of literacy in newly mobile communities. Among the people of Latin America, as among the Puritans of sixteenth-century England, equality of access to sacred knowledge laid the foundation for a claim to equality in general. Participation as equals in religious life provided a groundwork for a practical theory of rights manifest in the creation of an active citizenry that can play a continuing role in democratizing society and politics over the long haul.

See also *Brazil; Liberation theology.*

Daniel H. Levine

BIBLIOGRAPHY

Azevedo, Marcelo. *Basic Ecclesial Communities in Brazil. The Challenge of a New Way of Being Church.* Translated by John Drury. Washington, D.C.: Georgetown University Press, 1987.

Berryman, Phillip. *Religious Roots of Rebellion: Christians in the Central American Revolutions.* Maryknoll, N.Y.: Orbis, 1984.

Bruneau, Thomas C. *The Church in Brazil: The Politics of Religion.* Austin: University of Texas Press, 1982.

Burdick, John. *Looking for God in Brazil: The Progressive Catholic Church in Urban Brazil's Religious Arena.* Berkeley: University of California Press, 1993.

Hewitt, W. E. *Base Christian Communities and Social Change in Brazil.* Lincoln: University of Nebraska Press, 1991.

Levine, Daniel H. *Popular Voices in Latin American Catholicism.* Princeton: Princeton University Press, 1992.

Belgium

See *Low Countries*

Bhutto, Zulfiqar Ali

See *Pakistan*

Bonhoeffer, Dietrich

German Lutheran theologian, pastor, and leader of church resistance to the Third Reich who was executed for

Dietrich Bonhoeffer

steps beyond its legitimate sphere, as it had in dealing with the Jews.

Correcting the Church, Resisting the State

Bonhoeffer was among the relatively few to recognize the complicity of the conventional religion of his time with Hitler's strategy of using religion as an instrument of his policies. Bonhoeffer's approach to the task of correcting the church and resisting the encroachments of the state was more clear-headed and down-to-earth than most. No less theological because practical, he sought to allow God to enable the church to act responsibly in the contingencies of political struggle. Engaging with major theological influences, he concluded that God had in Christ bound himself to human social life in history with definite consequences for responsible social life (the scriptural "mandates" of labor, marriage, government, and church). For Bonhoeffer, these were not abstract theological considerations but decisive for the "Confessing Church" (a church that confesses itself to be for its Lord and against its enemies) as it formed itself in resistance against the "German" church that succumbed to Hitler's strategy. His own thought emerged in fragmentary form as he responded to the urgencies of the struggle.

What was particularly remarkable about Bonhoeffer's thought was the depth of his critique of religious rationalizations of church and state ("cheap grace"), and his recognition of the involvement of God in the sufferings of people in the world where they found freedom in living responsibly for each other ("costly grace"). In this, and in his attempts to work out the ethical and political consequences, he was convinced that in Christ God was always nearby and active in the human social struggle for justice.

It is clear that Bonhoeffer's capacity to live "outside" himself in his duties to Christ, church, and social order gave his life an extraordinary Christian integrity. This capacity is visible in his activities as university teacher, spokesman for the confessing church (and for those endeavoring to stop Hitler and his regime) abroad, director of the community in which confessing church pastors were educated, pastor in England and underground in Germany, and—in conscious opposition to Lutheran tradition—participant in the conspiracy on Hitler's life. It is also seen during his year-long imprisonment before his execution only three weeks before Hitler's suicide. This integrity, which shines through Bonhoeffer's writings and biography, accounts for his wide influence since then.

conspiring against Hitler. Bonhoeffer (1906–1945) was the sixth son of a professor of neurology at the University of Berlin. His family's tradition of responsibility in scientific and public life took an unexpected form as he chose to study theology and later to be ordained. His research into the church as the worldly reality in whose formation and witness God is active in the world, unusual for its time, qualified him as a university teacher. It gave him a distinctive Christian voice and also sensitized him to the perversion of society by Hitler. He came to a fresh understanding of how the state is circumscribed by its Creator and of the prophetic responsibility of the church. Its task is to care for social order, declaring the limitations of the state—especially where it

During his year in prison, freed of direct responsibilities and made accountable to secular authorities, he began to see how drastically modern life undercut "religion" in its usual forms (teaching, piety, and "exploiting human weakness or human boundaries"). This realization led him to ask himself what Christianity and the lordship of Christ might then mean. There is yet hope that God will then be "not on the boundaries but at the center," "not in death and guilt but in human life and goodness," revealing true human freedom in discipline, action, suffering, and death.

These remarkable views gave rise to far-reaching discussions about God, Christ, church, world, and human responsibility. Bonhoeffer was in effect resituating God in the historical situation of the world and taking modern atheism as an opportunity to investigate the Christian concept of God anew—not, as some claimed, advocating the death of God.

Concentration of Influence

Bonhoeffer's influence has been concentrated in two main arenas: among those concerned with the position and intelligibility of the Christian faith and church in modern thought and life and among those confronted by oppressive regimes. In the first, his insights about God, Christ, community, and sociopolitical responsibility in a post-Enlightenment world have figured importantly in the work of those reconsidering God and identifying God's activity in the achievement of just social life in history, but his ideas are not easily reconstructed or transferred.

In the second arena, Bonhoeffer's influence is seen where the churches must reconsider their role in society, as in Eastern Europe, Latin America, and South Africa. His conception of the church was particularly influential in the German Democratic Republic. His claim that there is no disjunction between the reality of the world and the reality of God, and that the brokenness of this world is reconciled with God through Jesus Christ, enabled the church to move from opposition to critical dialogue in its relations with the state. Bonhoeffer's view of the church as "for others," that it is not so much concerned for itself as for society as a whole, allowed the church to participate in the political process in such a way as to make the kingdom of God visible without legitimating an unjust socialism.

See also *Fascism; Genocide and "ethnic cleansing"; Germany; Holocaust; Lutheranism.*

Daniel W. Hardy

BIBLIOGRAPHY

Bethge, Eberhard. *Dietrich Bonhoeffer: A Biography.* New York: Harper and Row, 1970.

De Gruchy, John, ed. *Bonhoeffer for a New Day: Theology in a Time of Transition.* Grand Rapids, Mich.: Eerdmans, 1997.

Floyd, Wayne Whitson, Jr., ed. *Dietrich Bonhoeffer Works.* Vols. 1–16. Minneapolis: Augsburg Fortress, 1996–.

Kelly, Geffrey B., and F. Burton Nelson. *A Testament to Freedom: The Essential Writings of Dietrich Bonhoeffer.* San Francisco: Harper San Francisco, 1990.

Botswana

A landlocked democracy of 1.4 million people, Botswana is located to the north of South Africa. Until it gained independence from Great Britain in 1966, it was known as the Bechuanaland protectorate. Since gaining independence, it has become one of Africa's wealthiest nations. Although a multiethnic society, with more than a dozen language groups, the country has long been dominated by Tswana-speaking people.

Botswana today is predominantly Christian. There are no organized religious movements that seek to influence policy in the country's two main places of power—the legislature and the government bureaucracy. Indeed, since independence, the government and all major political parties have rarely consulted or worked with religious organizations in any formal way.

This emphasis on secular politics is not a long-standing practice. During the previous hundred years, mission churches played a central role in buttressing the powers of the Tswana chiefs, each of whom patronized a single church and refused to allow competitors in his territory. As a result, Christianity was linked closely to the chiefs. And because the chiefs lost practically all their power after independence, the churches have since lacked a formal role in Botswana's government.

Religious freedom, which came with independence, encouraged the introduction of large numbers of small churches, thus further diminishing the role of religious institutions. Formal religious influence on politics has therefore been restricted to lobbying, although in recent years many small denominations have begun to forge relationships with opposition politicians in a bid to win greater recognition for their congregations.

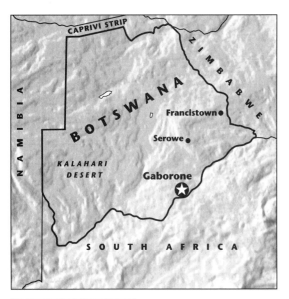

Traditional Religion and Colonization

Traditionally, the various people of Botswana were animists, whose worldview was similar to that of many other Africans. They believed in witchcraft and sorcery and generally thought that many events were influenced by the spirits of their ancestors, who were thought to punish those who failed to live by custom. Traditional leaders, the chiefs of the various Tswana groups, played an important role in sacred practices, such as rainmaking, and held a preeminent spiritual role in society.

When Christian missionaries began to evangelize the Tswana peoples in the mid-1800s, they found a receptive audience among the elite—particularly the chiefs, their relatives, and the traditional doctors. After being adopted by the elite, Christianity spread downward to the commoners and slaves. This process occurred among the five major Tswana chieftaincies: the Bangwato, Bakwena, Bangwaketse, Batawana, and Bakgatla. Once the chiefs and the elite became Christians, they began to replace animist practices. Rainmaking, for instance, was replaced by formal prayer sessions just before the plowing season. "Heathen" practices involving marriage, rites of passage, inheritance, and the like were gradually outlawed and replaced by Christian ones.

By far the most important of the Christian groups working among the Tswana was the nondenominational London Missionary Society, which sent missionaries into Botswana as early as 1824. The London Missionary Society gained a re-ligious monopoly among four of the major Tswana chieftaincies, and because of its links to the leading chiefs it became dominant across the country. This situation was strengthened by the arrival of colonialism in 1885, when the British system of "indirect rule" required the British colonizers to rule through the traditional chiefs. As a result, British authorities supported the chiefs' attempts to retain a single church within each of their territories. Colonialism thus cemented the ties between the chiefs and their "state" churches.

For a long period the London Missionary Society used its position to promote social change. It successfully persuaded chiefs to banish traditional practices and to institute Christian practices and ritual in their place. For the dominant Tswana especially, Christianity became part of their daily lives.

Close ties between the London Missionary Society and the chiefs meant that independent, African-run "Ethiopian" and "Zionist" churches were slow to spread in Botswana. Chiefs like Khama III of the Bangwato (1875–1923) routinely expelled preachers and converts of these churches, because they viewed them as potentially hostile political factions. Only during the mid-1930s did British authorities intervene to end the London Missionary Society's monopoly by allowing Seventh-day Adventists into several regions where the Adventists offered to build the country's first hospitals.

During the 1950s and 1960s independent churches, particularly Zionist ones, emerged—though they continued to be banned by all the major chiefs until 1966. These new churches were particularly popular among ethnic minorities, many of whom resented their subjugation under Tswana rule. The first vibrant independent churches were established by the Kalanga, especially those living on government land outside the control of the Tswana chiefs. Such groups as the Spiritual Healing Church and St. John's Apostolic Faith Healing Church were well established by 1960, after which they surreptitiously moved into Tswana regions. Another important group was the Zion Christian Church, many of whose adherents had to live on government-owned land to avoid persecution by the chiefs.

Modern Botswana

After 1966 the newly elected independent government drastically altered the status quo, first by gutting chiefly power and second by allowing complete religious freedom for the first time. Power moved away from British officials and chiefs and ended up with the ruling Botswana Democratic Party, which created a large new bureaucracy. Although elections have been held regularly since 1966, the Botswana Democratic Party did not face serious opposition until the 1990s.

The weakness of the opposition was mirrored by a weakness in civil society generally. Power came to be centered within the government bureaucracy. Popularly elected politicians in the legislature had little influence, and there were few private organizations to counteract government dominance. Until the mid-1980s, for instance, there was no independent press or media.

Whereas in the past the London Missionary Society (now the Botswana synod of the United Congregational Church of South Africa, or UCCSA) and other sanctioned churches had direct access to chiefs and government officials, they now lacked formal avenues to the government. Moreover, the rapid growth of dozens of small independent churches after 1966 allowed groups like the Zion Christian Church and Spiritual Healing Church to outstrip the UCCSA in membership. Christians in the country thus became divided into a large number of denominations, none of which had the clout formerly held by the London Missionary Society. Although a national body called the Botswana Christian Council, which incorporates all Botswana's churches, has the potential to wield political influence, it has nonetheless avoided any open political role since its inception in the 1960s.

The UCCSA continues to have some influence in the ruling party because of its historical role in education and health. One of its missionaries, Dr. A. M. Merriweather, for instance, was the country's first Speaker in parliament. Botswana's second president, Sir Ketumile Masire (who took office in 1980), is also a life-long UCCSA member; both he and his predecessor, Sir Seretse Khama, the country's first president, were educated in its schools.

Although churches since independence have eschewed any formal role in elections and in formal government, there can be no doubt that they have influenced the government to practice a range of socially conservative policies and have prevented the introduction of liberal ones. This situation is most clear in the case of pornography: the government prohibits the distribution of sexually explicit material. Abortion is another area in which groups like the Zionists and the UCCSA have taken a strong stand. In 1994, when government officials tried to legalize abortion, they met with strong opposition from church leaders. This is one of the few instances in Botswana's history where public protests led to the government's withdrawing proposed legislation.

In the 1990s, although mainline religious groups like the UCCSA have tended to be implicit supporters of the government, smaller churches have come to identify with the opposition. The left-leaning Botswana National Front, which dominates the urban vote, has to some extent courted ministers of independent and Zionist churches capable of delivering votes. In particular, the registration of smaller churches has been an important factor for the Botswana National Front because the government will recognize only registered churches. To register, a church must formulate a constitution and go through a cumbersome administrative process. Tedious registration formalities have often led aspiring churches to feel that they are being victimized by the government and thus have led them to identify with the opposition. In a large number of cases, independent ministers have continued to work with the opposition, even after registration finally is complete.

It is likely that in the future two religious-political blocs will coalesce: a mainline church allied with the Botswana Democratic Party, on the one hand, and an independent church and Botswana National Front partnership on the other. At present, though, Botswana's large Christian population is disorganized and split. As the rest of the country's civil society becomes more sophisticated, it is probable that the country's churches will assume a greater role in national politics.

See also *Africa, Christian; African traditional religion.*

Barry Morton

BIBLIOGRAPHY

Amanze, James. *Botswana Handbook of Churches: A Handbook of Churches, Ecumenical Organizations, Theological Institutions, and Other World Religions in Botswana.* Gaborone: Pula Press, 1994.

Boschman, Don. *The Conflict between New Religious Movements and the State in the Bechuanaland Protectorate prior to 1949.* Studies on the Church in Southern Africa. Vol. 3. Gaborone: Department of Theology and Religious Studies, University of Botswana, 1994.

Landau, Paul S. *The Realm of the Word: Language, Gender, and Christianity in a South African Kingdom.* Portsmouth, N.H.: Heinemann; London: J. Curry, 1995.

Schapera, Isaac. *Tribal Innovators: Tswana Chiefs and Social Change, 1795–1940.* London: Athlone, 1970.

Setiloane, Gabriel M. *The Image of God among the Sotho-Tswana.* Rotterdam: Balkema, 1976.

Bourguiba, Habib

Leader of the Tunisian nationalist movement and first president of Tunisia after independence from France, in 1956. After attending secondary schools in Tunis, Bourguiba (1903–) earned a law degree from the University of Paris. Returning to Tunisia, he renewed an earlier association with the nationalist Dustur Party but became an outspoken critic of party leaders' unwillingness to challenge French rule. Expelled from the Dustur in 1934, Bourguiba formed the Neo-Dustur Party, which supplanted the older party as the vehicle of nationalist sentiment and, in 1957, assured its popular leader a victory in the first postindependence presidential elections. After he won reelection in 1964 and 1969, the National Assembly appointed him president for life in 1974.

Bourguiba initiated a sweeping program of social change designed to foster the emergence of a secular, Westernized state. Many of his reforms targeted Muslim customs that he viewed as impediments to progress and development. He spearheaded campaigns to restore to their original owners properties held as religious trusts and to bring all education under state rather than religious control. He oversaw the introduction of a legal system that minimized the influence of Islamic law, most dramatically exemplified by the enactment of a code radically altering traditional practices (such as outlawing polygyny and legitimizing marriages between persons of different faiths). The government, accusing religious leaders of trying to preserve their power at the expense of the national good, forcefully curbed protest demonstrations.

Despite Bourguiba's enormous popularity and the considerable powers vested in the president by the constitution, some aspects of Islam remained impervious to change. In 1960, for example, Bourguiba failed to persuade his countrymen to ignore the religious obligation to fast during the month of Ramadan, despite his ingenious assertion that all Tunisians were waging a *jihad* (struggle) against underdevelopment and that Islam exempted persons engaged in *jihad* from observing the fast.

An uneasy truce developed as the religious establishment was brought to heel, but memories of Bourguiba's assault on Islam, combined with the conviction that his policies had created serious social and economic ills, gave rise in the 1970s and 1980s to a potent religiously based opposition epitomized by the Islamic Tendency Movement. Although the constraints of a single-party state and Tunisia's faltering

Habib Bourguiba

economy simultaneously engendered secular opposition movements, Bourguiba responded to his religious adversaries with vehemence. In 1987 Islamic Tendency militants were tried on charges of plotting to overthrow the government, and several received capital sentences. Bourguiba acceded to his advisers' pleas to commute the death sentences to deprive the movement of additional martyrs, but his abhorrence of the Islamists soon led to a disavowal of this pragmatic decision and a demand that the executions be carried out.

The prime minister, Zine el-Abidine Ben Ali, attributed Bourguiba's erratic behavior in this, as in other matters, to his failing health. Following the provisions of the constitution, Ben Ali convoked a team of physicians who declared the president unable to fulfill his duties. The ailing Bourguiba retired to his home town of Monastir and withdrew from public life.

See also *Jihad; Secularization; Tunisia.*

Kenneth J. Perkins

Brazil

The largest and most populous country of South America, the Federative Republic of Brazil is home to three major religious families: Roman Catholicism, Protestantism (especially its Pentecostal forms), and spiritism. Each of these religious families—and we must note wide variations in belief and practice within them, not least between popular and educated forms—has a claim to dominance in Brazil's social and cultural life. Catholicism was brought by the Portuguese who colonized the area in the sixteenth century. Protestantism is more recent, arriving with missionaries over the past one hundred years but developing strong local roots in the latter half of the twentieth century. The popular forms of spiritism, often designated Afro-Brazilian spiritism, have developed from the religions of the African slaves.

Catholicism looms large as the foundation religion of colonial Brazil: the calendar is organized around its feast days, and, despite separation of church and state since the constitution of 1891, dignitaries of the Catholic Church still preside over public occasions as though Catholicism were the established religion. In a population approaching 160 million, more than 80 percent describe themselves as Catholic. Nominally Brazil is the largest Catholic country in the world, but numerical preponderance and public presence are not accompanied by any kind of hegemony exercised by the church, and even on the numbers the other religions mount increasing challenge. The Pentecostal churches are growing at an extraordinary rate, and the number of Protestants attending church regularly now far exceeds the number of Catholics, though a best estimate of their proportion in the population is 13 percent. In any of the poorer suburbs and shantytowns of Brazil's great cities it may be difficult to locate the local Catholic church, but there will be a dozen or more Pentecostal temples—the Assemblies of God, Brazil for Christ, the Four Square Gospel Church (among others) and now, the fastest growing of them all, the Church of the Universal Reign of God.

In coastal cities the hymns and sermons of the Protestants, broadcast on loudspeakers for all to hear, may be drowned out by the sound of drums and chanting from the Afro-Brazilian religions, Candomblé (more traditionally African) and Umbanda (more of a blend). These religions are part of a larger family of spiritist religions, distinguished by belief in a world of spirits to which the living, through mediums, may have recourse in order to obtain strength, wisdom, and pro-

tection. The spiritist family includes forms of spiritism of European provenance. But the African elements of Candomblé, in particular, remind us that Afro-Brazilian spiritist religions were brought from Africa by African slaves and kept alive by them and their descendants since the abolition of slavery in 1888. Because many devotees of spiritism consider themselves to be Catholics as well, and so report themselves in the census, it is difficult to guess their proportion in the population. But if we include with practitioners of these religions the millions of Brazilians who periodically consult a spirit medium, then spiritism too has its claim to dominance over hearts and minds in Brazil.

The Role of the Catholic Church

The three religious traditions are woven deeply, and intricately, into the fabric of political life in Brazil. The most obvious and direct involvement occurs when religious leaders enter into the political arena or mobilize the faithful for political ends. The Catholic Church's political involvement was especially intense during the years of the country's military dictatorship from 1964 to 1985. The Brazilian Conference of Bishops endorsed the coup of April 1964, judging it necessary to restore order and defeat communism. But from the early 1970s the church gradually became the major institutional source of opposition to military authoritarian rule and the social injustices believed to be worsened by its policies.

This political radicalization occurred for a number of reasons. One was reaction to the imprisonment and torture of clerical and lay Catholic radicals who sought democracy and social justice. Another was the diffusion of critical social analysis and pastoral initiatives, including the fostering of grass-roots base communities, which were inspired by the liberation theology movement. According to liberation theology, the vocation of the church is to struggle for justice on the side of the poor and oppressed and to prefigure the biblical Kingdom of God in its own practices and structures. The base communities, consisting of groups in poor neighborhoods brought together by clergy, were an attempt, meeting varying degrees of success, to realize that vocation. By the early 1980s, in the years of gradual restoration of democracy in Brazil, Catholic clergy as well as laity were frequently involved in mobilizing support for parties of the opposition. The Catholic contingent in the coalition of radical groups that came together to form the new socialist Workers' Party was substantial.

It should not be concluded, however, that the Catholic

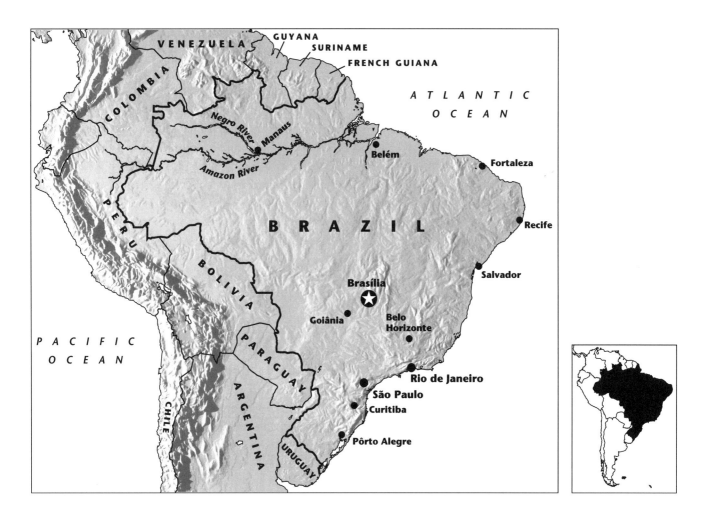

Church has been uniform or entirely effective in mobilizing support for the political left. Although there have been instances of individual radical clergy urging a vote for left-leaning candidates and parties, the closest the church has come to direct support for the left has been in a few dioceses like São Paulo where voter education programs have been organized. These programs reach only a small proportion of Catholics. Since the return of democracy to Brazil, Catholics of the left often have been disappointed to discover that those Catholic citizens who could be mobilized to support political initiatives expressing the church's "preferential option for the poor" in the early 1980s now distribute their votes across the political spectrum. This outcome appears to be how the majority of the bishops in the 1990s would want it: they are persuaded that with the military returned to the barracks, the clergy should return to the sacristy and the church should refrain from direct involvement in politics. Among politicians, the designation "Catholic" conveys nothing about an individual's policies or allegiances.

There is no Catholic party even of the unofficial kind like the Christian Democrats in Chile.

New Directions

For a while in the mid 1980s, following the restoration of democracy, it seemed that Protestants, and the Pentecostal churches in particular, would enter the political arena as a coherent and influential bloc, just as the Catholic Church, in effect, was leaving. Pentecostal pastors became active in national politics for the first time. Previously, although pastors might intervene in local politics, most were apolitical, engaged with their congregations in the defining practices of Pentecostals: celebrating and cultivating the gifts of the Holy Spirit, mutually supporting a strict Christian morality, proselytizing, and providing social services to members of the congregation. In 1985, however, leading pastors of the Assemblies of God organized to have members of their church elected to the federal legislature. In the Constituent Assembly (the Senate and House of Deputies combined) that produced the 1988 constitution for postmilitary Brazil, a Protestant caucus of mainly Pentecostal politicians (eighteen of the thirty-three Protestant deputies) was extremely influential for a time. The caucus did not survive, however. It received bad press, in part because of the political inexperience of the Pentecostals but mainly because it could all too easily be depicted as selling its votes for various benefits to the churches. Toward the end of the 1980s and into the 1990s, leaders of the Pentecostals were able to mobilize votes against the Workers' Party candidate for the presidency and at local levels to win support for Pentecostals or candidates prepared to extend patronage to their churches. At the grassroots, however, there are reports of Pentecostals who actively support the Workers' Party and take political positions for social justice not so different from those espoused by Catholics of the base communities.

The direct involvement of Afro-Brazilian spiritism in the political arena has been largely at the local level. The leaders of spiritist centers frequently enter into the exchanges of urban patronage politics. But, like the other two major religious families of Brazil, spiritism connects to politics in less direct ways. In some Afro-Brazilian groups religious engagement has led to involvement in something like a black civil rights movement. But in others belief and practice dispose members to accept the political and economic status quo.

Similar divergent tendencies can be seen in the other two religious families. Affinities between popular Catholicism and rural patronage politics, and the connection between Pentecostal belief and an attitude of aversion to all political engagement, have long been observed. On the other hand, certain forms of Catholicism and Pentecostalism dispose the faithful toward what might be called social movement politics. From the Catholic base communities various residential movements of the urban poor have emerged. The most important movement of the late 1990s, the Movement of the Landless, developed from the church's pastoral work with the rural poor and its sustained advocacy of land reform over three decades. In dioceses where communities have been fostered by church authorities, these primarily religious associations have motivated members and provided them with the means to participate in struggles for land tenure and basic services in such areas as health, education, and transport. In the course of these struggles, new forms of local exchange and cooperation have developed. In this way, forms of participation in the religious sphere have generated transforma-

tions in civil society which arguably enrich and strengthen Brazilian democracy.

Several case studies of Pentecostalism have shown that out of many a local temple come new citizens critical of the gender, racial, and class inequities of contemporary Brazil and disposed to challenge them, at least at the local level. Certain forms of Pentecostalism encourage and empower followers of the new faith to seek improvement for their families and neighborhoods and to invent new forms of local cooperation for achieving it. Further, Pentecostalism as a way of life, involving the reining in of machismo, scrupulous self-discipline, and consequent transformations of family life, may be transforming civil society as effectively as the base communities, but more pervasively and with similar long-term political consequences.

There is much debate among students of the religions of Brazil about these more indirect links between religion and politics, and that debate is fed by uncertainty regarding developments within each of the religious families. What will be the effect of the decline in the bishops' support for the Catholic base communities? In the Protestant family, what are the implications, religious and political, of the spectacular rise of the Church of the Universal Reign of God? Which of several streams of Afro-Brazilian spiritism, if any, will appeal to a generation of Brazilians who move to the beat of the global black diaspora? Among all the uncertainties and through the debates surrounding them, one thing is clear. Brazil remains a society in which neither politics nor religion can be understood except in their intertwining.

See also *Base communities; Catholicism, Roman; Latin America; Liberation theology; Pentecostalism.*

Rowan Ireland

BIBLIOGRAPHY

Burdick, John. *Looking for God in Brazil: The Progressive Catholic Church in Urban Brazil's Religious Arena.* Berkeley: University of California Press, 1993.

Chesnut, R. Andrew. *Born Again in Brazil: The Pentecostal Boom and the Pathogens of Poverty.* New Brunswick, N.J.: Rutgers University Press, 1997.

Cleary, Edward L. "The Brazilian Catholic Church and Church-State Relations: Nation Building." *Journal of Church and State* 39 (spring 1997): 253–272.

Ireland, Rowan. *Kingdoms Come: Religion and Politics in Brazil.* Pittsburgh: University of Pittsburgh Press, 1991.

Mainwaring, Scott. *The Catholic Church and Politics in Brazil, 1916–1985.* Stanford: Stanford University Press, 1986.

Korean sculpture of Yakushi, the healing Buddha. Buddhism has been practiced in Korea since the late fourth century.

Buddha

According to legendary history the person known to most of the world as the Buddha—the "enlightened one"—was before his enlightenment a prince living in northern India. This prince is remembered as having had the name Siddhartha Gautama, as belonging to a tribe or clan known as the Sakyas, and as having been born and raised in the northern Indian city of Kapilavastu. Most followers of Buddhism believe Prince Siddhartha was born in 624 B.C.E., but some Buddhist scholars argue that his birth was probably not before 566 B.C.E. The Buddha is believed to have lived a long life, dying at the age of eighty. The Buddhist calendar begins with the date of his death, traditionally calculated as 543/544 B.C.E.

Little in the popular stories of the life of the Buddha can be historically verified, but scholars agree that behind the legends there existed a historical person who as an adult renounced secular life, assumed the life of an ascetic, and left behind a set of teachings that have profoundly shaped the lives of millions of people in what are today South, Southeast, and East Asia.

Legends surrounding the Buddha depict him as having had the potential to be a *chakravartin,* a world conqueror, that is, one who would have wielded exceptional power. He is believed to have been reared in a royal palace, to have married as a young man, and to have become a father. When he was twenty-nine he witnessed the "four sights"—a man suffering from illness, an elderly man, a corpse, and a religious ascetic. This experience shattered his sheltered life within the confines of the court. From reflection on these sights he realized that there could be no escape from suffering (*dukkha*) even as a powerful ruler and vowed to follow the path of a homeless seeker of a way to transcend suffering. He left his wife and son and the luxury of the palace and for three years pursued the life of a wandering ascetic.

The Dharma

After having rejected the extreme practices of others, he discovered the "middle way." At the end of a period of intense meditation, he gained deep insight into the fundamental nature of human existence. Having been enlightened, he set forth at the age of thirty-three to teach the *dharma,* the truths he had learned, to others.

The dharma is predicated on the "Four Noble Truths": that suffering is fundamental to human experience, that the cause of suffering is desire (or craving), that the cessation of desire will release one from suffering, and that the way to achieve such cessation is the "Noble Eightfold Path." By cultivating wisdom (*prajna*), or right understanding and right thought, morality (*sila*), or right speech, right action, and right livelihood, and mental discipline (*samadhi*), or right effort, right mindfulness, and right concentration, one can ultimately escape from the wheel of suffering to which one is bound by *karma,* or "the consequence of one's actions," and achieve Nirvana.

The Sangha

The Buddha acquired a following of men, and subsequently a few women, who subjected themselves to the "discipline" that he established. Those who followed this discipline came to be known collectively as the *sangha*. Members of the sangha, distinguished still today by their distinctive robes and shaven heads signifying nonattachment to possessions or to bodily adornment, did not, however, separate themselves from society. Rather, they remained in close relationship to society in order to teach the dharma to others and to exemplify the dharma in their own actions. The Buddha, the dharma, and the sangha (those who maintain and teach the dharma) constitute the "Three Gems" upon which all Buddhist congregations are based.

The Buddha made the sangha, through the discipline he instituted, dependent for their food, clothing, shelter, and medicines on the generosity of the laity. Such generosity would be forthcoming only if lay people recognized the sangha as being a source of religious merit. Herein lies an apparent paradox: while the Buddha's message entails renunciation of the world, the survival of his message depends on the support of those who remain in the world, especially those with wealth and power.

Religious and Secular Authority

So long as the Buddha was alive, he held the authority to determine whether a member of the sangha was, indeed, a "field of merit" for the laity. When he died, however, the question became who could ensure that the sangha would adhere to the discipline and would embody his dharma. By the time the Mauryan ruler Asoka, who reigned from 270 to 230 B.C.E., became emperor of much of India, sectarian divisions had developed within the sangha. Asoka used his secular authority to call a council of Buddhist monks to resolve conflicting interpretations of the Buddha's teachings. He also assumed responsibility for keeping the memory of the Buddha present in the world through the construction of "reminders" of his presence in the form of stupas, tumulus structures housing relics of the cremated Buddha, and by spreading the message of the Buddha abroad through a program of missionization.

The moral authority—also called dharma—of the righteous monarch thus was joined with religious truths of the Buddha to create a distinctive symbiosis between religious and secular authority. Buddhists in South and Southeast Asia would follow the model of the "two wheels of the dharma" until modern times. The model was first adopted in East Asia but was subsequently undermined as Chinese and Japanese rulers looked to religious sources other than Buddhism for legitimating their power. In the Himalayan areas, another model would emerge, one that united the two types of dharma, that is, both religious and secular authority, under one theocratic system. Nowhere has the dharma of the Buddha prospered without the patronage of those holding secular power.

See also *Buddhism, Theravada; Buddhism, Tibetan.*

Charles F. Keyes

BIBLIOGRAPHY
Carrithers, Michael. *The Buddha.* New York: Oxford University Press, 1983.
Lamotte, Etienne. "The Buddha: His Teachings and His Sangha." In *The World of Buddhism: Buddhist Monks and Nuns in Society and Culture,* edited by Heinz Bechert and Richard Gombrich. London: Thames and Hudson, 1984.
Reynolds, Frank E., and Charles Hallisey. "Buddha." In *The Encyclopedia of Religion,* edited by Mircea Eliade. Vol. 2. New York: Collier Macmillan, 1987.
Thomas, Edward J. *The Life of Buddha as Legend and History.* Rev. ed. London: Routledge and Kegan Paul, 1975.

Buddhism, Theravada

As an institutionalized religion Theravada Buddhism has had since its beginnings a marked interdependence with the political structures in the societies in which it has become the dominant religion. Today it is the Buddhist tradition dominant in Sri Lanka, Burma (now also known as Myanmar), Thailand, Laos, Cambodia, and in some small communities elsewhere. The relationship between Buddhism and politics has, however, undergone radical changes in all these societies since the emergence of modern political systems.

Basic Characteristics

Theravada Buddhism is one of the major divisions of Buddhism, the others being Mahayana and Tibetan Buddhism. *Theravada* means the "way of the elders," a term that points to the centrality of monks, who collectively make up the *sangha,* or "clergy," in this religious tradition. The sacred language of Theravada Buddhism is Pali rather than Sanskrit. Pali, like Sanskrit, is an ancient Indian language believed to have been used at the time of the Buddha. Thus the Pali forms of Buddhist terms, such as *dhamma* rather than *dharma* and *kamma* rather than *karma,* are used here.

Theravada Buddhists commit themselves to "take refuge" in the "Three Gems," the Buddha, the *dhamma* (the teachings of the Buddha), and the sangha. The Buddha was Siddhartha Gotama believed to have died in the sixth century B.C.E. after having discovered and taught for nearly half a century the way to transcend the human condition of suffering that all experience. The Buddha is remembered through images and the tumulus structures known as stupas, which even if they contain no actual relic represent the mound in which his remains were enshrined after his death. These stupas are found not only in monumental forms at major shrines such as at Anuradhapura in Sri Lanka or Paga in Burma but also in more modest forms at thousands of local Buddhist centers throughout Sri Lanka and Southeast Asia.

Members of the sangha are the exemplars of the way taught by the Buddha by virtue of their adherence to the "discipline" that he laid down during his lifetime and as the propagators of the way through their communication of the Buddha's teachings in rituals and sermons. Most monks and novices in Theravada Buddhist societies, easily recognizable by their distinctive robes (which are usually yellow, but sometimes are brown or even red), do not remain within the sangha for life. Monks not only must abide by the basic moral precepts incumbent on all Buddhists but also must follow a cloistered life characterized by chastity, poverty, and asceticism. Although there has been no order of female members of the sangha in any Theravadin society since about the eleventh century, some women still take religious roles as nuns. Often wearing distinctive plain robes, they leave the life of a householder, and, like monks and novices, forgo any sexual relations, reject ornamentation for the body, eat only what is necessary for sustenance in meals consumed before noon, and live a life without gold or silver or entertainments. Nuns have become more noticeable in the twentieth century as a consequence of changing ideas about religion and gender.

The foundation of the dhamma is the doctrine of *dukkha,* by which it is understood that all who are born will experience "suffering" directly as pain or indirectly as the cessation of that which is pleasurable, with death, often a combination of both pain and cessation of pleasure, being its culmination. The Buddha taught that suffering can be transcended through following the "way" or "path" that includes the practice of "morality," mental concentration, and cultivation of wisdom.

For lay Buddhists, morality is understood primarily as entailing the offering of *dana,* or "alms," to the sangha in the form of food, clothing, shelter, and medicines and following the "five precepts." In return for alms, lay persons accumulate "merit," or "positive," kamma. By adhering to the moral precepts to refrain from taking life, stealing, lying, and improper sexual relations, one avoids accumulating "demerit," or "negative" kamma. The balance of one's kamma will condition the relative degree of suffering one will experience in both this life and in future existences. The kamma one inherited at birth is understood to have generated some of the physical and social conditions of one's present life.

The fifth precept—a commitment to refrain from ingesting substances (notably, alcohol and drugs) that lead to heedlessness—represents a step toward the cultivation of "mindfulness." Through such cultivation as well as the practice of "mental concentration" (meditation) one seeks to acquire the ability to detach oneself from those desires that lead to increased suffering. If one is successful in practicing mental concentration, one will gain that insight into the self that is a basic form of wisdom.

Buddhist Monarchies

Theravada Buddhism exists as a major religion not only because of the "truths" discovered by the Buddha and propagated by him and his "sons," the members of the sangha, but also because of the patronage of rulers. Theravada Buddhists trace the origin of such patronage to Asoka, the great emperor who extended his authority over much of India in the third century B.C.E. From this period to the nineteenth century, Theravada Buddhism depended on what is referred to as the "two wheels of the dharma," one being the sangha and the other the Buddhist monarch.

Buddhist rulers were expected not only to be the chief patrons of the sangha but also assumed responsibility for ensuring that members of the sangha adhered to the discipline that was made the basis for religious life by the Buddha. Although the sangha in turn was the source of symbolic legitimacy for Buddhist rulers, it lacked the ability to impose any real sanctions on a king who was an unbeliever or who acted against the tenets of Buddhist morality. While Buddhism failed to receive the patronage in India that would have ensured its success in competition with other religions in the subcontinent, Theravada Buddhist kingdoms were established in Sri Lanka and subsequently in Southeast Asia.

In Sri Lanka in the first century C.E., monarchs provided patronage for monks, who were the first to write down the teachings of the Buddha, previously transmitted only through oral traditions. These writings came to constitute the canon for all Theravada Buddhists. The canonical collection known as the Tripitaka, or "three baskets" (of the dhamma), and written in the Pali language includes the discourses of the Buddha, the record of the origin of disciplinary rules for the sangha, and a compilation of metaphysical summaries of the teachings of the Buddha.

Although Buddhist (as well as Hindu) religious thought and practices spread to Southeast Asia from at least the beginning of the Christian era, Theravada Buddhism had a very limited following until the eleventh century. In the eleventh to the fifteenth centuries, kings in what is today Burma, Thailand, Laos, and Cambodia became patrons of missionizing monks and of monks writing in vernacular languages, who made Theravada Buddhism the popular religion throughout much of mainland Southeast Asia. The religion also spread to neighboring areas in northeastern India and Bangladesh, southern China, northern Malaya, and southern Vietnam, although it always remained the religion of a small minority in these countries primarily because in these areas royal patronage was absent. By the fifteenth century, several distinctive forms of Theravada Buddhism had become established in mainland Southeast Asia, each associated with a different written language and a different set of principalities.

The Challenge of Colonialism and Christianity

Beginning in the sixteenth century, but especially in the nineteenth, Buddhism in Sri Lanka and Southeast Asia underwent radical change in the wake of challenges posed by Christian missionaries and colonial rulers. Sri Lanka (then known as Ceylon) was the first of the Theravadin countries to be strongly influenced by the West. The Portuguese established a colonial foothold on the island in the sixteenth century, and Catholic missionaries gained a small following in areas under Portuguese rule. Then in the seventeenth century the Dutch replaced the Portuguese and introduced Dutch Reformed Christianity in the expanded area under their control, although an independent kingdom controlled most of the island from the capital of Kandy in the highlands. The political turmoil of the period, however, almost led to the disappearance of the sangha in Sri Lanka. In the late eighteenth century Kandyan kings had reestablished the sangha with aid from monks from Siam (as Thailand was known before 1939) and Burma. But in 1815 the British conquered Kandy, abolished the monarchy, and ended forever the patronage of the religion once provided by the monarchy in Sri Lanka.

In 1824, soon after this conquest, the British began a series of wars with the Burmese. By 1885 the whole of Burma was under British rule, and, as in Sri Lanka, the British abolished the monarchy. They also, again as in Sri Lanka, disestablished the Buddhist religion.

The political upheavals in these countries and the efforts of Christian missionaries to convert local people posed significant challenges to Buddhism. In both countries in the late nineteenth and early twentieth centuries, religious leaders emerged who instituted significant reforms of the religion. In Sri Lanka reformed Buddhism has been termed "Protestant" Buddhism because it emerged in direct response to the efforts of Protestant missionaries and because, as in Protestant Christianity, reformed Buddhism also rejected many premodern rituals as hindering the practice of the true faith. In Burma, where Christian missionaries were far less successful, reformed Buddhism continued to coexist side by side with ritual-centered traditions.

In both countries nationalist leaders succeeded in promoting the premise that colonial rule was a threat to Buddhism. Although Buddhist nationalism was more militant in Burma prior to independence, militant Buddhism in Sri Lanka would, after independence, come to be a defining influence on the politics of that country.

Thailand was never colonized, and the encounter with Christianity was never seen as a serious threat. Nonetheless, Christian missionaries played a significant role in stimulating the reforms undertaken in Thai Buddhism through their encounters with the princely monk who spearheaded these reforms in the middle of the nineteenth century. This monk would later become King Mongkut, who reigned from 1851 to 1868. The reformed Buddhism that he began became the basis for an established religion that from 1902 on placed all monks under the authority of a state-sponsored hierarchy.

Cambodia and Laos were both incorporated into French Indochina in the period from 1863 to 1907, and although monarchies in both countries were left in place, they were allowed no real power throughout the colonial period, which lasted until 1954. In neither country did an autonomous reform Buddhist movement emerge, but a French-sponsored Buddhist Institute in Cambodia provided the breeding ground for a radical nationalism that was eventually taken over by communists.

Buddhist Politics in Postcolonial Societies

The radical changes imposed on Buddhist polities during the colonial period laid the groundwork for the distinctive Buddhist politics that have developed in the postcolonial period. In Sri Lanka, despite the fact that approximately one-third of the population is not Buddhist, those who have held power since the mid-1950s have succeeded in promoting a constricted Buddhist nationalism that relegates those who are not Buddhists or speakers of Sinhalese, the dominant language in the country, to a marginalized place within the national community. This narrowly defined and often militant Buddhist nationalism, supported by some leading monks and opposed by others, has been a major cause of the ongoing violent conflict between the Sinhalese majority and the Tamils.

S. W. R. D. Bandaranaike, who was elected prime minister in 1956, set forth a nationalist program that would shape Sri Lankan politics for the next four decades. Bandaranaike was a convert to a reformed Buddhism linked to a nationalist agenda. As prime minister he succeeded in having Sinhalese made the national language to the exclusion of English and Tamil, made the myths concerning Sri Lanka being the chosen land of Buddhism central to the nationalist ideology, and, in his role in the celebration of the 2,500th anniversary of the Buddhist era, emulated former Buddhist kings in providing patronage for the religion.

During Bandaranaike's premiership, monks became actively involved in politics for the first time in the postcolonial period, one tragic consequence being the assassination of Bandaranaike himself by a monk. This act did not lead to a change in nationalist policy, and Bandaranaike's successors, including his wife, Sirimavo Bandaranaike, continued to promote policies favoring the Buddhist Sinhalese majority. Even when the main opposition party succeeded in wresting power away from Sirimavo Bandaranaike in 1977, the government of Junius R. Jayawardene instituted changes in economic, not nationalist, policies. Supported by certain leading monks, the Jayawardene government took a hard line toward the Tamil minority.

The increasing rift between Tamils and Sinhalese erupted into violence in 1983 when the Liberation Tigers of Tamil Eelam began a war to gain independence for a Tamil state in northern Sri Lanka. In response, and with the tacit backing of the government, a reign of terror was loosed on Tamils living in Sinhalese-dominant areas.

The intensity of violence in Sri Lanka since 1983, which had claimed the lives of at least 40,000 by the mid-1990s, including that of President Ranasinghe Premadasa in 1992, has seemed to many to make a mockery of Buddhist ideals of nonviolence. Although a significant number of Buddhist monks have denounced the violence, others have offered moral justification for the killing of non-Buddhists to ensure that the religion will remain dominant in the country. Since taking power in 1994, the government of President Chandrika Bandaranaike Kumaratunga, the daughter of the two previous Bandaranaike prime ministers, has attempted to open negotiations with the Tamil nationalists, but the legacy of violence has proven too great for these negotiations to succeed.

In Burma efforts by the first independent government to make Buddhism a state religion exacerbated ethnic conflicts that had erupted even before independence. Although a nominally secularist government was installed after the military, under General Ne Win, staged a coup in 1962, Ne Win and his associates still drew heavily on Buddhism in promoting the "Burmese Way to Socialism." Ne Win's government also provided conspicuous support for many of the major shrines throughout the country, and members of the ruling elite were also prominent among the followers of leading meditation monks.

In 1988, after Ne Win nominally retired and socialist policies were abandoned, significant public opposition to the continued rule by a military oligarchy developed. Daw Aung San Suu Kyi, who has provided the charismatic leadership of this opposition, draws her moral authority not only from being the daughter of the revered leader of the independence movement but also from her strong links to reformed Buddhism. Monks have also played a significant role in the opposition. In reaction, the ruling military junta placed Daw Aung San Suu Kyi under house arrest for many years, used coercive force against opposition monks (as well as against others opposed to the regime), and has sought legitimacy through patronage for compliant monks, support for revered shrines, and sponsorship of significant rituals.

The military has continued to control Burma since Ne Win's "retirement" despite clear evidence that emerged in a 1990 election that the vast majority of the population would prefer the creation of a new political order under Aung San Suu Kyi's guidance. In the continuing tensions, and sometimes open conflict, between followers of Aung San Suu Kyi and the military junta, both sides have looked to Buddhism to provide legitimacy for their political visions.

The radical communist revolutionaries referred to as the Khmer Rouge, who succeeded in taking power in Cambodia in 1975, attempted to eliminate the Buddhist sangha and eradicate Buddhism from Khmer culture and society altogether. This extreme cultural revolution (strongly influenced by the Chinese prototype) was undertaken despite the fact that Prince Sihanouk, the successor to the premodern Buddhist monarchs, had allied himself with the Khmer Rouge after being ousted from power in a coup in 1970. But Sihanouk was allowed no role in the new order, although he, unlike at least two million of his compatriots, survived the Khmer Rouge period. The Khmer Rouge sought to build a wholly new order without links to the Buddhist monarchies of the past.

In late 1979 Vietnamese forces pushed the Khmer Rouge out of most of Cambodia and installed a new government made up of more moderate communists. This new government allowed Buddhism to be reestablished but strongly restricted its role for many years.

Throughout the 1980s the Vietnamese-backed government led by Hun Sen was treated as a pariah by all countries but those in the Soviet bloc. Despite the atrocities committed by the Khmer Rouge, the government actually gained some international support by entering into an alliance with royalist and republican groups. In the early 1990s negotiations carried out under the auspices of the United Nations compelled the government in Phnom Penh to agree to the holding of elections in which all factions would compete. In anticipation of a new electoral-based politics, Hun Sen and other erstwhile members of the Cambodian Communist Party assumed a major public patronage role toward monks and shrines, culminating in their making Buddhism the state religion.

In 1991, after the UN-sponsored accord was reached, Sihanouk returned to Phnom Penh as king, and political leaders who had been in exile for many years organized new political parties. All factions have sought to associate themselves publicly with leading monks and with patronage of the religion. Maha Ghosananda, a senior monk who was outside Cambodia when the Khmer Rouge took over, has emerged as a charismatic leader of a movement, unaffiliated with any political faction, that seeks to make Buddhist ideals the basis for transcending the violence of Cambodia. This movement has, however, been eclipsed by the continued violent conflict between the Hun Sen faction and that of Prince Ranaridh, a son of Sihanouk who has led the royalist political party.

A government led by a communist party also took control of state power in Laos in 1975. Although this government initially sought to ban some of the most popular traditional Buddhist rituals and to restrict significantly any new recruitment to the sangha, the Laos Communist Party did not attempt, as did its counterpart in Cambodia, to eradicate Buddhism. By the late 1970s most Buddhist rituals were once again permitted, and in the 1980s the sangha was allowed to recruit new members. By the mid-1980s the government had done an about-face and had begun actively to promote some Buddhist activities and even to use monks in carrying out the educational role of the state. But the sangha in Laos remains very much under the control of the state, and the only politics involving the religion is that allowed by the government.

Because Thailand remained independent politically throughout the colonial period, appeals to Buddhism as the foundation for Thai nationalist identity have been promoted by the state rather than in opposition to the state. In the early decades of the twentieth century, some opposition to the imposition of a central authority on areas that had previously enjoyed relative autonomy coalesced around certain local Buddhist leaders; this opposition was eliminated, however, by a combination of coercive force and cultural policies. The latter, carried out primarily through both monastic and secular education, eventually succeeded in inculcating in the populace an identification with a nation based on a shared Buddhism and the monarchy. In contrast to the situation in all other Theravadin countries, in Thailand Buddhism became, in effect, the state religion, and the religious establishment was co-opted in state-sponsored efforts to integrate the nation and modernize the society.

The very success of these efforts created the conditions for a new politics in which Buddhism has been a significant factor. Through a coup carried out in 1932, members of a small, nonroyal elite succeeded in establishing a constitutional monarchy. The "promoters" (as they were known) of the 1932 coup were educated in secular schools and shared a modern perspective on the world. But the ideal of "democracy" in the name of which the coup was staged held little meaning for the vast majority of the populace, who still lived in rural communities where life was organized around the agricultural and Buddhist ritual cycles. By the late 1930s the old monarchical absolutism had been replaced by a new authoritarianism, which was legitimated, in part, by state-sponsored Buddhist ritualism.

After World War II the economy of Thailand began to grow significantly, and from the 1960s until the late 1990s was one of the fastest growing in the world. This growth led to the emergence of a middle class. By the late 1960s, many, especially students, from this middle class had begun to question the right of a military oligarchy to exercise unchecked power. In the early and mid-1970s, the challenge to military rule was predicated primarily on secular, including communist, ideologies. This challenge initially succeeded on October 14, 1973, when a student-led movement forced the military junta to resign and, with the backing of the king, a new constitution was written. But this constitution was soon eclipsed as right-wing forces mobilized to support the reinstitution of an authoritarian regime. These forces acquired backing from both the Buddhist establishment, which allowed a former dictator to be ordained temporarily, and from a charismatic monk who offered moral justification for the killing of "communists."

A bloody coup on October 6, 1976, which resulted in the killing or imprisonment of many in the student movement and which led many others to flee to the jungle to join a communist-led insurrection, seemed to mark the triumph of a militant Buddhism. This proved, however, not to be the case; some military leaders for whom Buddhist values of tolerance were more compelling succeeded in taking power away from the most radical right-wing elements and insti-

tuted an amnesty for communist insurrectionaries. This, coupled with the loss by the Communist Party of Thailand of its external backers, led to the ultimate collapse of the communist challenge.

In the 1980s, as the Thai economy continued to boom, the political system evolved into what has been termed a "demi-democracy." Groups representing diverse interests among the now even larger middle class were able to exert increasing influence on policymaking through the parliament, through the media, and through a growing number of nongovernmental organizations. Some of these organizations based their mission explicitly on Buddhist critiques of materialism and social inequalities. One politician, who became mayor of Bangkok and the leader of the opposition to yet another effort to reinstitute military rule in 1991–1992, was closely associated with a new movement whose leader was expelled for heterodoxy from the established sangha. A junta that held power for a year in 1991–1992 attempted but failed to legitimate its role by linking itself with establishment Buddhism.

In the 1990s the Thai people faced the worst HIV/AIDS epidemic in Asia, environmental degradation and pollution, especially in Bangkok, and, in the late 1990s, an unprecedented economic crisis that began with the collapse of the value of the currency. In confronting these modern forms of suffering, the Thai people have often turned for guidance to monks, who have offered a significant diversity of interpretations of the Buddhist way. Among the most conspicuous are the "commercial" monks, who seem to offer shortcuts to reducing suffering to those who make large gifts in support of the religion. Other monks have rejected such religious materialism and have called for moral regeneration through the cultivation of spirituality centered on meditation. Yet others advocate a "socially engaged" Buddhism that emphasizes joining together with others, sometimes in opposition to governments, to address problems of social injustice, poverty, illness, and destruction of the environment. In such a pluralistic environment, it is no longer possible for any government to claim for itself, as did governments prior to the 1970s, the sole mantle of Buddhist legitimacy.

The militant Buddhist nationalism of Sri Lanka stands in marked contrast to the much more open and tolerant Buddhist politics of Thailand. So, too, does the Buddhist socialism sometimes espoused in Burma and, in a different way, in Laos and Cambodia and what might be called the Buddhist capitalism of Thailand. As these cases demonstrate, although

Theravada Buddhism has influenced and been influenced by the political cultures of the societies in which it is the dominant religion, there is no single type of Buddhist politics.

See also *Buddha; Buddhism, Tibetan.*

Charles F. Keyes

BIBLIOGRAPHY

Evans, Grant. "Buddhism and Economic Action in Socialist Laos." In *Socialism: Ideals, Ideologies, and Local Practice,* edited by C. M. Hann. New York: Routledge, 1993.

Gombrich, Richard. *Theravada Buddhism: A Social History from Ancient Benares to Modern Colombo.* London: Routledge and Kegan Paul, 1988.

Jackson, Peter A. *Buddhism, Legitimation, and Conflict: The Political Functions of Urban Thai Buddhism.* Singapore: Institute of Southeast Asian Studies, 1989.

Keyes, Charles F. "Buddhist Economics and Buddhist Fundamentalism in Burma and Thailand." In *Remaking the World: Fundamentalist Impact,* edited by Martin E. Marty and R. Scott Appleby. Chicago: University of Chicago Press, 1993.

———. "Communist Revolution and the Buddhist Past in Cambodia." In *Asian Visions of Authority: Religion and the Modern States of East and Southeast Asia,* edited by Charles F. Keyes, Laurel Kendall, and Helen Hardacre. Honolulu: University of Hawaii Press, 1994.

Schober, Juliane. "Buddhist Just Rule and Burmese National Culture: State Patronage of the Chinese Tooth Relic in Myanmar." *History of Religions* 36 (1997): 218–243.

Smith, Bardwell L., ed. *Religion and Legitimation of Power in Sri Lanka.* Chambersburg, Pa.: Anima Books, 1978.

———. *Religion and Legitimation of Power in Thailand, Laos, and Burma.* Chambersburg, Pa.: Anima Books, 1978.

Swearer, Donald K. "Fundamentalist Movements in Theravada Buddhism." In *Fundamentalisms Observed,* edited by Martin E. Marty and R. Scott Appleby. Chicago: University of Chicago Press, 1991.

Tambiah, Stanley Jeyaraja. *Buddhism Betrayed? Religion, Politics, and Violence in Sri Lanka.* Chicago: University of Chicago Press, 1992.

Buddhism, Tibetan

Tibetan Buddhism is the predominant religion of Tibet, of bordering areas in the Himalayan plateau, and, today, of Tibetan refugees living in India and elsewhere. From about the seventh century C.E. until the early 1950s, when the People's Republic of China incorporated Tibet as a province (Xizang), Tibetan Buddhism was the primary organizing principle in the development of Tibet's unique political system.

The Tibetan Buddhist Tradition

Beginning in the seventh century, with the spread of Mahayana Buddhism and esoteric forms of Buddhism from In-

dia, several kings of central Tibet became patrons of the faith. Following the suppression of Buddhism by one king in the ninth century, and his subsequent assassination, there followed a period of decentralized authority that lasted until the thirteenth century. Although political authority was in the hands of local rulers, scattered Tibetan monks and pious lay people continued to invite Buddhist scholars and teachers from India and Nepal. From these teachers the important Mahayana doctrines and practices of the period were received, and major portions of Buddhist scripture were translated from Sanskrit into Tibetan.

The four main sectarian traditions of Tibetan Buddhism today trace their origins to different Indian teachers. With the power vacuum in central Tibet created by the demise of the kings, petty Tibetan rulers sought to increase their political influence by forming relationships first with Indian and then with Tibetan religious authorities (called lama). At the same time, some lamas sought the protection and support of political leaders against their rivals from other Tibetan Buddhist sects. This trend was to continue, with far-reaching results, for most of Tibetan history. Beginning with the patron-priest relationship between the lama Sakya Pandita and the Mongol king Godan in the thirteenth century, Tibetan lamas from various sects received patronage from foreign powers. These included the lords of different Mongol tribes as well as the Mongol, Han, and Manchu emperors of China.

In Tibet the ideal of the bodhisattva, a spiritual adept who deliberately seeks to be reborn in the world in order to aid suffering beings, led to the religious and political institution of reincarnate lamas, beginning in the thirteenth century. Such a person is usually recognized when a young child as the rebirth of a previous spiritual master. There were several hundred recognized reincarnate lamas in Tibet, some of whom held considerable political power as the spiritual heads of large monasteries or sectarian traditions. The Dalai Lamas eventually became the most powerful of these, though other reincarnation lineages, such as the Panchen Lama, also held considerable religious and political authority.

In the seventeenth century, during the reign of the powerful fifth Dalai Lama, central Tibet became unified as a state explicitly governed by the principle of religion and politics combined. Yet even after the time of the "Great Fifth" Dalai Lama and his centralization of power in Lhasa, large, semi-independent monasteries owned vast estates, collected taxes on them from peasant landholders, and even raised their own military forces. Thus lamas from these important monasteries had considerable political as well as religious influence on what was often a weak central government. In short, the lay nobility and the monastic rulers were the twin poles of power in Tibetan politics. From the seventeenth century onward, both lay and monastic officials were appointed as government ministers. This system was institutionalized in the late-nineteenth century, and the long-standing political clout of certain clergy was incorporated into the central Tibetan government.

In the centuries following the fifth Dalai Lama's reign, patron-priest relationships between the Dalai Lamas in Lhasa (as well as other high-ranking lamas) and foreign monarchs were vital in the political climate of the Tibetan state. These relationships were described in both political and religious terms, with the Dalai Lamas as spiritual preceptors to the political rulers. When Mongol and later Manchu emperors were strong, the Chinese empire's political influence on Tibet was equally strong. Contemporary Chinese historians see this as evidence of Tibet's subservience and dependence on the Chinese state. But many Tibetan and Western historians point to Tibet's independence from Chinese political influence at other points in history, stressing that the patron-priest relationship did not militate against the temporal power that the Dalai Lamas held in their own domains.

Chinese Rule and Resistance

After the Communist revolution in China in 1949, the People's Liberation Army entered eastern Tibet, claiming it had come to "liberate" Tibet from feudal serfdom. Many Tibetans regarded the Chinese army as a foreign invader; this perception was reinforced by the profound differences between the atheistic communism of Mao Zedong, the Chinese leader, and their own Buddhist faith. After the flight of the fourteenth Dalai Lama to India in 1959, Tibet's religious-political system was dismantled and replaced by institutions under the direction of the Chinese government in Beijing. Since 1959 approximately 130,000 Tibetans have followed their leader into exile. Most settled in India, where the Dalai Lama's government was reconstituted as a government in exile. One of the principal aims of this exile government was to see that the religious culture of Tibet would be preserved among the refugees. Refugees continue to leave Tibet today, and more Tibetans have now settled in Europe and North America. Despite this geographical dispersal, faith in the Dalai Lama and Tibetan Buddhism have linked Tibetan exiles worldwide. For many Tibetans, Buddhism is one of the most important markers of their ethnic and national identity.

In the decades following the Chinese invasion of Tibet, the institutions and even the practice of Buddhism were suppressed. This political repression reached its height during the Cultural Revolution (launched in 1966), in which Mao's directive to eradicate old and outmoded systems of thought led to the destruction of thousands of Tibetan (as well as Chinese) Buddhist shrines and monasteries, which were believed to be strongholds of superstition and feudal society. When Chinese policy changed in the early 1980s, allowing for the return of Tibetan customs and religious practice, it was obvious that years of political reeducation and social reorganization introduced from Beijing had not weakened the beliefs of many Tibetans. The harsh slogans brought against the exiled Dalai Lama and religion had the opposite effect. Both the Dalai Lama and Buddhism became symbols of Tibet's cultural and political independence from China. Despite linguistic, historical, and cultural differences between Chinese and Tibetans, religion has proved to be the primary means through which Tibet's cultural uniqueness, and indeed its political sovereignty, is articulated.

In the autumn of 1987 the first popular Tibetan protests against Chinese rule were witnessed by Western tourists in Lhasa. Since then protests have continued in Lhasa and in other areas of Tibet, despite China's massive military presence and the Chinese government's willingness to crush all opposition. After Tibetan independence protests in the spring of 1989, martial law was imposed in Lhasa; it was not lifted until more than a year later.

During this time the figurehead of the struggle for an independent Tibet, the fourteenth Dalai Lama, was awarded the Nobel Peace Prize for his efforts to bring a solution to Tibet's ongoing crisis. Tibetans both within Tibet and those in exile reacted with jubilation. In 1995, in accordance with Tibetan Buddhist protocol, the Dalai Lama recognized a boy found in Tibet as the rebirth of the Panchen Lama, who had died in 1989. The government in Beijing rejected the Dalai Lama's candidate and replaced him with its own choice, thus indicating Chinese attempts to control Tibetan politics by way of its religion. Despite his worldwide acclaim, no world government has ever recognized the Dalai Lama as the legitimate political leader of an independent Tibetan nation. Because of Chinese pressure, he is treated at best as a religious dignitary, never as Tibet's head of state.

Many of the pro-independence demonstrations, which

A Tibetan monk holds the flag of his country while listening to protest speeches at a November 1997 rally, in Vancouver, British Columbia, demanding independence for Tibet. Buddhist monks and nuns have been at the forefront of the movement to end the Chinese occupation of Tibet.

have aimed at bringing China's repression in Tibet to the attention of the world, have been led by Buddhist monks and nuns. Monasteries and nunneries represent an autonomous sphere of Tibetan culture, despite Chinese attempts to reconfigure them as merely religious places in service to a unified China. Instead, monastics have exemplified the cultural, religious, and political autonomy of Tibet in relation to the People's Republic. Drawing on their pre–Chinese invasion role as upholders of tradition, monks and nuns have come to symbolize, once again, the unity of religion with politics that is part of Tibet's history and culture. Tibetan Buddhist symbols, practices, institutions, and clergy have become the most potent way of asserting Tibet's cultural and political independence in the face of Chinese rule.

See also *Communism; Dalai Lama.*

Peter K. Moran

BIBLIOGRAPHY

Goldstein, Melvyn. *A History of Modern Tibet, 1913–1951.* Berkeley: University of California Press, 1989.

Schwartz, Ronald. *Circle of Protest: Political Ritual in the Tibetan Uprising.* New York: Columbia University Press, 1994.

Shakabpa, Tsepon W. D. *Tibet: A Political History.* New Haven: Yale University Press, 1967.

Stein, R. A. *Tibetan Civilization.* Translated by J. E. Stapleton Driver. Stanford: Stanford University Press, 1972.

Burke, Edmund

British politician and political theorist. In opposition to the royal absolutists for whom the king's will was the ultimate principle of government, Burke (1729–1797) joined with the moderate Whig Party for whom the settled customs of the people constitute the fundamental law of the land. His political perspective, contrasting sharply with dominant intellectual trends of the time, has been variously classified over subsequent centuries, perhaps most significantly as the archetype of classical conservatism.

During his early years Burke became well acquainted with diverse religious communities throughout Great Britain. He was born in Dublin in a religiously divided family. His father and brothers were Protestant; his mother and sister were Roman Catholic. He attended a Quaker school and graduated from Trinity College. Contrary to rumors, unverified, of a secret liaison with the Jesuits, Burke was a devout communicant of the established Anglican Church throughout his life. In 1756 he married Jane Nugent, daughter of a Roman Catholic doctor and a Presbyterian mother. In Burke's judgment, religious sensibilities, while assuming various forms, constitute an indispensable means of comprehending the fundamental meaning of life and of sustaining social stability and growth throughout history.

Burke was a prominent member of the House of Commons for nearly three decades (1765–1794), addressing the critical issues of his time in speeches, pamphlets, and letters through which his political understanding was developed. He opposed the rationalism of the French *philosophes* (Voltaire, Denis Diderot, and others), whose principles of natural rights—rights derived by reason from human nature rather than dictated by social custom or legislative decision—were influential in stimulating the French Revolution. Instead, Burke invoked the ancient wisdom of humankind transmitted through long-standing cultural and social institutions. In matters of fundamental political judgment, the prejudices and prescriptions of our common history—most profoundly present in established religions and conveyed through an aristocracy of the wise and virtuous—are, according to Burke, more to be trusted than the speculative reasoning of the solitary individual.

Divine Providence, in Burke's assessment, works its way through the processes of history, but not uncritically, given the concern of Providence for the true happiness of all humankind. On the strength of that conviction, Burke vigorously opposed the oppressive practices of the East India Trading Company in South Asia as inconsistent with the traditions of that ancient civilization. He strongly supported moves to relieve Roman Catholics in Ireland and England of arbitrary restrictions on their religious practices and political

Edmund Burke

participation, and he promoted the cause of the American colonies in their struggle against King George III, despite his lack of sympathy with the natural rights appeals of the revolutionaries. Social change, Burke avowed, if it follows the insights of an informed prudence, does not run contrary to the principle of prescription.

But there are limits. In his most famous tract, *Reflections on the Revolution in France* (1790), Burke denounced the archindividualism and atheism of the French revolutionaries—the intellectuals as well as the monied interests—as destructive of the foundations of European civilization and productive of social anarchy. Whereas the Glorious Revolution of 1688 in England (in which the Roman Catholic king was ousted and replaced by Protestant successors at the invitation of parliamentary leaders) resulted in a restoration of the prescriptive rights of the English, the French Revolution threat-

ened the dissolution of ancient bonds of the European commonwealth. Burke's support of military action against revolutionary France as a religious war led to his rupture with
the prevailing powers in the Whig Party. Their support for
the new French regime manifested, from Burke's perspective, profound ignorance of the dynamics of human history.

See also *Conservatism*.

Douglas Sturm

BIBLIOGRAPHY

Burke, Edmund. *Reflections on the Revolution in France,* edited with in-
troduction by J. G. A. Pocock. Indianapolis: Hackett, 1987.
Cobban, Alfred. *Edmund Burke and the Revolt against the Eighteenth Cen-
tury.* London: Allen and Unwin, 1929.
Macpherson, C. B. *Burke.* New York: Hill and Wang, 1980.
Stanlis, Peter J. *Edmund Burke: The Enlightenment and Revolution.* New
Brunswick, N.J.: Transaction Publishers, 1991.

C

John Calvin

Caliphate

See *Islam*

Calvinism

Calvinism, a widely adopted theological system largely based on the teachings of John Calvin (1509–1564), has significantly influenced political developments in the modern Western world. In the sixteenth century John Calvin, inspired by the new Protestant Reformation set in motion by Martin Luther, sought to reform Roman Catholicism. He developed a theological system based on belief in biblical authority, divine sovereignty, predestination, and the responsibility of Christians to serve God in all areas of life. Born in France and educated in theology and law, Calvin was forced to flee from Paris in 1533 because of his radical views. He went to Switzerland, first to Basel and then to Geneva, where, after a period of exile, he helped Protestant leaders establish control over the civil government. By pastoring the Protestant congregation in Geneva, training numerous Protestant leaders, publishing many theological works, and maintaining an extensive correspondence with both church and governmental officials, Calvin had a substantial impact on political events during his lifetime.

In the next three centuries his followers helped shape political theory and practice in several Western nations, especially in England, Scotland, Holland, and the United States.

Some scholars argue that because he espoused an authoritarian concept of government, opposed the right of individuals to worship as they chose, persecuted "heretics," and endorsed theocracy (a system of government in which God rules), Calvin provided little support for modern notions of democracy. They claim that individual liberty and democracy were neither a logical implication nor an explicit teaching of Calvinism but instead developed accidentally from the competition and conflict between Catholics and Protestants during the sixteenth and seventeenth centuries. Other scholars counter that, because liberal democracy first arose precisely in the places where Calvinism was most deeply rooted and had the greatest influence on national life, a connection must exist between the two. They contend that Calvinist convictions helped prepare the way for, or convinced people to accept, modern democratic principles and practices.

Calvin's Theology

Although Calvin did not publish any treatises on politics, his theological teachings and writings had powerful political implications, and he was deeply involved in contemporary political events. He campaigned for governmental policies favorable to Protestants and frequently offered advice to kings. He played a major role in political affairs in Geneva, a city that sought to create a Christian commonwealth in the years after 1541. Although he never held a political office in the city, Calvin codified its civil and constitutional laws and had a tremendous influence on its development as a republic admired by his contemporaries for its administration of justice, hospitality, and civic righteousness. The congregations Calvin helped establish were based on representative and democratic principles and provided a model for republican governments. At the same time, though, Geneva was a paternalistic community that enforced the observance of the Christian faith through extensive regulations and rigorous surveillance of private life.

Unlike Lutheranism and Anabaptism, the other major movements associated with the Protestant Reformation, both of which placed little emphasis on temporal affairs, Calvinism insisted that Christians must participate in political life as part of their calling to glorify God in all areas of life. Calvin rejected views that Christians should shun political involvement because the state existed solely to restrain humanity's sinful nature. He and his followers considered the state to be an instrument of God, a positive good, not a necessary evil, and sought whenever possible to create a holy commonwealth. Calvin argued that civil government was ordained by God to serve his purposes and that magistrates, whether they acknowledged it or not, were under God's authority.

While arguing that the Bible did not mandate any particular form of government, Calvin was critical of monarchy, the prevailing political system in his day. He contended that the best form of government was a mixture of aristocracy and democracy (a form of representative government) like that which governed Geneva. He feared that a completely democratic government would degenerate into mob rule and anarchy. Rule by an aristocracy, by the most talented and politically astute citizens, not a hereditary class, would ensure the most just society.

In the midst of the political upheaval produced by the Reformation's break with the Catholic Church, Calvin strove to assure magistrates that Protestants were loyal citizens, not political revolutionaries. He urged all Christians to obey their rulers and advised Protestants living under unjust governments to pray for their rulers and even suffer persecution rather than to engage in civil disobedience or revolt as private citizens. He argued, however, that Christians could criticize their civil leaders and that they had a right, even a moral duty, to depose a wicked ruler, if led by the lesser magistrates who stood between themselves and kings. In the 1550s and 1560s, when the Catholic Counter Reformation threatened to exterminate Protestants, Calvin asserted that magistrates who exceeded their power violated their office and were reduced to the status of private citizens. Individual Christians could, therefore, disobey them. These teachings prepared the way for rebellions, led by the people's representatives, of largely Calvinist populations in Holland, Scotland, England, and the United States.

Deeply influenced by the medieval views of the relationship of church and state, Calvin did not believe in religious toleration, ideological pluralism, or the separation of church and state as it has developed in many Western nations since the late eighteenth century. Although he insisted that the church and state must have different leaders, he argued that their work must complement one another and that civil government must protect "the outward worship of God," defend "sound doctrine" and the position of the church, and help promote civil righteousness. To accomplish these ends, magistrates must compel citizens to adhere to all of the Ten Commandments and ensure that true religion was practiced in their jurisdictions.

Both Calvin and Luther believed that church and state should work closely together and argued that the state should promote true religion. Luther, unlike Calvin, however, asserted that God ruled only indirectly over the secular world, prohibited revolt against tyrannical government, and did not seek to create a distinctively Christian state.

Calvinist Expansion and Influence

Calvin's teachings and his political policies in Geneva inspired and served as a model for his followers in France, Scotland, England, Holland, and America. New political situations led Calvinists in these nations to alter and apply Calvin's political views to fit their contexts. In the 1570s and 1580s, for example, the Huguenots, a Calvinist minority in France, devised a theory of religious and political freedom that went beyond Calvin's more restrained position and had a substantial impact on other nations. In a series of revolutionary tracts, the Huguenots asserted that liberty was based on both a divinely ordained covenant and a concept of popular sovereignty that gave people the right to select and depose their rulers.

Calvinist thought was embodied most fully on a national level in Scotland. In numerous political pamphlets, John Knox (1513–1572), a Scottish Protestant reformer, insisted that Christians had the right to rebel against ungodly tyrants even without the leadership of lower elected officials. By stressing religious concerns, especially eternal salvation, Knox galvanized the Scots to political action that made the nation a Calvinist stronghold, and Calvinism became the basis of the Scottish Presbyterian Church. Three important concepts that developed in Scotland in the late 1500s were widely accepted in Great Britain by the early 1700s: the church has an equal legal right and standing with the civil state, citizens have the right to hold political officials responsible for performing their duties as prescribed by transcendent law, and democratic structures based on Presbyterian polity provides for the participation of ordinary people in government.

In the 1640s a civil war in England deposed the king, Charles I, and established a Commonwealth (1649–1660) under the leadership of the Puritan leader Oliver Cromwell. The Puritans were English Calvinists who wished to "purify" the church of Catholic doctrine and liturgy. The war stemmed in large part from the Puritans' opposition to Charles's belief in the divine right of kings and their resistance to the harsh persecution they suffered. In 1643 the Scots and English approved a Solemn League and Covenant that sought to balance individual and national liberty with the necessity of state authority and guaranteed the right of Presbyterians to worship freely in Scotland, England, and Ireland. The Westminster Confession, adopted by English and Scottish Calvinists in 1646, urged magistrates to maintain piety, justice, and peace and protect the church without giving preference to any denomination; it counseled citizens to pray for rulers, honor them, and obey their lawful commands.

The "Glorious Revolution" of 1688 was based in part on the principles of the Scottish Covenanters. It replaced the Catholic king of England, James II, with his Protestant daughter, Mary, and her husband, William III of Holland. The justification for this action rested largely on the teachings of Knox and fellow Scots Andrew Melville and Samuel Rutherford who argued that kings who violated their covenant with God and their people could justly be deposed.

Across the Atlantic, Calvinism helped shape the American political system and inform its values. Although three major streams of thought converged to direct the development of the U.S. Constitution and government—the ideas of the Commonwealth men of seventeenth-century England, the several varieties of the European Enlightenment, and the Judeo-Christian tradition—the Calvinist contribution to American independence and democracy was substantial. It is evident in the ideological similarities between Calvinist theology and American political theory, the historical leadership and models provided by Calvinist leaders and groups, and the role that Calvinists played in the American Revolution.

The Puritans who had settled New England in the seventeenth century wanted to create a biblical commonwealth that glorified God and adhered to divinely revealed norms. Their society acknowledged its dependence on God, recognized that God ordained government to promote the common good, and affirmed the rule of law. The state established a church, required church attendance, prevented other religious groups from worshipping, banished dissenters, and limited the vote to church members. More rigorously than almost all other religious groups, the Puritans applied the law of God to all aspects of society, including the state. The law was God's means for ordering a sinful world and helping to restrain the unregenerate and redeem the elect.

Scholars have stressed the role that seventeenth-century natural law theories and the eighteenth-century Enlightenment had on shaping the American understanding of civil authority and responsibility in the colonial period. Nevertheless, it is clear that the Puritans had a direct and powerful effect on the spirit of American democracy. Puritanism taught that government is under divine law and that people are capable of self-government. These concepts, combined with the Calvinist emphasis on self-discipline, individual calling, and education, helped inspire citizens to participate actively in politics, care deeply about civic righteousness and the structure and practice of government, and live responsibly under the law.

Calvinists contributed to the American Revolution that began in 1776 in a number of ways. During the 1730s and 1740s the First Great Awakening, a colony-wide revival based largely on Calvinist theology, helped unify colonists and prepare them for their break with England. In sermons and pamphlets numerous Calvinists argued that God's law was higher than the decrees of kings or the acts of Parliament. Because people were created in the image of God, Calvinists declared, they possessed certain inalienable rights. Calvinists joined other patriots in asserting that the success of a republic depended on the virtue of its citizens. Because of human depravity, written constitutions defining, limiting, and balancing power were necessary. Congregationalists and Presbyterians, the most influential denominations in America in 1776, supplied much of the ideological support, political leadership, and soldiers for the Revolution.

To a significant extent, the political foundation for the American Revolution and the U.S. Constitution, ratified in 1789, rests upon the thought of John Locke (1632–1704). Locke, however, was substantially influenced by his Puritan forbears. His ideas were acceptable in America largely because they restated familiar principles forged by Calvinists during the English Civil War. Samuel Rutherford, in *Lex Rex* (1644), had used almost every argument later employed by Locke, including the claims that the people were ultimately sovereign, government originated in a contract between the governor and the governed, and citizens had a right to revolt when this contract was broken. Even Locke's influential views on religious toleration restated Puritan convictions that human beings were fallible, church and state had different objectives, and government depended on the consent of the governed.

Calvinists in all nations emphasized the sovereignty of God and insisted that the state existed to promote the common good, not that of any individual or group. Because God had designed different institutions to direct other areas of life—the family, school, business, church—the powers of government, Calvinists argued, were limited to preserving the peace, ensuring justice, and advancing the corporate welfare. These convictions, coupled with Calvinism's emphasis on human sinfulness, contributed to the U.S. Constitution's principles of limitation and balance of power.

Modern Calvinism

Since 1790 Calvinism has influenced political life in a variety of ways. It produced the outstanding Dutch statesman and leader Abraham Kuyper (1837–1920). Kuyper published dozens of analyses of political issues, edited a daily newspaper, founded and led a Christian political party, and served several terms in the Dutch parliament. As prime minister from 1901 to 1905, he fought to expand voting rights to all social classes, improve education, and ensure that all religious groups were treated equally. Negatively, in South Africa Calvinism helped to provide a theological foundation for Boer nationalism and apartheid (racial segregation and inequality) by teaching that the Dutch who settled the area in the nineteenth century were God's chosen people, superior to indigent Africans. In the twentieth century the Reformed Church in South Africa did little to protest the nation's rigid racial segregation.

The stance of American Calvinists toward political activism during the nineteenth century varied greatly. Northern Presbyterians and Congregationalists provided extensive support for the benevolent societies spawned by the Second Great Awakening (1800–1840) that strove to abolish slavery, reduce drunkenness, improve education, and help the indigent. Reformed Presbyterians, a group rooted in dissenting Scottish Covenanters that formally organized in the United States in 1833, refrained from political participation because the United States refused to amend its Constitution to recognize Christ's lordship over the nation. After 1860 most Southern Presbyterians adopted the position that the church in its organized capacity should not attempt to influence government. By contrast, President Woodrow Wilson, son of a Presbyterian minister, practiced a "missionary diplomacy" designed to help developing nations become stable democracies. During his presidency (1913–1921), he attempted to base international relations on ethical principles, most notably by devising his "Fourteen Points" as a foundation for a treaty to end World War I and helping create the League of Nations.

Contemporary Calvinists, who reside primarily in the Netherlands, Scotland, the United States, and South Africa, hold varying positions about government and political life. Some espouse Christian reconstructionism, the belief that Old Testament law, moral and civil, except as it is specifically canceled by the New Testament, should be rigorously applied to present-day nations. Others, adhering to the national confession position, contend that all nations should officially declare allegiance to Jesus Christ in their constitutions and devise governmental structures and policies based on general biblical tenets. A third group of Calvinists, strongly influenced by Kuyper and Herman Dooyeweerd, a Dutch philosopher, advocate principled pluralism. They argue that God has established several basic independent structures—state, society, school, workplace, church, marriage, and family—that must work together to accomplish his designs in the world (structural pluralism). They also contend that governments should accept the presence of differing faith communities within their borders and ensure that all citizens, regardless of their religious convictions, receive equal rights (confessional pluralism).

Despite these fundamental differences, contemporary Calvinists agree that God's word is authoritative for all areas of life, including government and politics, and that the Bible provides transcendent norms for governing political life. They also affirm that political authority ultimately stems from God, not the consent of the governed, and that all earthly rulers are therefore subject to him. Finally, they believe that governments exist to enhance and enrich the lives of their citizens, especially by preserving order and ensuring justice.

See also *Anabaptists; Enlightenment; Lutherans; Natural law; Presbyterians; Reformation; Theocracy; Weber, Max.*

Gary Scott Smith

BIBLIOGRAPHY

Davies, A. Mervyn. *Foundation of American Freedom.* New York: Abingdon, 1955.

Gamble, Richard C., ed. *Articles on Calvin and Calvinism.* Vol. 3: *Calvin's Work in Geneva.* New York: Garland, 1992.

Hunt, George L., ed. *Calvinism and the Political Order.* Philadelphia: Westminster Press, 1965.

Kelly, Douglas F. *The Emergence of Liberty in the Modern World: The Influence of Calvin on Five Governments from the Sixteenth through the Eighteenth Centuries.* Phillipsburg, N.J.: Presbyterian and Reformed, 1992.

Kingdon, Robert, and Robert Linder, eds. *Calvin and Calvinism: Sources of Democracy?* Lexington, Mass.: D. C. Heath, 1970.

McNeill, John T. *The History and Character of Calvinism.* New York: Oxford University Press, 1954.

Reid, W. Stanford, ed. *John Calvin: His Influence on the Modern World.* Grand Rapids, Mich.: Zondervan, 1982.

Smith, Gary Scott, ed. *God and Politics: Four Views on the Reformation of Civil Government.* Phillipsburg, N.J.: Presbyterian and Reformed, 1989.

Stone, Ronald H. *Reformed Faith and Politics.* Washington, D.C.: University Press of America, 1983.

Wallace, Ronald F. *Calvin, Geneva, and the Reformation.* Grand Rapids, Mich.: Baker Book House, 1990.

Canada

Canada, like its much more populous neighbor to the south, the United States, has since its earliest days experienced close connections between religion and politics, although not in the same way or for the same reasons. The modern history of Canada began in the early seventeenth century with French settlements in what is now the province of Quebec. Unlike in the United States, Catholicism was important politically from the first. Even today, the corporate conception of civic life that characterizes Roman Catholic societies continues to exert an especially strong influence in Quebec, although levels of religious practice in the province have fallen dramatically.

Indeed, the Catholic factor loomed large in almost all major Canadian political developments until recent times. After the Treaty of Paris (1763), which granted Britain control of Quebec, British success at accommodating the province's Catholic establishment prepared the way for Catholic loyalty to the Crown during the American Revolution. When patriots invaded Canada in 1775, Bishop Briand of Quebec labeled support for the Americans "heresy," and most of his fellow religionists took the message to heart.

The tragic career of Louis Riel, who twice attempted to set up quasi-independent governments in Manitoba for the *métis* (mixed bloods of French Canadian and Indian parentage), also involved religion in several ways. Riel's execution in 1885, after his second rebellion failed, fueled bitter conflicts between Protestants eager to extend British religious hegemony and French-speaking Catholics who felt Riel had been wronged. Ill-will generated by the Riel episode came

to an end only when Wilfrid Laurier, the Liberal Party leader in the 1896 national election, successfully assuaged the wounded sensibilities of both sides.

Even with the easing of Catholic–Protestant antagonism over the past half-century, Catholicism still makes a difference in Canadian electoral politics. In the mid-1980s Richard Johnston found that Catholic–Protestant differences explained electoral variance more than any other social structural trait and, moreover, that these differences were not just a reflection of Anglophone–Francophone differences. In the 1995 Quebec referendum, active Francophone Catholics were much less likely to vote in favor of sovereignty for Quebec than were nominally Catholic or secular Quebecois.

Rejecting Revolution

Religion has played an important role in the persistent Canadian rejections of revolution as a means of altering the political system and of American liberalism as the sole norm for political life. Catholic gratitude for the Quebec Act of 1774, which secured civil rights for Canadian Catholics that their co-religionists in Britain did not gain until 1829, helps explain Quebec's rejection of American pleas to join the War of Independence. In the Maritimes, a much smaller, more Protestant population also refused to join the patriot cause. In that case, at least part of the reason was the apolitical pietism fostered by Henry Alline and other leaders of the revivalist "New Light Stir" that began about the same time as the war.

The greatest stimulus to the creation of an anti-American Canadian nationalism, however, was the War of 1812. When undermanned militia and British regulars repelled the attacks of American troops in the Niagara peninsula and on the Great Lakes in 1813 and 1814, Canadian ministers hailed God's providential rescue of his people from tyranny with the same assurance that Americans had employed after their struggle against Britain a generation before. Loyalty to the king and trust in God constituted the Canadian "Shield of Achilles" that frustrated the despotic plans of the American democratic mob.

The rejection of revolution, commemorated by the descendants of the fifty thousand loyalists who eventually settled in the Maritimes and Ontario and sealed decisively by the War of 1812, encouraged a spirit that several scholars, most famously Seymour Martin Lipset, have described as the critical element in Canadian politics. It is not as though the individualism, free market advocacy, and democratic principles that have meant so much in the United States are absent in Canada. Rather, in Canada liberalism always has been balanced by the corporate visions of the left and the right, and often with significant religious support. For example, the fundamentalist preacher William "Bible Bill" Aberhart embodied populist and communitarian principles in Alberta's Social Credit Party, which he led to power in the 1930s. A Baptist minister and contemporary of Aberhart, Tommy Douglas, exploited principles from the Social Gospel in organizing the Cooperative Commonwealth Federation in the prairies during the same Great Depression years. That movement eventually was transformed into the New Democratic Party, Canada's socialist alternative to the Liberals and Progressive Conservatives; this party has held power in several provinces at various times since the 1960s. The redoubtable Christian philosopher George Parkin Grant was only the most forceful of several prominent spokespersons in the 1950s and 1960s for a kind of statist conservatism that excoriated Canada's drift into American economic, political, and intellectual orbits.

Contrasting Approaches

Catholic corporatism as well as several varieties of Protestant loyalism have together encouraged in Canada an approach to questions of church and state that differs from the strict separation characterizing the U.S. system. The Catholic establishment in Quebec relinquished control of the school systems, hospitals, and labor organizations of the province only in the decades after the end of the Second World War. In the Maritimes and Ontario, the Anglican and Presbyter-

ian Churches never received quite the same levels of governmental support that their established counterparts enjoyed in England and Scotland, but direct forms of aid to the churches did not end until the Clergy Reserves (land set aside for the use of the churches) were secularized in 1854. Even after that contentious event, indirect government support continued for many religious agencies. Denominational colleges, for example, were folded into several of the major provincial universities so that to this day a few such colleges exist as components of the universities. In addition, varying kinds of aid are still provided to at least some church-organized primary and secondary schools in every Canadian province. As late as 1997, the Newfoundland school system was still operated on a denominational basis (but with proposals in place to set up a "public system" for the first time).

Canadian distinctives are suggested by other differences with the United States—for example, stricter enforcement of Sunday closing laws and much stricter restrictions on independent religious broadcasters. By contrast, the religious views of major political leaders are much less subject to public scrutiny than has become customary in the United States. Thus national political campaigns have been little affected by the fact that Canadian prime ministers Alexander Mackenzie (1873–1878) and John G. Diefenbaker (1957–1963) were practicing Baptists; John Turner (1984) was a serious Catholic; William Lyon Mackenzie King (1921–1926, 1926–1930, 1935–1948) was a Presbyterian spiritualist who enjoyed talking to his long-dead dog and mother; Pierre Eliott Trudeau (1968–1979, 1980–1984) and Brian Mulroney (1984–1993) were nominal Catholics; and John A. Macdonald (1867–1873, 1878–1891) was a casual Presbyterian who (late in life) established a close connection with the evangelists H. T. Crossley and John E. Hunter. In recent years, only the evangelical connections of Preston Manning, head of the Reform Party—and the son of Edward Manning, who succeeded William Aberhart as both Social Credit premier of Alberta and preacher for a radio Bible class—have made a stir in Canadian public life, but nothing on the scale of American preoccupation with the new Christian right.

One of the most important reasons for structural differences in religion and politics between the two nations arises from the varied proportions of religious adherence. A major cross-border survey conducted by the Angus Reid group in October 1996 revealed that although about the same proportions of the populations were adherents to mainline churches (15 percent in the United States, 16 percent in

Canada), in the United States a much higher proportion of citizens belonged to conservative Protestant churches (26 percent to 10 percent) and to African American Protestant churches (9 percent to less than 1 percent). In addition, a higher proportion of Canadians were adherents to the Roman Catholic Church (26 percent to 20 percent), and a much higher proportion were secular or only nominal in religious attachments (40 percent to 20 percent). The fact that each of these large blocs is constituted differently in the two countries—with, for example, the Mennonites and Dutch Reformed relatively more important among Canadian conservative Protestants and Baptists much more important in the United States—helps further to explain different religious tendencies.

At the same time, however, contrasts between Canada and the United States on questions of religion and politics are intriguing precisely because they coexist with so many similarities between the two nations. Those similarities include an active evangelical voluntarism that in the nineteenth century (outside of Quebec) came close to establishing an informal Protestant hegemony. Part of the dominant nineteenth-century Protestant culture was a propensity to use biblical imagery for the aspirations of Canadian nationalism that also mirrored practices south of the border. For example, when the Dominion of Canada was formed in 1867, it seemed only natural for the Methodist Leonard Tilley of New Brunswick to apply the words of Psalm 72:8 to his country ("He shall have dominion also from sea to sea"). Also like the United States, Canada had a dismal record of Protestant-Catholic violence in the nineteenth century, fueled sometimes by Catholic resentment of Protestant missionaries and sometimes by demonstrations of the Irish Protestant Orange Order.

In the immediate past, social scientific research has provided another way of comparing Canada and the United States. In both countries a "God's party" vote appears to be associated with politically conservative moments, but that association is considerably stronger in the United States than in Canada. Whereas 72 percent of self-identified fundamentalists and evangelicals who regularly attend church voted for the Republican presidential candidate in 1992, only 41 percent of church-attending adherents to conservative Protestant denominations voted for the Reform Party in Canada's 1993 parliamentary election.

The Angus Reid poll of October 1996 showed that on some issues Canadians and Americans are virtually the same—for example, in percentages who take a religiously motivated stance on abortion or who report that their clergy speak out on social issues. But Americans are considerably more likely (by at least ten percentage points) to say that Christian values should influence politics, to express confidence in organized religion, to belong to a church or a religious group, to say that Christians should get involved in politics to protect their values, and to affirm that religion is important for political thinking. By contrast, Canadians are more likely (again, by at least ten percentage points) to say that churches and religious organizations should be required to pay taxes, to express confidence in the news media, and to vote for a self-described atheist running for high political office. Such polling results suggest that processes of secularization have moved more rapidly in Canada than in the United States. They also suggest that, though Canadians and Americans share many social attitudes and experiences, historical differences in approaching questions of religion and politics continue to make at least something of a difference.

See also *Nationalism; Revolutions; Secularization; Social gospel.*

Mark A. Noll

BIBLIOGRAPHY

Adamson, Christopher. "God's Continent Divided: Politics and Religion in Upper Canada and the Northern and Western United States, 1775 to 1841." *Comparative Studies in Society and History* 36 (July 1994): 417–446.

Desrosiers, Yvon, ed. *Religion et Culture au Québec.* Montreal: Fides, 1986.

Gauvreau, Michael. "Protestantism Transformed: Personal Piety and the Evangelical Social Vision, 1815–1867." In *The Canadian Protestant Experience,* edited by George A. Rawlyk. Burlington, Ont.: Welch, 1990.

Grant, George Parkin. *Lament for a Nation: The Defeat of Canadian Nationalism.* Princeton, N.J.: Van Nostrand, 1965.

Johnston, Richard. "The Reproduction of the Religious Cleavage in Canadian Elections." *Canadian Journal of Political Science/Revue Canadienne de Science Politique* 18 (March 1985): 99–114.

Lipset, Seymour Martin. *Continental Divide: The Values and Institutions of the United States and Canada.* New York: Routledge, 1990.

Rawlyk, George A. "Politics, Religion, and the Canadian Experience: A Preliminary Probe." In *Religion and American Politics from the Colonial Period to the 1980s,* edited by M. A. Noll. New York: Oxford University Press, 1990.

Westfall, William. "Voices from the Attic: The Canadian Border and the Writing of American Religious History." In *Retelling U.S. Religious History,* edited by T. A. Tweed. Berkeley: University of California Press, 1997.

Capitalism

The word *capitalism* is contentious and impossible to define without offending the many vested interests that have disputed for, against, or about this system of economic activity, the dominant reality of our time. For present purposes, capitalism may be defined as an economic system that sanctions the private and corporate accumulation, exchange, and deployment of wealth as a means of organizing the work of others from whose labor it is possible to extract a surplus—a profit that may in turn be reinvested in the original or another enterprise or that may be otherwise directed.

Development

Classical capitalism appeared in the course of the eighteenth century and was first fully theorized by Adam Smith, a Scottish economist, in the *Wealth of Nations* (1776). Max Weber, a German sociologist, later argued that capitalism understood simply as great individual financial undertakings is as old as history, whereas capitalism as an economic system is a modern phenomenon. Since the publication of Weber's *Protestant Ethic and the Spirit of Capitalism* (1920) the capitalist system has developed enormously and diversified. There are many new markets in the globalized economy and innovative ways of manipulating capital for profit; and there are, besides, many cultural adaptations of capitalism.

According to Weber, the mentality associated with the capitalist mode of production had historical connections and affinities with Protestant asceticism, which developed as a result of the sixteenth-century Reformation. It is therefore a customary (but not undisputed) idea to link the nascent "spirit of capitalism" with the much disputed "Protestant ethic," and, above all, with the Reformed Christian tradition. Weber explored the affinities between the single-minded and ascetic pursuit of God and an equally focused desire for profit. Recent work by Donald Hay, Douglas Meeks, and others has provided Christian theologies of "God the Economist" and discussions of the ethics of distribution. In North America, "prosperity theology," with its relatively uncritical endorsement of capitalism, has remained a popular theological genre.

Theologically informed and critical evaluations of capitalism were rare in the period between the First and Second World Wars. It was only after the Second World War, and with a gradual thaw in the ensuing cold war, that this situation changed. In Germany, "political theology," which linked Protestant theology with various strands of revisionist Marxism, developed in the 1960s and 1970s. Insights from political theology were transplanted to Central and Latin America, where, after the Second Vatican Council (1962–1965) and the Conference of Roman Catholic bishops at Medellín, Colombia, in 1968, the liberation theology movement arose. This theology drew perspectives from the Marxist analysis of capitalist society, in particular, the class struggle and the need to liberate the poor, but side-stepped the atheistic aspects of Marxism. It attained its most radical critique of capitalism by representing the imbalanced distribution of wealth in the global economy between rich and poor nations as a religious issue.

Since the late nineteenth century Roman Catholic social teaching has provided a sustained, if limited, critique of capitalism and its chief antagonist, Marxist socialism. In 1891, after lengthy discussions, the pope produced the encyclical *Rerum Novarum,* the first modern papal document on social issues. The church's position with regard to the historic struggle between capital and labor was defined in terms of a conflict between the competing rights and obligations of owners and workers, over which the church was to exercise a moderating role. Both parties were to recognize their mutual rights and obligations while acknowledging the Beatific Vision (the state of the blessed in heaven who enjoy direct knowledge of God) as the sole and legitimate goal of humankind. During the pontificate of John Paul II a deeper level of cultural analysis became apparent in the encyclical *Centesimus Annus* (1991). In this encyclical the integrity of the human agent is defended against the depredations of both unrestrained capitalism and Marxist socialism, each of which is represented as an aspect of a destructive, secular modernity in need of comprehensive reevangelization.

New Directions

During the 1980s, when Margaret Thatcher was prime minister of England and Ronald Reagan was president of the United States, resurgent capitalism was driven by a new right version of political economy. The collapse of Marxist socialist regimes in Eastern Europe in 1989–1990 removed what was regarded by some as the final barriers to the triumph of capitalism. This encouraged Francis Fukuyama to proclaim the "end of history" (in *The End of History and the Last Man,* 1992) in which the unfettered enactment of victorious capitalism is attended by the managerial regularization of the whole world. An exceptional few, the enterprise heroes and "last men," must lead a mass humanity happily domesticated by capitalism. Fukuyama's vision of historic closure leaves unasked the many questions that first arose in Karl Marx's much-maligned critique of capitalism. As a rebellious, atheistic Jew, Marx had attacked both the alienated theology of the West and its displaced surrogates, the state and the accumulated power of money in dynamic, world-transforming capital. By the end of the twentieth century there seemed to be few, if any, constraints upon such power.

In recent years the market has expanded and commodification has correspondingly extended in ways scarcely foreseeable. Information technology has increased the speed with which capital can circulate to the point that time is to all effect abolished. Globalization has displaced the class struggle within nations with a world system that pits developed countries against developing nations. This is the era of what the Roman Catholic writer Michael Novak has called "magic capitalism." In his comprehensive inversion of Marxist socialism, Novak has argued that humankind has to abandon the naive and infantile "dream" (that is, the false consciousness) of Marxist socialism and recognize the universality of necessary alienation. Experience of the latter is a universal rite of passage in which each must encounter the "empty shrine" of "democratic capitalism." So, matured through alienation, humankind may then draw upon spirituality, theology, and religious values (supremely those of Christianity and Judaism) for strength to compete and survive in the face of the inner emptiness of capitalism.

There are, however, further dimensions of contemporary capitalism. In a globalized world system in which the consciousness of humanity (and its virtual enhancement) is refracted through the World Wide Web and the Internet, the parameters of the human and the natural are displaced in ways only remotely foreshadowed by Marx and others.

There is no one single "new" spirit of capitalism; but it is safe to assert that there are many and increasingly intimate synergetic interactions between religions, innovative spiritualities, and the cultures of capitalism. Moreover, any vestiges of ascetic denial have largely disappeared and have been replaced by a celebration of the consuming self in an expanding global market of human—and inhuman—opportunities.

See also Globalization; Liberation theology; Protestantism; Reformation; Weber, Max.

Richard H. Roberts

BIBLIOGRAPHY

Duchrow, Ulrich. Global Economy: A Confessional Issue for the Churches? Translated by David Lewis. Geneva: WCC Publications, 1987.

Fukuyama, Francis. The End of History and the Last Man. New York: Free Press; London: Heinemann, 1992.

Hay, Donald A. Economics Today: A Christian Critique. Grand Rapids, Mich.: Eerdmans; Leicester: Apollos, 1989.

Meeks, M. Douglas. God the Economist: The Doctrine of God and Political Economy. Minneapolis: Fortress Press, 1989.

Novak, Michael. The Spirit of Democratic Capitalism. New York: Simon and Schuster; London: IEA, 1991.

Ray, Larry "The Protestant Ethic Today." In Classic Disputes in Sociology, edited by R. J. Anderson, J. A. Hughes, and W. W. Sharrock. London and Boston: Allen and Unwin, 1987.

Roberts, Richard H, ed. Religion and the Transformation of Capitalism: Comparative Approaches. London and New York: Routledge, 1995.

Schumpeter, Joseph A. History of Economic Analysis. New York: Oxford University Press; London: Allen and Unwin, 1954.

Thrift, Nigel. "The Rise of Soft Capitalism." Cultural Values 1 (1997): 29–57.

Weber, Max. The Protestant Ethic and the Spirit of Capitalism. Edited and with an introduction by A. Giddens. London: Allen and Unwin, 1977.

Carter, Jimmy

See Presidents, American

Catholicism, Roman

Led by the pope, the bishop of Rome, Roman Catholicism is the faith of nearly nine hundred million people, making it by far the largest church body within Christianity and putting it on a scale similar to that of Islam and Hinduism among the world's major religions. Whatever Catholics may affirm about the church's immunity to substantive historical change, there is such a thing as modern Roman Catholicism. Indeed, the construction of Catholicism's modern identity began at a particular moment in history, in the immediate aftermath of the French Revolution. It gained momentum with the papal condemnations of liberalism and republicanism in the first half of the nineteenth century and reached initial culmination in the pontificate of Pope Pius IX (1846–1878).

A hostile, defensive attitude toward secular, post-Enlightenment philosophies and political developments defined this first phase of modern Catholicism. Known as "fortress Catholicism," the attitude was exemplified in Pius IX's "Syllabus of Errors" (1864), a list of purportedly misguided notions compiled from erstwhile papal condemnations of modern science and evolutionism, liberalism, democracy, and the secular idea and ideal of "progress." In this mode the church viewed itself as a persecuted and suffering but ultimately triumphant "eternal society," the spotless bride of Christ. It alone possessed the truth that could save the world from its own sinful excesses.

The fortress mentality served to alienate the church from an increasingly secular and atheistic world and to parochialize a faith that had previously projected itself as universal and open to all that was good in the realms of politics, art, science, and religion. While the Roman curia and conservative bishops waged a war against modernity, however, some Catholic intellectuals set about to develop an alternative to Catholic anti-modernism, thereby launching a second phase of modern Roman Catholicism.

These progressive or liberal Catholics, whose number eventually included bishops and cardinals as well as priests, women religious, and laity, believed that the church had much to learn from, as well as teach, the modern world, and they sought to effect a type of rapprochement or even a synthesis between the ancient faith and modern thought. An attitude of hopeful openness toward modern science (including evolution), democratic polities, religious liberty, and other liberal ideals informed their research, writing, preaching, and teaching. Known as "liberal Catholicism," this attitude was personified by Pope John XXIII (served 1958–1963), who convened the Second Vatican Council in 1962 as a dramatic and decisive way to pursue *aggiornamento* ("updating" the church) through *ressourcement* (selective retrieval of neglected but newly relevant Catholic theological and spiritual traditions). In this mode the church portrayed itself as an imperfect pilgrim on the path to salvation rather than as a heavenly kingdom aloof from and untouched by the errors and sins of the world.

It would be inaccurate to portray these overlapping phases of modern Roman Catholicism as strictly sequential; from the early nineteenth century, the two Catholic "parties" actually developed through interaction with one another as well as with the outside world. The progressive mentality was apparent as early as the 1820s in the writings of Félicité Robert de Lamennais (1782–1854), the French Catholic champion of liberalism, and it informed at least some aspects

Pope John XXIII

of the social teaching of Pope Leo XIII (served 1878–1903), but it did not gain full ascendancy in the church until the pontificate of John XXIII.

In the decades following the Second Vatican Council, furthermore, liberal Catholicism was itself transformed according to the mind and example of Pope John Paul II (served 1978–), the Polish actor, theologian, and mystic who reigned longer than any pope of the twentieth century, wielded papal power with extraordinary skill, and exercised enormous influence over the internal life and geopolitical influence of the postconciliar church.

Other articles in this encyclopedia provide detailed information on the reforms of Vatican II and the social teaching of the modern popes. This overview focuses on four themes—religious, cultural, socioeconomic, and political—that together describe the two-hundred-year transition from fortress Catholicism in its Europeanized mode to the global, multicultural Catholicism of the late twentieth century. In each case the examples are necessarily illustrative rather than comprehensive.

From Transcendence to Immanence: The Religious Turn

Prior to the Second Vatican Council the Roman Catholic Church considered itself an institution set apart from the world for the purpose of saving the world from damnation through its sacred teachings, offices, and rituals. The official Catholic theology of priesthood provides a window into this worldview. No human office is more important than the priesthood, wrote the Rev. John A. O'Brien in a popular 1943 textbook. He reminded seminarians that St. Thomas Aquinas (1225–1274) had declared the consecration of the eucharist to be the greatest act of which man is capable. In presiding over the transformation of the sacramental bread and wine into the body and blood of Christ during the Mass, O'Brien explained, the priest speaks with the authority of Christ himself. The Catholic priest was, in the theological terminology of the day, *alter Christus,* "another Christ."

The intellectual framework within which this conception of priesthood made sense was known as "neoscholasticism." Derived originally from the summas of the scholastics (or "schoolmen") of the thirteenth century, especially Thomas Aquinas, neoscholasticism was a formalized and routinized version of the medieval synthesis of philosophy and theology; it was, that is, an attempt to apply medieval thought to modern problems. The neoscholastic application, however, was often formulaic and driven by institutional needs (for example, the production of standardized manuals of moral theology for confessors) rather than by intellectual curiosity and creativity. By the nineteenth century it had taken on numerous accretions and was less historically minded than Thomas's own theology (Thomism).

Neoscholasticism was nonetheless presented in Catholic seminaries as an absolute, unified, and self-contained system of thought identical with Catholic orthodoxy. Its most ideologically driven proponents were sometimes called "integralists," for they affirmed the literal truth of each Christian doctrine (in its neoscholastic formulation) as necessary to the integrity of the whole, and they saw scholasticism's emphasis on divine revelation, grace, and the centrality of the church as the perfect antidote to agnosticism, Marxism, and a host of related irreligious modern philosophies.

By the dawn of the twentieth century the integralists feared that such philosophies were gaining sympathizers within the church itself. To challenge the doctrine of the virgin birth of Christ or the Mosaic authorship of the Pentateuch on the basis of the latest findings of the higher criticism of the Bible—as a handful of European Catholic biblical scholars and theologians seemed to be doing—was, in their minds, to threaten to unravel the web of Catholic doctrine, each strand emanating as it did from divine revelation as communicated in Scripture and apostolic tradition. In 1907 Pope Pius X (served 1903–1914) condemned as "modernists" the Catholic priests who were experimenting with non-scholastic methods and ideas.

The official Catholic theology of the time posited an unchanging spiritual essence as the principle of identity: a person is a human being by virtue of a soul, a priest is a priest by virtue of an indelible mark on the soul. The modern enemies of the church, by contrast, identified human history with the history of matter or consciousness, denying it a transcendence or spiritual significance compatible with Christian theism. In formulating an authoritative response to this theory, the Vatican's theologians rejected the notion that ordinary human experience is an arena for God's self-revelation—an ironic decision in that it undermined Catholicism's ancient commitment to salvation in and through this world.

Enshrined in Vatican I's document on revelation, this dictum was known as "extrinsicism." Its proponents denied that the human subject is inherently a "hearer of the word." Rather, divine self-revelation is an event entrusted to the church and utterly foreign to the everyday experience of the individual. The philosophy of extrinsicism was the integralists' attempt to protect the "objective, external fact" of revelation and to preserve the unique and irreplaceable role of the church in the saga of human redemption. It was, in other words, a defense against the modern turn to the human subject (what the integralists called "Kantian subjectivism") which led inevitably, the Vatican warned, to "vital immanence," the belief that the Spirit is indwelling, intimately present to each individual prior to and apart from any concrete apprehension of a specific revelation.

The notion of vital immanence, by shifting the locus of divine redemptive activity to the individual, called into question the institutional church's claim to be the exclusive or even a privileged mediator of saving grace. The acceptance of immanence as a defining theological model therefore carried significant ecclesial and political consequences. It spelled doom for hierarchical, monarchical, and any other systems of governance of church or state that failed to take into account the inherent dignity and "godliness" of every individual, baptized Catholic or otherwise. And it promised to shift the church's gaze, and orientation, from heaven to earth as the arena of redemptive action.

Resisting the turn to the subject and thus to history as the vehicle of religious "progress," the neoscholastic theologians promoted a kind of church-world dualism that shaped European and American Catholic sensibilities during the early decades of the twentieth century. In this view history, which had produced Protestants, materialists, and atheistic communists, was merely the chronicle of a fallen, secular world. Born to such a world, the faithful were predisposed to sin, unworthy to approach the altar of the living God. Their one recourse was to the church, a perfect society untainted by the sin of its members and possessed of an objective moral law and sacraments of saving grace legitimated in and of themselves (*ex opere operato*) rather than by the personal, subjective qualities of the priest. The church enjoyed this objective authenticity, the reasoning went, by virtue of the commission, promise, and perfect holiness of its founder, Jesus Christ.

While the Catholic hierarchy emphasized God's remote majesty and the necessity of the church's mediating role, the laity continued to experience the sacred more immediately in their daily lives—and daily devotions. If the mystifying transcendence of God stood behind the elaborate formalism of the Latin liturgy, a palpable sense of divine immanence inspired a "devotional revolution" in late-nineteenth- and early-twentieth-century Europe and America. Lay Catholics rejoiced in the delights or recoiled from the terrors of the supernatural world by means of constant access to familiar patron saints and the Virgin Mary, whose association with humanity was uninhibited by the burdens of full divinity.

This balancing act was accomplished within the system of transcendence developed by the integralists. Catholic social outreach, for example, was conducted within the parameters of the neoscholastic worldview. The emphasis was on saving souls, not transforming the world. Charitable organizations such as the St. Vincent de Paul Society helped the poor and underprivileged recover from, or cope with, the debilitating consequences of life in an unjust society and sinful world. They did not, however, bring the resources of faith to bear upon the intractable situation or complex economic structures that had left the neighbor homeless or penniless in the first place.

As the twentieth century unfolded, however, the concept of immanence—and the religious worldview it implied—gradually made a remarkable comeback. A moderate version even re-entered the official theology in Vatican II's document on divine revelation. The recovery of the Catholic belief in a strikingly catholic (universal and inclusive) Holy Spirit, a God who is always already present to laity as well as priests, and even to non-Catholics as well as Catholics, was revolutionary in its implications. It stood behind Vatican II's embrace of religious liberty, ecumenism, and a new ecclesiology that saw the church as the "People of God."

Immanence made its comeback, ironically, with the help of neoscholasticism. It began when Pope Leo XIII called for a renewal of scholasticism by a return to its original sources in the thought of St. Thomas. Only on the "safe" grounds of Thomism could a Catholic intellectual revival serve as an antidote to modernism. By encouraging the serious study of history, however, neo-Thomism opened the possibility that the entire history of the church (not just the High Middle Ages) would become the subject of inquiry. German Benedictine monks began to study the earliest Catholic liturgies, for example, and theologians influenced by their work argued that the modern church should look not to the medieval model of Christendom but to the apostolic church, which thrived at a time when much of the surrounding society was pagan (or "pre-Christian," in ways roughly analogous to the "post-Christian" beliefs and practices of the twentieth century).

Two encyclicals of Pope Pius XII (served 1939–1958), who died five years before Vatican II, also fostered the kind of theological creativity that led to a new appreciation for historical development and the dynamism of the Spirit in the life of the church. *Divino Afflante Spiritu* (1943) gave conditional approval to Catholic study of the Bible using critical methods. Among other advances, this encyclical allowed Catholic scholars to examine the New Testament Christian community in its historical context. *Mystici Corporis* (1943) drew upon St. Paul's letters to describe the church as the "Mystical Body of Christ," a scriptural image rich in implications for a new understanding of the church defined by a shared faith and spirituality, rather than by visible boundaries. This noninstitutional view of the church opened the way to reconceptualizing the relationship of Roman Catholicism to other Christian denominations and, indeed, eventually to other religions and even to nonbelievers.

In 1950 Pius attempted to forestall further innovation by promulgating the encyclical *Humani Generis,* which seemed to condemn the "new theology" emerging in postwar Europe in the writings of priests such as M. D. Chenu and Henri de Lubac. But those theologies would triumph at the Second Vatican Council.

Vatican II reflected and refined these developments by describing the church as the "People of God," a biblical rather than an institutional description (in its dogmatic constitution, *Lumen Gentium),* by declaring the church's openness to and respect for human cultures (in its pastoral constitution, *Gaudium et Spes),* and by affirming the right of every person, regardless of religious affiliation, to worship God (or not) according to his or her conscience and without coercion from church or state (in the decree on religious freedom, *Dignitatis Humane).* Thus Roman Catholicism embraced religious pluralism as a good in itself. In official teaching Roman Catholic Christianity remains the true and most complete human expression of the love and will of the Creator, but it acknowledges the holiness of many other religions as well.

From Mission to Dialogue: The Cultural Turn

The Second Vatican Council had enormous impact on the way the church conceptualized and lived its dual identity as a universal communion with its center of authority in Rome and a network (or "mystical body") of thousands of local churches, each rooted in its own "cultural horizon of self-understanding," as the theologian Karl Rahner (1904–1984) put it. In the years following the council, *inculturation* became the code word for the church's new understanding of its evangelical mission to the world.

Informed by a sophisticated awareness of the diverse social forms Christianity has taken over the two millennia of its history, the concept of inculturation describes the process by which the Gospel is adapted to a particular culture. With Rome's recognition that a monolithic European model was ill-suited to a culturally diverse church thriving on five continents, Catholics began to rethink their methods and purposes in preaching the Gospel to people inside and outside the church's visible institutional borders. After Pope John XXIII's revolution, Catholic missionaries no longer presumed to introduce the living God to pre-Christian or non-Christian peoples. Rather, believing itself to be blessed with

the clearest and fullest revelation of God's redemptive activity in the world, the church strove "merely" to lift up, embrace, purify, and clarify all that is good and productive of holiness in the diverse cultures of its peoples. (This formula is found in *Lumen Gentium,* Vatican II's "Dogmatic Constitution on the Church in the Modern World.")

Popes, bishops, theologians, and missionaries gradually worked out the pastoral and ecclesiological implications of inculturation after the concept was discussed in *Gaudium et Spes,* Vatican II's pastoral constitution. In his 1975 apostolic exhortation, *Evangelii Nuntiandi* ("On Evangelization in the Modern World"), Pope Paul VI (served 1963– 1978) described evangelization as comprehensive of the entire mission of the church and provided a blueprint for pastoral initiatives carried on from within the cultures of humankind. Evangelization is about liberation from every form of sin and oppression, the pope wrote. It occurs when Christians give "witness to an authentically Christian life" through lives of poverty and detachment from the world, through the liturgy and popular piety, and through the pursuit of justice.

The emergence of a movement known as liberation theology also shaped the new Catholic understanding of evangelization. Gustavo Gutiérrez, Jon Sobrino, and other Latin American theologians fostered the movement by wedding social scientific (and, in some cases, "Christian Marxist") analyses of political and social structures to a retelling of the New Testament message that portrayed Jesus as a radical revolutionary ("Christ as Liberator"). In 1968 the Latin American bishops meeting at Medellín, Colombia, lamented the massive poverty of the continent and focused attention on the social and political factors responsible for the oppression of the poor. Citing Vatican II's embrace of a "new humanism" in which human beings were defined primarily by their joint responsibility for history, the bishops denounced what they saw as the "institutionalized violence" of Latin American society and demanded "urgent and profoundly renovating transformations" in the social structures of their countries. The bishops urged each episcopal conference to present the church as "a catalyst in the temporal realm in an authentic attitude of service" and to support grassroots organizations for the "redress and consolidation of their [the poor's] rights and the search for justice." Finally, the bishops called for Catholics worldwide, in exercising their political and religious responsibilities, to adopt a "preferential option for the poor."

These events transformed Roman Catholicism's presence

in the postcolonial developing nations in two ways, one following upon and more profound than the other. First, the traditional goal of converting souls to Catholicism in the European mode gave way to inculturation, by which indigenous customs and rituals that did not contradict or undermine the doctrine of the faith were incorporated into the Roman liturgies and other religious practices. In Africa, for example, there was notable success in blending African tribal rituals and dances into the celebration of the Roman Catholic Mass. The conciliar respect for the integrity of cultures thereby resulted in the promise of a new, truly globalized Catholicism. It did not result, however, in a repudiation of the church's claim to be the "privileged instrument" instituted and raised up by Christ to work within the world and within history to help prepare humankind to become the Kingdom of God.

The second and deeper transformation entailed a change of attitude toward the very nature of missionizing itself, a radical calling into question of its purposes and methods.

Ad Gentes Divinitus, Vatican II's "Decree on the Church's Missionary Activity," categorically stated that the "pilgrim church is missionary by her very nature." This declaration raised a pivotal question, however: What attitude best suits a "pilgrim missionary"?

Religious orders such as the Maryknoll missioners were deeply influenced not only by theologies of inculturation but also by the liberation theologians' scathing indictments of the church's historical alliances with colonial governments and imperialist projects. These alliances, it was charged, had served to keep native peoples in economic and social subjugation. In response to such critiques, missionaries began to emphasize the demands of justice at least as much as the necessity for doctrinal orthodoxy.

Coupled with this emphasis on the need for social solidarity with the poor and oppressed was a new respect for non-Catholic Christians and for non-Christian religions. In part this attitude was an effect of the church's formal participation in the ecumenical movement after Vatican II; in part it was due to the immanentist and experience-based theologies achieving prominence within the church itself, such as various forms of feminism and liberation theologies. In any case, the postconciliar generation of Catholic missionaries and catechists pioneered a radical rethinking of the nature and purpose of their vocations.

In the Philippines, for example, Roman Catholic missionaries encountered both Filipino Catholics in Manila and other parts of Luzon, and a Muslim majority throughout the nation's numerous southern islands. If inculturation was the appropriate response to the former, conversion was no longer seen as an appropriate goal in dealings with the latter. In the 1980s and 1990s proselytization was replaced by dialogue, a difficult and delicate process of mutual self-disclosure, sharing, and self-criticism designed not to create new Catholics but to build peace and trust between peoples of different faiths, classes, and races.

According to promoters of dialogue-as-mission in the Philippines, the church's task was not mainly to convert postcolonial peoples but to promote their total human liberation. For this purpose, the Episcopal Commission for Tribal Filipinos and other social justice organizations were established. In addition, Catholic women religious, lay women, and priests working among the poor in the southern Philippines founded dialogue groups like Silsilah ("chain") dedicated to living among the people in a spirit of service, humility, and shared prayer across religious and cultural boundaries. In such groups there has been a growing interest in understanding the dynamics of folk religiosity in the hope of harnessing its potential for popular political mobilization in the cause of liberation.

Evangelization continues to exist alongside dialogue, but the traffic between the metropolitan churches of the old world and the younger churches of the colonies is no longer in one direction. In the postconciliar era every local church must be a sending church, a conviction that emboldened the Catholic Church in the Philippines to establish the Philippine Missionary Society.

The postconciliar experiences of Catholic missionaries in the southern Philippines and in similar contexts elsewhere in Asia and Africa raised the question: What happens to Catholic theology when it is conducted in an interfaith context? Aloysius Pieris, a Sri Lankan Jesuit, has been one of the most prominent advocates of genuine dialogue with other religious traditions as a resource for Christian theological reflection. Father Pieris's writings also emphasize the importance and applicability of liberation theology outside the Latin American context. They demonstrate that "liberation" and "inculturation" are two names for the same process in the Asian context, thereby posing a challenge to the Catholic Church in Asia to become a fully inculturated Church of Asia and no longer the outpost of a European colonial mission.

The Catholic turn from proselytization and "soul winning" to inculturation, dialogue, and political activism rests on the conviction that the extent and depth of structural injustice in the world requires Christians to speak and act in full solidarity with those who are suffering. Most Catholic missions after Vatican II have continued to provide "traditional" relief work to alleviate suffering, and many have strived to support economic development and political change as well. Thus the building up of the local Catholic Church has taken on a new and different meaning: Success in the mission field is to be judged not by the number of converts or new Catholic churches planted but by progress toward genuine evangelization, which encompasses a dialogue with the other local religious communities and solidarity with the masses of the poor and oppressed in the region. In this conceptualization evangelization is integral, historical, and social, involving the whole person (not only the soul). The Catholic evangelist asks how the church can become present to the people in question, with their particular history and culture and in their present specific economic, political, and cultural situation.

From Charity to Social Justice: The Economic Turn

The cultural turn coincided with and informed the church's changing relationship to modern states and their economic systems. Throughout the early modern period Catholic religious orders and laity dedicated to serving the poor focused on the works of mercy—feeding the hungry, caring for the sick, educating the ignorant, visiting the prisoner. They established hospitals, schools, orphanages, and other such institutions to counter the debilitating effects of the industrial age. Analysis of the social, political, and economic structures and "causes" of poverty, racism, and economic exploitation—what a later age would call "social injustices"—was rare.

A new awareness and approach emerged in 1891, with the appearance of the first official statement of modern Roman Catholic social doctrine, Pope Leo XIII's encyclical letter *Rerum Novarum* ("The Condition of Labor"). By systematically addressing the pressing social and economic questions of the day, such as the strengths and weaknesses of capitalist and socialist economic visions, the desirability of labor unions, and the plight of the industrial worker, *Rerum Novarum* set Catholics on a pathbreaking, century-long intellectual journey that prepared them to articulate and espouse not only the rights of workers but the liberation of all peo-

ples from every form of oppression and discrimination based on race, religion, or class.

The era of Vatican II saw enormous strides in Catholic social teaching. Pope John XXIII's social encyclical, *Mater et Magistra* (1961), revisited Catholic social teaching on property, the rights of workers, and the obligations of government in light of the new interdependence of peoples bound together by a global network of technology, mass communications, and big business that threatened to accelerate the division of the postcolonial world into prosperous nations on one side and their developing clients on the other. Vatican II's pastoral constitution, *Gaudium et Spes,* aligned the church with the social, political, and economic aspirations of all people seeking equality and opportunity for self-improvement. In 1971 a synod of Catholic bishops meeting in Rome to reflect on the legacy of Vatican II developed a memorable formula, in *Justice in the World,* expressing Catholicism's commitment to political and social change. Action on behalf of justice, they proclaimed, is a constitutive dimension of the Gospel and of the church's mission for the redemption of the human race and its liberation from every form of oppression.

The church's prescriptions for economic development were distinctive, rooted as they were in the Catholic understanding of the moral obligations imposed by the laws of nature, which were seen as being continuous with revealed truth and the divine will. In 1968, for example, Pope Paul VI reaffirmed the prohibition by the magisterium (the church's teaching authority) of artificial birth control. Rather than advocate population reduction as a primary means for addressing the perceived shortage of resources in the developing world, as many liberal foundations and relief agencies chose to do, the church pointed to the gross inequalities in wealth within and among nations and criticized the exploitation of workers by the new and powerful multinational corporations.

Speaking before the UN General Assembly on October 4, 1965, Pope Paul VI argued that the church, as "an expert in humanity" by virtue of its divine mandate and its long historical experience, has a special, indeed unique, role to play in the formulation of social policy. He identified the church with the voice of the poor, the dispossessed, the suffering, and all those who seek freedom and justice commensurate with the dignity of human life.

The social magisterium of Pope John Paul II has further deepened the church's commitment to global leadership. In

1991, on the centennial of *Rerum Novarum,* he issued *Centesimus Annus* ("The Hundredth Year") A celebration of Leo's (and the church's) decision to engage the moral aspects of political economy, the encyclical both summarized and advanced the modern tradition of Catholic social teaching by addressing the realities of the post–cold war world and the apparent triumph of the free market economy over Soviet-style state socialism. Its central affirmation, however, was the priority of the moral and cultural dimensions of human existence over specific political and economic systems. The correct view of the human person, the pope wrote, is the guiding principle of the church's social teaching.

In *Centesimus Annus*'s closely reasoned argument about the proper relationship between the political, economic, and cultural spheres of the social order—which has been described as a blueprint for "the economics of human freedom"—one encounters a fresh and dynamic application of Catholic social doctrines. This occurs in the creative conjoining of disparate principles in such a way as to reveal their overall coherence. Thus, for example, the right to own private property (established, against the socialists, in *Rerum Novarum)* is considered in light of the church's equally profound commitment to a preferential option for the poor (also known as the principle of solidarity). The interaction and synthesis of such principles yields corollary truths. Hence, the possession of goods is not an absolute right, the pope argued, and work should be directed not to the accumulation of personal wealth but to the service of others.

Debate continues over whether *Centesimus Annus* signals an unqualified endorsement of democratic capitalism, or what the pope referred to as "the free economy." Prior to its promulgation, some people read Catholic social doctrine as sympathetic to a Christian socialism, while others have construed Catholic social teaching as promoting a "third way" between socialism and capitalism. Catholic neoconservatives in the United States argued, however, that with the 1991 encyclical the pope and the church definitively acknowledged the superiority of a laissez-faire capitalist economy. They pointed to the pope's criticisms of the excesses of the "welfare state" as a clear violation of the principle of subsidiarity (established by Pope Pius XI in the 1931 encyclical *Quadragesimo Anno).* The principle of subsidiarity holds, against the encroachments of the modern state, that a community of a higher order should not interfere in the internal life of a community of a lower order, depriving the latter of its appropriate functions. Also protected by this principle is the

Catholic affirmation of the family as the primary educator of children.

Yet the thought of John Paul II was subtle and not easily categorized. Addressing the cultural community at the University of Latvia, once a Marxist academic center, he noted that church social teaching is neither a third way between capitalism and socialism nor a "surrogate for capitalism." *Centesimus Annus* is replete with qualifications of its support for democratic capitalism as practiced in the contemporary world. While the free market appears to be the most efficient instrument for utilizing resources and effectively responding to needs, the pope acknowledged, many human needs are not addressed by it. It is therefore necessary to go beyond the market, he continued, to help needy people acquire expertise and develop their skills. Clearly, the encyclical continues, the state has a right and obligation to intervene when and where lower forms of government and community organization are unwilling or unable to meet these needs.

In the same vein, wrote the pope, the church acknowledges "the legitimate role of profit" but cautions that profitability is secondary to the human dignity of the people employed by the firm, which is, in the final analysis, "a *community of persons.*" Capitalism should be promoted as the model for countries of the developing world, he maintained, only if economic freedom is circumscribed within a strong juridical framework that places it at the service of human dignity.

Even democratic capitalism can fail to serve legitimate human aspirations, the pope taught, if it is allowed to develop outside and apart from the encompassing vision of humanity proclaimed by the church. Catholicism has proven itself to be the bane of economic and political regimes that ignore or reject this vision. Without claiming that it was the sole actor in the fall of oppressive regimes in some Latin American, African, and Asian countries in the 1980s, or in the liberation of Eastern Europe from the grip of Soviet totalitarianism in 1989, Pope John Paul II praised the church's commitment to defend and promote human rights as the "decisive contribution" to such developments.

Whatever history's final apportioning of credit for the wave of democratization that swept over parts of the world in the eighties and nineties, it is true that the Catholic Church was a tireless promoter of human rights, especially religious freedom, in these decades. During his pontificate the charismatic John Paul himself carried this message to five continents, dozens of nations (including Poland, Russia, the United States, Cuba, France, Zaire, and Korea), and millions of Catholic and non-Catholic admirers. And *Centesimus Annus* rightly acknowledges the heroic witness to the inviolability of human dignity and rights borne by pastors, Christian communities, and other people of good will.

From State Church to Pillar of Civil Society: The Political Turn

The credibility of the church's social doctrines, including its teachings on economic justice, received a powerful boost when Catholicism formally renounced any claim to temporal sovereignty or political authority over states (beyond the tiny Vatican city-state). By virtue of this historic shift from a state-oriented "foreign policy" to a global, transnational approach based not on concordats with regimes but on the goal of strengthening the church's role in civil society, the church became a "disinterested" or nonpartisan player in local—and global—politics.

"Civil society" refers to the nongovernmental mediating institutions situated between the state and the individual citizen. Democracies tend to thrive when and where a strong civil society exists. A stable configuration of schools, labor unions, political parties, a free press, and other voluntary associations contributes significantly to the process of moderating the competing claims of ethnic, religious, and socioeconomic groups within pluralist societies. In the spirit of Vatican II and subsequent synods, the Catholic Church in recent decades has played a vigorous leadership role in civil society in nations as different as Poland, Spain, and the United States.

In Poland workers, inspired by the Polish pontiff, John Paul II, joined together under the banner of the outlawed labor union Solidarity to agitate for economic justice, civil liberties, and human rights. Polish cardinals, bishops, and priests gave moral and tactical support to the "nonviolent revolution" and served as effective mediators between the people and the Soviet-backed government in the dramatic events leading to the fall of the communist government and the transition to democracy.

In Spain Catholicism reversed itself after years of supporting the fascist regime of General Francisco Franco. Imbued by the spirit of Vatican II, priests and religious helped found the voluntary associations and political organizations that contributed mightily to the renaissance of civil society and strengthened the traditions of democratic action.

For more than a century Catholics in the United States have sponsored and staffed the kind of institutions associated with civil society. In the 1990s the work continued in nongovernmental organizations as Catholic Charities' extensive network of fourteen hundred charitable agencies served eighteen million people; Catholic Health Association's six hundred hospitals and three hundred long-term care facilities served twenty million people; and Campaign for Human Development's two hundred local antipoverty groups empowered the poor by improving policies, practices, and laws affecting low-income individuals.

In 1968 the National Conference of Catholic Bishops created a prominent social action and public policy office to influence the nation's debate about the common good and to lobby for political change in Washington. On the one hand, this decision merely continued the public witness the bishops had begun in 1917 with the establishment of the National Catholic War Council. On the other hand, the bishops brought to this new initiative a keener sense of the necessity of acting in a fully collaborative and consultative manner within the church (which Vatican II described as "collegiality") and a new appreciation for the art of persuasion in the pluralistic American political arena. In the 1980s the bishops put these virtues on display during the writing of two controversial pastoral letters, one assessing (and criticizing) U.S. policy on the arms race and nuclear deterrence and the other strongly implying that the economic policies of President Ronald Reagan's administration amounted to a preferential option for the rich.

While bishops' conferences and other official organs of the Roman Catholic Church have been quite active in shaping civil society in their respective countries, social movements of lay Catholics (often with some element of clerical leadership) have arisen as a dynamic response to Pope John Paul II's call for a more vigorous engagement with the political cultures in which Catholics find themselves.

A New Vision of "Evangelical Catholic Power": Comunione e Liberazione

Within Italy this development unfolded in a typically culture-specific pattern. Secular movements seeking democratic reform and political unity in the eighteenth and nineteenth centuries eroded much of the church's cultural and political influence, especially among the urban working classes. From ancient times Catholicism had been an urban reality in Italy; by the dawn of the twentieth century it was in full retreat, reduced to a minority culture. This dismal period culminated in the Catholic hierarchy's ineffectiveness in the face of the fascist regime. In the generation following the Second World War a succession of Catholic movements attempted to revitalize the church and return Italian society to some measure of religious-moral commitment. They did so amidst the general disarray in postwar Italian politics that saw a series of failed political experiments and governments, the cumulative effect of which was to weaken Italian culture, customs, and traditional ways of life.

In this context Luigi Giussani, a Catholic priest and theologian, founded Comunione e Liberazione (CL) in Milan in 1956. By the 1990s the movement had spread to thirty countries, including the United States, with particularly vibrant chapters in Brazil, Uganda, Germany, Spain, and Switzerland. CL is a Christian revivalist movement whose intrinsic moral authority comes from its members' experience of "saving grace" and their belief in the actual presence of Jesus Christ in their lives. Members learn to recognize the event of grace by imitating a person who already lives the values of the movement.

As Catholics they naturally seek social, corporate, and political expression of this experience, which they see as the central source of inspiration for the renewal of culture, economy, politics, and all of life. Thus CL developed a network of diverse economic, cultural, and political organizations, at the center of which are the *Scuole di Comunita* centers ("schools of community"), the local branches of the movement where members are educated and formed in Giussani's version of Catholicism.

With considerable support from the hierarchy, CL opposes the cultural form of secularization which has led to the marginalization of the church in Italian society. According to the movement's ideology, the church itself provides the principle of authority in society, the principle by which the moral quality of freedom is to be judged. By embodying the presence of Christ, CL claims, the church wields authority that is binding on society at large.

Dario Zadra, a sociologist who has studied the movement extensively, has documented Comunione e Liberazione's diverse and flexible forms of membership. Approximately one hundred thousand middle-class high school and university students and young adults take part in the Scuole di Comunita. In these groups priests or older laymembers of CL lead discussions of social and cultural problems and identify Christian solutions. Other CL members join related inter-

national organizations, the Fraternita and the Memores Domini. The Fraternita is a lay secular association recognized in 1983 by the Catholic Church as a canonically constituted entity within the jurisdiction of the church. In 1991, according to Zadra, the Fraternita had twenty thousand members, mostly between twenty-eight and thirty-five years of age. Members of the Memores Domini take vows of perpetual poverty, celibacy, and obedience.

Each CL member contributes a portion of his or her income to the international missions and the national organizations of the movement, attends several annual meetings and retreats, and participates in the weekly activities of the Scuole di Comunita, in the Sunday liturgy in their parishes, and in the social enterprises of the group. Members of CL often refer to each other as *militanti* ("activists").

Le Opere ("the Works")—the social and cultural activities and institutions of the movement—include the religious schools, workshops, and businesses that CL members see as the building blocks of a new Christian society. They bolster the finances of the movement and enhance its political influence. These initiatives are formally independent of the diocese, parish, or other levels of church organization. Rather, they are coordinated by two main institutions of CL, namely, Compagnia delle Opere, and the political arm, Movimento Popolare. Compagnia delle Opere, a nonprofit organization founded in 1986, promotes cooperation among companies and cooperatives to reduce unemployment and share resources. The main Milan office, Dario writes, is organized like a service center, with departments for sales, finance, marketing and communication, foreign development, employment and training, and for the startup and development of companies. The Compagnia has thirty-two branch offices in Italy and others in Brussels and Warsaw. Although each local CL group is financially independent, ideology and organizational policy are centralized around a council established by Giussani in Milan, also home of the related international organizations—the Fraternita and the Memores Domini.

CL's diverse panoply of charitable, economic, cultural, financial, and educational endeavors numbers approximately four thousand member companies and institutions exercising impact at both the local and national levels. Its national networks include a center that assists the homeless and drug addicts, centers for health care and for the study of health care legislation, an organization that provides humanities teaching materials to primary schools and teachers, a parliamentary lobby for legislation affecting the family, and a cooperative that provides student housing, cafeterias, and student centers in the major universities (and receives government funding). The movement also owns and staffs professional centers that offer consultations on technical, architectural, and environmental aspects of private and public development projects. Finally, the *associazioni professionali* bring together professionals such as engineers, doctors, lawyers, and scientists for religious study and philanthropic work.

In the realm of culture CL established the Italian Association of Cultural Centers in 1983 to contribute to the cultural, social, and artistic development of Italian society. Since 1988 a CL research center for social change has organized the International Academy of Science and Culture, which promotes ties with foreign universities and institutes. The movement also runs Jaca Books, a large and respected academic publishing house based in Milan; *Il Sabato,* a popular weekly political and cultural magazine; the monthly periodical *30 Giorni,* which is published in six languages; and literary works and treatises dedicated to the defense of human rights in the former Soviet Union. Among the most visible of CL's national activities is the Meeting of Peace (at Rimini), a major cultural event in Italy that is televised nationally. It features major European political and cultural figures and attracts approximately 150,000 people.

Comunione e Liberazione is emblematic of late modern Catholic social movements in that it takes full advantage of Roman Catholicism's redefined role in contemporary society. In the Catholic world of postwar Italy, several such movements have arisen among the 85 percent of the adult Italian population who identify themselves as Catholic, 10 percent of whom—approximately 4 million people—claim to belong to a religious group, association, or movement. These religious associations, groups, and movements are diverse in organizational structures as well as in purpose. Some are dedicated solely to spiritual renewal, while others give their energies to voluntary charitable works or to missionary activity. Some, such as the prolife movement, are specialized or single-issue movements. Others have a more comprehensive religious goal which is pursued in collaboration with the Italian Bishops' Conference (for example, Italian Catholic Action) or with the Vatican itself (for instance, international movements such as Opus Dei and Focolari). Comunione e Liberazione, by contrast, has an autonomous international status recognized by the pope, but it also enjoys a direct connection with each diocesan bishop and local parish organization.

CL sees culture as its primary arena of influence: By means of the education and formation provided in the Scuole and the economic and social initiatives of the Opere, the movement hopes to reshape society for the long term. It does not form theologians, scholars, or religious specialists; rather, it prepares lay people for cultural leadership and social action.

CL's entry into the Italian political arena came in 1974 with its participation in the national referendum on divorce. Yet CL did not attempt to establish a Catholic political party. It pursued specific political goals through Il Movimento Popolare [MP], a support organization for individuals and groups that promote the Catholic tradition in local and national political institutions and cultural organizations. MP also functions as an independent power broker and shaper of public opinion; it nominates and campaigns for candidates who favor the Compagnia delle Opere and its initiatives. Although MP has allied itself with the Christian Democrats, CL has criticized the party harshly for supposedly capitulating to the unacceptable cultural and political principles of the modern state. The party failed to transform its political hegemony into cultural hegemony; Il Movimento Popolare is CL's response. It has proved effective at every level of the electoral process and has become an influential insurgent within the Christian Democrat party by electing its representatives in every major local and national election.

Tension and Diversity in the Modern Church

Comunione e Liberazione is a fascinating mixture of both types of modern Catholicism discussed in this article. Ideologically, its antimodern and countercultural spirit has more in common with the preconciliar Catholic attitude toward the modern world and the secular political realm. By denying the "fact" of the Christ event, CL maintains, modernity is atheistic and divested of any viable spiritual value. Movement ideology holds that the modern state has attempted to usurp the power that rightly belongs to the religious and moral foundations of a just political order, namely, the church. Communism was one inevitable result of this error, in Giussani's view, but even democracy can become an illusory morality, he warned, if it marginalizes religion.

In its organizational structure and social location, however, CL is clearly a product of the Second Vatican Council. It is primarily a lay society dedicated to bringing about change "from below" through cultural renewal complemented by direct political action on social issues facing the Italian electorate. The political program of Il Movimento Popolare is encapsulated in the slogan "less state, more society"—an ironic twist on the old secular motto. CL promotes religious authority as the guide for both the individual conscience and the state, especially on matters pertaining to morality, faith, education, and family legislation.

Yet CL clearly resists certain aspects of Vatican II's program of liberalization. In the view of many CL leaders, the Second Vatican Council's endorsement of church-state separation and religious pluralism undermined the church's constitutional position in areas of family life, morals, and education. Instead of demanding greater pluralism and popular participation, CL seeks what its critics call a new type of Catholic hegemony. While stopping short of calling for a Catholic state (a move that would violate the letter as well as the spirit of Vatican II), CL makes no secret of its conviction that the church should wield political influence and exercise public power. Only the church, it believes, can legitimately establish normative structures which govern human existence.

This is not to be confused with the political model of church-state union associated with the old regime. Giussani assumes that cultural pluralism will continue to exist, but he and his movement wish to restore decisive cultural power to the church. This is not primarily a matter of the official position and role of religion vis-à-vis the state, Dario explains. It is rather a new social ethos based on Catholic solidarity and sustained from within by hierarchical authority. Presumably, political change will follow. Giussani has denied that he holds a confessional state to be the political ideal, but he does envision a state guided by religiously observant leaders.

Many Italian Catholics, fearing any form of hegemonic religion, reject CL's political and cultural agenda. They prefer to see Catholicism thrive as an apolitical moral and spiritual force in a genuinely pluralist society. Such open and sometimes vehement disagreements among Catholics living in the same society reflect a striking diversity of Catholic political and cultural orientations. This is one of the most important legacies of the Second Vatican Council.

In relocating its public presence rather than abandoning its commitments to the commonweal and the public good, Roman Catholicism is perhaps the preeminent example of a powerful world religion that refuses to become "privatized" in the late modern era. More than a few commentators have noted an irony in the fact of the Catholic Church, with its decidedly nondemocratic patterns of internal governance, standing as a powerful champion of pluralist, democratic so-

cieties in the modern world. Yet this is one striking result of the creative tension, built up over two centuries, caused by the two radically different attitudes and approaches to the modern world coexisting and competing for dominance within the church itself.

See also *CELAM; Christian Democracy; Civil society; Liberation theology; Maryknoll; Papacy; Vatican; Vatican Council, Second.*

R. Scott Appleby

BIBLIOGRAPHY

Alberigo, Giuseppe, and Joseph Komonchak, eds. *History of Vatican II.* Vol. 2 of *Announcing and Preparing Vatican Council II: Toward a New Era in Catholicism.* Maryknoll, N.Y., and Leuven, Belgium: Orbis/Peeters, 1995.

Burns, Gene. *The Frontiers of Catholicism: The Politics of Ideology in a Liberal World.* Berkeley and Los Angeles: University of California Press, 1992.

Casanova, Jose. *Public Religion in the Modern World.* Chicago: University of Chicago Press, 1995.

Gremillion, Joseph, ed. *The Church and Culture since Vatican II: The Experience of North and Latin America.* Notre Dame, Ind.: University of Notre Dame Press, 1985.

———. *The Gospel of Peace and Justice: Catholic Social Teaching since Pope John.* Maryknoll, N.Y.: Orbis Books, 1976.

Gutierrez, Gustavo. *Theology of Liberation.* Maryknoll, N.Y.: Orbis Books, 1976.

Hastings, Adrian, ed. *Modern Catholicism: Vatican II and After.* Oxford: Oxford University Press, 1991.

Himes, Michael J., and Kenneth R. Himes. *Fullness of Faith: The Public Significance of Theology.* Mahwah, N.J.: Paulist Press, 1993.

John Paul II. *Centesimus Annus.* Reprinted in *First Things* (August/September 1991).

McBrien, Richard P. *Lives of the Popes: The Pontiffs from Saint Peter to John Paul II.* San Francisco, Calif.: HarperCollins, 1997.

McBrien, Richard P., ed. *The HarperCollins Encyclopedia of Catholicism.* San Francisco, Calif.: HarperCollins, 1995.

Novak, Michael. *The Catholic Ethic and the Spirit of Capitalism.* New York: Free Press, 1993.

Zadra, Dario. "Communione e Liberazione. A Fundamentalist Idea of Power." In *Accounting for Fundamentalisms: The Dynamic Nature of Movements,* edited by Martin E. Marty and R. Scott Appleby. Chicago: University of Chicago Press, 1994.

CELAM

The Consejo Episcopal Latinoamericano (or CELAM), known in English as the Latin American Bishops Conference, is the regional organization of Roman Catholic bishops from twenty-two Latin American and Caribbean conferences. CELAM studies common issues, proposes practical approaches, and coordinates transnational activities among the Latin American nations. Its four general conferences have established the Catholic Church's policy for the region.

Latin American bishops met for the First General Conference in Rio de Janeiro, Brazil, July 25–August 4, 1955. The Vatican, especially through Italian archbishop Antonio Samoré, then the pope's chief of staff, had encouraged the bishops to form a permanent organization for the Latin American church. In September 1955 the new body set up a general secretariat in Bogotá, Colombia. During the 1950s CELAM served as the example for many national churches organizing similar permanent secretariats. CELAM influenced Latin American and developing world churches through a shift from emphasizing traditional piety and individual charity to concern for political and social issues affecting the lower classes. The Latin American conference also emphasized much broader participation of lay Catholics within the church and in politics.

Early assemblies took place in Rome during the years of the Second Vatican Council (1962–1965), which Pope John XXIII convoked to revitalize the Roman Catholic Church and which became the symbol of the church's openness to the modern world. Vatican II's renewed visions of the church—emphasizing a new ecumenical openness toward other Christian churches, the collective responsibility of the bishops in the church's mission, more acute concern for political and social issues, reform of priestly education, and partial diversity in theology and local practices—strongly influenced the Latin American bishops. Vatican II's final document, *The Church in the Modern World,* provided a this-worldly method that CELAM has followed for many years: a description of reality, biblical and theological reflection, and proposals for action.

Before the council concluded, Pope Paul VI (who became pope in 1963) accepted CELAM's proposal that it apply the teachings of Vatican II to Latin America. Liberation theologians and progressive advisers strongly influenced an important set of documents, which were modified and approved by the bishops at the Second General Conference at Medellín, Colombia (1968). Several Protestant observers attended, helping other churches understand the Catholic renewal movement.

The Medellín conference was a landmark meeting for church renewal. Theological and pastoral innovations such as liberation theology, base Christian communities, and preferential option for the poor were emphasized, especially in the documents on justice and peace. These issues and the bish-

ops' analysis of economic and social inequalities brought moderate and progressive church leaders into conflict with military governments and conservative Catholics and Protestants over repressive political governance and human rights abuses.

The Third General Conference at Puebla, Mexico (1979), by and large, ratified positions taken at Medellín. But the election of Archbishop Alfonso López Trujillo as president of CELAM the year before signaled a conservative shift within the organization that lasted for more than a decade. Under the imprint of John Paul II (who was elected pope in 1978) conservative leadership was evident at CELAM's Fourth General Conference at Santo Domingo, Dominican Republic (1992). But moderate and progressives were elected to major CELAM posts in the mid-1990s. They renewed attention to the economic system's failure to benefit a growing number of poor people and lack of respect for human rights in incipient democracies.

See also *Base communities; Central America; Human rights; Liberation theology.*

Edward L. Cleary

BIBLIOGRAPHY

Cleary, Edward L. *Crisis and Change: The Church in Latin America Today.* Maryknoll, N.Y.: Orbis Books, 1985.
Hennelly, Alfred T., ed. *Santo Domingo and Beyond.* Maryknoll, N.Y.: Orbis, 1993.
Second General Conference of Latin American Bishops. *Position Papers and Conclusions: The Church in the Present-Day Transformation of Latin America in the Light of the Council.* 2 vols. Bogotá: General Secretariat of Consejo Episcopal Latinoamericano, 1970.

Censorship

Censorship, the prohibition of public expressions of ideas and opinions, has three components. First, it is concerned with ideas and opinions, not with conduct. Banning communist parties or unconventional sexual practices, for example, is not censorship, but banning the advocacy of either activity is. Second, censorship is not concerned with ideas or opinions that individuals might express in the privacy of their homes but with the public expression of them. The term "public expression" refers to what is in principle accessible to others and includes ordinary utterances; philosophical, literary, scientific, and other works; and artistic performances. Third, censorship implies prohibition—that is, an official ban accompanied by a threat of sanctions.

There are two kinds of prohibition: preventive, in which certain ideas are denied public expression, and punitive, in which ideas are allowed to be published but authors of them are subject to prosecution and punishment. Mere disapproval, however strong, of a body of ideas or vague threats of undesirable consequences to those who articulate them do not amount to censorship. The disapproval must be explicitly expressed by the governing authority, and the threats must be clearly specified and enforceable.

Censorship can be imposed by anyone in a position of authority. Today, in its most obvious form, it is imposed by the state, but it can also be imposed by educational and religious institutions. Publishing houses, libraries, theaters, cinemas, television companies, and museums can exercise censorship by refusing to publish or circulate books or to display certain kinds of material. Powerful social, economic, and religious groups exercise censorship when they threaten to boycott certain products or programs as a way of imposing their views on others. Individuals too can engage in self-censorship by voluntarily refraining from publicly expressing their ideas for fear of unpleasant consequences.

Because all societies seek to reproduce themselves, and see certain sets of ideas as threats to their survival and identity, censorship in one form or another has existed in every society. In the West it was introduced by the Greek city-state Sparta, which banned not only unconventional ideas but also some forms of poetry, dancing, and music that were thought likely to encourage licentiousness and effeminacy. Classical Rome was far more tolerant, but it too instituted censorship; indeed, the term itself is Roman in origin. Censors, the guardians of Roman virtues, wielded considerable power. Although their primary duty was to ensure manliness and probity in public life, and thus to regulate personal and public conduct, they also banned ideas likely to undermine faith in Roman values and the traditional way of life.

Unlike Sparta and Rome, which were primarily concerned with regulating conduct and took only a limited interest in censoring ideas, the Roman Catholic Church emphasized the latter. The Church, which began to consolidate itself in the third century after Christ, was deeply concerned with developing and imposing a theological orthodoxy and banned heretical writings. Its censorship was largely punitive and consisted in punishing transgressors in various ways. (The medieval practice of inquisition is the best known.) It also issued a list of forbidden books, the *Index Librorum Prohibitorum,* first published in 1559. Catholics were forbidden to read these books on the grounds that they spiritually and morally corrupted their readers and undermined their allegiance to the only "true faith." Later, with the emergence of Protestantism, advances in the natural sciences, and the popular fascination with black magic, the *Index* was expanded to include Protestant writings; some scientific, medical, and philosophical works; books on magic and astrology; some Jewish writings; manuals on exorcism; and some pacifist books.

Challenges to State Censorship

With the disintegration of the medieval Church's power and the rise of the nation-state in Europe, governments began to assume the function of censorship. Initially, state censorship was preventive. No work was allowed to be published without the prior approval of government officers, and no one was allowed to set up a printing press without obtaining a strictly controlled government license. Over time, the practice was relaxed and censorship became punitive. Anyone could set up a printing press and authors could publish books, but both alike were subject to prosecution and punishment.

State censorship covered a wide range of books and artistic expressions, though it concentrated on three kinds of writings—the subversive, the blasphemous, and the obscene. The authoritarian—and insecure—early states banned works critical of the institution of government, the ruling dynasty, and the dominant political ideology. Such works, it was believed, weakened the authority of the government, threatened civil disorder, and encouraged disloyalty and disobedience. Because these states were religiously based, attacks on Christianity were banned in the interest of that faith, the state, and social and personal morality. Obscene works were banned on the grounds that they corrupted public morality, violated and weakened the established norms of decency and good taste, offended public sentiments, and encouraged licentiousness and prurience.

Almost from its beginning, and especially from the eighteenth century onward, state censorship came under considerable criticism. Although the criticism was mounted by different groups on different grounds, most critics drew their inspiration from liberalism, a body of ideas that had begun to emerge in the seventeenth century and acquired philosophical coherence in the eighteenth. Liberalism, which stressed individual autonomy, rationalism, progress, and the omnipotence of truth, articulated a vision of society in which self-determining individuals, pooling together their rational resources in public debate, could discover moral truths on which to base their personal and collective lives. Freedom of expression, which encompassed artistic and other forms of self-exploration as well as freedom of speech, was crucial to human progress and well-being.

Basing their objections on these and related ideas, liberal writers challenged all forms of censorship. Censorship was unacceptable to them for several reasons. Truth and progress resulted from a clash of ideas; so to suppress the latter was to foreclose the possibility of either. Because it was impossible to know what ideas were false except by openly confronting and criticizing them, censorship perpetuated ignorance and falsehood. Because new ideas could not be suppressed forever, all censorship ultimately was futile. Indeed, suppressed ideas acquired glamour and the halo of martyrdom and were widely embraced even when wrong, thereby rendering censorship counterproductive. Finally, censorship treated people as children unable to think for themselves, thus at the same time insulting them and arresting their intellectual growth.

Having questioned the basic presuppositions of censorship, liberals went on to challenge its three dominant forms. Political censorship was bad because it concealed the misdeeds of government, led to abuse of power, prevented the emergence of enlightened public opinion, and hindered the growth of responsible citizenship and democratic culture. Freedom could be misused, but the remedy lay not in restricting but expanding it.

Religious censorship was considered bad for similar reasons. God was too great to be blasphemed, and in any case he did not need the protection of human law to maintain his honor. Furthermore, theological truths could be interpreted in several different ways, and each individual had to decide which one was rationally most acceptable. Because religion was a matter for individual conscience, the state had no right to interfere with it. Although people could be swayed by wrong ideas, the best way to counter those ideas was not to suppress them but to refute them in public debate.

Censorship of obscenity was the last type to be attacked. Although critical of the prevailing economic, political, and religious ideas, liberals—who were generally drawn from the ranks of the middle classes—were often conservative and even puritanical in sexual matters. Only in the last few decades of the twentieth century did they begin to mount a radical critique of the censorship of obscenity. Obscenity, they argued, is a matter of individual opinion and cannot be objectively defined. Besides, there is no evidence that pornography corrupts public morals. Indeed, it can be shown to act as a safety valve, to offer vicarious gratification to unconventional sexual desires and fantasies, and thus to lead to moral health. The human mind is complex, and reading the right kind of wrong book has advantages the narrow, puritanical imagination cannot appreciate. What is more, it is up to self-determining adults to decide what sexual material to read; the state has no right to act as their guardian.

Political censorship today is almost nonexistent in liberal states, the major exception to it being the widely accepted need to protect vital state secrets. Religious censorship has declined considerably. Some states, such as Great Britain, still have antiblasphemy laws, but these are largely defunct and there is considerable pressure to abolish them. Some forms of censorship on pornography and obscenity remain, but they are increasingly being relaxed.

Many non-Western countries believe they have a right to uphold moral and religious values that are necessary to their survival as a particular kind of society. Those values represent a collective inheritance, a sacred trust, which society has a duty to transmit to succeeding generations. Censorship is therefore considered wholly legitimate. It is a form of collective self-discipline and as essential to building national character as moral discipline is to cultivating individual character. For these societies, which include many Muslim and some East Asian countries, the West has taken its liberal antipathy to censorship too far and is paying the price in the form of moral confusion and social disintegration.

Unresolved Questions

Moral and political questions are never completely resolved. Feminists in recent years have reopened the question of censorship of obscenity, and several religious leaders, especially Muslim migrants to the West, have reopened that of religious censorship. Some feminist writers have demanded a ban on pornography, especially material that depicts female bodies in exploitative and demeaning ways. Pornography, they argue, degrades women, undermines their self-respect, violates their dignity, and represents them as mere sex objects. Furthermore, it encourages men to believe that they may take sexual liberty with women and that women welcome this behavior. Many feminist writers argue that unless pornographic material has redeeming features, which it

Muslims protest in London against Salman Rushdie's 1988 novel The Satanic Verses. *The novel in 1989 prompted Iran's Ayatollah Khomeini to issue a fatwah, or legal opinion, sentencing Rushdie to death, and the author has lived in hiding ever since.*

rarely has, it should be banned. Pornography may rightly be curtailed when the liberal doctrine of self-expression comes into conflict with the liberal respect for persons.

The question of religious censorship was dramatically placed on the public agenda with the publication in 1988 of a novel by Salman Rushdie, a well-known Indian writer of Muslim descent who lives in England. Although Rushdie defended *The Satanic Verses* as an allegorical work, Muslims in England and abroad declared it to be "a form of religious pornography" that had taken unacceptable liberties with their religious heritage. It presented the prophet Muhammad as an unscrupulous businessman doing shady deals with the archangel and God and as a debauchee who married women out of lust. It treated the Islamic holy book, the Qur'an, as a collection of politically convenient verses, not a divine revelation.

For Muslims, *The Satanic Verses* insulted, trivialized, and told lies about their faith; demeaned them in their own and in others' eyes; crossed all limits of decency; and gratuitously insulted the Prophet, his wives, and followers. They demanded that the book be banned or at least purged of the offending passages. They argued that, while free speech is vital to the pursuit of truth, Rushdie's book was abusive and insult-

ing and did not provide a rational critique of Islam. Free speech promotes progress, they agreed, but it is difficult to see how a book of this kind promotes either intellectual or moral progress. Free speech is necessary to expose crude exploitation of religious beliefs; however, Rushdie had instead pandered to crude prejudices against Islam. The right to self-expression is important, but so are the rights of every individual to self-respect and of every religious community to the integrity of its beliefs and heritage. Muslims believed it was wrong, even irrational, to give precedence to self-expression and to allow it always to trump other rights. They appealed to the principle of equality and demanded that Britain's antiblasphemy law cover not only Christianity but also Islam and other religions.

Although some of these arguments are unconvincing, others have force. The liberal response that *The Satanic Verses* was a work of fiction, that Muslims were oversensitive about their religion, and that free speech was a more or less absolute value does not address some of the important questions that were raised. The issues remain unresolved. In 1989 the Iranian leader, Ayatollah Ruholla Khomeini, issued a death sentence on Rushdie, and Rushdie has since then been in hiding.

Because of feminist and other challenges, the liberal doctrine of minimally restricted freedom of expression has become a subject of public debate. The consensus built up over the past two centuries has weakened, requiring us to think the issue afresh. State censorship is not the answer. We need to find other ways of dealing with gross misuse of the freedom of self-expression.

See also *Conservatism; Fundamentalism; Inquisition, Khomeini, Ruholla Musavi; Liberalism.*

Bhikhu Parekh

BIBLIOGRAPHY

Ernst, Morris L., and Alan U. Schwartz. *Censorship: The Search for the Obscene.* New York: Macmillan, 1964.
Haiman, Franklyn S. *Freedom of Speech.* Skokie, Ill.: National Textbook Co., 1976.
MacKinnon, Catharine A. *Feminism Unmodified: Discourses on Life and Law.* Cambridge: Harvard University Press, 1987.
Mill, John Stuart. *On Liberty and Other Writings.* Edited by Stefan Collini. Cambridge: Cambridge University Press, 1989.
Parekh, Bhikhu, ed. *Free Speech.* London: Commission for Racial Equality, 1990.
Webster, Richard. *A Brief History of Blasphemy.* London: Orwell Press, 1990.

Central America

Forming an isthmus that bridges North and South America, Central America is predominantly Roman Catholic and includes the countries of Belize, Costa Rica, El Salvador, Guatemala, Honduras, Nicaragua, and Panama.

In the mid- to late-1970s revolutionary movements emerged and gained ground in Nicaragua, El Salvador, and Guatemala in response to long-standing poverty and decades of repressive rule. When the leftist Sandinista National Liberation Front (FSLN) took power in Nicaragua in mid-1979, successful revolution seemed possible in the region. Throughout the 1980s revolutionary and counterrevolutionary forces—with heavy outside intervention, especially by the U.S. government—made Central America a battleground. Unlike what had happened at the time of the Cuban revolution (1959), church people were significantly involved in these revolutionary struggles.

Nicaragua, El Salvador, and Guatemala were alike in many ways. They were small, agroexport countries under repressive rule (the Somoza family's dictatorship in Nicaragua

since the 1930s and de facto military control in El Salvador and Guatemala for decades). Over time, large agricultural producers expanded their operations, taking large tracts of the best land. The rural poor had less and less land, often of poorer quality, to pass on to their children. In each country several leftist guerrilla groups had been operating with little success for a number of years. In the 1970s mass political organizations of peasants, labor, the urban poor, and students emerged; these were Marxist-inspired and, as it eventually became clear, had ties to the guerrilla organizations that began to show new strength by the late decade.

In the period of renewal of the Roman Catholic Church following the Second Vatican Council (1962–1965)—with its emphasis on humanity and the world, marriage and family, cultural, social, and economic life, the political community, war and peace, and international relations—and the meeting of the Council of Latin American Bishops in Medellín, Colombia (1968), Catholic clergy and lay workers began new pastoral experiences with the poor (for example, setting up base communities or small religious study groups). In all three countries there were connections between such pastoral work and the emergence of the popular organizations, some of which were founded by church activists.

Nicaragua

The Catholic Church, which had largely accepted the Somoza dictatorship since its inception in the 1930s, began to move toward a more critical stance—for example, in 1970, Archbishop Miguel Obando y Bravo refused President Anastasio Somoza Debayle's gift of a Mercedes-Benz. When Somoza and his circle shamelessly profiteered from international aid arriving after the 1972 earthquake, opposition began to spread even among the elites. Archbishop Obando was called on to mediate after a daring Sandinista hostage operation in 1974 (and again in 1978). Catholic Church representatives documented and publicized the killing and disappearance of hundreds of peasants by Somoza's National Guard. In 1977 the Sandinistas took the offensive, and mass opposition developed, with significant church participation. After a year and a half of a struggle that cost an estimated 30,000 lives, the dictator departed, and the first successful Latin American revolutionary movement in twenty years took power.

Some believers were convinced that the Nicaraguan revolution represented a unique new opportunity for the church, a chance to embody the option for the poor in an

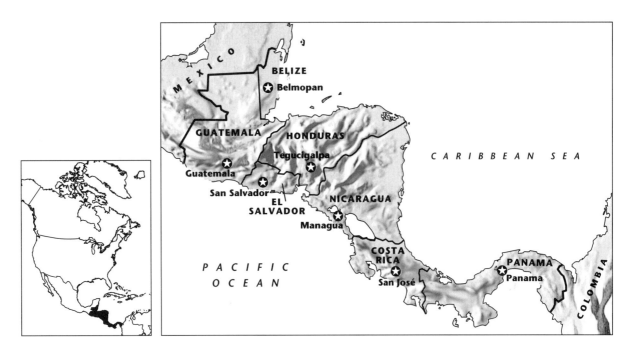

effort to make structural change and to create a new kind of society. In this view, it was not only legitimate for Christians to be involved, but such involvement also followed from their commitment to the Gospel. Others were concerned that the Sandinista revolution was Marxist and hence inevitably antireligious, whatever the Sandinistas might claim. As a rule, Protestants felt less impelled to take public stands, in part because they were regarded as a minority in a society considered Catholic.

Despite some initial misgivings, the Catholic bishops seemed to accept the revolutionary government during an early honeymoon phase, especially in a widely commented November 1979 pastoral letter in which they accepted socialism. Three hundred members of religious orders were active in the 1980 Sandinista-sponsored literacy campaign. But the honeymoon lasted less than a year. Over a number of years, the bishops expressed their fear that the Sandinistas would set up a Marxist regime that would put constraints on the church. They said that Catholics, and especially priests, who openly supported the revolution were causing division in the church. Shortly after the two members representing the business elite resigned from the government junta, the bishops went into opposition, ordering four priests in ministerial positions to resign.

In the early 1980s much of the public debate between Sandinista partisans and adversaries was presented in theological terms. In October 1980 the Sandinistas published their "Statement on Religion," which consciously broke away from a century of Marxist opposition to religion, noting that Christians had been active in the fight to overthrow the dictatorship and that this fact opened new possibilities "in the phase of building a new society."

By 1982 the U.S.-supported *contra*—for *contra revolucionario* or counter revolutionary—army (made up initially of former Somoza troops) was staging major attacks in Nicaragua, killing and terrorizing civilians. The Catholic bishops refrained from condemning these actions while opposing the Sandinistas repeatedly.

In a 1982 letter Pope John Paul II had admonished Nicaraguan Catholics to follow their bishops, seemingly endorsing their anti-Sandinista stance. On his arrival at the airport for his 1983 visit and in front of the world's television cameras, he wagged a finger at Father Ernesto Cardenal, the poet and minister of culture, and told him to leave the government and resume a normal priestly life. At an afternoon Mass before several hundred thousand people, Sandinista supporters who had hoped in vain for some word of comfort over the recent killing of seventeen young people began to chant for peace. The pope shouted back "Silence!" three times. Whether the shouting was indeed spontaneous, as Sandinista supporters claimed, or an orchestrated insult to the pope, the images transmitted around the world fueled the notion that the Sandinista regime was hostile to the church.

Through the rest of the decade lines remained firmly drawn as the conflict played itself out. The Sandinista government, forced to combat the contras and maintain a military capable of withstanding a potential U.S. invasion, diverted resources to defense and put its ambitious development programs on hold. The bishops, far from condemning the contra war, seemed to endorse it, especially when Archbishop Obando appeared in Washington in 1986 in apparent support of $100 million in U.S. aid to the contras. In mid-1986 the Sandinistas expelled one prominent bishop for supporting the contras.

The Central America peace plan (1987) prepared by the presidents of the region finally established guidelines for reversing the ever-deepening conflict. Cardinal Obando and Baptist leader Gustavo Parajon were appointed to the peace commission. Hundreds of pastors, sisters, and priests served on local reconciliation commissions around the country. Obando was later dismissed from the commission by the Sandinistas, who accused him of being a contra partisan.

Starting in the mid-1980s living standards began to drop, and inflation turned to hyperinflation. A disenchanted electorate voted the Sandinistas out of office in 1990, surprising most pollsters. The winning coalition under President Violeta Chamorro was split between moderates, who strove for an accommodation with the Sandinistas, and more hard-line members of her coalition, who urged harsher policies. Cardinal Obando and the bishops inclined to side with the hard-liners, but over time the public political role of the Catholic Church declined.

El Salvador

El Salvador had been under harsh military and oligarchical control since 1932, when the army had killed 10,000 to 30,000 peasants in suppressing an uprising. Very high population density made rural landlessness even more acute. As early as 1970, repression was being used against priests working with the rural poor. Popular organizations formed in the mid-1970s became militant. When the Catholic University supported a mild government-proposed land reform in 1976, bombs were set off in the institution as warnings. Conflict became extreme in the first several months of 1977. Several priests were expelled, others beaten; Fathers Rutilio Grande and Alfonso Navarro were killed. Outside the cathedral opposition figures protesting the electoral fraud were beaten, and several dozen were killed. Security forces swept the area around the town of Aguilares, abducting dozens of people and taking over the town church and holding its Jesuit staff captive. This was the setting of the first few months of Oscar Romero's tenure as archbishop of San Salvador. By

1980 approximately a dozen priests had been murdered by official forces or right-wing death squads.

As tensions rose, Archbishop Romero came to be seen as the "voice of the voiceless." In 1979, observing what had happened in Nicaragua, a group of officers overthrew President Carlos Humberto Romero and installed a junta, which immediately announced its intention of carrying out reforms. In practice, however, the level of violence increased until a thousand people a month were being killed or "disappeared" in early 1980. Archbishop Romero insistently called for dialogue to head off the civil war that seemed imminent. He himself was murdered by a right-wing assassin in March. The country slid toward civil war. In December, shortly after the brutal murder of six opposition figures, four North American women—three nuns and a lay worker—were abducted by National Guard troops, raped, and murdered. Only after intense American pressure and substantial delay were some lower-ranking solders sentenced to jail terms for this crime.

In January 1981 the leftist FMLN (Farabundo Marti National Liberation Front) formally launched an insurrection, but it failed to ignite great popular support among an already terrorized population. The guerrillas then withdrew to rural areas in the hills along the northern border with Honduras. Some priests, sisters, and lay people carried out pastoral work in guerrilla-controlled areas.

Romero's replacement, Archbishop Arturo Rivera y Damas, repeatedly urged that the war must be resolved through dialogue or negotiations. Pope John Paul II angered the right and the military by also using the word "dialogue" in his 1983 visit, thereby giving it respectability. Although Rivera's approach was more evenhanded than Romero's had been (Rivera insisted, for example, that the church human rights office document violations by guerrillas as well as official and right-wing forces), he and his associates earned the ire of the army by denouncing the frequent human rights abuses. The other bishops did not support Rivera, and, at least by default, supported the government.

The United States played a major role in funding the Salvadoran government and military and pressuring the military toward at least formal democracy. In 1984 José Napoleón Duarte, who had been defrauded of the 1972 election, was elected, but his role was largely that of executing an overall plan designed by the Americans, in which the primary objective was to prevent a guerrilla victory and to isolate the FMLN.

Throughout the 1980s Catholic University, under its rector, Ignacio Ellacuría, a Jesuit theologian, philosopher, and anti-war activist was a major center of independent research and analysis. In public forums it became a place where representatives of all political sectors—from right to left—could present their views. Although the government did little to carry out the Central America peace plan, repression abated somewhat, and the leftist opposition could have at least a minor political presence.

In November 1989 the FMLN launched an offensive in the capital, San Salvador. In response, army troops went to Catholic University and murdered six Jesuits, including Ellacuría, as well as a housekeeper and her daughter who had taken refuge there. The offensive again failed to spark a general uprising, and both sides were forced to face the fact that the war was at an impasse and could not be resolved militarily. The killing of the Jesuits by the U.S.-trained elite Atlacatl Battalion hastened the end of U.S. patience for the war, especially after an ensuing attempt at a cover-up. In October 1991 several lower-ranking officers were put on trial, but only two were found guilty. Shortly afterward, a formal peace accord was signed.

Guatemala

After a 1954 CIA-organized overthrow of its democratically elected government, Guatemala was under military rule. A complex guerrilla movement arose in the 1960s and was put down at the cost of six thousand to eight thousand civilian lives. Church workers came under suspicion when an attempt by two Maryknoll priests and a sister, along with a number of students, to join a guerrilla group was foiled in late 1967. In the early 1970s hundreds of labor union members and other activists were murdered each year. In the mid- to late-1970s guerrilla groups began to operate again, and there arose new mass popular movements, particularly of labor and peasants. A number of pastoral workers were involved in these. At least three priests jointed the guerrillas, and one was killed in combat.

Although the Guatemalan bishops' conference made several eloquent statements condemning injustice and violence, they were generally offset by conservative Cardinal Mario Casariego of Guatemala City. After Casariego's death in 1983 his replacement, Archbishop Prospero Penados, became more forthright in opposition to official violence.

As in El Salvador, approximately a dozen priests were murdered during 1978–1982 by the army or right-wing death squads. Repression was so acute in the Quiché diocese

that in June 1980 all Catholic Church personnel decided to leave the diocese, and the bishop went into exile outside the country (although in fact a few priests managed to maintain a low-key presence). In 1981–1983 the army launched a dirty war in areas of guerrilla influence, carrying out well-documented massacres of sometimes more than two hundred or three hundred people in a single village. In 1982 the bishops said that more than a million Guatemalans (out of a total population of seven million at that time) had been forced to leave their homes.

Such brutal tactics were effective, and by the mid-1980s the guerrillas had lost civilian support and were reduced to a minor presence. Very slowly, new organizations for human rights, labor, and indigenous rights began to form. Of particular interest was Rigoberta Menchú, a young Quiché Maya woman who as a teenager had gone from being a catechist to a peasant organizer before having to flee the country (her father, mother, and two brothers were all murdered by the army). Menchú carried on her work on behalf of Guatemalan human rights from her refuge in Mexico, and in 1987 she began to make occasional visits to Guatemala, in the wake of the Central America peace plan. In 1992, the five hundredth anniversary of the European discovery of the Americas (also proclaimed the Year of the Indigenous), she was awarded the Nobel Peace Prize, to the chagrin of the Guatemalan military.

Protestants also came to play a public role. By the 1980s they may have constituted 15 percent of the population, and in terms of actual church attendance were on a par with Catholics. General Efraín Ríos Montt, who took over the government in the wake of a military coup in 1982, was a member of the neopentecostal Church of the Word (based in Eureka, California). He was often blamed for the massacres in the highlands. His public moralizing and authoritarian attitude and actions (for example, setting up special courts for quick verdicts and even executions with no legal safeguards) made him increasingly a liability, and he was deposed in 1983. In the 1990 election Jorge Serrano Elias's Protestant identity helped him win the election (and become the first Protestant elected head of state in Latin America). He was forced out of office in 1993 after he attempted to close the congress and shut down the judicial system.

When on a 1985 visit to Nicaragua Brazilian theologian Leonardo Boff said that the revolution there embodied "all our utopias," he was expressing a shared hope that the struggles in Central America were a sign of Latin America's future, that is, that it was possible to create a different kind of society. In hindsight, however, those struggles apparently marked not the beginning of a utopia but the end of the 1960–1990 period in which revolution seemed possible. Many people, including Christians who had wagered their lives on revolution, were left perplexed by the world of the 1990s, which seemed to offer no alternative to a globalized economy that aggravated extremes of wealth and poverty. Both the FMLN and FSLN coalitions split, and many of their supporters, including prominent Christians, were left disillusioned.

The witness of Archbishop Romero, the murdered church women, the Jesuits, and many thousands of other martyrs remains alive in the groups that continue to defend human rights and to seek forms of development that are valid for the poor.

See also *Base communities; CELAM; Genocide and "ethnic cleansing"; Human rights; Latin America; Liberation theology; Maryknoll; Romero, Oscar A.; Sanctuary.*

Phillip Berryman

BIBLIOGRAPHY

Berryman, Phillip. *The Religious Roots of Rebellion: Christians in Central American Revolutions.* Maryknoll, N.Y.: Orbis Books, 1984.
———. *Stubborn Hope: Religion, Politics, and Revolution in Central America.* Maryknoll, N.Y.: Orbis Books, 1984.
Dunkerley, James. *Power in the Isthmus: A Political History of Modern Central America.* London and New York: Verso, 1988.
Hennelly, Alfred T., ed. *Liberation Theology: A Documentary History.* Maryknoll, N.Y.: Orbis Books, 1990.
Kirk, John M. *Politics and the Catholic Church in Nicaragua.* Gainesville: University of Florida Press, 1990.
O'Brien, Conor Cruise. "God and Man in Nicaragua." *The Atlantic Monthly,* August 1986, 50–72.
Whitfield, Teresa. *Paying the Price: Ignacio Ellacuría and the Murdered Jesuits of El Salvador.* Philadelphia: Temple University Press, 1995.

China

The cultural and geographic center of East Asia, China comprises a population of approximately 1.2 billion, characterized by considerable religious and ethnic diversity. This article traces the relationship of politics and religion in this vast nation from the late imperial period to the present day.

The Late Imperial Period

The relationship of politics and religion in late imperial China (1368–1911) differed from the European experience in that secular and spiritual power were never split between the state and an autonomous church. Instead, the state monopolized both functions, legitimizing its rule by reference to a state religion strongly shaped by Confucianism. It advocated a tripartite cosmology in which the emperor mediated the cosmic relationship of humanity with heaven and earth by means of a complex system of rituals and sacrifices. Imperial rule was legitimized by the conferral of "the mandate of Heaven" upon the emperor, who was regarded as "the son of Heaven." A concept of sacral kingship thus endowed the state with cosmic significance and gave the social and political order upheld by it a sacred and inviolable quality.

This state religion ideally was to structure all of society, defining the social, moral, and religious obligations of every class, from the emperor downward to the commoners. In fact, the traditional state was neither strong enough to enforce its orthodoxy throughout the empire, nor was this orthodoxy, geared as it was toward the state and the collective good of society, ever able to satisfy the religious needs of the individual. Thus the state always had to deal with the presence of religious alternatives within Chinese society. These alternatives can be grouped into two basic categories: on the one hand, there existed institutional religions with their own sacred literature and professional clergy, such as Buddhism, Daoism, Islam, and Christianity; on the other hand, we find a popular religion whose beliefs and practices were diffused through all the secular institutions of the society of commoners.

The state's approach toward both religious categories was a combination of control and co-optation. The institutional religions were denied any autonomous status and were subjected to strict control. For example, the state regularly decreed caps on the number of Buddhist and Daoist clergy permitted in any area of the empire and enforced these regulations through specialized government agencies under the Ministry of Rites, the department responsible for the state cult and court ceremonial affairs. Within this framework of administrative control, the institutional religions were allowed to practice their respective faiths without much government interference—as long as they did not question the legitimacy and inviolability of the state orthodoxy. Unwillingness to integrate into the officially sanctioned ethical and political order never failed to trigger a heavy-handed reac-

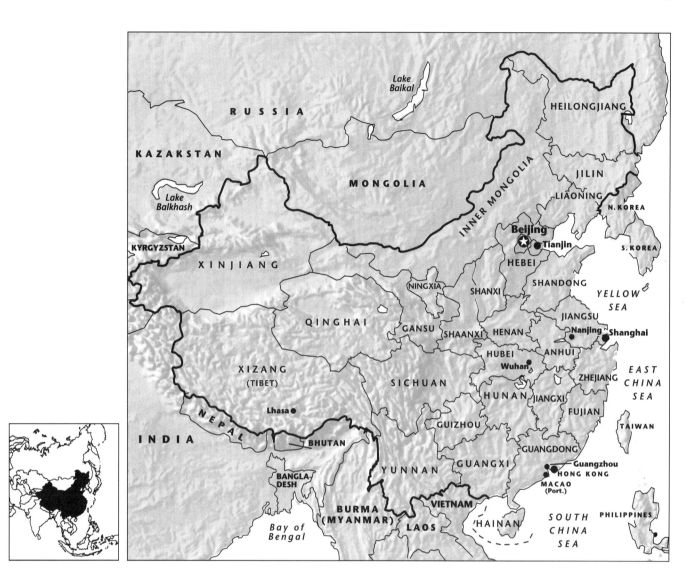

tion from the state. The power of the state was felt, for example, by the Jesuit mission in the early eighteenth century, when the pope's refusal to allow Chinese Catholics to venerate their ancestors, a vital expression of the Confucian cardinal virtue of "filial piety," led to the imperial prohibition of all missionary work in China.

Suppression was the routine response of the state toward any radical religious challenge of its orthodoxy. In the history of late imperial China, such a challenge was put forth principally by popular sects, whose millenarian preoccupations often led them to compare the perfections of the kingdom to come unfavorably with the shortcomings of contemporary society. The state frequently moved to suppress these sects even if they did not pose any immediate political threat but were content to await the millennium in an atti-

tude of quietistic pietism. Sometimes, however, sects did take violent political action, attempting to hasten the advent of the millennium by overthrowing the temporal order. The history of China's last dynasty, that of the Qing (1644–1911), records numerous bloody campaigns against so-called religious bandits. The greatest of these sectarian rebellions, that of the Taiping, lasted from 1850 to 1864. During the course of the rebellion huge areas were devastated and millions of lives lost. The state's tolerance of religious diversity ended whenever its orthodoxy was questioned in a radical manner and the offender refused to join its fold.

The state's relationship with popular religion was predicated upon the same assumption of official orthodoxy, and the state could move against any popular cult that it classified as "licentious" or "excessive." A basic problem faced by the state in this domain, however, was that most of the deities and religious practices of popular religion were strictly speaking noncanonical and thus theoretically heterodox. They grew out of and answered the religious needs of commoners for whom little provision was made in the official rosters of permissible and prescribed sacrifices. Furthermore, the deities at the center of village and township temples were focal points of local identity, and the determination of their status in relation to the official orthodoxy thus always involved a balance between local and national interests. As markers of local identities and interests, the status of local deities often became a matter of negotiation between state authorities and local elites. The latter championed the local cults, which defined their power base, while trying at the same time to interpret their meaning in a manner compatible with the state orthodoxy from which these elites, too, drew their legitimation. The state, on the other hand, was interested in assimilating local society into its ritual hierarchy by giving its gods the stamp of official approval and weakening their status as carriers of local identity.

Revolution, Communism, and the Two Chinas

Imperial rule ended in China with the revolution of 1911. The emperor was replaced by a series of regional warlords and eventually by a unified republican government. The new government adopted Western concepts of the separation of church and state, though it interpreted them in the light of Chinese political experience. This principle was taken to mean a separation of politics and religion: religion was to be banished from the public realm of a thoroughly secularized state and not allowed to "meddle" in politics.

Although the state thus effectively barred religion from legitimate participation in the political realm, the principle of separation did not work the other way around to shield religion from state interference. The traditional subordination of religion to the state was maintained and even strengthened by the increasing effectiveness of state control in a modernizing society. The traditional state orthodoxy was replaced by a modern one, a radical secularism that could take a decidedly antireligious turn. In the years following the revolution, Buddhist monasteries were taken over, Christian institutions secularized, and village temples turned into army barracks or primary schools.

Such antireligious zealotry was discouraged after the consolidation of the republican regime under Gen. Chiang Kai-shek, leader of the Nationalist Party. From about the early 1930s, we see the beginnings of a more careful approach to the nation's religions that attempted to enlist religious support for purposes of nation building. The national emergency created by the war with Japan (1937–1945) left little time for the further development of this approach, though it became dominant again at the end of the Chinese civil war that broke out after the defeat of Japan.

The civil war erupted when the uneasy coalition of Nationalists and Communists, who had made huge gains in numbers during the 1930s and 1940s, broke apart. It ended with a Communist victory and the declaration of the People's Republic of China (PRC), in 1949. The defeated Nationalists under Chiang Kai-shek withdrew to the island of Taiwan, off the southeastern coast of China, and established the provisional capital of their Republic of China (ROC) in Taipei. These "two Chinas" henceforth followed separate trajectories of development, creating a national division that persists to the present day. Both regimes—as far apart as they were ideologically—adopted similar policies toward religion. A clear line was drawn between the institutional religions and popular religion, with official recognition being extended only to the former. In the People's Republic the recognized religions were Buddhism, Daoism, Islam, Roman Catholicism, and Protestantism; the Republic of China recognized these "big five" plus a number of smaller indigenous religions.

Both regimes, the Communists in mainland China and the Nationalists in Taiwan, tried to co-opt these institutional religions into a united front to work along with other social forces in the great task of national reconstruction. The agenda to be followed was to be set by the state, and the religions were to propagate this agenda among their adherents. To facilitate communication of policy directives, national associations of the officially recognized institutional religions were formed. Following the corporatist model, these associations had a monopoly on the representation of their respective constituencies. The purpose of these associations was not to lobby their respective governments but to serve as channels for the transmission of government policies toward their members. To deal with the day-to-day business of maintaining tight administrative control over the religions, both regimes established Bureaus of Religious Affairs. This approach restricted religious liberty by subjecting religious organizations to tight state control, but it also created a legitimate space for religion in the new society and shielded it from the zealotry of the radical secularists in both regimes.

The size of that space differed between the two regimes, with the ROC generally allowing a much greater degree of religious freedom. An important difference in policy application was, for example, the PRC's insistence on the "Three-Self Movement": Religious bodies had to be self-funded, self-guided, and self-propagating. This policy excluded any support from foreign sources and led to the expulsion of all foreign missionaries. In the case of Catholics, for example, it resulted in the establishment of a national Catholic Church without any ties to the Vatican. As a result, Chinese Catholics were split between an officially recognized Catholic Patriotic Association and an underground church loyal to the pope, who denied the sacramental authority of the "patriotic" priests and bishops. The ROC, by contrast, did not require its religious associations to cut international relationships but, quite to the contrary, used these links to counteract its increasing diplomatic isolation. Thus the Catholic Church on Taiwan has always maintained close contact with the Vatican, which, to this day, maintains diplomatic relations with the ROC.

The united front collapsed in the PRC with the onset of the Cultural Revolution in 1966. The Cultural Revolution was Communist Party chairman Mao Zedong's campaign to create a new society overnight by eradicating all vestiges of the old. Along with intellectuals and government officials, innumerable clerics and lay believers of all religious traditions suffered, with untold thousands killed, thrown into prison, or forcibly secularized by the Red Guards. The Cultural Revolution ended officially in 1976 with the overthrow of the radical Maoists known as the Gang of Four and the assumption of power by the reformist wing of the Communist Party.

New Approach to Religion

The following period brought with it a significant relaxation of the suppression of religion and a return to the united front approach of the 1950s and early 1960s. It was now believed that religion still had a useful function to fulfill within Chinese society and that religious organizations should therefore be allowed to contribute to the construction of China. The new approach was sanctioned in the so-called Document 19, issued by the Party's Central Committee in 1982. It was enshrined as well in Article 36 of the PRC's 1982 constitution, which stated that citizens had freedom of religious belief. Since 1982 this more liberal approach has dominated PRC policy, granting the officially

recognized religions again a legitimate, though restricted, sphere of activity.

With this new freedom the 1990s have witnessed a "religion fever," which has widely been interpreted as a sign that the decay of Communist values and of the Party's ideological credibility has produced a spiritual vacuum that may be filled with religious content. Official sources claim that in 1997 there were more than 100 million religious believers in the PRC. Specific figures given for the five officially recognized religions, however, are much lower. There are said to exist 18 million Muslims, 10 million Protestants, and 4 million Catholics. For Buddhism and Daoism only the number of full-time clergy is given: 200,000 for the Buddhists and 25,000 for the Daoists. These official statistics, which often differ widely from unofficial estimates, are to be treated with caution.

In the ROC, some restriction was continued until the lifting in 1987 of the rule of martial law, which had first been imposed in 1949, shortly before the arrival of the Nationalist government on Taiwan. Since then, Taiwan has been undergoing a process of rapid democratization that has done away with many aspects of the authoritarian one-party regime, including the corporatist handling of religion. This new freedom has resulted in the growth of the number of officially recognized religions, including previously banned "heterodox sects" like the Way of Unity (Yiguan Dao), a modern successor to an ancient Chinese tradition of popular sectarianism focusing on the worship of a primordial mother deity.

With the gradual development of democratic pluralism, state ideological control of religions is becoming weaker, and religious groups now have much greater leeway to play a role in all aspects of social life, including politics. The strict secularist separation of politics and religions is being watered down, and the two realms of discourse are beginning to merge. For example, some political leaders have sought endorsements from prominent Buddhist clerics, while others have demonstrated their sensitivity to grassroots concerns by actively participating in popular religious festivals and pilgrimages. In the 1990s efforts were under way to adopt a new comprehensive "religion law" that would replace the old administrative regulations, some of which date back to the 1920s. According to government statistics, among a total population of roughly 21 million, Taiwan currently counts 4,863,000 Buddhists, 3,852,000 Daoists, 942,000 Yiguan Dao adherents, 726,000 Christians (both Catholic and Protestant), and 748,000 followers of other faiths.

Popular and Minority Religions

Many studies of religion and politics in the PRC tend to neglect the importance of popular religion. This is due in large part to the fact that popular religion is not recognized as religion at all but is relegated to a hazy category of "feudal superstitions." This means that popular religion is not protected by the constitutional guarantee of religious freedom, which applies only to the five institutional religions recognized by the state. In spite of its legally insecure status, popular religion has made a strong comeback in some areas of China, in particular in the south and southeast of the country, where active village temples and earth god shrines are again a common sight. Popular practices such as ancestor worship have been reevaluated by the authorities: ancestor worship, previously regarded as "feudal superstition," is now seen as an expression of positive moral values and thus in principle permissible. On the other hand, popular religious practices such as shamanism, fortune telling, and geomancy continue to meet with censure and are subject to intermittent suppression. Although popular religion operates in a legal gray zone and is vulnerable to shifts in government policies, it is reestablishing itself in some areas of China as a forum for local and national identities, much as it functioned in late imperial China.

The political dimension of popular religion has received more scholarly attention in Taiwan, where tensions between the Taiwanese majority and the small ruling elite of Nationalist mainlanders who fled to the island in 1949 has constituted a persistent political undercurrent. While remaining disdainful of the "irrationalism" of Taiwanese folk religion, the government never suppressed it violently; instead, it followed an only moderately successful approach of administrative control and interpretative co-optation. In the absence of genuinely democratic political channels of expression during the period of martial law, Taiwanese popular religion played an important role as a realm of symbolic protest. The Taiwanese, for example, could express their identity by holding lavish traditional temple festivals in the face of government efforts to curb the attending "superstition" and "waste of resources." In addition, popular religious cults continued to figure prominently in village and township politics, even though secularism dominated at the national level.

A final area of great importance to Chinese policymakers is the role of religion in the state's relationship with ethnic minorities. This is a significant issue primarily in mainland China, where many minority groups live in sensitive border areas and have historically been treated with a mixture of strict control and careful accommodation. Religion is usually a significant element in these minorities' ethnic self-identity and thus must be given special consideration. Even in the chaotic years of the Cultural Revolution the religious sensibilities of minority peoples were often shielded from the worst excesses of the Red Guards. Also out of respect for the role of religion in minorities' cultural self-definition, minority cadres are exempt from the general prohibition of membership in any religion for Party members. On the other hand, the state does not hesitate to come down heavily on any attempt to use religion to further political aims of minorities that are incompatible with the state's interests.

The limits of religious freedom are made very clear every time the authorities quell Muslim demonstrations in the predominantly Muslim autonomous region of Xinjiang in western China or conduct mass arrests of Tibetan Buddhist monks supporting the exiled Dalai Lamai. In spite of the more relaxed climate since the late 1970s, religion in the PRC remains vulnerable to periodic shifts in the state's policy agendas. The PRC thus continues a long-standing Chinese political tradition by resolutely insisting on the subordination of religion and religious freedom to the overriding interests of the state.

See also *Buddhism, Tibetan; Christianity in Asia; Communism; Confucianism; Dalai Lama; Millennialism; Separation of church and state.*

Philip Clart

BIBLIOGRAPHY

Ahern, Emily Martin. *Chinese Ritual and Politics.* Cambridge: Cambridge University Press, 1981.

Dean, Kenneth. *Taoist Ritual and Popular Cults of Southeast China.* Princeton: Princeton University Press, 1993.

Gladney, Dru C. *Muslim Chinese. Ethnic Nationalism in the People's Republic.* Cambridge: Council on East Asian Studies, Harvard University, 1991.

Luo Zhufeng, ed. *Religion under Socialism in China.* Translated by Donald E. MacInnis and Zheng Xi'an. Armonk, N.Y.: M. E. Sharpe, 1991.

MacInnis, Donald E. *Religion in China Today: Policy and Practice.* Maryknoll, N.Y.: Orbis Books, 1989.

Munro, Robin, ed. and trans. "Syncretic Sects and Secret Societies: Revival in the 1980s." Thematic issue of *Chinese Sociology and Anthropology* 21 (1989), no. 4.

Pas, Julian F., ed. *The Turning of the Tide: Religion in China Today.* Hong Kong: Hong Kong Branch of the Royal Asiatic Society, in association with Oxford University Press, 1989.

Seaman, Gary. *Temple Organization in a Chinese Village.* Taipei: Orient Cultural Service, 1978.

Wickeri, Philip L. *Seeking the Common Ground: Protestant Christianity, the Three-Self Movement, and China's United Front.* Maryknoll, N.Y.: Orbis Books, 1988.

Yang, C. K. *Religion in Chinese Society: A Study of Contemporary Social Functions of Religion and Some of Their Historical Factors.* Berkeley: University of California Press, 1961.

Christian Coalition

See *Conservatism*

Christian Democracy

Christian Democracy is a political orientation and party movement that has arisen largely, though not exclusively, among Roman Catholics in response to the liberal, democratic, and anticlerical impulses of the nineteenth and twentieth centuries. It has been an important political force in twentieth-century Europe and Latin America. Intellectually, it is rooted in the social teaching of the Catholic Church and in the writings of Catholic social thinkers such as Luigi Sturzo (1871–1959), who founded the Italian Popular Party, and French philosophers and writers Emmanuel Mounier (1905–1950) and Jacques Maritain (1882–1973). Politically, Christian Democracy grew out of Catholic involvement, alongside secular liberals and leftists, in antifascist activities prior to and during the Second World War.

Christian Democratic parties have offered a reformist alternative to the defensive conservatism with which Catholicism was identified from the sixteenth through the nineteenth centuries. In the years since their emergence most of these parties have gravitated rightward, standing for democracy and social justice but opposing the economic and cultural radicalism of Communist, Socialist, and Social Democratic rivals. Most, however, continue to defend economic regulations and social welfare programs that promote the "common good," despite the claims of some that such things negatively affect economic growth and job creation.

Of the twenty-two Christian Democratic parties in Western Europe, eight (in Austria, Belgium, Germany, Greece, Ireland, Luxembourg, the Netherlands, and Spain) command more than 20 percent of the seats in the national legislature (or of the national vote); a ninth (the Swiss Christian Democratic People's Party) has almost that many seats (17 percent); and five (in France, Italy, Norway, Portugal, and Sweden) are significant minor parties, with 5–10 percent of the seats independently or in coalition with others. In Eastern Europe, the numbers are smaller but the Christian Democrats have a distinct presence. These parties are supported by 10–15 percent of the voting population in Romania and Slovakia, and by 5–10 percent in Poland, Hungary, and the Czech Republic. In Latin America, Christian Democratic parties have more than 20 percent of seats (or of votes) in six countries (Chile, Costa Rica, the Dominican Republic, Ecuador, El Salvador, and Venezuela); they have minimal representation or impact (1–3 percent and only scattered seats) in five others (Brazil, Nicaragua, Panama, Peru, and Uruguay). In nine others (Argentina, Belize, Bolivia, Colombia, Cuba, Haiti, Honduras, Mexico, and Paraguay) they exist but are insignificant.

Christian Democratic parties coordinate with one another internationally through the loosely structured Christian Democrat International, headquartered in Brussels, Belgium. Among its affiliates are the European People's Party, a bloc in the Parliament of the European Union.

Origins

The notion of a Christian democracy was first embraced by Pope Leo XIII (reigned 1878–1903), who hoped to rescue elements of democracy and reform from the philosophically skeptical and individualistic foundations to which they were usually tied in the nineteenth century. In his encyclical *Rerum Novarum* (on capital and labor) in 1891, Leo called for social justice and improvements in the lot of workers and the poor and for active lay participation in politics wherever liberal and socialist currents were threatening the values and interests of the church (for example, calling for separation of church and state and the legalization of divorce). Tensions quickly arose, however, as lay activists pushing for reform ran afoul of conservative bishops and other authorities. In a second encyclical, *Graves de Communi Re* (1901), Leo so redefined the concept as to practically abandon it.

The church then was left dependent, by design as much as by default, on piously conservative Catholic parties. For the most part, these parties were the electoral arms of aristocratic elites bent on defending the status quo from religious, socioeconomic, and political challenges. As reform-minded working and popular-class elements emerged politically in the late nineteenth and early twentieth centuries, these parties grew weaker, and church leaders began to look to new strategies.

Gradually and unevenly, they distanced themselves from their elite allies and patrons. They also abandoned the notion of obligatory political unity for Catholics and accepted, reluctantly at first, "liberal" demands for religious freedom, separation of church and state, lay autonomy in political affairs, and greater social and political democratization. In addition, with an eye to reclaiming the fallen-away Catholic masses, Church authorities gave renewed emphasis to the church's social teaching. In 1931, on the fortieth anniversary of *Rerum Novarum,* Pope Pius XI issued the encyclical *Quadragesimo Anno* (on reconstructing the social order). The church began training and assigning lay men and women to apostolic activities through the Catholic Action movement and Young Christian Workers and Young Christian Students groups. Church authorities thus came to rely on the leavening impact of lay people in their parish communities and places of work. The experience of many middle-class and some working-class Catholics in these organizations helped them to reconcile their faith with their increasingly progressive social inclinations. It also led some of them to join with other, largely secular, forces in opposing Nazi parties in the 1930s and in resisting German occupation during the Second World War.

These developments formed a breeding ground in which "liberal" Catholic sentiments could arise and exert appeal. They also provided a context in which reform-minded Catholic parties were the logical next step. And so it was, in the late 1940s and 1950s, that Christian Democratic parties emerged in both Europe and Latin America. Blessed with extraordinary lay leadership, and with a ready constituency among former Catholic Action and anti-Nazi resistance activists, Christian Democratic parties quickly became major players in the politics of the postwar period. Notable in helping to found Christian Democratic parties in these years were Robert Schuman in France, Alcide De Gasperi in Italy, Konrad Adenauer in Germany, and Eduardo Frei in Chile.

European and Latin American Parties

In Europe, Christian Democratic parties attracted Catholic voters in Germany, Italy, Belgium, and the Netherlands, where traditional right-wing groups were weak and more progressive responses to Marxist and anticlerical forces were possible. In France, on the other hand, the initially promising Popular Republican Movement was eclipsed by Gen. Charles de Gaulle's triumphal return to the political arena in the late 1950s, and it later merged with other groups in a loosely fashioned centrist coalition. In Spain, Christian Democrats became leading elements in the Popular Party (which considers itself a Christian Democratic party). The Spanish Popular Party is a center-right alliance that emerged in 1989 and now governs Spain, under José María Aznar López, after fifteen years of rule by the Spanish Socialist Workers' Party.

European Christian Democrats have generally appealed to wide-ranging social forces by generating growth and helping to sustain a prosperous, if less than ideal, socioeconomic status quo. The German party is a union of the larger Christian Democratic Union and the staunchly Catholic Christian Social Union of Bavaria. It has headed the country's government for most of the period since 1949 and is widely credited with the economic growth and social benefits that its social market economy has produced. In contrast, the Christian Democrats in Italy, which also dominated that country's postwar politics, collapsed in 1994 under the weight of almost fifty years of scandal and corruption. It survives as the Popular Party, a junior partner in a coalition headed by former Communists. Christian Democratic parties are frequent partners in ruling coalitions in both Belgium and the Netherlands as well.

Each of the European Christian Democratic parties has clear ties to the Catholic Church and the tradition of its country, using them to substantial political advantage. But these parties also have made a point of operating independently of Catholic authorities. They remain open to Catholic and non-Catholic members alike, and, while acknowledging their inspiration in Catholic social teaching, claim a rightful autonomy in deciding upon its practical application. For the most part, local Catholic authorities have been willing to accommodate them, albeit more readily on socioeconomic and political issues than on moral and cultural concerns.

In Latin America, widespread poverty and the intransigence of socioeconomic and political elites pushed some socially conscious Catholics in a reformist direction, at least initially. Christian Democrats came to power in Chile (1964–1970), Venezuela (1969–1974), El Salvador (1984–1988), Ecuador (1981–1984 and 1984–1988), the Dominican Republic (1986–1996), and Costa Rica (1990–1994), in opposition to secular left and populist forces and, where it had been strong, against the right as well. Their economic and political performances generally compare favorably with preceding and ensuing governments. In most of these cases, however, tensions arose between rival moderate and progressive factions. The latter usually favored more thoroughgoing transformations and urged alliances with left-wing groups, but they invariably lost out to those suspicious of the left and concerned with not alienating local or international economic elites. In the process, these parties, and the smaller Peruvian party as well, lost members to Christian-Marxist splinter parties and to conservative Social Christian offshoots.

Venezuela's Social Christian Party (COPEI), which encompasses a widely disparate range of views, and Chile's Christian Democratic Party (PDC) are the region's most prominent and successful parties. The PDC has headed two center-left governments since 1990. Its appeal reflects its ability to combine steady, high-level economic growth with some progress in reducing poverty. In addition, it has benefited from socialism's decline as a credible economic and political alternative and from the unwillingness of most Chileans to take or support actions that might threaten economic or military elites and thereby risk another military coup. In Venezuela, COPEI's founder, Rafael Caldera Rodríguez, was again elected president in 1994 (he had served previously in the late 1960s and early 1970s), but he ran as a political independent against both COPEI and Democratic Action rivals and their neoliberal programs. Since his election, deteriorating economic conditions have forced Caldera to abandon his initially popular stance.

Current Directions

During the late 1980s and early 1990s Christian Democratic parties in both Europe and Latin America were beneficiaries of the collapse of Marxist economies and regimes in Eastern Europe and the former Soviet Union. In Germany, in 1990, the appeal of immediate reunification of East and West Germany and the votes of disillusioned East Germans carried Helmut Kohl and the union parties—the Christian Democratic Union and Christian Socialist Union alliance—to victory in an election that many observers initially expected them to lose. In Latin America, Christian Democrats found it easier to operate with reduced pressure from the left. Marxists and other leftists have become more willing to form alliances with centrist forces and are less likely to insist on policies that might alienate either local or foreign investors or potential export markets.

For much of their histories the diverse, multiclass constituencies to which Christian Democratic parties have appealed have had trouble agreeing on monetary and economic policy, social spending, tax burdens, wage levels, labor rela-

tions, and the like. Lacking a common vision, they tended to interpret and apply the same social Christian principles and ideals quite differently. Intellectuals and trade unionists, for example, were generally at odds with the center-right policies of their party's government and were more likely to agree with its leftist critics. They were willing to remain dissenting but ultimately loyal minorities because they thought their chances of maneuvering for what they wanted from within were better than if they abandoned the party and started over elsewhere. With the new free market consensus, however, divisions over issues of both economic policy (the need for low taxes, minimal deficits, deregulation, privatization, and increased exports) and political strategy (alliances and alignments) appear to have declined significantly.

But Christian Democratic parties are not entirely free of conflict. Their liberal and conservative wings continue to disagree on issues of personal morality (divorce, abortion, euthanasia, artistic expression, homosexuality, AIDS prevention, and sex education). In most instances, party leaders have sided with those backing restrictive policies—less from conviction, it seems, than from an unwillingness to alienate Catholic authorities whose informal blessings they hope to continue receiving.

See also *Anticlericalism; Catholicism, Roman; Conservatism; Liberalism; Vatican.*

Michael H. Fleet

BIBLIOGRAPHY

Baum, Gregory, and John Coleman, eds. *The Church and Christian Democracy.* Edinburgh: Clark, 1987.

Cary, Noel D. *The Path to Christian Democracy: German Catholicism and the Party System from Windthorst to Adenauer.* Cambridge: Harvard University Press, 1996.

Einaudi, Mario, and François Goguel. *Christian Democracy in Italy and France.* Notre Dame, Ind.: University of Notre Dame Press, 1952.

Fleet, Michael H. *The Rise and Fall of Chilean Christian Democracy.* Princeton: Princeton University Press, 1985.

Fogarty, Michael P. *Christian Democracy in Western Europe, 1820–1953.* Notre Dame, Ind.: University of Notre Dame Press, 1957.

Hanley, David, ed. *Christian Democracy in Europe: A Comparative Perspective.* London: Pinter; New York: St. Martin's, 1994.

Maritain, Jacques. *Integral Humanism.* New York: Scribner's, 1968.

———. *Man and the State.* Chicago: University of Chicago Press, 1951.

Mounier, Emmanuel. *Personalism.* Notre Dame, Ind.: University of Notre Dame Press, 1970.

Sturzo, Luigi. *Church and State.* New York: Longmans, Green, 1939.

Christian Science

Christian Science is the name applied to the teachings of the Church of Christ, Scientist, a sometimes politically controversial religious organization established in 1879 in Boston, Massachusetts. It is based on the writings of its founder, Mary Baker Eddy (1821–1910). Her book *Science and Health with Key to the Scriptures* summarizes major elements of the religion. Since its publication in 1875 it has served as the key writing that distinguishes the church from other Christian-based churches.

Theology and Practice

Christian Science theology places a strong emphasis on the spiritual in contrast to the material. The primary teaching of Christian Science is that God is at once omnipotent, omnipresent, and omniscient Divine Principle, Mind, Soul, Spirit, Truth, and Love. Creation, it is taught, is the spiritual expression of God, and man and woman are made in "God's image and likeness." The thrust of this theology is unitarian, the healings of Jesus being defined as examples of applying the scientific truth that Eddy discovered and began to practice following her own apparently spontaneous healing after a serious accident.

Perhaps the best known and most controversial concept from Christian Science theology concerns *spiritual healing.* The term refers to the treatment of physical ailments, depression, grief, stress, business problems, and marital crises through prayer alone. Christian Science teaches that healing will result if one will but depend completely on God and accept the basic truths of Christian Science theology.

In any healing situation the Christian Scientist focuses on establishing a proper relationship between the individual patient and God. A person seeking spiritual healing through Christian Science will often turn for help to specially trained *practitioners* or *teachers,* who have an established record of healing and are fully dependent on their healing ministry for their livelihood. Christian Science practitioners are reimbursed under some private insurance plans, although they have never received payments under any state or federal government programs.

In recent years much controversy has erupted over spiritual healing in the United States, especially as it is used with seriously ill children, some of whom have died. People have become relatively accustomed to spiritual healing, a factor contributing to the fact that for such healing many states

Mary Baker Eddy

have granted formal exemptions to laws concerning child endangerment and neglect. Children's deaths in the last two decades, however, have led to criminal charges being filed against parents in a few cases. Some of the cases have led to convictions, although most convictions have been overturned on appeal. The cases have brought about much negative publicity for the church, which has had a difficult time getting the media and the public to accept its explanations. These cases have led to some reexamination of Christian Science theology and practice concerning spiritual healing.

Sociology and Organization

Today the Mother Church in Boston has more than twenty-two hundred branches located in more than sixty countries. Most of the branches are in the United States. The estimated number of church participants worldwide is 350,000 to 450,000. This estimate reflects a decline in church membership in the United States and some European countries in recent decades but a growth in some developing countries. A high proportion of members are middle-aged and elderly women from middle- and upper-class origins. Females make up nearly 85 percent of the more than two thousand practitioners and about half of the higher-status teachers.

Members have active social and political lives and are not encouraged to be reclusive or ascetic, although little emphasis is put on communal life or collective living. They do not use tobacco or alcohol, believing that such substances impair moral judgment and spiritual development. Members also eschew gambling, which, they believe, would indicate that one depended on chance instead of God's law and will. Marriage is sanctioned and celibacy is neither promoted nor scorned.

The church has no ordained clergy and few overt rituals. It does not, for instance, practice baptism or celebrate Easter or Christmas through special services. Because of the lack of official clergy, marriage ceremonies are not performed in the church. In regular church services lay readers present material from the Bible and *Science and Health* selected by the church authorities in Boston. The same material is used in all branch churches for the week. Services, held in austere surroundings, tend to be unemotional. They include silent and audible prayer and readings and some hymn singing. Midweek testimonial meetings are also held in branch churches. Most of the churches have a Sunday School for younger participants, and each one operates a "reading room," which is open to the public and which contains all church publications and works by biblical commentators acceptable to the church.

The church and its branches are still governed by principles laid down by Eddy in the *Manual of the Mother Church,* published first in 1895 and revised by her several times. The Mother Church is governed by a five-person self-perpetuating board of directors that develops broad policy for the church, consistent with the *Manual.* Local branches operate on democratic principles. Members who desire to do so can participate in governance of the local church by being elected to a local church office.

A church Committee on Publication in each state monitors the media and state legislatures to make sure the church is not dealt with unfairly. The church also has a legal arm in Washington, D.C., that monitors federal cases and legislation to some extent.

The church has several major regular publications, the best known of which is the *Christian Science Monitor,* a daily newspaper of high standing among journalists and the general public. The newspaper is known for its lack of sensationalism and its thorough coverage of international issues. Eddy began the paper in 1908, two years before her death, as a way of making a statement about the practical implications of her spiritual philosophy.

The other major regular publications of the church are the *Christian Science Journal,* which appears monthly, the weekly *Christian Science Sentinel,* and the weekly *Herald of Christian Science,* which is published in many different languages. Included in these publications are articles on various aspects of Christian Science faith and practice; reports on the work of the church; reports of spiritual healings; and lists of Christian Science churches, reading rooms, organizations on college campuses, and practitioners and teachers around the world. More than fifty thousand reports of spiritual healings have appeared in these publications during the past hundred years.

See also *Medicine.*

James T. Richardson

BIBLIOGRAPHY

Christian Science Publishing Society. *Christian Science: A Sourcebook of Contemporary Materials.* Boston: Christian Science Publishing Society, 1990.

Eddy, Mary Baker. *Science and Health with Key to the Scriptures.* Boston: Christian Science Publishing Society, 1934.

Gottschalk, Stephen. *The Emergence of Christian Science in American Religious Life.* Berkeley and Los Angeles: University of California Press, 1973.

Peel, Robert. *Spiritual Healing in a Scientific Age.* San Francisco: Harper and Row, 1987.

Richardson, James T., and John DeWitt. "Christian Science Spiritual Healing, the Law, and Public Opinion." *Journal of Church and State* 34 (summer 1992): 549–562.

Christianity

Christianity, the religious movement that grew out of the ministry and crucifixion of Jesus of Nazareth two thousand years ago, has spread in a variety of forms and churches across the globe. Jesus was a Jew; his followers never abandoned the Jewish scriptures, though little by little they added to the Jewish "Old Testament" a further collection of writings that became the "New Testament" of their Bible. Christian beliefs and practices in every area have to be understood as a mix of elements and influences in part derived from their Hebrew ancestry, in part the product of the teachings of Jesus or the situation in which Christianity subsequently developed.

Judaism was the religion of a single people, claiming to be uniquely chosen by God and to have been given a particular territory as its own. Its sense of political identity was reinforced by the way in which so many of its sacred books were historical in character, relating to the rise and fall of a kingdom of Israel centered upon Jerusalem. Inevitably, this sort of political focus was entirely lost in a religious movement that contrasted itself with Israel precisely in terms of not being a "people" in a national sense but being instead a "new people of God" chosen from all peoples of the world. Whether or not this universalism was implicit in the teaching of Jesus himself, it was a decisive characteristic of the Christian Church within a generation of his death and was at the heart of the teaching of his most influential follower, St. Paul.

The politicism inherent in the Judaism from which Christianity came could have no possible place in a community stressing in theory and achieving in practice a rapidly growing "catholicity," that is to say openness on equal terms to people of every race and language. While Jesus must undoubtedly have spoken in Aramaic or Hebrew and never, so far as we know, left Palestine, the books about him and early Christian literature as a whole were written in Greek—the most widely spread language of the time. Christianity's very adoption of Greek expressed its claim to a nonethnic, nonnational, nonpolitical identity, especially as Greek was all the same not made into the one privileged language of the community. Once it had spread into western Europe among non-Greek speakers, its scriptures and liturgy were translated into Latin. In Syria they were translated into Syriac, in the interior of Egypt into Coptic, in Armenia into Armenian. The claim to universality extended well beyond the borders of the Roman Empire, and Christianity grew as naturally in Armenia or Persia as in the former.

Jesus was someone who had exercised no political power, who was quoted as distinguishing fairly clearly between the claims of religion and politics—give to Caesar the things that are Caesar's and to God the things that are God's—and who had died as a condemned criminal. Here was no glorification of political power but rather an assertion that "the Kingdom of God," which Jesus proclaimed, could be attained in a totally apolitical way, by turning the power system of the world on its head. After Jesus' crucifixion, the cross, a particularly cruel instrument of execution, a symbol of oppression and ignominy, became instead a symbol of liberation and glory. This was possible only because of the intense other-worldliness of the early Christian movement: the victory being sought was one not of this world but of the next. Enthusiastic early Christians had to be discouraged by the church from actually seeking martyrdom.

Nevertheless, some aspects of Old Testament political religion, the prophetic aspects especially, passed at once into Christianity—its highly ethical disposition, its concern for justice, the poor, and the oppressed. In a sense, taking for granted this prophetic concern, Jesus positioned himself and his movement as identified with the oppressed. Because the oppressed were politically powerless, this attitude could seem a withdrawal from the political, but in the long term it proved not to be. Instead it established as first priority an inescapable foundation for the reshaping of the political with the needs of the poor. It did so by proclaiming an authority in some way vested in the church, something in no way identical with normal political authority—Caesar—but nonetheless sanctioned to speak out about the world of political power and its misuse. The Christian tradition is thus intrinsically dualist: It recognizes the secular authority of Caesar, derived from God and the natural order, but it also asserts that there is within the church an independent, more directly God-given authority which can and must carry on the prophetic concern for justice, and Jesus' own identification with the most innocent and the most oppressed, by challenging the state in a vast range of matters which the state considers political and not religious.

The Constantinian Revolution

Until the beginning of the fourth century, the apolitical character of Christianity must have seemed overwhelmingly obvious. It had spread with striking rapidity yet without any political or military support whatsoever. On the contrary, it had undergone numerous persecutions because Christians refused to take part in emperor worship and had never responded by any sort of organized resistance. Most of its members were pacifists and few belonged to a governing class. Nevertheless, in various parts of the eastern Mediterranean world Christians had become so numerous that it was increasingly difficult for government to function effectively without their cooperation. The last great persecution, which began under the emperor Diocletian and lasted from 303 to 311, was a huge failure. Christians, by and large, refused to return to traditional worship, the numerous executions of harmless people discredited the state, and society was disrupted. In 313 the young emperor of the Western empire, Constantine, identified himself and his cause with Christianity. He proved stunningly successful, defeated all rivals, and established a new Christian capital for the empire at Byzantium on the Bosporus, renamed and rebuilt as Constantinople. He died in 337, having transformed the entire relationship between Christianity and politics.

Why did Constantine become a Christian? It remains hard to know. The pragmatic answer makes little sense. At the time, Constantine was struggling for control of the Latin West where Christians still formed a small proportion of the population. His religious background had been one of solar monotheism. Somehow, by vision, inspiration, or contact with Christians this religious inclination was transmuted into a Christian faith that included the conviction that his own victorious career depended upon it. Constantine's conversion led to the principles of the Edict of Milan (313), agreed to with his eastern rival, Licinius, whereby all religions were to be tolerated. Only at the end of the fourth century, under the emperor Theodosius, did Christianity become formally the one official religion of the empire. But already Constantine was giving the church privileges in all sorts of ways and, particularly after his conquest of the Eastern Empire in 324, incorporating it within the machinery of government.

It is understandable enough that Christians for the most part went along enthusiastically with this revolutionary change of status. It was not only that wealth and power had their attractions, or even that it was hard to question the propriety of a development that encouraged an enormous increase in the number of church members; it was also that in the eyes of men like Eusebius, bishop of Caesarea, the outstanding church historian of his age, and the Latin theologian Lactantius what had happened seemed to reflect the designs of divine Providence: church and empire were meant for each other. Luke's Gospel had already stressed how Jesus was born at a moment when the whole world was united as never before under the authority of the emperor

Constantine I

Augustus. Where hitherto persecution had held the two apart, intensifying an apolitical otherworldliness in Christianity and negating any claim that the empire could truly be part of God's benign providence, Constantine had joined the two together. No wonder Constantine was acclaimed as the thirteenth apostle, providing the church with an overt political dimension it would ever after have the greatest difficulty in escaping. Some of the early Christian ideals, like the tradition of pacifism, simply faded away in consequence, while the high social status accorded the bishops, incorporating them into the class of the powerful, set them apart from other Christians and deeply affected the church-state relationship, by partially encapsulating it inside a single ruling class.

There were other consequences as well. Christians outside the Roman Empire were put at once in an invidious position. If Rome was officially Christian, and if Christianity was indeed now in some sense Roman, then Persian Christians might be seen as agents of Rome. With the development of Constantinople as a completely Christian capital, an explicitly Greek form of Christianity became preeminent within what we can begin to call a Byzantine Empire. Christians at odds with the Eastern emperor and his Greek-centered world, whether within or without the borders of empire, became inclined to opt for a form of Christianity different from that patronized in Constantinople.

It was Constantine who had endeavoured to resolve the Arian controversy in 325 by calling the bishops together in a council at Nicaea. Arius, a priest in the church at Alexandria, Egypt, and his followers held a view on the nature of Christ that deviated from that of the majority. At Nicaea, Constantine had paid the bishops' expenses, he addressed them in person, and he expected them to agree to a line of doctrine that would not be politically divisive. Disagreement was to be punished by exile. Although neither Constantine nor most of his successors claimed to make doctrine, they expected the bishops to do so in the way they directed. What grew up in consequence was a monist system of control of the church by the state that was appropriate to the Roman tradition but profoundly alien to the Christian.

If this imperial control never fully took root, it was because the authority of the bishops was already too well advanced. While in practice bishops might often be chosen by an emperor, in principle their consecration and source of authority came from elsewhere—the apostolic succession. This doctrine maintained that the bishops derived their authority through the apostles as direct descendants of Jesus. Already in the time of Constantine and his immediate successors, Athanasius, bishop of Alexandria, had incurred exile after exile for not conforming to imperial policy. By his obstinacy and clarity of mind, Athanasius did much to maintain a sense of surviving dualism, which was in danger of disappearing within the privileged servility of an imperial church.

Dualism, however, survived even more emphatically in the West for two reasons. The first was the existence of the See of Rome, which claimed apostolicity in the fullest sense because its founders were the apostles Peter and Paul. The emperors were inclined to regard the undoubted superiority of the Roman church as due to its being the church of the first imperial capital and to claim that, for the same reason, the church of Constantinople should be next in importance. For the church in Rome, however, its imperial connection had no significance at all. Its authority came from the apostles. In consequence, the papacy (the bishopric of Rome) remained a bulwark against a creeping monism. Pope Gelasius,

in particular, formulated the theory of the two swords given by God: the earthly to the emperor, the spiritual to pope and church. Basically, this idea represents simply a reformulation of Christianity's traditional position: to recognize the validity of secular authority but to deny that such authority could be exercised over the church and to assert the claim of the church to challenge the misdeeds of the secular, as the prophets of Israel had once done.

The second reason that the leanings toward a unified church and empire of Constantine, Theodosius, and Justinian—the greatest Eastern emperor of the sixth century—failed to take root in the Latin world was that the empire itself collapsed in the West under invasion from Germanic tribes moving west across the Rhine. In consequence, the mirage of a single universal community of church and empire faded fast. In the early fifth century Augustine of Hippo, facing the collapse in morale occasioned by the sack of Rome by the Goths in 410, wrote his *City of God,* in which he took the Roman Empire to pieces as a work of man, no more privileged than any previous empire and wholly to be distinguished from the church as the City of God, which would continue across whatever change of political regime might occur.

Although the ideal of a unified Christian empire continued to haunt the West, stimulating the revival and survival of a "Holy Roman Empire" effectively limited to Germany and parts of Italy, the reality was moving toward a multitude of separate states. In each of these the church had to find a home and a measure of freedom.

The Papacy, Nationalism, and Protestantism

The attempt of the papacy in its most venturesome period, from the eleventh to the thirteenth century, to provide political leadership for a Christian community still imagined as single provided a watershed in Christian political history. To the pope, it was now claimed, both swords—the temporal and the spiritual—had been confided. The political role of a king was essentially inferior to that of the pope.

This attempt to achieve a Western kind of monism, unified not in a royal but clerical form, could not conceivably succeed. In reality, the power of the popes, bureaucratically far more efficient than anyone else, was simply too limited. Even at the level of a universalist ideology, they were continually challenged in the thirteenth and fourteenth centuries by people like the Florentine poet Dante and Marsilius of

Padua, who continued to believe in the dominating role of a universal emperor. But far more decisively were they defeated by the rising power of national monarchies, which were actually fortified by the underlying sentiment of Christian dualism, something that had been dangerously impaired by the papal claim to a sort of universal monarchy. The latter's supreme military embodiment, the Crusades, had also proved disastrous in religious terms and a long-term failure in political ones. The popes had drawn a religion that began as largely committed to pacifism and that had then been driven by political circumstances to allow a "just war" to fling itself into something very different, "holy war." Holy war is an expression of monism. Both the Crusades and the papacy of the high Middle Ages reflected a disastrous abandonment of the inherent dualistic balance between the religious and the political, and they were to lead in reaction to the large-scale lay and national takeover of the church in the following period.

As this happened, however, a new side of Christianity's political impact was revealed: its nation-building propensity. If on one side a united church, glorying in a single "communion" open to every people and language, naturally linked itself with a universal empire, which at its best cherished similar aspirations, on the other side the church retained in its Bible the Hebrew Scriptures, which evoked a quite different political model, one that can be not absurdly described as that of a national state, keen to defend its identity against invading powers. Western Christians, as they forged a series of national identities—English, Scottish, French, German, and the rest—were greatly assisted both by the political model of Israel they found in their Bibles and by the encouragement that the church gave to the development of literature in the vernacular languages. Christianity from the start had been a religion of translation, and this activity continued, despite the high value accorded to the role of Latin by the political and clerical elites.

The early emergence of vernacular literature in Welsh and Irish, English and French, German and Dutch was not accidental. It was inherent in Christianity's relationship to language—a relationship stressed still further at the Protestant Reformation in the sixteenth century. The extensive writing of a given vernacular solidified the community that possessed it, particularly when this literature included the Bible. The national state was the result, and it came to claim somewhat inevitably the sort of control over its own church that

Constantine had exercised over the universal church. It is striking that when Henry VIII declared himself to be supreme ruler over the church in England in 1534, he did so by asserting England to be an "empire," and he appealed explicitly to the example of Constantine and Justinian.

All Protestants did not, however, sit down quietly to the consequence of such a claim—a multitude of monist church-states, in each of which the ruler claimed to control the church by divine authority and the subjects followed the religion of their ruler (a doctrine known as *cuius regio, eius religio*). If this formula was effectively endorsed in Germany and England by the Lutheran and Anglican traditions, as it had been for centuries by the Eastern Orthodox, so that in all three a state church became the norm, it was not at all the case in regard to Calvinism or to any other of the more radical wings of the Reformation. Here, on the contrary, the essential freedom of the church from the state was asserted, though since this could lead on (as in John Calvin's Geneva) to the effective subordination of the state to the church, the bonding of the two might look much the same to the outside observer. With time, however, the Calvinist position led in practice as well as in theory to the reemergence of a "Free Church," that is to say, a church uncontrolled by the state. This pattern was evolving very notably in seventeenth-century England and in its overflow to New England in North America. Although the English Puritans, for the most part, had wanted to impose their own model of church upon everyone, and to a large extent did so during the years of the Commonwealth after the civil war and abolition of monarchy, the very dividedness of their own views rendered this prospect impossible. If the authority of the state to impose uniformity upon the church was denied, no other entity could do so, and the unity of church and state was bound to come to an end.

Historically, the Christian tradition thus presents a whole range of models for the relationship of religion and politics, models deriving from different periods and circumstances. This diversity was possible and remains possible largely because of the lack of any overt political dimension in early Christianity. In consequence, it has remained highly malleable to cultural circumstances and pressure from the state. That pressure, characteristic of almost all Christian history subsequent to Constantine, was first systematized within the Eastern Orthodox tradition, both in the Byzantine Empire and then in the Russian empire and elsewhere. It was later systematized in the West as the modern state system developed, claiming sovereignty even in the field of religion.

Nevertheless, the basic dualism always implicit within Christianity was not suppressed. This is most obvious in the cases of Roman Catholicism and Calvinism. It is true that in practice the state governments within Catholic Europe, such as Spain and France, exercised almost as great a control over the running of the church as happened in Lutheran and Anglican countries. But the existence of the papacy maintained in principle a distinct religious source of authority. Moreover, even in Orthodoxy, Lutheranism, and Anglicanism the claims of monism remained to some extent restricted by the recognition that fundamental doctrine could not be altered by the state. When in England a Roman Catholic, James II, ascended the throne in 1685 an inherently contradictory situation resulted. The bishops could neither obey him nor disobey him. To obey him could lead to the overthrow of the established Protestant church; to disobey him meant reneging on their religious obligation to accept royal authority. The result was revolution, which the bishops could not sanction but could also hardly deplore. A subsequent law confined the crown to Protestants.

The Modern Period

If the Constantinian model of a single church controlled and protected by a single emperor ceased to be practical once the empire broke apart in the centuries following his death, the resurrection of that model in national terms characteristic of the Reformation, in which the state holds authority over religion, has also been discredited. The modern church is back very largely with a clear dualism—the separation of church and state, whether the church itself is conceived of in unitary, more or less Roman, terms, or whether it is seen as a more fragmentary network of diverse groups. On the one side, such a fragmentary network may not be wholly unfaithful to the sort of decentralized communion of churches existing in the pre-Constantinian era; on the other, the World Council of Churches, in full existence since 1948, has endeavoured to make the network less fragmentary and more comparable to what in the Catholic communion is achieved by the Vatican in Rome.

When in modern times we consider the relationship of Christianity to politics, we must look at four levels: denominations, leaders, laity, and intellectuals. The first is the denominational level. Although in most parts of the world—the major exception being Eastern Europe—the specific approach of the various denominational traditions has greatly weakened, these still provide an underlying point of departure, alike for church leaders, the laity, and intellectuals. Anglicans continue to look at the political dimension of religion with preconceptions a little different from those of Lutherans or Catholics, though these differentiations that were still strong at the start of the twentieth century were enormously weakened by its close.

When a political problem arises with religious or moral implications people often say, "The church should speak out," meaning almost always the bishops or other church leaders. An analysis of the relations between Christianity and politics must distinguish carefully between church leadership, the laity, and intellectuals. All three are important. In a traditional but little educated society, the political leadership of bishops may remain all important in an emergency. Yet what is striking is the caution of bishops even in circumstances where one might expect them to give a strong lead. It may well be, nevertheless, that more political guidance has been offered in the late twentieth century by the Catholic episcopate, in particular in the form of pastoral letters, than ever before.

The central relationship between Christianity and politics remains a lay one. Even during the time of the Reformation it was claimed that kings, in excluding the power of the papacy and altering the doctrine and practice of the church, were acting by virtue of a basic lay responsibility for the church and its relationship to society. The state's control of the church was justified in terms of the church membership of those exercising control. It could be seen as a necessary piece of anticlericalism, the only way to curb the huge power bishops and popes had exercised hitherto. Thus a certain kind of lay role shaped the way in which the relationship between religion and politics was conceived. When it was challenged, it was mostly by other lay people. In the early twentieth century where the Catholic Church was often discriminated against on account of the dominance of either Protestantism or anticlericalist feelings, Catholics developed new forms of lay activity, particularly Catholic Action, a network of lay groups active in the social arena, together with lay-organized but religiously based political parties, chief among them the Christian Democratic parties that were powerful in Europe and Latin America after the Second World War. But lay Christian involvement in politics in the modern world, especially in democratic societies, is often and increasingly on a purely individual basis. Although it may be important that a Christian witness is brought to bear in regard to political issues, this generally happens in almost anonymous ways so that it becomes difficult to analyze the interaction of Christianity and politics. Where Christians continue to be mobilized within a pluralist society on a specifically political platform, it is usually on a basis of single-issue politics and may well be symbolic of a feeling of weakness.

Fourth, there is the level of intellectual or charismatic leadership. For the twentieth century one may think of Reinhold Niebuhr, Jacques Maritain, Barbara Ward, Paulo Freire, Martin Luther King Jr., and Gustavo Gutiérrez. Perhaps even more poignantly one can recall the roles of Karl Barth and Dietrich Bonhoeffer in challenging Nazism. None of these people could in a formal way speak in the name of the church, and what they said was repudiated at the time by many Christians. Nevertheless, it is the teaching of such individuals that has very largely shaped the subsequent attitudes of Christians toward politics. These are the people who can most aptly be called the heirs to the prophets of Israel. Free to speak less cautiously than ecclesiastical authority, capable of analyzing both Christian faith and contemporary circumstances, they provide the sharp edge of the encounter between religion and politics. It could be claimed that the church as a politically conscious community is guided largely by the inspiration of such action-orientated thinkers, so long as they keep sufficiently in touch with the grass roots and with a popularly recognizable expression of faith.

Finally, beyond the four basic levels, there is the role of the subgroup to consider. Quite often it is in this form that Christianity is most effective in relating to the political order. Consider, for example, the Jesuits, especially as they were before the dissolution of their order in 1773 and as they are again today, or the Clapham Sect, a group of upper-class Anglican evangelicals who did much to bring about the British abolition of the slave trade in the early nineteenth century. Consider the way a century later the Anglican Church Missionary Society lobbied successfully for the establishment of a British protectorate over Uganda, or the influence of the Quakers on legitimizing pacifism and conscientious objection. Maryknoll, the London Catholic Institute for International Relations, and Opus Dei are other contemporary examples of relatively small, well-organized groups with a consistent outlook or lobbying policy operating at the interface of religion and politics with an effectiveness generally unobtainable either by charismatic individuals, able as they may

be, or ecclesiastical authorities bound to represent and be restrained by the apathy and mixed viewpoint characteristic of any larger group of Christians.

Five Contrasting Tendencies

Post-Reformation Christianity has made an impact on the shaping of politics principally in five different, yet overlapping, directions, all of which have survived into the late twentieth century. These five directions may be described as tendencies toward autocracy, nationalism, imperialism, democracy, and, socialism.

Autocracy. To start with autocracy: kingship was sacralized and idealized in the Middle Ages, but it was held in check by various other things no less important—the church and the papacy, natural law, even parliaments of various sorts. Ultimate authority in medieval eyes, at least nonpapalist eyes, was usually conceived in terms of the supremacy of law. The Renaissance downplayed everything except the king. Catholicism, Lutheranism, and Anglicanism all went in this direction, though the absolutist tendencies in Anglicanism were rendered ineffectual by the seventeenth-century victory of Parliament over king. Nevertheless, in general, at the beginning of the modern period Christianity's political doctrine appeared to be one supremely justificatory of authority, especially royal authority. Romans 13 was its prime text: "The authorities that exist have been established by God. Consequently he who rebels against the authority is rebelling against what God has instituted." In a democratic age such a text could, of course, apply to democracy, but in a Europe still overwhelmingly autocratic it appeared to justify absolute monarchy and to condemn anyone who sought to change it. The fearfully antireligious consequences of the French Revolution greatly strengthened this conviction in most Catholic minds but, perhaps, hardly less in Lutheran or Orthodox ones. Throughout most of the nineteenth century, in consequence, the central political sympathy of Christianity appeared to be toward autocracy. Even in England most ecclesiastics supported the Tory Party in opposing moves toward a liberalization of the state.

In the nineteenth century some Catholics, like the French priest and philosopher Félicité-Robert de Lamennais, saw already how dangerous a policy of crown and altar could be, and, despite the extreme antiliberalism of Pope Pius IX, they were encouraged to some extent by his successor, Leo XIII. The Catholics who formed the Center Party may well have been the best democrats in Germany from the 1870s to the 1930s, and they were followed by the Catholics led by Luigi Sturzo, a priest and political leader who formed the Italian Popular Party in 1919, but both were sacrificed by the Vatican in a vain bid to placate Adolf Hitler and Benito Mussolini. From the age of France's Louis XIV to that of Hitler, the majority Christian view favoured autocracy as a political system. It was protective of the no less autocratic character of the pope's rule in the Papal States, which survived until 1870, when they were incorporated into the newly unified Italy, and within the church itself. If the French Revolution had pressed church leadership into the autocratic embrace, so did the coming of communism. It is striking how willing even leading English Catholics were in the 1930s to sympathize with Mussolini and Hitler, seen as comparable with Portugal's António de Oliveira Salazar and Spain's Francisco Franco, because they were all enemies of communism. Only with the Second World War did the preference for autocracy effectively disappear.

Nationalism. Next comes a fostering of nationalism. Here too the roots are ancient. The English nation-state, proto-model of Europe's political nations, was being fostered by the great monk historian Bede no later than the eighth century. When Joan of Arc encouraged Frenchmen to repel the English invaders of France in the fifteenth century, she had no hesitation in declaring "all those who fight against the holy kingdom of France fight against the Lord Jesus." When John Milton appealed to the English Parliament in 1640, he did not hesitate to ask "Why else was this Nation chosen before any other?" In each case a linked reading of the Bible and national history had fostered the conviction that God had chosen France, England, or Spain, Russia or America as his "elect people," to whom he had confided a unique destiny and whose cause, in consequence, had a special sanctity. The Reformation immensely enhanced England's consciousness of being an elect nation, a consciousness carried in the seventeenth century across the Atlantic. Nationalism backed by religion from then to the late twentieth century in its Serbian and Croatian forms has proved a formidably ruthless tool for eliminating enemies and the unwanted.

In many cases, a religious nationalism that started defensively later turned into an offensive force and, in doing so, stimulated counter-nationalisms among its neighbours. Thus Russian and German nationalism have stimulated Polish nationalism, and English nationalism triggered Irish nationalism. It is when conflicts of this sort are exacerbated by a religious frontier that the religious undergirding of nationalism is most acute. The English invasion of Ireland from the reign of Elizabeth I onward was very much a Protestant invasion intended to ensure that Ireland remained in Protestant hands. As the Irish insisted for the most part on remaining Catholics, their nationalism took on a predominantly Catholic character. Church and nation went together in self-defense against the linked domination of the English and Protestantism. Although English Protestant nationalism eventually faded at home, in Ireland it remained very much alive. The Ulster unionism of the twentieth century is essentially the last continuation of an English Protestant identity forged in the years after the Spanish Armada, when England was threatened by invasion from Catholic Spain and Ireland was seen as in danger of falling to Spanish power. The Catholic character of Polish nationalism was forged in much the same way as a reaction to Orthodox Russia and Protestant Prussia partitioning Catholic Poland.

Nationalist fervour is almost universally heightened by a somewhat mythical reading of history. Nowhere has this been clearer than in Serbia. Here, national identity was for centuries maintained by the institutions of the Serbian Orthodox Church, while the nation itself was divided between the Muslim Ottoman Empire and the Catholic Habsburg Empire. The foundation myth was that surrounding the Battle of Kosovo in 1389, when the Serb prince Lazar died in battle with an invading Ottoman army. The figure of Lazar eating his last meal before the battle and prophesying that one of his lords would betray him was transformed into the image of Christ, a mystical identity stressed in literature and art, particularly in the nineteenth century when the modern Serb state was coming into existence. No nationalism has had more intense a religious undergirding able to stimulate the most powerful hostility toward Muslims and Catholics.

Imperialism. An aggressive nationalism turns naturally into imperialism, and here close connections with Christianity must be noted. Imperialism expresses the dominance of the Christian West over the rest of the world from the sixteenth to the twentieth century. Europe's sudden, highly successful expansion was seen by Catholic and Protestant alike as best explicable in providential terms. It was perhaps forgotten how many defeats had been suffered in previous centuries, how many previously Christian lands had passed to Islam. If they were remembered, it seemed merely to highlight what was then happening.

It was the Spaniards, as the vast extent of the new world of America dawned on them, together with their own rather easy conquest of huge tracts of it, who first developed a belief that all this must be intended by God. They were, it seemed, uniquely favored. The division of all newly discovered lands between Spain and Portugal by Pope Alexander VI, in 1494, simply confirmed the religious significance of their empire, proclaimed again and again as a tool for evangelization. However badly the native inhabitants of America were treated, however bitterly Bartolomé de Las Casas, a sixteenth-century Dominican, denounced the behavior of the Conquistadores, there never was a closer link between government and church than in Spanish America. The king of Spain entirely controlled the church in his overseas dominions even more than he controlled it at home. Nor in this was the Portuguese empire any different. Christianization was conceived as Portugalization even into the second half of the twentieth century. The religious undergirding of Portuguese imperialism, reconfirmed by, for instance, the Concordat and Missionary Agreement with the Vatican of 1940, was a matter at once of ideology, of the political organization of Portuguese overseas territories, and even of the methodology of missionary activity.

As economic and political power in Europe shifted away from the Iberian peninsula to Britain, France, and, later, Germany, something similar happened, though Christianity was seldom tied quite so closely to their forms of imperialism. Nevertheless, the British Victorian sense of being a chosen people, providentially destined to carry the Gospel and its benefits throughout the world precisely through imperial and economic power was clear. As Edward Benson, archbishop of Canterbury, declared in 1894, "The Church of England is now charged with the world's Christianity."

The scale of the British Empire and the diversity of churches within nineteenth-century Britain made it impossible, however, to establish the sort of relationship between the British Empire and the Church of England that Spain had established between its empire and Catholicism. Britain, on the contrary, early learned the benefits of religious tolerance. It knew that it could rule Catholic Quebec, Hindu and Muslim India, only if it did not push Protestantism down the throats of its imperial subjects. Moreover, its willingness to admit Christian missionaries of all nationalities as well as many churches into its dominions ensured a further watering down within the imperial-Christian alliance. Nevertheless, it was also true that the churches were offered in many ways a privileged position in India and elsewhere—the Church of England above all—and that in a subtle if unde-

finable way Christianity validated imperialism in moral terms, while imperialism offered Christianity what looked like an open door to most of the world and encouraged Asians and Africans to respect Christianity as the religion of both civilization and power. If the effect in Asia was relatively limited, in Africa it proved overwhelming.

Only in the second half of the twentieth century has this relationship faded away in regard to Europe, and that only because the empires of Europe have faded away while that of the United States—less formal but still more world-embracing—has replaced them. Here too a relationship between imperialism and Christianity has been unmistakable. While European missions have declined, American missionaries have greatly increased in number since the 1950s, above all from the most emphatically Protestant denominations, evangelical and fundamentalist. Although it is not the case that all American missionaries are in some way agents of American imperialism, some have been so, even in organizational terms. But far more important than the latter is the ethos they spread, an ethos that sees America as God's chosen people so that the fortunes of Christianity everywhere are in some way tied to American success, just as in earlier ages they were tied to Spanish or British success. The face offered by Christianity in many parts of Latin America, Asia, and Africa remains a distinctly imperialistic one. What has changed is that the imperialism in question is now American.

Democracy. From imperialism we may turn to democracy. If Christianity was in many ways a foundation stone for autocracy, it has been no less a nurse for democracy. Both have roots in the Middle Ages. If the church's episcopal government had assumed a highly autocratic form by then—though bishops remained controlled by a canon law of exceptional complexity—Christian life had long had its more democratic side, which took the form in the late Middle Ages of lay confraternities and guilds. It may be in these urban associations that we can find the most lively roots of Western democracy, but they were naturally linked with the medieval development of parliamentary institutions. Although many withered during the Renaissance, the English Parliament weathered royal autocracy and retained its sense of a tradition that dated back at least to Magna Carta (1215). When civil war broke out in England in 1642, both sides claimed religious sanctioning. King Charles I based his claim on the divine right of kingship; Parliament, and, still more, some of its radical supporters, developed a theory of government based on the Bible as seen through Calvinist eyes and on English medieval and parliamentary tradition. What followed the Restoration of Charles II was a mixed constitution upholding both the theory of kingship and the effective primacy in power of Parliament, representing for the most part the landed and the urban middle class. Although this was certainly not a recognition of democracy, the claims of democracy rising to the surface in Oliver Cromwell's army during the civil war years were carried implicitly across to New England and came to prevail in America before being recognized in England.

If modern Western democracy owes most to the American experience and example, that experience would hardly have been possible without its matrix in New England Calvinist Protestantism. It is noticeable that in Europe the countries where democracy, even if still somewhat limited in scope (especially in regard to women), first flourished are almost all ones with a religious culture, either Calvinist or closely comparable—for example, Switzerland, Holland, Scotland. A Presbyterian or Congregationalist form of church government prepared the way for a democratic form of state government. The more divided Protestantism became, as in the United States, the more democracy flourished. This was not merely a matter of forms of government but rather of a whole program of what can be described as the liberal reform of society. It is noticeable how closely the Free Churches in England became linked to the Liberal Party and then to the early Labour Party, which, it has been claimed again and again, owed more to Methodism than to Marxism.

By the late nineteenth century it was probably taken for granted by many that Protestant Christianity made for a liberal and parliamentary government, Catholic Christianity for an illiberal autocracy. Yet, even for that time, this would be a simplification. Catholics in Britain, America, or Germany could be as much at home with parliamentary government as Protestants. Indeed, in Germany the Protestant identity of the kaiser and the political doctrine of Lutheranism kept Lutherans far happier with a rather autocratic state than it did Catholics. Only after the Second World War, however, did the Vatican and European Catholics as a whole become reconciled to a democratic system. This change occurred under the impact not only of the war and the discrediting of right-wing Catholic politics represented by Marshal Henri-Philippe Pétain and the Vichy regime in France but also of influential Catholic theorists like Jacques Maritain and

Christopher Dawson. From this point, any large contrast between Catholic and Protestant forms of Christianity in relation to democracy and autocracy disappears, even though it would continue to exist for a few more years in what were at the time culturally backward areas such as Spain, Portugal, and much of Latin America. Yet it may still seem ironic, in the light of past history, that Christians in the late twentieth century have so often taken it for granted that Christianity and democracy go hand in hand.

Socialism. Beyond liberalism, one may say, lies socialism. The Christian encouragement of socialism across the past hundred years is as important as anything in shaping the modern political face of Christianity. William Temple, archbishop of Canterbury (1942–1944) and one of the great Anglican leaders of the twentieth century, once remarked while still a young man that there was only one choice to be made: between socialism and heresy. Socialism can be defined and practiced in many different ways, but the most interesting political question as regards modern Christianity is whether Christianity can avoid being socialist without losing its own soul. Temple's close friend, R. H. Tawney, became the leading theorist of the Labour Party and wrote several of its manifestos and an immensely influential book, *Equality* (1931). He was also a devout Anglo-Catholic. The symbolic model behind Christian socialism is the account in the first chapters of Acts where the first believers "held everything in common. Selling their possessions and goods, they gave to anyone as he had need" (Acts 2, 44–45). It was an ideal that many Christians have sought to implement across the ages, mostly in monasteries or in other forms of "alternative community" removed from the inequalities of the ordinary world. Instead of opting out, however, should one not struggle to realize a greater measure of equality in the whole of society?

If such was the thrust behind various socialistic movements in the nineteenth and early twentieth centuries in Europe, and still more recently in the liberation theology of Latin America, one may come to recognize in retrospect that the great social tragedy of the twentieth century was the hijacking of socialism by Marxism and its consequent wide discrediting. Nevertheless, the concern for social justice apparent in a series of papal encyclicals beginning in 1891 with Leo XIII's *Rerum Novarum* (on capital and labor), in the Second Vatican Council's *Pastoral Constitution on the Church in the Modern World* (1965), and in numerous documents of the World Council of Churches makes sense only within what one can best call a socialist approach. Despite the denunciation of socialism in the 1980s, the age of Ronald Reagan and Margaret Thatcher (both of whom could appeal to Christianity when it suited them), it seems unlikely that the churches will entirely abandon this approach, which appears in the context of the twentieth century the most plausible reembodiment of the message of the Old Testament prophets Amos and Isaiah. It is countered by those who claim that the true social message of Christianity is one that encourages individuals to be successful and then to be charitable in their success, rather than one focused on the public protection of the poor and the unsuccessful.

These two views may provide the terrain on which the future relationship of Christianity to political society will be fought. The one side is grounded upon a tradition that condemned usury in the Middle Ages, that stimulated the trade guilds with their meticulous control of commercial processes, and that has insisted upon concepts like the just wage and the just price—the belief that the determination of wages and prices should depend not only on market forces but on the responsibility of society to ensure that work is rewarded according to the reasonable needs of workers. The other side looks back on the way in which Protestantism provided the ground for the rise of capitalism through its release of the values of individualism and the pursuit of prosperity. It is significant that Tawney, whose *Equality* has been for many the bible of a non-Marxist socialism, was also a historian who wrote the hardly less well known work, *Religion and the Rise of Capitalism* (1926). It may be that Max Weber's attempt (in *Protestant Ethic and the Spirit of Capitalism,* 1920) to link Protestantism and capitalism is too simplified at the theoretical level, but it is not open to question that the modern capitalist economy largely began in Protestant England and expanded first to other predominantly Protestant countries.

The deep theological contrast between Catholic and Protestant approaches to the church, to salvation, and moral life can hardly not be reflected in approaches to public justice and the right ordering of society. It could well be that continental Europe remains primarily shaped by Catholic approaches, modern America by Protestant ones. If so, while the one will seek what in a large sense can be called socialist solutions, the other will remain wedded to capitalist ones. But a socialist Christianity as represented most recently by liberation theology goes deeper than that because it challenges the covert collusion between church leadership and the class of the rich that has dominated Christian history, both Catholic and Protestant, ever since the Constantinian revolution.

Christianity and the Political Order

The impression left by a review of the relations between Christianity and political reality is their flexibility and the near impossibility of considering any one relationship normative. Although Islam began its history in a highly public and military way, which has always provided a normative model for the ideal Muslim political order, no such thing exists in Christianity. In many ways this absence of a model is characteristic of every side of Christianity. Just because Jesus wrote nothing, and what was written about him was written by many different hands in a language other than his own, there is a lack of precision from the start that has enabled Christianity to reshape itself time and again. This is particularly true of its relationship with the political order. Although the intense politicization of the Constantinian era has never quite been thrown off, it cannot obliterate the fact that for centuries before Constantine Christian life could be characterized by its strongly apolitical and otherworldly values. Christianity's incarnational tendency has made it enter into the culture and sociopolitical construction of remarkably different peoples and periods, and the resulting diversities in the political face of the church can seem overwhelming.

What is there in common? Four elements seem fairly constant. First comes the dualism that separates religious from secular authority. While, as we have seen, this element has frequently been under threat, it has quickly reemerged again and again, and where it has been denied, the authenticity of Christianity itself can be seen as imperiled. Second, and linked with the recognition that Caesar has rights in an order derived from God but independent of the Christian dispensation, goes a wider recognition of natural law. Although some Christians, especially within the Protestant tradition, have dismissed the claims of natural law, nevertheless their recognition has been one of the most central and characteristic marks of Christian political thought, and it explains why much of the latter is universalist by its nature. It is thought about the world—God's world—as a whole and not just about Christian societies. Third, there is in the Gospels a hard-to-interpret balance between present and future, between what may be called this-worldliness and other-worldliness. This balance—or, perhaps, jerky pursuit of a balance—leads to quietism on the one hand, to social activism on the other. The central Christian tradition has perennially laid claim to both. Finally, there is the voice of the prophets. Christianity inherited Amos, and Amos refuses to be silenced. In vastly different ages and circumstances the simple duty to speak out in favor of the poor and the oppressed has regularly demonstrated the vitality of the tradition. An absence of such prophetic activity may provide the litmus test as to whether in this or that place the subtle ability of the state and secularity to emasculate Christianity or replace it with a counterfeit model, more congenial to the powers of this world, has indeed succeeded.

See also *Africa, Christian; Anticlericalism; Calvinism; Capitalism; Catholicism, Roman; Christian democracy; Christianity in Asia; English revolution; Enlightenment; Europe, Eastern; Europe, Western; Jesus; Natural law; Protestantism; Reformation; Social gospel; State churches; Vatican; Vatican Council, Second; Weber, Max; World Council of Churches.* See also specific countries and denominations.

Adrian Hastings

BIBLIOGRAPHY

Barnes, T. D. *Constantine and Eusebius.* Cambridge: Harvard University Press, 1981.

Baum, Gregory. *Theology and Society.* New York: Paulist Press, 1987.

Brayshaw, David. *The First America.* Cambridge: Cambridge University Press, 1991.

Brouwer, Steve, Paul Gifford, and Susan D. Rose, eds. *Exporting the American Gospel.* New York: Routledge, 1996.

Burns, J. H., ed. *The Cambridge History of Medieval Political Thought, c. 350–c. 1450.* Cambridge: Cambridge University Press, 1988.

Cullmann, Oscar. *The State in the New Testament.* London: SCM, 1955.

D'Entrèves, A. P. *Natural Law.* London: Hutchinson, 1951.

Frend, W. H. C. *The Rise of Christianity.* London: Darton, Longman, and Todd, 1984.

Hastings, Adrian. *Church and State: The English Experience.* Exeter: University of Exeter Press, 1991.

———, *The Construction of Nationhood: Ethnicity, Religion, and Nationalism.* Cambridge: Cambridge University Press, 1997.

Kee, Alistair. *Constantine versus Christ.* London: SCM, 1982.

Morris, Colin. *The Papal Monarchy.* Oxford: Clarendon Press, 1989.

Norman, Edward. *Christianity in the Southern Hemisphere: The Churches in Latin America and South Africa.* Oxford: Oxford University Press, 1981.

Temple, William. *Christianity and Social Order.* London: SCM, 1942.

Troeltsch, Ernst. *The Social Teaching of the Christian Churches.* London: Allen and Unwin, 1931.

Christianity in Asia

From the first century the Christian faith entered portions of Asia, which is defined as South Central Asia (Afghanistan, Bangladesh, Bhutan, India, Kazakstan, Kyrgyzstan, Maldives, Nepal, Pakistan, Sri Lanka, Tajikistan, Turkmenistan, and Uzbekistan), Southeastern Asia (Brunei, Cambodia, East Timor, Indonesia, Laos, Malaysia, Myanmar, Philippines, Singapore, Thailand, and North and South Vietnam), and East Asia (China, North and South Korea, Japan, Taiwan, Macao, and Mongolia).

According to tradition, Christianity first entered Asia in India with the arrival there in A.D. 52 of the Apostle Thomas. Nestorian Christianity, which derived its name from Nestorius, fifth-century patriarch of Constantinople, came to China in 635. In the next several centuries its missionaries also went to India and Central Asia. Roman Catholic missionaries reached China for a short period in the thirteenth century. However, their greatest impact came from the fifteenth to nineteenth centuries as they introduced Christianity into India, Indonesia, Cambodia, Vietnam, the Philippines, China, and Korea.

The Protestant form of Christianity was brought to Taiwan by the Dutch in the early seventeenth century. In the nineteenth and twentieth centuries Protestant missionary representatives from several Western colonial powers went to many Asian countries where the Roman Catholics had preceded them. Orthodox Christianity came to Russia in 988, but its message did not reach Central Asia, which throughout most of the twentieth century belonged to the Soviet Union (and in the early 1990s, with the fall of communism there, became several independent nations). Indigenous Christianity, often an offshoot of earlier Catholic and Protestant efforts, has spread widely in many countries since World War II. Early missionization had been closely associated with the expansion of the colonial empires of Western countries. As a consequence, Christians in Asia were frequently considered as representatives of colonial powers.

The response to the Christian message in Asia has varied. Before World War II the most receptive audience were people who previously had adhered to folk religions not intimately associated with one of the major historic religious faiths. This was because, in part, there was no text-based religion with a formal hierarchy among these peoples. Often marginalized culturally, economically, religiously, and politically as ethnic minorities in modern states, they sometimes found Christianity to offer them a path to self-identity and self-esteem.

In the last half of the twentieth century the Christian faith has spread dramatically among the majority population groups in Korea, China, Singapore, Indonesia, and Vietnam. These new Christians, unlike those from the more marginal minorities, have come from those whose ancestors adhered to the traditional Asian religious traditions, usually a mixture of Buddhism, Confucianism, Daoism, and nominal Islam.

South Central Asia

Since the time when Christianity first entered India in the first century, both Roman Catholic and Protestant mission groups have been active. Best known of the Catholic missionaries were Francis Xavier (1542–1545), the first foreign missionary to India, and Robert de Nobili (1605–1645), an Italian Jesuit, who concentrated on winning the higher castes to the Christian faith. William Carey and Alexander Duff are considered among the most significant of the Protestant representatives. Active missionary work was prohibited by the East India Company in its territories (1706–1823), but much more freedom came for evangelization when India came under British control in 1858. With independence from Great Britain in 1947, India declared itself a "secular" state, guaranteeing equal protection for all religions and noninterference by the state in matters purely religious. Although there is freedom for local Christians, the government has made it difficult for expatriate missionaries to enter the country.

Despite many instances of local persecution, Christianity has been able to spread freely, particularly by movements of mass conversion in Andhra Pradesh in the southeast, very early in the Portuguese colony of Goa, and among tribal groups in the north among the Khasi, Garo, Mizo, and Naga peoples. Catholic, Protestant, and Orthodox Christians constitute only about 4 percent of the total population of India, but in the small northern states of Mizoram, Meghalaya, and Nagaland the percentage is a dominant 85 percent. Despite the relatively small number of Christians, nearly two hundred indigenous Indian mission societies have sprung up with a total of eleven thousand missionaries.

The Apostle Thomas may also have introduced Christianity to Sri Lanka. Subsequent Christian influence came through colonial efforts by the Portuguese in 1505, the Dutch in 1655, and the British in the nineteenth century. During the past 275 years the Christian population de-

creased from 21 percent to 8 percent, largely because of the influence of nominalism, a weak form of Christianity, and the anti-Christian attitude of Buddhism, which was declared the state religion in 1972.

Although the Christian message came early to Pakistan through the Nestorians in the eighth century and through the Jesuits in 1594, no lasting results were achieved. Modern Catholic Christianity began in 1842, after the conquest of Sindh by the British. At present, the work of the Catholic Church, whose members constitute less than 1 percent of the population, is maintained by three indigenous congregations of sisters and ten foreign orders and congregations of priests, brothers, and sisters.

Protestant Christianity was introduced to Pakistan in 1833. A large revival that occurred in 1904 ultimately resulted in six of the thirty "scheduled" Hindu castes becoming Christian by 1930. Despite the fact that Pakistan declared itself an Islamic republic in 1956, nine years after independence, many new Protestant agencies entered the country. At present, Protestant Christianity numbers no more than 2 percent of the population, and adherents of all Christian persuasions face the pressure of increasing Islamization.

Bangladesh, formerly East Pakistan, became independent from Pakistan in 1971, and, after a period when it was a secular state (1971–1988), became an Islamic republic. Both Catholics and Protestants came into this area in the nineteenth century, but growth of Christianity was minimal except for mass movements among the tribes of the Chittagong Hills. The total Christian population of the country is less than 1 percent.

Whatever Christian influence existed early in Afghanistan's history was wiped out by Timur, a Mongol conqueror, in the fourteenth century. Currently, the Christian community, slightly less than 0.1 percent of the population, is composed largely of foreign technicians, diplomats, and visitors. Very few of the local populace have dared to make a Christian commitment in the face of fierce opposition by radical Islamic factions fighting for control of the country.

The Himalayan region along the northern boundary of India has a population of about twenty-two million and is composed of Nepal, a Hindu kingdom; Bhutan, with Buddhism as the state religion; and Sikkim, formerly a Buddhist hereditary monarchy and now an Indian state. All of these states have traditionally been resistant to the Christian faith, but within the past five years revival movements have occurred, so that nearly 15 percent of Sikkim's population and

10 percent of Nepal's people have committed themselves as Christians. Proselytization is forbidden by the government in both Nepal and Bhutan.

The five states—Kazakstan, Kyrgyzstan, Tajikistan, Turkmenistan, and Uzbekistan—that were formerly part of the Soviet Union are now independent and seek to overthrow, often with internal conflict, the yoke of communism. Although declaring themselves to be secular or undetermined, they are in varying degrees influenced by Islam. Christians, largely Orthodox of immigrant minorities, number as low as 4–5 percent in Tajikistan, Turkmenistan, and Uzbekistan and as high as 11 percent and 27 percent in Kyrgyzstan and Kazakstan, respectively.

Southeastern Asia

Although Buddhism was declared the state religion of Myanmar (Burma) in 1961, this government edict was withdrawn in 1965, and there is now freedom of religion, albeit under a totalitarian government. For nationalistic reasons, the government expelled all foreign missionaries in 1966. It has not interfered directly with the work of the churches.

Nestorians reached Myanmar in the tenth century, Catholics by 1544, and Protestants by 1813. Today Baptists, whose founder in Burma was Adoniram Judson, and Catholics are the two largest Christian groups. Most of the Baptist Christians are not found among the Burmese peoples but among the Karen, Chin, and Kachin ethnic groups in the northern section of the country. Protestants number 5 percent of the population and Catholics 1 percent.

Christianity first reached Indonesia when Portuguese traders and missionaries came to the Moluccan isles (Maluku) in 1512. Several Catholic missionary orders came later in the sixteenth century and gained many converts, often promising them Portuguese protection against enemy neighboring kingdoms. Dutch traders expelled the Portuguese, including missionaries, in 1605, thus inaugurating the eras of the Dutch East Indies Trading Company (1605–1800) and Dutch colonial control (1816–1945). Dutch ascendancy in the area resulted in the arrival of many European and, sometime later, American mission agencies. Some of the established churches, largely Dutch Reformed, were under state control. The Dutch colonial administration occasionally prohibited missionary work in socially and politically sensitive areas.

The growth of Christianity has been uneven, with large people movements to Christ in areas dominated by traditional folk religion. Beginning in the mid-1960s, some of the greatest growth of both Protestant and Catholic Christianity in the world has occurred in Indonesia. A revival, sparked largely by lay people, occurred on the island of Timor in the eastern part of the archipelago in the early 1960s. Other movements to Christ resulted from the violent anticommunist repression following the abortive attempt by communist rebel forces to take over the Indonesian government in 1965. The Indonesian constitution, formulated in 1945 after the country's independence, granted freedom of religion despite the country's overwhelming Muslim majority. This was reinforced in 1965 by the "five principles" (pancasila), which made it necessary for every citizen to embrace a belief in Islam, Protestantism, Catholicism, or Hindu-Buddhism. The easiest, least politically complicated option for many was to choose the Christian faith.

Areas that have experienced the greatest growth in Christianity are east and central Java, Karoland in north Sumatra, and east and west Kalimantan. For all of Indonesia Protestants average 9 percent of the total population of two hundred million, and Catholics represent 3 percent. Christians number 30–85 percent in many of the island provinces such as East Timor (annexed in 1975), Irian Jaya (annexed in 1963), Maluku, and the E. Lesser Sunda Islands.

The Philippines are the only predominantly Christian country in Asia. Catholic priests reached these islands under the protection of Spanish armor in 1565. After five decades of evangelization directed toward the Malayo-Indonesian inhabitants, the entire country nominally embraced Christianity. Many Protestant mission agencies, with the door opened by American annexation of the Philippines in 1898, sent their representatives in the early 1900s. As a group they were outnumbered by the predominantly Catholic population. Nevertheless, they established comity agreements—plans for dividing the territory and work in such a way as not to compete directly with one another.

About 1 percent of the population, largely mountain dwellers dispersed through the nation, continue to believe in traditional folk religion. Muslim believers, tracing their origin to 1380, number about 8 percent and live largely in the southwest, Mindanao, the Sulu islands, and Palawan. Roman Catholicism, including the Philippine Independent Church, remains the dominant faith of nearly 80 percent of the population. Adherents of Protestant Christianity number 8–9 percent but have grown dramatically in the last decade. Since the time of American rule, church and state in the Philippines have been separated.

After the Philippines, Vietnam is the most Catholic country in Asia. In the first sixty years of missionary work, beginning from 1580, there were eighty thousand Catholics in the north and fifty thousand in the south. Growth continued at a slower pace until the late 1800s, but always with much persecution, until 1884, when France imposed a protectorate as French Indochina (including what is now Vietnam, Laos, and Cambodia). Catholic Christianity continued to grow in both North and South Vietnam, although with the victory of communism in the north, as many as six hundred thousand Catholic believers took refuge in the south, where they formed an influential anticommunist bloc supporting the government. With the fall of the regime in the south in 1975, and reunification of South and North Vietnam under the communists, the church, 9 percent Catholic and less than 1 percent Protestant, has continued to exist but with the repression characteristic of a Marxist regime.

Growth of Christianity in both communist Laos and Buddhist Kampuchea (Cambodia) has been very slow, with Christians numbering 2 percent and less than 1 percent of the population, respectively. In Thailand the Christian faith, with no more than 1 percent of the population classified as adherents, has not been able to penetrate the Buddhist world. Most of its converts have come from the Vietnamese, the Chinese, the Montagnards, and other ethnic minorities in the north of the country.

Catholic Christianity arrived in Malaysia with the Portuguese in the sixteenth century, and Protestantism was brought later by the Dutch and the British. The most responsive group has been the Chinese, followed by the Indians and aboriginal minorities. Very few Christians are found among the Malays, who are almost entirely Muslim. Protestants number about 5 percent and Catholics 4 percent. With similar ethnic and linguistic composition, the Republic of Singapore is 8 percent Protestant and 6 percent Catholic, with adherents largely from the Chinese and Indian populace. Because of Singapore's multiethnic and multifaith composition, the government has imposed restrictive legislation limiting overt evangelism.

East Asia

Christianity first entered East Asia during the Tang Dynasty in 635, with the arrival of Nestorian missionaries in China. A Franciscan Catholic missionary reached Beijing in 1294, but Catholicism did not establish itself until the Jesuits, led by Matteo Ricci (1552–1610), came at the end of the sixteenth century. Protestant Christianity commenced in 1807 with the arrival of Robert Morrison (1782–1834) of the London Missionary Society.

Both the Protestant and Catholic missionary movements were hindered greatly by being associated with the "unequal treaties" arising out of British efforts to import opium into China. (These treaties were imposed on China by Great Britain, which defeated it in 1840, and by other nations. When missionaries followed foreign diplomats and business people entering China under the terms of the treaties, the missionary movement came to be linked with imperialism and militarism.) Subsequently, Christianity was known as the foreign religion. With the coming of the Communist People's Republic of China in 1949, Christian missionaries were forced to leave China, and Chinese Christians, with both Catholics and Protestants numbering about two million, faced a difficult period of persecution, forced unity, loss of denominational identity, and destruction of meeting places and Bibles. This persecution was particularly intense during the Cultural Revolution (1966–1976). Churches began to reopen in the late 1970s, and since that time the number of Christians has increased spectacularly, with estimates placed anywhere from fifteen to sixty million. Catholic believers are divided between the government-approved Catholic Patriotic Association and those many congregations that retain their loyalty to the pope in Rome. Protestant Christians are found in the China Christian Council, related to the Three-Self Patriotic Movement, in thousands of autonomous house churches, and in student Christian fellowships on many college and university campuses. Technically, the constitution guarantees freedom of religion, but this has been interpreted diversely in many parts of the country. In some areas, freedom does indeed exist; in other sections, persecution and harassment continue. In the southwestern areas of China—Yunnan, Guangxi, and Guizhou—Christians from among the minority nationalities outnumber Han Chinese (culturally Chinese) Christians.

Christianity in both its Protestant and Catholic forms first came to Taiwan in the early 1600s. At this time about six thousand of the tribal people converted to Christianity under the Dutch, but this movement ceased with the Dutch expulsion by the Chinese in 1662. Protestant and Catholic missionaries returned to the island in the mid-1860s, and, apart from the World War II period, have been engaged in evangelism and nurturing of churches. Despite a great influx of missionaries coming after the fall of China's mainland to the Communist People's Republic of China in 1949, Christian growth for both Catholics and Protestants has not exceeded 5 percent of the population. Among the mountain tribal people, now labeled original inhabitants, Christianity is espoused by at least 50 percent of the population of three hundred thousand.

Christianity came to Hong Kong in 1842 after the territory was ceded to Great Britain. Christians are estimated to be about 15 percent of the population. With the return of Hong Kong to China in 1997, its churches were promised continued freedom of religion within their own territory as long as they did not interfere with churches on the mainland. A vigorous Hong Kong Evangelism 2000 program was promoted by Protestant churches.

Catholic missionaries reached Macao, a tiny peninsula about forty miles west of Hong Kong, in 1557, and used it as a base to send missionaries into China. Protestants arrived in 1807. About 10 percent of Macao's people are Christian. Much effective evangelism has been done in recent years among workers who have come from mainland China. With Macao's reversion to China in 1999, its churches were expected to be under the same guidelines as those in Hong Kong.

Catholicism entered Korea in the last decade of the eighteenth century, largely through Koreans who had learned of the faith in China. Korean scripture portions—translations of various books of the Bible—were distributed in Korea from China in 1831 and, one year later, the first Protestant missionary entered the country. These various Catholic and Protestant contacts led to many efforts of indigenous evangelization among the populace whose major religious faith was shamanism, which centered on spirits and spirit mediums. When religious freedom was gained in 1882, as a result of a treaty with the United States, many Koreans openly asked for baptism. Protestant Christians in Korea actively resisted the former Japanese colonial regime in 1919 and participated in moves to strengthen the country's national identity.

Today the Christian population of South Korea, with nearly twelve million Catholics (6 percent) and Protestants (28 percent), exceeds that of all other nations in Asia except the Philippines. Church growth continues at a rapid pace of nearly 6 percent annually in the south, bolstered by vigorous evangelistic efforts and also by the favor of the government, which views Christianity as an ideological means of resisting the encroachment of communism. In North Korea, a strong center of Christianity before its separation from the south following Word War II, all religions have been harshly suppressed, and the number of Christians is unknown.

The Catholic presence in Japan commenced in 1549 with the visit of Francis Xavier. By 1593 Catholic Christians numbered three hundred thousand, but with government prohibition in 1611, a severe persecution occurred. The church went through two hundred years of silence, emerging only when Catholic missionaries returned in 1859. Protestant missionaries arrived in Japan the same year and engaged in medical and educational activities. When the government removed all anti-Christian activities in 1878, both Catholics and Protestants were able to engage actively in evangelism. The Japanese constitution of 1889 made Shinto, the ancestral religion of Japan, the state religion. In December 1945, as a result of Japan's defeat in World War II, Shinto was separated from the state, and freedom of religion was guaranteed to all. More Protestant and Catholic missionaries, proportionally to the population, have been working in Japan than in any other country. Despite this, Christians number only seven hundred thousand, about 3 percent of Japan's total population.

See also *Colonialism; Missionaries.*

Ralph R. Covell

BIBLIOGRAPHY

Athyal, Saphir, ed. *The Church in Asia Today: Challenges and Opportunities.* Singapore: The Asia Lausanne Committee for World Evangelization, 1996.

Covell, Ralph R. *The Liberating Gospel in China: The Christian Faith among China's Minority Peoples.* Grand Rapids, Mich.: Baker, 1995.

Hoke, Daniel E., ed. *The Church in Asia.* Chicago: Moody, 1975.

Hunter, Alan, and Chan Kim-Kwong. *Protestantism in Contemporary China.* New York: Cambridge University Press, 1993.

Johnstone, Patrick. *Operation World.* Grand Rapids, Mich.: Zondervan, 1993.

Church Property

See *Taxation*

Citizenship

Citizenship refers to the liberties, rights, and obligations that define an individual's membership in the nation-state.

The terms of membership and participation in the nation-state evolved in Europe and North America in the nineteenth and twentieth centuries. The conditions for membership in society are on the whole framed in terms of the rights and obligations of individual citizens in their relations with one another and with the state authority. Together with struggles over the place of the church (or different religions) in national public life and the issues of distributive justice, the terms of citizenship—that is, the admission of the lower strata into full civic, political, and economic national membership—have been and remain the defining issue of the modern era.

Definitions of Citizenship

With the emergence of the modern nation-state, the medieval traditions of corporatism and privileged classes gave way to the principle of the direct relation of each and every citizen to the authority of the state. The legal and institutional codification of this relation took the form of equality before the law for even previously excluded groups such as those defined as dependent persons (wage laborers) and certain religious "out groups" such as Jews, who in most Western European countries gained full legal citizenship only after the French Revolution (1789–1799). Indeed, from John Locke's *Letter on Toleration* in 1689 through the end of the nineteenth century, the issue of equal rights for religious minorities (whether Catholics and dissenters in seventeenth-century England or Jews in nineteenth-century Germany) was at the center of the raging debate over the meaning of citizenship in Western Europe.

As the nineteenth century progressed the legal equality of citizens came to be perceived as the right of the franchise. In Europe the struggles over the right to vote were the single most important aspect of political integration in the nineteenth century. By the turn of the twentieth century and in the years following the First World War when universal male suffrage was granted in most Western European nations, the terms of citizenship were being increasingly perceived as containing a certain modicum of economic welfare and maintenance. These changing and expanding definitions of citizenship became political issues, often subject to struggle. In Western Europe these issues were at the center of often violent conflict throughout the nineteenth and early twentieth centuries.

In lectures delivered in 1949 in Cambridge, England, the British political scientist T. H. Marshall framed the historical evolution of the nature of citizenship in terms that since have become classic. Marshall distinguished among the civil, political, and social aspects of citizenship. The civil element of citizenship comprised those rights necessary for individual freedom: liberty of person; freedom of speech, belief, and faith; and the right to private property and so to contract and due process. The political aspect of citizenship was the right to participate in the decision-making process of society and so the right to exercise political power as an elector. The social aspect of citizenship was defined as the right to share in the material standards of society and to live a life that would partake of that society's full material and social heritage. The historical "benchmarks" used by Marshall to identify the founding moments of the first and second aspects of citizenship in England were the Reform Act of 1832 and the Electoral Act of 1918. In many countries people continue to struggle over the social aspects of citizenship such as welfare and other entitlements. For Marshall, however, the trajectory of social citizenship in England ran from expansion of the Workmen's Compensation Act in 1906 to the Old Age Pension Act of 1908 to the National Insurance Act of 1911 and the Unemployment Insurance Act of 1920 to the National Health Service Act of 1946.

The attributes of citizenship are nowhere fully institutionalized nor have the concrete implications of these criteria ever been fully agreed upon. In the United States struggles over, among other things, welfare entitlements, labor relation laws, minimum wage agreements, women's rights, and the place of homosexuality in American culture—that is, struggles over the place of diversity and public recognition of diverse cultural and ethnic groups and traditions as well as the legal representation of that recognition—are all, to no small degree, struggles over the definition of citizenship. Significantly, in many parts of the world struggles over citizenship continue to revolve around issues of religion. These struggles may take the form of tensions between religious law and secular constitutionalism (in Israel and in the Islamic world from Turkey and Iran to Pakistan and Indonesia) or efforts to gain toleration and equal rights for religious minorities, especially when the minorities also share a unique ethnic designation (for example, the aboriginal cultures in the United States, Canada, and Australia—countries that have dealt with the claims of these groups in very different ways).

Current debates in Western Europe and the North Atlantic contexts over the meaning and extent of social entitlements as well as over the very principles of national integration (as in the province of Quebec's relationship to Canada or Scotland's relationship to Great Britain) highlight the degrees to which the different definitions and criteria of citizenship are contested in different parts of the world. For example, throughout Eastern and East Central Europe the emerging civic polities are all struggling to define new principles of social organization and solidarity along a fault line of so-called principles of "demos," which establish absolute individual equality among the citizenry, or principles of "ethnos," which privilege one or another ethnic group as more "representative" of the nation, its values, and social heritage than other groups. The exclusive and exclusionary aspects of the ethnos model have been especially attractive to the political elites in many of the Balkan states and the states of the former Soviet Union.

Similarly, many of the exclusionary definitions of citizenship and of membership and participation in the nation-state are predicated along religious lines, which in fact often overlap with ethnic divisions with tragic results such as the 1992–1995 war in the former Yugoslavia. Unfortunately, precedent can be found for such exclusionary practices, ultimately belying any possible integration. One need only look at the 1947 breakup of India and Pakistan following the end of colonial rule and at the formal division of Ireland in 1920 into a self-governing, predominantly Catholic south and a British-governed, predominantly Protestant north.

No given polity can be defined solely by its acceptance of one or the other of these models. Rather, a polity, especially ethnically and religiously heterogeneous societies, should be defined by a mix of both—that is, by differential definitions of the terms of mutuality, solidarity, and obligations and rights of citizenship of different ethnic groups within society.

Citizenship and Historical Development

The very existence of multiple definitions of citizenship in different parts of the world and even in different parts of Europe lends credence to the claim that the definitions of citizenship reigning in the West are not universally relevant and are, moreover, rooted in the particular path of historical development that characterized Western European societies. Thus citizens and scholars increasingly have realized that the trajectory of the West was unique and not repeatable, and that, to understand the particular developmental paths of different societies, it is more and more important

to understand the models of citizenship evolving in those societies.

In contemporary Europe the historical trajectory of nation building and state formation is of major importance to understanding the terms of citizenship. The long, drawn-out process of state making and nation building in Western Europe was characterized by the only gradual integration of different ethnic and religious groups into one national identity (characterized by its own territory; economy; legal, educational, and cultural systems; and historical memories). Central to this process were the different features of linguistic assimilation, social mobilization, and, at a much later date, mass education and the effects of mass media. In this process, and as the American sociologist Daniel Lerner noted more than thirty years ago, the formation of "psychologically mobile personalities" enabled the establishment of "empathy" between individuals of different ethnic and religious traditions. This empathy rested on the replacement of traditional, often religiously defined, criteria of solidarity and collective membership and participation with the "modern" values of individual rights and universal citizenship.

Providing the background for these developments was a unique set of historical features. These included large autonomous cities which provided independent locales for the organization of different social interests; an autonomous legal system (rooted in the legacy of Roman law) with traditions of legal reciprocity; and a recognition of representative institutions (the medieval *Standen*). These factors, together with the critical separation and independence of the church from the empire and the relatively little overlap among ethnic, religious, class, and political groups, all provided a degree of pluralism and recognition of social interests independent of the state and its rulers that tended to be unique in world history. As a result, to different extents the countries of Western Europe saw, first, the crystallization of a national identity out of different ethnic groups. In England, France, and Spain this development occurred around an ethnic core group and in Greece or Switzerland without such core groups. The formalization and universalization of the criteria for membership and participation in this national entity followed, based on the principles of citizenship and mass participation in the social and political life of the nation.

In other parts of the world this process was very different. In Eastern Europe, for example, the nation-state—or more precisely the administrative-bureaucratic structures of state rule—emerged (after the First World War) before the nation itself. Contributing to this process were the political elites who in the nineteenth century, while leading the nationalist movements in East Central Europe, did not identify national independence with more than their own corporate interests. Moreover, the democratic component of national movements was submerged in these corporate interests; social reforms were minimal. Indeed, the very ethnic fragmentation of these societies led to the view that the state itself produces national sentiment and not the other way around. By the mid-nineteenth century all the ruling elites had agreed that the nation stemmed from the state and were focusing solely on the state's role as a cultural, administrative, or coercive producer of nationalism. Thus the type of mass mobilization around social reforms that characterized Western nationalism and, indeed, united diverse communities into one national identity did not come to pass.

The pattern of development in Eastern Europe had clear implications for the problem of citizenship in contemporary East Central Europe. The necessary preconditions for modern forms of citizenship—based on the legal autonomy of the individual agent (freed from communal, religious, or ethnic identities) and existing in legal and political equality with other citizens—did not develop. Rather, the historical development of this region has seen the continued existence of strong ethnic and group solidarities which have continually thwarted the emergence of those legal, economic, and moral individual identities on which modern democratic forms of political identity are founded.

Thus in the most general of terms the existence of the individual social actor—freed from ascriptive identities—who was the foundation of Western, democratic models of social citizenship stemmed from the twofold historical moment of national integration and then the universalization of citizenship within the nation-state. In East Central Europe, the first process took place in only a partial and mediated manner. The second process of universal citizenship was never realized.

Eastern Europe is not, however, a unique case, and latecomers to the process of modern state building and the formation of a democratic citizenry face daunting tasks in institutionalizing the principles of citizenship that are identified with Western European regimes. High dependence on an external (extraterritorial) center of power, low levels of elite and social unification, and equally low levels of institutional readiness for the demands of mass participation in the political process, together with high demands for a politics of eco-

nomic redistribution, all combine to make the implementation of citizenship on a Western model highly problematic.

Contemporary Debates over Citizenship

Even more important than the structural and historical differences of different societies in understanding current debates over citizenship is the very ideological rejection of some of the tenets of Western citizenship that began to emerge in the final decades of the twentieth century in different parts of the world. Principles of individual autonomy and liberty, which have been strongly identified with the citizenship process, are being increasingly questioned from the perspective of different national or even civilizational heritages. From areas as diverse as Southeast Asia and the Islamic Middle East new political elites are offering very different ideas of what the principles of citizenship may mean. Certainly the Islamic militancy movement that has spread to different parts of the world is questioning the universality of the Western model. With its rejection of secularization as part of the "package" of modern citizenship and its reaffirmation of the relevancy of sometimes ethnic, sometimes religious criteria to the terms of citizenship, the Islamic world (including Muslims in Western European societies) is challenging Western conceptions of citizenship in new ways with as-yet-untold results.

This is true not only in those parts of the world that one typically thinks of as Muslim—the Middle East, for example—but also in many of the countries of the former Soviet Union. From the reemergence of shamanism among the Yakuts in northeastern Siberia to the importance of Orthodox Christianity to postcommunist Russian nationalism, religious identities continue to serve as the center of people's individual and collective senses of self, providing them with the core terms of membership and participation in the political and social orders. Moreover, these modes of membership contrast and often conflict with more civic ideas of a liberal political order founded on the equality of the citizenry before the law. Thus, while the 1980s saw the Soviet leadership alarmed at the growth of Islamic ritual and belief within its central Asian republics, the 1990s witnessed growing ethnic competition and conflict in the region, intensified by the various religious commitments of the parties involved.

To some extent the contention over the terms of citizenship and participation in the nation-state taking place in such parts of the world is echoed within Western European societies as well. For example, the overriding value of secularization, once identified with liberal ideas of citizenship, seems increasingly problematic. The important role played by the Catholic Church in the transition to democratic rule in Spain as well as the continual resistance waged by the Catholic Church to the Communist Party in Poland point to very different types of political action than those associated with the more conservative role of Catholic Church before the Second Vatican Council in the 1960s. Likewise, the role played by the clergy in the overthrow of the apartheid regime in South Africa and, indeed, in the processes of democratization in other African countries (such as Kenya) have led scholars to reassess the role of religion in the modern world.

The growth of religious, especially Christian pentecostal, affiliations in Latin America, Asia, and the United States also have increased social conflict over fundamental issues of citizenship such as individual rights, autonomy, and what is known in the United States as individual choice. Debates over abortion, school prayer, homosexuality, and most especially the role of religion in public life, all refer in one way or another to the fundamental terms of individual citizenship and the role of the state in organizing and directing the life of its citizenry.

Some observers have described these debates as ones over liberal versus republican visions of citizenship—that is, a vision of the state as a morally neutral realm where its citizens are free to pursue their own vision of the good versus a vision of a "moral community" of citizens dedicated to a particular vision of good, a vision that takes precedence over that of any particular member (citizen) of the community. As this debate is influenced by and draws on the changing nature of religious affiliations in the United States and the world at large, it becomes clear that the idea of citizenship is as conflict-ridden and problematic at the close of the twentieth century as it was at its onset.

See also *Civil society.*

Adam B. Seligman

BIBLIOGRAPHY

Arjomand, Said, ed. *The Political Dimensions of Religion.* Albany, N.Y.: SUNY Press, 1993.
Bendix, Rienhart. *Nation-Building and Citizenship.* Berkeley and Los Angeles: University of California Press, 1977.
Dahl, Robert. *Polyarchy: Participation and Opposition.* New Haven: Yale University Press, 1971.
Eisenstadt, S. N. *Modernization, Protest and Change.* Englewood Cliffs, N.J.: Prentice Hall, 1966.
Hall, John, ed. *States in History.* Oxford: Blackwood, 1986.
Lindsay, A. D. *The Modern Democratic State.* New York: Oxford University Press, 1962.
Maier, Charles, ed. *Changing Boundaries of the Political.* Cambridge: Cambridge University Press, 1987.
Marshall, T. H. *Class, Citizenship, and Social Development.* Westport, Conn.: Greenwood Press, 1973.

Civil disobedience

Civil disobedience is the act of nonviolently disobeying a state-imposed law or command on grounds of conscience. Nonviolence distinguishes civil disobedience from armed rebellion or revolution. Conscience distinguishes it from mere law breaking. Other traits are sometimes added to the definition: that the disobedience must be public and the legal penalty accepted, that only unjust laws may be broken, or that the goal must be reform and not overthrow of the state.

These additional traits do not always apply. Civil disobedience cannot always be public and the penalty accepted—consider those conveying slaves to freedom and those who hid Jews in Nazi-occupied Europe. The act cannot always be violation of an unjust law—those protesting nuclear arms testing could not violate the authorizing laws directly, so they violated admittedly just trespass laws in order to bring the issue to the public. The goal has not always been reform—Mohandas Gandhi's campaigns in India from 1920 until Indian independence in 1947 aimed not at reforming British rule but at getting rid of British rule. Even nonviolence has not been invariable: consider war protestors' destruction of draft records and other property to oppose U.S. involvement in the Vietnam War in the 1960s and 1970s.

There are, then, different types and strategies of civil disobedience depending on the goals sought and practical considerations of effectiveness. Rescuers in oppressive states must act secretly. Reformers utilize public, nonviolent, opinion-mobilizing techniques. Those aiming at the fall of a regime may engage in large-scale acts of noncooperation with state commands.

Moral Foundations

Civil disobedience is grounded in the understanding that there are obligations superior to the obligation to obey the commands of a state. Typically these are obligations to God, to natural law or natural right, or to a community. In this vein, Jewish midwives, during Israel's captivity in Egypt, fearing God more than Pharaoh, disobeyed Pharaoh's command to kill all newborn males (Exod. 1:15–17). Shadrach, Meshach, and Abednego braved death by fire rather than obey idolatrous commands by Nebuchadnezzar (Deut. 3). Christians, commanded to "render . . . to Caesar the things that are Caesar's" (Matt. 22:21), and informed that the powers that be are of God and should be obeyed (Rom. 13:1–7), nevertheless held that, in case of conflict, God must be obeyed rather than Caesar (Acts 5:29). The early Christians followed this understanding even to martyrdom.

In other traditions, Gandhi, drawing on certain aspects of his Hinduism and traditions East and West, led a movement of noncooperation with the British colonial rulers. In classical Greece this understanding was embodied in literature in Sophocles' heroine Antigone, who defied the Theban king when he forbade her to bury her brother, and in philosophy in the distinction between what is right by nature and what is merely conventional. In classical Rome it was embodied in the natural law tradition. Marcus Tullius Cicero (106–43 B.C.E.), statesman and philosopher, gave this tradition its classic expression, holding that there is a true law, right reason, which accords with nature, applies to all, is unchangeable and eternal, and cannot be invalidated by human law. God is the author of this law. This tradition paralleled that in the Christian tradition of the Apostle Paul (c. 10–62) and cohered with that of St. Augustine (354–430) and St. Thomas Aquinas (1225–1274). It was continued by the Dutch jurist Hugo Grotius (1583–1645), modified by the English political theorist John Locke (1632–1704) into a theory of natural rights, and in this form given expression in the American Declaration of Independence (1776), the French Declaration of the Rights of Man and of the Citizen (1789), and the United Nations Universal Declaration of Human Rights (1948).

Notable examples of civil disobedience include religious resistance to idolatry or persecution from ancient times to the present, religious and secular conscientious objection and resistance to military service, and opposition to war taxes, to war itself or to particular wars, and to arms races and types of arms, such as nuclear weapons. Slavery evoked civil disobedience. In the United States slaves were spirited out of the South by sympathizers who assisted them on the Underground Railway, and there was resistance in the North to the fugitive slave laws, which would have forced them back. Similarly, in the era of Nazi conquest in Europe in the 1930s and 1940s, Jews were sometimes hidden or aided in their es-

The antinuclear weapons movement was invigorated in the fall of 1981, when the North Atlantic Treaty Organization reaffirmed its 1979 commitment to deploy a new generation of medium-range nuclear weapons in Western Europe. As many as 100,000 protesters took to the streets in London's West End October 24, 1981. Similar marches were held in other parts of Europe.

cape and in a few instances defended by mass noncooperation. Civil disobedience was a major part of Gandhi's efforts for civil rights in South Africa in the early years of the twentieth century, as it later was to free India from British rule. Civil disobedience was employed as well in other nationalist movements, and it has been a mainstay of labor and environmental movements around the globe.

In the United States civil disobedience was a galvanizing force in the civil rights movement of the 1950s and 1960s. At the beginning of World War I it played a significant role at a crucial time in the women's suffrage movement, and it has been used, to a greater or lesser degree, in virtually all civil rights movements since then, including those for homosexuals and the unborn. Civil disobedience has become a standard part of protest against injustice and has been used even in totalitarian and authoritarian societies. Indeed, massive noncooperation with state commands played a major role in the collapse of the communist governments in Eastern Europe in 1989, though it failed spectacularly in China in the Tiananmen Square Massacre in the same year.

Theory and Practice

Objection to slavery was the impetus for the best-known defense of civil disobedience in the nineteenth century—Henry David Thoreau's essay entitled "Civil Disobedience" (1849). In the twentieth century, the principal theoretical expositions and the most admired and emulated movements came from Gandhi and Dr. Martin Luther King Jr. Each of these men captured the imagination of the world even as they helped produce dramatic change. Gandhi, drawing on his interpretations of Hinduism, and combining those with like elements he found in Christianity and Buddhism (as well as Thoreau), developed the concept of *satyagraha,* which he defined as "truth-force." *Satyagraha,* which employed civil disobedience, aimed to achieve justice and reconciliation without violence or hatred. King was an ordained Baptist minister whose public life, from 1955 until his assassination in 1968, spanned a period of tense years of race relations in the United States. He drew on Gandhi, as well as his own interpretation of the proper social applications of Christian love and Jesus' Sermon on the Mount, the tradition of natural law, and the principles of the American Declaration of Independence, to provide moral direction to the civil rights movement.

King believed that unjust privilege is rarely given up without a struggle. He was more ready than Gandhi to acknowledge that a degree of coercion must be used in the struggle for civil rights. But the goal is both justice and reconciliation, so the means must be nonviolent and persuasive. Typically, King would pick a symbolic site for protest, one that would capture the public imagination or present a clear conflict between justice and injustice. After trying for negotiation—rarely effective without coercion—he would prepare his protesters for a campaign of nonviolent protest, usually involving civil disobedience. Protesters were to accept voluntarily the penalty for disobedience of the law to show that there was no disrespect for law as an institution. Nonviolence was necessary on principle (good ends require pure means) and as a tactic (nonviolence helps to defuse the issue of "law and order," while any harsh or violent reaction to the protesters, which was common, poses the moral issues in the clearest possible terms). The result of King's use of nonviolence was to present a kind of morality play highlighting the confrontation between justice and injustice, reasonable protest and unreasonable resistance. Such a campaign was both coercive and persuasive. It created a crisis that required a decision or response. And, by presenting the confrontation as a contest between good and evil, it was often effective in gaining political action against the injustice and in delegitimizing the injustice.

The anti–Vietnam War movement of the late sixties and early seventies increasingly practiced civil disobedience. Among the more prominent members of that movement were the Berrigan brothers, Daniel and Philip, Roman Catholic priests (though Philip soon left the priesthood). Perhaps their most famous tactic was raiding draft board offices and destroying draft files. This tactic was used in two well-publicized protests. The first occurred October 27, 1967, at the Baltimore Customs House, where Philip led a group of four in pouring blood on draft records. The second protest took place May 17, 1968, at Catonsville, a Baltimore suburb, where Philip and Daniel led a group of nine in burning draft files with homemade napalm. Using dramatic tactics, fleeing from authorities, and appearing in famous trials (the "Baltimore Four," the "Catonsville Nine"), the brothers helped merge the secular and Roman Catholic antiwar movements and contributed to a rethinking, by many Roman Catholics and others, of their support for the Vietnam War and "just war" theory.

Civil disobedience soon became a tactic in other protest movements, including the antiabortion and sanctuary movements. In 1973 the U.S. Supreme Court decided, in *Roe v. Wade,* that the U.S. Constitution protects abortion. The decision provoked protest that continues a quarter of a century later, conducted mainly by Roman Catholics and evangelical Protestants. The best-known organization employing civil disobedience in this protest movement was Operation Rescue, initially headed by Randall Terry. Following the biblical injunction to "rescue those who are being taken away to death; hold back those who are stumbling to slaughter" (Prov. 24: 11), this group made efforts to peacefully block entry to abortion clinics. By the early 1990s federal legislation—including legislation designed to curb racketeering—and strong penalties had largely curbed these "rescues." Joan Andrews Bell, convicted of felony trespass more than fifty times and imprisoned for more than five years, displayed the strength of resolve that characterized participants in this movement.

In the early 1980s civil disobedience was employed by the sanctuary movement in its attempt to shelter political refugees illegally in the United States from potentially dangerous deportation back to their conflict-ridden homelands, usually El Salvador or Guatemala. Individual congregations, loosely linked nationally, would formally declare their churches sanctuaries for the refugees, many of whom were attempting to get to Canada. This movement drew on an ancient tradition of churches offering sanctuary or shelter to those fleeing civil punishment.

Critics note that civil disobedience may fail and that rebellion, revolution, and war are sometimes justified or required. Others argue that civil disobedience may produce disrespect for law and that it may even lead to general lawlessness and to eruptions of violence and anarchy. Still, it has become an often effective part of the arsenal of protest, in both democratic and nondemocratic nations.

See also *Civil rights movement; Colonialism; Gandhi, Mohandas Karamchand; Human rights; Justice, Social; King, Martin Luther, Jr.; Natural law; Pacifism; Sanctuary; Slavery; Violence; War.*

William R. Marty

BIBLIOGRAPHY

Childress, James F. *Civil Disobedience and Political Obligation: A Study in Christian Social Ethics.* New Haven: Yale University Press, 1971.

Cohen, Carl. *Civil Disobedience: Conscience, Tactics, and the Law.* New York: Columbia University Press, 1971.

Gandhi, M. K. *Non-Violent Resistance (Satyagraha).* New York: Schocken Books, 1961.

King, Martin Luther, Jr. *Why We Can't Wait.* New York: Signet, 1964.

Moskos, Charles C., and John Whiteclay Chambers II, eds. *The New Conscientious Objection: From Sacred to Secular Resistance.* New York: Oxford University Press, 1993.

Pateman, Carole. *The Problem of Political Obligation: A Critical Analysis of Liberal Theory.* New York: Wiley, 1979.

Thomas, Owen, ed. *Henry David Thoreau, Walden, and Civil Disobedience: Authoritative Texts, Background, Reviews, and Essays in Criticism.* New York: Norton, 1966.

Walzer, Michael. *Obligations: Essays on Disobedience, War, and Citizenship.* Cambridge: Harvard University Press, 1970.

Civil religion

Civil religion is a set of cultural symbols that draw connections between a nation and some conception of the sacred. These symbols usually consist of beliefs and practices that make explicit reference to a divine being (for example, prayers for the well-being of the nation or acknowledgment of God on the currency). Some treatments also include symbols that legitimate the nation with reference to the transcendent or with some other idea of ultimate reality (such as fundamental human rights, the laws of nature, or a Marxist notion of universal class struggle).

The idea of civil religion was first advanced by the French philosopher Jean-Jacques Rousseau (1712–1778) in his effort to understand the social principles underlying democratic societies. Rousseau argued that it was in the self-interest of individual citizens to form cooperative relationships with

Jean-Jacques Rousseau

one another but that the resulting restrictions on individual freedoms required certain beliefs that would render the new relationships legitimate. In traditional societies a common religion had often provided such beliefs, but in modern nations a unifying set of beliefs needed to be found that would not exclude citizens who ascribed to minority religions or who were nonreligious. The religious wars between Protestants and Roman Catholics that devastated seventeenth-century Europe persuaded Rousseau that organized religion was likely to be divisive and therefore should be replaced, or at least augmented, by beliefs that pertained to the entire nation but that also inspired devotion in the way that organized religion had done in the past. Rousseau suggested that nations would (and should) develop a civil religion that would embrace all citizens, giving them reasons to practice civic virtue and to be patriotic.

The ingredients of civil religion, according to Rousseau, were to be relatively simple so that citizens could agree upon them and remember them. They should include belief in the existence of a divine being or order characterized by its power, wisdom, and goodness. They should also include some conception of the future, of justice, and of punishment, and they should emphasize the sanctity of the social bonds that link people together and the laws to which they are subject. Rousseau emphasized that civil religion should promote tolerance. The divine being in Rousseau's conception is thus a symbol that crystallizes the qualities people should admire in their nation and willingly commit themselves to upholding. Insofar as the divine being is both benevolent and just, and insofar as the life to come (whether on this earth or in heaven) is regarded positively, citizens will presumably be motivated to think well of their society.

Together, these ingredients provide a concept of reality in relation to which the specific activities of leaders can be assessed, for example, by providing cause for ending a particular regime but giving continuity to the nation's higher values and traditions. This concept of reality nevertheless legitimates the basic institutions of the nation by encouraging citizens to realize their dependence on a sovereign power, the ways in which their dependence on one another is conducive to achieving their highest values, and their need to be tolerant of one another.

Contemporary Views

Interest in the idea of civil religion was rekindled in the 1960s, in particular by the work of sociologist Robert N.

Bellah. Focusing primarily on the United States, Bellah stressed that civil religion exists to some extent among all people as the way in which each nation interprets its historical experience in the light of transcendent reality. The most important aspect of civil religion is thus a "myth of origin" that explains how a people came into being, who their heroic leaders were, and what the principles were on which their nation was founded. A myth of origin unifies citizens by pointing to common ancestors and a shared heritage. It also emphasizes times of crisis during which citizens worked together or perhaps engaged in conflict in order to resolve some fundamental ambiguity in their vision of who they should be. For the United States, stories about the early colonists, about the War of Independence and the Civil War, and about such figures as George Washington, Benjamin Franklin, and Abraham Lincoln provide a myth of origin in which current events can be interpreted in light of a time when sacred principles were perhaps especially clear. Following Mircea Eliade, a historian of comparative religion, Bellah suggested that ordinary time is often distinguished from mythic time, the latter being a period set apart in which humans communicated directly with the gods or took on characteristics that made them larger than life. In civil religion, mythic time is the period of founding or prehistory of a people.

Besides a myth of origin, civil religion includes beliefs that legitimate who is or who is not regarded as eligible for the full rights and privileges of citizenship. By drawing distinctions between citizens and noncitizens, civil religion reinforces loyalties among the former and encourages them to exercise their civic responsibilities; it also provides reasons for excluding certain groups from participating in civic activities. As definitions of citizenship are redefined (for example, to include people who do not own property or to permit women or eighteen year olds to vote), the civil religion is generally reinterpreted to legitimate these changing definitions. More negatively, the civil religion stigmatizes certain groups deemed to be threatening to the sanctity of the nation (for example, conspirators, witches, communists, aliens, subversives).

Civil religion also includes ideas about the goals, purposes, or destiny of a nation. These ideas help to mobilize the energies of citizens, especially when they are called on to sacrifice for their country. The goals specified by civil religion range from those that are quite specific (such as waging war against an ungodly foe) to more general or abstract values (such as upholding freedom or promoting world peace). The civil religion undergirds the nation's purposes by showing that its goals are not arbitrary or mean-spirited but are indeed consistent with sacred ideals and moral absolutes. Because political leaders are charged with the task of setting national goals and mobilizing commitment to those goals, civil religion is often articulated in the speeches of the leaders.

In contemporary discussions of civil religion, commentators have paid considerable attention to the rituals that maintain it. National holidays, state funerals, elections, and speeches by major leaders provide special occasions for reinforcing the civil religion. In the inaugural addresses of U.S. presidents, for example, some explicit reference to God is not uncommon; inaugurations typically include prayers and swearing of oaths on the Bible. Some rituals also provide citizens with an opportunity to reenact parts of the myth of origin, thus reminding them of its importance and altering it in light of present circumstances. Enactments of major battles are one example. Rituals are important because they bring people together physically or through mass communication, encouraging them to recognize that they are a people with a collective identity and stirring their emotions so that abstract symbols and historic narratives become personally meaningful.

Research on civil religion suggests that it is not as consensual or unified as earlier writers assumed. The effective functioning of civil religion depends on its capacity to incorporate themes and traditions that are meaningful to different segments of the population or that have been prominent at different periods in history. Western countries typically incorporate themes from Judaism and Christianity into their civil religions, but they also draw on ideas about republicanism or democracy that stem from Greek and Roman traditions or the Enlightenment. A study of Italy suggests that its civil religion is composed of several historic layers, including popular Christianity, Roman Catholicism, democratic liberalism, socialism, and activism. Japan's civil religion combines elements of Shinto and Buddhism. Muslim countries generally combine elements both of Islam and of modern secular political theory in their civil religions. The new nations that have emerged from the former Soviet Union have had to draw together democratic and Eastern Orthodox ideas with other themes to forge legitimating myths of origin. Because of the different traditions from which civil religions are generally composed, it is often helpful to distinguish the unifying (and often implicit) values on which they are based from "public theology," which articulates a particular tradition or vision of what the nation should be.

The Connection with Organized Religion

The relationships between organized religion and civil religion appear to vary considerably. On the one hand, many instances can be found in which the strength of one reinforces that of the other. For example, societies with large numbers of clergy are more likely to include specific references to God in their public commemorations than are societies with relatively few clergy. On the other hand, religious leaders who push for a specific interpretation of the civil religion sometimes find themselves with few resources when these interpretations fall into disfavor with particular regimes. In either case, it is important to acknowledge the differences between civil religion and organized religion. The former is more likely to represent a "least common denominator" faith, whereas the latter can emphasize the traditions of particular groups. The former may not be compelling because it focuses on the entire nation, whereas the latter (especially when it is organized around congregations) can reinforce local understandings and loyalties.

In general, the process of political modernization has resulted in greater differentiation between organized religion and political institutions, but it has not led uniformly to a weakening of civil religion. Because civil religion is largely cultural, rather than institutional, strong symbolic links can be maintained between the nation and various conceptions of the sacred, even when formal separation of religion and politics is present. In such conditions, the civil religion provides a way to legitimate the separate activities of religious and political functionaries, encouraging them to fulfill their particular roles and thus permitting organized religion to be a voice in the public arena without presuming it to be the only voice. Recognizing the continuing presence of civil religion is important in scholarship on modern societies because it shows that religion is not entirely "privatized" or relegated to the personal lives of individuals.

Current Approaches to Scholarship

The study of civil religion has mostly taken the form of qualitative research focusing on a single country over a period of time. Studies of this kind are valuable for sorting out the complex threads of a particular civil religion and for showing how it changes in response to new economic or political realities. For example, research on civil religion in

South Africa shows how it has been shaped by British and Dutch colonialism, by indigenous religions, and by the country's experiment with the racial segregation of apartheid. A few studies have examined civil religion comparatively, and some have done so by developing quantitative measures. For example, it is possible to examine constitutions, national anthems, and presidential speeches to determine the presence or absence of religious content.

Current scholarship appears to be shifting away from an emphasis on civil religion toward concepts such as national identity; public religion, ritual, and theology; and civil society and civic engagement. One reason for this shift is that civil religion may have fairly limited value as a concept for understanding the complex relationships between religion and politics, especially when it is defined narrowly to mean the use of religious language in reference to the nation. Conversely, civil religion becomes too broad a concept to be useful when it is defined as any transcendent event used in relation to the nation. In addition, scholars have sometimes objected to the idea of civil religion because it appeared to be used as a prescription for a certain kind of cultural renewal rather than as an analytic concept.

Concerns have also been raised about civil religion from a normative perspective. These concerns indicate that the study of civil religion often focuses on established or elite views, rather than on the folk religion or popular beliefs and practices of ordinary people. Some writers point to the importance of sectarian civil religion—that is, beliefs about the relationship between sacred teachings and civil authorities that are espoused by religious groups outside the social mainstream. The civil religions evident in teachings of American Quakers, Mennonites, or Jews are examples. Other writers emphasize the need for a more diverse conception of civil religion, especially one that moves beyond tolerance toward a more positive evaluation of diversity itself. In these treatments, civil religion is said to benefit from internal conflict and disagreement that encourages it to change or to engage in self-criticism.

Recent discussions about the decline of civic engagement in a large number of advanced industrial societies nevertheless point to the continuing importance of examining some of the core ingredients of civil religion. Civil society is strengthened not only by specific networks of social interaction, or by instrumental norms that tell people how to work together, but also by unifying symbols that define them as having a common history and sharing a common destiny.

Engaging in cooperative pursuits and working for the public good is often difficult to justify in terms of self-interest alone. Rousseau's insight that people need to know that it is legitimate to sacrifice some of their own freedoms in order to work together remains valid.

Although recent scholarship often does not refer explicitly to civil religion, the debate to which the idea of civil religion remains most relevant is that between writers who argue in favor of procedural agreements as the basis for democratic society and those who argue for substantive agreements. The former suggest that deep symbols, values, and traditions of the kind embodied in civil religion are likely to be disruptive and should thus be replaced by greater emphasis on laws, governmental procedures, and rational modes of public discourse. The latter argue that commitment to the common good cannot be sustained by procedures alone but must be reinforced by citizens' identification with the community, collective memory, and shared values.

The Utility of Civil Religion

The most specific application of the foregoing debate has to do with contemporary concerns about the spread of individualism and an alleged breakdown of community. These concerns are fueled by the observation that civil religion itself has helped to legitimate individualism and has, in turn, been redefined to focus more on individual rights than on collective responsibilities. Critics of individualism argue that a different form of civil religion needs to be rediscovered, in particular one that promotes deliberation about moral obligations, social justice, and equality.

The question that remains most open about civil religion is whether it promotes acceptance of the status quo or whether it provides ethical principles that transcend the status quo and serve as a basis for critical evaluations of social arrangements. On the one hand, it is relatively easy to find unifying symbols that give citizens a basis for communicating with one another and even to believe that what they are doing has some mandate that transcends themselves. These symbols may pertain to a divine being but are perhaps more likely to focus on realities that are so taken for granted that in effect they achieve a form of sanctity. Economic laws, nature, science, technology, national competition, efficiency, rationality, and even the appeals of advertisers may all be examples of such realities. On the other hand, civil religion has in the past upheld standards of freedom that helped to legitimate campaigns against slavery or to promote standards of compassion and social justice that encouraged efforts to provide private charity or pass ameliorative welfare legislation. These standards, it appears, depended not only on the inertia of cultural tradition to be perpetuated but also on the skills of advocacy groups capable of bringing them to the public's attention.

See also *Citizenship; Civil society; Communitarianism; Holidays; Individualism; Nationalism; Nativism; Presidents, American; Public theology; Tocqueville, Alexis de; Traditionalism; Voluntarism.*

Robert Wuthnow

BIBLIOGRAPHY

Bellah, Robert N. *Beyond Belief: Essays on Religion in a Post-Traditional World.* New York: Harper and Row, 1970, chap. 9.
———. *The Broken Covenant: American Civil Religion in Time of Trial.* New York: Seabury, 1975.
———, and Phillip E. Hammond. *Varieties of Civil Religion.* New York: Harper and Row, 1980.
Liebman, Charles S., and Eliezer Don-Yehiya. *Civil Religion in Israel: Traditional Judaism and Political Culture in the Jewish State.* Berkeley and Los Angeles: University of California Press, 1983.
Mathisen, James A. "Twenty Years after Bellah: Whatever Happened to American Civil Religion?" *Sociological Analysis* 50 (summer 1989): 129–147.
Moodie, T. Dunbar. *The Rise of Afrikanerdom: Power, Apartheid, and the Afrikaner Civil Religion.* Berkeley and Los Angeles: University of California Press, 1975.
Rousseau, Jean-Jacques. *The Social Contract and Discourse on the Origin of Inequality,* edited by Lester G. Crocker. New York: Washington Square Press, 1967.

Civil rights movement

The modern civil rights movement in the United States arose in the mid-1950s around the initial aim of dismantling the system of Jim Crow segregation, which had developed in the South in the decades following the abandonment of post–Civil War Reconstruction in 1877. Although resistance to white domination has been a constant of the African American experience in the United States, the modern civil rights movement can be said to have begun in December 1955, with the onset of the bus boycott in Montgomery, Alabama. The civil rights phase of the struggle gradually gave way in the mid-1960s to what has been termed the "black power" movement and was then dealt a critical blow with the assassination of Martin Luther King Jr. in April 1968.

The role of religion in social movements constitutes one of the notable "silences" in the study of collective action. What causes this silence is not clear. What is clear, however, is that the neglect of the topic seriously understates the often close connection between religion and collective protest activity. Religious institutions have long been among the most common social settings within which protest is likely to develop. Throughout history, religious groups have been the key source of animating ideologies, leaders, rank and file activists, and other organizational resources for countless social movements.

This connection between churches and protest movements has been especially true in the United States, where rates of church attendance and professed religiosity have remained high in the face of the trend toward secularization in virtually all other Western democracies. From the nineteenth-century abolition movement to the present-day Nation of Islam, from pro-life activism to the enduring tradition of religious pacifism, a long and varied list of American social movements have been nurtured and shaped by their roots in an equally long and varied list of American religious traditions. But perhaps no social movement better illustrates the close connection between religion and collective action in the United States than the modern civil rights movement. This essay highlights the role of the black church in the movement and, by extension, its influence in setting in motion other instances of religiously inspired activism around the globe. The example of Archbishop Desmond Tutu in the South African anti-apartheid struggle is only one prominent instance. Tutu was awarded the Nobel Peace Prize in 1984.

The Black Church as the Organizational Center

It would be hard to overstate the black church's central role in the civil rights movement. As the opening act in the civil rights struggle, the Montgomery bus boycott illustrates, even as it helped to cement, the close relationship between the movement and the southern black church. On December 1, 1955, Rosa Parks, a black woman, was arrested for quietly defying Montgomery's policy of segregated seating on city buses. E D. Nixon, the head of the state chapter of the NAACP (the National Association for the Advancement of Colored People), the country's oldest and most influential civil rights organization, posted bail for Parks. The next morning he called Martin Luther King Jr. and Ralph Abernathy of Montgomery's First Baptist Church, to apprise them of the events of the previous evening. The three men

Rosa Parks's December 1955 refusal to move to the back of a Montgomery, Alabama, city bus, in violation of seating regulations for black people, led to the Montgomery bus boycott. The boycott sparked the American civil rights movement.

agreed to organize a meeting of church and other civic leaders that evening at the Dexter Avenue Baptist Church. The purpose of the meeting was to call for a one-day symbolic boycott of Montgomery's buses. The boycott was to take place the following Monday, December 5.

The proposal was enthusiastically endorsed by Montgomery's black leadership, and the ministerial elite who formed the core of the leadership agreed to use their pulpits on Sunday to call for support for the boycott. The call worked. On Monday, between 90 and 95 percent of Montgomery's black bus patrons stayed off the buses. Buoyed by the unprecedented show of solidarity by Montgomery's black community, the leaders laid plans that evening at yet another meeting at Dexter Avenue to continue the boycott until the group's demands were met. The civil rights struggle had been joined.

The events in Montgomery illustrate the four organizational contributions made by the black church to the movement. These contributions were the provision of "free space" in which to mobilize, a group of established leaders, a com-

munications network, and members of the congregation to serve as the movement's "foot soldiers."

Free space. Scholars of social movements and organizers alike have long stressed the importance of free space to the embryonic beginnings of collective action. Free spaces are the social settings controlled by prospective insurgents and within which they can safely engage in the activities necessary to launch a protest movement. Within the oppressive confines of the Jim Crow South, the black churches—and, in particular, the largest and best-heeled, urban black churches—were the most significant institutional free spaces available to the burgeoning movement. In Montgomery, even though an NAACP official initiated action, his first move was to mobilize the black clergy and secure the sponsorship of the church. From that moment on control and direction of the movement and of the organization it spawned (the Montgomery Improvement Association) passed to a network of black ministers and the churches they headed. As sociologist Aldon Morris has noted (in *The Origins of the Civil Rights Movement*, 1984), what was true in Montgomery was true for the movement as a whole. Organized protest activity was centered in local networks rooted in the black church. The reason was simple: the black church was the central organization and the only truly independent institution in the southern black community.

Leaders. The church also provided the movement with a large share of its formal leadership. Martin Luther King Jr., who first achieved national prominence in Montgomery, is only the most obvious example. But without denying King's unquestioned centrality to the movement, it is important to note that his leadership was a reflection of the more general pattern. King was only the most prominent of a host of black ministers who spearheaded the struggle. In fact, he was not even the first to do so. In 1953 the Reverend Theodore Jemison of Baton Rouge, Louisiana, had organized a bus boycott on which the Montgomery campaign was modeled. Considering that the movement was so closely tied to the church, the dominance of black clergy in formal leadership roles is hardly surprising. Established ministerial leadership was only one of the organizational resources the movement appropriated by tying itself closely to the church.

Communications. Although we tend to think of social movements as large-scale national events, in fact most movements are collections of local campaigns, knit together by a dense communication network to create a semblance of national breadth and coordination. Such was the case with the civil rights movement. The black church served as the basis for the communications network that transformed Montgomery into a regional coalition of local movements that eventually garnered national support and attention. The nature of this communications network is suggested by the previous reference to the Baton Rouge bus boycott. When King, Abernathy, and the other leaders in Montgomery were laying plans for the boycott, they knew to talk with Jemison. They knew to do so because they were linked to Jemison through a series of formal and informal ministerial networks that connected black clergy throughout the South.

Similarly, King's ties to other locally prominent black ministers facilitated the spread of the boycott tactic well beyond Montgomery. The Reverend Charles Steele visited King in the winter of 1956 and returned home to Tallahassee, Florida, to organize a boycott there. In short order, other campaigns, patterned along the lines of the Montgomery movement, were organized in Atlanta, New Orleans, Birmingham, Chattanooga, and Rock Hill, South Carolina. As in Montgomery, all were church-based operations headed by a minister. From this collection of local campaigns the Southern Christian Leadership Conference (SCLC) was forged at a January 1957 gathering held in Atlanta. With King at the helm, SCLC was to spearhead the national movement through the 1960s.

Church members. Perhaps the single most remarkable feature of the Montgomery campaign was the extraordinary rate of compliance of black bus riders with the demands of the boycott. The key to the 90–95 percent compliance rate lies in the church's imprimatur, which legitimized the boycott. More generally, throughout its heyday the movement was able to mobilize large segments of the black community because of the fundamental embedding of the struggle in the black church. By centering the movement in the church, civil rights leaders were able to recruit congregations virtually en masse, thereby sparing themselves the much more difficult task of developing a membership from scratch.

In his 1963 book *Why We Can't Wait,* King likened the recruitment of movement volunteers at church-based mass meetings to the "invitational periods that occur every Sunday morning, when the pastor projects the call." Indeed, it may be more accurate to say that participants in church-based campaigns were not so much recruited from the ranks of active churchgoers as it was a case of church membership itself being redefined to include civil rights activity as a primary requisite of the role.

The Black Church as Cultural "Tool Kit"

Ann Swidler (in "Culture in Action: Symbols and Strategies") has described culture as a kind of "tool kit" that facilitates action. This analogy points to another set of functions performed by the black church in the civil rights movement. These functions relate to the church's role as a repository of cultural materials, ideas, and symbols that motivated and legitimated protest activity. We can distinguish three cultural resources that the church afforded the movement: an ideology that legitimated the movement, the mass meeting that became the movement's basic building block, and a rhetorical style that arose from the imagery and language of black preachers. We will look at each of these in turn.

Ideology. The civil rights movement drew ideological inspiration from a number of sources. No one embodied the unique combination of these sources better than did Martin Luther King. In his blending of familiar Judeo-Christian themes, conventional democratic theory, and the philosophy of nonviolence, King brought to the struggle a compelling, yet accessible, mix of ideas. At the core of this rich ideological stew was Christian theology. In employing traditional Christian themes, King not only rooted the movement in one of the ideological bedrocks of American culture but diverged sharply from the more conservative theological stance that had tended to mark the southern black church in the early decades of the twentieth century. In part, this orientation can be seen as little more than the temporary ascendance of one perspective in black theology over another—a stress on "other-worldly reward" over an emphasis on the everyday demands of the social gospel. This conservatism, however, must also be seen as a rational adaptation to a repressive system of caste restrictions. That is, whites' efforts at social control during this period encouraged an "acceptable" content in the overt teachings of the black church.

The fact that King and other young black ministers saw fit to break with the dominant "accommodationist" tradition was due both to their youth and the theological perspectives to which they had been exposed and to the relative freedom from white control they enjoyed by virtue of the large, urban congregations they headed. Regardless of the factors that allowed them to make the break, however, their reappropriation of the traditions of the social gospel served the movement well in a number of ways.

First, it resonated with the experience and values of the southern African American community, steeped as it was in the church and its teachings. Any account of the movement's ability to mobilize the black masses must begin with its foundation in the language and imagery of traditional Christian theology. Second, the themes of Christian forgiveness and redemptive healing that were central to King's philosophy were instrumental in gaining the broad support the movement received in white America. These themes were deeply reassuring to a white America burdened (as it still is) by guilt and fear of black anger and violence. King's emphasis on Christian charity and nonviolence promised a redemptive and peaceful healing of America's long-standing racial divide. In so doing, he invited a level of white support for the struggle that had until then been unimaginable. This support included the active backing of a host of religious institutions (for example, the National Council of Churches) and prominent figures outside the world of black Protestantism (among them Reinhold Niebuhr and Abraham Heschel). Finally, when coupled with the movement's appropriation of Christian themes, the practice of nonviolence effectively tied the hands of southern segregationists. That is, by embodying the image of peaceful, Christian petitioners, the movement drastically reduced the options of social control that had been open to its opponents. The free hand that southern authorities had once enjoyed in repressing civil rights forces was gone.

Mass meetings. From Montgomery onward, the mass meeting was the movement's basic organizational building block. Almost always held in a church, the mass meeting became the principal vehicle by which people were mobilized for action. In its basic form, it was but a transparent variant on the Sunday church service. Each meeting opened with announcements and the singing of "freedom songs," often included the kind of invitational period described by King, and generally closed with singing and one or more rousing "sermons" by movement leaders.

Although the form was initially adapted by King and other activist ministers for use in the movement, it became a staple of civil rights organizing more generally. Organizers in such nominally secular groups as the Student Nonviolent Coordinating Committee (SNCC) and the Congress of Racial Equality (CORE) readily adopted the mass meeting as well. In this way, the cultural familiarity and resonance of the congregational-style meeting was appropriated by the movement.

Rhetoric. During its heyday, the dominant rhetorical style associated with the movement was that of the black preacher. The dominance of this style is hardly surprising. Indeed, rooted as the movement was in the language and images of the black church, the surprise would have been if the rhetoric had been something other than ministerial. Then, too, the disproportionate role played by ministers in formal leadership positions in the movement made the adoption of this style logical and culturally comprehensible. Finally, once the mass meeting form had been firmly established within the movement, yet another pressure for adoption of this rhetorical style emerged. The strong cultural affinity between the mass meeting and the ministerial style of address prompted even secular organizers to adopt the style and mannerisms of the black preacher.

The southern black church, then, was both the organizational base and cultural template for much of the civil rights struggle. Indeed, so functional was the marriage of church and movement that a case could be made that the increasing secularization of the struggle during its black power phase contributed to the decline of the movement during the late 1960s and early 1970s. With its emphases on black pride, "self-defense," and the mobilization of the political and economic resources of the black community, the turn toward black power and the geographic shift northward (where the church was not the central institution it was in the South) deprived the movement of its strong foundation in the church. The movement was left with neither the central organizational vehicle nor the resonant cultural "tool kit" it had enjoyed in the South.

See also *African American experience; Civil disobedience; Heschel, Abraham; Human rights; King, Martin Luther, Jr.; Niebuhr, Reinhold; Prejudice; Slavery; Social gospel.*

Doug McAdam

BIBLIOGRAPHY

Findlay, James. F. *Church People in the Struggle: The National Council of Churches and the Black Freedom Movement, 1950–1970.* New York: Oxford University Press, 1993.

Garrow, David. *Bearing the Cross.* New York: Morrow, 1986.

King, Martin Luther, Jr. *Stride toward Freedom: The Montgomery Story.* New York: Harper and Brothers, 1958.

———. *Why We Can't Wait.* New York: Harper and Row, 1963.

McAdam, Doug. *Political Process and the Development of Black Insurgency, 1930–1970.* Chicago: University of Chicago Press, 1982.

Morris, Aldon. *The Origins of the Civil Rights Movement.* New York: Free Press, 1984.

Payne, Charles M. *I've Got the Light of Freedom.* Berkeley: University of California Press, 1995.

Swidler, Ann. "Culture in Action: Symbols and Strategies." *American Sociological Review* 51 (1986): 273–286.

Watters, Pat. *Down to Now: Reflections on the Southern Civil Rights Movement.* Athens and London: University of Georgia Press, 1993.

Civil society

Civil society is the realm of social voluntarism, the organization of interests outside of the state, and the existence of intermediary associations, mediating between the individual citizen and the state. The idea of civil society as a political concept expressing liberal and democratic norms gained currency in the eighteenth century, only to be revived in the 1980s in East Central Europe and later in many other parts of the world.

In response to the disruption of old certainties of territorial, kinship, and religious-based obligations and expectations, the notion of civil society emerged in the eighteenth century as thinkers sought to find a new basis for collective life, for social solidarity, and for trust among members of society. Eventually, the idea of civil society provided one of the earliest formulas for the modern, democratic form of political life that would, by the twentieth century, be identified with citizenship within the democratically organized nation-state.

The Modern Idea of Civil Society

While the idea of civil society has a long history in the traditions of Western political thought—its roots go back to Christian natural law—its modern emergence dates to the writings of the Scottish moralists. For the eighteenth-century thinkers of the Scottish Enlightenment, civil society was primarily a vision of society held together by the force of "moral sentiments" and "natural affections." In the writings of Francis Hutcheson, Hugh Blair, Adam Ferguson, and Adam Smith, the establishment of civil society came to be identified with the realization of the moral sense within humankind. As a form of sociability this sense would provide the foundation for the moral community. Consequently, this moral sense would assure mutuality, compassion, and empathy among individuals, all of which would take them beyond calculation of purely economic interests in their dealings with one another.

Thus for these writers and publicists of mid-eighteenth-century Scotland, the idea of civil society was primarily a new principle for the organization of society and the expression of men and women's fundamental ties with one another. In that sense, it replaced the medieval idea of the Catholic Church as a *universitas fidelium* (university of the faithful) with a new, more inclusive definition of membership in society based on the moral sense within humankind. No

longer able to conceive of society in the hierarchic terms of medieval orders and estates but rather as a grouping of discrete and autonomous individuals, the thinkers of the day had to find a new bond among these individuals.

For Scottish thinkers such as Adam Ferguson and Adam Smith this bond was based on the assumed need of people for recognition and consideration by others. At the epistemological level the notion of civil society is thus an attempt to ground the very idea of society in an intimately human propensity to mutuality, to something that in fact rather closely approximates the idea of friendship. Building on the social nature of human existence, the writers of the Scottish Enlightenment saw the essence of civil society in the continuing need of people to be validated and recognized by their fellow citizens. Eschewing the explanation that society and social interaction were organized solely by the pursuit of material goods and interest (that is, by market exchanges), these eighteenth-century thinkers recognized that mutual approbation was no less critical in explaining the transactions of the marketplace and counting house.

What stood at the core of all attempts to articulate a notion of civil society in the eighteenth century were the increasingly problematic relations between the private and the public, the individual and society, public ethics and private morals, individual passions and public concerns. More to the point, the question of civil society was, and still is, how could individual interests be pursued in the social arena and, similarly, how could the social good be pursued in the individual or private sphere? Scottish thinkers looked to the idea of natural sympathy and innate mutuality to resolve these contradictory tensions by positing the natural propensity to sociability within the breast of civilized man.

This "solution" to the problem of society, this "formula" for a civil society with its particular reading of civility as something quite beyond polite manners, was not, and indeed could not be, a lasting one. Very quickly in fact the idea of an innate propensity to goodness and sociability was countered—most especially in the writings of Scottish philosopher and historian David Hume—with an argument for society organized solely by the mutual pursuit of individual interests. Bernard Mandeville's *Fable of the Bees* (1714), in which the British philosopher and satirist maintained that private vices produced public goods, gained acceptance, and David Hume's famous argument that the exchange of services was based not on any kindness but rather solely on self-interest (in the mutual exchange of such services) became the reigning theory by which the organization of society was explained.

By the time German philosopher G. W. F. Hegel wrote his *Philosophy of Right* in 1821, the idea of civil society had indeed lost its moorings in any idea of natural sympathy or mutual benevolence, and for Hegel, as for the social philosopher Karl Marx after him, civil society was identified solely with that realm of social action where the interests of different social groups compete with one another. Thus by the turn of the nineteenth century, civil society was, for Hegel, Marx, and others, made up of a heterogeneity of classes, social groups, professional associations, and the like, each with its own interests and agendas, each competing with the others in pursuit of its own particular good. In many ways civil society became almost totally identified with that society of free competitors that one immediately correlates with the logic of the marketplace. For both Hegel and Marx this contradictory and tension-filled existence of society had to be resolved. Their solutions, however, were very different. For Hegel the conflict of particular wills that made up civil society would be resolved in the ethical entity of the universal state; for Marx the resolution of civil society's tensions could be accomplished only by the establishment of a classless society.

By the mid-nineteenth century civil society had taken on a whole new set of meanings. As it became increasingly identified with what was privately owned and market regulated, so it was also contrasted to the state. In fact, thinkers began to conceive of civil society and the state as dichotomous social realities, and among certain thinkers such as American political philosopher Thomas Paine and, later, French writer and politician Alexis de Tocqueville, a healthy civil society was seen as necessary protection against the development of a despotic state.

Civil Society and Citizenship

This evolving understanding of civil society as a phenomenon existing apart from and often in opposition to the state had much to do with the retreat of the concept from scholarly use and public debate in the second half of the nineteenth century and first half of the twentieth. For it was in this period that the problems originally viewed as remedied by civil society—that is, the problems of providing a new basis for the organization of societal interests and the establishment of new criteria for membership and participation in society—became, on the whole, subsumed under the devel-

oping idea of citizenship. The great struggles at the end of the nineteenth century and early in the twentieth century over workers' rights, unionization, and, most essentially, the right to vote and establishment of universal suffrage became the arena where the institutionalization of any idea of civil society was played out. Civil freedom, economic autonomy, and the moral agency of the individual man and woman became, to a great extent, identified with the rights and obligations of citizenship as defining the terms of membership in the social and political orders.

In this period, therefore, the idea of citizenship became more or less conterminous with that of civil society. Indeed, the extension or universalization of the rights of citizenship and the legal and institutional spheres of its workings (from equality before the law, to the right to vote, to different forms of social entitlement) became the concrete and practical forms taken by the idea of civil society in the nineteenth century. The social problems that, in the eighteenth century, had been discussed in terms of civil society were in no small measure transformed into problems that people in the nineteenth and twentieth centuries would discuss (and struggle over) in terms taken from the lexicon of citizenship.

This was the case until sometime in the 1980s, when the idea of civil society enjoyed a renewal and resurgence that have continued unabated. This more contemporary revival of the idea of civil society began in Eastern Europe, especially in Poland in the 1970s during the struggle between the Polish workers' movement and the coercive apparatus of the state. There, civil society reentered the lexicon of political and social usage—this time, however, more as a political slogan and as a cudgel to batter the totalitarian state than anything else. Its strong civic associations and resonance of social voluntarism and activities and spheres of action free of state regulation and intervention made it an especially favorable political slogan within the context of the Soviet-style totalitarian regimes of Eastern and Central Eastern Europe. Indeed, use of the term spread from Poland to the revolutionary movements under way in all the countries of the area.

With so much of social life regulated by the state and with private life rendered virtually meaningless in so many Eastern European countries, the banner of civil society presented a potent rallying point for those wishing to reclaim from the state a social (and indeed a private) space free from the state and its regulative agencies. Freely organized voluntary organizations of a civic, religious, and political nature became focal points for new demands to implement a civil society around what became the new political parties and employer and employee associations—and often religious organizations—of the post-1989 revolutions in Eastern Europe. Here too, civil society gave itself over, when circumstances finally permitted, to the dynamics of citizenship and of interest representation within a democratically organized political order.

Although the concept of civil society proved useful as a political slogan and rallying call under totalitarian and repressive regimes, many in Eastern Europe found in the post-1989 period that its usefulness in constructing an institutional order was limited. The drafting of new constitutions and rules of public order, the growth of free political parties, and the development of new market economies—each with their own dynamics, tensions, challenges, and sets of problems—have tended to reorient debate around more familiar concepts such as liberalism and democracy.

The Ambiguities of the Idea of Civil Society

A look at the changing role of the Catholic Church in Poland illustrates the ambiguity at the heart of the notion of civil society. In the period of communist rule (1945–1989) the Polish church was the center of protest to the regime, preserving in its very existence the meanings, identities, and commitments that had been suppressed by the communist state. In its role as a symbol of resistance to the regime and as an association that was to a great degree successful at preserving its independence and autonomy from the state, the Polish church became a model to many of the phenomenon of civil society.

Yet today the Polish church is not what it was before the triumph of the workers' union Solidarity and the overthrow of communism in 1989. The major battle lines in contemporary Poland are in fact between Catholicism and liberal democracy, and the church may be poised to reassert its lost privileges in the realm of state making and policy promulgation. Certainly the role of the church in the development of Polish policy on religious education and abortion in the 1990s would lead one to question its continuing role as supporter of universal human rights, individual autonomy, and, in fact, civil society. It is one thing to assign the church a role as political actor within a pluralist civil society—a role akin to that of any other interest group—but it is quite another to identify the church with the very essence of that national entity that supposedly finds expression in the workings of civil society as often is the case in contemporary Poland.

There, where the idea of civil society has a markedly national cast, where it resonates strongly with the Polish people, with national independence, and with national institutions, the role of the church is very different from its role in the West. The very political strength of the church and its public and deprivatized position in society as a political actor in its own right raise in fact serious questions about the role of such an institution within civil society. Similar questions can be raised about the organization of xenophobic political movements and parties within the multiethnic and nationally heterogeneous societies of Eastern Europe, and in Western Europe as well.

All these phenomena lead to the question: just how civil, or how representative of civil society, are organizations whose political programs are by nature antidemocratic, socially exclusive, or even racist? If civil society is the realm of social voluntarism, in which associations representing interests apart from the state mediate between the individual citizen and the state, then organizations such as the Montana militias and the Ku Klux Klan in the United States, the Muslim Brotherhood in Egypt, and fundamentalist terrorist groups such as Hamas on the West Bank also would qualify as examples of civil society. One could therefore conclude that civil society is not always an unmitigated good thing. While people may like to believe that voluntary associations and civic groups are all based on liberal individualist assumptions and honor universal human rights, that often is not the case. Civil society, then, must refer to something more than just a generous number of different forms of association. A vibrant civil society also must include associations dedicated to and organized around certain principles of tolerance and recognition of civility that may not be far at all from the original ideas of the Scottish moralists in the mid-eighteenth century.

To be sure, this understanding has not yet been accepted by all users of the term *civil society*. Indeed, the idea of civil society continues to be used by political groups and thinkers on both the right and the left, although in Europe it most often is the province of the left, whereas in the United States it has been appropriated by both groups to advance their political agendas. Thus for right-of-center thinkers as well as for libertarian followers of the Austrian economist and philosopher Friedrich von Hayek, the quest for civil society is a mandate to deconstruct many of the powers of the state and replace them with intermediary institutions based on social voluntarism.

Many of these thinkers and followers, however, refuse to recognize that voluntary organizations can be of a particularly nasty nature and based on primordial or ascriptive principles of membership and participation that put to shame the very foundations of any idea of civil society. For many liberals civil society is identified with social movements, also existing beyond the state. But they are blind to the fact that the Achilles heel of any social movement is its institutionalization which, one way or the other, must be through the state and its legal (and coercive) apparatus. In the meantime, both communitarians and liberals continue to assimilate the idea of civil society into their own terms, invest it with their own meanings, and make of it what they will as the term is identified with everything from multiparty systems and the rights of citizenship to individual voluntarism and the spirit of community.

The present confusion in the use of the term notwithstanding, the idea of civil society continues to be usefully invoked as a political slogan in the quest for more democratically organized societies that give greater scope to individual freedom and self-determination. Interestingly, Muslim societies in the Middle East and beyond (Indonesia, for example) have adopted this concept not only as a slogan in protest of existing institutional arrangements but also as the basis of a more theoretical and critical attitude toward the Islamic tradition itself, which has its own sources and unique potentialities for the formation of modern associations out of Islamic religious traditions and even kinship structures. Within Muslim societies there are many indigenous forms of association, from tribal forums, to the traditionally male *diwaniyyah* where people gather in the homes of leading citizens to discuss social issues, to the religiously endowed organizations of the *Awqaf,* all of which can and have played a role in the exponential growth of civic associations in Muslim countries. Indeed, in the Middle East, with its authoritarian, autocratic, and patrimonial regimes, demands for a civil society of freely organized citizens seem to have as much resonance now as they did earlier in the communist countries of Eastern Europe.

See also *Citizenship; Europe, Eastern.*

Adam B. Seligman

BIBLIOGRAPHY

Bell, Daniel. "American Exceptionalism Revisited: The Role of Civil Society." *Public Interest* 95 (1989): 38–56.

Bobbio, Norberto. *Democracy and Dictatorship.* Minneapolis: University of Minnesota Press, 1989.

Casanova, Jose. *Public Religions in the Modern World.* Chicago: University of Chicago Press, 1994.

Hall, John A., ed. *Civil Society, Theory, History, Comparisons.* Oxford: Polity Press, 1995.

Keane, John. *Civil Society and the State.* London: Verso Press, 1988.

Norton, Augustus R., ed. *Civil Society in the Middle East.* Leiden: E. J. Brill, 1995.

Seligman, Adam B. *The Idea of Civil Society.* New York: Free Press, 1992.

Taylor, Charles. "Modes of Civil Society." *Public Culture* 3 (1990): 95–118.

Colonialism

Colonialism involves extension of political and economic control by a usually technologically or organizationally superior people or state over a foreign area—populated or unpopulated. It has existed since antiquity and can be driven by motives as diverse as the desire to expand and control trade, the search for land and resources, the quest for freedom from religious persecution, and the zeal to convert indigenous peoples to the colonial power's faith.

Modern European colonialism virtually emerged from the Crusades, the military expeditions Western European Christians undertook between 1095 and 1270 to recover from Muslim control Jerusalem and the other Palestinian places of pilgrimage known to Christians as the Holy Land. The first forms of modern colonialism were created by Portugal and Spain in South America beginning in the sixteenth century. The central purpose was to extract gold and silver, bringing great wealth to the Iberian kingdoms and money for the foremost maritime power in Europe. Spanish America's own supremacy over the Low Countries did not go unchallenged by the Dutch and British, however. A series of raids by English navigator and explorer Sir Francis Drake (1540?–1596) and other adventurers siphoned off much of the Spanish and Portuguese bullion. The Dutch had a much larger fleet than did the English and so built it up as to take control of port cities in South East Asia. The British tried to challenge the Dutch but were repulsed. In the early seventeenth century the British relocated in ports in India. France was also active in several parts of India, and both countries were reduced to a state of intermittent war. Because India was so vast, these conquered areas were quite restricted and most of the subcontinent remained under Indian control.

At the end of the Napoleonic Wars (1799–1815), in which

the Netherlands had been a French auxiliary, British claims were asserted in the Cape Colony in Africa and Dutch sugar colonies in the Caribbean. Most of the Dutch possessions in Indonesia were returned to them, although Britain retained Singapore and Penang. These changes left most of the developing world still under its own rulers. The other European powers entered the colonial race after 1870. Britain and France secured their colonial possessions by sea. Other powers absorbed territory by landward expansion—hence Russia absorbed the Islamic states of Central Asia, and Japan took over Korea and much of China. It can be argued that the area the United States occupied in Mexico in 1846 was a similar landward acquisition of empire. The colonizing powers followed different patterns of government. Britain left indigenous rulers in charge of vast tracts, where they remained powerful. The French largely ruled directly, introducing their own officials as the colonial rulers. Both kinds of colonization left the new rulers in supreme control.

For the most part, colonial powers worked out their rivalries without direct antagonisms. The boundaries between the colonial regimes bore only a casual resemblance to their previous territorial divisions, and peoples with different languages were often put together. Because of these agreements between the colonial powers, there were seldom major wars between them. At most there were minor frontier conflicts. The main period of rivalry was from about 1890 to 1914.

When World War I erupted in 1914, African and Asian troops were employed not only in their own areas but also in Western Europe. The French deployed African soldiers on the Western Front, and the British brought in Indian troops. Although these encounters produced no immediate political consequences it has been argued that serious political awareness among colonial peoples can be dated from this wartime experience. The 1920s and 1930s witnessed a much greater demand for autonomy, particularly in India. Latin America had attained formal independence from Spain and Portugal, although political power was the monopoly of a small minority of whites, such as Simón Bolívar. The United States retained ultimate political power, however, and whenever it was deemed dangerous for American interests, the Marines were dispatched to restore order. British policy in Asia looked forward to eventual self-government for the Asians but in a time-scale so distant as to be quite unrealistic.

Africa, however, was not seen as producing nationalist feelings. The Africans were believed to be limited by concepts of tribalism that inhibited all but local and regional

groupings, and there was no thought of changing the existing social forces. The only major change was that the former dominance of hunters gave way to the landed classes. Groups without land were at the very bottom of the social scale and were not able to rise. In general land ownership was on traditional lines, although in a few, very limited areas traditional agriculture gave way to modern forms of cultivation. Thus in West Africa there was a move into the production of cocoa, and in East Africa, into tea and coffee. These changes gave greater wealth to some among the landed groups who moved into commerce, law, and other commercial activities. In a way they had become the allies or customers of the colonial overlords. This was the main change in the social deployment. There were few attempts at directly challenging the Western overlords, the most notable being the Zulu rebellion that involved the defeat of a British force. Generally the superior weapons technology of Westerners meant that the Africans stood no real chance.

It might have been supposed that the colonial relationship would continue indefinitely, but colonialism came to an end more because of world forces than because of the local pattern. With the rise of the ideas of national sovereignty and self-determination in the twentieth century, quite suddenly the deployment of colonial military power symbolized not an advanced role in international relations but, on the contrary, appeared as a sign of international backwardness. Different Western countries came to this view at rather different times. The United States and Britain were the first to understand that in the new circumstances of the world after World War II ended in 1945, there was no longer a place for colonialism. The French and Dutch were slower to change their attitudes. The first to take up colonialism, the Portuguese were also the last to discard it. All this happened between 1950 and 1970. There was also the phenomenon of colonized states that in turn had become colonizers. They were mainly in the South of Africa—notably Rhodesia (Zimbabwe) and South Africa. Here colonialism had been on strictly racial lines, but in a few short years it also disappeared.

Spanish and Portuguese conquests in South America witnessed a massive interaction of church and state. Every colonial city was dominated by a striking church of great size and splendor. The head of the church community, the archbishop, was also sometimes the head of secular affairs. In fact, the ordinary people remained largely unaffected by the new religion, but formally the tone of society was Catholic.

In British colonies the religious spirit was much less in evidence. Indeed, before 1800 Christian missionaries were excluded from India and some other areas of British control. Thereafter, as the spirit of religion became even stronger in Britain, there was a greater degree of Christian activity in India and other colonies. During the first half of the nineteenth century many Christian values were introduced in India and elsewhere. Higher education was much influenced by Christian thinking, and the colleges in Calcutta, Madras, and other cities were explicitly Christian in tone. All this was modified by the end of the century. There was a good deal of conversion to Christianity, but this was mostly among the poorer elements in society.

Only in the Philippines was the whole population converted to Christianity during three centuries of Spanish Catholic rule. Although the Spaniards were replaced by American forms of government, the existing system of society and politics was sufficiently well established to maintain the status quo.

French colonial possessions were second only to those of the British in size and importance, and of course France is a Catholic country, but the spirit of the French Revolution (1789–1799) was sufficiently pervasive to maintain the secular system to a large extent. The institutions of government and administration in French colonies were therefore not greatly influenced by Catholicism. The lawyers and landlords who dominated the new politics in British colonies were also dominant in those ruled by France. Although the increased democratization of forms of government brought new elements into the administrative structure, these did not fundamentally affect the nature of the system of control. Hence the interaction of politics and religion remained limited in Asia and Africa.

What difference, then, did colonialism make to the developing world? It advanced the movement of Asia and Africa into modernity somewhat. There were terrible injustices in colonialism, but there was also an overall quiet advancement that nevertheless brought Asia and Africa into the modern world. The stains, such as the slave trade, are striking; the gains are not. What seems clear is that colonialism did not contribute to the division of the world into advanced and backward sectors but in general led to the evolution of one world, which however stark its differences contributed to wholeness.

See also *Conversion; Missionaries; Nationalism.*

Hugh Tinker

BIBLIOGRAPHY

Brunschwig, Henri. *French Colonialism, 1871–1914: Myths and Realities.* London: Praeger, 1966.

Emerson, Rupert. *From Empire to Nation: The Rise of Self-Assertion of Asian and African Peoples.* Cambridge: Harvard University Press, 1960.

Fieldhouse, D. K. *The Colonial Empires: A Comparative Survey.* London: Weidenfeld and Nicolson, 1966.

Furnivall, J. S. *Colonial Policy and Practice.* Cambridge: Cambridge University Press, 1948.

Lapping, Brian. *End of Empire.* New York: St. Martin's Press, 1985.

Smith, Tony, ed. *The End of European Empire: Decolonisation after World War Two.* Lexington, Mass.: Heath, 1975.

Tinker, Hugh. *Men Who Overturned Empires: Fighters, Dreamers and Schemers.* Basingstoke: Macmillan, 1987.

Communication

Communication, broadly defined as the exchange of information between individuals or groups, plays an important role in American religion and American politics. Communication encompasses sources that are both formal or structured, like a daily newspaper, and informal and unstructured, like the exchanges between friends at church about who to vote for in an upcoming election. In addition, communication sources are both secular and religious in content.

The importance of both formal and informal sources of religious communication is growing in the United States as the millennium approaches. This development is tied to the flourishing of religious institutions in American society. Church attendance remains high, charitable giving is growing, and voluntary activity in the church and in church-related institutions is high as well. Despite some evidence of secularization in American society, the "religious factor," as scholar Gerhard Lenski called it a generation ago, remains strong.

In addition, the role of religious communication in determining the public's political beliefs may be stronger than ever, relative to other, more traditional sources of influence. Political party organizations at the local level no longer have the clout that they once did; local precinct workers knocking on doors and asking support for their candidates are far less common than in the past. Into that vacuum, lobbying for the voter's attention, proceed political candidates themselves, the national media, or local networks of the voter's friends, neighbors, and fellow churchgoers. Indeed, the latter act as sources of personal influence and have great potential for making an impact on the political attitudes and behaviors of the mass public. Given the strength of religious identifications and local church bodies, the potential for religious influence is great, relative to other sources. In addition, churches serve as mobilizing environments, as places where people gather, with vote-seeking politicians never far behind.

Despite strong indications that religious communication has political consequences, the relationships between religion, communication, and political behavior remain problematic because a systematic body of literature has yet to develop in this area. Scholars of religion have tended to ignore these relationships, except when they have been important to an understanding of the television evangelists and the role of the media in the careers of American evangelists like Aimee Semple McPherson and Billy Sunday. Similarly, experts in the field of political communications have tended to overlook the role of religion.

This discussion begins by examining the sources of communication, both secular and religious, including the mass media and other forms of communication. Next it looks at the receipt of communication, especially among religious people. Finally, it explores the impact of communication on the political behavior of the public. Throughout, special attention is given to evangelical Protestantism, the religious tradition that is both the source of and the object of many religious communications. In fact, it is reasonable to suggest that religious radio and television have made a major contribution to the development of evangelicalism as a self-conscious religious movement.

Sources of Communication

What are the sources of communication that affect political behavior? There are the familiar secular sources like newspapers, radio, television, and magazines. But there are also numerous sources of religious communication such as religious periodicals, radio, and television. These religious sources of communication have grown significantly since the 1920s. Religious publishing houses flourish in America, representing the variety of denominations. Religious periodicals abound, from narrowly focused denominational publications to interdenominational magazines like *Christianity Today,* the unofficial voice of American evangelicalism. *Christian Century* serves mainline Protestantism, while *Commonweal* is but one of many publications directed mainly toward a Roman Catholic audience. Finally, a variety of Jewish media are available, from the more general publications like *Moment* to the more intellectual *Commentary* and *Tikkun.*

Almost from the beginning of the radio boom in the 1920s, American religious broadcasters made their mark, from the hyper-energetic Aimee Semple McPherson (1890–1944) to the demagogic Father Charles Coughlin (1891–1979). The latter began on a single station in Detroit in 1926 but by 1930 had a national program on CBS Radio. From the start, religious broadcasting was viewed as a service in the public interest. As a result, both networks and local stations offered religious groups access to the airwaves. But Father Coughlin's strong attacks on President Franklin D. Roosevelt led to a reassessment of this policy by his network. CBS set up an in-house advisory board for religious broadcasting and sought the outside guidance of the Federal Council of Churches (today's National Council of Churches) to advise the network on religious programming. For a ten-year period ending with the conclusion of World War II, only the Mutual Broadcasting System offered commercial time without restriction to religious broadcasters. Evangelicals were effectively shut out from the airwaves during this period, leading to the founding in 1944 of the National Religious Broadcasters, which lobbied the Federal Communications Commission (FCC) for airtime for religious programming that was fair to all groups. Differences between religious groups were never settled, but a 1960 FCC ruling opened the door for paid religious broadcasting on both radio and television stations at the local level. Prior to the ruling 47 percent of all religious broadcasting was free, whereas by the late 1970s that figure had dropped to 8 percent.

Although networkwide religious broadcasting in America is sparse today, local radio and television stations offer a wide variety of religious programs. In this environment of paid religious programming, individuals and churches representing the evangelical religious tradition and its associated movements—fundamentalism and the charismatic or pentecostal movement—have been at the forefront. In terms of religious radio, an evangelical presence was a fixture in almost every community in the nation in the late 1990s. Some local stations had an exclusive or predominantly evangelical focus. The Moody Radio Network, for example, blanketed the nation with programs. Such personalities as the radio psychologist James Dobson became household names in Christian circles. Partly as a result of his radio show, *Focus on the Family,* Dobson became a leader in "Christian right" politics. Christian radio, then, has been a pervasive presence in American society. Although spreading the Gospel of Jesus Christ has been its first priority, promoting traditional conservative values has been a close second. It has been estimated that three-quarters of religious broadcasting (radio and television) comes from the evangelical religious community.

The story of religious media would be incomplete without a careful examination of religious television. The precursors of modern televangelism were the nineteenth-century American revivalists Charles Grandison Finney (1792–1875) and Dwight Lyman Moody (1837–1899) and their twentieth century American counterpart Billy Sunday (1863–1935). These leaders established evangelistically focused organizations that were separate from traditional denominations, developed successful techniques for mass evangelism, and brought sound business principles to their ventures, along with rhetorical gifts of persuasion. They serve as exemplars for religious television and its practitioners today.

Religious television began to make its mark in the United States in the 1950s with the network program of Roman Catholic Bishop Fulton Sheen and the televising of the Billy Graham crusades. Since Sheen went off the air in the late 1950s over a dispute with New York's Cardinal Francis Spellman, and in the aftermath of the 1960 FCC ruling noted above, the field has been left increasingly to evangelicals who have successfully raised the money to put and keep programs on the air. Mainline Protestantism has only a limited presence on religious television, compared with that of its evangelical brethren.

As a result, almost all of the best-known televangelists have been evangelicals, from Graham, Rex Humbard, and Oral Roberts to Robert Schuller, Jerry Falwell, Pat Robertson, Jimmy Swaggart, and Jim and Tammy Bakker. Despite scandals associated with Swaggart and Bakker, programs like Falwell's *Old-Time Gospel Hour* and Robertson's *700 Club* continue to play to sizable audiences, dispensing the now familiar mixture of oldtime evangelism and conservative politics. Both Falwell and Robertson were leaders of national political movements that had their beginnings in their religious television programs, with the media exposure helping to secure them a national following. In good measure, then, Falwell's Moral Majority and Robertson's Christian Coalition are the products of religious television. But the organizations of the Christian right, as important as they are, may not be the most important contribution of the religious media. As noted earlier, religious media contributed a sense of identity to an interdenominational movement, American

evangelicalism, with implications not only for politics but for other aspects of life as well.

Other sources of religious communication exist apart from the mass media. The growth of religious interest groups like the Moral Majority and the Christian Coalition has made these organizations influential participants in the political process. Groups such as these and the Washington offices of the major American denominations have altered the face of national politics. Many of these groups have networks that extend to the local level with participants meeting regularly, and they are often actively involved in politics.

Local churches are also locations for frequent political communication. The Roman Catholic Church in America has never been hesitant to send political messages to its member congregations; the pastoral letters from Catholic bishops are only the most recent form of this activity. The African American church has always been a place for local political activity, and it became the organizational focus for the civil rights movement. White Protestant clergy, particularly the mainline variety, were also active in the civil rights and peace movements, although neither movement had broad grassroots support within mainline denominations. White evangelical pastors have joined the fray in recent decades, pushing a moral reform agenda with a particular focus on abortion and gay rights. Both pastors and religious activists are in strategic positions to influence the politics of active laity within their congregations. This influence can take the form of pastoral communications from the pulpit, or it may find expression in one of the many informal means that pastors and other leaders use to communicate their views to the flock. For example, many pastors may feel uncomfortable about endorsing candidates from the pulpit but might be comfortable with Christian Coalition voter guides being handed out after the service.

Receiving Political Communication

The sources of political communication are many, but how important are they to the mass public? Recent research has attempted to answer this question. A national sample of Americans was asked to assess the importance of various sources of voting information. Sixty-six percent of a national sample of approximately twenty-four hundred respondents mentioned newspapers as a key source; 64 percent cited television news; 57 percent noted "this year's political campaign"; 46 percent mentioned radio; and 30 percent noted coworkers or friends. All of these, of course, are secular sources. Smaller percentages referred to religious sources: 14 percent mentioned their church or place of worship; 12 percent cited religious publications; another 10 percent noted religious television, with 8 percent mentioning religious radio; and, finally, 9 percent cited mail from religious groups. These figures increase significantly, however, when only the target group for most of these religious sources, white evangelical Protestants, is examined. The percentages increase even more when the examination is limited to "traditionalist" evangelicals—in other words, those with strongly orthodox Christian beliefs and very high levels of religious practice. Traditionalists, who make up almost 10 percent of the population, are much more likely than the public at large to regard religious radio as an important source of voting information (29 percent). Other important sources for traditionalists include religious publications (27 percent), religious television (24 percent), information obtained at their place of worship (21 percent), and mail received from religious interest groups (21 percent). In other words, a significant portion of the population both receives religious communications and regards them as important to their political behavior.

Impact of Communication on Political Behavior

Although secular sources of communication outnumber the religious, the latter are more important for evangelicals than for most other Americans and are particularly influential with the most orthodox and observant among them. Do these religious communications matter in terms of voting decisions, and do they matter more than the secular communications? In terms of the secular sources of communication, respondents that regarded newspapers and television news as important factors in their voting decisions were more likely to have voted for Bill Clinton than for Bob Dole and for Democratic as opposed to Republican House candidates in the 1996 election. In contrast, individuals that relied on radio and interest group mail in making their voting decisions were somewhat more likely to have voted Republican. Communications from the political campaign itself and from friends and coworkers made no difference in voting choices. The secular sources, then, exhibited no consistent pattern in relationships with the vote in 1996.

Communications from religious sources, however, consistently benefited the Republicans. Religious radio made the most difference: the 8 percent of the population that regarded religious radio as important to their vote choice gave 65 percent of their votes to Dole in 1996, while those who did not rely on this medium gave Dole only 42 percent. Comparable figures for voting for Republican candidates for the U.S. House of Representatives were 83 and 50 percent. Percentages for the other religious sources were not as striking but still in the same direction. This Republican bias among those who regarded religious sources of communication as important held up for evangelicals as well. The impact was less significant, but still present, among traditionalist evangelicals. Among the latter, ties to the local church and the evangelical community are so strong (84 percent of them claimed to be in church the weekend before the 1996 presidential election compared with 58 percent of the nation as a whole) that they lessen the dependence on external sources of religious communication. As documented in the scholarly literature, many forces are pushing evangelicals in the direction of the Republican Party, and religious sources of communication are certainly part of the explanation.

Is there evidence about the content of pastoral political communication? The classic studies of Protestant clergy emphasized the liberal bias of pastors in communicating with their congregations. But there is evidence of change. In recent research on the Protestant clergy, mainline and evangelical pastors were asked what political subjects they talked about in church. Their theological positions predicted their responses, with the theologically orthodox emphasizing a moral reform agenda focusing on abortion, gay rights, sexual promiscuity, and moral decline; the theologically liberal, on the other hand, emphasized a social justice agenda focusing on race, poverty, equal rights, and the environment. Clerical conservatives, the research showed, were as politically active as their liberal counterparts. In a 1996 survey the mass public was asked what political issues their clergy had spoken about in the past year. Seventy-four percent said their pastors had talked about hunger and poverty, 55 percent mentioned abortion and sexual behavior, while just 19 percent noted "candidates and elections," and only 9 percent said their clergy had spoken about foreign policy or defense-related issues. For traditionalist evangelicals the percentages increased significantly on the abortion, sexual behavior, and "candidates and elections" items while declining on the other two items.

This evidence indicates that both pastors and the mass public agree about the content of clerical communications. Do these communications make an electoral difference? The 1996 survey found that when clergy discussed abortion or sexual behavior, their congregations tended to side with the Republicans. When they discussed poverty and hunger or foreign policy and defense issues, congregations leaned toward the Democrats. Somewhat surprisingly, if candidates and elections had been discussed in the previous year, individuals leaned toward the Democrats. So there is evidence that the content of pastoral communications is related to the vote choices of those who receive the messages.

Finally, in the same survey, a series of questions were asked about secular and religious contacts made during the campaign itself. Here the disparity between secular and religious contacts was much less pronounced than that between secular and religious media communications. In terms of campaign contacts, 26 percent of Americans claimed to have been contacted by a candidate for office, 23 percent by a political party, and 19 percent by either a business or labor group. Among evangelicals, the percentage contacted by a business or labor group fell to 15 percent, but the other percentages were about the same. These secular contacts made little difference in how evangelicals cast their votes. Twenty-five percent of them said that they had had discussions about the election with friends at church, while 21 percent claimed that information on candidates and parties had been made available in their place of worship before the election. These figures rose to 44 percent and 33 percent, respectively, among traditionalist evangelicals. Smaller proportions of the mass public claimed to have been contacted by "a religious group, like the Christian Coalition or the Interfaith Alliance" (12 percent), or to have had their clergy or church leaders urge them to vote a particular way (10 percent). But 31 percent of traditionalist evangelicals said the Christian Coalition or some other religious interest group had contacted them, although only 11 percent of traditionalists had been given voting advice by their pastor or other church leader. It is not surprising that talking with church friends and finding materials about candidates and parties in church were related to voting for Republican candidates in 1996 and that being contacted by the Christian Coalition or another outside religious interest group had the largest GOP impact of all. Clergy vote recommendations did not have much impact one way or the other.

The evidence supports the conclusion that secular contacts had little effect on the outcome of the 1996 election. Religious contacts, however, did have an impact, especially among evangelicals. These findings are far from conclusive but suggest that targeted contacting efforts can pay off in

election campaigns. Traditionalist evangelicals are a natural target because their political attitudes are relatively homogeneous and they are easy to reach in the church setting.

Audiences for Communication

The secular and religious media clearly communicate to different audiences. Secular communications are received by large segments of the population, including the highly religious, while religious communications are rarely if ever received outside religious circles. Increasingly, many religious communications are received by the evangelical community only. In that community their impact is greatest among traditionalist evangelicals and is closely related to their voting decisions.

See also *Conservatism; Evangelicalism; Fundamentalism; Graham, Billy; Pentecostalism.*

Paul M. Kellstedt and Lyman A. Kellstedt

BIBLIOGRAPHY

Green, John C., et al. *Religion and the Culture Wars: Dispatches from the Front.* Lanham, Md.: Rowman and Littlefield, 1996.

Guth, James L., et al. *The Bully Pulpit: The Politics of Protestant Clergy.* Lawrence: University Press of Kansas, 1997.

Hadden, Jeffrey K. *The Gathering Storm in the Churches.* Garden City, N.Y.: Doubleday, 1969.

Hadden, Jeffrey K., and Anson D. Shupe. *Televangelism, Power, and Politics on God's Frontier.* New York: Henry Holt, 1988.

Hertzke, Allen D. *Representing God in Washington: The Role of Religious Lobbies in the American Polity.* Knoxville: University of Tennessee Press, 1988.

Horsfield, Peter G. *Religious Television: The American Experience.* New York: Longman, 1984.

Quinley, Harold E. *The Prophetic Clergy: Social Activism among Protestant Ministers.* New York: Wiley, 1974.

Schultze, Quentin. "Evangelical Radio and the Rise of the Electronic Church, 1921–1948." *Journal of Broadcasting and Electronic Media* 32 (1988): 289–306.

Sweet, Leonard I., ed. *Communication and Change in American Religious History.* Grand Rapids, Mich.: Eerdmans, 1993.

Wald, Kenneth D. *Religion and Politics in the United States.* 3d ed. Washington, D.C.: CQ Press, 1997.

Communism

Communism set out—in theory—to bring about a society in which all would be equal: everyone would contribute to it according to ability and everyone would draw upon its resources according to need, a prelude to the withering away both of the state and of religion. However, in practice every communist or Marxist regime promoted hostility to, often persecution of, religion as one of its defining features. Karl Marx, the founding father of communism in the nineteenth century, did not write extensively about religion, but he defined it as "the opium of the people"—an unhealthy palliative necessary during the painful transformation of society to its "socialist" phase. Religion, Marx believed, would die a natural death when economic conditions improved to the point that all humanity shared the world's economic bounty. Not until October 1917, with the accession to power of Vladimir Ilyich Ulyanov, the Russian revolutionary known to history as Lenin, did communism execute a program of active persecution of religion.

Lenin and Stalin

Lenin's intentions were soon made clear. The Russian Orthodox Church was forced not only to dissociate itself from its tsarist past, when it had been a subservient state religion, but it was to be extirpated from society forthwith. Since the time of Peter the Great, tsar from 1682 until 1725, the state had nominated its own lay representative as head of the church, but the collapse of the tsarist regime in March 1917 provided an opportunity for the assertion of independence. The church elected a supreme head, Tikhon, the first patriarch since Peter the Great's abolition of the office two hundred years earlier.

Lenin's first legislative act was to abolish private ownership of land, including land that belonged to monasteries and churches. The Law on Separation of Church and State and of School from Church followed in January 1918. Although Lenin's constitution proclaimed the right of individuals to religious liberty, believers nevertheless were bereft of their religious heritage, and violent persecution followed. Church leaders (including Tikhon as well as the minority Roman Catholics and later the Baptists), along with uncounted millions of ordinary believers, were harassed, imprisoned, often murdered, or starved to death.

When Stalin (Joseph Vissarionovich Djugashvili) succeeded Lenin in 1925, the lot of believers deteriorated further. The assertion of unconditional loyalty to the state by the intimidated acting head of the church, Metropolitan Sergi, in 1927, was unavailing, even though this vow of loyalty became the theoretical standard for church-state relations until 1985, when Mikhail Sergeyevich Gorbachev became Soviet leader. Stalin's constitution replaced Lenin's right to "free-

dom of religion" by the much more restrictive phrase—"freedom of religious worship." But even that right was severely limited by compulsory state registration of places of worship, which in practice the authorities usually refused. The continued proclamation of separation of church and state was no more than a legal fiction.

The suffering of believers in Stalin's purges of the 1930s was the most comprehensive and organized persecution in Christian history, not excluding that of the early Christians under the Roman Empire. The church, both as an institution and as a worshipping community, virtually ceased to exist by 1941. The results of that devastation are still visible—the ruined relics of countless churches and monasteries—in nearly every town and village in Russia, Belarus, and Ukraine.

World War II and Its Consequences

The Great Patriotic War, as the Russians call the Second World War, had a positive effect on the life of the Russian Orthodox Church; however, the effect on all the territories that fell under Soviet domination at its conclusion was negative. The beneficial effect worked in two ways. Western areas of the Soviet Union (Belorussia and huge tracts of Ukraine and of Russia itself) were temporarily liberated from Soviet domination by the incursion of the Nazi German army in June 1941. Almost everywhere behind the German lines there was an immediate revival of religion. Churches reopened and, as from nowhere, clergy and laity emerged, ready to maintain them. This very fact would soon become a contributory factor to increased persecution, for when the Soviets reconquered these territories they were looking for scapegoats who could be accused of collaboration with the enemy.

In the Russian heartland and even in the non-Russian republics of the Soviet Union, Stalin used the call to patriotism to revive the morale of a nation that had been duped into a feeling of security by the Ribbentrop-Molotov pact. (This pact supposedly guaranteed nonaggression between the communist and fascist regimes.) After having abused religious believers for a decade and a half, Stalin called on their church to promote patriotism. Priests and pastors were released from prison on condition that they take an oath of loyalty to the Soviet state.

Stalin even received the surviving rump of the church leaders in 1943 and rewarded them for their loyalty with the promise of concessions as soon as practicable. Until recently, the substance of this meeting was unknown. But with the fall of communism and the opening of Soviet records, researchers have been able to dig through the archives and locate the protocol. It is evident that Stalin exhibited a benign face, making far-reaching promises about the reopening of churches, monasteries, and theological seminaries; the publication of a journal; and the election of a patriarch for the first time since the death of Tikhon, in 1925. Stalin generally kept to the promises he made, though his price was continuing political loyalty on the lines of Metropolitan (later Patriarch) Sergi's assertion of 1927, particularly offering moral support for the subjugation of the new parts of the Soviet empire acquired by conquest at the end of the First World War.

This unofficial concordat between church and state lasted until the accession to power of Nikita Sergeyevich Khrushchev in 1958. Khrushchev instituted a new period of active persecution, with the reclosure of many churches, from 1959 until his ousting in 1964.

Soviet Expansion and Cold War Policy

The Soviet Union expanded westward at the end of the war in 1945, to encompass the Baltic states (Estonia, Latvia, and Lithuania), which had been independent in the 1920s and 1930s. A huge swathe of territory, stretching from the Arctic to Moldavia in the south, was incorporated, in every part of which the church was flourishing. Protestant areas (predominantly Lutheran Estonia and Latvia) came under Soviet domination for the first time. There were millions of indigenous Roman Catholics in Lithuania, parts of Belorussia, and Ukraine. In Moldavia the Orthodox Church had a vigorous parish and monastic life. Every one of these areas had to be sovietized in its own way, but without exception subjugation of the church was a key issue and the brutality with which this was done contrasted with the improved situation in the Russian heartland.

A special case was Western Ukraine, where the Eastern Rite Catholics flourished—a church with developed education, a strong hierarchy, and an identification with Ukrainian nationalism. Its origins went back 250 years, and its development as a Catholic Church loyal to Rome but using the Slavonic liturgy and Orthodox Church order (allowing priests to marry, for example) had always been somewhat contentious. In 1946 Stalin's commissars forcibly incorporated it into the Russian Orthodox Church. Even this latter name was anathema to those upholding such a strong tradition of Ukrainian nationalism, but any who protested—many clergy, all the bishops, and the redoubtable Metropolitan Slipyj—immediately lost their liberty and some even their lives. The Ukrainian Catholic Church regained its legitimacy only at the time of Gorbachev's visit to the pope in December 1989.

From the end of World War II, Soviet influence spread further, as the parameters of the cold war were established. The new Communist bloc of Eastern and Central Europe presented a massively diversified religious picture. While each regime had limited autonomy to deal with the religious question in its own way, nowhere did the new rulers relinquish the basic communist tenet of state atheism.

Of all these countries Poland experienced the least direct persecution. After an unsuccessful attempt to gag Cardinal Stefan Wyszynski, an outspoken opponent of the government's repression of religious freedom, by imprisoning him from 1953 to 1956, the regime had burned its fingers in the fire of popular dissent. From then on a variety of even less successful antireligious tactics, all negated by the election of Cardinal Karol Wojtyla as pope in October 1978, were to occur. The new pope, John Paul II, was to become an instrumental figure in Poland's move toward liberation. Never before had the College of Cardinals elected a pope from Eastern Europe. The immediate effect, from the moment of his first visit back to his homeland in 1979, was to destabilize the country in a political sense, leading directly to the founding of the Christian trade union Solidarity.

Other Catholic leaders faced longer imprisonment than Cardinal Wyszynski, the best known of whom were Cardinals József Mindszenty in Hungary, Josef Beran in Czechoslovakia, and (in a country never fully incorporated into the Soviet bloc) Aloysius Stepinac in Yugoslavia. However, despite the temporary rise of various "peace priest" movements, which sought to reconcile Communism and Christianity and promote pro-regime sentiments among the populace, nowhere did the Catholic Church capitulate to the political demands of the ruling faction.

One cannot make such a generalization of the Protestant or Orthodox churches. In the Soviet Union the Baptists, who had been present in Russia and Ukraine in small numbers since the 1860s, at first appeared to do the political bidding as required, but from the early 1960s, in response to the renewed persecution under Khrushchev that affected all denominations, a resistance movement evolved uniting many congregations. The leaders of the *Initsiativniki* (initiators of a movement to set up a free congress) as they were called, or

Reform Baptists, put up decades of resistance to brutal treatment, but they succeeded in a way no other religious group in the Communist bloc ever did in attracting worldwide publicity and international support. The leadership of the registered Baptist congregations meanwhile made strenuous efforts to undermine the credibility of these reformers, both inside the Soviet Union and worldwide.

In Hungary a compromised but strong leadership of the Reformed Church, smaller than the majority Catholic Church, predominated over the anticommunist opposition in 1948 and again after the uprising of 1956. The resulting "diaconia theology," which was in effect a New Testament phrase for accommodation with the powers that be, exercised a telling influence on international bodies such as the World Council of Churches and the World Alliance of Reformed Churches, which, in their turn, were diverted from any front they might have established against Communist atheism. The Orthodox Churches of Eastern Europe played an even more prominent part in defining such a policy.

In the German Democratic Republic the majority Lutheran Church evolved a much more critical stance, never abandoning its determination to criticize the regime if it intruded too crassly into the administration of church affairs. Nevertheless, Christians found themselves to be second-class citizens, suffering discrimination in education and career opportunities.

The situation was very different in neighboring Czechoslovakia, where the minority Church of the Czech Brethren evolved its policies under the leadership of Josef Hromadka. As well as accepting the Soviet worldview, promoted by the Christian Peace Conference, which Hromadka established in 1958, the Czech Brethren put a unique emphasis on dialogue with the Communists. This effort drew together theologians from East and West in a series of meetings in the 1960s. The meetings ended abruptly when the Soviet invasion of August 1968 annihilated the so-called Prague Spring, the attempt under Alexander Dubček to introduce "communism with a human face." Those who had promoted the dialogue found themselves persecuted, but they, as well as the more traditional opposition to Communism, undoubtedly contributed to the evolution of a civic consciousness.

The Orthodox Church outside the Soviet Union unquestionably played a role in pacifying the people and, directly or indirectly, persuading them to accept their lot under the new regime. In Bulgaria, Communism in its early years instigated brutal persecution of all believers, especially the small Protestant and Catholic Churches, but Patriarch Kiril sacrificed independence of speech in order to preserve the structural unity of the Orthodox Church. From 1971 his successor, Patriarch Maxim, built relations that might almost be described as cordial.

In Romania the situation was not that different, though on the world stage the Orthodox Church, as the second largest after the Russian, played a more prominent role. Patriarch Justinian exercised his office for almost the first thirty years of the Communist state, evolving his own, less compromised version, of diaconia theology. The massive popular support for Orthodoxy was never confronted by the closure of churches such as happened in the Soviet Union. The Romanian Orthodox Church was the strongest visible Christian presence in a Communist country, even though the price, as a small number of dissenters and many Protestants discovered to their cost, was political conformity.

A total contrast to these countries was Albania, a predominantly Muslim country, though there was a significant Catholic and Orthodox presence as well. Following the precept of Chinese leader Mao Zedong, who never finalized the plan of closing every place of worship in China, Enver Hoxha, the Albanian premier, alone totally outlawed religion (1967), closing more than two thousand mosques and churches and imprisoning all religious leaders.

Many Albanian Muslims who lived on the Yugoslavian side of the frontier, in Kosovo, were at that time better off (though they were to suffer more after the breakup of Yugoslavia in 1989). Muslims in Bosnia (then part of Yugoslavia) were also treated tolerantly, which could not be said of Muslims in Azerbaijan and the five Soviet republics of Central Asia (nor of other Muslim enclaves in Russia). Although Islam was never outlawed, Soviet Muslim institutions collapsed in the early days of Communism and there was a massive closure of mosques.

Other Communist Countries

After the consolidation of Soviet power in Eastern and Central Europe, other countries in a wide diversity of geographical locations went over to the Communist sphere of influence. Although their relations with Moscow varied considerably, every one of them adopted state atheism in some form or other.

The most significant of these was China, which signaled its adoption of communism under Mao by the immediate expulsion of all foreign missionaries. The local churches had

Pope John Paul II and Cuban president Fidel Castro in January 1998, after the pope said Mass in Havana. The pope's visit marked an official thaw in Cuba's anti-religion policies, which had grown more hospitable to the practice of religion since Castro's pronouncement, in the early 1970s, that he saw no contradiction between religion and Marxism.

to become indigenous almost overnight, and political loyalty was demanded after the Soviet model. This situation led to a split in the Catholic Church between those who remained loyal to a "foreign regime" (Rome) and were forced to go underground and a new Chinese Catholic Church. Among Protestants of various denominations, who were forced to unite, there was a similar development. During the Cultural Revolution of the late 1960s and early 1970s, Christians, especially those belonging to the unofficial "house churches," suffered appalling deprivation, along with many other sectors of the population. The traditional Chinese religions such as Confucianism were less structured and survived with a low profile, though Islam, strong in the less populated western region of Xinjiang, suffered repression.

A special case was Tibet, which lost its independence as a result of the Chinese invasion of 1959. From that year on, following the escape of the Dalai Lama, Tibet's spiritual leader, to India, the Buddhist faith, which embraced the whole nation, was locked in a life-or-death struggle to survive. Buddhist monasteries and cultural institutions were under daily attack. The spirit of the people and their loyalty to the exiled Dalai Lama never succumbed, however.

Even Cuba, far distant from the hub of Communist power, became a loyal satellite of Moscow. In 1959 Fidel Castro demonstrated his intentions, after seizing power, by expelling all foreign, particularly American, missionaries. The majority Catholic Church was subjected to pressure and discrimination, if not open persecution. In more recent years Castro has shown himself to be more positive to issues such as Bible distribution, and the visit of Pope John Paul II to Cuba in 1998 seems finally to have reversed Cuban antireligious policies. North Korea, slavishly following Chinese policies, has come close to eradicating public religious life, though doubtless there is much below the surface which will one day be revealed. The African states of Angola, Mozambique, and Ethiopia all operated antireligious policies of one kind or another in the 1970s and 1980s, but in none of these were they systematic enough to have much beyond a short-term effect on religious life.

The Collapse of the Berlin Wall

The churches contributed to the rapid and relatively bloodless collapse of communism in Eastern Europe at the end of 1989 and two years later in the Soviet Union. While the events are still to be fully evaluated, what happened in Poland is clear. The election of the Polish pope led directly to the open resentment expressed by the tens of millions of Catholic Poles at the domination of their country by an alien ideology. Pope John Paul II visited his country in the summer of 1979 for the first time since his election and encouraged his people to take the initiative in the struggle for full religious liberty and their independence from false ideologies. Following the pope's visit, Lech Walesa (who would later be the first president of an independent Poland) gained massive support when he established Solidarity as a Christian trade union. Bishops, priests, and working laity were united. Fr. Jerzy Popieluszko became a Christian spokesman for political reform and attracted the attention of the nation before his murder by the police in 1985. The imposition of martial law could only fail to suppress freedom of thought, unless backed by a Soviet invasion, something that became unthinkable after the accession of Gorbachev.

In the German Democratic Republic the Protestant church began to provide a remarkable safe haven for political protesters in 1989. The churches in Czechoslovakia and Hungary were involved in the popular protests that led to increasing demands for the freedom to travel. The removal of the first brick from the Berlin Wall, which had stood as a symbol of a divided Europe since 1961, released a flood tide that no political edict could stem. Gorbachev and his right-hand man, Eduard Shevardnadze, the foreign minister, chose a policy that saved Europe from a bloodbath: the Soviet army would not intervene, as it had done in Hungary in 1956 and in Czechoslovakia in 1968. In Romania, which by then had an especially tough regime under Nicolae Ceausescu, a leader of the Reformed Church, Laszlo Tokes, led the first popular protests in Timisoara. These protests eventually resulted in the deposition and execution of the dictator.

In the Soviet Union the role of the churches in the period of glasnost and perestroika, Gorbachev's watchwords for examining the past and restructuring society, had been less dramatic but not insignificant, as they moved into the public domain for the first time since 1917. From 1988, when the state permitted—even encouraged—the Russian Orthodox Church to celebrate the millennium of its founding in Kiev, believers established social work in prisons, hospitals, and orphanages. In 1990, a year before the collapse of the Soviet Union, new laws were passed that guaranteed complete religious liberty and brought to fruition the efforts of thousands of all denominations who, in the 1970s and 1980s, had risked their freedom and even their lives to achieve religious liberty and transform the face of a repressive regime.

See also *Atheism; Balkan states; Buddhism, Tibetan; China; Cuba; Europe, Eastern; Hungary; Marxism; Orthodoxy, Russian; Poland; Russia; Yugoslavia.*

Michael Bourdeaux

BIBLIOGRAPHY

Beeson, Trevor. *Discretion and Valour.* 2d ed. London: Collins, 1982; Philadelphia: Fortress Press, 1982.

Bourdeaux, Michael. *Gorbachev, Glasnost, and the Gospel.* London: Modder and Stoughton, 1990; published in the United States as *The Gospel's Triumph over Communism.* Minneapolis: Bethany House, 1991.

Ellis, Jane. *The Russian Orthodox Church: A Contemporary History.* London and New York: Routledge, 1988.

Pospielovsky, Dimitry. *The Russian Church under the Soviet Regime, 1917–1982.* 2 vols. Crestwood, N.Y.: St. Vladimir's Seminary Press, 1984.

Walters, Philip, ed. *World Christianity: Eastern Europe.* Monrovia, Calif., and Eastbourne, Sussex: MARC, 1988.

Weigel, George. *The Final Revolution: The Resistance Church and the Collapse of Communism.* New York: Oxford University Press, 1992.

Communitarianism

Communitarianism, a contemporary social movement and political philosophy, developed in reaction to the individualist tendencies of Western culture. Its proponents seek to find remedies to the crisis of social disintegration, evidenced by the breakdown of family life, poverty, violence, and political fragmentation, through the development of communities. They advocate a renewed sense of responsibility for persons as parents, workers, employers, neighbors, and citizens.

Philosophically, communitarianism defines itself against liberalism, the dominant Western view that highlights individual liberty in personal, economic, and political life. Communitarianism holds that exaggerated individualism is the root cause of society's moral and social problems. It is distinct from communism in that it does not seek to subsume the dignity of the individual under the collective whole. Communitarianism aims to create a balance between persons and community, individual freedom, and the social good. It is most developed in the United States and Great Britain.

Philosophical Characteristics

The fundamental argument of communitarianism is that liberal individualism presents a distorted description of what it means to be a person. Communitarians describe persons as social beings. They hold that persons are formed within relationships and have no identity apart from relationships. Personal autonomy, the ability to choose freely, is dependent in many ways on human relationships. People, born within traditions, develop their own identity—who they are, what they think and feel—in relation to other people. Communitarians thus use such phrases as "the socially embedded self" or "the dialogical self" or "persons-in-community" to describe the essential social nature of persons.

Liberals defend a stance of neutrality on the notion of social good: it is up to individuals or businesses to define their own good. It is thus inappropriate for society to define social good in a way that would limit individual or corporate liberty. Communitarians hold that society can and must seek a shared meaning of the good. They believe the well-being of society is the element that should determine morality and social policy. Communitarians defend a strong notion of participatory democracy. The public good, to be truly a public good, must be discussed publicly.

In contrast to liberals, communitarians are suspicious of "rights" language, which in contemporary culture dominates moral discourse. Rights, by definition, are moral claims that individuals make against society. Communitarians argue that rights are proclaimed independently of particular social contexts and without concern for related responsibilities. Communitarians, although split on the significance of rights, as we shall see, are united in their concern for the priority of responsibility and the social nature of persons.

Types of Communitarians

There are two forms of communitarians, moderate and radical. Moderate communitarians are postliberal in that they build on the strengths of liberalism, especially its concern for social equality, while challenging its lack of social integration. They defend basic human rights but argue that the liberal understanding of rights is impoverished. Moderate communitarians call for a balance between rights and responsibilities. Their political positions do not fit neatly into categories. For example, they advocate strengthening the structure of the family by such politically diverse means as making divorce less accessible than it is now and by ensuring that employers provide maximum support for working par-

ents. They support teaching values of tolerance, conflict resolution, personal responsibility, and democracy in schools. They believe a healthy society is built on healthy institutions and thus promote participation in local institutions, schools, places of worship, and neighborhood groups. Radical communitarians reject the notion of human rights because they reject any attempt to develop an ethic that is applied universally to all communities and cultures. They hold that moral standards arise within particular communities as expressions of their history and tradition.

Both forms of communitarianism tend toward a relativistic morality. They typically reject transcommunal, or objective, moral claims in favor of a morality developed by consensus within a particular community. On the other hand, moral relativism within a community, they argue, is ultimately destructive to the community. Moderate communitarianism looks outward and focuses on civic responsibility. Radical communitarianism looks inward and focuses on preserving the identity of a particular community.

Role of Religion

Communitarianism has allies in Christianity and Judaism. Roman Catholic social thought, with its strong sense of people as social beings, its moral tradition of promoting the common good, its hierarchical structure that directs local communities to focus on larger communities, and its natural law tradition (moral truth is open to all persons of good will), has strong affinities with moderate communitarianism. The Biblical notion of covenant, as found in some Protestant and Jewish theology, corresponds with the communitarian notion of persons being bound in community, united by a common morality, and directed toward a good beyond the self.

The communitarian public virtues of rational dialogue, diversity, toleration, and a commitment to the social well-being resonates with fundamental concerns of contemporary Jewish and Christian life. Some forms of Protestantism, which stress the place of the individual against larger social structures, would be critical of the communitarian emphasis on the secular community. There is a strong affinity between radical communitarianism and some forms of Protestant and Jewish thought. Just as radical communitarians seeks to promote particular communities, some Jewish and Christian groups advocate forming alternative communities distinct from the world.

Criticisms

A tension between communitarianism and organized religion lies in the question of moral authority. Although contemporary Christianity and Judaism support democracy in political organization, there is concern about defining all moral value through a democratic method of a particular society—that is, moral relativism. Other critics note that community ought not to be an end in itself and that many communities have oppressive histories. It has been suggested that communitarianism is a nostalgic philosophy, recalling a simpler time, and that the radical pluralism of modern societies makes it impossible to speak of a substantive social good.

See also *Communism; Covenant; Human rights; Individualism; Liberalism; Natural law; Pluralism.*

Bernard V. Brady

BIBLIOGRAPHY

Bellah, Robert, Richard Madsen, William Sullivan, Ann Swidler, and Steven Tipton. *Habits of the Heart: Individualism and Commitment in American Life.* Berkeley: University of California Press, 1985.

Daly, Markate, ed. *Communitarianism: A New Public Ethics.* Belmont, Calif.: Wadsworth, 1994.

Dyck, Arthur. *Rethinking Rights and Responsibilities: The Moral Bonds of Community.* Cleveland: Pilgrim Press, 1994.

Etzioni, Amitai. *The Spirit of Community: Rights, Responsibilities, and the Communitarian Agenda.* New York: Crown, 1993.

———, ed. *New Communitarian Thinking: Persons, Virtues, Institutions, and Communities.* Charlottesville: University of Virginia Press, 1995.

Glendon, Mary Ann. *Rights Talk: The Impoverishment of Political Discourse.* New York: Free Press, 1991.

MacIntyre, Alasdair. *After Virtue: A Study in Moral Theory.* Notre Dame, Ind.: University of Notre Dame Press, 1984.

Sandel, Michael. *Liberalism and the Limits of Justice.* Cambridge: Cambridge University Press, 1982.

Community organizing

Community organizing encompasses a wide variety of efforts to empower residents in a local area to participate in civic life or governmental affairs. Most community organizing efforts operate in low- or middle-income areas and have adopted at least some of the tactics and organizing techniques pioneered by Saul Alinsky (1909–1972), a controversial American community activist and reformer, which focus on building the political power of an organization of local residents and using that power to influence issues the organization defines as important.

Community organizing has taken many forms, often differentiated according to whether they are "neighborhood-based," "issue-focused," "church-based," or "race-based or multiracial." From the 1940s to the 1960s Alinsky drew on the previous experience of labor unions to pioneer neighborhood-based confrontational tactics in Chicago and elsewhere. The federal government funded some community organizing in the 1970s, and several local governments sponsored community organizations in the 1990s. Today most community organizing is sponsored by nongovernmental organizations funded by charitable organizations, foundations, and individuals. Religious organizations including the Campaign for Human Development of the U.S. Catholic bishops and various mainline Protestant denominations have been leading nongovernmental funders.

Church-based community organizing is of greatest interest to scholars of religion and politics, and probably the most influential form of community organizing in American civic life today. It draws on the social ties within religious congregations to build a base of participants and draws on religious beliefs and symbols to motivate participants' engagement in civic life. Through "actions"—large public gatherings at which officials are asked to commit to a specific course of action—these organizations strive to exert leverage on the political system. These actions may be sponsored by a single religious congregation, by a citywide federation of congregations, or by a statewide network; they draw from a hundred to several thousand participants. They typically incorporate music from the congregations, prayer led by local pastors, and religious language invoked by lay leaders to define a specific issue as important and suggest an appropriate role for religious believers in the public realm. The action serves to highlight a specific issue and pressure political or corporate leaders to respond to the organization's concern. By negotiating with officials, an organization may also seek to shape public policy in long-term ways.

In the United States four large networks bring together most of the local federations engaging in church-based community organizing. These are the Industrial Areas Foundation (based in Chicago), the Pacific Institute for Community Organization (based in Oakland, California), Gamaliel (Milwaukee, Wisconsin), and Dart (Florida). Federations affiliated with these networks have addressed issues of public safety, city services, government block grant programs, educational reform, housing policy, bank lending practices, economic development, and minimum wage levels. Many have gained significant influence on local policy regarding these issues and, in some cases, on state-level policy; none have yet played decisive roles in shaping national policy.

Church-based community organizing has drawn the attention of scholars of religion and politics for two reasons. Those interested in democratic theory and social movements have studied church-based organizing to understand its successes and limitations in changing public policy and empowering low-income urban residents. Those interested in the importance of religion in the public realm have studied such efforts as one example of how Christians participate in the secular political world.

See also *Base communities; Civil society; Economic development; Lobbying, Religious; Maryknoll; Nongovernmental organizations; Philanthropy.*

Richard L. Wood

BIBLIOGRAPHY

Alinsky, Saul D. *Rules for Radicals: A Pragmatic Primer for Realistic Radicals.* New York: Vintage Books, 1971.
Boyte, Harry. *Commonwealth: A Return to Citizen Politics.* New York: Free Press, 1989.
Cortes, Ernesto, Jr. "Reweaving the Fabric: The Iron Rule and the IAF Strategy for Power and Politics." In *Interwoven Destinies: Cities and the Nation,* edited by Henry Cisneros. New York: Norton, 1993.
Greider, William. *Who Will Tell the People.* New York: Simon and Schuster, 1992.
Horwitt, Sanford. *Let Them Call Me Rebel: Saul Alinsky—His Life and Legacy.* New York: Knopf, 1989.
Wood, Richard L. *Faith in Action: Religion, Race, and the Future of Democracy.* Forthcoming; 1995 Ph.D. dissertation, University of California at Berkeley.

Conference of Latin American Bishops

See *CELAM*

Confucianism

Based on the teachings of Chinese political and ethical philosopher Confucius (551–479 B.C.), Confucianism is a set of institutional practices grounded in the centrality of familial relations. By the second century B.C. this guide to state-craft and moral teaching had become the official creed of China.

Confucianism has undergone any number of alterations since its inception. Throughout these transformations, however, it has remained remarkably consonant with the original teaching of Confucius. As a philosophic or religious vision, Confucianism has been expressed through a line of scholars who have continued to elaborate on the canonical texts (*Analects*) passed on after Confucius's death, thereby extending the way of living that the "Master" had begun.

Although the influence of Confucius was felt soon after his death, thanks to a number of dedicated disciples, it was not until the Han dynasty (206 B.C.–A.D. 220) and the establishment of Confucianism as the state ideology that his school of thought became unchallenged orthodoxy. From this period on, the fundamental insights of Confucius's thought—the importance of family, friendship, education, and community—were central to the Chinese cultural and political experience.

The Terms of Confucianism

Use of oneself as a measure for gauging others describes *shu,* the standard by which both self-realization and social harmony may be attained. As Confucius characterizes *shu*: "Do not impose on others what you yourself do not desire" (*Analects,* 15/24). *Shu* is an act of comparison in which one takes oneself as starting point and attempts to discover the desires of others.

If one is able to act in accordance with *shu,* it is essential that the standard from which one begins—one's self as socially constituted—be expressive of appropriate moral character. In other words, it is essential that one be truly human. The notion expressive of such humanity is *ren,* often translated as benevolence or human-heartedness. This term also alludes to the process of becoming human. Human-heartedness involves both the sense of being fully human and the sense of acting humanely toward others.

Ritual activity (*li*) provides the more or less formal structure that permits the embodiment of *ren* and *shu. Li* comprises the various roles and relationships making up the family and the sociopolitical order beyond. The most important relationships for Confucius are those of father and son and elder brother and younger brother. These hierarchical relationships help to establish the grounds for respect within both the biological and the broader political families. Much of the ritual activity associated with the Confucian vision is modeled on familial relationships. Thus *li* constitutes a code of formal behaviors for stabilizing and disciplining life situations.

Charting a harmonious path within and among the world of others is a principal task for those who want to achieve real humanity. Such an effort leads to a search for the proper way, or *dao,* a crucial term in Confucianism. Confucius characterizes *dao* in terms of cultural inheritance. In this sense *dao* is a cultural resource specifiable in terms of particular individuals or ritual forms. The *dao* of a particular person, or a particular social situation, is a specification of this general inheritance. Thus there is a *dao* of music, and of archery, a *dao* of the bureaucrat, as well as a *tian dao*—a way of heaven. All these ways have their source in the rituals, actions, institutions, and writings that have survived in the cultural memory. *Dao,* then, is not some specific norm in accordance with which a person acts; rather, *dao* is realized in the performance of appropriate conduct. The person of *ren* acting with *shu*—within the context provided by *li*—is therefore able to discern the proper way of conducting himself or herself.

Confucianism in a Broader Context

One characteristic of Confucianism that flies in the face of most Western understandings of its vision is its porousness and adaptability. Confucius called himself a transmitter, not a creator, of cultural traditions—that is, he simply adapted the wisdom of the past to his own historical present. Confucius's principal resource was the institutions of the Duke of Zhou who lived some five hundred years earlier. It was from the Duke of Zhou that he inherited the insight of employing the family as the model of all sociopolitical relations.

Just as Confucius reinvented the culture of the Zhou and earlier dynasties for that of his own era, the disciples of Confucianism sought to accommodate many of the ideas of its competing schools (among others, Mohism, Daoism, Legalism, and emerging Buddhism), and in doing so to interweave elements of these sensibilities into its own. This same process of accommodation was to take place after the decline of the Han dynasty. From the third to the tenth centuries Daoist and Buddhist elements began to exert renewed intellectual influence, often strongly competing with Confucianism. Thus since its inception in the eleventh century, a neoclassical form of Confucianism has expressed an interweaving of Confucian, Daoist, and Buddhist ideas.

In either its traditional or neoclassical form, Confucianism dominated Chinese thought after the Han synthesis and largely remained the unchallenged orthodoxy of the Chinese empire until the fall of the Qing dynasty in 1911. Indeed, perhaps this continues to be true today, for a strong argument can be made that just as a composite of Daoism, Buddhism, and Confucianism produced neo-Confucianism, the combination of Marxism and Confucianism in the twentieth century created but another kind of neoclassical Confucianism. Evidence of this development has been China's renewed interest in Confucianism beginning in 1976 just after the death of Communist Party chairman Mao Zedong. Ideological Marxism is fading under the impact of foreign capitalism, but that same impact has led to a reemphasis on the classic Confucian values of discipline, thrift, and task orientation, which harmonize well with the capitalist sensibility. Such an appeal to traditional values could make the transition to a capitalist society much less traumatic.

Meanwhile, the values of Confucianism have had a far-ranging impact on the educational and political institutions of numerous Asian countries—notably Korea, Japan, and Vietnam. Elsewhere in Asia, Singapore has made a conscious attempt to reform its political and educational institutions along traditionally Confucian lines. South Korean schools require formal exposure to Confucian values. Everywhere in Asia where the impact of Western individualism has been felt, there has been a return to Confucianism as a means of reasserting the communitarian model of society.

See also *Confucius.*

David L. Hall

BIBLIOGRAPHY

Chan, W. T. *A Source Book in Chinese Philosophy.* Princeton: Princeton University Press, 1963.
Confucius. *The Analects.* Translated by D. C. Lau. Hong Kong: Chinese University Press, 1992.
———. *Mencius.* Translated by D. C. Lau. Hong Kong: Chinese University Press, 1984.
De Bary, W. T., et al. *Sources of the Chinese Tradition.* New York: Columbia University Press, 1960.
Graham, Angus. *Disputers of the Tao.* La Salle, Ill.: Open Court Press, 1989.
Hall, D. L., and R. T. Ames. *Anticipating China—Thinking through the Narratives of Chinese and Western Culture.* Albany, N.Y.: SUNY Press, 1995.

Confucius

No philosophic or religious visionary, whether Plato or Aristotle, Jesus, Buddha, or Muhammad, is more significant than Confucius (551–479 B.C.) who founded in China an entire culture. Even today, in a China nominally influenced by Marxism, Confucianism remains the foundation of the society and culture.

Confucius (K'ung Fu-tzu) was born in the state of Lu (Shandong province in contemporary China) during the decline of the Zhou dynasty (1027–267 B.C.). For much of his life he was an itinerant scholar who traveled among competing Chinese states, offering advice on the art of rulership. But Confucius never achieved real practical influence, either in his home state of Lu, where he was for a short period police commissioner, or in any of the other states in which he briefly resided. Somewhat frustrated, Confucius returned to Lu late in life, serving as a councilor of the lower rank, while he continued teaching a small number of disciples who later would begin to disseminate his ideas more broadly.

Among his other accomplishments, Confucius established a school in the state of Lu for the education of future "statesmen"—Plato's academy would not appear until more than a century later. The curriculum of Confucius's school was based on a collection of poetry, music, historical documents, and annals that chronicled the events at the Lu court, along with an extensive commentary on the *Book of Changes,* a divination book containing all the permutations of a six-line figure made up of straight (*yang*) and broken (*yin*) lines and consulted to understand the best action in a particular situation. These works, which provided a shared cultural vocabulary for his students, would become the classics of Chinese culture and the standard curriculum for the Chinese literati in the centuries to come.

The principal source of Confucius's own thinking is the *Lunyu*—traditionally translated as the *Analects* or sayings—which records his life and teachings. The earlier-written portions of the work contain disciples' remembrances of Confucius the man, recording his personal habits and interests. Later portions, particularly the last five of the twenty chapters, were likely recorded by disciples well on their way to becoming mature interpreters of Confucian thought. In these chapters, though Confucius remains the focus, the disciples often speak in their own voices.

Confucius's vision of the means to social and political harmony was grounded in the rites and institutions originated by the Duke of Zhou some five hundred years before Confucius. The Zhou feudal system made family relations the basis of political loyalties. Thus Zhou feudal lords were both vassals and blood relatives of the king.

Building on the vision of the Duke of Zhou, Confucius articulated and elaborated on the importance of the family as a sociopolitical model. The family provides the context within which an individual becomes who he or she is. Moreover, the state itself is patterned on the model of the family. One does not, as Aristotle asserted, move out from the privacy of the family to become a public person, a "citizen"; rather, one is always a member of a family—both of the biological unit into which one is born and of the political "family" which urges a broader set of allegiances. The importance of the family as a model for all sociopolitical relations was the grounding principle from which Chinese civilization was to emerge.

See also *Confucianism.*

David L. Hall

BIBLIOGRAPHY

Confucius. *The Analects.* Translated by D. C. Lau. Hong Kong: Chinese University Press, 1992.

Confucius. *Mencius.* Translated by D. C. Lau. Hong Kong: Chinese University Press, 1984.

Graham, Angus. *Disputers of the Tao.* La Salle, Ill.: Open Court Press, 1989.

Hall, David L., and Roger T. Ames. *Thinking through Confucius.* Albany: State University of New York Press, 1987.

Consejo Episcopal Latinoamericano

See *CELAM*

Conservatism

Conservatism, at least in the West, is a political position that seeks to reduce the role of government in the economy and to reestablish moral order in the face of a culture deemed too secular and too permissive. Whether characterized as capitalist, industrialized, or simply modern, Western societies inevitably generate problems of moral order, community, and meaning, to which conservative religious politics is one response. In the United States, for example, the New Christian Right is an independent conservative political movement rooted primarily in theologically conservative white Protestant religious groups.

Although other Western societies face problems and issues similar to those in the United States, their problems and issues are not framed in the same religious terms. Societies such as those in Great Britain, France, and Germany have strong rights of various kinds, but independent, religion-based political movements play relatively little role in them. Perhaps this is why scholars looking for cross-national analogies compare the New Christian Right to "fundamentalist" political movements primarily in the non-Western, less industrialized, less modern world. Yet Islamic fundamentalism in Iran and Hindu fundamentalism in India are clearly different: their critique of secularism is tied to the rejection of Western influences and occurs in a far different political context. It thus has quite different implications. The American New Christian Right stands alone.

The distinctive role of religion in the American right becomes clearer when it is compared to the rights of two otherwise very similar societies, those of Great Britain and Canada. In each country the right has sought to cut back big government, enliven free markets, and restore the entrepreneurial spirit and "traditional" values. And in each case the issues have been cultural as well as economic. Only in the United States, however, has "cultural" become tied so closely to "religious." In Great Britain under Prime Minister Margaret Thatcher (1979–1990), the cultural battles focused in complicated ways on social class. The right wing of the Conservative Party fought against an upper-class Tory paternalism as well as working-class union militancy. In Canada the Reform Party became prominent in the 1990s by focusing on the linguistic and regional issues that have pitted French-speaking Quebec against the rest of English-speaking Canada, especially the western provinces, where the Reform Party built its base. The British and Canadian rights certainly have invoked traditional or Judeo-Christian values, but they have not generated an independent religious movement.

The New Christian Right Defined

The New Christian Right emerged in the late 1970s, and by the mid-1990s it had become a central part of the American right and a fixture of American politics. Its main organizations have included Moral Majority and the Religious Roundtable, and more recently the Christian Coalition and the Family Research Council. The New Christian Right has supported the entire political agenda of American conservatism, including cuts in government social spending and economic regulation and (until the late 1980s) militant anti-communism, but it has emphasized the moral element of the right's agenda.

The constituencies on which the New Christian Right draws have been variously called evangelical, fundamentalist, charismatic, and Pentecostal. In this article the term *evangelical* refers to these groups generally, meaning by that term all those who combine a relatively literal reading of the Bible, regarded as the final authority in all moral matters, with an emphasis on individual salvation through a personal relationship with God and a born-again experience. Some groups in this category may place more emphasis on biblical authority; others on religious experience. Some may belong to relatively large, mainstream denominations; other may belong to independent churches. The New Christian Right also draws strength from the strong set of evangelical religious networks that developed in the decades after World War II, from the broader religious polarization of Americans, and from other forces on the right.

Central to the politics of the New Christian Right is the idea that most of America's many problems stem from the dominance of a secular humanist culture, purveyed by elites in government as well as in the media, universities, and other cultural institutions. This culture fundamentally denies God or any transcendent source of morality and thus removes religion and any moral moorings from public life. As a result, this culture leads to a general moral crisis and is tied to a host of specific "problems" as well: the decline of the conventional family, feminism, homosexuality, pornography, and even the growth of government. In addition to attacking this secular culture and calling for the reassertion of religious values in politics, the New Christian Right has supported, among other things, a variety of specific measures to outlaw abortion; prevent the spread of gay rights; permit religious activities in schools and other public places; ensure that public school curricula praise capitalism, the conventional family, and the virtues of America; support the expansion of private schools; and reinforce the traditional one-wage-earner, male-centered family.

Significance of the New Christian Right

Religion is no newcomer to conservative politics in democratic capitalist societies. Generally, devout members of established or high-status churches have tended to support conservative political parties, whereas members of lower-status churches have voted for more liberal or leftist parties. Historically, struggles over the relationship between church and state sometimes have coincided with class conflict between right and left. As a result, the religious bases of voting often have overlapped with the class bases of voting.

The New Christian Right, however, represents a different and currently more significant kind of religious involvement in conservative politics. Although closely allied with the broader American right, it is an independent movement with its own leaders, organizations, and agenda. It is rooted not in the highest-status churches, but in ones that, historically at least, have been lower status. It speaks not with the quiet voice of privilege, but with a loud, moralistic voice, condemning sin wherever it sees sin.

The New Christian Right is unique to the United States among democratic capitalist nations. Politics has moved to

the right in nearly all these countries since the 1970s. As global economic competition has heated up and as welfare state expenses have outrun the ability of governments to pay for them, conservative governments such as those of U.S. president Ronald Reagan (1981–1989) and British prime minister Margaret Thatcher have come to power seeking to cut government spending and regulation, weaken unions, and generally promote "free enterprise." (In the meantime, social democratic parties have generally moved to the center, forsaking any ambitious programs for building democratic socialism.) Conservative regimes also have often emphasized a return to "traditional" values centered on individual responsibility, self-control, and hard work. And, until the end of the cold war, they often featured a militant anticommunism. Only in the United States, however, has an independent, religion-based political movement played a significant role in promoting this agenda.

The New Christian Right may seem akin to "fundamentalist" political movements that have proliferated in recent years, particularly in the Islamic and Hindu worlds, in former communist countries, and to some extent in Latin America. It is true that the New Christian Right shares with these movements a rejection of a fully secular society and an effort to reorganize political discourse at least in part around a belief in a transcendent moral authority. To this end all such movements selectively retrieve and redefine beliefs and practices from a putative sacred past. To place the New Christian Right in this context, however, is to reemphasize how unique it is. These other political movements have developed chiefly in non-Western societies. Their antisecularism often is characterized by an anti-imperialism, an opposition to the legacies of Western or communist domination. And these movements occur in societies in which the secular state they attack is weak or relatively new, or in which religious issues are tied closely to ethnic conflicts over political boundaries and rights. Indeed, the only other Western countries that can be said to have independent fundamentalist political movements—Northern Ireland and Israel—are precisely the ones still rent by ethnic conflict over political identity.

Many observers have sought to explain the rise of the New Christian Right by referring to the broad social changes common to all democratic capitalist societies. Some have argued that the New Christian Right is a reaction to "modern" society—that is, a society that as it industrializes (and postindustrializes) becomes not only increasingly secular but also increasingly specialized (with different societal activities carried on in different institutional settings) and rationalized (with more and more of life organized by formal rules). Other observers have argued, in a somewhat different vein, that the New Christian Right is a response to what neo-Marxist philosopher Jurgen Habermas calls the "colonization of the lifeworld"—that is, the growing intrusion of market forces and government rules into everyday life. Whatever one makes of these explanations, they cannot be the whole story because Christian right movements have not sprouted up everywhere these forces are at work. At best these theories describe endemic discontent with the impersonal, meaningless, and materialistic nature of life in the West; they do not explain how under some circumstances some people channel their discontent with the moral quality of life into a particular kind of religious movement. To understand why the New Christian Right emerged in the United States when it did, one must look at what makes U.S. society different from those of other countries as well as what it shares with them.

The Salience of America's Religious Past

Some of the roots of the contemporary New Christian Right lie deep in America's religious past, especially in the strength of religious institutions in civil life and the beliefs propagated by certain religious groups. The United States always has had a relatively high degree of separation of church and state. This separation has not meant that religious issues have not been important politically, or that religious institutions have not been involved in political life, or that government has not acted at times to favor one religion or another. It does mean that there has not been an established church, one that enjoys consistent official recognition and substantial public subsidies.

The lack of public recognition and support, ironically perhaps, has encouraged, not discouraged, the proliferation of religious institutions and activities because churches have had to compete to get and hold members. Since the early nineteenth century, foreign observers of life in the United States such as French writer and politician Alexis de Tocqueville have noted the large percentage of Americans attending churches and the strength of these institutions in everyday life. Compared with the citizens of other countries, Americans have allocated a relatively large share of the fruits of economic growth to religious institutions, with several results. First, churches are easily available to would-be mem-

bers and are more likely to become the focus of a civic life that in other countries might be dominated by political parties and unions. Second, a vast array of seminaries and theologians are available to articulate religious ideas. Third, Americans have, with relative ease, developed the habit of attending church and orienting themselves to religion. In short, religious institutions in America occupy a central place in everyday life. This does not mean that U.S. churches necessarily provide a basis for political mobilization but that they are well placed to do so.

A significant part of this religious activity always has been oriented toward a distinctive kind of Protestant moralism. This moralism has emphasized several themes that remain important among evangelical Protestants today: the importance of individual salvation gained through a born-again experience and a personal relationship with God; an emphasis on "Christianizing" and otherwise reforming a sinful world; a belief in the Bible as the sole source of moral authority; and the idea of America as a "new Israel" destined to play a special role in the divine plan for humanity. Together these beliefs do not necessarily encourage political activism. (Indeed, they may encourage radical withdrawal from a society deemed irretrievably corrupt.) They do, however, provide a powerful basis for a thorough critique of the secular tendencies of modern societies.

In the early twentieth century this Protestant moralism took the form of fundamentalism, and its adherents began to formulate this critique. In reaction to scientific advances, especially the Darwinian theory of evolution, and the rapid industrialization and urbanization of America, some American Protestants—later called "modernists"—argued that interpretations of the Bible had to be adjusted in the light of modern scholarship, science, and historical conditions. They also argued that the social conditions in urban industrial America required more emphasis on social reform and improvements in the material conditions of life and less on individual salvation. In response, those Protestants who came to call themselves "fundamentalists" renewed their strict emphasis on a literal reading of the Bible and on the importance of individual salvation.

The fundamentalist-modernist conflict began largely as theological debates over how to read the Bible and the relative importance of individual salvation and social reform. After World War I, however, the debates became broader and more politicized. Fundamentalists believed that America was facing no less than a spiritual crisis brought on by the growth of a secular culture and manifested in such things as political radicalism, growing crime rates, and the materialism of an increasingly consumer-oriented society.

Although fundamentalists lost the battles they fought in the 1920s over control of specific Protestant denominations as well as over the teaching of the theory of evolution in public schools, they provided later generations with a distinctive religious culture focused on a critique of a secular society and a drive to recover from the past a set of putative religious fundamentals. Furthermore, the fundamentalist impulse continued to express itself in two distinctive directions. Those going in one direction continued to call themselves "fundamentalists." They split off from the modernist-dominated major Protestant denominations and created independent churches. Many of these churches helped to form the American Council of Christian Churches in 1941. Those going in the other direction called themselves "evangelicals" or "neoevangelicals." They founded the National Association of Evangelicals (also in 1941), which sought to speak for and to supporters within the major denominations.

These groups were somewhat active politically from the 1940s into the early 1970s, but, more significant, they built an intricate network of religious institutions. Evangelical and fundamentalist Bible institutes, colleges, seminaries, journals, and publishing houses flourished. Evangelical radio and television programs, youth organizations, and mass revival meetings (notably those of Billy Graham) enjoyed considerable success. Above all, evangelical and fundamentalist Protestant churches continued to grow, even in the 1970s when theologically moderate and liberal churches were losing members.

By the late 1970s two elements of this institutional network had become especially important, the superchurch and the electronic ministry. A superchurch or megachurch, often wholly independent of established denominations, had thousands or even tens of thousands of members, was located on a large campus with multiple buildings, and offered a wide array of activities and services beyond church services—typically, schools, daycare, athletic facilities, and social programs for everyone from children to senior citizens. Electronic ministry refers to the use of cable television by ministers to reach millions of viewers. Direct-mail technologies were employed to raise funds from those viewers.

Superchurches and electronic ministries were the direct sources of the leadership of the New Christian Right. They also were a powerful way of disseminating the ideas of this movement and an especially suitable base for mobilizing evangelical Christians into politics.

Mobilization of the New Christian Right

By the early 1970s, then, an organizational base for a Christian Right existed, but this in itself did not lead to political mobilization. Indeed, from the 1950s through the early 1970s, evangelicals, if anything, were relatively depoliticized. They participated less in politics than other Americans and were less likely to condone the participation of their churches. In the 1960s and 1970s religion in politics took the form of the active involvement of the liberal churches in the civil rights and anti–Vietnam War movements.

This picture changed dramatically in the mid-1970s. From then on, according to most surveys, evangelicals became more politically active than other Christians. They registered to vote and voted in increasing numbers; they lobbied their elected representatives and worked on political campaigns. They also increasingly approved of their clergy becoming politically involved, and their religious leaders were eager to oblige. Above all, a network of leaders and political organizations dedicated to mobilizing this constituency rapidly developed.

Why this happened can be understood in terms of the emergence of both new issues and new political opportunities. Although evangelical and fundamentalist Christians for a long time had condemned the secularism of American culture and identified it as a cause of many important social problems, from the 1960s on a host of new issues emerged in American society that made that critique especially salient. Commentators have called these "social" or "cultural" issues. They were not economic—that is, they were not primarily about how the costs and benefits of economic growth were distributed and what role government played in this. Rather, they concerned matters of social order and morality such as crime and drug use, sexuality, family and gender roles, affirmative action, and the values taught by America's cultural institutions (schools, mass media, family).

These social issues emerged in part because of broad changes in American society and in part because of liberal social movements. For example, the rise of women's rights issues such as equal rights and abortion partly reflected long-term changes in the family and gender roles: the increasing percentage of women (especially those with young children) working outside the home, rising rates of divorce and single parenthood, and more permissive sexual mores. But the emergence of these issues also stemmed from the rapid growth after the mid-1960s of the women's movement, which placed these issues on the political agenda.

New political opportunities also encouraged the mobilization of the New Christian Right, of which three stand out in particular. First, the involvement of largely nonevangelical religious leaders and organizations in the liberal social movements of the 1960s, especially the civil rights and antiwar movements, legitimated the mixing of religion with politics. The 1976 presidential campaign of Democrat Jimmy Carter, himself an evangelical Christian, stressed the need to return morality to government and appealed in particular to evangelicals, albeit from a centrist position. This development too gave evangelicals a heightened sense of political legitimacy and entitlement.

Second, a series of changes in the religious world made it easier for evangelical Christians to find sympathetic allies and form cross-denominational alliances. Beginning in the 1950s, boundary lines between the various traditional religious denominations in the United States, especially within Protestantism, blurred as the old regional and ethnic differences that once distinguished them declined in importance. At the same time, the religious world became somewhat polarized along secular/religious lines as the ranks of both the religiously unaffiliated and the more theologically conservative churches grew, while those of moderate and liberal churches declined. Moreover, within many religious denominations a growing cleavage developed between the more orthodox and more progressive elements. This general realignment in the religious world provided the basis for political polarization on social issues (what some observers described as "culture wars") and thus created a conducive political terrain for the New Christian Right.

Third, the New Christian Right benefited from the support of other conservative elements in American politics, which also became ascendant in the late 1970s and early 1980s. Apparently dead in the water after the Watergate scandals of the early 1970s and the 1974 midterm elections (which returned huge Democratic majorities to Congress), the Republican Party rebuilt itself into a potent political force. The party used direct-mail fund-raising techniques to develop a mass base of contributors. Their donations allowed the party to develop strong national organizations which systematically cultivated new generations of political candidates and provided them with sophisticated political technology and other resources.

At about the same time, large corporations began mobilizing to push American politics to the right. Concerned about increasing government economic regulation in particular and a political system that seemed hostile to capitalism in general, business leaders and large corporations formed new organizations (such as the Business Roundtable) for high-level lobbying, directed an increasing percentage of corporate campaign donations to conservative Republican congressional candidates, and poured money into conservative think tanks.

Most important, a secular conservative political movement came of age at the same time. Born with the founding of the journal *National Review* by William F. Buckley Jr. in 1955, this movement had by the mid-1970s developed into a vast network of political activists and organizations. Several of the most important leaders of this movement at the time, including Howard Phillips (head of the Conservative Caucus) and Paul Weyrich (leader of the Committee for the Survival of a Free Congress), played a formative role in cultivating the first leaders and creating the first organizations of the New Christian Right. Having identified white evangelical Christians as a largely untapped constituency for the right, they approached several television preachers and helped one of them, Jerry Falwell, establish Moral Majority. They also helped to create Christian Voice and the Religious Roundtable, the other two organizations with broad political agendas, and to bring other TV evangelists, notably Pat Robertson, into politics.

Growth of Political Activism

The political activism of the New Christian Right that began in the mid-1970s focused on specific issues of concern to evangelical Christians: the proposed Equal Rights Amendment, gay rights initiatives, the tax status and rights of private Christian schools, and the content of public school textbooks. These initially disparate efforts fed at the end of the decade into the formation of Moral Majority, Christian Voice, and the Religious Roundtable.

These organizations drew on preexisting religious networks and leaders. Each was associated with a major TV preacher—Moral Majority with Jerry Falwell, Christian Voice with Pat Robertson, and Religious Roundtable with James Robison. Moral Majority also featured ministers from some of America's largest superchurches on its board of directors, and it recruited most of its state leaders from the ranks of the Baptist Bible Fellowship, an organization of independent fundamentalist churches. It drew on the computerized mailing list of Falwell's television show, *Old-Time Gospel Hour,* to raise money.

More generally, the New Christian Right relied especially on evangelical church congregations and the networks of ties these produced to mobilize its rank-and-file membership. Only those evangelicals heavily involved in their churches—not evangelicals generally—were politicized and moved to the right. In the politically pivotal years of the early 1980s, evangelicals as a whole shifted their political allegiances sharply to the Republican Party. A closer look, however, shows that this shift occurred wholly among those evangelicals who attended church frequently—and not at all among nonattendees. Frequent church attendance correlated as well with conservative positions on issues such as abortion and the Equal Rights Amendment. Evangelical congregations provided both a religious ethos and a network of social ties conducive to conservative political mobilization.

The organizations of the New Christian Right lobbied Congress on a variety of issues in the 1970s and 1980s, including the SALT II nuclear weapons treaty (which they opposed) and school prayer legislation and the Family Protection Act (which they supported). More important, they systematically threw their support behind Ronald Reagan and Republican candidates for Congress in the 1980s elections.

When Reagan won the presidency and Republicans took control of the Senate in 1980, the New Christian Right gained considerable notoriety and many commentators came to regard it as a decisive force in American politics. Others, however, questioned how much substance there was to the image. They pointed out that few Americans had heard of Moral Majority in 1980 (and most of those who had were opposed to it), that evangelical Christians were not a monolithically conservative force, and that there was little evidence that the New Christian Right had had an independent effect on the 1980 elections.

By 1984, however, the impact of the New Christian Right had become unambiguous. That year, 80 percent of white evangelical Christians voted for Ronald Reagan, and subsequent Republican presidential candidates enjoyed similar majorities even as their overall shares of the popular vote fell. Polling data showed that white evangelical Christians in all regions of the country, especially those who attended church frequently, were shifting their political allegiance significantly to the Republican Party. In addition, they were be-

coming the most important source of new conservative grass-roots political activism. Clearly, then, white evangelical Christians were a new political force for right-wing politics.

Yet, if the mid-1980s were good years for evangelical Christians politically, they were mixed for the organizations and leaders that represented them. Perhaps killed by success, all three major New Christian Right organizations were moribund by 1986, as were a number of others, including the National Christian Action Coalition, the Freedom Council, and the American Coalition for Traditional Values. Many of the television evangelists from whose ranks New Christian Right leaders had come found their electronic ministries beset by financial problems and had to retrench; a few faced moral scandals as well. Most significant, the well-financed campaign of Pat Robertson for the 1988 Republican presidential nomination fell flat, failing even to gain strong support among all evangelicals, let alone expand beyond those ranks.

This malaise, however, turned out to be only a brief downturn in the fortunes of the New Christian Right. After 1987 a new generation of organizations (most notably, the Christian Coalition, but also the Family Research Council and the American Freedom Coalition) and new leaders (Ralph Reed and Gary Bauer) emerged to push the religious right's agenda. These new organizations sought to develop a broader base of support for their agenda and to present their position less in sectarian religious rhetoric and more in pluralist secular language. Thus organized prayer in school was justified as a matter of student rights and religious liberty, as was putting religious values back into education. Battles over the content of school textbooks were presented as a matter of securing parental rights to control curriculum and countering a secular humanist culture.

The mid-1990s saw Americans more polarized than ever along secular/religious lines and the New Christian Right apparently perfectly at home in American politics. White evangelicals, especially those who attended church frequently, were the most conservative group in America on a wide range of issues, and religious conservatives in particular seemed ever more willing to cross denominational lines to form political coalitions. The New Christian Right's concern with the corrosive effects of a secular culture continued to have plenty of targets. Abortion remained a powerful issue, and there were a host of others: school choice, school prayer, government funding of the arts and the humanities, gay marriage. Talk about "culture wars" and a "new kind of party alignment" might have been overblown, but they contained a strong kernel of truth.

See also *Evangelicalism; Fundamentalism; Pentecostalism; Secular humanism; Secularization.*

Jerome L. Himmelstein

BIBLIOGRAPHY

Bruce, Steve, Peter Kivisto, and William H. Swatos Jr. *The Rapture of Politics: The Christian Right as the United States Approaches the Year 2000.* New Brunswick, N.J.: Transaction Publishers, 1995.

Himmelstein, Jerome L. *To the Right: The Transformation of American Conservatism.* Berkeley and Los Angeles: University of California Press, 1990.

Hunter, James Davison. *Culture Wars: The Struggle to Define America.* New York: Basic Books, 1991.

Martin, William C. *With God on Our Side: The Rise of the Religious Right in America.* New York: Broadway Books, 1996.

Marty, Martin E., and R. Scott Appleby. *Fundamentalism and the State: Remaking Polities, Economies, and Militance.* Chicago: University of Chicago Press, 1993.

Wilcox, Clyde. *God's Warriors: The Christian Right in Twentieth-Century America.* Baltimore, Md.: Johns Hopkins University Press, 1992.

Wuthnow, Robert. *The Restructuring of American Religion.* Princeton: Princeton University Press, 1988.

Constitution, U.S.

The U.S. Constitution, the world's oldest surviving written constitution, is the fundamental law of the country, simultaneously specifying a structure of government and limiting the power of that government. In contrast to patterns of government in European nations in 1787, when the Constitution was adopted, and even in variance with the Declaration of Independence of 1776, the Constitution is strictly secular; that is, it does not claim an explicit theological or religious base. This omission was primarily because its framers limited the federal government to a few areas of defined powers, mostly regarding interstate and international commerce and defense. The individual states remained responsible for determining any government relation to religion. Thus the Constitution addressed religion in only the briefest terms.

Article Six, Clause Three, of the Constitution prohibits religious tests for individuals holding federal office. This clause was adopted because the framers thought religious affiliation should not be a bar to service to one's country. Several state constitutions did have bars to public office, ex-

cluding nonbelievers, Catholics, and Jews. Maryland and Massachusetts, for example, at first stipulated that only a Christian could become governor.

The most significant reference to religion in the Constitution was added after its adoption, in the First Amendment of the Bill of Rights, which was ratified in 1791: "Congress shall make no law respecting an establishment of religion or prohibiting the free exercise thereof." These religion clauses affirmed that Congress has no power to establish religion nor to interfere with the exercise of religious faith. This position was extraordinary for its time, contravening the pattern that had prevailed in Europe for one and a half millennia, since the fourth century, when the Roman emperor Constantine adopted Christianity (312) and his successor, Theodosius, made it the official religion of the state (390). James Madison and other founders at the Constitutional Convention had carefully read the history of religion and state patronage, finding that the fusion debilitated both. Thus, for the first time in Western history, they decided to establish a government that was neither legitimated by religion nor was the patron of religion. The two spheres would be separated from the onset.

In 1970 the Supreme Court, in *Walz v. Tax Commission,* noted that the relationship between religion and government must be one of "benevolent neutrality." This means that American government, though secular in purpose, is not hostile to religion but is generally sympathetic to religious faith. Determination of the precise parameters of religion-state relations has not been easy; therefore, this task has usually been left to the courts.

The Nineteenth Century

Before the twentieth century, jurisdiction over most religion cases rested in the states rather than the federal government. Thus the highest court, the Supreme Court, heard only a few cases. In two cases that dealt with disputes in U.S. territories, *Reynolds v. United States* (1879) and *Davis v. Beason* (1890), the Supreme Court said that freedom of religion did not reach to the Mormon practice of polygamy. *Watson v. Jones* (1872) declared that the federal government had no power to intervene in disputes between competing Christian sects or congregations. Justice Samuel Miller, writing for the Court, stated emphatically, "The law knows no heresy, and is committed to the support of no dogma, the establishment of no sect."

In *Bradfield v. Roberts* (1899) the Supreme Court, for the

first time, addressed establishment of religion. *Bradfield* held that congressional funding to a religiously affiliated organization (in this case a hospital in Washington, D.C.) that accomplished a secular purpose of providing medical care for the indigent did not constitute a case of establishment of religion in violation of the First Amendment.

The Twentieth Century

During the twentieth century the Supreme Court began incorporating provisions of the Bill of Rights into the Fourteenth Amendment as a restraint on state actions. *Cantwell v. Connecticut* (1940) witnessed the incorporation of the free exercise clause. The Court ruled that Connecticut could not prohibit Jehovah's Witnesses from distributing literature in support of their faith. On the matter of incorporation, the Court stated, "The fundamental concept of liberty embodied in the [Fourteenth] Amendment embraces the liberties guaranteed by the First Amendment. . . . The Fourteenth Amendment has rendered the legislatures of the states as incompetent as Congress to enact laws" prohibiting the free exercise of religion. The Court incorporated the establishment clause seven years later, in *Everson v. Board of Education of Ewing Township*. In this decision the Court upheld a city's subsidizing the transportation of students to and from both public schools and private religious schools, reasoning that the aid went to students and their parents and not to the support of religious instruction. *Everson* also included a broad definition of the unlawful establishment of religion, setting a significant precedent for establishment clause jurisprudence.

Incorporation of the religion clauses ushered in a new era of federal jurisdiction in religion cases. The Supreme Court has since then heard more than one hundred religion cases. Faced with the challenge of balancing the demands of ensuring freedom from the imposition of religion by law (no establishment) and freedom for religion (free exercise), the Court has found religion cases to be among the most difficult to decide with consistency.

Free Exercise Clause Jurisprudence

The Supreme Court, in *Sherbert v. Verner* (1963), held that South Carolina's denial of unemployment benefits to Adell Sherbert, who had lost her job because of her refusal to work on Saturday, her day of worship, was an unconstitutional restriction on Sherbert's free exercise of religious rights. This case is notable for broadening free exercise claims and establishing the precedents that a state must show a compelling state interest to justify infringing religious rights and that its method of enforcement of that interest must be the least restrictive means available.

A major shift in jurisprudence came in *Employment Division v. Smith,* decided in 1990. In this case the Court abandoned the compelling-interest test for a rule of neutral applicability, upholding a law prohibiting unemployment benefits to employees fired for drug use, even when associated with religious worship. In 1993 Congress responded specifically to the *Smith* decision by passing the Religious Freedom Restoration Act. The act, in holding that the government could "substantially burden" free exercise of religion only when a law furthered a compelling state interest and was the least restrictive means for doing so, reinstated the test principles enunciated in *Sherbert* thirty years previously. In *Boerne v. Flores* (1997), the Court found the act unconstitutional, not because of its insistence on the compelling interest–least restrictive test, per se, but because the act was found to violate the constitutional separation of powers.

Free exercise questions have often arisen in relationship to education. *West Virginia State Board of Education v. Barnette* (1943) upheld the right of Jehovah's Witnesses to abstain from pledging allegiance to the American flag, warning against making use of governmental means to coerce religious and ideological unanimity. *Wisconsin v. Yoder,* decided in 1972, upheld the right of Amish parents to withdraw their child from school after the eighth grade, to avoid worldly influences. In *Widmar v. Vincent* (1981) the Court ruled that a public university could not bar religious groups from meeting in buildings in which the school allowed nonreligious groups to meet. *Rosenberger v. Rector and Visitors of the University of Virginia* (1995) determined that a public university could not withhold funding from a Christian-oriented student newspaper when the school also funded other publications. In a 5–4 decision, the majority of the Court applied the general notion of neutral treatment of all speech, whether religious or nonreligious, rather than deciding the case strictly as an establishment issue.

Tax policy has, on occasion, clashed with religious liberty claims. In *Murdock v. Pennsylvania,* decided in 1943, the Court held that states could not condition the distribution of religious literature on the payment of a licensing fee. In *Murdock* the Court considered an ordinance of Jeannette, Pennsylvania, which conditioned door-to-door solicitations for merchandise of any kind on payment of a licensing fee. The

Walter Gobitas and his children, William and Lillian. The Gobitases, Jehovah's Witnesses, challenged the U.S. government's flag salute requirement as an infringement on their religious beliefs in Minersville School District v. Gobitis *[sic] (1940).*

The U.S. Supreme Court's ruling upholding the requirement was overturned in West Virginia State Board of Education v. Barnette *(1943).*

Pennsylvania borough held that Jehovah's Witnesses, who were distributing literature and soliciting people to purchase their books, were subject to the ordinance. The Court determined that application of the ordinance to the Witnesses was unconstitutional, finding that it would amount to a tax on free exercise of religion. In *Christian Echoes National Ministry v. United States* (1973) the Court upheld rules from the Internal Revenue Service that did not allow any religious organization involved in political activities to declare a tax exemption. In *Bob Jones University v. United States* (1983) the Court upheld the IRS policy disallowing tax exemption to any religious organization that practiced racial discrimination. *Swaggart Ministries v. California Board of Equalization* (1990) held that requiring religious organizations to collect sales tax on the sale of religious literature did not violate free exercise. The Court's reasoning was that the tax was applied generally and was only an incidental burden on religion.

Establishment Clause Jurisprudence

In 1968 the Court considered how to apply the *Everson* precedent on funding of religious education, in *Board of Education v. Allen,* ruling that the loan of secular texts to private religious schools did not establish religion. More direct aid to private religious schools was first rejected in 1971, in

Lemon v. Kurtzman. Lemon determined that state funding of secular instruction in private religious schools was an unconstitutional establishment of religion. *Lemon* was also notable in that it was the first establishment case to combine the secular purpose, primary effect, and entanglement tests developed in *Abington and Walz* (discussed later). These three components have since been referred to as the *Lemon* test.

In 1973, in *Committee for Public Education and Religious Liberty v. Nyquist,* the Supreme Court struck down, as unconstitutionally advancing religion, a New York program that provided grants to religious schools that served low-income families, gave tuition reimbursement to low-income parents with children in nonpublic schools, and allowed tax deductions for middle-income parents with children in nonpublic schools. In *Mueller v. Allen* (1983) the Court upheld Minnesota's policy of providing a tax deduction to parents with children attending any school, private or public. *Tilton v. Richardson* (1971) allowed funding under Title I of the Higher Education and Facilities Act of 1963 for financing buildings on the campuses of church-related colleges and universities, but only if the buildings were used for nonreligious purposes.

Several disputes over religious exercises in public education have ended up in federal courts. *McCollum v. Board of*

Education (1948) ruled that public schools could not allow religious instruction during the school day, even though participation was voluntary and the instruction was given by local religious leaders who were not paid from tax moneys. The ruling in *Zorach v. Clauson* (1952) clarified the limits of *McCollum,* however, holding that public schools could release students early to attend religious instruction off campus.

A controversial ruling in 1962, *Engel v. Vitale,* held that student recitation of a government-written prayer was unconstitutional, noting that a showing of compulsion to participate in a practice was not required to reach an establishment prohibition. *Abington Township School District v. Schempp* (1963) prohibited both the daily recitation of the Lord's Prayer and the reading of ten Bible verses, allowing, however, the study of religious documents in an academic, nondevotional manner, as literature or comparative religious history. *Abington* reasoned that a policy must have a secular purpose and that its primary effect must neither advance nor inhibit religion. In *Wallace v. Jaffree* (1986) the Court extended that rationale to the "minute of silence" proviso some state legislatures and school boards had adopted as an alternative to school-sponsored prayer. An Alabama statute (1978) had provided for a time of silence which could be used "for meditation." When it was amended in 1981 to add "voluntary prayer," the Court held it unconstitutional, reasoning that this would characterize prayer as a favored practice, a violation of the secular purpose test in *Lemon. Lee v. Weisman* (1991) dealt with prayer at school graduation. The principal of a Rhode Island middle school had invited a rabbi to give opening and closing prayers and to do so with guidelines set by the school board. The majority opinion set aside the argument that graduation prayer was simply a long-held tradition favored by most people, finding instead an unconstitutional "psychological coercion" of those at the ceremony who disagreed with the practice.

Under the Equal Access Act of 1984, schools that provided a limited open forum where student organizations could meet must also allow student-initiated and student-led religious organizations to meet. The Supreme Court upheld the Equal Access Act in *Board of Education of the Westside Community Schools v. Mergens* (1990).

Does granting of tax exemptions to churches constitute an unconstitutional establishment of religion? In *Walz v. Tax Commission* (1970) the Court upheld New York's policy of allowing property tax exemptions to churches, finding that the policy was not an unlawful establishment of religion be-

cause it applied broadly to charitable institutions. Also the Court noted an important rule that has become a major factor in establishment clause jurisprudence—the entanglement test. This test prohibits government interference with religious activities when interference would create an excessive entanglement with religion.

Government-supported religious traditions have given rise to numerous legal challenges. *Marsh v. Chambers* (1983) reviewed state funding of legislative chaplains; rather than applying the *Lemon* test, the Court opted to uphold the practice as a long-established tradition. In *Lynch v. Donnelly* (1984) the Court allowed a city's sponsorship of a nativity scene, accompanied by secular symbols of Christmas.

Challenges to religious exemptions from labor laws have resulted in several cases that defined the relationship between labor laws and religion. In *National Labor Relations Board v. Catholic Bishop of Chicago* (1979) the Court ruled that a religious school was not subject to the National Labor Relations Act. In 1972 Congress amended Section 702 of the Civil Rights Act of 1964, to allow religious organizations to discriminate in employment on the basis of religion. Subsequent decisions in *Southwestern Baptist Theological Seminary v. Equal Employment Opportunity Commission* (1980) and *Alamo Foundation v. Secretary of Labor* (1985) determined that religious exemptions from labor laws do not apply to nonministerial employees or employees engaged in commercial employment. In *Church of Latter-day Saints v. Amos* (1987) the Court upheld the dismissal of an employee working in a Mormon-owned gym, a nonprofit service related to a religious mission of the Mormon church.

A lively debate over the proper relationship of religion to government has continued for two hundred years. Although the fine points of this relationship will never be entirely resolved, the U.S. Constitution will continue to offer a framework for peaceful discussion of church-state issues.

See also *Education; Freedom of religion; Separation of church and state; Taxation; United States of America.*

Derek Davis

BIBLIOGRAPHY

Ariens, Michael S., and Robert A. Destro. *Religious Liberty in a Pluralistic Society.* Durham, N.C.: Carolina Academic Press, 1996.

Cord, Robert L. *Separation of Church and State: Historical Fact and Current Fiction.* New York: Lambeth Press, 1982.

Curry, Thomas. *The First Freedoms: Church and State in America to the Passage of the First Amendment.* Oxford: Oxford University Press, 1986.

Davis, Derek. *Original Intent: Chief Justice Rehnquist and the Course of American Church-State Relations.* Buffalo, N.Y.: Prometheus Books, 1991.

Miller, Robert T., and Ronald B. Flowers. *Toward Benevolent Neutrality: Church, State, and the Supreme Court.* 5th ed. Waco, Texas: Baylor University Press, 1996.

Pfeffer, Leo. *Church, State, and Freedom.* 2d ed. Boston: Beacon Press, 1967.

Stokes, Anson Phelps. *Church and State in the United States.* 3 vols. New York: Harper, 1950.

Conversion

Religious conversion is the process by which the identity, relationships, and personal values of an individual or group are reformulated as new religious ideals. Although today many people think of it as a uniquely individual event, throughout history broad changes in politics and society have prompted religious conversion. In ancient times the incorporation of tribal and nonstate peoples into multiethnic empires was often accompanied by their conversion to more socially expansive and doctrinally formalized religions, including those known today as the world religions. In modern times religious conversion has assumed new forms, in a manner deeply influenced by world politics, global communications, and the accelerated pace of social change.

Christians and Muslims in the Modern Macrocosm

More than most other religions, Christianity and Islam have demonstrated a remarkable ability to adapt to the modern era and communicate their message to growing numbers of believers. Restricted to Europe and portions of the Middle East during the Middle Ages, Christianity in the early modern era benefited from the colonial ascent of western Europe, extending its reach to all corners of the globe. Some scholars have argued that the often close collaboration of mission and colonial authorities during this time amounted to a "colonization of consciousness." Although they often did facilitate mission establishment and compel conversion, the attitudes of colonial authorities toward missionaries varied widely. In Mexico, East Africa, and Sumatra, authorities promoted the establishment of missions in recently colonized territories but later restricted missionary privileges when church leaders sought to defend native populations from exploitative labor programs. Elsewhere, as in Muslim portions of Africa and the Dutch East Indies, colonial officials barred missions outright, on the grounds that proselytization among Muslims might provoke unrest and jeopardize European economic concerns.

Christian missionaries in colonial times, therefore, were not everywhere agents of European domination. What is clear is that Western expansion presented a forceful challenge to localized and politically vulnerable religions. On some islands in the South Pacific, nineteenth-century natives discarded their cults shortly after European contact, hoping that adoption of the new arrivals' religion would allow them to tap into European military and economic power. Elsewhere, as in portions of Southeast Asia and sub-Saharan Africa, missionaries required converts to adopt European dress, worship, and etiquette. As a result, many natives rejected Christianity as "the religion of Europeans." Not coincidentally, the ranks of native Christians in Asia and Africa swelled dramatically after World War II, when church leadership devolved from European to native clerics, and the identification of Christianity with European colonialism weakened.

Since the end of that war, Christian conversion has continued in large portions of the developing world in a manner that again reflects changing political realities. In contemporary Africa, Christian conversion has been accompanied by the growth of "African" and independent churches. Some of these new religious movements maintain orthodox belief and ritual, but many draw on indigenous styles of leadership and worship. More dramatic yet has been the recent expansion of evangelical Christianity in Africa, eastern Europe, Latin America, and Southeast Asia. In Latin America, upward of 15 percent of the population has converted to the new faith since 1960. Although North American missions pioneered the movement in many countries, today evangelicalism's grass roots are locally sustained. As with Methodism in nineteenth-century England, many poor and marginalized urbanites view evangelical Christianity as an avenue to direct religious participation and social dignity. Women converts look to the faith to provide checks on abusive macho males. In societies plagued by political violence, evangelicalism also provides believers a means to express alternative ethical values without encoding that alternative in a political form and thereby inviting repression by local authorities.

In parts of the Old World, the European expansion also accelerated the process of Islamic conversion. When, in the sixteenth century, the Portuguese seized "spice island" entrepôts in Southeast Asia (in what is today the island nation of

Indonesia), Muslim rulers responded by attacking and converting their Hindu neighbors, whom the Muslims saw as potential allies of the Europeans. As nineteenth-century colonialism improved roads and economic infrastructures in Asia and Africa, Muslim preachers often followed in their wake. Like their Christian counterparts, Muslim preachers were identified by native peoples as the carriers of a powerful and cosmopolitan religion. Islam appealed to many converts because colonial penetration undermined local authorities and ideals, unleashing a desire for a religion capable of responding to the challenge of an expanded social universe. In numerous instances, too, Islam was drawn into the struggle against European colonialism.

At several points in modern history Islamic conversion came about through political conquest. Islam's contemporary growth, however, has more to do with the Muslim community's voluntarism, proselytizing zeal, and grassroots organization, qualities that it shares with evangelical Christianity. Still, the usual process of conversion differs between the two religions. Unlike mission Christianity (especially its Protestant variant), Islam rarely requires converts to demonstrate early in the process a comprehensive knowledge of theology; conversion is effected through a simple profession of the faith. As a community of believers grows, however, Muslim practices of almsgiving, collective worship (required of all males on Fridays), pilgrimage, and religious education create strong pressures for a deepening orthodoxy. Islam has no centralized church structure or even a formal clergy; religious leadership is instead assumed by jurists or religious scholars known collectively as *ulama*. Unlike nineteenth-century Christianity, mainline Islam has allowed converts in new Muslim lands to rise quickly to leadership positions. In newly converted regions of Africa, South Asia, and Southeast Asia, the permeability of Islamic leadership to local recruits has allowed converts quickly to identify their new faith as indigenous, discouraging the development of nativist sects like those that have proliferated in African Christianity.

Internal Conversion

Islam and Christianity have been the two most powerful agents of religious conversion in modern times. However, an equally significant reformulation of religious identity has occurred among other believers, not through the adoption of a new faith, but through the reconfiguration or "rationalization" of the religion with which individuals have long been affiliated. Scholars refer to this reformulation of identity

within an already-professed religion as "internal conversion."

In the modern era internal conversion has often been prompted by Muslim or Christian challenges to other faiths. In early twentieth-century India, for example, Christian and Muslim success in converting untouchables led Hindu leaders to develop their own programs of religious proselytization. In so doing, the Hindu leadership standardized and simplified their religion's organization and doctrine in a manner that showed strong Protestant influences. Elsewhere, as in Muslim Southeast Asia, the recent Islamic revival has prompted the adherents of minority religions to defend their faith by adopting educational and organizational reforms similar to those promoted by reformist Muslims. In the majority Buddhist nations of Burma, Sri Lanka, and Thailand, finally, government officials have supported efforts by reform-minded Buddhists to convert minority populations within their borders.

Not all cultures are equally susceptible to conversion appeals. In the eighteenth and nineteenth centuries, as they reshaped their diverse populations into a more homogeneous citizenry, many western European countries developed ethnonationalist traditions that diminished religion's role in political life and dampened popular interest in formulating expressly religious public identities. In premodern China and Japan, too, ruling elites discouraged the development of exclusive religions in favor of a civilizational tradition in which confessional religion played a secondary and nonexclusive role. In the twentieth century, the bitter experience of Japanese colonialism, civil war, and cultural disorientation led many Koreans to depart from this East Asian pattern and convert to Christianity in large numbers. More recently, Japan, Taiwan, Hong Kong, and even mainland China have witnessed the development of proselytizing religions promoting conversion and exclusive affiliation. Evangelical Christianity has figured in some of these new religious movements, but confessional sects of Buddhism and Daoism, as well as assorted "new religions," have emerged as well. Despite these developments, East Asia remains a region in which conversion and the idea of exclusive religious affiliation are less prevalent than in many other parts of the world.

Modern politics, economics, and communications have drawn growing numbers of people into a fast-changing and multicultural macrocosm. In many communities, this development has also increased social differentiation, accelerated the collapse of locally organized traditions, and unleashed aspirations for voluntarism and popular participation in religious affairs. Having originated in the empires of the ancient world and been reformulated through their encounter with modernity, Christianity and Islam developed values and organizations well suited to the challenges of the modern era. Other religions have followed suit, promoting widespread movements of religious renewal and conversion. Inasmuch as world events continue to challenge popular morals and identity, conversion will likely remain a central feature of contemporary politics, contradicting forecasts of modern religion's demise.

See also *Colonialism; Evangelicalism; Islam, Southeast Asian; Missionaries.*

Robert W. Hefner

BIBLIOGRAPHY

Geertz, Clifford. "'Internal Conversion' in Contemporary Bali." In Clifford Geertz, *The Interpretation of Cultures.* New York: Basic Books, 1973.

Hefner, Robert W., ed. *Conversion to Christianity: Historical and Anthropological Perspectives on a Great Transformation.* Berkeley: University of California Press, 1993.

Keyes, Charles F., Laurel Kendall, and Helen Hardacre, eds. *Asian Visions of Authority: Religion and the Modern States of East and Southeast Asia.* Honolulu: University of Hawaii Press, 1994.

Kipp, Rita Smith. *The Early Years of a Dutch Colonial Mission.* Ann Arbor: University of Michigan Press, 1993.

Lewis, I. M. *Islam in Tropical Africa.* 2d ed. Bloomington: Indiana University Press, 1980.

Martin, David. *Tongues of Fire: The Explosion of Protestantism in Latin America.* Oxford: Blackwell, 1990.

Sanneh, Lamin. *West African Christianity: The Religious Impact.* London: C. Hurst, 1983.

Van der Veer, Peter. *Religious Nationalism: Hindus and Muslims in India.* Berkeley: University of California Press, 1994.

Covenant

Covenant, a political idea whose sources are deep in Western religion and rooted in biblical monotheism, defines political justice, shapes political behavior, and directs humans toward a civic synthesis of the two within a context of what theologians know as federal liberty. Covenant is one of the seminal political ideas of humanity. It is particularly significant for its political and religious origins and its theo-political character. It may also be the oldest political idea providing for human liberty, with law antedating the idea of natural law by centuries.

The term "federal" is from the Latin *foedus,* which means

covenant. Hence federal liberty is the liberty to do that which is right and proper by the terms of a particular covenant, thereby providing a basis for resolving the problem of balancing liberty and authority with which every society must grapple. As such, covenant is an idea whose importance is akin to natural law in defining justice and to natural right in delineating the origins and proper constitution of political society. This is especially true in periods of crisis or transition, such as transition from the late medieval period to the modern epoch, which took place from the Reformation early in the sixteenth century to the great revolutions of the eighteenth century. Although somewhat eclipsed since the shift to organic and then positivistic theories of politics, which began in the mid-nineteenth century, covenant persists as a factor shaping political behavior in those civil societies whose foundations are grounded in the effort to translate covenant ideas into political reality and in others attempting to build a democratic order on federalist rather than centralist principles.

Since its beginnings, political science has identified three basic ways in which polities come into existence: conquest, organic development, and covenant. In *Federalist* No. 1 (1787), one of the defining documents of American constitutionalism, these were referred to as force, accident, and reflection and choice. These questions of origins are not abstract; the mode of founding of a polity does much to determine its subsequent political life. The covenant worldview is one of the two or three "mother" views shared by humanity. It may even be rooted in the very psyches of people, in the sense that every personality, as formed by nature and culture, has a tendency toward hierarchical, organic, or covenantal perceptions of human relationships.

The uses of covenant demonstrate how political conceptualization and expression go hand in hand. In ancient Israel the Jews—and during the sixteenth and seventeenth centuries, the Scots, Dutch, and English Puritans—not only conceived of their worlds in covenantal terms but wrote national covenants to which loyal members of the body politic subscribed. Similar covenants were used in the founding of many of the original colonies in British North America. Covenantal thinking was the common mode of political conceptualization and expression during the American Revolution, where it was reflected in any number of constitutional documents. More recently, such examples as the call for a social contract in England to create a new set of relationships between labor and management and the covenant inaugurated in Boston, Massachusetts, by the city's major religious groups in 1979 in an attempt to bring racial peace to that city are but two of many examples of the continuing use of covenant and its derivations as forms of political conceptualization and modes of political expression.

As a source of political ideology, covenant shapes the worldviews or perspectives of whole societies, defining their civil characters and political relationships and serving as a touchstone for testing the legitimacy and often even the efficiency of their political institutions and those who keep them going.

Perhaps most important is the role of covenant as an element in shaping political culture and behavior. This element is the most difficult to measure, and yet it is operationally the most significant dimension of covenant.

The Idea of Covenant

A covenant is a morally informed agreement or pact between people or parties having an independent and sufficiently equal status; it is based on voluntary consent and established by mutual oaths or promises witnessed by the relevant transcendent authority. A covenant provides for joint obligation and action to achieve defined ends (limited or comprehensive) under conditions of mutual respect that protect the individual integrities of all the parties to it. Every covenant involves consent. Most are meant to be of unlimited duration, if not perpetual. Covenants can bind any number of partners for a variety of purposes, but in essence they are political in that their bonds are used principally to create relationships best understood in political terms.

In its original biblical form, covenant embodies the idea that relationships between God and humanity are based on morally sustained compacts of mutual promise and obligation. God's covenant with Noah (Genesis 9), which came after Noah had harkened fully to God's commands in what was, to say the least, an extremely difficult situation, is the first of many examples. In its political form, covenant expresses the idea that people can freely create communities and polities, peoples and publics, and civil society itself through morally grounded and sustained compacts (whether religious or otherwise in impetus), establishing thereby enduring partnerships.

In all its forms the principal focus of covenant is on relationships. A covenant is the constitutionalization of a set of relationships of a particular kind. As such, it provides the basis for the institutionalization of those relationships; but it would be wrong to confuse the order of precedence.

It is possible that covenant ideas emerged spontaneously in various parts of the world. If covenant thinking is rooted in human nature as well as nurture, it is to be expected that some people everywhere would be oriented toward the idea. For an idea to take root and spread, however, it is not sufficient for random individuals to be disposed to it. Somehow a culture or civilization must emerge that embodies and reflects that idea.

All the evidence points to the existence of certain covenantal peoples whose political cultures are informed by covenantal and related concepts, which in turn influence their political behavior. Those people emerged from two nuclear concentrations. The first was at the western edge of southwestern Asia three to four thousand years ago in what was once known as the Fertile Crescent, especially in Israel. Its principal manifestations were the Bible and the Jewish people, who were to foster the covenant idea and its practice through the introduction of monotheism.

The second concentration was in northwestern Europe, especially in Switzerland and the region stretching northward up the Rhine River valley through what is today western Germany, Alsace, Belgium, and the Netherlands, extending across the North Sea to Scotland, and continuing along the western coast of Scandinavia. These peoples, who drew their covenantal ideas from the Hebrew Bible, subsequently settled and shaped various "new worlds" from Iceland and North America to South Africa and Australia.

From these covenantal peoples emerged Judaism and Christianity with their biblical covenantal base, Reformed Protestantism with its federal theology, federalism as a political principle and arrangement, modern constitutionalism, civil societies based on interlocking voluntary associations, and almost every other element that reflects social organization based on what has loosely been called "contract" rather than "status." Moreover, these covenantal peoples seem to have internalized a covenantal or federalistic approach to life to a greater or a lesser extent.

The first such civilization or culture area was that of ancient Israel whose people transformed and perfected a device originally developed among the Amorite and Hittite peoples who inhabited the area. The first known uses of the term "covenant" (biritum in Akkadian) were the treaties through which the empire builders of southwest Asia secured the fealty of conquered peoples and their domains through pacts secured by oath before their respective deities. These pacts laid out the form which covenants have taken ever since. They included four elements: a prologue indicating the parties and purposes involved, a preamble stating the general purposes of the covenant and the principles behind it, a body of conditions and operative clauses, and an oath to make the covenant morally binding. The oath stipulated the agreed-upon sanctions to be applied if the covenant was violated. These first covenants simultaneously established the political purposes and moral bases for covenanting.

The domestic political and religious usages of covenant emerged either parallel to or derived from these ancient vassal covenants. The two were connected in the Bible to transform the idea of covenant into the classic covenant tradition. God's covenant with Israel established the Jewish people and founded it as a body politic, while at the same time creating the religious framework that gave that polity its purpose, its norms, and its constitution, as well as the guidelines for developing a political order based on proper, that is, covenantal, relationships.

Biblical adaptation of the forms of the vassal covenants involved a transformation of purpose and content so great as to mean a difference in kind, not merely degree. A covenant was used to found a people, making their moral commitment to one another far stronger and enduring than that of a vassal to an imperial overlord. The Bible draws a distinction between "children of the covenant," *bnei brit* in Hebrew, and "masters of the covenant," or *ba'alei brit*. Children of the covenant is used where the covenant has established a new entity whose partners are bound together as children within a family. The covenant that unites and forms the Jewish people in the biblical account and in all subsequent Jewish history makes all Jews *bnei brit*. On the other hand, where the term used is *ba'alei brit*, it is essentially an international treaty. It does not create a new entity but establishes a relationship of peace and mutual ties between separate entities that remain for all purposes separated despite the limited-purpose pact.

This new form of covenant brought God in as a partner, thus informing it with religious value and implication for the Israelites, who saw no distinction between its religious and political dimensions. The covenant remained a theo-political document with as heavy an emphasis on the political as could be. The strong political dimension reflected God's purpose in choosing one people to be the builders of a holy commonwealth that would be a model for all others.

It was only later with the rise of Christianity and the beginning of the long exile of the Jews from their land that covenant took on a more strictly religious character for some. The political dimension was downplayed, if not ignored, by Christian theologians and diminished by Jewish legists. Christianity embraced the covenant idea as one of its foundations, but Christians reinterpreted the old biblical covenant establishing a people and a polity to be a covenant of grace unilaterally granted for individual humans and mediated through Jesus. Jewish legists simply took the basic covenantal framework of Judaism for granted and concentrated on the fine points of the law as applies to daily living or the expected messianic redemption.

Within the Jewish world, the political dimension of covenanting received new impetus in the eleventh through the fourteenth centuries to provide a basis for constituting autonomous local Jewish communities throughout Europe. That effort ran parallel to the establishment of municipal corporations throughout the Continent that were legitimized by royal charter, usually negotiated between the municipality and the throne. Although these efforts found some expression in political thought, it was really not until the Reformation that covenant reemerged as a primary political category, first in political theology and then in political philosophy.

The Reformation and Federal Theology

It was then that the covenant idea emerged as a powerful force in the second major cultural area, that of western and, most particularly, northwestern Europe. What cultural predispositions lay behind the receptivity of the peoples of that area to covenant as a concept remain to be uncovered, if they can be. It cannot be an accident that the federal theology emerged simultaneously in the sixteenth century in four separate places in Switzerland (Zurich, Basel, Berne, and Geneva), where confederal political arrangements had been dominant since the late thirteenth century. The other major covenantal polity was the United Netherlands, formed as a confederation by its revolt against Spain inspired by Reformed Protestantism.

The Reformed churches turned to the covenant concept with relish, finding in it the most appropriate expression of their theological ideas and expectations for church polity and the new search for religious and political liberty. The first great use of the concept in an overtly political manner in this period was the *Vindiciae contra Tyrannos* (Claim against kings, 1579), thought to be written by Philippe Du Plessis-Mornay, a Huguenot leader, and based on scriptural discussions of the legitimate right of resistance to tyrannical kings.

The very term "Huguenot," which was applied to French Calvinists, is from the German *eidgenossen,* meaning "covenant."

Drawing heavily on biblical sources, the foundations of religious and political freedom were established through the federal theology developed by these theologians and political thinkers such as Johannes Althusius, a German political theorist, who, as the intellectual father of modern federalism in the late sixteenth century, stimulated the systematic political application of the covenant idea. In the next century, covenant was given secular form by Thomas Hobbes, John Locke, and Benedict de Spinoza. By the late-seventeenth century, the concept had taken on an independent life of its own in the ideas of political compact, civil society, and modern constitutionalism.

From northwestern Europe, covenantally grounded civilization spread to the new worlds opened by northwestern European colonization. Those covenantal societies ranged from Iceland, settled by Danes and coastal Norwegians in the tenth century, to the United States, settled in the early seventeenth century by Scots and Puritans from the British Isles and Netherlanders and Huguenots. Where settlers from those traditions were dominant, new peoples were established by covenant, and they in turn wrote constitutions that realized the covenantal dimension through a network of political institutions. At the end of the eighteenth century the American Revolution translated the concept into a powerful instrument of political reform, but only after merging it with the secularized covenantal idea of compact. American constitutionalism is a product of that merger.

Covenant, Compact, and Contract

Covenant is tied in an ambiguous relationship to two related terms, *compact* and *contract.* On one hand, both compacts and contracts are in a sense derived from covenant, and sometimes the terms are even used interchangeably. On the other hand, there are very real differences that need clarification.

Both covenants and compacts differ from contracts in that the first two are constitutional or public and the last is private in character. As such, covenantal or compactual obligation is broadly reciprocal. Those bound by one or the other are obligated to respond to one another beyond the letter of the law rather than to limit their obligations to the narrowest contractual requirements. Covenants and compacts then are inherently designed to be flexible in certain respects as

well as firm in others. As expressions of private law, contracts tend to be interpreted by each party as narrowly as possible as to what is explicitly mandated by the contract itself.

A covenant differs from a compact in that its morally binding dimension takes precedence over its legal dimension. In its heart of hearts, a covenant is an agreement in which a higher moral force, traditionally God, is either a direct party to or a guarantor of a particular relationship. When the term *compact* is used, moral force is involved only indirectly. A compact, based as it is on mutual pledges rather than on guarantees by or before a higher authority, rests more heavily on a legal—though still ethical—grounding for its politics. In other words, compact is a secular phenomenon.

This statement is historically verifiable by examining the shift in terminology that took place in the seventeenth and eighteenth centuries. While those who saw the hand of God in political affairs in the United States as a rule continued to use the term *covenant,* those who sought a secular grounding for politics turned to the term *compact.* Although the distinction was not always used with strict clarity, it does appear consistently. The issue was further complicated by the eighteenth-century French theorist Jean-Jacques Rousseau and his followers who talk about the "social contract," a highly secularized concept that, even when applied for public purposes, never develops the same level of moral obligation as either covenant or compact.

Covenantal Relationships

Over the centuries the ideas of covenant, natural law, and constitutionalism became intertwined. In 1776, for example, when the Americans formally declared themselves an independent people in the Declaration of Independence—itself a covenant establishing a new relationship based on precepts of natural rights—they saw constitution making as a way of further covenanting or compacting together to form civil instruments designed to carry out the premises of the Declaration. The resulting state and federal constitutions were seen as compacts embodying the principles of natural law, especially in their Declarations of Rights. The propriety of subsequent legislation was, therefore, to be judged in light of its "constitutionality," or, in other words, its conformity to both the natural law and the covenant, one step removed.

Normally, a covenant precedes a constitution to establish a people or civil society, which then proceeds to adopt a constitution of government for itself. Thus a constitution involves the implementation of a prior covenant into an actual structure of government. The constitution may include a restatement or reaffirmation of the original covenant, as does the Massachusetts Constitution of 1780 in its preamble: "The body-politics is formed by a voluntary association of individuals: It is a social compact, by which the whole people covenants with each citizen, that all shall be governed by certain laws for the common good."

Covenant relationships have often been compared to marriages in their permanency, promise of trust, mutuality of responsibility, and respect for the integrity of each of the partners within the community created by wedding (an ancient Anglo-Saxon term for sealing a contract). The analogy also highlights the way in which covenant links consent and kinship. In the biblical-covenantal view of marriage, two independent and otherwise unrelated persons consent to become "one flesh" and establish a family.

In politics, covenant connotes the voluntary establishment of a people and body politic. The Declaration of Independence is an excellent example of this kind of covenant. Through it, the diverse inhabitants of the thirteen colonies reaffirmed that they consented to become a people. It was not without reason, therefore, that President Abraham Lincoln fondly described the union created by that act as "a regular marriage." The partners do not unquestionably live happily ever after, but they are bound by covenant to struggle toward such an end, a commitment well understood and made explicit by Lincoln during the Civil War years in the 1860s.

To the extent that covenant is both a theological and political concept, it is also informed by a moral or ethical perspective that treats political relationships in the classical manner. That is, it links power and justice—the two faces of politics—and preserves the classic and ancient linkages between ethics and politics. Again, the emphasis is on relationships rather than structures as the key to political justice. Structures are always important, but ultimately, no matter how finely tuned the structures, they come alive (or fail to) only through the human relationships that inform and shape them.

Parallel to the theological and philosophic dimensions is the sociopolitical aspect of the covenantal founding of new societies. A principal, although not necessarily universal characteristic of new settlements, is that they tend to promote equality. People come together in a new place, away from the established civil order and must organize their own political life. The natural inclination is for them to do so on

the basis of equality because of the equal risks involved. Moreover, they can do so only through some contractual means whereby each agrees to accept the jurisdiction of the whole. They are likely to do so only if each preserves those liberties deemed essential and acquires some share in the common decision-making processes. The further removed a new settlement is from older political orders, whether physically or in other ways, the more likely it is that this will be the model for its founding. Where previously existing political authority can effectively be extended over new territories, and older constitutional arrangements enforced, there is less room for the application of this model than otherwise, although even in such cases the very fact of new settlement tends to bring some of its elements into play. Where the old order cannot be effectively extended, or where it actively encourages a contractual founding in the new territory, the model is more likely to be implemented in its fullness.

The case of Switzerland illustrates this point. The territories of what is today Switzerland were for many generations wild lands at the peripheries of the various royal, imperial, and feudal domains of Europe. People seeking to be free of autocratic rule fled to those lands, where they organized themselves into communities of equals with a minimum of outside interference. When the Habsburg emperors sought to impose their rule on those communities, the Swiss fought back, organizing to do so by applying the same federal principles to the confederation of communities that they had to earlier unions of individuals and families.

The covenant idea has been important for the growth of democratic government and society, whatever the starting point. It presupposes the independence and worth of each individual and the truth that each person possesses certain inalienable rights because only free people with rights can enter into agreements with one another. It also presupposes the necessity for government and the need to organize political society on principles that ensure the maintenance of those rights and the exercise of power in a cooperative or partnerlike way.

On the other hand, covenantal or federal liberty is not simply the right to do as one pleases. Federal liberty is the liberty to pursue the moral purposes for which the covenant was made. This latter kind of liberty requires that moral distinctions be drawn and that human actions be judged according to the terms of the covenant. This does not preclude changes in social norms, but the principles of judgment remain constant. Consequently, covenantal societies, founded as they are on covenantal choice, tend to emphasize constitutional design and choice as a continuing process, whether in the form of state constitutional referendums in the United States or the recurring referendums in Switzerland or whatever.

The Dynamics of Covenant

The dynamic dimension of covenant emphasizes relationships and their proper shaping, which finds expression in the language of covenantal peoples. All covenantal peoples have appropriate covenantal language. The Hebrew examples discussed here present only a few samples, drawn from a rich covenantal terminology.

To take one example, a central Hebrew term for defining human relationships is *haver*, which means friend, partner, or comrade. This term is developed extensively in the Talmudic literature of Jewish civil and religious law and in medieval Jewish thought in ways that have clear covenantal connotations. The modern Zionist pioneers transformed the term into the Hebrew equivalent for "comrade," deepening its built-in connotation of partnership. Most covenantal societies have a similar term. It is significant that the form of address of the archetypical American folk figure, the cowboy, is "pardner," and "partnership" is the term of choice for describing American federalism. In Australia, the term is "mate" and "mateship" is a basic concept in Australian society.

The essence of covenantal dynamics lies in three biblical terms expressed in Hebrew as *brit* (covenant), *hesed,* and *shalom* (peace). *Biritu,* the original Semitic term for covenant itself suggests a dynamic process and relationship. It reflects two actions, cutting and binding—that is, the separating of something into parts and its reunification in such a way that the parts remain separate in their identities. Indeed, the biblical term for making a covenant is *lichrot brit,* to "cut a covenant." In the ancient Near East, the original covenant ritual involved the division of a sacrificial animal, the parties passing between it, and the animal being reunited through a rebinding. This imagery can be found in other covenantal rituals and ceremonies among Jews and other peoples. Thus both the language and the ritual reflect the dynamics of the covenantal way.

Hesed, which is sometimes translated as "grace" and sometimes as "lovingkindness" is not really translatable into English. It is best understood as the loving fulfillment of the obligations flowing from a covenant bond. Here we shall use the term "covenant obligation" as the equivalent of *hesed.* The Bible recognized the problem of all contractual relationships; namely, the tendency of the parties to a contract to interpret it as narrowly as possible in their own interests. *Hesed* is a dynamic concept designed to reinforce mutuality. Every *brit* creates a *hesed* relationship, whereby the obligation of the parties to it is not narrowly contractual but broadly covenantal. Thus they are required to go beyond the letter of the law in dealing with covenantal matters. The Bible is a record of God's *hesed* toward Israel, his constantly going beyond the letter of the law in dealing with his people who, despite their basic loyalty to the covenant, persistently violate its strict standards in one way or another. At the same time, it is a record of the equivalent response of the people or at least some important segment of the people to God and to each other. A person who acts in the way of *hesed* is called a *hasid,* that is to say, one who builds one's life around the rendering of *hesed* to the covenant partners. The whole concept of Hasidism in Jewish life, both in the biblical period and subsequently, is an outgrowth of this dynamic approach to covenantal relationships.

The Supreme Constitutional Court of the German Federal Republic has developed the concept of *bundestreu* or *bundesfreundlichkeit* as a civil equivalent of the biblical idea of *hesed* and has applied it to adjudicate intergovernmental issues. It calls for a kind of federal friendship and loyalty among the federal government and the constituent states of the German federation, requiring them to go beyond the letter of the law in certain issues, so as to promote more effective intergovernmental cooperation. There are situations in which the federal government or the states may be able to claim that the federal constitution does not require them to respond to their partners. But since such a stance reflects a lack of cooperative spirit, which could paralyze governance, the court has developed this concept as a constitutional norm which it will apply to ensure that the parties go beyond the letter of the law in order to fulfill its spirit.

In the United States the term "partnership" is the American quasi-constitutional equivalent of *hesed.* Although it has not gained similar legal status, it has tremendous normative power. Even its misuse is revealing; every effort of linkage is labeled partnership even when hegemony of one "partner" is the goal.

Shalom, the third term, means peace. Etymologically, it suggests completeness, wholeness, coming together; that is, it is covenantal in its echoes and implications. Thus peace itself, in biblical terminology, is dynamic; it involves the completing of something, bringing things together to create a new whole. Peace is obtained through a *brit shalom,* a covenant of peace, which can be maintained only through the *hesed* of the parties to it.

See also *Civil society; Communitarianism; Judaism; Natural law; Reformation.*

Daniel J. Elazar

BIBLIOGRAPHY

Elazar, Daniel J. *The Covenant Tradition in Politics.* 4 vols. New Brunswick, N.J.: Transaction, 1995.
Elazar, Daniel J., ed. *Kinship and Consent: The Jewish Political Tradition and Its Contemporary Uses.* 2d ed. New Brunswick, N.J.: Transaction, 1997.
Elazar, Daniel J., and John Kincaid, eds. *The Covenant Connection: Federal Theology and Politics.* Forthcoming.
Hillers, Delbert R. *Covenant: The History of a Biblical Idea.* Baltimore: Johns Hopkins University Press, 1969.
Miller, Perry. *The New England Mind.* Boston: Beacon Press, 1961.
Niebuhr, H. Richard. "The Idea of Covenant and American Democracy." *Church History* 23 (1954).
Snaith, Norman H. *The Distinctive Ideas of the Old Testament.* New York: Schocken Books, 1966.
Thundyil, Zacharas P. *Covenant in Anglo-Saxon Thought.* Madras: Macmillan, 1972.
Walzer, Michael. *The Revolution of the Saints.* Cambridge: Harvard University Press, 1965.

Crime and criminal justice

A crime is any act deemed an offense against the state and that is punishable according to law. Criminologists consider religion a deterrent to conventional crime and a factor in shaping criminal justice policy.

The interdisciplinary field of criminology studies the making of laws, the breaking of laws, and the formulation of responses to the breaking of laws. Religion plays a role in all three processes. For example, in the United States, religious motives and organizations have been active in writing laws concerning alcohol, pornography, drugs, abortion, homosexuality, and race relations. Furthermore, religious beliefs can both increase the volume of crime by motivating adherents to break the law on behalf of their convictions (as in the case of civil disobedience) and decrease the volume of crime by serving as a deterrent and as a reinforcer of secular laws. Finally, religion often is a central ingredient in the formation of public opinion and eventually public policy concerning the goals of punishment and the methods used to treat offenders.

Two issues have received considerable attention in criminological research: the importance of religion as a deterrent to conventional crime and delinquency and the relationship between religious beliefs and views about the appropriate response to criminal offenders.

Religion as a Deterrent

Perhaps surprisingly, religion was not recognized as an important variable in most theories of social control developed in the 1950s and 1960s. These theories were aimed at identifying forces that deter people from violating the law. Though one of the early statistical studies in criminology in the United States reported in 1950 that only 40 percent of a sample of juveniles with court records attended church regularly, compared with 67 percent of a matched sample of nondelinquents, religion still was not considered a prominent variable in control theories developed over the next two decades.

The most influential control theory, presented by Travis Hirschi and supported by research conducted in the late 1960s on a large sample of California junior and senior high school males, found no evidence that religious beliefs and religious participation were factors in deterring people from engaging in illegal behavior. Although acceptance of conventional moral values and respect for the law (measured with reports from research subjects and juvenile court records) did inhibit delinquency, frequency of church attendance was not related to acceptance of conventional values or to respect for the law. Furthermore, while church attendance fostered a belief in supernatural sanctions for violating the law, the belief in sanctions had no effect on involvement in delinquency.

Hirschi's findings seemed to defy common sense and sparked a flurry of research that continues today. After all, sacred proscriptions and prescriptions typically overlap with secular laws so that commitment to sacred teachings should reinforce one's commitment to the legal order.

Charles Tittle and Michael Welch in 1983 identified sixty-five studies containing information on the relationship between religiosity (measured by either frequency of church attendance or the strength of persons' religious beliefs in their daily lives) and rule breaking. Of these, fifty-five found a significant positive association between religiosity and compliance, at least under some conditions: those who were more religious were more compliant with rules. Although most of these studies concerned juveniles, six examined adult crime and deviance, and all of the adult studies found that religiosity deterred people from violating conventional laws and norms.

The importance of the findings concerning adults should be stressed. Among juveniles, measures of religiosity such as frequency of participation in religious activities might reflect parental coercion rather than the juvenile's true level of religiosity. Research on adults potentially provides more conclusive evidence concerning the deterrent effect of religion.

By the end of the 1980s scholarly opinion had shifted, and criminologists generally agreed that at least in some conditions religion was a deterrent to crime. During the two decades after Hirschi's conclusion, research and theory were targeted at specifying the conditions in which religiosity had its greatest deterrent effect on illegal behavior. Three themes emerged in the literature.

One line of research focused on the nature of the community. Researchers partially replicated Hirschi's study in Atlanta, Georgia, where they found a significant inverse effect of church attendance on self-reported delinquency among high school students. In other words, in a southern city where religion presumably was a more central part of people's lives, and contrary to Hirschi's findings from California (presumably a more secular region of the country), as church attendance increased, delinquency decreased. A theory that emerged from this and other studies was that religiosity had a stronger inhibiting effect on conventional illegal behavior in communities where religion was a more prominent force in day-to-day life ("sacred communities") than in communities where religious convictions generally were weak ("secular communities").

Not all research, however, supported this conclusion, and in fact the inconsistent research findings prompted Tittle and Welch to develop a different theory. They noted that religion is but one of many social institutions and sources of values that promote compliance with the law. According to their theory of secular social disorganization, religion has its strongest deterrent effect when secular moral guidelines are weak or have lost their authority. In these kinds of communities, where the institutions of family, education, and politics are in disarray and fail to provide clear moral guidelines, the institution of religion serves as a last resort to instill compliance with the law.

A second attempt to understand the relationship between religiosity and illegal behavior addressed the nature of particular laws and came to be called the anti-asceticism hypothesis, which is similar to the secular social disorganization theory. Scholars noted that some acts are more consistently condemned throughout all societal institutions than are others. According to the anti-asceticism hypothesis, behaviors that are consistently condemned, such as murder or robbery, are not strongly influenced by religious beliefs. The messages from secular institutions are sufficient to deter people from these kinds of behavior, whether or not they have religious convictions. But there are other behaviors, labeled anti-ascetic forms of deviance, for which secular condemnation is weaker or ambiguous—underage drinking, drug use, tax fraud, employee theft, traffic law violation, and so on. According to the anti-asceticism hypothesis, religiosity should have its greatest deterrent effect on these kinds of behavior for which secular proscriptions are not as compelling. Much like Tittle and Welch's secular disorganization theory, the anti-asceticism hypothesis proposed that religiosity serves as a deterrent to crime and deviance primarily when other forces have failed to elicit conformity.

A third approach to specifying conditions in which religiosity affects deterrence emphasized religious denomination; it has been called the norm qualities hypothesis. The argument focuses primarily on the distinctions between more and less conservative denominations. Conservative denominations expect total commitment and uniform interpretation of sacred teachings, leaving little room for individual discretion in decisions concerning compliance or noncompliance with rules. Consequently, it might follow that religiosity, viewed either as personal religious commitment or frequency of participation, would be a stronger deterrent to crime and deviance among people affiliated with conservative denominations than among those affiliated with less conservative denominations. The extent to which religiosity deters crime depends on the content of the religious norms to which one adheres. With some exceptions, however, research has failed to support this theory, finding instead that religiosity is a significant deterrent regardless of religious affiliation.

By the end of the 1980s the search for conditions in which religiosity has an impact on deterrence seemed to have run its course. Scholars almost unanimously reached the conclusion that religiosity had at least some, though not an extremely strong, deterrent effect on conventional crime and delinquency in nearly all conditions. Prominent scholars such as John Cochran and Ronald Akers called for an end to this line of inquiry. Attention then shifted to the processes through which religiosity had its deterrent effect on crime.

Harold Grasmick and his collaborators resurrected Hirschi's earlier concern with religion as a possible sanctioning system and attempted to link religion to the rational-choice theory of crime that was gaining respect in criminology and other areas. According to the theory, criminal behavior is like any other behavior—it occurs when the rewards for it outweigh the costs.

Religion potentially contributes to the cost side of the equation in two ways. First, to the extent that sacred norms overlap with secular law, those people for whom religion plays a prominent role in everyday decision making would be more likely than others to feel ashamed if they violate the law. Shame is a self-imposed sanction, enhanced by the importance of religion in one's life and occurring even when others are unaware of one's transgression. Second, to the extent that participation in religious organizations brings one into contact with others who endorse legal norms, individuals actively involved in religious organizations risk greater embarrassment if they choose to violate the law. Embarrassment is a socially imposed sanction, experienced as a loss of respect from others who become aware of one's transgression. Rational-choice theory, therefore, has shifted attention away from attempts to specify conditions in which religion is a deterrent to concern with how religion functions as a deterrent. From this theory's perspective, the multiple dimensions of religiosity, religious commitment and organizational participation, which were not clearly distinguished in earlier research, receive special attention.

The consensus seems to be that religion serves at least as a modest deterrent to conventional crime and delinquency in most conditions. The process through which this effect occurs stems from both the personal and the social dimensions of religiosity.

Religion and Responses to Criminal Offenders

Public opinion concerning preferred societal reactions to criminal offenders is an important topic because policy makers take public opinion into account when formulating criminal justice policies. Since about the mid-1970s Americans have become increasingly punitive in their reaction to crime. For example, in the 1960s the majority of Americans

opposed the death penalty, but by the late 1990s an overwhelming majority (over 80 percent by nearly all estimates), when asked whether they generally favored or opposed the death penalty, said that they favored it.

At the same time there has been a growing disillusionment with rehabilitation and even deterrence as a goal of criminal justice policy and increasing public support for retribution (often called "just deserts") as the objective of the criminal justice system. The goal of punishment, according to the retributivist doctrine, is to punish offenders simply because they deserve it, whether the punishment rehabilitates them or deters others.

Earlier research examined the effect of standard socioeconomic and demographic factors (race, age, sex, education, and others) on attitudes toward punishment and justice, finding only weak relationships at best. Other scholars considered the possibility that America's increasing punitiveness was linked to an increasing crime rate, but studies failed to find evidence that victimization or fear of crime affected people's opinions about appropriate punishments.

Sparked in part by David Garland's work on the history of punishment, research in the 1990s explored the previously neglected link between religion and people's views about the goals of punishment and the appropriate punishment for offenders in American society. In contrast to the previously cited research on religion and involvement in crime, in which strength of religious commitment was shown to be more important in determining compliance with laws than religious affiliation or adherence to particular religious doctrines, research on attitudes toward punishment focused on religious affiliation and the nature or content of one's religious beliefs.

Evidence suggests that individuals affiliated with more conservative Protestant denominations are the strongest proponents of retribution as the goal of punishment. This effect of conservative Protestant affiliation is stronger than the effects of socioeconomic and demographic variables, and it appears that this support is linked to conservative Protestants' more literal interpretation of the Bible. Kenneth Wald has noted that conservative churches are especially well equipped to influence public policy, and it has been speculated that the movement toward retribution in the American criminal justice system, as well as in the juvenile justice system, is connected to the revival and growth of such denominations in contemporary American society.

Not only are conservative Protestants more inclined to

favor retribution as the objective of criminal justice policy, but they also appear to be more punitive in their response to crime. Compared with others, conservative Protestants are more supportive of the death penalty for adults and for juveniles; they are more likely to believe the courts should be harsher in their punishment and are more likely to favor stiffer laws. Again, the effect of conservative Protestantism is greater than the effects of socioeconomic and demographic variables and political party affiliation. Some evidence, however, suggests that the effect is restricted to whites, with blacks affiliated with conservative denominations being less punitive toward offenders than are other blacks.

Grasmick and his colleagues have attempted to explain why conservative Protestants are stronger supporters of retribution and more punitive in their response to crime, noting, as have others, that conservative Protestants are more punitive toward the transgressions of their own children. In the field of social psychology, attribution theory addresses variations in what people consider to be the causes of behavior. Some people are more inclined to think that behavior results from the "will" or character of the actors. These people are said to have a dispositional attribution style. Others who believe that the behavior is the product of forces in the actors' environment are said to have a situational attribution style. Dispositional rather than situational attributions of criminal behavior render the actor more blameworthy and thus, from the perspective of the one making the attribution, more deserving of punishment. Evidence is convincing that those who make dispositional attributions of criminal behavior are more punitive in their response to offenders.

Drawing on the work of Phillip Greven and Robert Wuthnow, Grasmick and his colleagues proposed that conservative Protestantism promotes a dispositional attribution style. A main ingredient in this religious perspective is an emphasis on the "character" of a person. Behavior consistent with religious prescriptions and proscriptions reflects good character; behavior inconsistent with such teachings reflects weak character. From this frame of mind, situational influences have little impact on what a person does.

Grasmick and his colleagues further argued that conservative Protestants, compared with more moderate Protestants, Catholics, and those with no affiliation, are more punitive in their response to crime because they are more likely to attribute criminal behavior to dispositional factors. They tested the argument by studying preferred responses to pun-

ishments for juvenile offenders. Their research yielded four conclusions. First, people who adhere to a literal interpretation of the Bible are more punitive in their preferred response to juvenile delinquents. Second, adherence to a literal interpretation of the Bible is closely linked with making a dispositional attribution—that is, with attributing the causes of delinquency to the character of delinquents rather than to environmental influences. Third, this dispositional attribution style strongly increases the punitiveness of people toward juvenile offenders. And, finally, the dispositional attribution style associated with interpreting the Bible accounts for more than half of the greater punitiveness among those who are biblical literalists.

See also *Civil disobedience; Violence.*

Harold G. Grasmick

BIBLIOGRAPHY

Cochran, John, and Ronald Akers. "Beyond Hellfire: An Exploration of the Variable Effects of Religiosity on Adolescent Marijuana and Alcohol Use." *Journal of Research in Crime and Delinquency* 26 (May 1989): 198–225.

Garland, David. *Punishment and Modern Society: A Study in Social Theory.* Chicago: University of Chicago Press, 1993.

Grasmick, Harold G., and Anne L. McGill. "Religion, Attribution Style, and Punitiveness toward Juvenile Offenders." *Criminology* 32 (February 1994): 23–46.

Grasmick, Harold G., Elizabeth Davenport, Mitchell B. Chamlin, and Robert J. Bursik Jr. "Protestant Fundamentalism and the Retributive Doctrine of Punishment." *Criminology* 30 (February 1992): 21–45.

Grasmick, Harold G., John Cochran, Robert J. Bursik Jr., and M'Lou Kimpel. "Religion, Punitive Justice, and Support for the Death Penalty." *Justice Quarterly* 10 (June 1993): 289–314.

Grasmick, Harold G., Robert J. Bursik Jr., and John Cochran. "'Render unto Caesar What Is Caesar's': Religiosity and Taxpayers' Inclinations to Cheat." *Sociological Quarterly* 32 (summer 1991): 251–266.

Greven, Phillip. *Spare the Child: The Religious Roots of Punishment and Psychological Impact of Physical Abuse.* New York: Random House, 1991.

Hirschi, Travis. *Causes of Delinquency.* Berkeley: University of California Press, 1969.

Tittle, Charles, and Michael Welch. "Religiosity and Deviance: Toward a Contingency Theory of Constraining Effects." *Social Forces* 61 (March 1983): 653–682.

Wald, Kenneth. *Religion and Politics in the United States.* 3d ed. Washington, D.C.: CQ Press, 1996.

Wuthnow, Robert. *The Consciousness Reformation.* Berkeley: University of California Press, 1976.

Crusades

The Crusades were military expeditions launched by various popes during the Middle Ages and beyond to achieve what were seen in the Christian West as righteous ends, most commonly but never exclusively to capture or establish control over Jerusalem. The city of Jerusalem, which was holy to Jews, Christians, and Muslims, had been under Muslim control since 638. In 1095 Pope Urban II launched the First Crusade, which captured Jerusalem in 1099.

This notion of holy war had no clear sanction in the Bible, which defines no particular attitude to violence. Rather, it arose from contemporary religious and political developments that led the church to interpret the Christian religion in new ways. Medieval churchmen knew that it was impossible to stop the violence of medieval society; instead, they tried to harness it to Christian ends.

In the latter part of the eleventh century, in what is known as the investiture contest, the popes threw off domination of Rome by the German emperors and established the principle that the church should be governed by the clergy. As a result, the Western church was centralized under the control of a papal monarchy that saw its role as reordering society to increase people's chances of salvation. A natural outcome was the use of war as an instrument of policy against opponents. The papacy was conceived of as universal, although the Eastern Orthodox Church—the dominant religious force within the Byzantine Empire centered in Constantinople—had always been reluctant to recognize papal supremacy. By 1071 this empire had lost Asia Minor to an Islam resurgent under the Turks. Two popes, Gregory VII (ruled 1073–1085) and Urban II, tried to reassert supremacy over the Orthodox Church by offering military aid against Islam.

Rise of the Crusading Movement

Urban II was able to mount a successful expedition, the First Crusade, for two reasons: He had cultivated good relations with the Byzantine emperor, Alexius I Comnenus (ruled 1081–1118), and he cast his appeal to European knights in the form of a pilgrimage to Jerusalem, offering to all who participated the hope of eternal life. The First and all subsequent Crusades were penitential wars in which every step forward and every blow was an act of penance that would free a man's soul from hell. It was this brilliantly original notion that created the special character of the crusading movement. The crusader was a soldier, but—rather like a monk—he was also under a spiritual discipline that would earn him forgiveness of his sins. From this idea sprang the Knights Templars and the Knights Hospitalers, military orders of monks sworn to a lifetime in the Holy Land in search of salvation by fighting those they considered the Muslim infidel. Ironically, the crusading eruption revived the Qur'anic injunction to *jihad,* the religious duty of Muslims to wage war for the spread of Islam. This imperative formed the rallying cry for the Muslim resistance to crusader conquest that ultimately would drive Westerners from the Holy Land.

The crusaders' establishment of principalities in the East created an obligation on Western Christians to support them, and after 1099 a stream of expeditions great and small went to the Holy Land. For the European upper class the idea of crusading became an integral part of the chivalric code, which supported knights in their role as the arms-bearers of the church. Crusading to the Holy Land reached a climax after the capture of Jerusalem by Saladin, the sultan of Egypt, in 1187, and in the thirteenth century the papacy gave the movement a new definition and organization. But Jerusalem was not the only goal of crusades.

Only the pope could launch a crusade, and although the idea was intimately associated with the Holy Land, it was open to the pope, as an assertion of his leadership in Christian society, to define other objectives. In the early twelfth century crusades were launched to Spain, much of which was under Moorish control. The Second Crusade was preached to rescue Edessa (in modern-day Turkey), which fell to Islam in 1044. Many German crusaders, however, were allowed the crusading reward for fighting the pagans of eastern Europe; others received the same benefit for wars in Spain and Portugal. In 1199 Innocent III promulgated a crusade against his enemy, Markward of Anweiler, in Sicily, and in 1208 against the Cathar heretics of southern France. His successors used crusades against the German Hohenstaufen emperors who were gaining strength in Italy.

Redirection

Scholars today tend to perceive these as "political crusades," rather than religious, and so did their victims at the time, but most people in Western Europe accepted papal authority—especially as the liberation of Jerusalem was widely desired. By the mid-thirteenth century, however, failure to retake Jerusalem caused Western thinkers to question whether God wanted them to succeed.

By the late thirteenth century greater forces were at work. The church developed means other than crusading to allow its followers to escape the burden of sin. The European world of 1095 had been dominated by relatively small principalities and kings with limited power, and among these the authority of the papacy towered. But by the mid-thirteenth century France and England had developed efficient monarchies that demanded allegiance from their subjects and had the means to enforce it. Monarchs disputed the right of the pope to take men and money for wars in the East and even tried to limit the power of the papacy to tax their subjects and regulate their lives in the name of the church. In a series of conflicts between the French monarchy and the papacy at the turn of the thirteenth into the fourteenth century, the role of the church was much more tightly circumscribed than ever before. Crusading continued to be an ideal of late medieval society, but the institutional decline of the papal monarchy deprived it of vitality. It became increasingly an idea dependent upon the initiative of individuals, particularly of secular kings.

The rulers of Spain and Portugal were influenced by the crusading ideal to encourage voyages of discovery in the hope of finding new ways of attacking Islam, but other factors, like hopes of commercial success, tended to become dominant. The Protestant Reformation, in full swing in the sixteenth century, delivered a fatal blow to crusading because it was as the leader of a united Christendom that the pope had launched the Crusades. Once that fundamental political condition of a united church had been shattered, the movement, which had been dogged by failure and eclipsed by new social and political developments, increasingly became an abstract ideal. However, the notion of crusade as a war inspired by moral righteousness lives on in the consciousness of the modern Christian world. Preaching missions are called crusades, and the cold war was often portrayed in the West as a crusade against communism. Conversely, there is an echo of the worst features of crusading in the use of the word as a synonym for fanatical, unreasoning belief, reinforced by Nazi invocations of the crusading spirit against their enemies.

See also *Jerusalem; Jihad; Muslim encounters with the West; Orthodoxy, Greek; Papacy; Reformation; Sacred places.*

John France

BIBLIOGRAPHY

Brundage, James A. *The Crusades, a Documentary Survey.* Milwaukee, Wis.: Marquette University Press, 1962.

Edgington, S. B. *The First Crusade.* New Appreciations in History, No. 37. London: Historical Association, 1996.

France, John. *Victory in the East: A Military History of the First Crusade.* Cambridge and New York: Cambridge University Press, 1994.

Maalouf, Amin. *The Crusades through Arab Eyes.* Translated by Jon Rothschild. London: Al Saqi Books, 1984; New York: Schocken, 1985.

Riley-Smith, Jonathan. *The Crusades: A Short History.* London: Athlone; New Haven: Yale University Press, 1987.

Cuba

Religious beliefs have historically permeated the Caribbean island of Cuba, whereas the influence of churches has waxed and waned. With the Spanish conquest of the island in the early sixteenth century, the indigenous population was decimated and pre-Columbian religions largely disappeared. Spanish colonial control established Roman Catholicism as the official religion, while the importation of Africans as slaves, primarily in the eighteenth and nineteenth centuries, spread Yoruban and Bantu beliefs, among others. Beginning in the 1880s Protestant churches targeted the island, intensifying their efforts after the United States intervened in Cuba's war of independence (1895–1898). The U.S. protectorate imposed in 1901 facilitated the penetration of North American churches, which regarded themselves as promoters of democracy and modernization.

By the 1940s both Catholics and Protestants were reassessing their growth strategies particularly in the face of increasing competition from secular groups, including Marxist political parties and labor unions. European imports such as the Federation of Young Catholics and Catholic Action promoted socioeconomic justice as a means of combating socialism, secularism, and Protestantism. A 1957 Catholic Action survey found that only 52 percent of 4,000 rural families identified themselves as Catholics, with 53.5 percent stating they had never laid eyes on a priest. Nevertheless, more than 96 percent expressed a belief in God. African spiritist beliefs, popularly known as Santería, were, however, prevalent in rural areas.

By the 1950s the Catholic Church in Cuba was widely regarded as the weakest in Latin America: only about 70 percent of the population identified with it, reflecting its failure to penetrate the rural areas and limited pastoral emphasis. Protestants were estimated at 3–8 percent, and Jews constituted less than 1 percent.

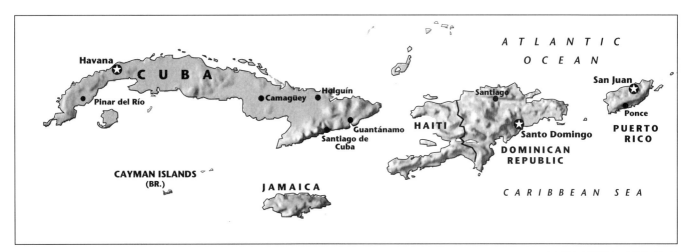

The Cuban Revolution

In 1952 Fulgencio Batista, the Cuban dictator from 1934 until 1944, seized control of the government. Fidel Castro, a lawyer and political activist, led a populist movement to overthrow Batista. Most church people supported the insurrection. They expected a multiparty reformist government to replace the dictator and were taken aback when Castro consolidated his power in 1959 and proposed extensive agrarian reform and increased state control of private school curricula. Such initiatives, together with a fear of communism, generated a backlash. In November 1959 an estimated one million Cubans gathered in Havana for a National Catholic Congress, where shouts of "Cuba, sí, comunismo, no!" rang out. As criticism of the government increased, both domestically and in the United States, Castro sought allies, including the Popular Socialist Party, the forerunner of Cuba's Communist Party, and the Soviet Union. In 1961 he declared himself a Marxist-Leninist in the immediate aftermath of the Bay of Pigs invasion, thereby cementing his identification with communism both nationally and internationally.

Tensions between church people and government supporters contributed to a growing exodus of Catholics, Protestants, and Jews from the island. Of approximately 700 priests in Cuba in 1960, 70 percent had left by 1963, including 8 percent who were expelled by the government for alleged counterrevolutionary activities. The Methodists, Presbyterians, and Episcopalians lost virtually all of their ministers and 40–70 percent of their congregations. By 1965 the Jewish community had declined from more than 12,000 to approximately 1,200. Such losses help explain why so many churches shut down and many denominations became

refuges for the disaffected. The nationalization of private schools in the aftermath of the Bay of Pigs, together with the induction of some clerics and seminarians into Military Units to Aid Production in the early and mid-1960s, confirmed the fears of many church people. Armed resistance to the revolution by small groups of fundamentalist Christians in the interior of the country in the mid-1960s fueled the government's suspicions of all religions.

In the late 1960s tensions began to lessen as Catholic and mainline Protestant denominations, as well as the government, sought rapprochement. In 1969 the Catholic Church issued two pastoral letters criticizing the U.S. embargo of Cuba, imposed after Cuba nationalized some U.S.-owned properties, and urging the faithful to support government programs that contributed to the common good. Several mainline Protestant denominations initiated dialogues with the government, with the Presbyterians and Methodists, in particular, praising state health and educational programs. Castro responded in the early 1970s by stating that he saw no contradiction between religion and Marxism and praising the emergence of progressive Christian groups throughout Latin America.

In 1976 a new constitution guaranteed freedom of conscience and the right to profess or practice any religion, although it was illegal to oppose one's faith or beliefs to the revolution. It also asserted that the state was obligated to educate all Cubans in scientific materialism, a commitment abandoned in 1992. Constitutional guarantees did not, however, end discrimination against believers, especially in schools and workplaces. The government continued to condemn such groups as the Assembly of God and the Jehovah's Witnesses, in part because of their opposition to universal military service and to work and school on Saturdays.

Easing of Church-State Tensions

By the mid-1980s church-state relations had been regularized through a special office of the Communist Party's Central Committee. Among other matters, it provided for the importation of materials necessary for religious activities and travel of church people to and from Cuba. Relations were also improved after Castro granted an interview on religion to a Brazilian friar that was published in 1985.

In 1986 the Catholic Church held a National Encounter in an effort to revitalize itself. It recommended greater lay participation, more intensive evangelization, and dialogue among all Cubans. The church hastened to affirm that it was not in competition with the government since it was promoting a religion, not an ideology; nor was it against socialism.

The end of the cold war and the breakup of the Soviet Union in 1989 ended foreign aid from that country and helped precipitate economic crisis in Cuba. Food subsidies and government welfare programs were cut back, causing the churches to seek international humanitarian assistance. Difficult economic conditions contributed to a new exodus of Cubans. As a result, the Catholic Church in 1993 called for a reassessment of public policies as well as the initiation of a dialogue aimed at reconciling all Cubans on the island and abroad. This declaration prompted a series of sharp responses from the government, which regarded it as overstepping the bounds of legitimate church activities. Church-state tensions intensified but were held in check somewhat by a desire not to exacerbate internal divisions as well as by a pragmatic interest in retaining assistance from religious aid organizations.

Ten years after the Catholic Church's first National Encounter, the faithful again gathered to assess the state of the church and the nation. Dialogue and reconciliation were seen as even more necessary than in 1986. The church criticized the government's repression of human rights activists and called for greater respect for the rights of all citizens. It reasserted its strong criticism of the U.S. embargo of Cuba and specifically condemned the 1996 Helms-Burton law, which tightened it. The government responded positively to this condemnation, while essentially ignoring the calls for dialogue and reconciliation. The Catholic Church received a boost when Pope John Paul II visited the island in 1998. Among his concerns were moral regeneration, greater freedom for evangelization, revitalization of the family, and power to influence the course of Cuba's future. The government was interested in having the pope condemn the U.S. embargo and lend legitimacy to a fading regime, which he did.

Since the late 1980s virtually all religions in Cuba have been growing, in part because of the pressures resulting from the economic and political crisis. A 1994 survey by the *Miami Herald* estimated that 20 percent of the population had attended services in the previous month, significantly higher than in 1958. In addition, a 1989 study by the Cuban Center for Psychological and Sociological Research found that 84 percent of the population professed some form of religious belief. These data suggest a remarkable survival of religious belief after many years of Marxist government and promotion of materialist atheism.

See also *Marxism; Revolutions.*

Margaret E. Crahan

BIBLIOGRAPHY

Castro Ruz, Fidel. *Fidel and Religion.* New York: Simon and Schuster, 1987.

Gómez Treto, Rafael. *The Church and Socialism in Cuba.* Maryknoll, N.Y.: Orbis Books, 1988.

Kirk, John M. *Between God and the Party: Religion and Politics in Revolutionary Cuba.* Tampa: University of South Florida Press, 1989.

Pérez-Stable, Marifeli. *The Cuban Revolution: Origins, Course, and Legacy.* New York: Oxford University Press, 1993.

Cults

Cults, as the term is generally understood today, are new and unconventional religious groups, many of which grew rapidly in the 1960s and gave rise to controversies about their teachings and practices. The term "cult" is problematic partly because its range of meanings is wide and partly because it has become pejorative. Its range extends from the practice of special veneration for holy figures or relics (as in the Christian cult of the Virgin Mary) to allegedly authoritarian religious movements (as in Sun Myung Moon's Unification Church, or "Moonies," founded in Korea in 1954). In addition, popular usage of "cult" refers to celebrities or cultural products that attract the unusually intense devotion

The April 1993 standoff between the Branch Davidians and the U.S. Bureau of Alcohol, Tobacco, and Firearms, in Waco, Texas, ended in a deadly blaze that engulfed the Davidians' compound. The fire killed eighty-eight members and their leader, David Koresh.

of admirers (as in cult movies or the cult of Elvis Presley). All meanings of the word emphasize intense devotion and commitment, but popular usage nowadays implies that intensity can degenerate into fanaticism and irrationality.

The Controversial Nature of Cults

The meaning of "cult" has changed significantly since about 1960. It used to mean a small group of enthusiasts for esoteric or spiritual beliefs whose activities were secretive or marginal to mainstream social life. Cult members were usually considered to have little interest in politics because they were preoccupied with their personal beliefs and practices. Very few cultic groups had enough resources to make an impact on public affairs. This particular conception of cults began to change in the 1960s, however, when a large number of new religious movements began to attract followers and public attention, initially in the United States and subsequently in other advanced industrial democracies. Many of these new movements such as the International Society for Krishna Consciousness, the Church of Scientology, the Unification Church, and the Neo-Sannyas movement of Shree Rajneesh were based on beliefs and values deriving from non-Western and non-Christian philosophies.

In addition to being charged with perverting or rejecting the main Christian traditions, religious groups regarded as

cults were accused of having harmful effects on the fabric of society and on the mental health of their followers. Accusations that cults "brainwashed" their recruits, exploited them, and ruined their education or careers became commonplace in the 1970s. The relatives and friends of some recruits fought hard to get them out of cults either by persuasion or by forcible "deprogramming."

By the mid-1990s about six hundred groups were probably identifiable as cults in the United States, with the number of their members being estimated at roughly 200,000. Although controversies have concerned only a dozen or so cults, the public image of all cults has been heavily influenced by the controversial ones. Since "cult" has become value-laden, most social scientists who study emergent, alternative, or unorthodox religious groups prefer the term "new religious movement."

Most marginal religious movements are not controversial, but a series of tragedies affecting a small number of so-called cults has kept them in the public eye. These events include the suicide or murder of more than nine hundred followers of Jim Jones at the People's Temple compound in Jonestown, Guyana, in 1978; the death of eighty-eight members of the Branch Davidian group led by David Koresh in Waco, Texas, in 1993; the murder or suicide of sixty-seven members of the Order of the Solar Temple at various sites in Canada,

Switzerland, and France in 1994 and 1995; and the death of eleven victims of the sarin gas attacks carried out on the Tokyo subway by followers of Aum Shinri-kyo in 1995.

The fact that the People's Temple and the Branch Davidians were Christian churches exploited by unscrupulous leaders rather than new movements with Asian or esoteric teachings did not prevent their critics and opponents from labeling them as cults. These collective tragedies, along with other, less well publicized, incidents involving death or damage to individual members of new religious movements, have helped to fuel the suspicion that any unorthodox religious movement outside the Christian mainstream might have cultic tendencies. At a time when levels of active participation in mainstream religious organizations are declining in most advanced industrial societies, unease about movements lumped together as cults shows no sign of abating.

Religious cults are politically significant for two main reasons. First, some cults have tried to exercise political influence directly. Second, cult controversies have raised interesting political questions about the public's response to challenging or unorthodox religious movements. The strength of public concern about cults fluctuates over time—though journalists keep cults in the public eye even when there is a shortage of newsworthy stories about them. But there have also been major scandals, disasters, and tragedies that not only have thrust cults into the headlines temporarily but also have provoked official investigations into the "cult phenomenon" in general.

Cults in Politics

Although most religious cults are rarely involved in organized politics, a few have been politically active in various countries. Virtually the only thing these political activities have in common is that they have been controversial. By comparison, the political activities of major Christian, Jewish, and other well established religious organizations have usually attracted little public interest and criticism.

The Unification Church, under its high-profile founder and leader Sun Myung Moon, stands out as one of the few cults that are known to have tried to exercise influence over politics in the United States, the Republic of Korea, and elsewhere. The Unification Church's teachings do not support the idea of a sharp distinction between the affairs of the everyday world and those of a transcendent, heavenly realm. Consequently, Unificationist theologians argue that it is a re-

ligious responsibility to work toward the perfection of human societies on earth. The Unification Church's ambitious and varied programs of social change and cultural improvement are therefore inseparable from political activity—especially campaigns against communism and in favor of free-market economics in a unified world. Numerous lobbyists for Unificationist ideals worked in Washington, D.C., in the 1970s and 1980s in support of various conservative issues, not only in the United States but also in the cult's place of origin and in Latin America. Moon's launch of a new daily newspaper, the *Washington Times,* in 1982, was further evidence of his intention to shape American politics. Two major controversies developed in response to this direct political activity.

First, the Unification Church was accused of lobbying U.S. political leaders on behalf of Korean companies that stood to suffer large financial losses if the U.S. administration withdrew American troops from South Korea in an attempt to reduce its budget deficit and to foster better relations with communist regimes in China and North Korea. Second, the Unification Church's links with right-wing regimes and political interests in Central and South America were furthered by one of its political front organizations, CAUSA (the Confederation of Associations for the Unity of Societies of the Americas), throughout the 1980s.

Similar accusations of political and economic influence peddling have been made against some of the massive new religions that mushroomed in Japan after World War II. The largest of them, Soka Gakkai, has been at the center of numerous controversies associated with the activities of the Komeito, a political party to which it was formally connected between 1964 and 1970. Soka Gakkai, a lay Buddhist movement of about sixteen million members, officially separated itself from Komeito (Clean Government Party), in order to reduce the risk of offending Japanese sensibilities about the mixing of religion and politics. The movement's leaders, however, did not refrain from trying to keep certain political issues in the forefront of members' minds, especially in relation to global peace, disarmament, environmental protection, and racial discrimination. Komeito's continuing ideological sympathy with Soka Gakkai's values and ideals also ensures that the movement remains in a position to influence Japanese politics indirectly.

Very few cults have matched the aspirations of the Unification Church and Soka Gakkai to exercise direct political influence on a national or international level, but some of them have occasionally been active in broadly political campaigns that cut across the boundaries of political parties. The Church of Scientology, founded by L. Ron Hubbard in 1953, for example, has campaigned for many years against what it considers to be the abuses of institutional psychiatry. The Scientologists' strategies have included direct lobbying of politicians and government officials, publication of campaigning literature, and attempts to gain control over voluntary associations in the field of mental health. Similarly, Scientology has sought to tackle drug abuse and crime by mounting programs to change public attitudes and conduct.

Regional and local administrations have necessarily interacted with cults that occupied premises in their areas. Questions about zoning applications, the education of the children of cult members, and public health concerns loom large in places where religious movements have residences or businesses. Local journalists have played an important role in alerting public authorities to alleged problems.

In the 1980s local and state officials in Oregon clashed with the followers of the Bhagwan Shree Rajneesh, who founded the Rajneesh Foundation International in India and expanded it to the United States. Controversy arose over the way in which the Rajneeshpuram commune constructed and ran its vast settlement in remote surroundings. There were allegations that the cult breached immigration regulations, tried illicitly to control local politics, brutally repressed critics, and plotted to kill at least one of its opponents. In Japan the official investigation into Aum Shinri-kyo's criminal activities raised the possibility that there had been complicity or negligence on the part of local officials or politicians in covering up the cult's potential threat to its own members and the public. In several countries similar allegations have been made about the complicity of politicians and police in the possibly illegal activities of the Order of the Solar Temple, including connections with well-placed neo-Nazi supporters in France. Luc Jouret, who founded this apocalyptic cult in 1977, led many of his followers to commit suicide and possibly murder in 1994 and 1995 in Canada, Switzerland, and France.

All these cases illustrate the general point that public attitudes toward the minority of religious cults that are directly involved in politics tend to be distinctly suspicious, if not hostile. The belief is widespread that new or controversial religious movements exploit their members and their fiscal privileges unfairly or deceptively for the sake of gaining power and wealth. On the other hand, there are also fears that strong criticism of cults has served as a stalking-horse to conceal broader attacks on the privileges enjoyed by most religious organizations.

The Politics of Cults

The central issue in the politics of cults is the extent to which democratic and pluralist societies can afford to tolerate religious beliefs and actions that may appear to be intolerant in themselves. As a classic dilemma of liberalism, the issue of the limits of tolerance in a tolerant society arises particularly in countries that recognize formally or informally the freedom of citizens to practice the religions of their choice.

This dilemma has arisen in an especially poignant and ironic form in countries of Central and Eastern Europe, which were under Soviet domination until the early 1990s. The opportunity for autonomy and democracy might have been expected to lead to an explosion of unorthodox and nontraditional activities in all spheres of social life. Instead, a concern to protect individual citizens and the social fabric from the dangers of exploitation has given rise to campaigns and formal proposals of law to prevent Christian churches and religious movements that did not have large followings or that had not been active in these countries for generations from operating legally. It is as if the advent of democratic political systems has convinced many people that complete freedom of religion would be an unacceptable risk to take in their newly democratic countries.

The fact that movements labeled "cults" in advanced industrial societies tend to originate in the United States or Asia and to involve ideas foreign to the former Soviet spheres of influence makes them especially vulnerable to political campaigns for the control of nonindigenous forms of religion. The vested interests of the Orthodox and Catholic Churches in these countries create still more obstacles to the implantation of cults. Yet the ideological vacuum left by state socialism offers a golden opportunity for new religious movements to achieve a rapid expansion of their sphere of operations.

The growth of extreme nationalistic sentiments has also created a political atmosphere of hostility toward religious organizations that have no association with the history of the nations concerned. For example, a new law enacted in Russia in 1997 is designed to halt the missionary activities of most mainstream and cultic religious groups originating outside the country.

Cults face the same legal disabilities as those faced by other "foreign" religious organizations in countries that restrict or prohibit any religious activity except that permitted by the state. But even countries that formally or informally guarantee freedom of religion—as in the regions of Western Europe, North America, and Australasia—the "problem of cults" is framed in such a way that new religious movements encounter obstacles ranging from the denial of fiscal privileges to the prohibition of some of their normal activities. The range of official and quasi-official investigations into cults extends from ad hoc inquiries to full-scale parliamentary reports such as those commissioned in the 1990s by the French National Assembly, the German Parliament, and the Japanese Religious Corporation Council. The French report aimed to take stock of the dangers allegedly presented by cults to individuals and society and to identify appropriate countermeasures. The German inquiry was concerned primarily with collecting information about new religious movements and analyzing the social background to their emergence and spread. The Japanese report was more narrowly focused on whether the official procedures for registering religious movements needed to be tightened in the wake of the Shinri-kyo incident.

Alongside these high-level initiatives are numerous voluntary anticult or cult-watching associations running campaigns to monitor or suppress the activities of new religious movements. In turn, groups concerned with protecting civil liberties and the separation of church and state are opposed to many of these cult-monitoring activities on the ground that they threaten religious freedoms.

It is important to keep the topic of cults in perspective. The number of cults involved directly in politics has never been large, and their effect has been negligible. Only a handful of highly controversial cults have attracted attention, but public opinion and journalistic practice tend to lump all cults together and to portray them as uniformly destructive and threatening. It is therefore important to emphasize that most cults display little interest in politics and prefer to turn their back on the world. The major political controversies concern a small number of religious groups that are not representative of other new religious movements but that have become embroiled in public controversies and political disputes. Controversial cults are politically significant mainly because they test the outer limits of religious toleration and the freedom of religion.

See also *Denominationalism; Millennialism; Religious organization; Survivalism; Unification Church; Voluntarism.*

James A. Beckford

BIBLIOGRAPHY

Beckford, James A. *Cult Controversies: The Societal Response to New Religious Movements.* London: Tavistock, 1985.

Melton, J. Gordon, and Robert L. Moore. *The Cult Experience: Responding to the New Religious Pluralism.* New York: Pilgrim Press, 1982.

Richardson, James T. "Legal Status of Minority Religions in the United States." *Social Compass* 2 (June 1995): 249–264.

Robbins, Thomas. *Cults, Converts, and Charisma.* Beverly Hills and London: Sage, 1988.

Shupe, Anson D., Jr., and David G. Bromley. *The New Vigilantes: Deprogrammers, Anti-Cultists, and the New Religions.* Beverly Hills and London: Sage, 1980

D

Dalai Lama

The highest ranking religious and political figure of Tibetan Buddhism. Tenzin Gyatso (1935–), the fourteenth Dalai Lama, was born in northeastern Tibet and now lives in exile in northern India. As a small boy he was recognized as the rebirth of the thirteenth Dalai Lama and was enthroned as the secular and spiritual ruler of Tibet. Like all Dalai Lamas (a title first bestowed by the Mongolian ruler Altan Khan in 1578), he is also believed to be an emanation of Tibet's patron deity, the Bodhisattva of Compassion. In 1950, when the fourteenth Dalai Lama was fifteen, Chinese troops entered Tibet and soon incorporated it as a province into the newly formed People's Republic of China. In 1959 he escaped to India, where he reestablished his government in exile.

Since the 1980s the Dalai Lama has traveled extensively in his capacity as a spiritual and political leader. In 1987 he presented his Five Point Peace Plan for Tibet before the U.S. Congress, calling for an end to the increasing Chinese immigration to Tibet; the establishment of Tibet as a neutral "zone of peace"; respect for Tibetan human rights; implementation of safeguards to protect Tibet's natural environment; and initiation of earnest negotiations leading to a resolution on Tibet's future. Such proposals have been denounced by the Chinese government as attempts to split Tibet from China, but in other statements the Dalai Lama has indicated that he is willing to forgo full independence for Tibet if he can be assured of real autonomy within the Chinese nation.

Tenzin Gyatso, the fourteenth Dalai Lama

The Dalai Lama was awarded the Nobel Peace Prize in 1989 in recognition of his attempts to work out a political solution for Tibet through peaceful measures. As a Buddhist monk, he is guided in his political work by principles of nonviolence; he has also cited Mahatma Gandhi and the Reverend Martin Luther King Jr. as exemplars of his political philosophy. A prolific author and lecturer as well as a strong proponent of interreligious dialogue, the Dalai Lama has become internationally known not only as a religious leader but also as a champion of human rights.

See also *Buddhism, Tibetan; Human rights.*

Peter K. Moran

Day, Dorothy

American reformer and journalist. Day (1897–1980) co-founded the radical Catholic Worker Movement in 1933 and published a monthly newspaper, the *Catholic Worker.* Her unique blend of pacifism, anarchism, and fidelity to Christian principles of charity and justice led her and the movement she founded to oppose many social policies. Whether criticizing child labor, the exploitation of blacks, and anti-Semitism during the 1930s or protesting the treatment of migrant workers, the Vietnam War, and the nuclear arms race in the 1960s and 1970s, the Catholic Worker consistently challenged Americans to think through the implications of public policy.

Born in Brooklyn, Day grew up in Chicago where she learned of the struggles of the labor movement in the decades preceding World War I. As a student at the University of Illinois, she rejected religion because of its lack of social vision and joined the campus socialist group. Arriving in New York in 1915 to pursue a career in journalism, she wrote for left-wing journals and newspapers and, during the war, participated in draft protests and marches for women's suffrage.

In the early 1920s Day lived with her common-law husband, had a child, and mingled freely with the political and cultural left wing of Greenwich Village. She became interested in Roman Catholicism, which satisfied her hunger for prayer and transcendence. It was her association with the French peasant-philosopher Peter Maurin, however, that enabled her to synthesize her radical political commitments and religious beliefs. Together they founded the Catholic Worker movement with the intention of reconstructing the social order in accordance with the norms of the Christian Gospels.

The Catholic Worker was as critical of capitalist economics as it was skeptical of Marxist revolutionary claims. Day's movement was also distinguished by its commitment to pacifism during the Spanish Civil War of the 1930s, the Second World War, and the cold war that followed. In the early

Dorothy Day

1940s Day and her colleagues sponsored the Association of Catholic Conscientious Objectors, which promoted alternative service rather than military combat. In the 1950s she was arrested for refusing to participate in compulsory air-raid drills. In the 1960s and 1970s the Catholic Worker supported critics of the Vietnam War and advocates of disarmament. Day's was an authentic religious pacifism, an opposition to violence and war that was rooted in the Gospels and tradition.

A second contribution of the Catholic Worker movement was the establishment of simple "houses of hospitality" to feed the hungry, clothe the naked, shelter the homeless, and promote interracial justice. Under Day's influence, some forty houses grew up across the country. Day herself lived a life of voluntary poverty among the destitute and the homeless on New York's Lower East Side. The task at Catholic Worker houses was to live out the Christian ideal of personal charity, respect for human dignity, and practical assistance to the needy. Day's movement thus combined political activism against injustice with direct assistance to the poor. As both a political radical and a Catholic, Day embodied a remarkable integration of religion and politics in twentieth-century American culture.

See also *Humanitarianism; Justice, Social; Pacifism; Vietnam.*

Mary C. Segers

BIBLIOGRAPHY

Day, Dorothy. *The Long Loneliness.* New York: Harper, 1952.

Ellsberg, Robert, ed. *By Little and by Little: The Selected Writings of Dorothy Day.* New York: Knopf, 1983.

Klejment, Anne. *Dorothy Day and the Catholic Worker: A Bibliography and Index.* New York: Garland, 1986.

Miller, William D. *Dorothy Day: A Biography.* San Francisco: Harper and Row, 1982.

Piehl, Mel. *Breaking Bread: The Catholic Worker and the Origins of Catholic Radicalism in America.* Philadelphia: Temple University Press, 1982.

Segers, Mary C. "Equality and Christian Anarchism: The Political and Social Ideas of the Catholic Worker Movement." *Review of Politics* 40 (April 1978): 196–230.

Denominationalism

Denominationalism, a system of institutionalized division among many, competing religious organizations, is made possible by a constitution that separates the affairs of government from those of the church, a culture of religious voluntarism, and societal differentiation. A denomination is a type of religious organization defined not so much by its internal characteristics as by the social milieu in which it is found. A denomination emerges in a society that has no established church but permits and encourages the practice of religion by the various organized religious communities. Unlike a church, it emphasizes voluntary allegiance. Unlike a sect, it makes no exclusive claim to religious truth. Although denominations tend to develop complex administrative structures (for example, to take care of mission work, education, fund raising, lobbying), this outcome is not inevitable and is not unique to this religious form.

Denominationalism sometimes refers to a constellation of religious organizations, whose forms have come to resemble each other (more than their own ancestors) and who coexist in a relationship of institutionalized division. At other times the term is used to refer to a normative system—a set of values and rules—undergirding a voluntary religious order. Denominationalism, in this sense, presupposes religious pluralism, accepts the claims to legitimacy of competing groups, and expects religious organizations to be "this worldly" and publicly engaged—although sectlike in the idea that individuals should obey their own conscience and should adhere voluntarily. Denominationalism provides space for individuals to exist outside or alongside any religious establishment, making it possible for them to join or not join. Each believer is responsible for his or her own faith, within the framework of the church, which he or she has helped to build.

Historical Relation between Denominationalism and Disestablishment

Denominations have flourished in the United States, but they are not unique to the United States and did not originate there. The theological idea that the church has no necessary earthly form can be traced to the Independents of seventeenth-century England. Ironically, many of the religious groups that settled the United States (especially Anglicans) did not share this view and considered themselves transplanted representatives of the true church in their homeland. They were soon to find that the idea of a state church was impracticable in the New World, where a wide variety of social groups existed and space abounded for the religiously discontented to move away and found a religion of their own. In eighteenth-century America, congregations were important focuses of community solidarity—the key to neighborhood stability, ordered family life, and the education of children. Denominations grew out of efforts by these scattered congregations to propagate the Christian faith independent of civil power. They become an important link between the local community and the emerging national society. All this happened before the colonies declared independence from Britain in 1776.

Revivalism also helped created conditions conducive to denominationalism. The Great Awakening, which occurred some thirty years before the War of Independence, was made possible by the liberties enjoyed in the more sparsely settled regions. It added a new pietistic element to the American religious life, giving birth to denominations such as the Disciples of Christ, attracted many new adherents to recent imports from England (for example, Methodism), and gave fresh energy to some of the more established denominations (for example, Presbyterians).

In short, the attempts to replicate European church-state relations in the New World had largely failed by the outbreak of the Revolutionary War. The separation of church and state was a result, as much as the cause, of denominationalism. Once in place it fostered and protected it. Independence, and the Constitution (1787) and Bill of Rights (1791) that followed, made it possible to distinguish between being a member of society and a member of a church—a distinction crucial to denominationalism.

Effect of Disestablishment

The granting of religious freedom and toleration was a political necessity that actually went against the principles and beliefs of many of the early settlers. It was the result of a tacit bargain between evangelicals, who wanted to keep politics out of religion, and rationalists, who wanted to keep religion out of politics. By denying the establishment of any religion and granting the free exercise of religion to all (in the First Amendment to the Constitution), the state could no longer support regulation that denied privileges to or imposed sanctions on specific religious organizations—or their members. Unshackled from government control, American congregations were free to choose whichever form of association they believed conforms most closely to the scriptural ideal.

It is important to note that disestablishment in the United States means freedom of religion, not mere toleration. This is different from the European model, which assumes that there is a favored church but allows others to exist—on sufferance. Tolerance in the United States—a society preoccupied with questions of national identity—has always been conditional: Jews, Catholics, Mormons, and many sects have at various times been excluded from the list. But there has been enough tolerance to allow social mobility of religious denominations, as their members' fortunes change or as they compete for new adherents in the religious market place, to a degree unknown in most other countries.

Not to be ignored in this account of the effect of disestablishment on denominationalism is the acknowledged legitimacy of secular claims for freedom of expression. This secular spirit not only prevents the state from playing favorites with particular religions but also discourages the state from overtly favoring religion in general. This ideal sits in uneasy tension with an equally powerful set of ideals that attach the founding of the United States to larger religious purposes. Ironically, the absence of an established church has made it easier for there to emerge an inchoate but nevertheless meaningful "civil religion" to which all or most of the established denominations contribute but which is reducible to none of them in particular.

Influence of Other Social Factors

The separation of church and state is a necessary, but not sufficient, condition for denominationalism. Church and state are separate in other countries (the Netherlands, for instance) without the same proliferation of denominations and

frequency of mergers and schisms. First, the social and ethnic diversity of the early settlers in the United States and subsequent immigrants encouraged great diversity of religious expression. Denominations came to express differences in ethnicity, community, and the social status of their clientele. Freedom of choice was thus somewhat limited—by ties such as race and ethnicity and by social class. Second, vast, unsettled spaces made it possible for people to find room for their own religious expression or no religion at all. Third, the economic needs of an expanding frontier and growing industrial sector—especially the need for cheap, mobile labor—provided a disincentive to religious discrimination and intolerance. Fourth, and perhaps most important of all, denominationalism resonates with American values, most notably those encouraging activism, pragmatism, reformism, individualism, freedom of choice, pluralism, and toleration. The denomination offers a way for Americans to be involved in a faith that is neither authoritarian nor privatistic.

Protestant, Catholic, Jew

The denominational form is associated most closely with Protestantism. However, it is a feature of denominationalism that the organization, beliefs, and practices of all religions become absorbed within it, and a process known as "structural isomorphism" occurs whereby religious organizations of many different persuasions come to resemble each other. With respect to Roman Catholicism, the immigration experience of Irish and Italians at the turn of the century, in the context of disestablishment, led many to "discover" their Catholicism and use it as a means of self-identification. Catholicism had become a source of group affiliation rather than a taken-for-granted ethnic or national identity. Subsequent generations of Catholics have enjoyed considerable social mobility, and the church has lost its "sectarian" position as a result. Although theological differences might remain, cooperation in dealing with civic problems at the grass-roots level is now common.

The denominationalization of the Catholic Church was accelerated by a political event, the election of John F. Kennedy as president, in 1960. No longer were Catholics outside the mainstream. The reforms of the Second Vatican Council enacted in the 1960s made it easier for the U.S. Catholic Church to involve lay people in the running of the church and to cooperate with non-Catholic organizations in religious and secular activities. As a result, the Catholic

Church became less distinctive, less mysterious, to outsiders. Today, the individualism, congregationalism, and pragmatism of denominational America has begun to replace the communal, hierarchical, and sacramental understandings of the original church. More and more Catholics see the church as just another voluntary association. This tendency goes along with the greater freedom enjoyed by Catholic bishops to enter "civil society" and speak as a group on social issues, such as poverty, social injustice, and abortion.

Judaism has also had to adapt to American realities. For Jews, the choice of denominational preference expresses what it means to be a Jew in the United States. A tripartite structure of national religious organizations has emerged resembling Protestant denominationalism in its representation of various shades of belief and practice and in the social differentiation of adherents into different religious communities. Reform Judaism (39 percent) embraces sacred-secular dichotomies and narrowly defines the arena of the sacred. Orthodoxy (6 percent) speaks for a Judaism with a strong continuity and sense of exclusivity. Conservatism (42 percent) occupies a midway point. Some argue that, given the strength of voluntarism and congregationalism in the Jewish community, the "denominations" are more akin to movements, little more than paper organizations, forced to tolerate a wide range of behaviors and attitudes between local synagogues. This is especially true of Orthodoxy. As in the Catholic and Protestant faiths, tolerance is a matter of degree in the Jewish community. To Orthodox Jews, Conservative and Reform Judaism are not legitimate expressions of the faith.

Denominations as Group Political Affiliations

The choice of denomination in the United States is based less on detailed knowledge of specific positions than on an awareness of where the denomination falls on a broad continuum, from conservative to liberal. Members of denominations develop particular political outlooks—even if their affiliation is nominal. Denominational preferences are systematically associated with political partisanship, issue positions, and voting patterns. Although denominational affiliations overlap with race, ethnic, and social class identities, they are also independent forms of group identification because they represent cultural traditions and personal attachments.

There are hundreds of religious denominations in the United States today. No single denomination constitutes more than 40 percent of the American population, and nearly half the U.S. population resides in counties in which no single denomination has majority status. It is common practice to group denominations into "families" or "traditions." Protestants are typically grouped into Evangelical Protestant (for example, Baptist, Adventist, Holiness, Pentecostal, some Lutheran, some Presbyterian); Mainline Protestant (for example, United Church of Christ, Methodist, Disciples of Christ, Episcopal, some Lutheran, some Presbyterian); Black Protestant (for example, National Baptist Convention, African Methodist Episcopal Church); Conservative Nontraditional (for example, Jehovah's Witnesses, Mormons); and Liberal Nontraditional (for example, Unitarians, New Age). The other two religious "families" are Catholics and Jews. White mainline, evangelical, and Catholic affiliates constitute about one-quarter each of the American population. The rest are black Protestants (10 percent), Jews (2 percent), and the unaffiliated (13 percent).

Denominational affiliation is stable over the life-course of individuals: 69 percent of evangelicals, 76 percent of mainliners, and 81 percent of Catholics surveyed in 1989 still belonged to the tradition in which they were raised. Switching from one denomination to another is more common—somewhere between one-third and one-half of all Americans will do this at least once during their lifetime. Many people switch to bring their politics and the politics of their denomination (on civil rights, abortion, and so forth) into line. Given the overlap between race and religious identification, it is no surprise that little switching occurs between white and black denominations, even within the same tradition.

There is a clear pattern of association between denominational family and political attitudes and behavior (differences between denominations within families are less predictable). In the 1994 congressional elections, 75 percent of white evangelicals voted Republican (an interesting pattern, considering that most evangelicals are drawn from lower social classes, which traditionally do not support Republican candidates). In comparison, 56 percent of the white mainline, 53 percent of Catholics, 39 percent among other religions, and 44 percent among those with no affiliation voted Republican. Hispanic Catholics largely support the Democratic Party, but they are less likely to vote than are other groups. Very little is known about the politics of the minor religious traditions. The Orthodox churches (Russian, Greek) tend to behave like traditional Roman Catholics;

Mormons and Jehovah's Witnesses resemble highly sectarian evangelicals, while Christian Scientists and Unitarians are close to the liberal mainline. Within Judaism, Reform Jews are the most liberal, followed by Conservatives, with Orthodox Jews being the most conservative.

Changing Alignments

During most of the twentieth century, white mainline Protestants constituted the core of the Republican Party. They shared a common north European ancestry, an impulse for moral and social reform, and support for the principles of the free market. Catholics were predominantly Democratic, as were the (mainly Baptist and Methodist) white Protestants in the South. Since the 1960s the core groups of the New Deal coalition—namely, white evangelicals and white Catholics—have begun to desert the Democratic Party. On the other hand, members of the mainline Protestants have left the Republican Party in large numbers. Evangelicals have moved into the Republican Party coalition, while mainline Protestants have become less solidly Republican than they were. The partisan attachment of evangelicals is magnified by their large and growing numbers, bolstered by high religious commitment, and fostered by the conviction that their religion is relevant to politics. During the same period, black Protestants have joined the Democratic coalition, Jews have remained loyal to it, and Catholics have become less Democratic than formerly as their social heterogeneity increases.

Do Denominations Matter Any More?

Some scholars believe that the day of the denomination is past. The denominational form is thought to be weakened by the membership losses of the mainstream denominations, the alienation of members and congregation from the national leadership (especially during the civil rights era), the resulting diversion of resources away from denominational coffers and into local projects, and growing divisions between liberals and evangelicals within denominations. Large, pluralistic denominations, such as the Methodists and Episcopalians, have lost adherents to the opposing forces of secularism and evangelicalism. Their replacements tend to be less committed than are those born into the faith. Internal dissension and organizational decline have further weakened them. Their ties to the state have atrophied, and more vigorous pandenominational organizations, such as the Christian Coalition, seem to command more political attention. The political stage is now occupied by a host of paradenominational groups (such as pro-life, environmental, and health reform groups), each pursuing its own issue-specific agenda. The fastest membership growth today is in the nondenominational sector of churches. These churches, which are generally evangelical, do not affiliate with larger bodies and prefer to call themselves "community churches."

Recent years have also healed many previously bitter social divisions upon which denominations were formed—the exception being race. This is the result of increased educational opportunities, social and geographical mobility, the civil rights movement, the culture of experimentation fostered during the 1960s, and the controversy over the Vietnam War. These trends not only blur the boundary around denominations but add to their internal heterogeneity. Partially as a result, religious belief and practice have become more personal, and the ties to the denomination have weakened. Individual congregations now actively seek a "niche" within their local religious community as they compete for survival in a culture where individual choice is prized as never before. This, in turn, creates much variation within denominations and makes them less viable.

It would be wrong to conclude from the erosion of strength and distinct identity of the mainline Protestant denominations that the denominational form is extinct. The past generation has witnessed a counterbalance to this decline: the emergence onto the political scene of a revitalized evangelical family of denominations, which have shaken off their southern and lower-class origins to identify with the Republican Party, especially on social issues. Evangelicals have grown richer, they have become more involved in their community as the result of becoming property owners, and their higher levels of education have imparted political self-confidence and sophisticated political skills. Although they skillfully use a variety of organizational forms to mobilize political action, they do not show any signs of abandoning the denominational form as a primary organizational tool. There is every promise, in conclusion, that denominationalism will continue to undergird religious freedom in the United States and sustain its contribution to cultural pluralism and political toleration.

See also *Civil religion; Constitution, U.S.; Freedom of religion; Pluralism; Separation of church and state; Voluntarism.*

John Wilson

BIBLIOGRAPHY

Carroll, Jackson W., and Wade Clark Roof, eds. *Beyond Establishment: Protestant Identity in a Post-Protestant Age.* Louisville, Ky.: Westminster Press, 1993.

Finke, Roger. "Religious Deregulation: Origins and Consequences." *Journal of Church and State* 32 (summer 1990): 609–626.

Lazerwitz, Bernard, J. Alan Winter, Arnold Dashefsky, and Ephraim Tabory. *Jewish Choices: American Jewish Denominationalism.* Albany: State University of New York Press, 1998.

Leege, David C., and Lyman A. Kellstedt, eds. *Rediscovering the Religious Factor in American Politics.* Armonk, N.Y.: M. E. Sharpe, 1993.

Mullin, Robert Bruce, and Russell Richey, eds. *Reimagining Denominationalism.* New York: Oxford University Press, 1994.

Richey, Russell. *American Denominational Organization.* Pasadena, Calif.: William Carey Library, 1980.

Wald, Kenneth. *Religion and Politics in the United States.* 3d ed. Washington, D.C.: CQ Press, 1997.

Wilson, Bryan. "Religious Organization." In *International Encyclopedia of the Social Sciences.* Vol. 13. New York: Macmillan, 1968.

Diaspora

See *Judaism*

Discrimination

See *Prejudice*

Douglass, Frederick

American abolitionist, writer, and orator. Douglass (1817–1895), born a slave in Tuckahoe, Maryland, became an ardent social reformer and a profound moral and political voice for most of the nineteenth century. His father a slave owner and his mother a slave, he stood between two different worlds bound together by a brutal institution.

Douglass's career can be divided into two interrelated phases: the pre–Civil War and wartime period (early 1840s–1865) and the period during and after Reconstruction until his death. The first phase marks Douglass as an impassioned abolitionist and early advocate of women's rights. Although often drawing on moral suasion to convince America of the

Frederick Douglass

evil of slavery, he parted company with those abolitionists who rejected out of hand the resort to force.

The latter phase consists of his activity within the Republican Party and the eventual waning of his sphere of political and moral influence. Douglass's journey from slavery to become one of the leading moral and political voices of the nineteenth century has been chronicled in his three autobiographies: *Narrative of the Life of Frederick Douglass* (1845), *My Bondage and My Freedom* (1855), and *Life and Times of Frederick Douglass* (1881, amended 1892). From the moment the *Narrative* appeared, Douglass took his place in America's literary imagination.

Douglass is often characterized as black America's first "Jeremiah." His activism, like that of the biblical Jeremiah, called attention to the failure of his community to live up to its stated ideals. Indeed, Douglass expressed deep dissatisfaction with the nation and urgently challenged America to rid itself of the evils that threatened it, particularly the evils of slavery and racism. Douglass worked within the most important tradition of public exhortation in America: the political sermon called the American Jeremiad, which joins social criticism with calls for moral renewal.

From his first encounter with the abolitionist William Lloyd Garrison in 1841, to the creation of his own newspaper, the *North Star,* to his death in 1895, Douglass consistently reminded the nation of its stated commitments to the ideals of democracy, freedom, and equality. He drew on the cultural repertoires and styles of black America, particularly the oratorical style of the black preacher, to exhort black Americans to act for themselves and to convince white Americans that slavery and racism threatened the nation and compromised Christian principles.

Douglass judged the South for its support of the institution of slavery, but he saved his harshest criticism for those in the North who professed themselves Christian but continued to allow the evil of slavery and racism to exist in the United States. For Douglass, it was more than a contradiction that a Christian nation would allow these two evils to exist: such practices were an abomination. Nevertheless, Douglass held an abiding faith in America. He even served the nation in his later years as the U.S. ambassador to Haiti. But, forever the Jeremiah, he continued to remind the nation—even when most would not listen—of America's promise and its failure to live up to it.

Eddie S. Glaude Jr.

BIBLIOGRAPHY

Douglass, Frederick. *Frederick Douglass: New Literary and Historical Essays.* Edited by Eric J. Sundquist. New York: Cambridge University Press, 1990.

———. *The Frederick Douglass Papers.* Edited by John W. Blassingame. New Haven: Yale University Press, 1979.

Pitney-Howard, David. *The Afro-American Jeremiad: Appeals for Justice in America.* Philadelphia: Temple University Press, 1990.

Quarles, Benjamin. *Frederick Douglass.* Washington, D.C.: Associated Publishers, 1948.

Waldo, Martin. *The Mind of Frederick Douglass.* Chapel Hill: University of North Carolina Press, 1984.

Druze

The Druze are a religious community of about a million people concentrated mainly in Lebanon, Syria, and Israel. The Druze faith was born within the Ismaili Shi'ite sect of Islam in Egypt during the reign of Bi Amr Allah al-Hakim (985?–1021), the sixth caliph of the Egyptian Fatimid dynasty. Although religion was and remains the primary cause of the cohesiveness of the Druze community, the group's status as a minority has also been a factor.

Al-Hakim and the New Faith

Although the Fatimids were Ismaili Shi'ites, Al-Hakim formulated a new faith that dissented from the Ismaili doctrine, and in 1017 he announced the new faith and proclaimed that he was the manifestation of God. The adherents of the new faith became known as Druze. The name came from Muhammad al-Darazi, an Ismaili missionary from Bukhara, who, with Hamza ibn Ali, an Iranian Ismaili theologian, and Hamza's disciple Baha al-Din al-Samuki, had responsibility for propagating the new religion. The new doctrine was first spread by missionaries in Lebanon and other parts of the Middle East.

Doctrinal divisions soon surfaced between Hamza and al-Darazi. Al-Darazi believed that *tawil* (the inner interpreted truth) is superior to the *tanzil* (the revealed outer truth) and attributed supernatural powers to al-Hakim. Al-Darazi advocated conversion by force, while Hamza believed in using persuasion to promote the faith. In 1019 al-Darazi was assassinated, and his name became anathema to the Druze, who refer to themselves as Muwahidun (unitarians) because of their emphasis on the oneness of God. Hamza, who now led the missionary movement, went beyond al-Hakim's concepts and proclaimed that al-Hakim was the incarnation of the divinity.

The spread of the Druze doctrine went on unabated until al-Hakim mysteriously disappeared in 1021. His successor, li I'zaz Din Allah al-Zahir, rejected the claim to divinity and persecuted the followers of the new faith, leading many to recant and others to go underground. Despite the persecution, Hamza and Baha al-Din continued to spread the message. Between 1027 and 1043, Baha al-Din collected into six books, known as *al-Hikmah al-Sharifa* (the Noble Wisdom), the epistles of the faith (written by al-Hakim and his close disciples) and the proclamation made by al-Hakim. The last epistle was added in 1042, after which no new adherents were accepted into the faith. The overwhelming majority of the Druze community today are the descendants of the original Druze.

The Belief System

The Druze faith was for a long time surrounded by mystery. Some parts of it remain so today. Its tenets were kept secret even from most Druze, except for a small number of initiates, known as Uqqal, or enlightened ones. The remaining group, known as Juhhal, are the uninitiated ones. The religion requires that all follow a simple code regarding moral and ethical behavior and loyalty toward each other.

Over the centuries the secrecy of the religion has been misunderstood by some Muslim religious scholars, who have generally considered the Druze heretics, even infidels, and sometimes people without religion. They have also been wrongfully accused of engaging in peculiar practices, such as worshiping a calf. The religion is believed to have been influenced by Greek and Hindu philosophies as well as Christianity and Islam. In response, the Druze practiced dissimulation (*taqiya*) and were outwardly allowed to deny their faith and to pose as adherents of the dominant religion to survive. In later periods the Druze practiced dissimulation to deny the principles of the faith to those whom they considered unfit to receive the wisdom.

The Druze have several main articles of faith, which must be accepted by all. In addition to a strict unitarian concept of God, they revere al-Hakim as the tenth, last, and most perfect manifestation of God. It is believed that al-Hakim has only temporarily gone from view and will reappear along with Hamza to establish universal justice, at which time the truly pious will rule the world.

The Druze believe in five divine messengers. These messengers represent specific theological concepts and are equated with major figures in the religious history of the Druze and with three lesser ones. There are also several precepts to which all Druze must adhere: truthfulness, the giving of mutual aid to all Druze, rejection of all other religions, maintenance of the secrets of the religion, detestation of evils, and submission to and acceptance of God's will.

The Druze also believe in reincarnation, or the transmigration of souls, which is foreign to Islam. The last judgment is the last transmigration and the last divine manifestation. After death the soul is reborn into another human body. The five pillars of Islam are not observed, and the revelations of al-Hakim are viewed as the ultimate truth.

A Druze boy raises the Syrian flag in the Israeli village of Majdal Shams to protest Israeli occupation of the Golan Heights. Although Druze inhabitants of Israel are expected to serve in the Israeli military, many remain loyal to Arab nations with sizable Druze populations, including Syria, Lebanon, and Jordan.

The Druze Emirate and Later

The twelfth century witnessed the emergence of a Druze emirate (principality) in Lebanon, but the Druze did not play a prominent role until the sixteenth century, when Fakhr al-Din al-Ma'ni allied himself with the victorious Ottoman Turks against the Egyptian Mamluks. Fakhr al-Din II greatly expanded the emirate and opened his country to Western influences. He was harassed, however, and ultimately defeated by the Ottoman overlords. The influence of the Druze declined under their successor, the Shihab dynasty, in the eighteenth century as rivalries emerged between different factions, one of which fled to the Hawran region of Syria, later known as the Druze Mountain. Ottoman and European meddling in the nineteenth century, as well as changing demographic and political patterns, led to confrontations between the Druze and their Christian neighbors and to massacres of Christians in 1860 in Lebanon and Damascus. These led to European, mainly French, involvement and to a new autonomous system of government in Lebanon under a governor who was required to be a Christian Ottoman.

Present-day Druze

Kamal Junblat, of the influential Druze Junblat family, played a major role in Lebanese politics from the 1950s and allied himself with the Palestine Liberation Organization. He was assassinated in 1977, and his son Walid replaced him. In Syria the Atrash family, which led the 1925 nationalist revolt against the French, and in Israel the Tarif family have been the leading Druze families. The Druze in Israel, unlike most other Arabs, serve in the Israeli military.

See also *Lebanon*.

Edmund Ghareeb

BIBLIOGRAPHY

Abu Izzeddin, Najla M. *The Druze: A New Study of Their History, Faith, and Society.* Leiden: E. J. Brill, 1984.

Betts, Robert. *The Druze.* New Haven: Yale University Press, 1988.

Chassaud, George Washington. *The Druze of Lebanon: Their Manners, Customs, and History.* London, 1855.

Hitti, Philip. *The Origins of the Druze People and Religion.* New York: Columbia University Press, 1928.

Makarin, Sami Nasib. *The Druze Faith.* Delmar, N.Y.: Caravan Books, 1974.

Najjar, Abdullah. *The Druze: Millennium Scrolls Revealed.* Translated by F. Massey. Atlanta: American Druze Society, 1973.

Durkheim, Emile

French sociologist regarded as one of the founders and giants of modern sociology. Durkheim (1858–1917) was born at Epinal, in the eastern province of Loraine. The son of a rabbi, and descended from a long line of rabbis on both sides of his family, he studied Hebrew, the Old Testament of the Bible, and the Talmud (the writings that constitute Jewish civil and religious law), while at the same time attending secular schools in his native city. Although at the age of thirteen

Emile Durkheim

he had a brief mystical experience under the influence of a Roman Catholic teacher, he soon thereafter turned forever from all religious involvement. Yet religious phenomena and the religious roots of societal forces remained at the center of his theoretical concerns throughout his life.

Durkheim studied philosophy at the Ecole Normale Supérieure, the traditional training ground of the French intellectual elite, and soon was regarded by fellow students and teachers as a man of great promise, though somewhat aloof. Graduating in 1882, he taught in a number of provincial academic schools from 1882 to 1887, when he moved to the University of Bordeaux. It was there that he first had the occasion to teach sociology, hitherto a taboo subject in the eyes of both pro- and anticlericalists. In 1902, by then a widely recognized student of society, Durkheim was called to the Sorbonne, the traditional first citadel of French academic life. Partly because of his position at the Sorbonne and partly because of the growing prestige of the *Année Sociologique,* a journal that he founded in 1898, Durkheim became the leading spirit of French sociology and attracted a gifted group of young French scholars and disciples. He remained until his death an eminent, though controversial, figure in French intellectual life and social thought.

Basic Teachings

In part in reaction to the turmoil and conflict-ridden early years of the French Third Republic (1870–1940), to which he was passionately devoted, Durkheim centered his teaching on a diagnosis of the ways in which common bonds could bind individuals together for the common good. Such bonds, he concluded, had in the past been provided by religious institutions but had largely eroded. What, then, he asked, could provide functional equivalents to the largely decayed religious commitments of individuals?

Among Durkheim's early contributions to the science of social thought was his distinction between mechanical and organic solidarity. In societies based on mechanical solidarity, which had predominated for most of human history, the social edifice is founded on the fundamental likeness of individual components and the minimization of individual differences. Organic solidarity, on the other hand, develops from differences rather than from likenesses. In the former, most people are engaged in a similar course of life and activities. In the latter, people's lives and activities vary, and they must cooperate with others engaged in different pursuits. With increasing differentiation of functions in modern society come increasing differences among its members.

A central concept in Durkheim's sociology is *anomie* (lawlessness or rootlessness), a term that denotes a state of affairs in which the social bonds that support the social body have so corroded that they can no longer control and guide individual action. Although human drives and propensities tend to be unlimited, social forces can counteract and control them. When social regulations erode, the controlling influence of society on individuals breaks down and leaves individuals to their own, insufficient, devices. Social scientists can use their knowledge to point to ways of overcoming societal crisis and breakdown.

The Role of Religion

In his early major works, such as *The Division of Labor in Society* (1893) and *Suicide* (1897), Durkheim did not focus on religious phenomena and the role of religious institutions. Only in the magisterial *Elementary Forms of Religious Life* (1912) did he concentrate on the religious bonds that he believed were necessary for social cohesion. In this volume, Durkheim analyzed the functions of religion in primitive societies, in particular, among Australian aborigines. He maintained that these functions are still central to the analysis of modern societies based on developed forms of labor and organic solidarity. Whereas previously he had focused on external factors of control, such as legal institutions, he now emphasized internal forces rooted in individual consciousness. Religion was the major force that created within individuals a sense of moral obligation to adhere to society's demands. What, then, if it was true that religious observance had decayed in the modern world? Was not Ivan Karamazov, in Fyodor Mikhailovich Dostoyevsky's novel *The Brothers Karamazov,* right when he asked in despair, "Once God is dead, does not everything become permissible?"

Many nineteenth-century thinkers had urged a return to religion as the remedy to Karamazov's despair. But Durkheim—an agnostic—searched for functional substitutes for religion. He argued that the deities that people worship are projections of the power of society. Religions are not just social creations but are society divinized. Durkheim did not follow his intellectual ancestors Saint-Simon and Auguste Comte, both French social reformers, in their attempts to institute new humanitarian cults. Instead, he searched for ways that would allow individuals to transform their puny egos in a new civic morality rooted in collective social phenomena. Religious ceremonies bring people together. Religion brings about cohesion; it is a vitalizing force in society. When Australian aborigines gather together, they celebrate the victory of collective existence over the dispersion of humdrum social life; they revitalize the social world of which they are a part.

This same revitalization occurs in many other social phenomena that are not obviously religious in character. Every effervescence in society, whether the revolutionary manifestations of the overthrow of the monarchy in the French Revolution or the ceremonial observance of Bastille Day on July 14, revitalizes the sense of collective bonds and moral cohesion by bringing into the collective consciousness the glory and the power of the bonds of social living. Every incidence of collective effervescence documents the force of social cohesion and rekindles the flames of solidarity in the face of anomic doubt and existential despair. The decline of formal religion then need not herald the dissolution of society. Durkheim urged collective engagement and communitarian revival as the cure to the sickness of modern society.

See also *Civil religion; Communitarianism*.

Lewis A. Coser

BIBLIOGRAPHY

Coser, Lewis A. "Emile Durkheim." In *Masters of Sociological Thought*. 2d ed. New York: Harcourt Brace Jovanovich, 1977.

Durkheim, Emile. *The Division of Labor in Society*. Translated by W. D. Halls. Introduction by Lewis A. Coser. New York: Free Press, 1984.

———. *The Elementary Forms of Religious Life*. New translation and introduction by Karen E. Fields. New York: Free Press, 1995.

———. *Suicide*. Edited and with an introduction by George Simpson. New York: Free Press, 1951.

Lukes, Steven. *Emile Durkheim: His Life and Work*. Stanford: Stanford University Press, 1985.

E

Economic development

Economic development is the process of generating a sustained rise in per capita incomes that leads to the elimination of mass poverty—the fate of humankind till the era of modern economic growth. This modern era of *intensive* growth, when per capita incomes have risen, can be contrasted with the much longer period of *extensive* growth, when per capita incomes stagnated—with output growing at a rate equal to the growth in population.

Limits on Economic Growth

Before the Industrial Revolution, output growth was limited by the fixed factor of production—land. The produce from such land supplied food, clothing, housing, fuel (charcoal), and the raw materials required for all economic uses in agriculture, industry, and transport. Also the mechanical energy needed in these "organic" economies depended on human or animal muscle, which again required nutrients provided by land. Once the land frontier was reached, returns diminished. The principle of population growth put forward by the English economist Thomas Robert Malthus in 1798 (that is, that population tends to increase faster than the means of subsistence) meant that, in the long run, the masses would languish at a near-subsistence standard of living.

Even in these organic economies there was some possibility of intensive growth through the greater division of labor made possible by international trade, as the eighteenth-century Scottish economist Adam Smith argued in *The Wealth of Nations*. But if the resulting growth in opulence led

to population increase, the per capita standard of living would revert to subsistence. "Smithian" intensive growth accounted for the prosperity of the Mauryan Empire in India, the Roman Empire, the Abbasid Empire of the Muslims, and the empire of the Chinese Sung dynasty. In each case a larger geographical area was economically integrated by imperial arms, creating a wider market. But the rise in per capita income could not be sustained, given the fixed amount of land, and these areas reverted to extensive growth.

The Industrial Revolution

It was not, however, till the Industrial Revolution in Europe, which led to the substitution of a mineral-based energy economy for the traditional "organic" economy, that "Promethean" intensive growth based on science and technology became possible worldwide. Coal and the steam engine allowed virtually unlimited supplies of mechanical energy, and the land constraint on the raw materials required to raise aggregate output was removed. The alleviation of mass poverty became possible, because, contrary to Malthus, the rising prosperity led to a fall in the birth rate as richer parents began to trade quality for quantity in their desired families. This "demographic transition" has occurred not only in the West but also in many developing countries—particularly in East Asia—that have been able to eliminate poverty by transforming their organic into mineral-based energy economies.

Religion and Politics

Given these contemporary possibilities, the relevance of religion and politics to economic development is twofold.

First, there is the historical question of why the Industrial Revolution occurred in Europe and not in China, which under the Sung had developed all the necessary technology and science well before the West. The German sociologist and economist Max Weber saw the materialist and individualist ethic promoted by Protestantism as being the spur for the creation of the new economy in Europe. His thesis is unpersuasive because all the economic institutions responsible for the rise of the West predate the emergence of Protestantism. More recent research, reported by Deepak Lal in *Unintended Consequences,* indicates that it was the revolutions first of Pope Gregory I in the sixth century A.D., which concerned the family and promoted individualism, and then of Pope Gregory VII in the eleventh century, which created all the institutions of a market economy, that are in large part responsible for the rise of the West.

Equally important was the decentralized nature of European polities after the fall of the Roman Empire, which forced rulers to grant various forms of property rights to feudal lords in return for revenue. By contrast, China for millennia maintained a system of bureaucratic authoritarianism that despised merchants and commerce—the lifeblood of a market economy.

More recently, the role of religion and politics in economic development has been raised in relation to the prospects of current developing countries. Confucianism is thought by many to be responsible for the spectacular development of East Asia. Others believe that without democracy economic development will be retarded. The available evidence does not support either position.

Lal and Hla Myint have found that the immediate causes of the differential postwar growth performance of twenty-one developing countries were the rate and efficiency of investment. Moreover, the latter depended on the policy environment. Countries that adopted central planning and state controls and whose economies were insulated from the world economy had lower growth rates than those with open, market-friendly economies. But these differences in policy were not associated with a particular type of government—for example, democracy—but rather with the countries' initial endowment of resources—in particular, the availability or lack of natural resources. Countries poor in resources—like the East Asian ones—irrespective of the nature of their government, were forced to develop their only resource—their citizens. The performance of such countries was much better than that of countries rich in natural resources, like Brazil and Mexico. This was because of the inevitable politicization of the income that natural resources yield, which damages economic performance as people scramble for this unearned income, rather than undertaking productive economic activities. Countries like India and China, whose endowments of resources fall between these extremes, swerved between following the policies of their resource-abundant and resource-poor cousins, with a resulting indifferent economic performance.

Economic performance could be affected in regions and countries where religion and politics have been combined—as by the Hindu fundamentalists in India and Islamic fundamentalists in the Middle East—to try to stop the process of modern economic growth in order to maintain the social systems associated with their old agrarian economies. But if they recognize, as Japan has done, that it is possible to modernize without westernizing, they may be able to achieve prosperity while keeping their souls.

See also *Confucianism; Individualism; Protestantism; Science and technology; Weber, Max.*

Deepak Lal

BIBLIOGRAPHY

Becker, Gary. *A Treatise on the Family.* Enl. ed. Cambridge: Harvard University Press, 1991.

Lal, Deepak. *The Poverty of Development Economics.* 2d ed. London: Institute of Economic Affairs, 1997.

———. *Unintended Consequences: The Role of Factor Endowments, Culture, and Politics on Long Run Economic Performance.* Cambridge: MIT Press, 1998.

Lal, Deepak, and Hla Myint. *The Political Economy of Poverty, Equity, and Growth: A Comparative Study.* Oxford: Clarendon Press, 1996.

Little, Ian. *Economic Development.* New York: Basic Books, 1982.

Marty, Martin E., and R. Scott Appleby, eds. *Fundamentalisms and the State.* Chicago: University of Chicago Press, 1993.

North, Douglass, and R. P. Thomas. *The Rise of the Western World.* Cambridge: Cambridge University Press, 1973.

Wrigley, E. A. *Continuity, Chance, and Change: The Character of the Industrial Revolution in England.* Cambridge: Cambridge University Press, 1988.

Education

Education, the provision of organized socialization and training conducted by formally qualified instructors, has been prominent at the intersection of politics and religion throughout the modern era. The learned personnel produced by the church's educational institutions figured prominently in the rise of the modern state in Europe. The church served as the primary model for state bureaucratic development and for the involvement of entire populations in society-wide structures and activities. Education in the early modern era was highly restricted, however, focusing mainly on the production of clergymen, lay professionals, and a small range of bourgeois occupations. For the vast majority of children and youth, especially peasants, learning was simply living.

This article focuses primarily on elementary education, particularly mass schooling; higher education is treated briefly. Secondary education is omitted because the religious issue has been much less prominent at the secondary level and systematic information about secondary schooling worldwide is relatively scarce.

Religion and Elementary Education in Citizen Formation

Two large-scale developments were of primary importance in the construction of broadly inclusive educational systems in Europe. The first was directly religious: the Reformation of the sixteenth and seventeenth centuries shifted the focus of religiosity from rituals conducted by the clerical elite to confessions of faith experienced in the heart of individual parishioners. As this "interiorized" view of religion took hold, both Protestants and Counter Reformation Catholics, especially the Jesuits, turned to schooling as a means of winning and keeping souls. Compulsory schooling laws formalized this notion as early as 1619 in Lutheran Weimar, Germany, and 1642 in Puritan Massachusetts, although these laws had more symbolic than practical consequences.

The second development of critical importance for mass schooling was the consolidation of the European state system in the seventeenth and eighteenth centuries, which led to rapidly expanding state administrative capacities and deliberate nation-building efforts by states, particularly from the eighteenth century onward. State expansion and nation building entailed the gradual displacement of the church by the state as the primary central institution in society, settling the long church-state struggle in the state's favor. Open conflict regarding the implications of this process for education occurred mainly at the university level; elementary education remained decentralized and sporadic until the nineteenth century, by which time the state's supremacy over the

church was far advanced even in strongly Catholic countries.

Religious groups played a major role in the expansion of schooling in some countries, most notably the United States and England, but for the most part the mass schooling systems that emerged after 1800 were essentially state creations. By this period, the driving motivation for schooling was no longer the struggle for souls; rather, it was a new, progress-oriented ideology that emerged as European countries began to formalize state-citizen relations, rationalize agricultural practices, industrialize production, and expand their cities. What would later be called "modernization" had taken firm root, and societal modernization implied extensive and, increasingly, state-directed restructuring.

Mass schooling became one of the central mechanisms for this restructuring. In line with emerging theories of childhood socialization, individual malleability, and the usefulness of formalized systems for the pursuit of specific goals, a vision of societal progress as dependent on the formation of carefully socialized citizens came to dominate the European arena and its colonial extensions. Schooling would endow children with new skills and capacities, imbue them with loyalty and commitment to the nation, and foster proper moral character. And it must do so for all children, because every individual, regardless of sex, social status, or future occupation, was a potential contributor to national development. In short, schooling was to fashion productive and committed national citizens of the entire population. National success was thus seen as contingent on educational success. While the potential of schooling to encourage rebellion among the "lower classes" was a concern among aristocratic and bourgeois elites, by the end of the century the imperative of schooling had become a self-evident and virtually unchallengeable tenet.

The mass schooling systems that spread rapidly in the nineteenth century were heavily secularized, emphasizing basic literacy skills, arithmetic, and rudimentary geography and history. Nevertheless, religion was deemed an indispensable element of schooling in most places. National (political and economic) citizenship had become the central focus, but religious citizenship—active and sincere participation in a religion—was a necessary complement. Religious piety and moral virtues would impel children, particularly those of the lower classes, to become conscientious, God-fearing adults, respecting authority and working diligently as agriculturalists, factory workers, and parents. Hence, although religious education as such typically occupied only a small portion of the school day, religious materials (above all, Martin Luther's Small Catechism and various abbreviated Catholic catechisms) were a mainstay of reading instruction in many European countries. In the latter half of the century, as labor unions formed and voting rights were extended to ever-larger segments of the population, elite concern for the potential unruliness of modestly educated but self-assertive lower classes made the importance of religion in the schools even more prominent.

Making religion a distinct "subject" in the elementary curriculum, and emphasizing the subjective character-building potential of religion, yielded a situation in the schools that faithfully reflected social development at large. Religion was being compartmentalized as a distinct social sector, subordinate to the state and the market; religion was narrowing its focus primarily to the level of individual faith and moral propriety. Secularization did not mean the end of religion but its circumscription as one among many institutions, and so it was in the schools of most countries.

With few exceptions, the major one being the United States, sectarianism in mass elementary education systems was not a problem. While most European and New World countries had made formal commitments to religious tolerance by the end of the nineteenth century, in the schools the predominant religion of the country was usually the sole doctrine propagated—whether it be Lutheran Protestantism in the highly homogeneous Scandinavian countries or Catholicism in the Mediterranean and Latin American countries. Hence, the principle of separation of church and state that became the object of so much struggle in the United States had little meaning for schooling elsewhere. The principle was largely ignored even in the United States until the latter part of the nineteenth century, when established Protestant denominations were challenged by the burgeoning populations of Catholic immigrants from Europe. Catholics objected to the entrenched Protestantism that prevailed in the schools; Protestants abhorred the papal threat and the Catholic capacity to build separate schools not subject to state control. Yet the imperative of enrolling Catholics in standardized public schools was great, for no other mechanism seemed able to ensure the Americanization of these polyglot immigrants. The pragmatic resolution eventually reached was the doctrine of absolute nonsectarianism in the public schools, so that Protestants and Catholics could attend side by side without the religiously based eruptions that explicit religious instruction would likely trigger.

Twentieth-Century Developments

In the twentieth century much of the institutional apparatus that had developed in Europe and the European-dominated independent countries of the New World became standard equipment for new states formed out of the collapsing colonial empires. Virtually without exception, the social imperative of schooling as essential to progress and modernization was accepted as self-evident truth: only modernized children could produce strong, progressive, wealthy societies. The striking breadth of this imperative appears in both national constitutions and legislation (which can be seen as embodying not only political philosophy but also social theory about how to build the good society). It also appears in data on school enrollments that show how this imperative yielded durable organizational practices. The right to education appeared in about two-fifths of the 39 constitutions in existence in 1870 (the earliest date for which collections of constitutional documents are available); in 1970 about two-thirds of the 141 national constitutions in force specified this right. Notably, newer countries are more likely than older countries to make education a constitutional right, and constitutions usually make of education not only a right but also a duty (57 percent of constitutions in 1970 obligated all children to attend schools). Where the right and duty to education are not constitutionally specified, they usually are legislatively enacted; the country without universally obligatory education is much more the exception than the rule.

School enrollment data demonstrate that this formalized commitment to mass schooling is hardly mere rhetoric. In the past hundred years, the expansion of schooling has been nothing less than astonishing. On average, in 1870 about a third of school-age children were enrolled in elementary schools in the 40 countries and colonies for which data are available. By 1940 the countries and colonies reporting data numbered 120 and average enrollment had risen to about 41 percent. By the latter date, practically all school-age children in most industrial countries were enrolled, so the rising average figure shows that new school systems were growing very rapidly. After World War II schooling exploded in every region of the world, as new states everywhere devoted large shares of their resources to educational development. By the 1990s average enrollment was above 90 percent for the more than 180 countries (and few remaining colonies) reporting enrollment data. As this state-controlled educational explosion has proceeded, traditional educational practices, often based on religious instruction (for example, in Buddhism and Hinduism) or on the spiritualistic practices of African and pre-Columbian American peoples, have largely disappeared or become entirely marginal activities almost everywhere.

Although the state has dominated in the worldwide expansion of elementary education, religion has remained a standard curricular concern, both in the older developed countries and in newer countries. Nowhere, however, is religion the primary curricular concern; modern schooling is decidedly secular. The most comprehensive information available regarding elementary school curricula throughout the world shows that, on average, religious education accounted for less than 5 percent of total curricular time in the 1970s and 1980s. Early in the century, during the 1920s and 1930s, the average share of school time devoted to religion was only slightly above 5 percent, and it was even lower in the middle of the century (under 4 percent in the 1950s and 1960s). In contrast, language, mathematics, and the natural and social sciences consume upward of two-thirds of curricular time in the world's schools, and their predominance goes back well into the nineteenth century.

Yet religious instruction has endured as a widespread element of the curriculum. Religion is taught in the public schools of about 60 percent of countries; this figure has been quite steady throughout the century. Wherever religion has entered the elementary curriculum, it has remained on the books almost without challenge. Regional variations are large, however. Religion is most prominent in the school systems of Islamic countries, concentrated in the Middle East and North Africa, accounting for nearly 12 percent of curricular time in the 1970s and 1980s. Religion is also relatively prominent in Western Europe and Anglo-America, taking almost 5 percent of curricular time in recent decades. Religion was entirely absent, however, from the curriculum of the countries of Eastern Europe (change is now under way, beginning with the collapse of communism in 1989), and it receives only scant attention in Latin American and Caribbean countries (about 2 percent of curricular time in each region).

These figures reflect the varied institutional role of religion in different societies. States in countries dominated by the Islamic faith not infrequently define themselves as formally Islamic and build their commitment to Islam into state-directed institutions. The most extreme case is Saudi Arabia, where nearly a third of the elementary school curriculum in the 1980s was devoted to religion. Northern and western European countries with an established state church have always seen religion in the schools as a matter of course—in England, religion has always been a compulsory subject—and this fact helps account for the relatively high proportion of curricular time given to religion in Western countries. In contrast, in Catholic countries where the French Revolutionary example has been followed (the state subordinating the church and building barriers to church influence in nonreligious matters), religion is quite rare in the curriculum. This mode of state-church relations applies most regularly in Latin America, which is the reason for the low proportion of school time reserved for religion despite the almost universal Catholicism of Latin American populations.

An additional dimension of importance with respect to elementary education is the parallel systems of religious schools that prevail in many countries. In Western countries in which religious groups played important roles in the general expansion of mass schooling, these parallel systems are still prominent. For example, in Ireland most schools are still directed by local boards with strong representation by the Catholic Church, and in the Netherlands a majority of all schools have either Protestant or Catholic affiliation. In Australia, Belgium, Britain, and France, religious schools are less numerous but equally durable, and in many Latin American countries the Catholic schools consistently enroll 10 to 20 percent of elementary students. The United States is unusual in that a great variety of denominational schools operate in a highly decentralized manner, enrolling in all some 5 to 6 percent of all elementary students. These U.S. schools are increasingly the province of children from affluent families and since the 1970s have witnessed a marked decline in enrollment.

Outside the Western sphere, most school systems are thoroughly state creations; parallel systems are limited to former or contemporary missionary schools that enroll a few percent of elementary pupils at best. The exception here is religiously infused states, such as Israel (where religious schools, most of which are formally within the state school system, enroll nearly a third of all pupils) and some Muslim countries. In the latter, traditional forms of schooling involving a scholar *imam* (a religious leader) and his associated pupils, often focused on the Qur'an, may be common; in Indonesia such schools enroll more than 10 percent of elementary students, and in parts of northern Nigeria they enroll more children than do state schools.

In most instances, however, the curricula of the religious schools have become increasingly secular, and state regulation and funding of these parallel systems have expanded considerably; often states provide the vast bulk of funds. Except in some Muslim countries, religious elementary schools are usually not very different from the public schools, even where they enroll large numbers of children. Religious schools include more direct religious instruction, of course, but religion is still only a small part of the normal school day.

Although religion remains a fixture in school curricula and religiously affiliated schools have a substantial presence in many countries, rarely is the relationship between state and religion strained with regard to elementary education. What is more, in recent decades the content of religious instruction has changed, especially in the liberal Western democracies. Cultural relativism and globalization have made tolerance and diversity important watchwords in many school systems, with the result that teachers typically teach about religion in general, not as advocates of a particular faith. The ideologies of individual rights and freedom of conscience lead states to avoid imposing religious beliefs on children, so religious advocacy is out of bounds. Religion courses are likely to include surveys of the major world religions and sometimes include brief forays into "primitive" religions such as totemism and shamanism. This sort of desacralization of religious instruction is not prevalent in many Islamic countries, however.

Higher Education

If religion in elementary education has been largely a subsidiary complement to the dominant secular focus, the same can hardly be said of higher (or tertiary) education. In Europe from the fourteenth century, the struggle between church and state was as evident in higher education as it was in the Vatican and royal courts. Early universities or their cathedral-school predecessors were church institutions whose establishment was prompted by the intellectualization of the church and the commitment of strong bishops to improving the training and piety of the clergy. As the Renaissance unfolded, humanistic subjects began to make inroads in the universities, but a convenient ideology of complementarity between Augustine's "City of God" and "City of Man" was maintained as long as the church remained a major landowner and social institution.

During the seventeenth and eighteenth centuries, however, when the church had been Protestantized or largely dispossessed in many places, this contingent complementarity began to erode as states undertook the expansion and secularization of higher education in earnest. Nation building was in process; rationalized knowledge (science) was coming to be seen as crucial for national success; a common national language was deemed necessary for internal cohesion, while the classic languages of Greece and Rome were considered all but dead. Thus states pushed to make secular subjects, especially science, medicine, and mathematics, elements of the core curriculum. Latin and Greek became optional languages of instruction and written expression, and the production of personnel useful to the state took precedence over the production of clergy. This process was hastened by a proliferation of universities founded by states and operated largely outside church control; it was opposed bitterly by many church officials but proved to be unstoppable.

As with elementary education, religion was gradually compartmentalized at the higher level. Seminaries and similar religious institutes did not necessarily decline; with the ongoing expansion of societal resources, they often expanded in absolute terms. But religion became the focus of distinct schools or faculties of theology in universities, and university faculty became increasingly lay and secular in orientation, even in Jesuit and other schools with strong religious affiliations. By the time of the great expansion of higher education after World War II, states were clearly the primary actors, both in the West and in new countries, which eagerly established state universities. Hence public universities of fully secular character accounted for the great majority of this worldwide expansion. Considerable variation persists in the degree to which tertiary institutions are formally linked to religion. In Catholic countries in particular, church-related universities have a sizable share of university enrollments and are often noted for their general excellence. Nevertheless, religion is almost always a small and optional part of the average student's curriculum, and little tension remains between states and religious bodies regarding the mainly secular orientations and purposes of higher education.

The major exceptions to this pattern of largely harmonious relations between states and religious bodies regarding higher education are various Muslim countries. In countries like Afghanistan, Algeria, Egypt, Iran, Pakistan, and even officially secularized Turkey, Islamicization advocates question such standard features of higher educational systems as equal access for women and coeducational instruction, and they urge the institutionalization of Islamic principles in all aspects of higher education. Secularists and religious minorities oppose such efforts, and the resulting conflicts are often harsh. Even where Islamicization has occurred, however, it generally appears to be more symbolic than substantive. Most students continue devoting nearly all of their studies to secular subjects oriented to secular occupations, and women's level of participation in higher education has not yet suffered significantly.

See also *Citizenship; Globalization; Individualism; Jesuits; Reformation; Secularization; Separation of church and state; State churches.*

John Boli

BIBLIOGRAPHY

Bereday, George Z. F., and Joseph A. Lauwerys, eds. *Church and State in Education.* World Yearbook of Education. New York: Harcourt, Brace and World, 1966.

Boyd, William, and Edmund J. King. *The History of Western Education.* 11th ed. London: Adam and Charles Black, 1975.

Cameron, John, Robert Cowan, Brian Holmes, Paul Hirst, and Martin McLean, eds. *International Handbook of Education Systems.* 3 vols. Chichester, England: John Wiley, 1983.

Cummings, William K., and Noel F. McGinn, eds. *International Handbook of Education and Development: Preparing Schools, Students, and Nations for the Twenty-first Century.* Oxford: Pergamon, 1997.

Meyer, John W., David Kamens, Aaron Benavot, Yun-Kyung Cha, and Suk-Ying Wong. *School Knowledge for the Masses.* London: Falmer Press, 1992.

Meyer, John W., Francisco O. Ramirez, and Yasemin Soysal. "World Expansion of Mass Education, 1870–1980." *Sociology of Education* 65 (1992): 128–149.

Mor, Menachem, ed. *International Perspectives on Church and State.* Omaha, Neb.: Creighton University Press, 1993.

Postlethwaite, T. Neville, ed. *The Encyclopedia of Comparative Education and National Systems of Education.* Oxford: Pergamon, 1988.

Reagan, Timothy. *Non-Western Educational Traditions: Alternative Approaches to Educational Thought and Practice.* Mahwah, N.J.: Lawrence Erlbaum Associates, 1996.

The State of the Art: Twenty Years of Comparative Education. Special issue. *Comparative Education Review* 21 (1977): 151–416.

Egypt

The Arab Republic of Egypt, located in northeast Africa and bordered by Israel, Libya, and Sudan, has a predominantly Sunni Muslim majority and a significant Coptic Christian minority. Of Egypt's sixty-four million people 90–93 percent are Sunnis, and 6–10 percent are followers of the indigenous Coptic Church, which separated from both Con-

stantinople and Rome in the early days of Christianity. Other Christian groups total about 1 percent of the population. With Islam as the religion of state, and the vast majority of the population Muslim, Copts have been unable to achieve full equality with Muslims. Only several hundred Jews remain in Egypt, compared with eighty thousand in 1948, when the new state of Israel was declared. With their loyalties often wrongly called into question after the establishment of the Jewish state, most Jews were forced to emigrate after the war over control of the Suez Canal in 1956.

Historical Background

Egyptian politics and religion have been bound together since the ancient pharaohs, considered semidivine by their subjects, ruled the land. In the early days of the Christian church, Egyptian Christians died for refusing to worship the Roman emperor. In Byzantine times, Egyptians expressed their distinct identity through the Coptic Church's resistance to dogma endorsed by the Greek-speaking Orthodox emperors of Constantinople.

The Arab Muslims who conquered Egypt in 640 made no theoretical distinction between religion and state. The caliph, or successor to the prophet Muhammad, was duty-bound to apply Islamic law *(shari'a)* and defend the Muslim state and community. Christians and Jews who did not follow the majority of Egyptians in converting to Islam obtained tolerated but inferior status under their own religious leaders. From the twelfth century through the Ottoman period that ended in 1882, Turkish-speaking military elites ruled. They depended on Islamic scholars *(ulama)* for legitimacy and ties to their Arabic-speaking subjects. As prayer leaders, preachers, teachers, *shari'a* court judges, and legal experts *(muftis),* the *ulama* were well placed to voice popular grievances. The Islam of the *ulama* was centered in the great mosque-university of al-Azhar, which drew students to Cairo from throughout the Islamic world.

Sufism (Islamic mysticism) offered an alternative to al-Azhar's formal, legalistic Islam. Permeating all levels of society, Sufism encompassed ecstatic rituals, celebrations of saints' birthdays and pilgrimages to their tombs, and charms against disease and infertility. By the eighteenth century even many Azhari scholars had joined Sufi orders.

To Muhammad Ali, who became governor of Egypt in 1805 and ruled until 1848, building a modern centralized state included seizing control of religious endowments and turning the *ulama* into salaried bureaucrats. But rulers and reformist *ulama* like Jamal al-Din al-Afghani and Muhammad Abduh had little success in modernizing al-Azhar. Sometimes al-Azhar was easier to bypass than to reform: the result was separate state and religious education systems, with Mixed Courts deciding cases involving foreigners and National Courts sitting alongside the old *shari'a* courts.

Nineteenth-century Egypt became an economic dependency of industrial Europe, with cotton as the cash crop for export. Political control followed when the British occupied the country in 1882. A national uprising in 1919 pressured Britain into granting limited independence, in 1922, though British interference and military bases lasted into the 1950s.

The Western-inspired constitution of 1923 articulated a new political framework. Egypt became a constitutional monarchy with elections and a parliament. Islam remained the religion of state. Turkey's abolition of the caliphate in 1924 led Egypt's King Fu'ad (ruled 1917–1936) and his successor Faruq (ruled 1936–1952) to bid unsuccessfully to revive the office. In 1925 Ali Abd al-Raziq, a *shari'a* judge, attacked the caliphate as a post-Qur'anic innovation lacking religious sanction and demanded separation of religion and state. Al-Azhar anathematized him as an atheist and drove him from his judgeship.

By the 1940s British interference, royal authoritarianism, and the inability of the Wafd Party—the main Egyptian nationalist party—to achieve either independence or socioeconomic reform had tarnished liberalism, capitalism, and constitutionalism in Egyptian eyes. Hasan al-Banna's Muslim Brethren surged forward with an Islamist challenge. Banna demanded a truly Muslim state and denounced colonialism, Zionism and the new state of Israel, and Egyptians who aped the decadent West. His was a truly mass movement, but government agents assassinated him in 1949.

Military Coup and Islamist Revival

After overthrowing King Faruq in 1952, Col. Gamal Abdel Nasser and a military group known as the Free Officers broke with the Muslim Brethren, one of whose members tried to kill Nasser. Mass arrests, torture, and executions shattered the Brethren. The secular-minded Nasser, who became president in 1956 after serving as prime minister, developed Arab nationalism and socialism as the ideologies of his authoritarian rule. He presided over the union of Egypt and Syria as the United Arab Republic from 1958 to 1961, when Syrian secession ended the union. In 1961 he struck at the *ulama,* forcing al-Azhar to admit women and to add medicine, engineering, science, and agriculture to its religious curriculum. Egypt's defeat by Israel, and the Israeli occupation of the Sinai peninsula in 1967, dealt a blow to Arab nationalism, paving the way for an Islamist revival throughout the Arab world and beyond.

Anwar al-Sadat, elected president in 1970 after Nasser's death, freed jailed Muslim Brethren, dubbed himself "the Believer President," enshrined the *shari'a* in the 1971 constitution as the main source of legislation, and fostered Islamist student groups to counter leftist groups. Even some leftists began going over to Islamism. Saudi oil money, both governmental and private, helped underwrite the Islamist surge. Islamists increased their appeal to students by offering them practical assistance at the overcrowded universities. By the late 1970s disciplined Islamists controlled many student organizations. Islamists broke with Sadat when he made peace with Israel, and one of them assassinated him in 1981.

Sadat was succeeded by Husni Mubarak, who set out to separate nonviolent from violent Islamists. The line proved difficult to draw, however. At first, in 1984 and 1987, Mubarak let Muslim Brothers win parliamentary seats under the banners of other parties. In the 1990s he squeezed most Islamists out of parliament, but they returned in leadership positions in student councils and professional syndicates. He purged these and rode herd on the press, only to have Islamists win several important cases in civil court. Mubarak enlisted the official *ulama* of al-Azhar to refute the radicals, but even the Azharis were not always reliable. Secularists and Copts complained that the government had already conceded too much to the Islamists.

In the 1990s Islamist extremists intermittently targeted and killed policemen, outspoken secularists, Copts, and foreign tourists. They also made attempts on the lives of Nobel Prize–winning novelist Naguib Mahfouz and President Mubarak himself. Mass arrests, torture, summary military trials, and executions ran the risk of radicalizing the uncommitted. Islamist militants often quoted Sayyid Qutb, a Muslim Brethren theorist who was executed in 1966. The radicals were mostly young, lower-middle-class provincials or recent immigrants to the urban slums. Outside Cairo, extremist Islamism was strong in underdeveloped Upper Egypt in Asyut and Minya Provinces, where there were also many Copts. A number of Islamist extremist leaders had studied science or technology but were only narrowly self-taught in religion. A few Azhar-educated *ulama* joined the extremists; among them was Shaykh Umar Abd al-Rahman, who was convicted on terrorism charges in connection with the bombing of the World Trade Center in New York City in 1993.

Although Egyptian religion and politics will remain closely intertwined, Egypt's strong tradition of religious tolerance is being severely tested. A breakthrough to general economic prosperity would likely foster more moderate interpretations of Islam than those now popular among the Islamist opposition. More discrimination in police crackdowns, less Egyptian dependence on the United States, a more balanced U.S. policy toward Israel, and a more peace-minded Israeli government would also help.

See also *Al-Afghani, Jamal al-Din; Banna, Hasan al-; Fundamentalism; Islam; Jihad; Muhammad Abduh; Muslim encounters with the West; Nasser, Gamal Abdel; Qutb, Sayyid.*

Donald Malcolm Reid

BIBLIOGRAPHY

Baker, Raymond William. *Sadat and After: Struggles for Egypt's Political Soul.* Cambridge: Harvard University Press, 1990.

Binder, Leonard. *Islamic Liberalism: A Critique of Development Ideologies.* Chicago: University of Chicago Press, 1988.

Delanoue, Gilbert. *Moralistes et politiques: Musulmans dans l'Egypte du XIXe siècle (1798–1882).* 2 vols. Cairo: Institut Français d'Archéologie Orientale, 1982.

Eccel, Chris. *Egypt, Islam, and Social Change: al-Azhar in Conflict and Accommodation.* Berlin: Klaus Schwarz, 1984.

Kepel, Gilles. *Muslim Extremism in Egypt.* Berkeley: University of California Press, 1985.

Moussalli, Ahmad S. *Radical Islamic Fundamentalism: The Ideological and Political Discourse of Sayyid Qutb.* Beirut: American University of Beirut, 1992.

Sagiv, David. *Fundamentalism and Intellectuals in Egypt, 1973–1993.* London: Frank Cass, 1995.

English revolution

The English revolution of the mid-seventeenth century refers to a diverse set of events that brought England through two civil wars, the execution of a king, a brief period of republican rule, and the Restoration of the monarchy. The near fusion of religion and politics during this period can be attributed to institutional and cultural contexts. Institutionally, disagreements over the future of the state church—the Church of England—defined political issues that divided rival political parties. Culturally, this was an age whose inhabitants saw the hand of Providence in all dimensions of existence, natural and social. Hence conflict over esoteric doctrines or minute organizational matters quickly became entangled with different views on a broad range of secular issues, including foreign policy, economic justice, and models of government.

The Civil War Years

The interweaving of religion and politics is evident in the events that led to the outbreak of civil war. After eleven years of ruling without the aid of Parliament, Charles I convened Parliament in 1640. His ability to rule alone ended when he tried to impose his religious policy on Scotland. The Scots refused to conform to the liturgy of the Church of England and give obedience to its bishops. Northern England was occupied by a Scottish army pledged to defend its Presbyterian model of John Calvin's church in Geneva, Switzerland. Confronted by an alliance between his rebellious Scottish subjects and domestic opponents of his rule, Charles summoned what was to be known as the Long Parliament, so called because it was not dissolved until 1660.

The issue that eventually drove members of Parliament into rival camps was Charles's unyielding opposition to the Puritans' demands for religious reforms. The Puritans were Calvinists who had left the Church of England and wanted to "purify" the church of its Roman Catholic traditions and practices. Among their demands were imposition of religious discipline (detection and punishment of "ungodly" behavior), repression of Catholics, and limits on the powers of bishops. Street demonstrations led to Charles's flight from London in 1642.

Religious issues remained central to subsequent developments. A broad consensus in the Long Parliament on the need for moderate religious and constitutional reforms led to intractable conflict between Royalist and Parliamentarian parties that culminated in civil war. The first civil war lasted until 1646. Royalists not only supported a prominent place for royal prerogative in political decision making but also regarded bishops and the established ecclesiastical order of the Church of England as an essential pillar of monarchy. Perhaps the strongest source of popular support for the Royalist cause was widespread attachment to the established liturgy and suspicion of its critics. Chief among supporters of Parliament was the main body of Puritans, religiously committed Protestants who rejected the bishops and liturgy of the Church of England but supported the ideal of a national church. An abortive coup against Parliament in 1647 was followed by a second civil war in 1648. The civil war ended with the execution of Charles and the abolition of the House of Lords in 1649.

Sectarian Divisions

During the first civil war Puritan support for Parliament disintegrated into rival factions, principally Presbyterian and Independent factions. The terms have distinct political and religious referents. Not all political Presbyterians, who advocated conservative social and military policies, were religious Presbyterians; not all religious Independents, who preferred a Congregationalist model to the coercive model of church discipline in Presbyterianism, sided with the policies of political Independents in Parliament.

Independent opposition to Presbyterian efforts to reconstruct a state church facilitated the appearance of many radical sectarian groups with a variety of political and religious commitments. Although it took many forms, radical religion upheld the possibility of spiritual perfection and the priority of inner spirit over rituals and organization. This view devalued precisely those aspects of religion that traditionalists thought made society orderly. For example, unyielding hostility to mandatory tithes to the established church and fierce anticlericalism among Quakers and other sectarian groups led traditionalists to equate sectarianism and sedition.

An ethos of egalitarian individualism in religious life pervaded radical sectarianism. Some versions, like the Levellers, Diggers, and Fifth Monarchy Men, combined this egalitarian spirit with an explicit, radical political agenda; others, like the Baptists, Ranters, and Seekers, generally did not. Moreover, radical politics exhibited great variation. Levellers such as John Lilburne advocated a greatly expanded franchise, religious toleration, and freedom of the press. Diggers, led by Gerrard Winstanley, advanced primitive communism as a means to a moral utopia. Fifth Monarchists, who expected the imminent return of Christ, were led by these millennial beliefs to participate in violent, abortive uprisings.

Quakers came from the middle reaches of society, especially its mobile, literate segments, such as artisans, yeomen farmers, and shopkeepers. In the 1650s they recruited members from mainstream Puritan denominations, its sectarian offshoots (Baptists, for example), and heretical groups that until then had led a furtive existence apart from Puritanism. Quakerism arose in the northern areas of England as George Fox and other itinerant preachers, in 1652, first mobilized followers who were united by economic as well as religious grievances. They opposed high rents as well as mandatory tithes. The New Model Army, like other radical political groups, was a fertile source of recruits to Quakerism. (Indeed, in the 1650s Quakers sometimes served in the Parliamentary party's New Model Army and the county militia; they did not adhere to pacifism as a principal tenet until after the Restoration.)

Like other radical sectarians, Quakers were not consistent in their political alliances and views, though they generally supported abolition of the monarchy and the House of Lords. Individual Quakers held government and military positions during Oliver Cromwell's Protectorate, which replaced an experiment in republican government that lasted until the end of 1653, despite Cromwell's suppression of millennial agitation to remodel England as a holy commonwealth. At the same time, Quakers supported republican proposals to institutionalize parliamentary democracy when this seemed the best option for preventing the return of the Stuart monarchy, the bishops, and a state church.

When the monarchy was restored, in 1660, under Charles II, in part because of widespread fear of Quakers and other sectarian groups, Quakers responded to defeat by retreating from politics and embracing pacifism as a doctrinal tenet.

Oliver Cromwell

Underdown, David. *Pride's Purge: Politics in the Puritan Revolution.* London and Boston: Allen and Unwin, 1985.
———. *Revel, Riot, and Rebellion: Popular Politics and Culture in England, 1603–1660.* Oxford: Clarendon Press; New York: Oxford University Press, 1985.

Enlightenment

The Enlightenment, a historical period and a European intellectual movement, radically redefined the relationship between religion and politics. The *Enlightenment* is an ambiguous term, and scholars debate its historical duration, geographical location, leading figures, and dominant characteristics.

In narrowest terms the Enlightenment, often identified simply as the French Enlightenment or the Age of Reason, was an intellectual movement in eighteenth-century France. It ended with the French Revolution of 1789 and the revolution's failure to achieve most of its Enlightenment-defined goals (many of which were achieved in the nineteenth century and continue to shape contemporary life).

In broadest terms the characteristics of the Enlightenment define the leading characteristics of modernity. Intellectual forerunners of the Enlightenment date to classical Greece and especially to the Renaissance and the Reformation. Viewed broadly, the Enlightenment began in seventeenth-century England, particularly with John Locke's approaches to knowledge, politics, and religion. English and Scottish Enlightenment thinkers included Joseph Priestley, Francis Hutcheson, Adam Smith, Edward Gibbon, David Hume, and Jeremy Bentham. The French Enlightenment was dominated by Voltaire, baron de Montesquieu, Denis Diderot, Jean le Rond d'Alembert, and Jean-Jacques Rousseau, while the leading figures of the German Enlightenment were Christian Wolff, Moses Mendelssohn, G. E. Lessing, and Immanuel Kant. The North American Enlightenment was led by Thomas Paine, Benjamin Franklin, and Thomas Jefferson and found expression in the American Declaration of Independence of 1776.

Characteristics of the Enlightenment

The dominant, medieval, European, pre-Enlightenment approach to politics and religion emphasized the hierarchical supremacy of supernatural religious authority. It upheld divine revelation, religious scripture and tradition, the church,

Under Charles, the Church of England and the House of Lords were restored. Modest legal and constitutional changes formally abolished lingering remnants of feudalism, limited the Crown's powers to raise revenue, required Parliaments to be called every three years, and took the first steps toward toleration of religious dissent.

See also *Anglicanism; Friends, Society of (Quakers); Protestantism; Reformation; State churches.*

David Zaret

BIBLIOGRAPHY

Finlayson, Michael George. *Historians, Puritanism, and the English Revolution: The Religious Factor in English Politics before and after the Interregnum.* Toronto and Buffalo: University of Toronto Press, 1983.
Hill, Christopher. *The English Bible and the Seventeenth-century Revolution.* London: Allen Lane; New York: Penguin, 1994.
———. *The World Turned Upside Down: Radical Ideas during the English Revolution.* London: Temple Smith; New York, Viking, 1975.
Lindley, Keith. *Popular Politics and Religion in Civil War London.* Aldershot: Scolar Press, 1997.
Morrill, John S. *The Nature of the English Revolution.* London and New York: Longman, 1993.
Reay, Barry. *The Quakers and the English Revolution.* London: Temple Smith; New York: St. Martin's, 1985.
Seaver, Paul S. *Wallington's World: A Puritan Artisan in Seventeenth-century London.* Stanford, Calif.: Stanford University Press, 1985.

and clerical authority. The monarchy and political institutions were derivative, receiving their legitimacy by appeals to supernatural and religious authority.

Proponents of the Enlightenment rejected this approach to politics and religion and upheld reason and nature, not the supernatural realm, as the primary sources of and authorities over objective knowledge and human progress. They emphasized critical reasoning, laws of nature, objectivity, and universality; a scientific outlook; progress; natural rights, liberty, and equality; utility; toleration; and freedom from superstition, irrationality, and dependence on religious and other forms of external authority.

According to Kant's famous definition of 1784, Enlightenment is characterized by the emergence of human beings from a self-imposed immature condition in which they lack the determination and courage to use their own capacity for understanding and instead depend on the external authority and guidance of another. Individuals must have the courage and will to think for themselves about politics and religion instead of depending for their views on political and religious authorities.

Moreover, human beings must be true to their nature and exercise their central capacity for reason as the sole means for gaining objective knowledge and understanding of politics and religion. Critical reasoning exposed irrational dogma and externally imposed, religious, and political structures of domination. Reason freed human beings from religious dogma and superstition, from irrational and oppressive legal systems, and from political and moral injustice and suffering. By developing their rational capacity, humans made progress and moved toward greater perfection.

Although many Enlightenment thinkers had confidence in the human rational capacity and in its potential for progress, others were more skeptical about human nature and focused on the conditions and limits of objective knowledge. Since these thinkers believed, along with their less skeptical counterparts, that rationality was a universal human capacity, they called for a new sense of egalitarianism in which individual human beings were free to exercise their own critical reason and to enjoy individual liberty, equality before the law, and equal toleration. There was and continues to be a huge gap between such Enlightenment ideals and their limited applications and actual practices in modern political and religious life.

According to these ideals, in studying politics and religion human beings must rationally investigate nature, including human nature. Nature has a rational structure exhibited through universal natural laws. Natural phenomena, religious and political institutions, and human behavior were to be investigated using the same fundamental conceptions and a common methodology. Nature, including human, scientific, religious, and political phenomena, were to be understood by breaking complex phenomena into simple component parts and by uncovering relations of cause and effect. For example, political authority could be analyzed in terms of rational individuals voluntarily coming together to form a social contract and then transferring power to a sovereign ruler. Enlightenment thinkers disagreed on the nature and content of the social contract, the extent to which power should be transferred to the sovereign, and the political relationship between the ruler and the ruled.

Politics and Religion of the Enlightenment

Unlike many counter-Enlightenment thinkers, proponents of the Enlightenment asserted that the methods of investigating and verifying the truth in politics and religion were the same. Uncritical dogma, superstition, and irrationality were to be uprooted, whether in religion or politics. At the same time and in contrast, natural law, natural rights, critical reasoning, and objective knowledge were to be upheld, whether in religion or politics.

The Enlightenment world view affirmed both religious and political tolerance. Toleration was necessary for human beings to develop their natural capacity to reason and to decide what to believe. Both political and religious intolerance restricted human beings' ability to develop their universal, natural, rational capacity for arriving at objective knowledge. It also prevented them from establishing political and other relationships that maximized their potential for human development and for the realization of liberty and happiness.

Compared with pre-Enlightenment figures, Enlightenment thinkers were critical of past interactions and intersections of politics and religion. Although they approached religious and political phenomena using the same fundamental conceptions and the same methodology, they tended to discourage the intersection of religion and politics and to affirm their separation. This tendency was clear in the formulations of atheists of the Enlightenment who saw no value in religion and were determined to free politics from religious authority, dogma, ignorance, and superstition. Other Enlightenment thinkers affirmed a natural and rational deism, a rational theology, and a natural religion over a religion of supernatural revelation. However, even these religious figures of the Enlightenment opposed religion's using supernatural revelation, dogma, scripture, and institutional and clerical authority to interact with and restrict political life.

Furthermore, any legitimate view of religion and politics was based on humans' critical understanding arising from their nature as rational beings. Religion, based on reason and nature, must respect the rational, natural foundation of politics and the universal, equal, and political rights and liberties of others, including those of nonbelievers and believers alike. Politics, also based on reason and nature, must ensure human beings' freedom from religious and other forms of domination. At the same time it should protect their liberties, including religious liberty, so that they could freely and critically pursue the truth of religious, political, and all other matters.

See also *Natural law; Secular humanism.*

Douglas Allen

BIBLIOGRAPHY

Cassirer, Ernst. *The Philosophy of the Enlightenment.* Princeton: Princeton University Press, 1951.

Gay, Peter. *The Enlightenment: An Interpretation.* 2 vols. New York: Knopf, 1966, 1969.

Hazard, Paul. *European Thought in the Eighteenth Century.* New Haven: Yale University Press, 1954.

Horkheimer, Max, and Theodor W. Adorno. *Dialectic of Enlightenment.* New York: Herder and Herder, 1972.

Im Hof, Ulrich. *The Enlightenment.* Oxford, England, and Cambridge, Mass.: Blackwell Publishers, 1994.

Manuel, Frank E. *The Eighteenth Century Confronts the Gods.* Cambridge: Harvard University Press, 1959.

Yolton, John H., ed. *The Blackwell Companion to the Enlightenment.* Oxford, England, and Cambridge, Mass.: Blackwell Publishers, 1992.

Environmentalism

The rise of environmentalism has been occasioned by the growing perception of a crisis in the relationship between modern societies and the natural environment, a crisis manifest in the threat of global warming already evident in the melting of the polar ice mass; in dramatic reductions in biodiversity caused by industrial farming and fishing methods; in deforestation, desertification, soil erosion, and atmospheric and water pollution; and in dangers from toxic and indus-

trial waste. Those most affected by environmental problems such as desertification, over-fishing, and deforestation are often poor rural and indigenous peoples in developing countries, where natural resources are often mobilized without regard to the needs or wishes of the local people.

The crisis therefore has a significant political dimension because it relates to local, national, and global decision making about wealth distribution, land use, resource allocation, economic development, and population control. There is also a religiocultural dimension to the environmental crisis. Some environmentalists argue that certain religious beliefs, rituals, and behaviors may be implicated in the growth of exploitative attitudes toward the natural world. But other environmentalists, and many religious adherents, also propose that the ritual systems, mythological beliefs, and moral and spiritual values of religious communities may provide a significant resource with which to challenge the global capitalism and values of secular consumer societies that drive environmental destruction.

Environmentalism and Political Thought

Environmentalists point to a fundamental conflict between the dominant values and practices of modern civilization—economic growth, technological progress, consumerism—and the fragile and finite character of the nonhuman world. Many environmentalists believe that the exploitative tendencies of modern life in relation to the natural world originated in religiocultural attitudes toward nature fostered by the Christian religion, including the biblical idea of human dominion over the creation and the influence of the ancient Greek dualism between soul and body in the Christian doctrine of salvation. Patriarchy and the Protestant work ethic are also said to have contributed significantly to the environmental crisis, providing a fertile ground for the modern industrial despoilation of natural resources.

Environmentalism may be seen as a pervasive reformist trend in modern political thought and practice. Environmentalism in this sense is a regional and global program of political, economic, even civilizational reform. For example, the 1987 United Nations Commission on Environment and Development report, *Our Common Future,* promoted the concept of sustainable development. And world leaders who met to discuss global environmental problems at the Rio Earth Summit in June 1992 adopted *Agenda 21,* which identified the deterioration of ecosystems and the worsening of poverty, hunger, and ill health as a defining moment in human history requiring remedial action by local communities and national governments, and by international cooperation and treaty.

Ecological economics is an important tool for local and national environmental reform. The central idea is that the full environmental costs—air, water, or land pollution; ecosystem disruption; natural resource depletion; global warming—arising from the industrial production of goods or services be met by producers and consumers through "green taxes," rather than deferred onto the state, the poor, or future generations.

Environmentalism has been less successful internationally than regionally or locally. The Montreal Protocol, signed by all developed and most developing countries in 1987, agreed to dramatic reductions in the production of ozone-depleting chlorofluorocarbons (CFCs) and initiated an international quest for less-damaging refrigerants. But similar efforts at the Rio Earth Summit to set globally agreed limits to tropical deforestation and industrial fishing or at the 1997 Kyoto Summit on Climate Change to reduce global production of gases associated with global warming—particularly of carbon dioxide—have been unsuccessful.

Environmentalism may also be seen as a countercultural or postmodern social movement whose proponents see the environmental crisis as representing the defining-limit problem of modern civilization. They seek to rebalance the utilitarian quest for maximum human welfare with the welfare of other species, and even of the planet, or *gaia*. James Lovelock, who originated the now widely accepted gaia hypothesis, proposes that the Earth is a total living system in which organic life forms modulate the atmospheric, climatological, geological, and marine environments necessary for life.

Ecocentric philosophers point to the Cartesian metaphor of the cosmos as machine as a major cause of the disharmony between modern technologically driven societies and the fragile and complex organic balances of ecological systems. Ecocentric environmentalism is manifest in a range of alternative political, economic, and lifestyle projects involving direct action, alternative communities, and a rejection of the core values of the dominant society. Countercultural environmentalists argue that, like the social and ritual systems of indigenous peoples, production and exchange systems should be fashioned not with the primary aim of reordering the natural world after human purposes, but rather of promoting human and nonhuman welfare by mirroring the balances and recycling patterns of ecological systems.

Ecocentric environmentalism has its origins in the nineteenth-century Romantic movement, which, in reaction to Enlightenment rationalism and early modern industrialization, sought to relocate ethical goods and spiritual values in the intrinsic beauty and order of the natural world. Ecocentric environmentalists argue that exalting wealth accumulation and luxury over ecological goods is a sign of the moral impoverishment of an urban industrial culture out of touch with the sustaining spiritual energies of the planet and that puts material acquisition before relationships of care and responsibility between people, and between people and their environment.

Environmentalism and Religion

The spiritual and religious dimensions of environmentalism are of growing significance to environmentalism as global political policy and as a new social movement. The environmental crisis is seen by many, particularly ecocentric, environmentalists and by many religious adherents as a spiritual crisis of modern civilization.

There is also a pragmatic motive that recognizes the continuing cultural power of religions as a resource for moral and social change in many parts of the world. In 1990 the World Wide Fund for Nature helped organize an ecological council of faiths in Assisi, Italy, at which religious leaders, including Pope John Paul II and the Dalai Lama, affirmed the need for radical change in the direction of modern civilization if the world is to be saved from environmental catastrophe.

The ecological turn in world religions first became evident in the Christian faith in the prophetic writings of North American theologians such as Joseph Sittler, Francis Schaeffer, Paul Santmire, and John B. Cobb in the 1960s, and in the efforts of international ecclesiastical organizations, most notably the World Council of Churches, to reexamine Christian social teaching and action in the light of the ecological crisis. Some theologians have argued that the Christian tradition contains within it significant resources for a more sustainable way of living on the Earth and have drawn on biblical motifs such as creation, covenant, reverence for life, and stewardship as crucial elements in a Christian ecological theology.

Other theologians have sponsored various ecological adaptations of Christian doctrine and ethics. Process philosophers, for example, propose that basic reality is characterized by creativity and flux rather than stasis. Theologians such as Charles Hartshorne and Cobb argue that instead of seeing God as an unchanging absolute being who is external to the world, we should see God in a caring and dynamic relationship with the evolving processes of the biophysical world. Christian ecofeminists and liberation theologians have sponsored ecojustice, which extends the ethical ideals of social justice and equality between people and genders to a concern for justice, and even equality, among all species on the earth. It is, however, in worship and spirituality that the most widespread influence of ecological concerns may be observed in contemporary Christianity. New liturgies, hymns, and credal affirmations in Christian worship connect reverence for the divine creator with care for the gifts of creation and encourage Christians to exercise daily ecological responsibility for the earth through simpler lifestyles.

The greening of religion is also evident in the religions of Asia and in Islam. Buddhist monks have fought illegal logging of the few remaining areas of tropical forest in Thailand. Criticizing the pact between statist Islam and Western capitalism fostered by Arab monarchs and political leaders, radical Muslims adopt simpler lifestyles. Westerners, who find in these Asian traditions an emphasis on the oneness of all life forms absent from Western religion and philosophy, adopt meditative practices and philosophical ideas from Daoism and Zen Buddhism.

Hindus draw on the philosophy and practices of Gandhi, as well as on the Upanishads, in deploring the depredatory effects of industrialization and international trade on the peoples, forests, and wild animals of South Asia. Perhaps the most ecological of all Asian religions, Jainism takes the Buddhist concept of *ahimsa* (nonviolence) with such seriousness that all Jains are vegetarians, and Jain monks take enormous care never to crush an insect inadvertently.

In the Americas the practices and religions of Native Americans recognize the interdependence of all life, and their deep ethical regard for the land and all its inhabitants prevented them from despoiling the wilderness as did later colonizers. Advocates of environmental ethics argue that modern civilization needs to recover this regard for land and nature and that for many, this recovery will involve a spiritual as well as a philosophical reorientation.

Environmentalism in its more radical ecocentric forms may be said to represent a new and growing ecological religion, perhaps the archetypal religion of post-Christian societies, and to have sponsored the recovery of pagan and primal religious styles. Ecological religion takes a variety of

forms, some of which are quite culturally diffuse. A growing number of vegetarians reject the killing animals for sport and food, for example, and ascribe equivalent moral value to all sentient life forms. Other forms of ecological religion—which may be variously described as New Age, pagan, ecofeminist, or Wiccan—reflect an explicit desire not just to prevent harm to the natural world but also to reconnect the rituals and rhythms of human life with reverence for the sacred spirit or spirits said to reside in natural elements, cycles, processes, beings, and events.

See also *Dalai Lama; Enlightenment; Feminism; Hinduism; Justice, Social; Paganism; Science and technology; Traditionalism.*

Michael S. Northcott

BIBLIOGRAPHY

Attfield, Robin. *The Ethics of Environmental Concern.* 2d ed. Athens: University of Georgia Press, 1991.

Nasr, Seyyed Hossein. *Religion and the Order of Nature.* New York: Oxford University Press, 1996.

Northcott, Michael. *The Environment and Christian Ethics.* Cambridge: Cambridge University Press, 1996.

Oelschlaeger, Max. *Caring for Creation: An Ecumenical Approach to the Environmental Crisis.* New Haven: Yale University Press, 1994.

Ruether, Rosemary Radford. *Gaia and God: An Ecofeminist Theology of Earth Healing.* San Francisco: Harper, 1992.

World Commission on Environment and Development. *Our Common Future.* Oxford and New York: Oxford University Press, 1987.

Episcopalians

See *Anglicanism*

Ethnicity

Ethnic identity is predicated on the assumption that one shares a heritage with others that can be traced to a common forebear. Ethnicity differs from kinship, however, in that the links are not traced through genealogy. Rather, certain cultural attributes are taken as signifying that one shares descent with those who also share these attributes. For those who affirm an ethnic identity, certainty is found in the heritage that is believed to link them to others with whom they share descent. This belief is embedded in cultural practices such as the stories heard in childhood, ceremonies and commemorations, the expression of ethnic stereotypes encountered in relations with others, the implementation of bureaucratic rules based on ethnic distinctions, and political acts, sometimes violent, that entail the assertion of ethnic boundaries. In all cases, an ethnic identity is validated by the authority of the past, a past to which one is linked through a nongenealogical line of descent.

Religion, like ethnicity, offers certainty with reference to the authority of the past, providing truths first enunciated by elders, prophets, and messiahs who lived in former times and followed by many successive generations. Such truths enable those who accept them to confront problems of suffering and death, chaos, and injustice that do not lend themselves to rational solutions. In a religion, like Judaism, that is followed by those who consider themselves a chosen "people," such truths may be traced to founders who are also thought to have been forebears. Most religions, however, are open to any who choose to act in accord with their tenets and to participate in the prescribed rituals. Some religions specifically require the follower to forgo the expectations associated with kinship or membership in an ethnic group if these conflict with the practice of the faith. This has been especially true of many proselytizing religions such as Islam and certain branches of Christianity.

Ethnic Movements and Modernity

The rise of ethnic movements in the twentieth century, especially in the latter half of the century, can be traced to some of the same causes as the resurgence of religious movements in that same period. Both are manifestations of a quest for certainty about one's self and the world in which one lives in the wake of the destabilizing forces associated with modernity. Bureaucratic and economic rationalization have undermined social cohesion based on kinship, locality, and patronage. Alienation has been intensified in many cases when modern governments have intruded deeply into everyday life. In the same period scientific successes in finding cures for or ways to prevent many of the afflictions that humans have long suffered from have also served to accentuate for many the lack of scientific means for confronting those physical afflictions that still lack cures.

The intensified uncertainty that has been the by-product of modernity has led many to turn to beliefs and practices that posit unchanging and unchangeable truths about their relation to the world. Both religious and ethnic movements offer such truths, but these are based on different premises. While ethnic identity may reinforce religious identity, it is also often the case that ethnicity and religion are in tension or even in conflict with one another.

Ethnicity, Religion, and the Politics of Cultural Diversity

Both ethnicity and religion are important factors in what can be termed the *politics of cultural diversity* in modern societies. Every ethnic group and every religion is associated with distinctive cultural patterns. Some cultural patterns have generated political interest because they are seen as being in conflict with the patterns of others. Major differences in cultural attitudes toward reproduction or property rights, for example, or even something seemingly unimportant, such as the clothes a student wears to school, have proved to be very divisive in some societies. The politics of culture can, and all too often do, turn violent when state power is used to curb or forbid some cultural practices considered to be central to a religious or ethnic identity.

If a modern state has made religion the basis for national identity, then ethnic divisions within the society may become associated also with religious divisions. This is evident in Sri Lanka, for example, where since the 1950s the state has promoted policies that accord a privileged position to the Sinhalese-speaking Buddhist majority. Although these policies have marginalized many groups, Tamil-speaking peoples in northern Sri Lanka, who are also predominantly Hindu, have felt especially discriminated against. Religious as well as ethnic differences have been used to justify violence by Sinhalese against Tamils in the mid-1980s and since then violence by Tamils against Sinhalese in support of a movement whose goal is the creation of an independent or autonomous Tamil polity in northern Sri Lanka. By the late 1990s, after tens of thousands of deaths, the conflict in Sri Lanka had assumed an endemic character that appeared to be beyond resolution. A comparable situation has also existed in Lebanon, with violent conflicts in that country resulting in an ethnoreligious partition of the country.

Links between religious, ethnic, and national identity have shaped the politics of Israel in fundamental ways. The definition of Israel as a Jewish state has generated many conflicts, not only with Palestinians living on the West Bank and in Gaza, but also among Christians and Muslims who hold Israeli citizenship and between secular Jews whose Jewishness is based primarily on their ethnic background and religious Jews who wish to see religious injunctions enforced by the state.

In some instances the political culture has prompted the reconstruing of religious identities as ethnic ones. A foremost example is in the former Yugoslavia, where despite markedly similar languages and cultures Serbs, Croats, and Bosnians are considered fundamentally different because of their religious heritage. Identities as Orthodox Christian, Catholic, or Muslim are taken as signifying the existence of deep historical differences that legitimate ethnonationalist divisions. The equation of religious with ethnonationalist differences also has occurred in Northern Ireland, where "Protestant" and "Catholic" have come to be seen as labels for distinct peoples.

Many indigenous peoples who have converted to Christianity or Islam have found in these religions and associated institutions sources of support for asserting their ethnic distinctiveness within the societies in which they live. A good example is that of the Karen people, found mainly in Burma but also in Thailand, who have built an ethnonationalist movement on Christian institutions and on a writing system that was developed in association with their conversion to Christianity. The Hui of China, who live among the Han Chinese and share the same language and much of the same culture but who trace their origins to Muslim converts, provide another example. In contemporary China many Hui have rediscovered their links to Islam and increasingly express their identity through religious actions.

For a religious affiliation to be construed as marking a distinctive ethnic or ethnonationalist identity, it must be understood as an essential element of one's heritage. Many religions explicitly reject such an assumption and, instead, insist that a person's faith can be demonstrated only through an act of commitment that could well entail a rejection of one's heritage. In many parts of Africa, for example, conversion to Christianity or Islam has made it possible for people to transcend local and tribal backgrounds and to find a new cultural identity, which they now share with others of diverse ethnic origins.

In any society in which a politics of cultural difference is significant, it can be anticipated that the relationship between ethnic and religious identity will for at least some people become a matter of political concern. At the same time, these relationships will always be shaped by the particular politics of the societies in which they are manifest.

See also *Genocide; Ireland; Israel; Prejudice; Yugoslavia.*

Charles F. Keyes

BIBLIOGRAPHY

Anderson, Benedict R. O. G. *Imagined Communities: Reflections on the Origin and Spread of Nationalism.* Rev. and expanded ed. London: Verso, 1991.

Bruce, Steve. "Fundamentalism, Ethnicity, and Enclave." In *Fundamentalisms and the State: Remaking Polities, Economies, and Militance,* edited by Martin E. Marty and R. Scott Appleby. Chicago: University of Chicago Press, 1993.

Geertz, Clifford. "The Integrative Revolution: Primordial Sentiments and Civil Politics in the New States." In *Old Societies and New States,* edited by Clifford Geertz. Glencoe, Ill.: Free Press, 1963. Reprinted in *The Interpretation of Cultures: Selected Essays,* by Clifford Geertz. New York: Basic Books, 1973.

Keyes, Charles F., Laurel Kendall, and Helen Hardacre, eds. *Asian Visions of Authority: Religion and the Modern States of East and Southeast Asia.* Honolulu: University of Hawaii Press, 1994.

Kotkin, Joel. *Tribes: How Race, Religion, and Identity Determine Success in the New Global Economy.* New York: Random House, 1993.

Europe, Eastern

In the post–World War II era, the term *Eastern Europe* often was used to refer to the Soviet bloc countries of Europe: Poland, Czechoslovakia, Hungary, Romania, Bulgaria, and the German Democratic Republic. Only after Soviet-imposed communism collapsed in 1989 in Eastern Europe did a real relationship between politics and religion begin to develop. The collapse of communism also marked the return of these countries' separate identities.

Eastern Europe is a mosaic of languages, cultures, denominations, and traditions; the imposition of the Soviet model had only made the countries of the region seem homogeneous. Indeed, "Eastern Europe" was a concept that could be understood only by reference to Soviet practices. The Soviet model presented the struggle against religion as dictate of ideology, and, as a result, it applied a strategy to the region aimed at eventually eliminating religion. It would be too simple, however, to reduce the history of relations between religion and politics to a matter of religious persecution alone. In fact, differences among countries of Soviet-led Eastern Europe on the place of religion in society and politics very quickly became apparent—for example, the constitutional prohibition of all religion imposed by the regime in Albania and the "church within socialism" mandated in the German Democratic Republic.

The Church in Communist Eastern Europe

The main function of religion in pre-1989 Eastern Europe was to provide proof of the permanence of historic na-

time in identifying a strategy that would call into question the solidity of communist power in terms of both social geography and time. This strategy was to be continued by Pope John Paul II who, as a former archbishop of Krakow, knew it well. Thus the whole interpretation of reality on which communist power relied was swept away by the emphasis on the long haul of civilization and on the historic and cultural unity of Europe rather than on the short life of political systems.

From this point of view, the pope's first visit to his native country in 1979 after becoming head of the Catholic Church had a considerable impact. John Paul II attracted huge crowds and proved that the legitimacy of political power had eroded. This proof, coupled with the pontiff's encouragement to Poles to have no fear, was largely responsible for the birth of the Solidarity movement in 1980, led by Gdansk shipyard worker Lech Walesa and supported by the workers' union Solidarity.

Although religion had the potential to play three liberating roles, it was up to the actors on the scene to grasp this potential and turn it into an effective weapon in the fight against state power. In Eastern Europe the actors used this opportunity in a variety of ways. The end in 1956 of the dark (and relatively uniform) days of repression fomented by Soviet Communist Party leader Joseph Stalin left the way clear for a variety of scenarios. In Poland the Catholic Church operated as the main sociopolitical force by coordinating the forces of resistance. But the Catholic and Protestant churches in Hungary followed the model of submission to the state that had been initiated by the Habsburg emperors. And while the Orthodox churches in Romania, Bulgaria, and Russia threw themselves into legitimizing state power with theological justifications (which objectively placed them in a compromising position), in Czechoslovakia all the churches, beginning in the 1980s, came down on the side of opposition.

Entering the Postcommunist Era

Pope John Paul II's visit to newly democratic Czechoslovakia in 1990 at the invitation of President Václav Havel was of symbolic value to the church and, indeed, the whole country. Sanctioning by his journey the role played by the Catholic Church in opposing the regime, the pope also endorsed religion as a provider of the ethical values required for the moral regeneration of those societies damaged on the moral level. To some extent, history gained its revenge by en-

tions, the existence of pluralistic societies, and, as time went on, the largely incidental character of communist systems. Religion was capable politically of playing three liberating roles regardless of the particular denomination in which it was practiced. At the level of individuals, confession of a faith could drive the faithful to abandon the schizophrenic attitude demanded by the communist system which forced people to keep their actions and thoughts separate. At the level of societies, religion could help to repair the fabric of communities that the political authorities had tried hard to destroy. And, at the level of nations, religion could be liberating by revealing the historical continuity of nation-states and thereby calling into question the legitimacy of the "revolutionary" break on which the Soviet system had been based.

When the Polish church celebrated one thousand years of Christianity in the country in 1966, it revealed publicly Poles' commitment to Catholicism. The church then lost no suring that liberation from communism was celebrated in the Cathedral of St. Vitus in Prague. (The capital is located in Bohemia, a region that previously had turned Catholicism into the very enemy of the nation's historical destiny.) But this event, which blessed the crucial role played by the faithful in resisting the regime, could not conceal the profound secularization of Czech society.

Some churches such as the Polish and Czech Catholic churches and the Protestant churches in the former East Germany and Transylvania emerged with prestige from their long confrontation with Soviet projects and practices. This was not the case, however, for the majority of Orthodox churches such as those in Romania and Bulgaria whose position vis-à-vis political authorities had been so compromised that they had to seek their own people's forgiveness. For this reason, the Romanian patriarch Theoctist had to resign just after the revolution. Likewise, the Hungarian churches appeared to have generally lost their credibility. Finally, churches that had survived in secret, such as the Uniate Church in Romania and Ukraine, began to revive and inevitably to see signs of hope and revenge in the fall of the regimes that had made martyrs of them.

Regardless of how the churches entered the postcommunist era, they were immediately confronted with many challenges from a sociopolitical modernity for which they were ill-prepared. The example of the West aroused fears of rationally disenchanted politics in which the social influence of churches would be lost. In fact, most religious leaders had, and continue to have, difficulty understanding what may turn out to be a provisional choice between, on the one hand, a policy of making churches the center of political life (the choice of several, mainly Protestant, churches) and, on the other hand, direct intervention in the political arena by using the prestige and institutional influence that flow from such intervention.

Analyzing Politics and Religion in Eastern Europe

Analysis of the relationship between politics and religion in Eastern Europe during the communist era relied for a long time on the use of numerous stereotypes that often said much more about the fantasies of those who used them than about the reality they were supposed to describe. The same could be said about the unrealistic image of a uniform and homogeneous "Eastern Europe" and the existence of the "Church of Silence" that was closely associated with it and

tended to lend credence to it. Yet, without denying that churches and believers were really persecuted in certain countries, those who made such a categorization, because of its very inclusiveness, could not account for the wide range of different situations among the countries of Eastern Europe. Moreover, a research project carried out in January 1990 by Median in Hungary, Demoskop in Poland, and the Institute of Public Opinion Polls in the Soviet Union, and coordinated by the French CSA Institute, discovered that 90 percent of Hungarians, 91 percent of Poles, and 89 percent of Soviets questioned denied they had ever been victimized because of their religious beliefs.

"Religious revival" eventually joined the original list of stereotypes and was applied to the years just before and after the collapse of communism. This stereotype tried, on the one hand, to explain both the erosion and then the fall of the Soviet system in terms of the force of religion, and, on the other hand, to give some meaning to the process triggered by this fall. It is clear how this stereotype gained credibility: everywhere and at different levels religion seemed likely to provide a privileged means of escape from communism. It did not matter whether this stemmed from, among other things, the religious symbols used by Solidarity and the presence of the church in the developments in Poland; or Augustin Navratil's petition for religious freedom in Czechoslovakia; or the position of Catholic and Protestant believers at the heart of the Charter 77 movement in the same country (a 1977 manifesto, Charter 77 denounced the lack of civil rights in Czechoslovakia); or the role played by Protestant churches in opposing the regime in East Germany or that played by Pastor Tökes in Romania in sparking the revolution.

Yet if religion really had potential as a liberating movement, it was not necessarily based on a renewal of faith; rather, it reflected the specific status granted to religion by the Soviet-type system. By making God the only category that it banned from its own ideology, this system raised God to the status of the only independent category capable of calling the system's own legitimacy into question.

Poland, which is of special importance in this context both because the pope was born there and because of his efforts to give it "model" status, countered the false belief that the legitimacy of the country's political system rested on consensus with an equally false belief, like an echo, that the whole of Polish society was united behind its church. When the first false belief disappeared, the second was bound to follow. The return to reality in the form of a pluralized political landscape brought to light an ambiguity that shaped the way in which the system of social resistance operated. By placing its own idea of totality in opposition to that which the state claimed to impose, the church, whether or not it was aware of the fact, was defending relative values. The church represented "real pluralism" as opposed to "real socialism." Various elements of society made symbolic use of the church, its pronouncements, and its values merely as ways of questioning the legitimacy of the regime. But the people who chose to refer to a totality did not necessarily have to belong to it.

In any case, this observation was supported by the participants themselves and particularly by members of the church hierarchy. In fact, the gap between reported membership in the Polish church and respect for its moral standards often has been noted, as much by bishops as by sociologists. Indeed, since the end of the 1970s there have been many instances in Poland in which the church's authority has declined when its views have moved too far away from representing the interests of society in favor of working out its own objectives and priorities, especially on the political front. Thus Poland created the original sociological type of the "practicing nonbeliever" who used religion for purposes that were clearly nonreligious. Today in Poland in the areas of human rights and relations with modernity, the differences between the church, on the one hand, and society, on the other, are becoming sharper. As early as 1991 a survey in Poland revealed that 74 percent of respondents thought the church played too large a role in public life, and this figure went up to 82 percent in November 1992. Fifty-seven percent thought the church should not participate in politics at all. More than 50 percent reported that priests gave political sermons, and 71 percent were in favor of separating church and state.

In general, then, the social influence of the church in Poland has continued to decline since 1989: 90 percent of Poles expressed satisfaction with its role in 1989 but only 45 percent in 1992. Since then the rate has stabilized at around 50 percent. In the same vein, the success of the former communists in the legislative elections of the fall of 1993 and the historic failure of all the parties claiming to represent Catholicism are viewed as running counter to the Polish church's attempts to perpetuate in a pluralist arena the kind of central control that it had acquired only because of particular circumstances bound up in the very nature of the Soviet-type

system. The victory of Aleksander Kwasniewski, a young communist turned social democrat, over Lech Walesa in the presidential elections of the fall of 1995 is in line with this thinking.

Although the use of stereotypical ideas like "Eastern Europe," "Church of Silence," or "religious revival" in writing about Eastern Europe led to a somewhat simplistic interpretation of reality, the introduction of a new stereotype, "the transition toward democracy and the free market," created even more confusion. Promoters of the idea of transition suggested that, with the dissolution of an "abnormal" situation (communism) and the gradual progression toward "normality" measured by Western standards, the conditions for a real "religious explosion" were fulfilled. The participants themselves were expecting it: in 1990 76 percent of Hungarians believed that democratization would boost religious activity.

By contrast, 57 percent of Poles believed at the same time that recent developments would make no difference or would bring about a decline in religious practice. The case of Poland may appear unusual, and indeed it is, precisely because of the special significance of religion and the church in the long exodus from communism. Moreover, Poles had a vague idea, which became clearer over time, that by abolishing communism as their central point of reference they also were getting rid of the central importance of struggle that they had entrusted to the church.

Above all, the situation in Poland took to an extreme conclusion certain tendencies that were found all over Eastern Europe, at least wherever religion had been used effectively as a means of escape from communism. In the mid-1970s, when reformers had to draw up a platform for attacking the legitimacy of the system without giving the appearance of entering directly into politics proper (access to this field was forbidden by the very nature of Soviet practices), the church was able to join a comprehensive resistance movement based on the fiction that all its protagonists agreed on the content of the movement for human rights. But as soon as the movement was no longer needed, the consensus disappeared with it, together with the ambiguity on which the church's potential for social influence rested.

The result was the ultra-rapid privatization of religion: as early as 1991, 81 percent of Poles thought that it was wrong for the church to get involved in the issue of contraception; 71 percent were against the church's involvement in problems relating to abortion (although the church itself, at the highest level, considers the fight against abortion to be one of its main priorities); and 63 percent rejected its stance on divorce. Moreover, the pluralization now affecting the whole sociopolitical scene in Eastern Europe is finding expression at the very center of the religious scene—and it is, to say the least, a spectacular development. In Poland, where perhaps more than anywhere else Catholicism had sought the image of a "citadel under siege," the splintering of the Catholic camp into different fragments has been brutal, leading, for example, to violent attacks by the church's hierarchy against the weekly Catholic newspaper *Tygodnik Powszechny* and a section of the Catholic intelligentsia.

Poland does not have a monopoly over privatization. Religious practice already was very weak in prewar Czechoslovakia. Even if at the end of the "Velvet Revolution" the churches, and in particular the Catholic Church, enjoyed real prestige, religion once more became a "private matter" in Bohemia. (In April 1990 half a million Czechs had traveled to see the pope during his visit to the country, whereas only fifty thousand turned up to meet the pontiff during his visit in May 1995.) In Hungary fewer than 10 percent of the population goes to church.

Debates and Uncertainty

The developments just described—the church's loss of social influence and the privatization of religion—are being aggravated by the debates about the return to the churches of assets confiscated by the communists. In Hungary where a July 10, 1991, law provided for the return of these assets (with the exception of land), the call for charity and generosity comes from the political sphere, while the declaration of the rights of property ownership comes from the church. In the Czech Republic, the trust accumulated by the church is being lost, just as it is in Hungary, precisely because of this issue of returning the church's assets.

One must not, however, be misled by a certain amount of turmoil. The growing number of new religious movements, the increase in popularity of certain groups (especially the Pentecostalists), and even upsets in the major long-established churches only show that it is difficult to find landmarks and to redefine individual and collective identities in the context of a violent transformation of scenarios from which all references to communism have been expunged.

Indeed, the withdrawal from communism has led to uncertainty and to the reconstruction of identities in all countries. In a very fluid situation, where most of the landmarks have disappeared, the temptation is strong to use religion to establish the membership of an organization and to fix a firm identity, as is the temptation to use this approach in legitimizing or managing a political clientele. Clearly, in Poland, Slovakia, and Hungary—and in Russia and in a particularly dramatic way in the former Yugoslavia—the potential to mobilize religion in the cause of nationalism has been used for political ends.

Religion as a privileged means of seeking identity also can be used as an instrument for legitimizing the nation-state with all the risks that such a function entails. Concern about Catholicism's potential for nationalist mobilization in Poland is relevant to the situations found elsewhere in Eastern Europe and the Balkans such as in Slovakia and Croatia. As for the Orthodox churches, whether through fear, passivity, or submissiveness, they have retreated into a conservatism and a ritualism that make it difficult to predict their attitude at a time of political change tending toward democratization. Even if the Orthodox hierarchy has avoided sliding toward anti-Semitism, there still is a risk in Romania and Bulgaria that religion will be exploited by political forces that adopt a program of excluding minorities and that the churches themselves will go one better than the nationalists in order to efface the memory of their compromises with the old order. In fact, in this part of Europe, where identification with a single state was the exception rather than the rule, religion can function as a means of marking out the nation, as happened during the interwar period, with the state deriving the legitimizing stereotypes it needs from religion.

The religious processions held in Slovakia to celebrate the end of the communist era undoubtedly showed some signs of taking over an evolution that the vast majority of people had undergone. Thus the aim of such processions was to confirm a personal and collective victory over an enemy against whom the people had not really fought for most of the time. Rather, participants in the processions were trying to take their revenge on historical events, to tame a past they had rewritten, and to overcome the frustration that had built up. Participation in the processions also allowed people to express an identity—an identity that their previous experience had supposedly sought to weaken—by using religion, the privileged guardian of the foundational myths of identity, to forge links with past traditions that the communist regime had allegedly destroyed. These processions also helped to reappropriate "national space" by making the geography of everyday life sacred. A final effect of these processions was the opportunity they presented Slovaks to affirm explicitly a Slovakian identity and to open up the possibility, which was rich in potential ways to achieve political goals, of formulating a view about the Czechs and, therefore, about the union of the two peoples within the same political entity—or about their separation.

The reevaluation of the importance of Cardinal József Mindszenty, the cardinal primate of Hungary who had staunchly opposed the communist regime there, shares this logic. The solemn transfer of his remains to Esztergom in May 1991 allowed the church to take on the appearance of a victim of the old order. Thus the history of the relationship between church and state in Hungary has been rewritten—in the 1970s and 1980s historians and commentators had deliberately omitted all reference to Mindszenty. Now it is Cardinal Lekai, Mindszenty's successor as head of the church in Hungary and the person who masterminded "one-step-at-time" politics, who is going through the trap door. The idea is to endow the church with a "resistance identity," so that political parties with an interest in maintaining a link to religion will be able to avail themselves.

In Poland the stereotypical idea that "Polish equals Catholic" has been reworked in ways have turned this very effective tool for delegitimizing the communist system into an instrument for disqualifying political opponents.

Religion can act as an indicator of a crisis of identity and as a means of handling the restructuring of identities brought about by the crisis because it is, first and foremost, an indicator of the state of advancement of a process aimed at defining a link with the change under way. (It often does this by referring to a tradition that is peculiar in the sense of having to be continually invented at the same time as it is supposed to be undergoing protection.)

Here the position of religion is neutral. This means that any religious contents can be used equally well as a way of encouraging change (be it social, political, or other), taming it, or denying it. Such an approach entails many ambiguities: in Poland the church was punished soundly in the 1993 legislative elections, in the 1995 presidential elections, and during the 1997 referendum on the new constitution because of its desperate attempts in a pluralist situation to perpetuate a form of central control that it had acquired in the first place as a result of communism. From this point of view, it is not surprising that from 1989 to 1993 public debate in Poland centered on questions such as the legal status of the church, the constitutional nature of the state, abor-

tion, the teaching of the catechism in schools, and divorce.

All these issues allowed Polish society to formalize its relations with pluralism, to establish the divisions necessary for forming (or beginning to form) a public space that the disappearance of communism—as a system and above all as an apparatus of legitimization in the last instance—had stripped of all its landmarks. The links with religion remain as they were before: a privileged indicator of the fact that a relation with pluralism has been established. But whereas the withdrawal from communism took place *with* the church (and, to a certain extent, thanks to it), the context has now changed, and democracy is advancing *against* the church.

See also *Catholicism, Roman; Havel, Václav; Hungary; Poland; Russia; Yugoslavia.*

Patrick Michel

BIBLIOGRAPHY

Michel, Patrick. *Politics and Religion in Eastern Europe.* Cambridge: Polity Press, 1991.

———. *Politique et religion: La grande mutation.* Paris: Albin-Michel, 1994.

———. "Religion and Democracy in Central Eastern Europe." In *Religion in Contemporary Europe,* edited by John Fulton and Peter Gee. New York: Gellen Press, 1994.

———. *Les religions à l'Est.* Paris: Cerf, 1992.

Ramet, Pedro, ed. *Catholicism and Politics in Communist Societies.* Durham, N.C.: Duke University Press, 1990.

Swatos, William. *Politics and Religion in Central and Eastern Europe: Traditions and Transitions.* Westport, Conn.: Praeger, 1994.

Europe, Western

Western Europe encompasses the countries of the European Union, Norway, and Switzerland; included here, in addition, are some references to those countries of the Western religious tradition that were under Soviet domination from 1945 to 1989 (that is, the Baltic States, Poland, Hungary, the Czech Republic, Slovakia, Slovenia, and Croatia). "Western," therefore, is used in the following sense: it includes those parts of Europe that found themselves within Western rather than Eastern, or Orthodox, Christianity at the time of the schism between Rome and Byzantium, a division that dates from the middle of the eleventh century. The particular arrangements of church and state that emerged in the West as a result of this schism facilitated a whole succession of nonconformist movements—notably the Renaissance, the

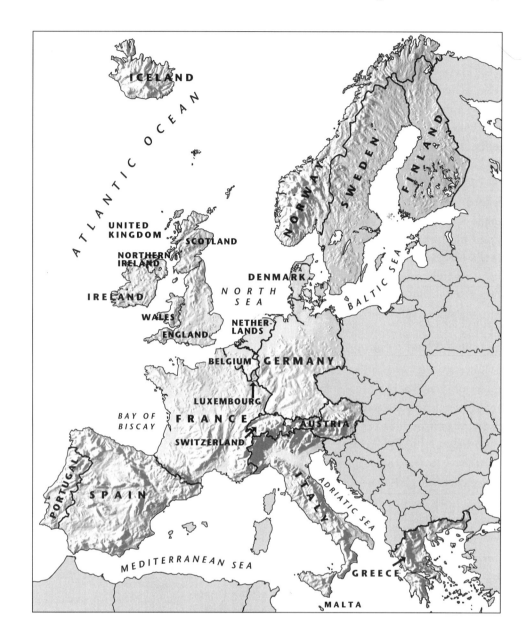

Reformation, the scientific revolution, and the Enlightenment. These are shared experiences that have colored the whole evolution of religious life in the West. None of these movements made a similar impact on the Orthodox world.

In contrast, the relatively recent division between communist and noncommunist Europe becomes almost a parenthesis to the central account, a matter of generations rather than a millennium. Indeed, the terms *eastern* and *central* Europe have significance in this respect, for the countries of eastern Europe (Bulgaria, Romania, and most of European Russia) belong to the Orthodox tradition, whereas the central European countries (Poland, the Czech Republic, Slova-

kia, Hungary, and what was East Germany) developed within Western Catholicism. The position of the Baltic states is equally revealing. Roman Catholic Lithuania and Poland are closely linked historically; in contrast, Estonia and Latvia belong essentially to northern (Lutheran) Europe. None of them faces East.

Such distinctions have significance with regard to the future of Europe and the European Union. The former communist countries that belonged—and continue to belong—to Western rather than Orthodox Christianity may well find it easier to realize their political and economic aspirations. Despite their real economic difficulties, their aim is to reestablish Western traditions; they are not learning something totally new. The vicissitudes in the Balkans in the early 1990s exemplify the same point. The postwar entity known as Yugoslavia combined within one country not only contrasting Christian traditions but a sizable Muslim presence as well. For a relatively short space of time the country held together under the personal authority of Marshal Josip Broz Tito. As that authority—and the creed that underpinned it—collapsed, it is hardly surprising that Yugoslavia's pseudo-unity began to fall apart. Ethnic nationalisms, bolstered by religious differences, interacted with a multiplicity of factors (linguistic, historical, and economic) to create an explosive situation. At the same time, the presence of sizable ethnic minorities within the borders of each state rendered the dissolution of the country as problematic as its retention. Long-term stability remains elusive.

Facts and Figures: Europe's Religious Profile

Europe's religious profile can be considered from several points of view. There is, first, a historical perspective that stresses the formative factors or themes that come together in the creation and re-creation of the unity that we call Europe: these are Judeo-Christian monotheism, Greek rationalism, and Roman organization. These factors shift and evolve over time, but their combinations can be seen forming and re-forming a way of life that we have come to recognize as European. The significance of the religious strand within such combinations is self-evident. It is equally important, however, to grasp the historical complexity of European identity. One way of doing this lies in identifying the interlocking and overlapping blocs that exist within the European whole. There are seven such blocs: the western islands, western (Atlantic) Europe, the Rhinelands, the Nordic/Baltic countries, the Mediterranean group, the former Ottoman territories, and the Slavic countries. Not all of these will be covered in this article, but the notion of building blocs underlines a crucial aspect of modern as well as historical Europe—its diversity. The religious factor is one dimension of this diversity.

One point in particular, however, requires firm underlining: the shared religious heritage of western Europe as one of the crucial factors in the continent's development—and, possibly, in its future—and the influence of this heritage on a whole range of cultural values. Other, very different sources reinforce this conclusion. One of these, the European Values System Study Group (EVSSG), provides a principal source

of data for this article. Using careful sampling techniques, the EVSSG aims at an accurate mapping of social and moral values across Europe. It has generated considerable data and will continue to do so.

Two underlying themes run through the EVSSG study. The first concerns the substance of contemporary European values and asks, in particular, to what degree they are homogeneous; the second takes a more dynamic approach, asking to what extent such values are changing. Both themes involve, inevitably, a religious element. The first, for example, leads very quickly to questions about the origin of shared value systems: if values in western Europe are shared (and it seems that many of them are), how had any such joint cultural experience been created? As the European Values study indicates, the answer lies in deep-rooted cultural experiences that derive from pervasive social influences that have been part of western European culture for generations, if not centuries. A shared religious heritage is one such influence.

Many of these findings are unproblematic and confirm the historical perspective already outlined. As soon as the idea of value change is introduced, however, the situation becomes more contentious. A series of unavoidable questions immediately present themselves. Is the primacy given to the role of religion in the creation of values still appropriate? Has this role not been undermined by the process known as secularization? Can it really be maintained that religion remains a central element of the western European value system? The influence of religion is becoming, surely, increasingly peripheral within contemporary European society. Or is it? These are the central questions facing the analyst of religious life in western Europe. The principal findings of the 1981 and 1990 EVSSG surveys provide a starting point for social scientific understanding in this field.

There are, broadly speaking, five religious indicators within the EVSSG data: denominational allegiance, reported church attendance, attitudes toward the church, indicators of religious belief, and some measurement of subjective religious disposition. Two types of variables, however, emerge with respect to these multiple indicators: on the one hand, those concerned with feelings, experience, and the more numinous religious beliefs; and on the other, those that measure religious orthodoxy, ritual participation, and institutional attachment. It is, moreover, the latter (the more orthodox indicators of religious attachment) that display, most obviously, an undeniable degree of secularization throughout western Europe. In contrast, the former (the less institutional indicators) demonstrate considerable persistence in some aspects of Europe's religious life. In particular, some form of "religious disposition" and an awareness of the moral concepts of Christianity continue to be widespread among large numbers of Europeans, even among those for whom the institution of the church has ceased to resonate.

It may, therefore, be more accurate to suggest that western Europeans remain, by and large, unchurched populations rather than simply secular. A marked falling-off in religious attendance (especially in the Protestant North) has not resulted, yet, in a parallel abdication of religious belief. (Seventy percent of Europeans continue to believe in God.) In short, many Europeans have ceased to belong to their religious institutions in any meaningful sense, but they have not abandoned, so far, many of their deep-seated religious motivations.

This relatively widespread—although fluctuating—characteristic of believing without belonging (if such it may be called) within European religion in the late twentieth century should not merely be assumed; it must be examined, probed, and questioned. A second point illustrates this need for questioning. It introduces two contrasting situations where believing without belonging is not always the norm. Indeed, in parts of eastern and central Europe prior to 1989, the two variables were reversed, for the nonbeliever quite consciously used church attendance as one way of expressing disapproval of an unpopular regime. The second, very different, contrast comes from the United States. Here religious attendance appears to maintain itself at levels far higher than those that prevail in most of Europe; about 50 percent of the American population report that they both believe and belong. Once again the situation should not be taken for granted; it must be examined, sociologically as well as theologically.

Returning now to western Europe, there is further evidence of consistency in the shapes or profiles of religiosity that obtain across a wide variety of European countries. One very clear illustration of such profiling can be found in patterns of religious belief. Levels of belief quite clearly vary from country to country, but irrespective of level of belief, the rank order among different indicators of belief is almost identical across Europe. The one exception to a consistent pattern, paradoxically, is the higher ranking given by English-speaking countries to heaven than to life after death. This kind of consistency is persuasive, the more so in that it is not easily predictable.

Correlations between different aspects of religion and socioeconomic variables confirm the existence of socioreligious patterning across national boundaries. Throughout western Europe, it is clear that religious factors correlate—to varying degrees—with occupation, gender, and age (social class as such is more problematic). The correlation with age is particularly striking, raising the question of the future shape of European religion. Indeed, the EVSSG findings (particularly the 1990 study) seem to indicate that western Europeans may be experiencing a permanent generational shift with respect to religious behavior. Markedly lower church attendance, institutional attachment, and adherence to traditional beliefs are found in younger compared with older respondents, a finding reinforced by other data. Such changes are difficult to explain simply by life-cycle differences. If this really is the case, the future shape of European religion may be very different indeed.

The EVSSG data—like all survey data—tell us some things and fail to tell us others. There is no way of grasping, for example, *why* a particular country should be similar to or different from its neighbors. Apparently similar statistical profiles can mask profound cultural differences. A second difficulty concerns the presence of religious minorities. The EVSSG sample sizes for each country are too small to give any meaningful data about such communities. It would be grossly misleading, however, to present an image of Europe at the end of the twentieth century without any reference to these increasingly important sections of the European population.

Religious Minorities

The first of these, the Jews, has been present in Europe for centuries; a presence, moreover, that has been inextricably bound up with the tragedies of recent European history. Nor can it be said, regrettably, that anti-Semitism is a thing of the past. It continues to surface from time to time right across Europe, itself an accurate indicator of wider insecurities. Estimations of numbers are always difficult, but there are, currently, about 1 million Jews in western Europe, the largest communities being the French (five hundred thousand to six hundred thousand) and the British (three hundred thousand). French Judaism has been transformed in the postwar period by the immigration of considerable numbers of Sephardim from North Africa. The causes of this immigration are multiple but include the Suez crisis of 1956 (when Britain and France supported Israel's attack on Egypt), the withdrawal of France from its former colonies in the Maghrib, and the repercussions of the Arab-Israeli conflict, especially in Muslim countries; Europe's religious life is in no way self-contained.

Former colonial connections also account for other non-Christian immigrations into Europe. The Islamic communities are, undoubtedly, the most significant in this respect, although Britain also houses considerable numbers of Sikhs and Hindus. Followers of Islam are, however, the largest non-Judeo-Christian population in Europe. Conservative estimates suggest a figure of 6 million; other commentators put this as high as 10 million. Such figures, however, depend largely on accurate information about immigration, information that is not at all easy to come by. Bearing this in mind, it is likely that Muslims make up approximately 3 percent of most western European populations. More specifically, the colonial links between France and North Africa account for the sizable French Muslim community (2 million to 3 million at least). Britain's equivalent comes from the Indian subcontinent (1.2 million). Germany, on the other hand, has absorbed large numbers of migrant workers from the fringes of southeastern Europe and from Turkey in particular. The fate of these migrants in the face of growing numbers of ethnic Germans from the former Soviet bloc looking for work within the new Germany remains to be seen.

Whatever the outcome of this particular situation, however, one fact remains increasingly clear: the Islamic presence in Europe is here to stay. It follows that Europeans can no longer distance themselves from the debates of the Muslim world. Whether they like it or not, the issues are present on their own doorstep. Admitting that this is the case is not easy for many Europeans, for the Islamic factor undoubtedly challenges the assumptions of European life, both past and present. Peaceful coexistence between Islam and Judeo-Christian Europe cannot—and never could be—taken for granted. Nor can Muslims accept unequivocally the live-and-let-live religious attitudes assumed by the majority of contemporary Europeans. This, surely, remains the problem at the heart of both the controversies surrounding the publication of Salman Rushdie's book *The Satanic Verses* and the disputes about wearing the Muslim veil in French schools that took place from 1989 onward. Rushdie's book was published in 1988; its text was considered blasphemous by many Muslims and led to death threats to its Indian-born author. The fact that both episodes remained effectively unresolved

almost a decade after their inception indicates the intractability of the underlying issues.

One further source of diversity should also be pointed out: the controversial presence of new religious movements in all European societies. There can be no doubt that new religious movements attract considerable media attention, which is often negative in tone; the numbers involved are, however, tiny. Be that as it may, such movements have inadvertently become barometers of the changes taking place in contemporary society, revealing—among other things—the limits of western European understanding concerning unconventional forms of religious life. This perspective can, moreover, be used to examine one of the most urgent questions facing Europe at the present time: the need to create and to sustain a truly tolerant and pluralist society, both in Europe as a whole and in its constituent nations. A society, that is, that goes well beyond an individualized live-and-let-live philosophy and that can accommodate that unusual phenomenon in contemporary Europe—the person (of whatever faith) who takes religion seriously. If a country fails in its tolerance of new religious movements, it is unlikely, or at least much less likely, to succeed with respect to other, more significant (numerically speaking) religious minorities.

Church and State

A broad-brush profile of religion in western Europe provides the background for a more detailed discussion of church and state relationships. It is helpful to set these within the following framework, taken from David Martin's seminal work on the evolution of secularization in the Western world, *A General Theory of Secularization*. Following Martin, Europe is a unity by virtue of having possessed one Caesar and one God (hence the commonalities of faith and culture set out above); it is a diversity by the existence of nations. The patterns of European religion derive from the tensions and partnerships between religion and the search for national integrity and identity. These tensions and partnerships are ongoing processes that have dominated four centuries of European history and have resulted in a bewildering variety of church-state relationships within the continent as a whole.

The first split within Christendom concerned the divergence of Catholic and Orthodox Europe in the eleventh century. The subsequent divisions of the West into areas or nations that are primarily Catholic or Protestant (or combinations of the two) are inseparable historically from the emergence of the nation-state as the dominant form of Europe's political life. The processes by which such division occurred are highly complex, involving economic, social, and political issues as well as religious ones. Which of these led to the others and how the whole thing was set in motion in the first place is the subject of an ongoing debate among historians, themselves of different persuasions. What remains indisputable, however, is an unprecedented upheaval in the ordering of Christian society in the sixteenth century, an upheaval that included the emergence of separate political entities, or nation-states, some of which expressed their independence from papal interference in the form of a state church. These state churches were increasingly underpinned not only by Protestant understandings of theology but by corresponding changes in the ecclesiastical order.

Part of the ambiguity regarding the whole historical process lies in the understanding of the term *Reformation*. Does this imply innovation and the breaking of new ground? Or does it imply a return to and rediscovery of primitive excellence? Were those who endorsed the theological changes taking place at this time looking primarily for radical change or for conservative independence? Motives were bound to be mixed. The more conservative interpretation, however, was bound to appeal to those political rulers who were anxious to establish independence from external authority but who kept a careful eye on stability within. Both were possible within the Lutheran concept of a "godly prince." Sometimes the prince had jurisdiction over a whole kingdom or kingdoms. Such was the case in Scandinavia, where Lutheranism became embodied in the state churches of northern Europe. Elsewhere the process was far more local and concerned relatively small patches of land. Germany exemplifies the latter process, which led to patterns that are not only extant but highly influential some four hundred years later.

The Reformation took different forms in different places. In addition to Lutheranism, some Europeans—notably the Swiss, the Dutch, the Scots, some Germans, some Hungarians and Czechs, and a small but significant minority of French people—were attracted first by the Swiss reformer Ulrich Zwingli (1484–1531), but then by John Calvin (1509–1564), toward a more rigorous version of Protestantism. Calvinism was both more radical and more restrained: radical in the sense of a new kind of theology based on the doctrines of predestination and redemption but restrained with regard to its stringent moral codes. The effect

of this particular combination on the subsequent economic development of Europe has provided inexhaustible material for an ongoing debate among historians and sociologists alike.

Broadly speaking western Europe divided itself into a Catholic south (France, Italy, Portugal, and Spain, but also including Belgium and Ireland) and a Protestant north (Scandinavia and Scotland), with a range of "mixed" countries in between (England and Wales, Northern Ireland, the Netherlands, and Germany). Central Europe exemplifies similar categories, although the geography is rather more complicated. Lithuania, Poland, Slovenia, Slovakia, and Croatia are firmly Catholic; Estonia and Latvia are Lutheran and relate closely to their Scandinavian neighbors (a commonality strongly reemphasized as the Baltic republics regained their political independence); the Czech Republic and Hungary, finally, are rather more mixed (primarily Catholic but with significant Protestant minorities). In other words, boundaries gradually emerged all over Europe dividing one nation from another, one region from another, and one kind of Christianity from another. Boundaries, moreover, imply dominance as well as difference. Majorities and minorities were, and still are, created as a result of the precise location of a political boundary line. One of the most arbitrary in recent years has been the line that divides Northern Ireland from the Irish Republic. The consequences of this division compound rather than resolve the Irish question.

The previous paragraphs have introduced the confessional map of western Europe that emerged in the early modern period and that has remained *relatively* stable ever since. It would be a mistake, however, to assume that church-state arrangements necessarily follow suit. What evolves in the latter respect is a bewildering variety of arrangements that are dictated for the most part by particular historical circumstances and that change over time as political necessity dictates or as economic or social shifts suggest. The following summary moves from north to south and covers the countries of the European Union together with Norway and Switzerland. The countries of central Europe are harder to deal with because their church-state relationships are part of newly established relationships in nations where independence remains a novelty. The point to recognize in all of them, however, is the significance of church-state relationships in an emergent democratic order. Freedom of belief and conscience is a universal aspiration, but how this works in practice, particularly for smaller, less recognized denominations, is much more problematic. The solutions are not self-evident.

The Nordic countries (Sweden, Norway, Denmark, Finland, and Iceland) are some of the easiest to deal with from a church-state perspective. Here are the Lutheran state churches of northern Europe, which have high rates of membership although practice is universally low; low, too, is the acceptance of orthodox Christian beliefs. It is worth noting, however, that in Sweden, the gradual unpicking of the church-state relationship has already begun; it is no longer thought appropriate in an increasingly—if modestly—pluralist society. The Netherlands and Belgium exemplify a pillarized society: that is, a society in which the vertical divisions between Catholic, Protestant, and secular have provided the parameters for daily living (traditionally from the cradle to the grave). The particular nature of the pillars varies in the two countries, themselves very different from a confessional point of view. In both, however, church and state are technically separate, although in neither case is the separation rigorous; it should be seen rather as a "mutual independence," implying at the same time a considerable degree of mutual respect.

The United Kingdom is a complex case, embodying as it does four distinct nations, each with its own religious history and constitutional arrangements. England has an *established* church (which is Anglican) and Scotland a *national* church (which is Calvinist); Wales has neither, and its important Nonconformist congregations are crosscut by linguistic differences. Northern Ireland exemplifies the most problematic entity in the European Union, given its divisive religious history, with a resolution still to be carried out. The Irish Republic, in contrast, is technically a secular state, although the preamble to its constitution is heavily Catholic and the practice of Catholicism remains unusually high compared with the European norm.

The German case is complicated by the reunification of the country after 1989. The Catholic-Protestant bi-confessionality of the country remains nonetheless the most significant feature of Germany's religious life, despite the growing presence of those with no religious allegiance (partly but not wholly explained by the population from the former East Germany) and of a sizable Muslim community. With regard to categories, Germany holds a middle position between state church and the separation of church and state. The Weimar Constitution (1919) ensured a constitutionally secured form of cooperation between church and state,

structured around three principles: neutrality, tolerance, and parity. Germany continues to operate a church tax system. Despite the leakage of membership in the postwar period, especially among Protestants, the numbers who contribute through this system to the churches' budgets are huge—so too are the budgets themselves. Austria also maintains an intermediate position between separation and state church; it is different from Germany, however, in that the population is overwhelmingly Catholic, at least in nominal allegiance.

France is a hybrid case in a different way; it is culturally part of Catholic Europe but far more like the Protestant north with regard to religious practice or patterns of belief. It is, moreover, the country of western Europe that embodies the strictest form of separation between church and state. The French state is conceived as a neutral space, privileging no religion in particular and effecting this policy by excluding the discussion of religion from all state institutions, including the school system. The incapacity of the French to accommodate the demands of young Muslim girls who wish to wear their *foulard* (or veil) in school exemplifies the limitations of this system in a rapidly changing Europe. Switzerland is entirely different. Not only is it made up of twenty-six independent cantons, but each of these has its separate arrangements regarding church and state; confessional (and indeed linguistic) boundaries crosscut cantonal ones, resulting in a highly complex but ultimately stable set of checks and balances.

Italy, Spain, and Portugal remain solidly Catholic, at least in culture. The presence of the papacy within Italy undoubtedly influences the evolution of Catholicism within the peninsula, despite the fact that the Italian state came into being in 1870 at the expense of the temporal power of the pope. Relationships have eased since then, giving the Catholic Church a privileged position in Italian society, followed by a large number of denominations recognized by the state (including the Waldensians, an early Protestant community). A third group, which includes Muslims and Jehovah's Witnesses—more numerous in fact than almost all the groups in the second category—are excluded from significant privileges. Spain exemplifies a rather different history, where the re-creation of democracy is relatively recent. Technically speaking there is no state church in Spain; in effect, however, the Catholic Church is privileged simply by its dominance in terms of numbers. Regional autonomy remains a life issue in Spain—it is not without relevance for the status of the churches. Portugal is in many ways similar to Spain, exemplifying once again a halfway stage between theoretical equality before the law and a certain degree of privilege for the dominant religion. The Concordat, or legally privileged, status of the Catholic Church, for example, still exists in Portugal, despite the constitutional changes of the 1970s.

Greece, finally, is the only Orthodox country of western Europe—the exception that proves the rule (Greece became part of the European Union for particular political reasons). In modern Greece Orthodoxy is almost identical with Greek identity; it is the official religion of the Greek state. Observance of the major festivals and the rites of passage is almost universal. Orthodoxy, moreover, is able by its very nature to contain a greater degree of diversity within itself than Catholicism; this is one reason for its relative success in a changing moral climate.

An overview such as this can only scratch the surface, beneath which lie layers of legal complexity concerning the financial arrangements of different churches; differential access to both education systems and the mass media; questions about divorce, abortion, and family life; and the legal protection of both religious communities and religious minorities. From a legal point of view, an interesting aspect to arise in recent years has been the recourse to European, as opposed to national, law on the part of some religious minorities. Crosscutting sociological themes are rather different: among them can be found the patterns of secularization in different parts of Europe (including the degree of conflict that might be embedded therein) and the likelihood or not that religion will be caught up in the destructive—rather than constructive—aspects of national identity.

Confessional Parties

Church-state relationships provide the stage set within which particular histories unfold. Like all stage sets, such relationships affect what is going on and how it is presented; particular forms of church-state relationships permit certain actions and prevent others. Only when the strain becomes intolerable do the relationships themselves alter, in, for example, the dramatic break between church and state in France in 1905 or in the reestablishment of the democratic process in Spain after the death of the dictator Francisco Franco.

The actors in such histories are many and varied; they are both collective (such as churches, religious organizations, po-

litical parties, and pressure groups) and individual (political and religious leaders and, in some cases, their followers as well). One collectivity with particular resonance in Europe is the confessional (usually Catholic) political party. Christian democracy can be understood within this context; it belongs to a particular, and probably passing, period in the history of western Europe.

The antecedents of Christian democracy go back to the nineteenth century as individual Catholics looked for ways in which to reconcile their faith to a changing world. Such initiatives were, however, heavily outweighed by the institutional—and especially Roman—dislike of democracy, whether in politics or in theology. The "natural" home for Catholicism remained the authoritarian political party until the collapse of fascism and National Socialism destroyed that possibility forever. It was, therefore, in the period immediately following World War II that Christian democracy proved the effective alternative for Catholics in large parts of western Europe. Despite a mixture of ideas at the outset, these Christian Democratic parties soon became parties of the moderate right. This was particularly true in Germany and Italy. In France the picture was more confused with the presence of a right-wing Gaullist Party, to which many Catholics were attracted.

Christian democracy varies from country to country. There are, nonetheless, common features in its political philosophy, many elements of which derive from a central emphasis on personalism, an approach that sees society as composed of persons rather than individuals. The person is a fundamentally social being with a significant place in different types of community, for example, neighborhood, church, family, or nation. Individualism, in contrast, is the primary emphasis within liberalism—a juxtaposition that leads Christian Democrats to be critical of the excesses of capitalism. Or to put the same point more positively, Christian democracy incorporates an emphasis on welfare. There is, however, an inherent tension in the politicization of welfare as a Christian Democratic philosophy in that it collides with the traditional Catholic emphasis on charity—an essentially apolitical theme. Be that as it may, the Catholic origins of Christian democracy underline its principal contrast with social democracy. The latter also emphasizes welfare within its political programs but without the formative influences of Christian teaching; indeed, social democrats (parties of the left) are, more often than not, rigorously secular in their outlook.

Christian democracy became for a time a significant political actor in many European countries (Austria, Belgium, France, Germany, Italy, and the Netherlands). It is important, however, to recognize its international dimensions. Christian democracy was an essentially European phenomenon, giving considerable impetus to the idea of a European Community. It is not entirely a coincidence that the treaty that brought the Community into being was the Treaty of Rome, for its architects were profoundly influenced by their religious as well as political backgrounds. The implications of the treaty's title provide, moreover, one explanation why at least some of the non-Catholic countries of Europe remain ambivalent toward the idea of a European Union, and not least to the notion of an external power that may threaten the sovereignty of individual nations.

Christian democracy is certainly less influential than it was. Why this should be so is not easy to discern, although one possibility must lie, surely, in the growing indifference of Europeans to their churches and to the centrality of Christian teaching, if not to "softer" versions of the spiritual (see earlier sections). Such an evolution was bound to affect parties claiming a confessional rather than a class constituency. It is not the whole story, however, for one of the most dramatic collapses of all Christian Democratic parties occurred in Italy, where the conventional indicators of religion remain relatively high. Here Christian democracy seems to have imploded partly through exhaustion (and the inevitable corruption that corrodes a party too long in power), but also through the even more spectacular collapse of its alter ego, the Italian Communist Party. Without the potential opposition of the latter, the checks and balances within the Italian Christian Democratic Party gave way, leading to a splintering of interests among many different groups.

It is important not to jump to conclusions about the future. The partial eclipse of the confessional party does not mean the eradication of religion as a significant influence in the political life of western Europe (or indeed elsewhere). The innovative commentator José Casanova is beginning to reformulate the question of religious influence in the modern world in his *Public Religions in the Modern World.* European churches of all kinds, despite the history of some of them as state churches, are increasingly operating as voluntary organizations—organizations that attract appreciable numbers of people and that become significant actors in the political sphere. At the level of *civil* society (as opposed to the

nation-state), such churches are, and will remain, important contributors to the political life of Europe. Indeed, as Casanova suggests, a healthy political democracy would be infinitely poorer without them, for they are effective—some would say the most effective—builders of social capital in societies that at times show signs of fragmentation.

Europe and Ecumenism

If the emergence of the nation-state, and the role of the religious factor within this process, has dominated European history since the early modern period, the possibility that the final decades of the twentieth century might indicate the beginnings of a reversal in that process requires serious consideration. In 1945 Europe had come close to self-destruction for the second time in a century. The idea of European unity was barely conceivable as individual nations struggled to come to terms with what had happened and to rebuild their devastated societies. Surprisingly quickly, however, the seeds of a European Community began to generate in the form of the Coal and Steel Agreements of the 1950s, European treaties that embodied the principle that the weapons of war should themselves be subject to supranational if not international control. Since then Europe has moved inexorably, if not very steadily, toward a greater common identity.

Coincidentally—or perhaps not—the Christian churches have made significant progress toward greater unity, in, for example, the agreements between the Anglicans and the Lutherans in Germany (the Meissen Agreement of 1991) and in the Nordic countries (the Porvoo Agreement of 1996), and in the ongoing conversations between Anglicans and Roman Catholics. Indeed, it could be argued that the building of a greater European identity and the growth of ecumenical endeavor are part and parcel of the same process. There is, once again, a greater (if by no means unanimous) emphasis on what Europe has in common rather than its differences. That some nations and churches find this process easier than others is part of the complexity of European religiosity. Britain, Denmark, and Greece are particularly interesting in this respect. Each of these countries is ambivalent toward the European Union: in all their hesitations the religious factor as an exemplar of particularity plays a significant role.

Europe remains, however, a rapidly changing place. From a religious point of view, one of the most significant evolutions of the late twentieth century has been the increasing representation of faiths other than Christianity. Analytical concepts will have to evolve accordingly. Europe's religion—essentially the legacy of Christendom—is giving way to the "religions of Europe"; Europe has become a continent that houses a significant representation of Muslims, Sikhs, Hindus, and Buddhists in addition to the Jewish communities that have played such a crucial role in Europe's recent history. It is paradoxical that at precisely the moment when Europe, and to some extent, the Christian churches of the continent, are attempting to draw themselves back together again, new forms of demographic and religious diversity are appearing. The tension between unity and diversity re-presents itself once again, although in forms that are peculiar to late modern rather than early modern society.

See also *Christian democracy; Secularization; State churches;* see also individual countries, religions / groups, and denominations.

Grace Davie

BIBLIOGRAPHY

Barker, David, Loek Halman, and Astrid Vloet. *The European Values Study, 1981–1990: Summary Report.* London: Gordon Cook Foundation on behalf of the European Values Group, 1992.

Beckford, James. *Cult Controversies.* London: Tavistock Publications, 1985.

Casanova, José. *Public Religions in the Modern World.* Chicago: University of Chicago Press, 1994.

Davie, Grace, and Danièle Hervieu-Léger, eds. *Identités religieuses en Europe.* Paris: La Découverte, 1996.

Ester, Peter, Loek Halman, and Ruud de Moor, eds. *The Individualizing Society: Value Change in Europe and North America.* Tilburg, Netherlands: University of Tilburg Press, 1994.

Hanley, David, ed. *Christian Democracy in Europe: A Comparative Perspective.* London: Pinter Publishers, 1994.

Martin, David. *A General Theory of Secularization.* Oxford: Blackwell, 1978.

Nielsen, Jørgen. *Muslims in Western Europe.* Edinburgh: Edinburgh University Press, 1995.

O'Connell, James. *The Past and Future Making of Europe.* Peace Research Report 26. Bradford, England: University of Bradford, Department of Peace Studies, 1991.

Robbers, Gerhard. *State and Church in the European Union.* Baden-Baden: Nomos Verlagsgesellschaft, 1996.

Van Kersbergen, Kees. *Social Capitalism: A Study of Christian Democracy and the Welfare State.* London: Routledge, 1995.

Vertovec, Steven, and Ceri Peach. *Islam in Europe: The Politics of Religion and Community.* London: Macmillan, 1997.

Vincent, Gilbert, and Jean-Paul Williame, eds. *Religions et transformations de l'Europe.* Strasbourg: Presses Universitaires de Strasbourg, 1993.

Webber, Jonathan, ed. *Jewish Identities in the New Europe.* London and Washington, D.C.: Littman Library of Jewish Civilization, 1994.

Evangelicalism

Evangelicalism describes the large "extended family" of Protestant denominations and religious movements bound together by common beliefs. Like many religious terms, however, *Evangelicalism* has a number of meanings, especially among those who adopt the label.

Evangelical, or *evangelical Protestant,* is a term commonly used to describe the largest Protestant tradition in the United States. Most simply put, evangelicals are Protestants who adhere to highly traditional Christian beliefs and practices and who focus on individual salvation. For this reason, evangelicals often are called the "private party" of Protestantism, as opposed to the "public party" of mainline Protestants and as distinguished from the historically black Protestant churches. The latter share many beliefs and practices with evangelicals but come out of very different historical experiences.

Origins and Development

In the New Testament the Greek word *euangelion,* often translated as *evangel*—and the Greek root of evangelize, evangelist, and evangelical—is used to describe the "good news" of salvation through Jesus Christ. In this sense, all Christians might be described as evangelical because, in theory at least, they believe and proclaim the evangel.

But in the sixteenth century *evangelical* took on a more specific meaning with the Protestant Reformation, when German theologian Martin Luther (1483–1546) used the word to describe his Protestant alternative to the Roman Catholic Church. Luther emphasized the evangel itself over church tradition, stressing the authority of Scripture (the source of the evangel) and salvation by grace through faith (the message of the evangel). These Protestant distinctives were shared by other reformers, including John Calvin (1509–1564), and the term *evangelical* eventually was extended to them as well. Many Europeans and Americans in Reformation-era churches—for example, the Evangelical Lutheran Church in America, the major mainline Lutheran denomination in the United States—still use the word in this sense today.

Ironically, the Protestant Reformation set in motion a process of periodic redefinition of the term *evangelical.* Luther, Calvin, and other reformers had rejected the institutionalized Catholic Church of their time, claiming that it had diluted the evangel by accommodating itself to secular culture. But over time the Lutheran and Calvinist movements became established churches in their own rights and, in doing so, drew close to the dominant powers of the secular world, thereby inviting new rebellions dedicated to recovering and proclaiming the evangel. This "church-sect" cycle has recurred many times among Protestants. Perhaps the best American example is the Methodists, who began as a sectarian movement within the Church of England but who gradually institutionalized to become the largest mainline Protestant denomination, spawning sectarian revolts along the way.

As a result of the various iterations of the church-sect cycle, the dawn of the twentieth-first century finds the meaning of evangelicalism changed once again. It encompasses both the first-century meaning of the "good news" of salvation through Jesus Christ and the Reformation meaning of the authority of Scripture and salvation by grace through faith. In addition, its meaning includes the necessity of personal conversion (the mechanics of the evangel) and the centrality of witnessing and missions (sharing the message of the evangel). These experiential aspects of evangelicalism are manifestations of the spiritual revivals (systematic efforts to bring "outsiders" into the ranks of the faithful) that swept through the United States at the end of the nineteenth century and that continue in a more limited fashion today.

Given this complex history, it is hardly surprising that Evangelicalism has had many meanings and that these could be applied with some validity to church institutions, sectarian movements, and beliefs. Indeed, scholars frequently employ all three to define Evangelicalism.

Denominations

The denominations generally assigned to the evangelical tradition had three sources. First, many evangelicals (or their religious ancestors) came to the United States to practice their religion freely. Examples include the Amish, the Dutch Reformed churches, some ethnic Lutherans, and Pietist groups. This kind of immigration continues today, notably among Latino Pentecostals. Second, many evangelical denominations were the product of revivals, especially the nineteenth-century Presbyterians and Baptists. And, third, many evangelical denominations arose from reactions within existing denominations and local churches, which attempted to recapture more fully spiritual excitement and which often were linked to sectarian movements. The Holiness churches (such as the Nazarenes and Salvation Army) and

many conservative Baptists are good examples. Immigration combined with the church-sect cycle has thus produced a diverse set of evangelical denominations.

Today scholars generally recognize four large evangelical subtraditions. The largest, the Baptist, includes the Southern Baptist Convention and a host of other denominations, many of them quite small and sectarian. As a group, Baptists are known for their intense individualism, stressing the "soul competency" of each believer in matters of doctrine. Typical of the Baptist subtradition—and perhaps of Protestantism as well—are the numerous independent Baptist churches. Scholars frequently include other, smaller groups in the Baptist subtradition because of similarities in belief and origin. These include the Adventists, of whom the Seventh-day Adventists are best known, and the Restorationists, within which the Churches of Christ is the largest denomination.

Another subtradition is the Reformed–Confessional, composed of other churches originating in the Protestant Reformation. The Reformed elements stress traditional Calvinist beliefs, such as the sovereignty of God and predestination. The Presbyterian Church in America, the Orthodox Presbyterian Church, and the Christian Reformed Church are the best-known bodies in this category. The Confessional elements, which largely originated in the Lutheran churches, stress traditional Lutheran beliefs. Major examples are the Lutheran Church–Missouri Synod, the Evangelical Lutheran Synod, and the Wisconsin Evangelical Lutheran Synod. Scholars often include in this subtradition other split-offs from Reformation-era families, such as the Reformed Episcopal Church and the Congregational Christian churches.

Pentecostal-Holiness, the third evangelical subtradition, is made up of churches stressing special kinds of religious experiences. Churches in the Holiness family emphasize personal sanctification and individual purity. The Church of the Nazarene, Salvation Army, and Church of God (Anderson, Indiana) are the best-known Holiness groups. Scholars frequently include in this subtradition other churches that split off from the Methodist family, such as the Wesleyan Methodists, and from the Pietist churches, such as the Evangelical Free Church. The Pentecostal movement had roots in many Holiness churches but emphasizes the "gifts of the Holy Spirit," such as speaking in tongues and faith healing. The largest white Pentecostal denominations are the Assemblies of God, the Four-Square Gospel churches, and the Church of God (Cleveland, Tennessee).

The fourth and smallest subtradition is the Anabaptist. Many of these denominations also date from the Reformation era and include the Amish, Mennonites, Brethren groups, and some Friends (Quakers). They combine traditional doctrine and lifestyle with opposition to serving in the military or swearing public oaths—beliefs that have earned them the label "peace churches." All of these evangelical subtraditions give at least some emphasis to separating themselves from modern society.

Sectarian Movements

The sectarian impulse is crucial to Evangelicalism, and it is what separates these churches from their mainline cousins. Indeed, evangelicals are far better known for their sectarian movements than for their denominations. Four such movements are important today. By far the best known is Fundamentalism, an early twentieth-century revolt against accommodation in the major Protestant denominations, especially the northern Baptists and Presbyterians. Named after *The Fundamentals,* a series of pamphlets published between 1910 and 1915 that defended basic Christian beliefs, Fundamentalism is characterized by strict doctrinal orthodoxy and strident ecclesiastical separatism. This movement influenced many evangelical denominations, created new denominations, and produced a myriad of nondenominational or independent churches and institutions. Most fundamentalists are classified with the Baptist subtradition, where the movement has had its biggest impact. The Reverend Jerry Falwell is perhaps the best-known fundamentalist leader, and Bob Jones University in South Carolina is a leading fundamentalist institution.

Another important movement is neoevangelicalism, which emerged in the 1940s as a conscious rejection by some fundamentalist leaders of the strictness, stridency, extreme separatism, and anti-intellectualism of Fundamentalism. Instead, these leaders, addressing American culture, emphasized outreach and "evangelism." (The "neo" is almost invariably dropped these days, producing some confusion of identity between this movement and the broader evangelical tradition.) Evangelical institutions and leaders, such as the National Association of Evangelicals and the Reverend Billy Graham, are somewhat better known than their fundamentalist counterparts. Their adherents are found across the denominational spectrum, in all four of the evangelical subtraditions, and as minorities in many mainline Protestant denominations, such as the Presbyterian Church (USA) and the United Methodist Church. This movement has been the source of numerous nondenominational churches, including many of the so-called megachurches.

The Pentecostal and charismatic (Spirit-filled) movements, the third sectarian grouping, stress the direct work of the Holy Spirit. Pentecostalism originated in a series of revivals at the beginning of the century that eventually produced denominations such as the Assemblies of God. (Pentecostalism gets its name from the Pentecost in the New Testament, when the Holy Spirit transformed the original followers of Jesus into the Christian Church.) Despite almost a century of existence, Pentecostalism still shows strong sectarian tendencies, and these helped to generate the charismatic movement in the 1960s (the term *charismatic* derives from the Greek word for gifts). Charismatics originated in denominations that did not emphasize spiritual gifts, although tensions with noncharismatics led many to form nondenominational churches. Television evangelist Pat Robertson is a charismatic, and many of his close associates are Pentecostals. It should come as no surprise that the Spirit-filled movements are usually classified with the Pentecostal–Holiness subtradition, although they have a broader reach.

Core Beliefs

Despite all this diversity, evangelical denominations, subtraditions, and movements share core beliefs that tie the "extended family" together. Scholars agree on four doctrinal distinctives, each closely linked to the historical development of Evangelicalism: salvation comes only through faith in Jesus Christ; a high view of Scriptural authority; an emphasis on witnessing and missions; and the need for personal acceptance of salvation, or personal conversion. The emphasis on the latter is so great that the common parlance for personal conversion—"born again"—often is used interchangeably with Evangelicalism.

Although each of these four distinctives is common among all types of Christians, they are combined with rare force among adherents to evangelical denominations and movements. As one might imagine, there is considerable dispute over the exact nature of each "doctrinal essential." For example, some evangelicals insist on a literal interpretation of Scripture and a sudden "born-again" experience, while others allow wider latitude in biblical interpretation and a gradual process of conversion. Similarly, some evangelicals understand witness and mission exclusively as a quest for converts, while others include social reform and charity. Such disagreements help to define the subtraditions and movements just described.

Politics

A religious tradition as diverse as Evangelicalism is bound to display some political diversity. This has been the case historically and remains true today—the differences between Baptists and Anabaptists on the issue of military service are a good example (Anabaptists, unlike Baptists, oppose conscription). The core beliefs and sectarianism of evangelicals have produced strong political tendencies at some times and abstention from politics at others. For example, in the nineteenth century evangelicals were vigorous proponents of both religious freedom and social reform, with many of the former preferring the Democrats and many of the latter joining the Whigs and, later, the Republicans. By the early twentieth century many evangelicals, especially in the South, were strong backers of the Democratic Party for regional, cultural, and economic reasons, while others withdrew from politics to concentrate on saving souls.

Evangelicals have come to public notice more recently as a result of their vigorous reentry into politics in the 1970s. The Christian right appeared as a major social and political movement whose key elements, from Jerry Falwell and the Moral Majority to Pat Robertson and the Christian Coalition, drew special support from sectarian movements. Such groups encouraged the movement of many evangelicals toward conservative ideology and identification with the Republican Party. In fact, by the mid-1990s evangelicals had become mainstays of conservative politics, especially on social issues, and had emerged as a core constituency of the Republican Party.

See also *Communication; Conservatism; Fundamentalism; Pentecostalism; Revivalism.*

John C. Green, James L. Guth, Lyman A. Kellstedt, Corwin E. Smidt

BIBLIOGRAPHY

Bebbington, D. W. *Evangelicalism in Modern Britain: A History from the 1730s to the 1980s.* London and Boston: Unwin Hyman, 1989.

Dayton, Donald W., and R. K. Johnson, eds. *The Variety of American Evangelicalism.* Knoxville: University of Tennessee Press, 1991.

Finke, Roger, and Rodney Stark. *The Churching of America, 1976–1990: Winners and Losers in Our Religious Economy.* New Brunswick, N.J.: Rutgers University Press, 1993.

Kellstedt, Lyman A., and John C. Green. "Knowing God's Many People." In *Rediscovering the Religious Factor in American Politics,* ed. David C. Leege and Lyman A. Kellstedt. Armonk, N.Y.: M. E. Sharpe, 1993.

———. "The Mismeasure of Evangelicals." *Books and Culture* (January/February 1996): 14–15.

Kellstedt, Lyman A., John C. Green, James L. Guth, and Corwin E. Smidt. "The Puzzle of Evangelical Protestantism." In *Religion and the Culture Wars,* ed. John C. Green, James L. Guth, Corwin E. Smidt, and Lyman A. Kellstedt. Lanham, Md.: Rowman and Littlefield, 1996.

Marsden, George, ed. *Evangelicalism and Modern America.* Grand Rapids, Mich.: W. B. Eerdmans, 1984.

Marty, Martin E. *The Righteous Empire: The Protestant Experience in America.* New York: Dial Press, 1970.

F

Fascism

Fascism, a political movement that seeks to induce the rebirth of the nation in a "new order" based on the coordination of all political, social, and cultural energies in a homogeneous national community, first arose as a radical alternative to liberalism and communism in some nation-states of the Christian world in the aftermath of the Great War (1914–1918). It went on to wreak immense destruction on human life and humanistic institutions as the ideology of Benito Mussolini's Italy and Adolf Hitler's Germany, especially during the Second World War (1939–1945).

The appeal of fascism, which, in the conditions of extreme economic hardship, social anxieties, and political crisis that prevailed in some liberal democracies during the 1920s and 1930s, could be considerable, derives from the core myth of the nation's imminent phoenix-like resurrection from the ashes of the decadent old order—a secular vision fundamentally antagonistic to any metaphysical religion. The antagonism was, however, generally obscured in the interwar period by fascism's success in presenting itself as an ersatz or civic religion based on the cult of the leader, the nation, and the state, and further obfuscated by the hostility to Marxism that it shared with Christianity (which in the past had been used to rationalize other European manifestations of authoritarianism and imperialism). These elements enabled fascist movements in several countries not only to appropriate the energies of Christianity as a moral authority but to convince many thousands (and, where they seized power, millions) of ostensibly devout Christians, including some high-ranking clergy, to become enthusiastic recruits to their cause and

hence prepared to connive with, or even participate personally in, acts of repression, violence, racial persecution, and war in blatant defiance of basic Christian values.

In the contemporary world some fascists still abuse Christian precepts and biblical references as part of the often phantasmagorical mix of ideas that they invoke to rationalize hatred, legitimize violence, and demonize the "other." Meanwhile, some radically fundamentalist forms of Christianity, Judaism, Islam, and Hinduism display several features reminiscent of interwar fascism, even if their underlying myth is distinctive, being based on a highly selective and politicized interpretation of revealed truth. But though the distinction between fascism and metaphysical religion can become blurred, a fundamental distinction remains: the belief of the fascist centers on the need for national or ethnic regeneration and not on obedience to a divine law.

Fascism as a Civic Religion

Although the precise definition of fascism has been the subject of considerable academic controversy, there are signs of a growing consensus outside the Marxist camp that it is best treated as a revolutionary form of nationalist ideology, with a specific dynamic of its own imparted by its profoundly antirational, self-consciously mythic character. The version of this approach that informs the present article identifies the ideological matrix underlying fascism's policies, propaganda, and actions as the fusion of the vision of imminent rebirth, or "palingenesis" (an archetypal human myth), with a virulently illiberal form of populist nationalism (a secular creed originating in modern Europe). This gives rise to a palingenetic variety of "ultranationalism" obsessed with the need for cleansing and renewal in every sphere of national life—political, social, economic, cultural, moral, and, in some cases, even biological (as in the case of the Nazi eugenics program). Accordingly, fascist activists believe that their political campaigning and paramilitary actions can arouse the latent patriotic fervor and sense of cultural belonging in the spiritually disoriented, disaffected, and "slumbering" masses to the point where the nation is rescued from the encroaching forces of decadence and given a new lease of life as the protagonist of an epic historical destiny.

In the aftermath of the Great War, in which mass mobilization in a climate of extreme patriotism and militarism had conditioned the lives of millions, it was all the more natural that fascism's pursuit of the utopia of national unity and greatness should lead it to adopt a militarized, overtly charismatic style of politics in which rhetoric, faith, and action prevailed over debate, understanding, and coherent party programs. Legitimacy of the state was no longer to be derived from constitutional procedures but from the intensity of the displays of mass enthusiasm that could be orchestrated in support of the movement. Fascism systematically replaced the "rational" processes of liberal democratic politics with a constant stream of carefully staged and deliberately ritualized events in which the general population could take part only as more or less fervent spectators.

The typical manifestation of this "spectacular" politics was the rally or "oceanic assembly" in which the scores of thousands who participated in person, and the millions more who listened to it on the radio or watched it in newsreels, celebrated both the symbolic deification of the leader as Providence's response to the plight of the nation and their own transformation into a national community united in mind and body within a single fate. When fascism held power in Italy (1925–1943) and Germany (1933–1945), the state itself became extensively "sacralized" through such techniques as the invention of national holidays and festivals to commemorate aspects of the fascist revolution; the mounting of propagandistic exhibitions sometimes attended by hundreds of thousands of people; the emphasis placed on sport, collective calisthenics, and choreographed parades; the pervasive use of symbols (the *fasces,* the swastika); the linking of all achievements in the technological, social, or political sphere with the nation's regeneration under fascism; the erection of civic buildings and creation of public spaces on a monumental and "timeless" scale; and the pervasive use of quasi-religious discourse in references to the new order, its institutions, leadership, and total claims on the life of the individual.

In anthropological terms, the goal of this concerted attempt to revolutionize the nation's culture within a generation was to induce all members of the national community to experience a sense of supra-individual, ritual, or "sacred" time in which the limitations and problems of individual existence were transcended. In this sense fascism not only sets out to overcome the atomization and skepticism fostered by liberalism, and to ward off the class division and internationalism fomented by socialism, but eventually to replace organized religion by becoming the sole source of social and ethical values in the modern age. Although it is legitimate to apply the term "civic religion" to fascism, it is misleading to treat it as a modern form of millennialism, since the fascist transformation of society is conceived as taking place imminently within secular historical time and solely through human—not divine—agency, however religious the discourse used to articulate it.

Fascists and the Church

Fascists can adopt three basic strategies in reacting to the presence of organized religion in the nation that they intend to "regenerate": persecution, compromise, and appropriation. The dominant Fascist tactic in Italy was compromise, while the policy of the National Socialist Party, or Nazis, in Germany, though ultimately geared toward persecution, oscillated between all three for reasons of expedience. A number of abortive fascist movements, however, arose in countries still dominated by Christianity to a greater extent than either Italy or Germany. Because they could not hope to gain a mass following by overtly repudiating Christian values, they set about appropriating them.

Thus the Spanish Falange and the Hungarian Arrow Cross embraced Catholicism, the South African Ossewabrandwag incorporated Dutch Reformed Christianity, the Finnish Isämaallinen Kansanliike (IKL) upheld the values of Lutheranism, while the Romanian Iron Guard stressed the role of the Orthodox Church to the point that its leader, Corneliu Codreanu, looked forward to the collective resurrection of all "true" Romanians on Judgment Day. In Belgium a radical form of reformist politics modeled on the style and ethos of Fascism arose that started as a form of right-wing political Catholicism, taking its name from the religious journal *Christus Rex*. When Belgium was occupied by the German Third Reich, Rexism's leader, Léon Degrelle, turned it into a fully Nazified movement and organized a volunteer legion of French-speaking Walloons in southern Belgium to fight alongside the Wehrmacht in the Third Reich's "European crusade" on the eastern front.

Even in France, where most fascist initiatives were secular in orientation, a leading ideologue of ultranationalist rebirth, Drieu la Rochelle, depicted the Third Reich as betokening the renaissance of the medieval age of Christian faith in a form perfectly adapted to the needs of the modern age, one which combined the spirituality of the First Reich (the Holy Roman Empire) with the industrial and military might of the Second Reich (1871–1918).

The attempted appropriation of Christianity by fascists to their own political ends should be seen in the context of three major currents in interwar Europe: first, the extensive conflation of "God" with "country" that had characterized the propaganda of all European states in the era of the First World War; second, the widespread rejection of laissez-faire capitalism, urban living, and individualism in favor of corporatist economics combined with a nostalgia for the apparent stability of rural life and traditional family values; finally, the crisis of belief in parliamentary democracy and party politics as the best basis of stable government and the search for a "third way" between liberalism and communism.

Mainstream Christianity was until 1945 closely associated with all three ideological currents—for example a papal encyclical of 1931, *Quadragesimo Anno,* officially endorsed the idea that the best economic basis for a Christian society was corporativism, a system in which sectors of economic activity were organized into corporations that harmonized the interests of workers, management, and the state. It thus became natural for every conservative regime (or, when it aped Fascism and Nazism, "parafascist" regime) to broaden its support by presenting itself as the upholder of Christian values and hence antimaterialist, anticommunist, and, not infrequently, anti-Semitic. As a result it was able frequently to win the all too often uncritical support of the church and much of the laity. Antonio Salazar's Portugal, Francisco Franco's Spain, Engelbert Dollfuss's Austria, Nicolas Horthy's Hungary, Joseph Pilsudski's Poland, Ion Antonescu's Romania, Ionnis Metaxas's Greece, Henri Pétain's Vichy regime in France, and most authoritarian regimes of the Balkan and Baltic states fit this pattern. Historians sometimes use the term "clerical fascism" to refer to regimes that fuse Catholicism with paternalistic authoritarianism, such as the corporate state established in Austria between 1933 and 1938. The

fact that its leader, Engelbert Dollfuss, was assassinated by Austrian Nazis underlines the necessity to distinguish modern forms of conservative dictatorship from fascism proper, which as a revolutionary movement is anticonservative and anticlerical at heart, despite its pragmatic need to forge alliances with conservative forces once in power.

Since the Second World War nonreligious forms of fascism have prevailed, whether neopagan (for example, based on Nazi Aryanism) or secular (for example, "scientifically" racist) ones. There are exceptions, however, such as the *Oeuvre Française,* a small fascist movement active in the 1990s, that defines the authentic Frenchness it wants to resurrect from the "chaos" of liberal democracy as a fusion of Christian faith with French language and culture. (This is clearly an attempt to brand Muslim fellow citizens as "aliens.") Meanwhile, building on a tradition established by the Ku Klux Klan, the United States has witnessed a proliferation of virulently racist forms of fascism partially rationalized through a highly selective and distorted interpretation of Scripture. Foremost among these are the Christian Identity movement, which fuses components of Christianity with Nazi Aryanism and some currents of the highly disparate survivalist and militia movements (not all of which are fascist).

The Catholic Church and Fascism

The response of Christians to fascism can take one of three basic forms. The most theologically consistent one, *opposition,* stems from the urge to act on the realization that fascism, however it seeks to disguise the fact and whatever enemies it has in common with organized religion, is the antithesis of everything Christianity stands for. The theologically and morally more questionable tactic of *collusion* is rooted in the pragmatic hope that in the prevailing historical circumstances the interests of the church may be better served by cooperating with a fascist regime than by adopting a hostile position, despite the radical divergence of the ultimate ends they serve. Finally, true to a long tradition in which divine precepts become conflated with an all-too-human creed of aggression and destruction, Christians may experience a deep-seated *confusion* of their faith with the fascist world view. An example is when the Slovak Republic—officially a "Christian national community" headed by a Catholic prelate—collaborated with the deportation of its Jewish population to the death camps during the Second World War. A parallel episode took place in another Nazi puppet regime, the Independent State of Croatia, where Roman

Catholic priests played a conspicuous role in the mass murder of Orthodox Christian Serbs, Jews, and gypsies by the Ustasha, a paramilitary organization dedicated to the cause of Croatian independence. This violent ultranationalist movement was underpinned by a mind-set and world view closely akin to those of fascists, but its goal was the creation of a nation-state through secession rather than the regeneration of an existing one.

All three permutations of the relationship are to be found under Italian Fascism. Although his movement was originally anticlerical, Mussolini quickly recognized that to establish the power base for the "new Italy" he had to compromise, which meant allying his vulnerable, numerically weak movement with the country's major conservative forces, foremost among which was the Catholic Church. As for his followers, only a few leading ideologues, notably Giovanni Gentile, the idealist philosopher of the "ethical state," were prepared publicly to attack Christianity as an obstacle to Italy's rebirth. The bulk of the Fascist leadership, though agnostic, instinctively embraced Catholicism both as an integral part of "Italianness" and as another manifestation of the "universal" civilizing mission of the Italian genius first displayed in the ancient Roman Empire. (Falangists cultivated an analogous myth about Spanish Catholicism.) Meanwhile, even the less secularized rank-and-file members of the Fascist Party and its affiliated mass organizations operated a sufficiently flexible, watered-down version of Christianity to experience no fundamental contradiction between their political and religious commitments or behavior as long as the church was prepared to endorse the Fascist revolution.

This the church was predisposed to do. A pact with Fascism offered the Vatican the unexpected opportunity to reoccupy the central place in the spiritual life of the nation, a role that had been denied it by the liberal *risorgimento,* or resurgence, which had finally unified Italy in 1870 in the teeth of papal opposition. The path to such a reconciliation was smoothed by the fact that it converged with Fascism on several core issues: antiliberalism, antisocialism, and a belief in family values, patriarchy, hierarchy, and imperialism. The result of Mussolini's eagerness to turn a potential antagonist into a major source of legitimacy at home and abroad (even if it flouted the "totalitarian" claims of his regime) was the Concordat and the Lateran Pacts agreed in February 1929 between the Italian state and the Vatican. In exchange for recognizing the Kingdom of Italy, and hence enabling Mussolini to take the credit for resolving the long-standing "Roman question" the papacy, among other things, exacted

recognition of the sovereignty of the Vatican state, the prerogative to assert its moral authority on issues such as divorce and abortion, and the right to teach Catholic doctrine in elementary and secondary schools. Perhaps most important for the future of Italy, the church was allowed to continue to run Catholic Action as a nationwide organization that, though strictly "nonpolitical," nevertheless had considerable potential for ensuring that a section of Italian youth grew up with non-Fascist values.

Whatever its fundamental misgivings about Fascism, the Vatican officially pursued a policy of active cooperation with it at least until the alliance between Mussolini and Hitler caused Italy to adopt racial and foreign policies that made further quiescence impossible. The attitude of individual Catholics to Fascism could vary considerably, however. In the 1920s an important constituency of anti-Fascism was formed by the radical faction of the Christian Democrat Italian Popular Party established in 1919. Seen as subversively socialist by both the Vatican and Mussolini, adherents of the Popular Party were first marginalized and then suppressed, and no significant anti-Fascist movement developed within the church to replace them. In July 1943 Mussolini was removed from power by the Fascist Grand Council and the king; he was imprisoned in a former hotel in a mountainous region of the Abruzzi in central Italy. Rescued in a daring SS operation four days after the armistice between Italy and the Allied forces was signed on September 8, he was installed on Hitler's orders as nominal head of the Italian Social Republic, which was effectively run by the Nazis as a puppet state. It was only then that anti-Fascist political Catholicism reemerged as a significant force by inspiring one of the most important partisan factions. The church thus helped to lay the ground for the domination of the new postwar Italian Republic by the Christian Democratic Party from 1946 to 1994.

At the other end of the spectrum, ardent ecclesiastical support for the regime in its formative years was provided by the Clerico-Fascists, a loose faction of Catholic clergy, intellectuals, and politicians who advocated collaboration with Mussolini's new Italy and helped prepare the ground for the Lateran Pacts. Their cause was taken up by high-ranking church dignitaries, such as Cardinal Schuster of Milan, who enthusiastically and unashamedly used his authority to contribute to the cult of Mussolini—the Duce—and the sacralization of the Fascist state. In the 1930s, however, except for an open rupture with Mussolini when he tried to curb the activities of Catholic Action, the Vatican itself came close to adopting a Clerico-Fascist position. Its representatives played a prominent part in the elaborate civic liturgy evolved by Fascism, and it gave its blessing to Italy's imperialist conquest of Abyssinia (now Ethiopia), in the name of Christian civilization, and to its participation in the Spanish civil war (ostensibly to defend Catholicism from Bolshevik atheism and anticlericalism).

Pope Pius XI, despite misgivings about the Fascist regime, was reluctant to compromise the Concordat, from which he expected so much, by using the creation of Italy's pact (Axis) with the overtly pagan Third Reich in the autumn of 1936 or the introduction in November 1938 of Italian anti-Semitic legislation as pretexts to condemn the regime outright. Something of the pope's true feelings can be inferred from his issue in 1937 of the encyclical *Mit Brennender Sorge* ("With burning sorrow") declaring the incompatibility of Nazi paganism and racism with Christianity, an implicit condemnation of Italy's Axis partner. The Vatican also vehemently protested against the Law for Defense of the Italian Race, but these protests centered on the way the veto on marriages between Italians and Jews constituted a violation of the Concordat, which recognized the primacy of the church on issues of marriage. Whether the pope's refusal to wage an all-out diplomatic and propaganda war on Nazism, the Axis, and Fascist racism is to be attributed to the legacy of Christian anti-Semitism and cowardice or prudence and pragmatism is still a matter of considerable scholarly controversy. The fact remains that by the death of Pius XI, in February 1939, the collusion between the Vatican and the Italian state had given way to open hostility.

The new pope, Pius XII, a germanophile, hinted at intentions to call a truce on the racial issue, raising hopes among Fascist leaders of *détente*. But though Mussolini's catastrophic decision to enter the Second World War as Hitler's ally prompted the same public displays of ecclesiastical approval and loyalty as had accompanied all of the regime's bellicose acts, behind the scenes the new pope had been using his authority to campaign against Italy's abandoning of its neutrality. His denunciation of racism—as in his first encyclical to the bishops of the world of October 1939—and sanctioning of thinly veiled polemics against the "pact of steel" in the Vatican organ *Osservatore Romano* led to a steady deterioration in the relations with the Fascist regime. In May 1940 Mussolini denounced the papacy as a "cancer which gnaws at our national life."

Pius XII, however, never took a public stand against the policies of the Third Reich, and although the Curia was kept meticulously informed about the mounting scale of atrocities being committed by the Third Reich, he never resorted to the weapon of excommunication against the many thousands of his flock (whose ranks technically included Hitler) directly or indirectly involved in genocide and state terror. The most explicit attack on the regime's expanding system of terror and mass murder was the papal message of Christmas 1942 that managed to condemn persecution on racial or political grounds without specifically mentioning the plight of the Jews.

The precise reason for the pope's reluctance to speak out unequivocally against the Third Reich's foreign and racial policies and Fascist Italy's participation in their implementation is still a matter of controversy. Certainly there is evidence that behind the scenes the pope had tried to dissuade Mussolini from entering the war and that in 1942 the Vatican initiated contacts with the British and U.S. governments as well as with anti-Fascist elements within Italy bent on overthrowing the regime and negotiating a peace treaty with the Allies. There were also moves by high-ranking church dignitaries to stop the deportations of Jews to the death camps from France, Croatia, and Italy. But direct appeals for the Vatican to use the full weight of its authority to condemn the extermination of the Jews, such as those made by the British ambassador to the Holy See, D'Arcy Osborne, fell on deaf ears.

The Christian Churches and the Third Reich

The failure of the Holy See to become a source of active resistance to the Rome-Berlin Axis did not help Germany's twenty-two million Catholics adopt an attitude of unequivocal opposition to Hitler, who was deeply conscious of the power of organized religion and took care in the formative stage of the regime to emphasize its commitment to "positive Christianity." In July 1933 a concordat was signed, mediated by one-time chairman of the by then dissolved (Catholic) Center Party and former chancellor, Franz von Papen, and the future Pius XII. Like the Italian Concordat, a degree of strictly apolitical autonomy was secured in return for recognition of the regime, thus making it all that much easier for patriotically inclined Catholics to experience no fundamental tension between their religious and their nationalist loyalties. Indeed, parts of the Catholic press called for active participation in the "national revolution," while the church gave official backing to the return of the occupied Saarland by France in 1935 and to the incorporation of Austria into Germany (the *Anschluss*) three years later. At no time did it avail itself of its still theoretically intact moral authority to mount a sustained campaign denouncing the regime's creation of a vast European empire based on organized, bureaucratized, and eventually industrialized inhumanity.

If the Catholic Church never became a major source of resistance to the Third Reich as a whole, however, it was prepared to show its opposition on specific issues. Such acts as the placing on the Catholic Index of forbidden books of Arthur Rosenberg's *The Myth of the Twentieth Century* (a major exposition of the Nazis' pagan, fiercely anti-Christian vision of the history of culture published in 1930) and the protracted struggle to defend the autonomy of the Catholic Action and the Catholic Youth League from state interference were sufficiently provocative to the regime for hundreds of clergy to be sentenced to terms in concentration camps during the thirteen-year reign of state terror.

A high point of coordinated Catholic opposition to Nazism was the nationwide reading from the pulpits of the encyclical *Mit Brennender Sorge* of March 1937. A minority of Catholics also took stands on their own initiative, often at great personal risk. The most famous examples are the three sermons preached in 1941 by the bishop of Münster, Clemens von Galen. (In fact, though the bishop's prominence protected him from retribution, several Catholics were executed for distributing his sermons.) In them he used theological arguments to attack the legitimacy of the police state, accusing of murder authorities which claimed the right to carry out the "mercy killing" of those deemed to have "a life unworthy of being lived." As a direct result of von Galen's intervention, the text of which was circulated throughout Germany, the euthanasia program was officially halted, and even in practice lost much of its momentum. The courage of the "lion of Münster" inspired many acts of heroism on the part of individual Catholics, a famous example of which was the abortive attempt by Hans and Sophie Scholl, a brother and sister who were leaders of the Munich University resistance circle, the White Rose, to stir their fellow students into revolt. They were arrested, tortured, and executed in February 1943. Meanwhile some former members of the Catholic workers' movement had joined forces with socialists to set up underground resistance to Hitler. In general, however, overt antisocialism and illiberalism combined with the covert nationalism and anti-Semitism of established Catholicism to preclude the possibility that German Catholics would turn against Hitler en masse.

Germany's Protestant churches were even less well placed to put up united resistance to Nazism. In the nineteenth cen-

Although the Vatican was criticized for failing to speak out against Nazi chancellor Adolf Hitler, many individual Catholics actively opposed Hitler's Third Reich, often at great personal risk.

tury, German Protestantism had closely identified itself with Prussian imperialism and the Second Reich. After 1918, with the exception of the weak liberal faction, its main groupings instinctively rejected the legitimacy of the "social democratic" Weimar Republic. Instead most aligned themselves with the ultraconservative, and fiercely antisocialist German National People's Party (DNVP) and with the presidency of Paul von Hindenburg, a First World War hero and incarnation of the nexus between army, aristocracy, monarchy, and Protestantism, which was the foundation of the Second Reich. They also hosted currents of ultranationalism and anti-Semitism, which associated the pluralism, individualism, materialism, and skepticism of modern urban existence with moral decay. As the republic started collapsing in the wake of the Great Depression in the 1930s, these tendencies predisposed political Protestantism to be drawn into the orbit of the National Socialist Party, not just as a shield against communism but as a party that campaigned for the rebirth of

Germany as an imperial power based on a healthy, organic, and spiritually reawakened national community. The path to collusion was smoothed by the influence of prominent Protestant academic theologians such as Gerhard Kittel, Paul Althaus, and Emanuel Hirsch. Their scholarship extensively rationalized the compatibility between belief in the reborn Christ and in the reborn German people, or *Volk*. As a result, the Executive Committee of the Protestant Churches, the *Kirchenausschuss*, saw no reason to use its authority to attack the National Socialists in the run-up to the crucial elections of 1933, in which the Nazis became the largest single party, hence securing Hitler the chancellorship. Its response to Hitler's victory was the promise of cooperation with the new government, which some members saw as a "gift of God."

Although Hitler feigned respect for the spiritual independence of the Protestant churches, in reality he intended to neutralize them as a rival claim on German "belief." At first he applied a covert strategy of "appropriation" *(Gleichschaltung)*, encouraging the "German Christians," a faction of Nazi activists who worked within the church and promoted an Aryanized perversion of Christianity, to infiltrate the Protestant hierarchy and help engineer the election of their candidate, Ludwig Müller, as the first "Reich bishop." However, the rigged victory of the German Christians in the church elections of July 1933 provoked a backlash led by two pastors, Martin Niemöller and Dietrich Bonhoeffer, who rallied the support of a third of the Protestant clergy in Germany to create the "Confessional Church," a name chosen to indicate that it intended to stay true to its "confession," or religious principles, and hence preserve its religious autonomy from the inroads of the state. Hitler's response was to turn to persecution. Between 1935 and 1938 several thousand pastors, priests, and nuns were arrested for criticizing Nazi neopaganism, for disloyalty to the regime, or on trumped-up charges of immorality. Indeed, the offensive launched against Christianity during the war in the new province of Germany, the "Warthegau," which had been carved out of occupied Poland, was probably a harbinger of the fate that eventually awaited the churches in Germany too had the Third Reich been victorious.

For the time being, however, the main weapon deployed against Protestantism was suppression: under the Reich Church Ministry set up in 1935 all church activities and publications were scrutinized for anything that could be construed as political interference with or veiled criticism of the regime. This muzzling tactic was generally successful. While infighting over theological issues between the increasingly factionalized German Christians and the Confessional Church continued until 1945, on only a few occasions did Protestantism take a principled stand against the inhumanity of the Third Reich. An important instance of this was the Confessional Church's detailed memorandum of June 1936 (not originally intended for publication) attacking the regime's racial ideology and anti-Semitism, the cult of the leader, and the unaccountability of the concentration camp system and the Gestapo to the rule of law. About a million copies were circulated, and three-quarters of Confessional pastors read it from the pulpit. Even more courageous was the memorandum of the Prussian synod of the Confessional Church of October 1943; it condemned the regime's policies to exterminate people on whatever grounds as "wielding a sword which is not given to the state by God" and declared the lives of the people of Israel to be "sacred to Him." Such rare moments when genuine Protestant faith triumphed over ideological and moral disorientation did little or nothing to slow down the Nazi juggernaut of mass destruction.

The Corruption of Religion by Fascism

A year into the Second World War, 95 percent of Germans still claimed to be members of a Christian denomination. Given the weakness of organized Christian resistance to the regime, this number suggests that compromise, denial, and double-think had become behavioral norms for the mass of the population. Only a minute proportion of theologians, clergy, and lay Christians, Catholic or Protestant, were prepared to draw the logical consequences of their faith by taking personal stands against the regime or joining the resistance movement. An outstanding exception was the Lutheran theologian Karl Barth, who scrupulously spelled out the logical consequence of the Christian faith, namely unequivocal rejection of Nazism, in his journal *Theologische Existenz Heute* ("Theological Existence Today") until he was forced to resign his professorship at the University of Bonn and return to his native Switzerland for refusing to declare an oath of allegiance to Hitler. It must be said that the cost of defying the regime was enormously high: although Clemens August von Galen, the bishop of Münster, was too famous to be touched, three priests who circulated the text of his sermons were executed and draconian punishments were imposed on some civilians suspected of tacitly supporting him. Even being in the public eye did not spare Niemöller seven years internment in concentration camps (1938–1945). Nor did it save Bonhoeffer, who, convinced that the defeat of his nation was to be preferred to the destruction of Christian civilization, joined the resistance, only to be arrested and condemned to death by the infamous "People's Court," a sentence carried out in the very last days of the war.

Bonhoeffer's personal courage and his efforts to formulate a doctrinal rationale for the resistance to the Nazi terror state were to help inspire the anti-authoritarian stands taken by some clergy in Latin America and the Soviet Empire in the years after the war. The overriding impression created by the responses of Christian communities in the face of fascist or parafascist regimes is less one of cowardice, however, than of a general failure of both the laity and the clergy at every level to adopt an appropriate moral position on them. This failure was openly acknowledged in the Stuttgart Confession of Guilt published by the Protestant churches at the end of the war, and although the Vatican has never formally conceded the inadequacy of its attempts to curb the inhumanities committed by the Axis powers, mainstream Catholicism has since 1945 flowed along democratic rather than authoritarian channels.

Symptomatic of the radical shift of postwar Vatican thinking toward a liberal humanist position was the publication of the papal encyclical *Nostra Aetate* ("In this age of ours") in October 1965. It declared a sense of solidarity with non-Christian religions, stressed the common heritage of Christians and Jews, and condemned "every form of persecution against whomsoever it may be directed." Nevertheless, the history of the Christian churches' relationship with fascism between 1922 and 1945 provides a disturbing case study in how insidiously easy it is for religious convictions to become corrupted into an ideological force that compounds rather than combats the organized inhumanity of the modern state.

See also *Anti-Semitism; Barth, Karl; Bonhoeffer, Dietrich; Christian democracy; Civil religion; Colonialism; Ethnicity; Fundamentalism; Genocide and "ethnic cleansing"; Germany; Holocaust; Italy; Millennialism; Nationalism; Papacy; Spain; Survivalism; Vatican Council, Second; Yugoslavia.*

Roger Griffin

BIBLIOGRAPHY

Buchanan, Tom, and Martin Conway, eds. *Political Catholicism in Europe, 1918–1965.* Oxford: Clarendon Press, 1996.
Chadwick, W. O. *Britain and the Vatican during the Second World War.* Cambridge: Cambridge University Press, 1986.
Eriksen, Robert. *Theologians under Hitler.* New Haven and London: Yale University Press, 1985.
Gentile, Emilio. *The Sacralization of Politics in Fascist Italy.* Cambridge: Harvard University Press, 1996.
Griffin, Roger D. *The Nature of Fascism.* London: Routledge, 1993.
———. *International Fascism: Theories, Causes, and the New Consensus.* London: Arnold, 1998.
Housden, Martyn. *Resistance and Conformity in the Third Reich.* London and New York: Routledge, 1997.
Michaelis, Meir. *Mussolini and the Jews.* Oxford: Clarendon Press, 1978.
Kent, Peter C. *The Pope and the Duce.* London: Macmillan, 1981.
Pollard, John. "Fascism." In *New Dictionary of Catholic Social Thought,* edited by J. Dwyer. Collegeville, Minn.: Michael Glazier.
———. *The Vatican and Italian Fascism, 1929–1932.* Cambridge: Cambridge University Press, 1985.
Scholder, Klaus, *The Churches and the Third Reich.* 2 vols. London: SCM Press, 1987–1988.
Wolff, R. J., and J. K. Hoensch, eds. *Catholics, the State, and the European Right.* Boulder, Colo.: Social Science Monographs, 1987.

Feminism

Feminism can be most simply defined as the belief that women have been thought to be (or have been treated as if they were) secondary or inferior to men and that this situation must change. This leaves room for many kinds of feminism, and indeed, feminist movements have been extremely varied in their diagnoses of the present situation and the prescriptions they offer for its improvement. But whatever the precise content they give to their agenda for social change, feminists have insisted that the full range of social institutions be confronted. Thus, although feminism is often thought of in reference to legal and policy issues (such as the Equal Rights Amendment, abortion rights, or educational opportunities for girls), feminists find work to be done elsewhere as well. As the feminist slogan goes, "the personal is political": social institutions make their impact felt in personal life, and vice versa. No sector of society, then, is off-limits for feminist reform.

Certainly, feminists have always targeted religion as one bastion of male power. Feminists have consistently demanded that male-dominated religions transform themselves such that women are given opportunities for religious leadership, theologies include the female or feminine, and scriptures be interpreted to emphasize women's equality within the religious tradition and before God. This effort to make organized religions more favorable to women is probably the most common way in which feminists have interacted with religion, but there are other ways as well. Some feminists have given up on traditional, patriarchal religions altogether, saying that they are nothing more than an elaborate cosmic justification for male dominance. Such feminists have sometimes worked to create new religions that they believe to be feminist at their core; at other times they have sought to eradicate the hold of religion on people's consciousness altogether. Finally, many feminists have used religion—traditional or otherwise—as a power base from which to demand social reforms in women's interest, stressing themes within a specific religious tradition that lend divine support to their struggle. These initiatives are not mutually exclusive; individual feminists often use one or more of these strategies simultaneously.

Early Feminism

These are approaches that have an extensive history. As long as there have been women seeking spiritual growth within religious communities or institutions, there has been some form of feminist agitation for women's rights. Early Buddhist women, for example, sought to establish spiritual orders for women and to ensure that women, like men, were given opportunities to pursue enlightenment. French poet Christine de Pisan (1364–c. 1430), writing in the late fourteenth century, argued for women's rights from a Christian standpoint. And in the United States, women such as the Puritan Anne Hutchinson (c. 1591–1643) exercised religious leadership, sometimes in vocal and controversial ways, even before this was generally considered proper.

In spite of these precedents, feminist criticism of religion as such did not gain significant momentum until the nineteenth century, and at that time it was monopolized by Christians. The rising tide of Christian evangelicalism gave women new opportunities to become involved in missionary societies and in social movements such as abolitionism and temperance. The demand for charismatic speakers meant that many women, both black and white, were preaching (although they were rarely formally ordained). This situation, coupled with the emergence of the women's movement in the mid-nineteenth century, left the field ripe for feminist religious activism.

The Declaration of Sentiments and Resolutions, written by the suffragist Elizabeth Cady Stanton (1815–1902) and adopted by the women's convention held in Seneca Falls, New York, in 1848, is often said to have launched the women's movement in America. Modeled on the Declaration of Independence, the connection of the Declaration of Sentiments to political activism in the United States has always been clear. But what has been perhaps less noticed, but equally significant, is that like the Declaration of Independence, the Declaration of Sentiments relies on religious lan-

guage to justify its advocacy of women's rights. "Woman is man's equal," the declaration claimed, and "was intended to be so by the Creator." And yet the Declaration of Sentiments does not spare the Christian Church from criticism; among the grievances it articulates against male dominance is the subordination of women within the church and the "perverted application of the Scriptures" in support of this subordination.

This combination of reliance on religious authority and critique of it was also present in *The Woman's Bible,* a scriptural commentary compiled by Stanton and others in the late nineteenth century (and which presaged later interest in feminist biblical criticism). Concentrating on those passages of the Christian Bible that had been most damaging to women's status, the authors offered commentary, wherever possible turning these texts to serve feminist interests. For example, Stanton interpreted the first creation story in Genesis—where God creates human beings in "his" own image, male and female—as an indication that God was "himself" both male and female.

In the suffragist politics of the late nineteenth and early twentieth centuries, feminists drew on religious resources to strengthen their cause. Some, favoring the approach pioneered by Stanton and her fellow activist Matilda Joslyn Gage (1826–1898), relied on a vision of women's religious equality in their demand for political equality, while others, like Frances Willard (1839–1898), longtime head of the Women's Christian Temperance Union, used more traditional stereotypes of femininity to argue that society needed the input—via the vote—of women's "special" perspectives. Suffrage, like the union's campaign for temperance, expanded to include other social reforms that we today would recognize as feminist, such as day care for young children, homes for unwed or impoverished mothers, medical clinics for urban women, and the "rescuing" of prostitutes. But the battle for suffrage was hard won, and once accomplished, feminist religious activism lay more or less dormant for several decades, only to break free again with new vigor in the late 1960s and early 1970s.

Twentieth-century Feminism

This wave of feminist activism, still flourishing today, has stressed the same points raised by nineteenth-century feminists, and added new ones as well. It has broadened to include women from religions other than Christianity—most prominently, Jewish women—and has increasingly been both strengthened and challenged by the feminist (or womanist, or *mujerista*) religious activism of African American, Hispanic, and Asian American women, who are dominantly Christian.

Attempts to secure equality for women within American churches and synagogues led in the 1970s to demands for women's ordination in Jewish and Christian movements and denominations. Some denominations, such as the Baptists, Congregationalists, and Unitarians, had begun to ordain women even before 1900, but most excluded women from the clergy well into the 1970s. By the late 1980s, however, most denominations—with the exception of Roman Catholicism, Orthodox Judaism, Eastern Orthodox Christianity, and some of the more conservative Protestant denominations (including Southern Baptists, Mormons, and Seventh-day Adventists)—began to ordain women. Once women were admitted to the clergy, they rushed in with perhaps more enthusiasm than had been expected, quickly forming significant minorities—and even majorities—in more liberal denominations.

This era also saw significant activism around the issue of inclusive language. Many prayer books, liturgies, and hymn books were rewritten in an effort to include women as equal spiritual seekers. Words like *mankind* were changed to *humanity,* and the ritual invocation of female religious figures (saints, matriarchs, and heroines of the faith) alongside that of male figures was encouraged. Particularly in the 1980s, these publications made their way into American congregations, where sometimes bitterly unhappy congregants were forced to learn new words to their favorite prayers and hymns. Feminist successes were abundant in this arena, but far from complete: many prayer books, hymnals, and the like have retained the male generic to this day.

Feminists also drew attention to Scripture, calling on the one hand for new translations, where these seemed warranted and, on the other hand, for biblical interpretations that, like Stanton's *Woman's Bible,* removed the sting of divine commands that subordinated women to men. Within Christianity this enterprise embraced an entire spectrum, from biblical literalists—who could soften but not eliminate blows against women—to textual critics who dispensed with any notion of direct divine authorship of Scripture, freely separating the wheat of those passages that supported women's freedom from the chaff of those that denied it. Jewish feminists, with a tradition of midrash (commentaries on Scripture) behind them, have had a relatively freer hand in reinterpreting and retelling key biblical stories but a perhaps more difficult task in working around Jewish biblical law,

which is still held to be authoritative by Conservative and Orthodox Jews.

Perhaps the greatest challenge for both Jewish and Christian feminists has been confronting the maleness of God. Although both traditions have, at times, emphasized that God is neither male nor female, they have also persistently referred to God with male pronouns, and even justified, with theological argument, the practice of doing so. For example, God has been said to be male in relation to humanity's femaleness, or to be uniquely paternal in his relationship to humans. Feminists have dealt with this situation in several ways. At times they have struggled to avoid the use of gendered pronouns altogether (repeating the word *God,* or using terms like *Godself*), making God as gender-neutral as possible. At other times, they have retained male pronouns for God but offered female ones for another member of the Christian Trinity, usually the Holy Spirit. They have also described God with female metaphors—some of them drawn from Scripture—saying that God is like a woman in childbirth or that God nurtures humanity as a woman suckles a child. Finally, there have been efforts to reconstruct female deities or divine powers, such as the Sophia of Hebrew and Christian Scriptures or the cabalistic Shechinah, and to worship God with these names.

In addition to working with preexisting materials, religious feminists have also improvised, creating new stories, rituals, and religious communities that they believe work to enhance women's spirituality. Noncanonical stories have been retold: for example, that Eve, the dutiful wife, was preceded in the Garden of Eden by Lilith, who was more of an upstart. Where male-only rituals have existed, religious feminists have created complementary ones for females. For example, in the Jewish tradition, where formerly only boys were honored with religious ritual at birth (circumcision) and puberty (bar mitzvah), girls are now frequently given ceremonies at birth (in which they are given their Hebrew names) and coming-of-age rituals (bat mitzvot) at puberty. Additional rituals with no male counterparts have been created by religious feminists, sometimes to celebrate women's life-cycle events such as childbirth, menstruation, and menopause. New, all-female religious communities, such as Women-Church (an egalitarian feminist group composed mainly of Roman Catholics) or Rosh Chodesh groups (which mark the Jewish new moon with a women's ritual), have been created broadly within the bounds of established religion.

Religious feminists have networked across denominations

to share existing resources and develop new ones, sometimes finding common cause across differing religions as well. Increasingly, American women have attempted to extend their feminist religious insights to other religions besides Judaism and Christianity. They have sought to build a more global network of religious feminists. Efforts in this direction are still preliminary, but there are growing international coalitions of feminists from a variety of religious backgrounds. In addition, some American women, raised as Jews or Christians, have taken up Eastern religions such as Buddhism and sought to reform these as well in a more feminist vein.

All these manifestations of feminist religious activism occur within the religions that feminists deem patriarchal. But some can find no compelling reason to stay within patriarchal religions, preferring a more secular (or less obviously religious) approach to feminism. For example, Sonia Johnson, who was branded a heretic by the Mormon Church, used her notoriety to launch an assault on patriarchal religions. Mary Daly, who in 1968 wrote *The Church and the Second Sex,* which attempted to make a home for women within Roman Catholicism, in 1971 led an "exodus" from Christianity when she preached a sermon at Harvard Memorial Church encouraging women to leave patriarchal religions behind them. Although both of these women were steeped in religious concepts and language as young women, and continue to draw on this background and interact with other religious feminists, neither has rushed to invent a new, more feminist religion.

Others, however, have done just that. Respecting the power of religion, they believe that it cannot be abandoned but must instead be recreated in new, nonpatriarchal forms. Such feminists work to create new religions or spiritualities that do not share what they believe to be the debilities of patriarchal religions. The most prominent example of this religious creativity in the United States is the feminist spirituality movement.

The feminist spirituality movement began in the early 1970s concurrently with feminist reforms within established religions. Drawing on neopagan and New Age religions, feminist spirituality's key innovations were to worship a goddess (or goddesses) and nature and to exclude men (at least initially). Insisting that feminist principles must be the cornerstone of religion, and not an elaborate patch on a fundamentally patriarchal structure, spiritual feminists designed their new religion with women's needs and interests as their first criterion. Although the feminist spirituality movement

has set itself up in opposition to established religions, it actually works to a large degree in concert with Jewish and Christian feminism (and, to a lesser extent, with Buddhist and other religious feminisms). Women sometimes participate in both a church or synagogue and in a ritual circle of goddess-worshiping women. And even though some individual women do not claim a joint allegiance to patriarchal religions and feminist spirituality, religious feminists as a group have worked across this divide. Jewish and Christian feminists have adapted theologies and rituals pioneered by spiritual feminists; in turn, spiritual feminists have often supported the work of Jewish and Christian feminists though not claiming it as their own.

Most religious feminism since 1970 has characterized itself as reforming patriarchal religions, but it has also seen religion itself as a power base upon which feminism can stand. Claiming that these religions are—or can be, or should be—fundamentally committed to human equality, feminists have sometimes used religious ethics and rhetoric in their organizing, hoping to mobilize religious congregations in the service of feminist political goals. In this area feminists have been inspired by the earlier example of black theology and the civil rights movement, which found in the very religions that were oppressing African-American communities the resources to call for an end to this oppression. As a consequence of this connection, no doubt, those feminists who have been most adept at seeing patriarchal religions themselves as agents of social change have been women of color. No less concerned about sexism than their white counterparts, African American, Hispanic, and Asian American feminists have constructed theologies that situate race more squarely in the middle as a concern every bit as pressing as sex discrimination (or more so).

Politics and religion can, of course, never be truly separated. Little can prove this better than feminist activism within and against certain practices of organized religion, religious feminism outside its boundaries, and the grounding of political feminism—at least at times—on religious principles.

See also *Gender; Paganism*

Cynthia Eller

BIBLIOGRAPHY

Daly, Mary. *Beyond God the Father.* Boston: Beacon Press, 1973.
Eller, Cynthia. *Living in the Lap of the Goddess: The Feminist Spirituality Movement in America.* Boston: Beacon Press, 1995.
Gross, Rita M. *Feminism and Religion: An Introduction.* Boston: Beacon Press, 1996.

Isasi-Díaz, Ana María, and Yolanda Tarango. *Hispanic Women, Prophetic Voice in the Church: Toward a Hispanic Women's Liberation Theology.* Minneapolis: Fortress Press, 1988.

King, Ursula. *Feminist Theology from the Third World: A Reader.* Maryknoll, N.Y.: Orbis Books, 1994.

Plaskow, Judith. *Standing Again at Sinai: Judaism from a Feminist Perspective.* New York: HarperCollins, 1990.

Ruether, Rosemary Radford. *Women-Church: Theology and Practice of Feminist Liturgical Communities.* New York: Harper and Row, 1985.

Schüssler-Fiorenza, Elisabeth, ed. *Searching the Scriptures: A Feminist Introduction.* New York: Crossroad, 1993.

Stanton, Elizabeth Cady, et al. *The Woman's Bible.* New York: Arno Press, 1974 [1895, 1898].

Williams, Delores. *Sisters in the Wilderness: The Challenge of Womanist God-Talk.* Maryknoll, N.Y.: Orbis Books, 1993.

Foreign Mission Society

See *Maryknoll*

France

France is a traditionally Roman Catholic country in Western Europe now adjusting to the growth of other religions among its population. The first phrase of the French constitution—"France is a secular and indivisible Republic"—confirms with exceptional solemnity that the secularism of the state is a fundamental part of the republican tradition. This notion may appear curious and sometimes contradictory to the ideal of tolerance of a democratic and pluralist society. To understand its true significance, one must remember that the secular ideal originated in the long struggle of French kings to escape the yoke of the Catholic Church. Secularism is not opposed to religion as such but to all the forms of clerical control that a particular religion wishes to exercise over a political power.

Catholicism and French Society

On the eve of the Revolution of 1789, Catholicism pervaded French society. It legitimated political institutions, governed collective life, and controlled the registry office and teaching, medical, and social service institutions. In a matter of months (May–September 1789) the Old Regime collapsed and the constitutional monarchy that followed immediately made the political system secular. The legitimacy of the monarchy lost its religious foundation—from then on it was based on a contract struck between the king and the people.

Citizens now defined themselves as belonging to the nation as a community, and their religious affiliation could not be used to prevent them from participating in politics. The proclamation of the principle of religious freedom in Article 10 of the Declaration of the Rights of Man and of the Citizen (1789), the preamble to the revolutionary constitution, was a decisive step in this political transformation. Religious minorities were gradually granted all the rights associated with citizenship. The rights of Protestants to vote and to be elected to public office—as well as their admission to all employment—were rapidly established. Jewish emancipation was effected in September 1791.

The constitution adopted in September 1791 guaranteed freedom of religion, but the very question of religious freedom raised the issue of the status of Catholicism in society. The national assembly repeatedly voted down church demands that Catholicism be recognized as the state religion. The long symbiosis between the Catholic institution and the absolute monarchy leant to political modernization a dimension of religious conflict that divided the church itself. Radicalization of the opposing positions came to mean for each the exclusion of its adversary—the republic could triumph only in bringing down the church, but this constituted a victory of one-half of France over the other.

But the revolutionaries did not question the importance of religion in society. Their objective was to join the ecclesiastical institution with civil society. The 1789 Civil Constitution of the Clergy obliged priests to swear an oath of loyalty to the new regime, splitting them between those who rallied around the new regime and those who increasingly fought it. French Catholicism divided into two factions. The hardening of resistance to the new regime, the increasing repression of those opponent clergy, and the authoritarian radicalization of the revolutionary regime drew France into a religious conflict of astounding violence. Many clergy were among those who lost their heads to the guillotine during the Reign of Terror (1793–1794).

Until the end of the nineteenth century, the struggle against the political and social power of the Catholic Church was at the center of the republican effort to build a nation. The 1905 Separation of the Church and the State law, approved in a climate of ideological war, constituted at the time the final struggle in this confrontation and the begin-

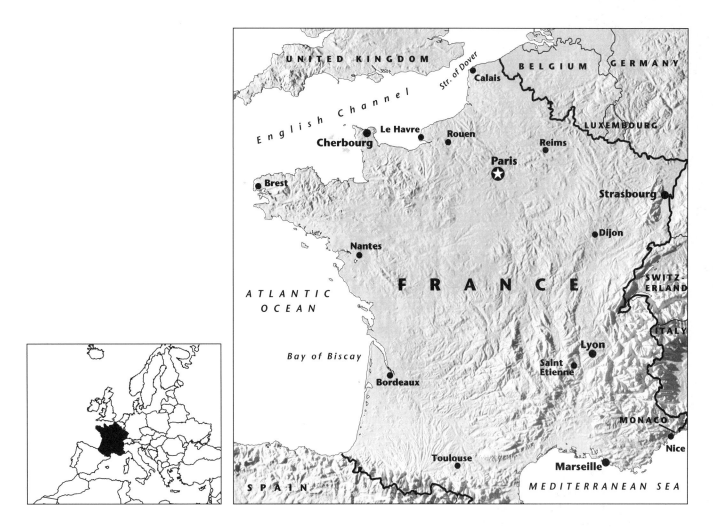

ning of a reconciliation made possible when the Catholic masses sided in force with the republic. Until World War II, however, French political life carried traces of this religious struggle. On one side was Catholic France, traditional and politically conservative; on the other was a republican and progressive France, where the Protestant French minority and the French Jews freed by the revolution found their place.

Paradoxically the republican culture born of opposition to the power of the Catholic Church was itself constructed along the lines of the Catholic culture that had typified the nation for centuries. The educational and moral work of the Third Republic (1870–1940) and the ceremonies, symbols, temples, and republican processions of the nineteenth century are a form of what British sociologist David Martin has called Catholicism without Christianity. The political victory of the republic did not signify the end of a religious France but the emergence of a specific identity: that of a secular country with a Catholic culture.

Modern France

What remains of this long and turbulent history today? The passionate episodes that regularly shake up French political life (the dramatic political conflict over the wearing of the Islamic head covering by Muslim students in the public schools, secular mobilization against the pope's 1996 visit to France to commemorate the baptism of Frankish king Clovis I in 496, and so on) should not be misunderstood—the war of two Frances is over. There are many reasons for this pacification. The first—along historical lines—was the stabilization of the republican regime and the definitive adherence of Catholics to the republic, which was pledged in the trenches of World War I. In this respect the Catholic hierarchy had clearly renounced all of its direct political role (no bishops have intervened in elections since 1965).

Even if the vote of regular, practicing Catholics normally goes to the conservative right and the center right, the distinguishing trait of the last thirty years has been the pluralistic politics of French Catholicism as a whole. Regions strongly associated with the Catholic tradition that moved politically to the left (Brittany, Alsace) were the deciding factor in the election of socialist president François Mitterand in 1981. Today the political role of the Catholic Church is identified with affirming moral values that Catholics believe should preside over public life. For example, French bishops have been driven to vigorously denounce the beliefs of xenophobes, protectionists, and the anti-Semites of the extreme right headed by National Front Party founder Jean-Marie Le Pen.

This moral judiciary advocated by the Catholic Church but also embraced by Protestant and Jewish minorities is important to the redefinition of relations between secularism and religion under way today. The principal question is no longer the independence of the state from the Catholic Church. It is how the state can function to integrate the republic in a multicultural France in which Islam, with four billion followers, has become the second religion in the nation. In this new age, new alliances are established that form new connections between religion and politics.

See also *Anticlericalism; Catholicism, Roman; Europe, Western; Islam.*

Danièle Hervieu-Léger

BIBLIOGRAPHY

Baubert, Jean. *Vers un nouveau pacte laïque?* Paris: Seuil, 1990.
Donegani, Jean Marie. *La Liberté de choisir. pluralisme religieux et pluralism politique dans le catholicisme français contemporain.* Paris: Presse de la Fondation Nationale des Sciences Politiques, 1993.
Hervieu-Léger, Danièle. "The Past in the Present: Redefining Laïcité in Multicultural France." In *The Limits of Social Cohesion: Conflict and Mediation in Pluralist Societies,* edited by Peter L. Berger. Boulder, Colo.: Westview Press, 1998.
Poulat, Emile. *Liberté, laïcité. La guerre des deux France et le principe de modernité.* Paris: Cerf-Cujas, 1987.

Freedom of religion

Religious freedom is a two-pronged idea, granting people the right to practice their faith as they choose and to be free from supporting an established religion. More than two hundred years ago Thomas Jefferson penned a classic description of religion freedom: "No man shall be compelled to frequent or support any religious worship, place, or ministry whatsoever, nor shall be enforced, restrained, molested, or burthened in his body or goods, nor shall otherwise suffer on account of his religious opinions or beliefs; but that all men shall be free to profess, and by argument to maintain, their opinions in matters of religion, and that the same shall in no wise diminish, enlarge, or affect their civil capacities." Jefferson's definition expresses an ideal yet to be realized.

From time immemorial religions—with their rites, rituals, moral codes, and creeds—have been an integral if not central component of every culture and thus a major concern of every government. Until the past three centuries of Western civilization, there was no such thing as a secular realm in which people had choices.

Religion and culture were so intimately intertwined through most of human history that it was inconceivable for any member of a society not to share its religion. Religion was the fabric of tribal life. Nonbelievers who spoke up were probably killed or driven out, but they were so few in number that we have no records. Conflicts between religious groups usually occurred when one people or tribe conquered another, as when Rome conquered Palestine in the first century B.C. or Muslims invaded Hindu India in the eleventh century A.D. Conflict occasionally arose when a new indigenous religion developed and gained adherents, as when Christianity arose within Palestine in the first century A.D. or Islam arose in Arabia in the seventh century. Normally, conquered people were required to accept the religion of the conqueror or, if they maintained their own religious beliefs and practices, to pay tribute. After a few decades uniformity was reestablished and conflict disappeared.

Christian Beginnings

When Christianity originated in Judaea and Galilee, it was a heretical sect that took root within a despised minority, the Jewish people, who had only recently been conquered by the Roman Empire. Early Christians had reason to respect, or at least accommodate the empire, if only to gain protection from Jewish leaders. Early Christians introduced a number of radical ideas, many attributed directly to Jesus. Among these was the admonition, "Give unto Caesar the things that are Caesar's and unto God the things that are God's." (Mark 12:17) It was Roman custom to have its emperors identified with the gods, so a split between the deity and the earthly ruler was a radical idea. This caused ambiguous relationships in the late Roman Empire. On the one hand, Christians could be loyal Roman citizens, for "their kingdom was not of this world" and therefore not in competition with Rome. On the other hand, it was a limited loyalty, a distinction between spiritual and temporal domains described and defended in St. Augustine's *City of God,* written in the early fifth century. Here were the seeds of a separation of church and state idea that took centuries to germinate.

When Christians gained hegemony in the fourth century, after the emperor Constantine's conversion, they reverted to traditional patterns by establishing Christianity as the official faith of the empire, albeit with a two-swords doctrine: the Holy Roman Empire theoretically consisted of spiritual and temporal realms that were separate but coordinate. Much of medieval history is the story of a struggle for supremacy between secular rulers and popes and between contending "Christian" nations, primarily France, England, Spain, and the Habsburg empire, with the Italian city-states, Portugal, and the small Germanic states playing lesser roles.

Heretics and schismatics were widely persecuted or protected, depending on the political circumstances of individual rulers and the power of various popes, cardinals, and bishops. Freedom of religion for individuals was not given serious consideration.

Reformation and Enlightenment

The Protestant Reformation in the sixteenth century, led by Martin Luther, John Calvin, Henry VIII, and others, initiated profound shifts in Western political thinking—particularly in the area of religious ideas. Luther's original protest was strictly against the established church, both its corruption and its doctrine. He preached the priesthood of all believers and each person's ability to interpret the Bible. He rejected the two-swords theory, substantially strengthening the hand of secular rulers. These new ideas reinvigorated an older notion of the divine right of kings, the belief that kings rule by direct authority from God, not from the will of the people. Early Calvinist thought followed in the same vein, although keeping the concept of separation of church and state, with each institution having distinct rights and duties.

Protestantism quickly spread and split into denominations—Lutheran, Calvinist, Presbyterian, Anglican, Puritan, Dutch Reformed, and the more radical Anabaptists. Ironically, the Reformation also triggered the Counter Reformation, a moral cleansing and rejuvenation of the Roman Catholic Church. The intellectual and spiritual turmoil of the period brought social upheaval and persecutions as people began to think and argue about their faiths. Lutherans and Catholics reached an accommodation in the Peace of Augsburg (1555), agreeing to the principle that each ruler could choose the religion of the people within his region *(cuius regio, eius religio)*. This strengthened belief in the divine right of kings and worked against any idea of individual freedom of religion. It also backfired.

The idea of toleration, a critical step on the way to freedom of religion, was all but inconceivable to rulers except as an expedient to be espoused in times of political weakness. It was in such a time that the Edict of Nantes, proclaiming toleration for Calvinists in France, was decreed in 1598, only to be revoked by Louis XIV in 1685. The French phrase *une roi, une loi, une foi*—"one king, one law, one faith"—captured the conventional wisdom of the time. All three elements were seen as essential to maintain national unity and identity.

Attempts to enforce uniformity of belief within political realms were simply not compatible with a core Protestant principle—freedom of each person to read and interpret the Bible for him or herself. Reformers naively believed all persons of good will would interpret the Bible the same. That was not the case. The principle that rulers could choose their citizens' religion led not to peace but to civil war, suppression of minorities, assassinations, forced conversions, emigrations, expulsions, and searing hatreds that poisoned Western civilization for generations. These disasters still influence our politics.

Religious wars and the ideas that caused them began to change in the seventeenth century as a flurry of writers, primarily but not exclusively English, began to rethink the relationships between kings and subjects. Political philosophers began thinking in terms of social contracts as a more legitimate basis for governing than divine right. Contracts imply mutual responsibilities and limits between ruled and ruler. Thomas Hobbes (1588–1679) and Jean-Jacques Rousseau (1712–1778) used the idea as a starting point for very different philosophies, but they helped the idea gain legitimacy. John Milton penned a plea for freedom of the press (except for Catholics and atheists) in his classic *Areopagitica* (1644). In a lesser known but influential work, *Treatise of Civil Power in Ecclesiastical Causes* (1659), he argued against a professional clergy and in favor of private interpretation of Scripture according to each person's conscience. His work was followed in short order by that of John Locke. In *Two Treatises on Government* (1689), published a year after the Glorious Revolution of 1688, in which the English Parliament replaced James II with William and Mary, Locke attacked the very idea of a divine right of kings. Substituting instead the idea of a social contract between ruled and rulers, he argued that religious freedom was a natural right which it was government's duty to protect.

Although these ideas did not immediately take hold in England or on the Continent, they were profoundly influential with another group of emerging leaders, the founders of the American Republic.

The American Colonial Experience

During their almost 170 years before independence, the American colonies participated in many of England's religious persecutions on a smaller scale. The first Puritans had come to the New World seeking religious freedom for themselves. They had no intention of extending that freedom to others with different religious views. The smaller scale was due partially to the ease with which dissenters could move to other colonies or to the frontier. But religious tensions and hostility were never far below the surface, especially as religious enthusiasts such as Baptists and Methodists engaged in proselytizing among adherents of the more established Anglican and Congregational Churches.

Two of America's classic religious documents grew out of this tension. Thomas Jefferson first wrote a bill for establishing religious freedom in 1779, but it was not passed by the Virginia legislature until 1786. It still reads so well as a general statement of religious freedom that it was used to begin this article.

The second document, James Madison's "Memorial and Remonstrance against Religious Assessments" (1785), was written as a circular to be signed by citizens in response to an effort by Virginia's governor, Patrick Henry, to raise tax money to support teachers of the Christian religion. It is a passionate treatise on why "the religion of every man must be left to the conviction and conscience of every man" and why a tax to support any religion violates that liberty. The two documents were forever linked after the "Memorial and Remonstrance" so successfully turned public opinion that Governor Henry's tax measure was defeated and Madison successfully substituted Jefferson's bill for religious freedom. Jefferson considered this one of his greatest accomplishments.

Widely circulated and studied, the two documents set the standard when the U.S. Constitution was written in the summer of 1787. Madison had helped organize the Constitutional Convention and was so influential during its proceedings that he is rightly called the father of the Constitu-

tion. During the convention he resisted all calls to add a bill of rights. The only mention of religion in the constitution is a prohibition against using a religious test as a qualification to hold office. Madison feared listing even major rights, lest future generations would infer that rights not listed were not protected. He also believed that the very structure and design of the national government spelled out in the Constitution, with three equal branches and limited to the exercise of delegated powers, was the best protection of rights. When it became clear during debates in the state ratifying conventions that a bill of rights was the price of ratification, he agreed to propose amendments during the first term of Congress. He kept his word, and the first ten amendments are now known as the Bill of Rights.

Madison made yet another contribution to our understanding of religious liberty. During the battle for ratification he, along with Alexander Hamilton and John Jay, penned the *Federalist Papers* to explain and defend the new Constitution. In *Federalist* No. 10, Madison argued that the best way to control the violence of factions (among which he included religious groups) is to have a multiplicity of parties and sects spread over a large republic. In that way no one party or sect can gain enough power to oppress the rest. Pluralism, as we now call it, has become a stable feature of American religions. It is accepted by the churches and has become a basis for cooperating in defense of religious liberty claims—even of competing sects.

The First Amendment to the Constitution reads in relevant part: "Congress shall make no law respecting an establishment of religion or prohibiting the free exercise thereof." These are respectively known as the establishment and free exercise clauses, and they form the basis for nearly all subsequent development of religious freedom in the United States. Although it is Congress that is prohibited from legislating in this arena, two developments have altered the thrust of this amendment. The first is that the Supreme Court has emerged as the ultimate interpreter of the Constitution, so Court cases have become the primary authority for defining what freedom of religion means. The second is that, beginning in the 1920s, the Supreme Court has gradually applied the Bill of Rights to the states, that is, mandating that states and not just Congress must abide by the standards set in the Bill of Rights. Because most religious liberty claims arise in local situations, the Court's rulings have had a huge effect on the development and spread of religious freedom in the United States.

The Role of the Court

The establishment and free exercise clauses sometimes appear to be in tension. The establishment clause is generally interpreted to mean that there can be no officially recognized or sponsored church (such as the Anglican Church is in England or the Roman Catholic Church once was in Spain), and that no government can support any religion either through monetary aid or display of religious symbols. The free exercise clause, on the other hand, is generally interpreted to mean that no government can prohibit religious expression or activity, discriminate against a person or organization because of their religious belief, or coerce anyone to do things their religion prohibits. Many contemporary scholars argue that both clauses are designed to protect religious liberty in its largest sense, one that includes equal treatment of all religions and of religious institutions with similar nonreligious (usually nonprofit) organizations. However, not every action can be allowed just because someone claims freedom of religion. There are hundreds of court cases that define the contours of constitutionally protected free exercise of religion. The following are discussed in chronological order to give an idea of the range of issues covered.

In the first major religious liberty case, *Reynolds v. United States* (1879), George Reynolds, a Mormon official, believed polygamy was required by his religion. He was convicted of practicing polygamy and appealed, arguing that his free exercise rights had been violated. The Supreme Court rejected his claim. The Court reasoned that a person is free to believe whatever he wishes, but actions can be regulated by government, and that polygamy violates social duties and is subversive of good order.

West Virginia v. Barnette (1943) considered whether Jehovah's Witness children could be required to salute the American flag, even though this act violated their religious beliefs. The Court noted that the children's refusal was peaceful and orderly and did not interfere with the rights of others. The justices were also troubled that the flag salute statute coerced children into professing a belief they did not hold. This case is particularly interesting because it reversed a decision the justices had made just three years earlier upholding a similar statute.

Twenty years later the Court heard *Sherbert v. Verner* (1963). Adell Sherbert, a Seventh-day Adventist, worked in a textile mill in South Carolina. When she refused to work on Saturday, because Saturday was her Sabbath, she was terminated. She sought unemployment benefits but was denied, again because she refused to be available for work on Satur-

days. In this case the Supreme Court began to work out a free exercise doctrine. After affirming that Mrs. Sherbert's beliefs were sincere and a central component of her religious faith, the Court looked to see whether South Carolina had a compelling state interest in denying her unemployment benefits. Finding that it did not, the Court ordered the state to accommodate the needs of religious people in its unemployment benefit regulations.

The U.S. Congress has since its inception provided conscientious objector status for citizens who oppose war in all circumstances because of their religious beliefs. Men granted C.O. status are not required to serve in the military, but they may be required to perform alternative service in noncombatant roles. *Gillette v. United States* (1971) presented a new issue. Mr. Gillette objected to the Vietnam War—though not to all wars—because he considered it unjust. He based his objection on a humanist approach to religion—his deeply held beliefs about the purpose and obligations of human existence. The Supreme Court ruled that Gillette did not qualify for C.O. status. Although Congress had indeed distinguished between citizens who oppose all wars and those who oppose only "unjust" wars, the Court ruled that there were pragmatic reasons for doing so (maintaining an adequate pool of candidates, showing fairness to all, and providing administrative clarity). The statute that grants C.O. status is neutral and secular; it does not discriminate between religions since it affects only individual believers. In brief, relief from the duty to serve in the military is limited to those who conscientiously oppose all wars. Individuals are not allowed to pick and choose which wars they will fight.

Unusual or minority religions have always had a difficult time in America. The Amish, descendants in the Anabaptist tradition, attempt to live simple, peaceful lives in rural areas, having as little contact with the outside world as possible. They do not use motor vehicles, electric motors, telephones, or other modern inventions. They send their children to school until they can read, write, and do arithmetic, usually through the eighth grade. The Amish lived for many decades peaceably among their neighbors in Wisconsin until the state changed its law to require all students to attend school through their sixteenth birthday, generally the ninth or tenth grade. Amish parents refused, arguing that their children not only did not need the extra years of schooling but that they might be tempted to abandon their faith if exposed to modern ideas not compatible with their way of life. Further, these were critical years in which children would learn the farming and housekeeping skills they needed as adults in the

Amish community. In *Wisconsin v. Yoder* (1972) the Supreme Court sided with the Amish, arguing that the state did not have a compelling state interest in the extra years of school and that there were alternative means to achieve its legitimate ends—the informal education given by Amish parents during their children's adolescent years. In this case the free exercise claim was upheld. Justice William Douglas raised the issue of whether this right of the parents was contrary to the right of children to be equipped to make other career choices when they became adults, but the Court was not willing to pursue this line of argument.

Goldman v. Weinberger (1986) dealt with a Jewish military officer who was told he could not wear his yarmulke indoors. Capt. Simcha Goldman argued that his religion required him to wear the head covering and that he had previously worn it without infringing on anyone's rights or disrupting military discipline. The Supreme Court reasoned that military life has unique needs for uniformity and discipline and that what might be considered an infringement on religious liberty in civilian life could be subordinated to military discipline in the armed forces.

Employment Division, Department of Human Resources of Oregon v. Smith (1990) is the most important case decided since *Sherbert v. Verner*. Two Native Americans who were counselors with a private drug rehabilitation agency were fired when their employer discovered that they had ingested peyote, an outlawed drug, at a religious ceremony in the Native American Church, of which both were members. Their applications for unemployment benefits were denied because they had been fired "for cause"—that is, for committing an illegal act—and were thus ineligible. The Supreme Court upheld the state of Oregon's right to refuse benefits, overriding the free exercise claim of the defendants.

What is most important about this case is not the outcome but the reasoning. Writing for the majority, Justice Antonin Scalia argued that so long as a state's criminal statutes were general in nature and neutral toward religion they did not have to accommodate religious beliefs. Although *Sherbert* required a government to show a compelling state interest as to why its laws should outweigh a religious liberty claim, the majority's opinion held that in the case of criminal statutes only a rational basis for the statute is required. The result is that religious liberty claims will always lose if the government can show that its laws are a reasonable way to achieve otherwise legitimate goals.

Religious interest groups and denominations from across the political and religious spectrums found this decision an alarming threat to religious liberty and combined in an extraordinary coalition to petition Congress for a law rejecting the *Employment Division v. Smith* reasoning and reinstating the *Sherbert v. Verner* rule. After intensive lobbying by these groups, Congress passed the Religious Freedom Restoration Act of 1993. But in a 1997 case, *City of Boerne (Texas) v. Flores, Archbishop of San Antonio,* the Supreme Court ruled, 6–3, that Congress exceeded its power to regulate state activity when it dictated that states and courts had to use a compelling interest and least restrictive means test in religious liberty cases. The current constitutional rule governing religious liberty cases is that statutes which are general in nature and not specifically written to burden religion do not have to accommodate religious beliefs. Many scholars see this as a serious erosion of religious liberty protection. Whether that will be the case in practice remains to be seen.

If we look to the future, it seems clear that the United States, as a relatively open, changing society that accepts immigrants from around the world and emphasizes individual liberties, will continue to see a stream of ever changing freedom of religion claims come before its courts. There will be numerous efforts to curtail religious liberty, particularly for unfamiliar minority groups with unfamiliar practices. Religious liberty enjoys a broader range of protection in the United States than anywhere else in the world, but it is never quite secure. Religious groups must be vigilant to maintain their freedom in its present form.

Global Dimensions

It is tempting to consider religious freedom in strictly American and European terms. That is a mistake, even though the roots of religious freedom are deeply embedded in these cultures. The ideals of peace, justice, and universal love are preached in all major religious traditions. The idea of toleration of others' religious beliefs can be found in Islam's sacred book, the Qur'an, which dates from the seventh century. Unfortunately, concern for freedom of religion did not become a matter of global concern until the mid-twentieth century.

Stimulated in part by a desire to protect their missionaries in colonial territories, an ecumenical group of mainline Protestants held a conference at Oxford, England, in 1937, during which they developed a common position on religious liberty as a global problem. The statement noted a close link between religious liberty and a just, stable international order. After World War II the first assembly of the World Council of Churches was held in Amsterdam in early

1948. This assembly issued a statement linking religious freedom to peace and urged that religious liberty become part of a new international bill of rights. Driven in part by widespread revulsion at the fate of Jews in Nazi-occupied territories, and input from the World Council of Churches, the United Nations General Assembly passed the Universal Declaration of Human Rights in late 1948. Article 18 may be considered the Magna Carta of religious freedom: "Everyone has the right to freedom of thought, conscience and religion; this right includes freedom to change his religion or belief and freedom, either alone or in community with others and in public or private, to manifest his religion or belief in teaching, practice, worship and observance."

Little was done to clarify or implement this declaration in the following years. The major world powers turned their attention to cold war issues, and colonized nations were caught up in winning their independence. The concept of religious liberty received a major boost in 1965, when the Second Vatican Council passed a Declaration on Religious Freedom that supported freedom of conscience for all people. Although the Catholic Church was the last major Christian church to embrace religious liberty for all, it was also the largest, and its statement added legitimacy to the idea.

Freedom of religion is now seen as an important universal human right, but attempts to define exactly what it requires in practice have run into a number of difficulties. Five very different, but sometimes overlapping cultures have such different ideas that this area has become a complex one to negotiate.

• A Western secular tradition sees religious freedom as rooted in separation of church and state and disestablishment along the American model. Secularists are concerned that nonbelievers be treated equally and that no tax monies or government influence be used to support religion.

• A Zionist Jewish tradition believes that Israel is a special case calling for government support of Judaism because of the close identification of the Jewish faith with the land of Israel, especially Jerusalem, throughout history. Further, the unique record of persecution of Jews in other lands supports the idea of Israel as a separate Jewish state.

• A Christian tradition holds that government support for religious ideas and institutions helps preserve important cultural values and identities and is not incompatible with religious freedom as long as other religions are protected and no individuals are coerced or disadvantaged because of their faith. Long prevalent in England and Latin America, this idea is emerging in Eastern Europe as newly freed nations try to return or compensate for religious properties confiscated during the Communist years and to reestablish their national cultures.

• A Marxist tradition, still powerful in China and several smaller nations, sees religion as a competitor to the state, a social institution to be controlled and limited, and at best a necessary evil to be tolerated only until it withers away. This tradition is willing to accept the freedom of conscience as an "inner freedom" but rejects any social role or rights for religious institutions.

• An Islamic tradition rejects the very idea of separation of church and state and in some cases even the legitimacy of a secular state. Allah is Lord of all, and where possible Islamic law, shari'a, is to be the primary source of justice. Of particular concern to Muslims is any acknowledgment of freedom for non-Muslims to proselytize or convert Muslims. The memory of the Christian Crusades and Western colonialism make this issue particularly sensitive and radically at variance with the Christian view that religious freedom entails the right of churches to evangelize and individuals to change faiths. A growing Hindu nationalism takes a negative view of evangelism parallel to that in Islamic tradition.

Freedom of religion remains an area filled with controversy and complexity. The very idea that there is any universal set of human rights has come under attack from nations whose religious and cultural traditions do not include such emerging rights as equality for women and protection of children. Another challenge comes from religion-based nationalism, essentially the idea that a particular religion, invariably that of those in power, is the "soul of the nation" and that religious minorities are disloyal or at best second-class citizens. A further tension comes from certain churches themselves, as their self-understanding increasingly requires them to criticize social injustice and political oppression wherever it is found.

Although great progress has been made in understanding and spreading the ideal of religious freedom as a universal human right, limits on religious expression and activities and even outright persecutions continue across the globe. The fight for freedom of religion is a story without end.

See also *Constitution, U.S.; Human rights; Nationalism; Secularization; Separation of church and state.*

Paul J. Weber

BIBLIOGRAPHY

Freedom of Conscience. Proceedings, Seminar organized by the Secretariat General of the Council of Europe. Strasbourg: Council of Europe Press, 1993.

Koshy, Ninan, "The Ecumenical Understanding of Religious Liberty: The Contribution of the World Council of Churches." *Journal of Church and State* 38 (winter 1996): 137–154.

Laycock, Douglas, "Continuity and Change in the Threat to Religious Liberty: The Reformation Era and the Late Twentieth Century." *Minnesota Law Review.* 80 (1996): 1047–1102.

Miller, Robert T., and Ronald B. Flowers. *Toward Benevolent Neutrality: Church, State, and the Supreme Court.* 5th ed. Waco, Texas: Baylor University Press, 1997.

"Religious Human Rights in the World Today: A Report on the 1994 Atlanta Conference." *Emory International Law Review* 10 (spring 1996).

Reynolds, Noel B., and W. Cole Durham Jr. *Religious Liberty in Western Thought.* Atlanta, Ga.: Scholars Press, 1996.

Weber, Paul J. *Equal Separation: Understanding the Religion Clauses of the First Amendment.* Westport, Conn.: Greenwood Press, 1990.

Witte, John, Jr., and Johan D. van der Vyver, eds. *Human Rights in Global Perspectives.* 2 vols. Amsterdam: Martinus Nijhoff, 1996.

Freemasonry

A fraternal order, known to outsiders primarily for its secrecy and ritual, Freemasonry has its greatest strength in Britain and the United States. Masonry played a central role in the transformation of American society from the colonial era to the rise of Jacksonian democracy in the late 1820s. Under President Andrew Jackson American society became increasingly egalitarian and became known as the era of the "common man."

The Freemasons, the largest and most influential fraternal order to come to America, trace their roots to England at the time of the Norman Conquest (1066), when building in stone was carried on with remarkable activity by stonemasons at the behest of kings, nobles, and churchmen. As early as the seventeenth century the membership of Masonic lodges began to shift from tradesmen skilled in the craft of masonry to noblemen and gentry who took an interest in planning and design. By 1717, at the time of the formation of the first Grand Lodge in London, "free," or independent, masonry had taken on the character of a nobleman's club, while continuing to employ remnants of a tradition-laden medieval institution, including a secret brotherhood; consistent identity from lodge to lodge; centrality of ritual, initia-

tion, and myths of origin; and explicit connection to an artisan culture.

In its migration to the Continent and to North America the newly formulated Masonic order continued to alter its beliefs and practices as larger social and political contexts framed the terms in which it was understood. In Europe, reaction against Masonry's trade origins was articulated most forcefully in the development of Templarism, or Scottish Masonry. Templaric Freemasonry offered a reinterpretation of Masonic origins that traced its birth from the orders of Crusader knights such as the Knights Templars. Templarism involved the creation of more exclusive and hierarchical subgroups within Masonry. In contrast, American Masonry underwent a limited democratization.

The Enlightenment and American Revolution

The first American Masonic lodges reflected the ideals of benevolence and sociability at the heart of eighteenth-century Enlightenment social theory. Established in eastern coastal towns during the 1730s and 1740s, and dominated by many of the colonies' most prominent men, American Freemasonry erected no formal barriers of religion or nationality to membership, yet it reinforced social divisions between gentlemen and others. In its rejection of religious and political disputes, and its support for "that Religion in which all Men agree," the order embodied a liberal view of religion as an institution that brings order and harmony to society. Similarly, fraternal men believed that the proper awareness of nature's harmony would act as a corrective to the individualism and greed that threatened the social and political order. Masonic references to God as the Supreme Architect reflect this Newtonian understanding of a harmonious and ordered universe. At the same time, the first American lodges believed in the Enlightenment's ideal of a cultivated, orderly community, where a benevolent elite would be recognized and honored for selfless devotion to the public good.

In the mid-eighteenth century, new directions in Masonry placed it at the center of revolutionary changes in definitions of power and hierarchy. Beginning in the 1750s large numbers of mechanics, small merchants, and military men, some of whom had been rejected by existing lodges, proposed a variant of Freemasonry, which they termed "Ancient Masonry." Preoccupied by issues of status in a rapidly changing society, these ambitious and politically active men reshaped the social and intellectual boundaries of the fraternity. Revolutionary concepts of disinterested virtue and equality lay at the heart of this transformation, helping to buttress Ancient Masonry's claims to social distinction and to identify the order as an archetype of the republican society based on virtue and talent they were attempting to build. In the 1790s, with the American Revolution fought and won, the order spread rapidly. Masons began to describe the fraternity as embodying the republican values of education, morality, and Christianity.

Ambiguous Relationship with Religion

The first quarter of the nineteenth century was marked by a growing convergence of Christianity and Freemasonry around ideals of the Enlightenment. Standing between Christian sectarianism and nonbiblical rationalism, Freemasonry attracted ministers and members from various protoliberal denominations with a high incidence of Congregationalists, Episcopalians, and Unitarians among its leaders. At the same time, its members began to invest Freemasonry with explicitly Christian values and beliefs. Lodge meetings were opened with Christian prayers and Bible readings, new rituals emphasized biblical narratives and settings, Christian ministers were admitted without charge, and, by 1815, lodges were appointing their own Christian chaplains. After the shift to republican ideals and symbols—in contrast to the colonial period, when civic ritual had centered on the British monarchy and the church, with Christian ministers called upon to bless public institutions—Masons were increasingly called upon to solemnize public enterprises, even going so far as to lay the cornerstone at the foundations of churches.

Despite this glowing public presence, an Anti-Masonic Party arose in the early nineteenth century. The Anti-Masons attacked the fraternity's secrecy and medieval trappings as exemplifying the evils identified by the new democratic and evangelical critique of society. The fraternity's secret brotherhood now appeared to undermine government: its exclusiveness was a sign of aristocracy, while its promotion of preference illustrated the wealthy's subversion of the open market. Masonic ideas were prominent among Joseph Smith's radically new Mormon sect whose stories of revelation threatened the "truth" of Christian beginnings.

Finally, Masonry's affinity for a religion that arises naturally from human reason, together with its liberal view of Christian doctrine, furnished grounds for believing it was incompatible with revealed religion. By the late 1820s and 1830s Freemasonry was effectively shut down, its membership dispersed and lodges closed. By the 1840s, however, the order was reborn as a private male world quite separate from an increasingly feminized Christianity.

See also *Enlightenment*.

David G. Hackett

BIBLIOGRAPHY

Brooke, John L. *The Refiner's Fire: The Making of Mormon Cosmology, 1644–1844.* Cambridge: Cambridge University Press, 1994.

Bullock, Steven C. *Revolutionary Brotherhood: Freemasonry and the Transformation of the American Social Order, 1730–1840.* Chapel Hill: University of North Carolina Press, 1996.

Carnes, Mark C. *Secret Ritual and Manhood in Victorian America.* New Haven: Yale University Press, 1989.

Clawson, Mary Ann. *Constructing Brotherhood: Class, Gender, and Fraternalism.* Princeton: Princeton University Press, 1989.

Dumenil, Lynn. *Freemasonry and American Culture, 1880–1930.* Princeton: Princeton University Press, 1984.

Goodman, Paul. *Towards a Christian Republic: Antimasonry and the Great Transition in New England, 1826–1836.* New York: Oxford University Press, 1988.

Jacob, Margaret C. *Living the Enlightenment.* New York: Oxford University Press, 1991.

Lipson, Dorothy Ann. *Freemasonry in Federalist Connecticut, 1789–1835.* Princeton: Princeton University Press, 1977.

Friends, Society of (Quakers)

The Society of Friends (Quakers) is a religious movement that arose out of radical Puritanism in the seventeenth century in northwestern England. The movement now includes about 135,000 English-speaking members worldwide, with larger numbers in East Africa and Latin America.

Though considered a Protestant denomination, the Friends require no creeds, outward sacraments, or ordained clergy for worship (meeting). Their worship centers on silent waiting together for the personal, direct experience of God—that is, divine guidance from an "Inner Light."

Friends have sought ethical perfection throughout their history. "Speaking truth to power," the watchword of a twentieth-century Friends committee, reflects early Friends' vision of a world ruled by evil yet conquered by the Spirit. Their experience of restoring primitive Christianity led them to pacifism, a refusal to take oaths, and simplicity in dress and speech. But it also led them into the "Lamb's War" to transform the social order as well as personal lives and to struggles throughout their history to balance sectarian purity and political responsibility.

Early Friends (see John 15:15) became known as Quakers

because they quaked upon "convincement" and because the founder of the movement, George Fox (1624–1691), urged English magistrates to tremble (or quake) before the word of God rather than that of the law.

The Early Years

The Society of Friends was born in England in the 1650s when civil war followed the overthrow of King Charles I, Anglican bishops, and the House of Lords by the parliamentary leaders, rising merchants, and Puritans among the parish clergy. Although Puritans saw God's hand in these events, their apocalyptic hopes were disappointed as their alliance fractured. Artisans' "separatist" congregations renounced the inclusive parishes of the Church of England.

Many became Friends, adhering to the teachings of George Fox, an English shepherd and shoemaker who felt divinely led to preach that a formal church structure with its rites and educated ministers was not necessary because God illuminated the inner soul of every person. The Quaker "Awakening" mushroomed as lay itinerants called on unchurched crowds in moorlands and cities to heed the searching "Light" or Spirit that shows all evil within: "Jesus Christ has come to teach his people himself."

Defensive gentry and some Puritans rejected Quaker claims of human perfectability. But as the Puritan Commonwealth and Protectorate established in 1649 fell apart in 1659, radical Puritans invited Quakers to hold public office.

The restoration of King Charles II, the House of Lords, and bishops in 1660 led to two bitter decades of persecution of all dissenters from the Anglican Church. Nevertheless, Friend Margaret Fell and Fox, who had organized the "First Publishers of Truth" across Europe and America, set up a network of meetings to support Quaker community life.

Meanwhile, mutual discipline patterns turned "testimonies" of speech and dress, which began as prophetic confrontations of non-Quakers, into badges of sectarian loyalty. Quaker theologians such as Robert Barclay (1648–1690) defended silent worship and the universality of the "Light." Cautions that each person must follow "the measure of Light" within provided Friends such as William Penn (1644–1718), an aristocratic convert to the movement, with a basis on which to appeal to the consciences of even non-Quaker persecutors. Indeed, the Friends' reliance on "spiritual weapons" and "friendly persuasion" became evidence that the Spirit would never lead them to violence. Finally, by openly but peacefully refusing to restrict their worship and ethics, Friends helped to secure passage of the Toleration Act

George Fox

of 1689, which freed worship (though not all civil rights) in England.

Quaker Settlements in the New World

Between 1656 and 1672 Fox and other traveling Quaker preachers had gathered to meetings settlers in Barbados, Jamaica, Rhode Island, New York, Maryland, Virginia, and Carolina. The persecution continued, however; in Massachusetts four Friends were hung. Even before the 1689 Toleration Act, William Penn, who had secured a royal land grant in the American colonies in payment of debts owed his family, had established the colonies of West New Jersey and Pennsylvania, which were based on his faith in the universality of the Light and conscience. Penn shared ideas with other Friends and, despite his landlord rights, placed power from the beginning in the hands of an elected assembly. But its leaders were able to maintain power and outward peace among the varied settlers and native American Indians until

1755 only by frequent compromises of "Truth" with successive British monarchs and ministers who continued to demand military defenses. Finally, in 1756, the Quakers relinquished control of the assembly.

In England and its American colonies Quakers always had been penalized for refusing militia service and tax support for clergy, but from 1790 to 1860 they escaped sectarian isolation by immersing themselves in commerce and pioneering programs for hospital and prison reform, public education, and efforts to abolish slavery. Indeed, to recover Quaker purity, John Woolman (1720–1772), a tailor from West New Jersey, and others persuaded Friends to "disown" slave owning. Quakers Benjamin Lundy (1789–1839) and John Greenleaf Whittier (1807–1892) published newssheets. Lucretia Mott (1793–1880), Sojourner Truth (1797–1883), and the Grimke sisters lectured, defending women's rights. Black sea captain Paul Cuffee repatriated freedmen to Africa. Levi Coffin (1798–1877) coordinated the Underground Railroad and Freedmen's Aid. And Elizabeth Fry (1780–1845) reorganized women's prisons.

Nineteenth-century American Friends migrated in great numbers from the South, where laws enforced slavery, to the farmland of the Midwest. There and in cities, increasingly influenced by non-Quaker neighbors and social pressures, the Friends became permanently divided in theology and worship between the Bible-centered evangelicals and quietists, who later became liberals. Moreover, they increasingly found their patterns of congregational discipline unable to handle intermarriages and those members who had enlisted in the Union Army during the Civil War to oppose slavery. In England, where since 1832 Quakers had been entitled to enter Parliament, Quaker reform politician John Bright (1811–1889) helped to maintain English neutrality in the U.S. Civil War, but lost his seat for opposing the Crimean War (1853–1856).

Relief and Reform

After the American Revolution, Friends embarked on what became long-term alternatives to sectarian purity and political compromise: alternative services in times of war, relief programs in times of natural disasters, and reform efforts at the national and international levels. For example, Friends undertook aid efforts during the Crimean War and the Franco-Prussian War (1870–1871). The outbreak of World War I in 1914 saw British and American Friends, who faced hostility for opposing the war and its conscription, form the frontline Friends Ambulance Unit and American Friends Service

Committee, which served in battle-ravaged northern France. In 1919 relief and reconstruction programs were extended to Germany, where until 1924 a million children were fed daily in cooperation with German teachers and social workers. Similar programs in central Europe and Russia (1917–1927) followed. In all these programs, Quakers worked with or under Red Cross and government officials such as Friend Herbert Hoover (U.S. president, 1929–1933).

The first Friends World Conference in 1920 called for disarmament and racial justice, and in 1922 and 1929 the American Friends Service Committee and the British Friends Service Council tackled economic social issues by aiding the families of striking textile workers and coal miners. Volunteer work camps, "peace caravans," and education programs enlisted students. Quaker senator Paul Douglas, a Democrat from Illinois, worked within Congress.

In World War II American Friends were barred by Congress from most of the ambulance, air raid, children's resettlement, and mining services open to British conscientious objectors. The historic peace churches (Mennonites, Brethren, and Friends) vainly opposed conscription and agreed to administer civilian public service camps, mostly for forestry and conservation. But frustrated with army oversight and the isolation of the work, the churches declined to administer similar pacifist service options during the Korean and Vietnam Wars.

The Friends' four-decade battle against conscription and for disarmament and the rights of Native Americans led to the establishment of the Friends Committee for National Legislation in 1943. Under Raymond Wilson and Edward Snyder it became the pioneer among Protestant lobbies. The American Friends Service Committee oversees the Quaker United Nations office. Elsewhere over the years, individual Friends have joined in vigils against nuclear weapons and power plants, chemical and biological weapons, and the Vietnam and Persian Gulf Wars, among other things, and Friends still lead the worldwide network of Alternatives to Violence Programs in dozens of prisons. Except among East African and Latin American Friends, at most Quaker monthly and regional yearly meetings of varied theologies committees present programs and resolutions for or against abortion, homosexuality, and capital punishment—issues on which Friends have no consensus nationally. Overall, the emphasis of most Quakers and their committees since the tumultuous 1960s has shifted from social service to social change.

See also *Pacifism; Protestantism.*

Hugh Barbour

BIBLIOGRAPHY

Barbour, Hugh, and J. William Frost. *The Quakers.* Richmond, Ind.: Friends United Press, 1994.

Brock, Peter. *The Quaker Peace Testimony, 1660 to 1914.* York, England: Sessions, 1990.

Fox, George. *The Works of George Fox.* 8 vols., ed. T. H. Wallace. State College, Pa.: George Fox Fund, 1990.

Jones, Rufus M. *The Later Periods of Quakerism.* London: Macmillan, 1921.

Marietta, Jack D. *The Reformation of American Quakerism, 1748–1783.* Philadelphia: University of Pennsylvania Press, 1984.

Mullen, Tom, ed., and Edward Snyder. *Witness in Washington: Fifty Years of Friendly Persuasion.* Richmond, Ind.: Friends United Press, 1996.

Fundamentalism

Fundamentalism is a modern form of politicized religion by which self-styled "true believers" resist the marginalization of religion in their respective societies. Fundamentalists identify and oppose the agents of marginalization (secularists) and seek to restructure political, social, cultural, and economic relations and institutions according to traditional religious precepts and norms.

"True believers" adopt different approaches and methods in pursuing their common goals. Some battle secularists gradually on the cultural and social fronts by establishing schools, religious academies, journals, newspapers, hospitals, and orphanages to serve, educate—and convert—people in need of such services. Other fundamentalists enter the political arena by forming political parties and contesting elections. Seeking power through established, conventional means, they hope to transform society in dramatic ways. Still other fundamentalists, abandoning rule by law and conventional politics, become militants who wage a religious war to overthrow the established political order or commit violent acts of terrorism designed to intimidate the enemy into making concessions.

Defining Fundamentalists

Use of the term *fundamentalist* for everyone who pursues one of these strategies can be misleading if other considerations are not taken into account. For example, some modern religious leaders eschew political power and concentrate on fostering a return to religious practices and lifestyles by fallen-away Muslims, Christians, or Jews. It is more accurate to call such apolitical leaders revivalists and see their move-

ments as expressions of religious revivalism. In other words, not every person who takes her religion seriously, practices it fervently, and organizes her life and career around it is a fundamentalist. Fundamentalists, by contrast, want to change the behavior of nonbelievers as well as believers; therefore, they strive to change the laws and structures of society that impede their mission of opposing the godless and converting the nonbeliever. At the other extreme, many terrorists and so-called religious warriors are not motivated by religious sensibilities at all; rather, they are mercenaries or secular ideologues exploiting religious fervor for their own irreligious ends. The genuine fundamentalist is both religious and political; indeed, he believes that circumstances require him to act politically (and perhaps violently) in order to fulfill his religious obligations.

If Fundamentalism is defined as a cross-cultural, religio-political pattern of thought and behavior rather than equated with a specific set of beliefs, rituals, or religious practices, it becomes clear that fundamentalists may be found within any historic religion that has sacred scriptures and basic teachings. They are defenders of a religious tradition that goes back centuries rather than promoters of a new religion or cult centered on one charismatic leader, such as David Koresh of the Branch Davidians, a cult centered in Waco, Texas, in the early 1990s. Although fundamentalists defend traditional beliefs and draw on the symbolic and organizational resources of their ancient religion, they are not merely conservative or orthodox believers. Being a conservative Christian, a devout Muslim, or an Orthodox Jew, in other words, does not necessarily make one a fundamentalist. Rather, fundamentalists are militant conservatives who see the world as a battleground between absolute good and absolute evil. Thus they are spiritual (and sometimes physical) warriors who oppose nonbelievers as well as the doubters or compromisers within their own religious community.

Most fundamentalists are neither uneducated, backward-looking people nor the credulous dupes of silver-tongued preachers. To the contrary, they are medical doctors, nurses, engineers, teachers, businessmen, and college-educated mothers and fathers, who readily use (or even invent) the tools of technology, mass communications, and modern science. Yet they feel strongly that Western societies erred grievously when they replaced God, religion, and divine law with human reason and secular political principles as the basis for the legal and social order. For such people, religiously derived morality is the only acceptable framework for discerning the common good, evaluating human behavior, and governing society. Moreover, for most Muslims, Western ideas and institutions were imposed by European outsiders who colonized and dominated their societies, converting many of their brothers, sisters, and children to their foreign "godless" ways.

Accordingly, fundamentalists oppose ideas and social movements that carry secular values. Whether Jewish, Christian, or Muslim, fundamentalists are, for example, antipluralist because they believe in the superiority of the one true religion (their own) and therefore reject the idea that the state should offer equal protection under law to all religions or philosophical positions. Fundamentalists also tend to be antifeminist because they believe that the movement for women's liberation from patriarchy (a society ruled by men) violates the will of God (Allah, Yahveh) who created males and females for different roles, with women destined to be subordinated to men in society and in the home.

Jewish, Christian, and Muslim fundamentalists may not share the same specific beliefs, but they do share a way of thinking about their beliefs. First, fundamentalists are selective. They are selectively traditional, choosing certain scriptures or theological teachings from the past and insisting that all true believers "fight to the death" (literally or figuratively) to protect these "fundamentals." And they are selectively modern, choosing certain twentieth-century technologies (such as television, computer, and fax machine) and processes (such as modern political parties and elections) as weapons against their enemies.

Second, the fundamentalist pattern of thought is absolutist (the truth we proclaim is perfect, complete, and irreformable); inerrantist (the truth we proclaim is free from any kind of error); and dualist (we who proclaim the truth are children of light; all others are children of darkness). Fundamentalists also believe that they are living in a special time in history, perhaps the last days, in which God is working in a new way among the true believers. This idea, known as millennialism in Christianity, helps fundamentalists to explain why they sometimes resort to violence even though their religion normally forbids it. In the final days, when the true believers find themselves in direct combat with the enemy, God wants them to retrieve teachings that justify violent action in defense of the faith.

Members of fundamentalist movements often live by strict rules of discipline; they dress, eat, drink, and perhaps marry according to rules prescribed by an authoritarian leader who always is male and also may be charismatic (gift-

ed with special powers, including the ability to inspire heroic action in others). And members devote a great deal of energy toward maintaining the borders between themselves and outsiders, whom they may portray as witting or unwitting agents of Satan.

Fundamentalists are found within the three great monotheistic faiths—Judaism, Christianity, and Islam. Many of the characteristics of fundamentalism also appear in twentieth-century South Asian religious movements, including Hindu nationalists in India, Sikh radicals in Punjab, and Buddhist militants in Sri Lanka. In the South Asian cases, the innovative and (ironically) antitraditional character of fundamentalism is especially clear: the political leaders of these movements, seeking to use religion as the basis for an ethnically and culturally exclusive nationalism, have found it necessary to "Westernize" the host religious tradition.

Hinduism and Buddhism do not readily lend themselves to the political dynamics of fundamentalism; they lack the necessary theological "raw materials"—a comprehensive religio-legal code, a concept of time as linear and progressive, and a salvation history prefigured in sacred scriptures and directed by an interventionist personal God. Thus Hindu nationalists created in the 1980s a synthetic fundamentalism by borrowing politically charged Western religious concepts and grafting them onto the diverse, local, folk-oriented traditions and practices known as "Hinduism." Members of the World Hindu Party (VHP, Vishva Hindu Parishad), the cultural wing of Hindu nationalism, staged a campaign in the 1980s and 1990s to promote the mythical deity Lord Rama to the status of a national patron of Hindustan, the imagined sacred nation whose citizens, whether they be Hindus, Muslims, Christians, Jains, Buddhists, or Sikhs, must conform to the cultural and political requirements of *Hindutva* (Hinduness). Seeking to project Rama as a historical figure with a clearly defined birthplace and political legacy, the VHP helped to popularize (and modernize) the *Ramayana,* the epic poem celebrating the deeds of the god-hero, by broadcasting it, in serial form, on national television.

The renewal of Rama's myth and cult served explicit political purposes: the secular government of India, led by the Congress Party, was at the time implementing the "affirmative action" recommendations of a national commission, and Hindu activists vigorously opposed affirmative action for "minorities" in India, especially Muslims. The most flagrant expression of the new Hindu chauvinism was the 1992 destruction of Babari Masjid, a mosque established in 1528 in the north-central town of Ayodhya by Muslim leaders of the Mughal dynasty. Hindu nationalists, claiming the site as the birthplace of Lord Rama, razed the mosque in hopes of re-building the ancient temple as a twentieth-century Hindu national shrine. In doing so, they unleashed a spiral of vio-lence across India that resulted in the death of thousands of Muslims and Hindus.

In whatever religious tradition they inhabit, fundamental-ists always are outnumbered by conservatives, moderates, and liberals who practice the religion without developing a prin-cipled hostility toward outsiders. Despite their relatively small numbers, however, fundamentalists usually capture the headlines and cause controversy by acting in a way that oth-er religious believers as well as the secular public find dra-matic and intentionally provocative. Fundamentalists would say that they are only fulfilling sacred obligations; such fideli-ty to orthodoxy (correct religious belief) or orthopraxis (correct religious practice) may seem defiant and even scan-dalous, they acknowledge, to people who have compromised their religious identities by cooperating with nonbelievers for political or economic gain.

Christian Fundamentalism

In 1920 Curtis Lee Laws, editor of the Baptist *Watchman-Examiner,* coined the term *fundamentalist* to describe the evangelical Christians of North America willing to do "bat-tle royal" in defense of the fundamentals of the faith. Evan-gelical Christians, to paraphrase historian Grant Wacker, are Protestants who believe that the sole authority in religion is the Bible and the sole means of salvation is a life-transform-ing experience wrought by the Holy Spirit through faith in Jesus Christ. And fundamentalist Christians, according to the liberal Protestant preacher Harry Emerson Fosdick, are "mad evangelicals."

At the turn of the twentieth century, when they first emerged from the Protestant churches, the fundamentalists were angry because new secular ideas and methods were threatening to discredit traditional Christian beliefs. English-man Charles Darwin's theory of evolution by means of ran-dom mutation and natural selection seemed to deny God's providence in creating and sustaining the world. When mid-dle ground–seeking Protestants like Lyman Abbot pro-claimed that evolution was simply "God's way of doing things," his bruising-for-a-fight coreligionists rankled. They saw an insidious link between evolutionism and the so-called higher criticism, a method of examining the historical

and literary character of the Bible as if it were just another book. To make matters worse, liberal Protestants were im-porting the new methods and ideas from Germany into American Protestant seminaries and colleges.

In what would become fine fundamentalist fashion, the angry evangelical Christians reacted by selecting certain tra-ditional beliefs—Christ's birth to a virgin, blood atonement for human sins by death on the cross, bodily resurrection, and anticipated second coming in glory—and fortifying them with a new way of describing the authority of the Bible. This fifth "fundamental," the strict inerrancy of the Bible, guaranteed that everything taught in Scripture, in-cluding science and history as well as religion, was absolutely true without qualification. Adherence to the doctrine of strict inerrancy served to separate the true believer from the moderate or merely conservative evangelical, whose judg-ment presumably was clouded by the seductive appeal of the prestigious new sciences. (Fundamentalists earned the name "come-outers" when they fled the mainline denominations and established their own independent churches in order to worship apart from their corrupted brethren.)

The fundamentalists also were innovative in their inter-pretations of the Bible's teaching about the end days. The Scofield Reference Bible (1909) presented their own unique form of apocalypticism. Called dispensational premillennial-ism, the widely adopted theory held that Christ would soon return to punish the nonbelievers, beginning with the liberal Protestants who accepted evolution and the higher criticism, and lift the true believers directly into heaven (rapture). After vanquishing the Antichrist in a terrible battle called Ar-mageddon, the triumphant Christ would establish a thou-sand-year reign.

Christian fundamentalism found its form through a series of Bible conferences held during the last quarter of the nine-teenth century. From 1910 to 1915 Lyman and Milton Stew-art, wealthy oil businessmen from California, financed the publication and distribution of a twelve-volume paperback series entitled *The Fundamentals,* authored by prominent evangelical thinkers who described their opponents within the churches as modernists. In 1919 these combative thinkers formed the World's Christian Fundamentals Association to oppose modernism. Charismatic preachers such as the col-orful Billy Sunday popularized their antimodernist message through well-publicized revival meetings.

After World War I (1914–1918) the United States experi-enced "a revolution in morals," celebrated by the eastern media, including the new tabloid newspapers. Women smoked and even danced in public; popular literature discussed Sigmund Freud (1856–1939), the Austrian founder of psychoanalysis, and aberrant sexual behavior; and communal enforcement of Victorian standards of personal behavior virtually collapsed. In response, Christian fundamentalists launched a moral crusade and aligned themselves temporarily with Catholics and other Protestants to campaign for laws banning the manufacture or sale of alcoholic beverages. This effort culminated in passage of the Eighteenth Amendment implementing Prohibition in 1919.

Despite this temporary victory in the battle against alcohol, the war for the enforcement of Victorian/Methodist behavioral standards was ultimately lost. The death knell sounded in 1925, when fundamentalists in Dayton, Tennessee—led by the legendary William Jennings Bryan and opposed by the celebrated criminal lawyer Clarence Darrow—charged schoolteacher John T. Scopes with teaching biological evolution and thereby violating Tennessee's anti-evolution laws. Although Bryan won the "Scopes Monkey Trial," the fundamentalists, depicted as superstitious rubes and hicks, were discredited nationally. After campaigning against Catholic presidential candidate Al Smith in 1928, they withdrew from the American cultural and political mainstream.

During their period of cultural separatism, Christian fundamentalists were not inactive. In the 1930 and 1940s they built a subculture of fundamentalist radio stations, periodicals, publishing houses, Bible colleges, missionary bands, creationist science institutes, and Christian day schools and academies. Their operative world view, a premillennialist expectation of Christ's imminent return, encouraged missionary outreach and soul winning, however, rather than political activism.

A change in attitude occurred in the 1960s, when dismayed Christian fundamentalists observed what they described as a conspiracy of secular humanists invading the nation's schools, Congress, and the Supreme Court (which banned prayer in the public schools in 1962 and 1963 and permitted abortion on demand in 1973). In 1979 the Reverend Jerry Falwell, a gifted preacher and pastor of an independent Baptist church in Lynchburg, Virginia, explained that Christians could no longer wait for Christ to do the dirty work of rolling back the tide of atheistic humanists serving Satan; Bible-believing Christians, whom Falwell called the "Moral Majority," must reinvest the public square

Jerry Falwell

with the "Judeo-Christian values" on which the nation had been founded (according to the fundamentalists).

Falwell's Moral Majority was only the most prominent of dozens of Christian political action groups that sprang up in the late 1970s and had their heyday during Ronald Reagan's presidency, lobbying against abortion, pornography, and feminism, among other social forces erosive of a Christian America and "traditional family values." Politicians on the secular right helped fundamentalists perfect their mass marketing and voter mobilization techniques in exchange for support of Republican Party candidates who did not necessarily pursue the rather narrow, and controversial, Christian agenda. In 1990 Falwell disbanded the Moral Majority, claiming it had accomplished its goals. But, in fact, Congress and the Supreme Court, in their lawmaking and jurisprudence, were arguably no closer to Judeo-Christian values than they had been in the 1970s.

Nonetheless, the demise of the Moral Majority signaled only the end of the first phase of renewed Christian activism. The second phase began almost immediately with the formation of the Christian Coalition, a political action group led by Pat Robertson, a Pentecostal preacher, the son of a former U.S. senator, and a successful television entrepreneur (*The 700 Club*) in his own right. Robertson, like Falwell, established his own university as a base of operations. But, unlike the fundamentalist preacher, the Pentecostal media mogul turned over political management of the movement to his savvy young protégé, Ralph Reed, a Ph.D. in American history with a knack for grass-roots politics. Reed shifted the focus of Christian politics from Washington, D.C., to thousands of communities across the United States, where his operatives organized local chapters of the Christian Coalition and trained candidates to run for the school board, state assembly, and Republican Party leadership.

The Christian Coalition quickly demonstrated its new political muscle by injecting strong antiabortion language into the 1992 Republican Party platform and then claiming credit for the 1994 congressional election results, in which 56 House seats, 10 Senate seats, 472 state legislature seats, and 11 governorships shifted from Democratic to Republican hands. Independent pollsters confirmed that the Christian right was indeed crucial to the electoral results. During the campaign the Christian Coalition, with 1.5 million members organized in 48 state units and 1,400 local chapters, had mobilized a network of 17,000 precinct coordinators, 30,000 local volunteers, and 23,000 "church liaisons," who distributed 33 million "nonpartisan" voter guides. Other organizations on the Christian right, including Concerned Women for America, Focus on the Family, and the Traditional Values Coalition, also helped to ensure that, for the first time, a majority of the nation's 50 million evangelical Protestants identified themselves as Republicans.

Meanwhile, the prolife movement Operation Rescue, led by Randall Terry, recruited fundamentalists and conservative Roman Catholics, whom they trained to participate in marches on abortion clinics. Acts of civil disobedience led to prison terms for some activists, who saw their jailing as a sign of God's unfolding plan of redemption for the United States.

Islamic Fundamentalism

In the twentieth century religious reformers within both major branches of Islam advocated adoption of a new practice by Islamists, or fundamentalist Muslims: identify and persecute the "infidel," or nonbeliever, including the person who pretends to be Muslim but has actually betrayed the faith by adopting Western attitudes and values. Muslim fundamentalists believe that the only remedy for the growing threat of apostasy (the renunciation of Islam) is to establish states governed exclusively by the *shariʿa*, the law of Allah, inscribed in the Holy Qurʾan and in the *hadith,* or traditions, of the prophet Muhammad (A.D. 570–632), the founder of Islam.

Muslim fundamentalists focus their rage first on lax members of the faith community itself and see the world as divided sharply between true believers and corrupt sinners. But Muslims are unique among the major monotheist traditions because they have never formally accepted and institutionalized a distinction between religion and the state, or between the "public" and "private" realms of society. Thus many radical Muslims believe that the real enemy is "Westoxification," the slow poisoning of Muslim purity by the insinuation of foreign ideas and practices imported from Western "imperialist" nations, especially the United States, Great Britain, and France.

In Sunni Islam, followed by nine-tenths of the world's one billion Muslims, the fundamentalist tendency first emerged in the work of Hasan al-Banna (1906–1949), an Egyptian schoolteacher who founded the Muslim Brotherhood in 1928 after concluding that the shaykhs, or religious scholars, of the Islamic religious establishment in Cairo had sold out to British interests, allowing night clubs, advertising, the consumption of alcohol, and other un-Islamic activities. After the Muslim Brotherhood combined religious education with social services (child care centers, medical clinics, orphanages, and schools), the movement spread quickly throughout the Arab world.

In the 1950s the Egyptian branch of the Muslim Brotherhood began to oppose the presidency of Gamal Abdel Nasser (1918–1970), who had jailed and tortured hundreds of young Muslim activists. One of them, a literary critic named Sayyid Qutb, developed a radical fundamentalist ideology before he was executed in 1965. Published in a little book called *Milestones,* it inspired a generation of violent radicals who accepted Qutb's notion that *jahiliyya* (pre-Islamic ignorance) had descended over Muslim societies, making it necessary for true Muslims to flee society, name the infidel, and attack the nonbeliever. One group inspired by this ideology, Islamic Jihad, assassinated Egyptian president Anwar Sadat (1918–1981) as retribution for the peace treaty he signed with Israel—the group saw the treaty as a flagrant betrayal of Islamic interests to the religion's greatest enemy. Shaykh Umar Abd al-Rahman, the blind religious scholar convicted in 1996 of conspiring to blow up New York City's World Trade Center and other U.S. landmarks, was one of Qutb's intellectual disciples.

Today the Muslim Brotherhood and its radical splinter groups are active in Egypt, Palestine, Sudan, Nigeria, Algeria, and several other Muslim nations. Some experts argue that the Muslim Brotherhood is a separate and distinct organization, no longer dedicated to the violent overthrow of corrupt regimes; it prefers instead to compete with secularists within the existing political system. In Jordan, for example, Islamists won election to parliament in significant numbers; in Egypt, while the Brotherhood itself was officially banned, its members were allowed to participate in the Labor Party and to operate their own press. But other analysts claim that the Sunni Islamic movement simply diversified in the 1980s and 1990s, with different levels adopting different tactics—the radical *jamaat* groups going underground and fomenting violent revolution, for example—in order to reach the same ultimate goal of replacing the existing states with Islamic governments and judicial systems based on *shari'a*.

In any event, Sunni Islam produced a variety of fundamentalist parties, movements, and activists in the final decades of the twentieth century. In 1992 the strongest such Algerian party, the Islamic Salvation Front (FIS), was poised to assume a commanding majority in the Algerian parliament. But President Chadhli Benjedid of the ruling National Liberation Front (FLN) resigned, thereby delivering the government into the hands of the military and effectively ending Algeria's three-year experiment in democracy. By winning 180 of the 231 seats contested in the December 1991 election—the first free national election since Algeria gained its independence from France in 1962—the FIS Islamists surprised their secular opponents. Exploiting widespread disgust with the FLN—the Marxist party that has controlled Algeria for thirty years despite a record of inefficiency and corruption—the Islamists mobilized the disgruntled and the zealous alike, including thousands of veiled Algerian women clad in traditional Islamic garb.

After Benjedid's resignation, a High Security Council composed of military and civilian leaders canceled the second round of elections and announced the creation of a five-man body, the High State Council, to rule the country. Described as a junta by FIS spokesmen, this ruling body was headed by a founding member of the FLN and dominated by army officials. A thoroughgoing crackdown on the FIS followed, with the arrest of hundreds of Islamists and the party's most prominent leaders. Since the government crackdown, civil war has raged between the government and tenacious radical factions such as the Armed Islamic Group, which adopted terrorist tactics (including the murder of unveiled Algerian women) in the wake of the failure of Islamic fundamentalists to gain power by legitimate means at the ballot box.

The one Sunni fundamentalist movement to have tasted significant political power, the Sudanese faction of the Muslim Brotherhood (called the National Islamic Front), hardly provided a model of Islam as a force for democratization. Its charismatic leader, the Sorbonne-educated lawyer Hassan Turabi, spoke in grandiose terms of the inevitable Islamization of Africa, the Middle East, and South Asia, but his considerable influence in the Sudanese government did not prevent, and may have abetted, the country's decline into a debilitating civil war waged by the government against Christian and animist rebels in the south. Marred by the excessive human rights violations committed by the regime he helped to govern, Turabi's carefully cultivated image as the enlightened spokesman for the "Islamic Awakening" failed to persuade Islamists in other countries, much less Westerners.

The reach of Sunni Islamic fundamentalism extends to South Asia. In Pakistan, established in 1947, the Jama'at-i Islami (Islamic Group) and other fundamentalist movements characterize Islam as a comprehensive way of life that covers the entire spectrum of human activity, be it individual, social, economic, or political. By contrast, the conservative religious scholars confine Islam to the observance of its five pillars (the profession of faith, prayer, fasting, alms giving, and pilgrimage).

Jama'at-i Islami seeks to acquire political power and establish an Islamic state on the prophetic model. Sayyid Abu al-Ala Mawdudi (1903–1979), the movement's founder, taught that Islam cannot be implemented without the power of the state. His commentary on the Qur'an reads like an Islamic legal-political text, providing guidance in the fields of constitutional, social, civil, criminal, commercial, and international law. By providing Islamic discourse with a political vocabulary, Mawdudi achieved a pervasive influence on contemporary Islamic fundamentalist groups. By defining the Islamic system of life, ideology, constitution, economic system, and political system, Mawdudi elaborated the total subordination of the institutions of civil society and the state to the authority of divine law.

Although Sunni Islamists are more numerous than their Shi'ite counterparts and are organized in many more countries worldwide, the most prominent and politically consequential example of Islamic fundamentalism emerged from within Shi'ite Islam, practiced by about 100 million Muslims concentrated in Iran, Iraq, and Lebanon, and scattered throughout several Persian Gulf states. Shi'ite Muslims have endured a long history of persecution by the majority Sunnis and by non-Muslim rulers; part of their unique belief system holds that the Great Imam, or spiritual leader, will return from self-imposed hiding to lead the Shi'ites to victory over their many enemies. When the Ayatollah Ruholla Khomeini (1900–1989) successfully led a Shi'ite revolution against the modernizing shah of Iran in 1979 and later established the Islamic Republic of Iran, many of his followers came to believe that Khomeini was the Hidden Imam returned, or at least his powerful precursor—an impression Khomeini did little to correct. Instead, he retrieved a little-known Shi'ite teaching and developed it into a politically useful doctrine: the Rule of the Jurist. This innovative interpretation of Shi'ite theology justified the establishment of an Iranian government run by Muslim religious scholars and presided over by the grand ayatollah, Khomeini himself.

While striving to consolidate the Islamic regime in Iran during the 1980s, the charismatic Khomeini and his authoritarian successor, Hashemi Rafsanjani, attempted to spread the Islamic revolution elsewhere, most successfully in Lebanon. In that fragmented nation, suffering the ravages of civil war, the Shi'ite guerrillas of Hezbollah (Party of God) carved out a homeland and launched suicide missions in 1983 against French and U.S. troops stationed in southern Lebanon. Hezbollah eventually exercised political and military control over the region and continues to hold sway there today.

The future of Islamic fundamentalism—and its influence on the development of political systems in Muslim-majority nations—remains a pressing question. Many of the Algerian supporters of the FIS, motivated more by a passion for Islam than for democracy, were obviously not preoccupied with working out a long-term alliance between the two. The

Qur'an and the *shari'a* provide a sociomoral framework rather than a detailed blueprint for the political order, and allow a measure of adaptation and flexibility in state building, as the history of Islam demonstrates. The Islamic Republic of Iran, while maintaining a virulent anti-Western discourse, has nonetheless entered into economic partnership with European and American corporations and with some European governments. In Palestine, Jordan, Nigeria, Algeria, and Saudi Arabia, Sunni Islamic fundamentalists have made great demands on their governments without yet developing coherent and sophisticated alternative economic and social policies; the emphasis has been on cultural and political authenticity and self-reliance.

But the quest for sovereignty and self-reliance does not rule out a gradual process of incorporation and Islamization of Western structures and mechanisms, including mass participation in democratic procedures. Indeed, this has been the pattern followed in the Islamists' appropriation of Western science and technology, a borrowing they describe as an act of "repossession" of a mode of discourse and production that originated, they claim, in the golden age of Islamic civilization.

Jewish Fundamentalism

Two messianic movements within modern Judaism approximate fundamentalist patterns of thought and political behavior. The religious Zionists known as Gush Emunim (Bloc of the Faithful) are found primarily in Israel, while the ultra-Orthodox, mostly Hasidic, Jews known as the haredim (those who tremble before God) live in communities in Israel, Europe, Canada, and the United States. Together these movements constitute a minority within a minority—that is, they are Jews (numbering only fifteen million worldwide) who practice their religion (80 percent of Israelis are nonobservant Jews). More than most other Orthodox Jews, the fundamentalists narrowly focus their energies on the eagerly awaited coming of the Messiah, the divinely sent king who will bring justice to earth and vanquish the enemies of the Jewish people (including a considerable number of lukewarm Jews).

These two groups take different attitudes toward the modern world in general and the Zionist state of Israel in particular. The six thousand hard-core members of Gush Emunim are religious Zionists; they believe that God inspired secular Jews like Theodor Herzl (1860–1904) to create a political movement of Jewish return to Zion, the name for the ancient Jewish homeland in Palestine. Even though the Zionist movement was not explicitly religious, the Jews of Gush Emunim believe that the Zionist political leaders were and are unwitting agents of the Messiah. For evidence of this divine plan, they point to the founding of the state of Israel in 1948 against all odds, and to the astounding victory of Israel against its hostile Arab neighbors in the Six-Day War of 1967, when Israel took control of the Gaza Strip and territories on the West Bank of the Jordan River (which members of Gush Emunim refer to by their biblical names, Judea and Samaria).

To advance God's plan, Gush Emunim members have pressured the Israeli government to annex the territories, which they consider to be part of "the Whole Land of Israel" promised by Yahveh to the Jewish people in the Book of Genesis. However, the Palestinian Arabs who were displaced by the creation of the modern state of Israel claim the same lands as their own home. These competing claims to the West Bank and Gaza have led to several violent confrontations and terrorist episodes between the Jewish settlers and Arab and Muslim militants. For their part, Gush Emunim, like all fundamentalists, reject the idea of religious pluralism, divide the world into realms of evil and good (they believe that all Jews embody a "sacred spark"), and selectively retrieve the most politically useful Orthodox Jewish teachings from the past. Indeed, they selected one of the 613 Jewish ethical obligations—"settle the land"—and made it paramount.

The haredim are the second candidate for inclusion in a category called Jewish fundamentalism. Many returned to Israel but not to participate in the Zionist enterprise. Indeed, haredi Jews denounce Zionism as an ill-advised effort by nonobservant Jews who seek to take God's work into their own hands. To them, it was not God but human pride that inspired Herzl and the other Zionist pioneers. Unlike the Jews of Gush Emunim, who wear jeans, work shirts, and other modern clothes, the haredim wear the long black coats and dress of the Jewish villages of early modern eastern Europe, their traditional home before the onset of the so-called Jewish Enlightenment and disasters such as the Nazi persecution and murder of six million Jews in the Holocaust.

Ultra-Orthodox Jews (known for their strict and unyielding adherence to the imperatives of Jewish law) include Hasidic, Polish, and Galician followers of a charismatic folk Judaism based on feeling, piety, and human attachments, and the Misnagdim, Lithuanian Jews who opposed the excesses of Hasidism and maintained a rigorous attachment to the letter of Jewish rabbinic law.

The haredim live uneasily, as exiles, wherever they are found—including in Zion (Israel), their religious and spiritual homeland. The various eastern European sects live crowded together in enclaves such as Jerusalem's Mea Shearim neighborhood, where the men spend years in yeshivas (religious schools) studying the Torah (the law, contained in the first five books of the Hebrew Bible) and shun the outside world, refusing to join the Israeli army or interact socially with other Israelis. (By contrast, members of Gush Emunim, some of whom studied in the same yeshivas as the haredim, have served in the Israeli army.) Haredi Jews are selectively modern, however; in New York City, for example, they own a photo shop where one can purchase the latest computer and communications technology.

The haredi political parties, such as Agudat Israel (Party of Israel) and Neturei Karta (Guardians of the Gate), were formed primarily to settle disputes within the haredi community itself. But in the 1980s and 1990s they were drawn into the larger world of Israeli politics, where they exercised influence disproportionate to their tiny numbers, often providing the votes needed to bring a larger political coalition to power. They sought to retain their privileges in the Israeli system and to promote the passage of laws to enforce the keeping of the Sabbath and other Orthodox Jewish norms.

Pluralism and Antipluralism

Fundamentalism today is one of several political forces vying for supremacy in the post–cold war world. In most cases fundamentalists represent the noncompromising, antipluralist elements in a conflict. In Israel, for example, both the radical Jewish settlers of Gush Emunim and the Sunni activists of Hamas (Islamic Zeal) violently opposed the peace process pursued by the Israeli government and the Palestine Liberation Organization. Throughout the Islamic world, radical fundamentalists are a destabilizing minority dedicated to the overthrow, by any means, of Western-supported governments. But in the United States, with its strong traditions of pluralism and democracy, Christian fundamentalists "play by the rules" and generally eschew violence. Their hope is to transform American society gradually into a Bible-believing republic, as they believe it once was. Fundamentalism, in other words, may exist in democratic as well as undemocratic societies, but it stands a much greater chance of dominating its enemies in states where pluralism and human rights do not enjoy strong protection under the law.

See also *Banna, Hasan al-; Conservatism; Evangelicalism; Gush Emunim; Herzl, Theodor; Hinduism; Islam; Judiasm; Khomeini, Ruholla Musavi; Mawdudi, Sayyid Abu al-Ala; Millennialism; Qutb, Sayyid; Zionism.*

R. Scott Appleby

BIBLIOGRAPHY

Appleby, R. Scott. "Religious Fundamentalisms and Global Conflict." Foreign Policy Association Headline Series booklet, 1994.

Heilman, Samuel. *Defenders of the Faith: Inside Ultra-Orthodox Jewry.* New York: Schocken Books, 1992.

Kepel, Gilles. *The Revenge of God: The Resurgence of Islam, Christianity, and Judaism in the Modern World.* University Park: Pennsylvania State University Press, 1994.

Marsden, George M. *Understanding Fundamentalism and Evangelicalism.* Grand Rapids, Mich.: Eerdmans, 1991.

Marty, Martin E., and R. Scott Appleby, eds. *Fundamentalisms Observed.* Chicago: University of Chicago Press, 1991.

———. *Fundamentalisms Comprehended.* Chicago: University of Chicago Press, 1995.

G

Gandhi, Mohandas Karamchand

A leading practitioner of civil disobedience and acclaimed as the father of India as a nation. Gandhi (1869–1948) was born in an upper-caste Hindu family and grew up in the religiously plural environment of western India. At nineteen he went to England to train as a lawyer. There he read two religious texts that had a deep and abiding influence upon him, the great Hindu poem the *Bhagavad Gita* and the Bible. He also read an account of the life and teachings of the Buddha. The Jain ideas of nonviolence (*ahimsa*) and nonpossessiveness (*aparigraha*), the Buddhist ethic of renunciation, the Hindu attitude of detachment (*anasakti*)*,* and the Christian values of selfless love and passive (nonaggressive) resistance to evil embodied in Jesus' Sermon on the Mount became the moral foundation of Gandhi's life and work.

On his return to India, Gandhi accepted a short assignment as a legal consultant to an Indian merchant in South Africa. He arrived in Durban in 1893 to discover that Indian settlers in the British colonies of Natal and Transvaal were the victims of vicious racial discrimination. When his contract expired, he decided to stay in South Africa to organize the Indians to fight for their personal dignity and political rights.

Gandhi developed a philosophy of action anchored in an unflinching insistence on truth, *satyagraha,* in thought and deed. He ruled out any compromise with evil but considered it morally obligatory to try to reform the evildoer through love. It was imperative that political actors should be moral individuals, ready to acknowledge their infirmities and atone for them. At the level of collective political action

Gandhi developed the techniques of nonviolent civil disobedience and passive resistance. He maintained that politics was a legitimate instrument, provided that it was subsumed under ultimate values. His religious vision was holistic: "For me, every, the tiniest, activity is governed by what I consider my religion" (1932).

Gandhi, who was a theist but not a ritualist or traditionalist, placed moral reason above scripture. In 1909 he wrote a confession of faith, which was followed by a political pamphlet on Indian self-governance. In these he argued that modern industrial civilization is evil.

Gandhi's efforts on behalf of Indians in South Africa were attended by both successes and failures. Between 1893 and 1915, when he finally returned home, he paid several visits to India and kept in touch with developments there. He became known as a leader in the heroic mold. Rabindranath Tagore (Nobel laureate in literature) acclaimed him as a *mahatma* (great or noble soul), and the title won ready and wide acceptance. It was only in 1917, however, that Gandhi plunged into political activity, championing, first, the cause of an exploited peasant community in northern India and, then, challenging the might of the British raj in Punjab.

During the 1920s and 1930s Gandhi emerged as the unquestioned leader of the Indian National Congress Party. He perceived quite early that two major obstacles impeded the struggle for freedom: the political differences between Hindus and Muslims and the moral and social degeneration of Hindu society, represented most critically by the practice of segregating the group known as untouchables.

In a bold move in 1920 Gandhi, in his first major noncooperation movement against the British, gave support to the

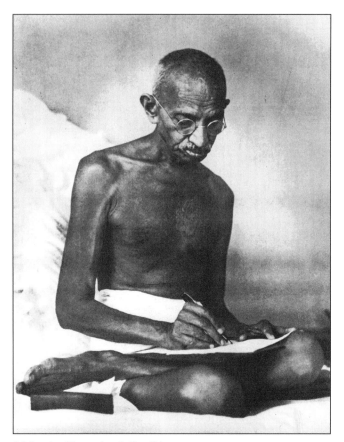

Mohandas Karamchand Gandhi

Turkish sultan. The sultan, recognized by Muslims world-wide as their caliph, or religious leader, had most of his territories taken away from him by the victorious powers at the end of the First World War. Gandhi hoped that his support of the cause of the sultan would bring the Muslims into the Indian national movement. His success in mobilizing Muslims was phenomenal, but it was short lived. His concessions to Muslim sentiments resulted in a right-wing Hindu backlash. Furthermore, conservative Muslims, who were the backbone of the caliphate movement, withdrew their support of Gandhi after the caliphate was abolished by Turkish nationalists. Thus the long-term consequence of his strategy was the strengthening of divisive religious nationalisms. Gandhi met with greater success in his crusade against caste discrimination in Hindu society.

Muslim separatism peaked in 1940, when the demand for partition of the subcontinent on a religious basis was formally made. Gandhi opposed the idea, calling it political folly and moral evil. In 1942 he launched the "Quit India" movement against British rule. All the senior leaders of the Congress Party were jailed. Their absence created an opportunity

for Muslim separatists to mobilize support. When the imprisoned leaders were released, they found that the political situation had changed significantly. India and Pakistan emerged as free nations in 1947 in the midst of unprecedented intercommunity violence and the movement of millions of refugees.

Old and frail, and deeply disappointed, Gandhi refused to give up his vision of religious concord in the subcontinent. He called for the establishment of a secular state in India. His efforts on behalf of the Muslims who stayed in India angered Hindu fanatics. One of them, Nathuram Godse, shot Gandhi dead on January 30, 1948, when he was on his way to an evening prayer meeting.

Gandhi's emphases on the moral foundations of society and on nonviolence in politics have won universal recognition. His influence has been acknowledged in major political struggles, notably that of African Americans under the leadership of Martin Luther King Jr. In a world that has woken up to the destructive dimensions of technology, consumerism, and religious fundamentalism, Gandhi's ideas of religious pluralism, limitation of desires, and living in harmony with nature have acquired a keen relevance.

See also *Hinduism; India.*

T. N. Madan

BIBLIOGRAPHY

Chatterji, Margaret. *Gandhi's Religious Thought.* Notre Dame, Ind.: University of Notre Dame Press, 1983.
Nanda, Bal Ram. *Mahatma Gandhi: A Biography.* London: Allen and Unwin, 1958.
Parekh, Bhikhu. *Gandhi's Political Philosophy.* London: Macmillan, 1989.

Gender

Gender, which derives from the Latin *gener* (genus, birth, race, kind, gender), has traditionally referred to a grammatical feature of Indo-European languages that classifies nouns, pronouns, and modifiers in arbitrary groupings (masculine, feminine, and neuter). A secondary meaning of the word equates it with biological sex. With the women's movement that took on new energy in the 1960s and 1970s, gender has become a key analytical term in feminist studies.

In Western societies two genders are thought to exist. They are understood as mutually exclusive and, at best, complementary: one is either a woman or a man but not both.

Generally, *male* and *female* classify beings primarily on the basis of anatomical differences; *men* and *women* connote social agents; and *masculine* and *feminine* or *man* and *woman* express cultural-religious ideals, values, and standards appropriate to one's gender. The cultural construct of male and female, masculine and feminine as both complementary and mutually exclusive categories constitutes the Western sex/gender system that correlates sex to cultural contents according to social hierarchies and values.

Gender then is a societal construct, a principle of classification that imposes psychological, social, cultural, religious, and political meaning upon biological sexual identity. In the 1970s women's studies distinguished social gender from biological sex; by the mid-1980s gender studies had emerged as a distinct field of inquiry that questions seemingly universal beliefs about women and men and attempts to unmask their cultural and societal roots.

Gender as an Ideological Structure

Language in general reinforces cultural-religious gender assumptions. If one does not distinguish between sex as a biological given and gender as a cultural construct but sees both sex and gender as sociocultural constructions that together constitute the Western sex/gender system, one can analyze this system as a cultural symbolic structure of representation that has become "naturalized" in people's way of thinking. As an ideological structure, gender actively naturalizes this sex/gender system through grammar, language, biology, and culture and makes its construction of sexual difference appear to be "common sense" views.

Moreover, in Western linguistic systems, masculine terms function as "generic" language. *Man, male, masculine,* and *he* stand for human and male, whereas *woman, female, feminine,* and *she* connote only femaleness. In other words, Western languages are androcentric, that is, male-centered. Grammatically androcentric Western languages explicitly mention woman only as the exception to the rule or as particular individuals. Unless women are specifically mentioned, one has to decide in light of contextual linguistic markers whether women are meant to be included or not.

Western androcentric languages and discourses do not just marginalize women or eliminate them from historical records. As kyriocentric (from the Greek *kyrios,* which means lord or master) languages, they also construct the meaning of being a woman or a man differently. What it means to be female does not so much depend on one's sex

but on one's location in the kyriarchal system. The meaning of *woman* is unstable and shifting: it depends not so much on its sex/gender relation but on the context of the time and place in which it is used.

For example, *woman* today is used interchangeably with *female* and thus has become a generic sex-based term, although until very recently it was applied to lower-class females only. One can perceive the historical ambiguity of the term *woman* much more easily if one compares it with the term *lady,* an appellation that readily reveals its race, class, and colonial bias. Not only has *lady* been restricted to women of higher status or educational refinement, until recently it also symbolized "true womanhood" and femininity. A statement such as "slaves were not women" offends our common-sense understanding, whereas a statement such as "slaves were not ladies" makes perfect sense in this context.

In most Western languages the lady, mistress, and mother is the "other" of the lord, master, and father. All other women are marked as inferior by race, class, religion, or culture, and as the "others" of the other are not mentioned at all. One can illustrate, for example, how such supposedly generic language works with reference to a famous biblical text, Galatians 3:28, which states that in Christ there is "neither Jew nor Greek, slave nor free, neither male and female." Generally, this statement is understood as referring to three different groups: Jew and Greek as religious-ethnic characterizations, slave and free as sociopolitical determinations, and male and female as biological sex/gender opposites. Such an understanding of the text carries the inference that "Jew," "Greek," "slave," and "free" pertain solely to men and that only the third pair, "male and female," refers to both men and women.

The social classification of gender, like the grammatical, does not always correspond to the biological classification of sex. Anthropologists have pointed out that not all cultures and languages know of only two sexes/genders, and historians of gender have argued that even in Western culture the dual sex/gender system is of modern origins. Thomas Laqueur, for instance, has argued that a decisive shift took place in modernity: a shift from the ancient one-sex model to the present dichotomous, two-sex model. Women were once believed to have the same sex and genitals as men except that women's were inside the body whereas men's were outside. In this one-sex model the vagina was understood to be an interior penis; the labia, the foreskin; the uterus, the scrotum; and the ovaries, testicles. Not biological sex but gender was the primary category determining the order of things.

What it meant to be a man or a woman in the ancient one-sex model was determined by social rank and by one's place in society, not by sexual organs. As man or woman, one performed a cultural role according to one's social status and was not thought to be organically one of two incommensurable sexes. Not sex but the social status of the elite, propertied male heads of household determined superior gender status. Hence the ancients did not need to resort to sexual difference for supporting the claim that women were inferior to men. Rather because women were subordinate beings, their "nature" was believed to be inferior.

Beginning with the Enlightenment in the eighteenth century, the two-sex model—the notion that there are two stable, opposite sexes—emerges. It was commonly believed that the economic, political, and cultural lives of women and men, their gender roles, are based on two sexes that are biologically given. Just as in antiquity the body was seen as reflecting the cosmological order, so in modernity the body and sexuality are seen as representing and legitimating the social-political order. But the social and political changes wrought by the Enlightenment produced the change from the one-sex to the two-sex model. Because the Enlightenment's claims for human liberty and equality did not exclude freeborn women, new arguments had to be fashioned if men were to justify their dominance over the public domain.

The promise of democracy, the promise that women and disenfranchised men could achieve civic and personal liberties, generated a new kind of antifeminist argument based on nature, physiology, and science. Those who opposed, for instance, the democratic participation of freeborn women sought evidence for women's mental and physical unsuitability for the public sphere by arguing that women's bodies and biology made them unfit to participate.

The doctrine of separate spheres for men and women thus arose together with the dual-sex model. It also shattered the notion of a male hierarchy. In Enlightenment discourses women are no longer construed as lesser men but as totally different from men, as beings of a "purer race," as an "angelic species" less affected than men by sexual drives and desires. With women excluded from the new civil society, the physical and moral differences between men and women were conceived to ensure that women and men did not resemble each other in mind any more than in body. Two incommensurable sexes are the result of these exclusionary practices.

Contemporary feminist work on gender has attempted to unravel the politics of this modern two-sex model. Teresa de Lauretis, for instance, argues that gender is the product of various social technologies, institutional discourses, and practices of daily life. Gender as a sociocultural construct does not connote a biological, anthropological, or psychological given but a semiotic difference that assigns meaning to individuals within a society.

The assumption of natural sex/gender differences serves as a preconstructed frame of meaning for individuals and cultural institutions. By presenting the sex/gender system of male and female or masculine and feminine as universal, this preconstructed frame of meaning obscures the reality that the very notion of two sexes is a sociocultural construct for maintaining domination rather than a biological essence. Feminist studies hold that gender classifies persons on the basis of conceptualized biological sex differences. Sexual differences depend on sociocultural communicative practices of self-recognition and therefore can be developed and changed.

Individuals recognize gender and appropriate ascriptions because they are real for them. Gender is thus a product and process not only of representation but also of self-representation. The recognition of women's own participation in the construction of gender makes it possible to see that gender, if it is constructed, can also be deconstructed or differently constructed. Understanding gender as a product and process makes it possible for feminist theory to analyze cultural masculinity and femininity with the idea of changing them.

Gender as a Sociopolitical Structure

Gender is a social institution as well as an ideological representation. Generally accepted gender expectations define the socially recognized genders in a given society. The gendered division of labor assigns work according to gender, whereas kinship spells out family rights and responsibilities for each gender. Gender scripts prescribe behavior and grant prerogatives. Social controls, which reward conforming behavior and stigmatize aberrant conduct, produce personalities that conform to gender roles. Finally, gender ideology and imagery, the cultural representations of gender in symbolic language and artistic production, legitimate and support dominant gender statuses.

For instance, the modern ethos of femininity, which prescribes that "good" women perform unpaid services inside and outside the family, therefore prescribes selfless love, nurturing care, and patient loving-kindness as feminine virtues. The ethos of "true womanhood," romantic love, and domesticity defines woman's nature as "being for others" in actual or spiritual motherhood. Whereas men are measured by the masculine standards of self-assertion, independence, power, and control, women are called to fulfill their true nature and destiny in self-sacrificing service and loving self-effacement. The cultural socialization of women to selfless femininity and altruistic behavior is reinforced and perpetuated by the Christian preaching of self-sacrificing love and humble service.

Although maleness and femaleness supposedly are biological givens, they are actually cultural norms that are backed by social sanctions. In antiquity, for instance, menial service was seen as appropriate to the nature of slaves and serfs; in modernity it is construed as a feminine ideal appropriate to the nature of women. Public political service in turn is conceptualized as masculine, appropriate to the nature of men. This separation between the public male sphere and the private female domain is at the root of an economic system that frequently leaves female-headed households destitute, a development that has devastating effects, especially on women and children of developing countries.

Gender as an individual identity structure rests on the ascription of a sex category from birth or even before birth. Gender identity constitutes a sense of self; it determines marital and procreative status as well as sexual orientation that patterns sexual desires, feelings, and identifications. The outcome is the gendered personality fashioned by socially normative patterns and emotions inculcated through family structure, parenting, and education.

Finally, gendered practices internalize learned social gender behavior, sexual cues, and gender socialization and interaction, while gender display presents the self as a masculine or feminine person through dress, cosmetics, and other permanent or reversible body markers. Thus the inferior status of women is achieved not by force but in and through individual socialization. Religion has played a major role in the construction and symbolic legitimization of such naturalized gender, race, class, and colonial relations.

Gender as a sociopolitical and psychological practice of domination and subordination is only one of several social ascriptions that promote the exploitation of women. Feminists argue that if one realizes that gender is modified by race, class, age, religion, sexual preference, and ethnicity, one is able to demystify naturalized gender oppositions. Conceptualizing gender as a practice that produces not only sex differences but also those of race, class, sexual preference, culture, religion, age, and nationality allows one to see that individual women are not just gendered but have other characteristics.

By the fourth century B.C., the Greek philosopher Aristotle argued that the freeborn, propertied, educated Greek man is the highest of moral beings and that all other members of the human race are defined by their functions in his service. Until the modern women's movement, political philosophy continued to assume that propertied, educated, elite Western man was defined by reason, self-determination, and full citizenship, whereas women and other subordinated people were characterized by emotion, service, and dependence. They were seen not as rational and responsible adults but as emotional and helpless children.

In short, kyriarchal societies needed a "servant class" or people—be they slaves, serfs, house servants, kulaks, or mammies. The existence of a servant class was maintained through law, education, socialization, and brute violence. It was sustained by the belief that members of a servant class are by nature or by divine decree inferior to those whom they are destined to serve.

Such relations of domination and subordination are articulated in Western political philosophy in the context of Greek patriarchal democracy. They have been mediated by Christian theological traditions and have determined modern kyriarchal forms and ideologies of democracy. Genevieve Lloyd, among others, has argued that modern (and postmodern) understandings of rationality and of the world have been articulated by white, European-American, elite, educated men. These men have not only defined white women as "others" but have also regarded all "others" as nonpersons who lack human, that is, masculine, qualities.

Nineteenth-century scientists constructed women, the "lower races," the sexually deviant, the criminal, the urban poor, and the insane as biological "races apart." Their differences from the white male, and their likeness to each other, explained their lower position in the social hierarchy. In this scheme the lower races represented the feminine aspect of the human species, and women represented the lower race of gender. Hence it is important to see gender as one among several structures of domination constructed to serve the division of power and wealth by sex, economics, race, culture, nationality, and religion.

Religion and Gender

If the ideological and social institution of gender is shaped by power relations, feminist theory and feminist studies aim not only to criticize and reconstruct perceived knowledge but also to dismantle powers of oppression and dehumanization. Since the industrial revolution in Europe and America at the beginning of the nineteenth century, church and religion have been pushed out of the public realm and relegated to the private sphere of individualistic piety, charitable work, and the cultivation of home and family. Nevertheless, both religion and women were crucial in shaping American identity. As a "missionary religion," Christianity had the same function as the "white lady." It was to "civilize the savages," who were understood as "untamed nature."

Because theology and religion are heavily gendered in masculine terms, they have reinforced cultural gender roles and concepts and legitimized them as ordained by God or as the "order of creation." As Judith Plaskow has argued, Christian male theologians have formulated theological concepts in terms of their own cultural experience, insisting on male language relating to God and on a kyriarchal symbolic universe in which women do not appear.

For instance, many Christian churches still exclude women from ordination to the priesthood on grounds of anatomy: it is female sex alone that disqualifies a woman from representing Christ. Whereas traditional theology had rationalized the exclusion of women on Aristotelian and scriptural grounds of subordination, modern theology argues that women cannot physically resemble Christ, the bridegroom of the church.

Feminist theologies insist that religious texts and traditions must be read in the framework of the promise of the Enlightenment—that women and other nonpersons could achieve full citizenship, human liberty, and radical equality. They argue that differences of sex/gender, race, class, and ethnicity are socioculturally constructed and not willed by God and must be changed. God, who created people in the divine image, has called every individual differently and is to be found in and among people who are created equal.

Replacing the one-sex model with that of a divine image that is neither male nor female, white nor black, rich nor poor but multicolored and multigendered would open up the possibility of moving beyond the masculine monism of the one-sex model and the asymmetric dualism of the sex/gender system. Such a process would offer the prospect of deconstructing gender and of fashioning identity and community in the variegated image of the divine in our midst.

See also *Feminism; Homosexuality; Sexuality.*

Elisabeth Schüssler Fiorenza

BIBLIOGRAPHY

Baron, Dennis. *Grammar and Gender.* New Haven: Yale University Press, 1986.

Butler, Judith. *Gender Trouble: Feminism and the Subversion of Identity.* New York: Routledge, 1990.

Cameron, Deborah. *Feminism and Linguistic Theory.* London: Macmillan, 1985.

Caraway, Nancy. *Segregated Sisterhood: Racism and the Politics of American Feminism.* Knoxville: University of Tennessee Press, 1991.

Chopp, Rebecca S. *The Power to Speak: Feminism, Language, and God.* New York: Crossroad, 1989.

De Lauretis, Teresa. *Technologies of Gender.* Bloomington: Indiana University Press, 1987.

hooks, bell. *Yearning: Race, Gender, and Cultural Politics.* Boston: South End Press, 1990.

Laqueur, Thomas. *Making Sex. Body and Gender from the Greeks to Freud.* Cambridge: Harvard University Press, 1990.

Lorber, Judith. *Paradoxes of Gender.* New Haven: Yale University Press, 1990.

Miller, Casey, and Kate Swift. *Words and Women.* Garden City, N.Y.: Anchor Books, 1977.

Moller Okin, Susan. *Justice, Gender, and the Family.* New York: Basic Books, 1989.

Plaskow, Judith. *Sex, Sin, and Grace: Women's Experience and the Theologies of Niebuhr and Tillich.* Washington: University Press of America, 1980.

Rothenberg, Paula S. *Race, Class, and Gender in the United States: An Integrated Study.* 3d ed. New York: St. Martin's, 1995.

Schüssler Fiorenza, Elisabeth. *But She Said: Feminist Practices of Biblical Interpretation.* Boston: Beacon Press, 1992.

———. *Jesus: Miriam's Child, Sophia's Prophet: Critical Issues in Feminist Christology.* New York: Continuum, 1994.

Genocide and "ethnic cleansing"

The terms *genocide* and *ethnic cleansing* were both coined in the twentieth century to describe the attempted extermination of a specific group of people by their own government. *Genocide* was first used in 1944 in regard to the Holocaust, and *ethnic cleansing* was first used in the early 1990s to describe the policies of Bosnian Serb militias against Muslim civilians after the breakup of Yugoslavia. The concepts and the practices have been in use for much longer, across the globe. But our era has earned the title Century of Genocide.

The 1948 United Nations Convention on the Prevention and Punishment of the Crime of Genocide defines that crime as "acts committed with intent to destroy, in whole or in part, a national, ethnical, racial, or religious group." From the point of view of international criminal law, genocide is a specific crime against humanity. But the convention has been criticized by scholars from two major, different points of view. Some argue that the genocide convention is too sweeping, allowing the serious charge of genocide to be leveled if just a part of a group, implicitly even a very small part, is targeted for destruction. Others argue that it is too narrow, failing to outlaw attempts to exterminate political or social groups. Conceivably, both could be correct.

Social scientists and historians have proposed, first, new typologies of genocide. For example, separate categories for religious, racial, and ethnic genocides have been established, those of colonial conquest and those prescribed by a political ideology. One typology includes "retributive" genocide, in which mass murder is perpetrated for revenge; "institutional" genocide, which accompanied military conquest in premodern history; "utilitarian" genocide, associated with colonial expansion or economic exploitation; "monopolistic" genocide, used to transform plural societies; and "ideological" genocide. Another uses the first and last of these categories, but substitutes "developmental" or "despotic" genocide for the others. And another typology distinguishes between genocides according to the motive of the perpetrator, whether it is to eliminate what is perceived to be a threat, to terrorize enemies, to increase wealth, or to impose an ideology.

The imprecision of the UN convention's terms raises questions about whether nonviolent or even forcible cultural assimilation constitutes genocide, or rather a distinct phenomenon sometimes called *ethnocide*. And the convention's restricted range of victim groups has led to the coining of *democide* for killings of any large populations. These issues have all provoked a search for new scholarly definitions. The terms *genocidal massacres* and *related atrocities* have been coined for mass killings of groups beyond the scope of the convention's definition of genocide, either because the perpetrators targeted social or political groups or because of their lack of intent to destroy a group. A term like *genocidal massacres* is also needed for killings that are sporadic and limited to a few towns or rural locations. As scholars have slowly converged on a new definition, the first international legal implementations of the convention—the Ad Hoc International Tri-

bunals on the Former Yugoslavia and Rwanda—have refocused attention on enforcing the 1948 definition.

Early and Modern Cases of Genocide

It is suspected that genocide was fairly common even in antiquity. The best-known but sometimes still contentious cases since earliest times include the Athenian destruction of Melos (416 B.C.) during the Peloponnesian War, the Roman obliteration of Carthage in 146 B.C., the ravages of the Mongols under Genghis Khan in the thirteenth century, the Albigensian Crusade in thirteenth-century Europe, the persecution of Christians in early modern Japan, the mass killings of Ndwandwe people by Shaka's Zulu armies in the 1820s, and the destruction of certain Native American and Aboriginal peoples in the New World and Australia. Critics of the British imperial regime also used the term *extermination* to characterize the Irish famine of the 1840s, during which at least a million people perished.

The twentieth century opened on a continuing theme, with the near extermination of the colonized Herero people of southwestern Africa by their German conquerors. Ten years later, during World War I, the Young Turk rulers of the Ottoman Empire deported the Armenian people from their homelands, causing the death of more than a million in forced marches and massacres. This was the first premeditated genocide in modern times. During World War II, in an escalating series of persecutions, deportations, mass shootings, and extermination in gas chambers, the Nazis (National Socialists) murdered nearly 6 million European Jews and 500,000 Gypsies. This—the Holocaust—became the archetypal genocide, the most extreme case in history if not a unique one. It has been fruitfully compared with the Armenian genocide. The Khmer Rouge genocide from 1975 to 1979 in Cambodia, then called Democratic Kampuchea; the Bosnian ethnic cleansing and concentration camps; and the ethnic Hutu regime's 1994 racial massacres in Rwanda, killing 1.5 million Tutsi and their Hutu defenders in four months, have all evoked similar memories of that first modern genocide.

Two other major series of mass killings have marked our century. Although not always described as genocide, these fall into the category of ideological or political mass murder of opponents or suspected opponents, sometimes called *politicide*. First, communist regimes, most particularly Joseph Stalin's Soviet Union and the later Soviet client state Ethiopia, as well as China and its client states North Korea and Cambodia, have targeted entire social and political groups for physical extermination.

In the Soviet Union the kulak class of rich peasants, almost the entire Soviet political class, religious and other dissidents, and various ethnic minorities—all were targets of Stalin's murderous purges, which took tens of millions of lives, especially in the 1930s. Mao Zedong's extermination of China's landlord class after 1949 killed several million people. Another 20 million to 30 million Chinese perished in the greatest human tragedy of the postwar world, the famine during the "Great Leap Forward" of 1958–1961. The evidence suggests that this famine, though man-made, was not deliberately instigated but was a disastrous result of rampant ideological arrogance and extraordinary economic mismanagement. The enforced starvation of Cambodians from 1975 to 1979 by the pro-Chinese Pol Pot regime, ostensibly pursuing a "Super Great Leap Forward," also involved ideological retribution and mass political killings (as well as ethnic exterminations), accompanied by the export of food amid nationwide hunger.

Second, political mass murder by anticommunist regimes, with links to the United States and an ideological obsession with guarding "national security" and preventing social reform, has been prevalent in Latin America and Southeast Asia. Such regimes instigated the "Matanza" massacres in El Salvador in the 1930s and the army-organized "death squads" that killed 70,000 people there in the 1980s, the state-sponsored slaughter of 150,000 indigenous Indian peasants of Guatemala beginning in the 1960s, the murderous 1973 coup in Chile, and the "dirty wars" and mass disappearances of civilians in Argentina, Brazil, Colombia, Peru, and Uruguay. This continental phenomenon may be compared to the killings of 500,000–800,000 communists and other civilians by the Suharto military regime in Indonesia in 1965–1966 and of similar numbers of Vietnamese, Cambodian, and Lao civilians by U.S. and allied forces in Indochina during the wars of intervention from 1954 to 1975. To these may be added the 200,000 East Timorese victims of the Indonesian army's continuing bloody campaign to annex and incorporate their territory since Jakarta's initial invasion of 1975.

Religion and Race

Perpetrators of genocide and ethnic cleansing are usually preoccupied with ethnic or racial visions—and divisions. But their concepts can be dissimilar, internally inconsistent, or combined with a range of other political features. They may be based on notions of religious heritage, racial purity, ethnic hierarchy, biological theory, geographical origin, national citizenship, or combinations of these and other ideological preoccupations.

In colonial genocides, racial divisions are usually clearcut. In other cases, religion has played an equally important role. The Armenian genocide, quickly followed by massacres of Greeks, was in part an attempt to eliminate Christian non-Turks from a newly defined Turkish Muslim nation. But it also involved forcible assimilation (or ethnocide) of Muslim non-Turks. Kurdish Muslims were mobilized to kill Armenians. They were then reclassified as "Mountain Turks," and forbidden to practice their separate culture—or even to speak the Kurdish language. In Cambodia, the majority religion, Buddhism, along with Islam and Christianity, was repressed by the antireligious Khmer Rouge regime. Minority and foreign languages were also banned, and Khmer became the only permitted language. The fiercest extermination campaign was directed at the ethnic Cham Muslim minority, who suffered a combination of genocide and ethnocide, and at the Vietnamese, all of whom were expelled or murdered. The Vietnamese Catholic cathedral in Phnom Penh was dismantled by a Khmer Rouge decision with explicit racialist overtones.

In the case of Germany, anti-Semitism was central to Nazism. Adolf Hitler's pathological hatred for the Jews was perhaps best illustrated in the Nazi film *Der Ewige Jude* ("The Eternal Jew"), which depicted Jews as rats.

Genocidal regimes, radical and often unstable, make decisions on pragmatic as well as ideological grounds, in order to maintain or secure their grip on power. For similar reasons, genocidal racialism often proves deadly to many members of the supposedly privileged or protected race. This was least true in the case of the Armenian genocide, where the number of Turkish victims was low. By contrast, in absolute numbers, most victims of the Khmer Rouge regime were from the country's ethnic Khmer majority. Under Nazism, Jews were the largest single group to be exterminated; no other large group was exterminated more systematically than Jews were. But the numerous other victims were not even limited to "non-Aryans" such as Gypsies and Slavs. Hitler targeted German homosexuals, communists, liberals, trade unionists, and others who opposed him. In the Nazi purge of German culture, books and paintings were burned, literary and film criticism abolished, and modern music banned. The day after

As allied troops advanced on Nazi concentration camps at the end of World War II, prisoners of the camps—not only Jews but also homosexuals, communists, liberals, and anyone opposing the Nazis—were forced to undertake extended, deadly marches. The "death marches," including this one from Dachau concentration camp, constituted the final initiative in the German army's campaign of genocide.

the *Kristallnacht* (Night of Crystal, or Night of Broken Glass) pogrom on November 9, 1938, Hitler speculated that if someday the intellectual classes in Germany became unuseful, he might exterminate them.

During the Nazi invasion of Poland, more than 750,000 ethnic Germans were put into camps. The SS investigated and interrogated them. The "racially unfit," those who opposed Nazism, and those whom the SS disliked for some other reason were killed. Thousands more were mistreated before the SS decided to send them either to Germany or the east. Thus many German settlements were demolished or turned over to the Poles. This illustrates how the individual was rejected in favor of the race. Individuals were not privileged by virtue of their membership in a particular race but, rather, their individual rights were suppressed and the idealized group given primacy.

Nazi "eugenics" eliminated 70,000 Germans with hereditary illnesses. This euthanasia forms a close link with the destruction of Jews: the Nazis considered both sets of victims to be unproductive and to have an unpleasing outward phys-

ical appearance and thus to be biologically inferior and unworthy of life. By the same token, Gypsies, although defined in 1935 as "alien to the German species," were in the early years of the war persecuted not on the basis of race but on the basis of an "asocial and criminal past" and their being a threat to security. Some more-assimilated Gypsies, known as Sinti, even became members of the armed forces, where they served until 1942, when all Gypsies were ordered to be sent to the concentration camp at Auschwitz.

The Nuremberg Laws, designed by Hitler and approved by the Nazis in 1935, defined a "mixed-blood" Jew (*Mischlinge*) as anyone who had one or two "fully Jewish" grandparents. "Fully Jewish" was defined as belonging to the Jewish religious community. It has been contended that an individual was considered Jewish only if he or she had three or four Jewish grandparents or if the individual had two Jewish grandparents and belonged to the Jewish religion or was married to a Jewish person. The most important issue always was the religion of the grandparents.

In Cambodia, Khmer Rouge racism was even more inconsistent, with no attempt at "scientific" precision. Formal Nazi and communist differences aside, the Khmer Rouge considered their captive urban populations "subhuman" (*anoupracheachun*), the same term (*Untermenschen*) the Nazis had used for conquered Slavs. Democratic Kampuchea referred to its enemies as "microbes"; the Germans had talked of "vermin" and "lice." Pol Pot considered his revolution the only "clean" one in history, just as the Nazis "cleaned" occupied areas of Jews. Both regimes were obsessed with the concept of racial "purity." Pol Pot called himself the "Original Khmer," but his preoccupations had precedents.

People and Land

Genocidal regimes often proclaim a need to "purify" not only a race but a territory. The Young Turks dreamed of a Pan-Turanian empire of Turkish-speaking peoples across Central Asia. As Christian provinces in the Balkans seceded from the Ottoman Empire in the years before World War I, there was an increasing call to make the remaining parts Turkish. The Young Turks initially chose to name their country Turkestan, with expansionist Central Asian connotations. Purification and expansion went hand in hand.

The Nazi attempts to expand their territory and to exterminate the Jews were similarly connected. Hitler initially envisaged individual German, Polish, and Jewish areas of population from west to east. Pragmatic considerations gave priority to exchanging populations of Poles and German settlers, then expelling or exterminating Jews.

First, idealization of the land itself played an important role. Enver Pasha claimed that it was the rural class that had given his Young Turk army its strength. National Socialism descended from the *Volkisch* (folk) tradition, a product of the romanticism of the late eighteenth century. It is believed that Nazi nationalism sprang directly from the doctrine of "blood and soil" (*Blut und Boden*), which sought strength for the *Herrenvolk* (master race) in German soil and in peasant virtues. Hitler declared the farmer "the most important participant" in the Nazi revolution. In *Mein Kampf* ("My Struggle"), he linked German peasant farmland with German racial characteristics. Then the Nazi peasant leader Walther Darré took up the concept of *Blut und Boden* and became the main theoretician of expansion and agricultural settlement to the east.

Prefiguring Pol Pot, Hitler proclaimed that a nation could exist without cities but not without farmers. He described modern industrial cities as "abscesses on the body of the folk [*Volkskörper*], in which all vices, bad habits, and sicknesses seem to unite. They are above all hotbeds of miscegenation and bastardization." The Khmer Rouge took this much further, evacuating the cities of Cambodia and seeing only the peasants as allies in their revolution.

The Nazis believed in the superiority and virtue of rural life. It has been asserted that *Blut und Boden* was one of National Socialism's very few consistent concepts. A film of that name made for use in Nazi Party meetings was subtitled *Foundation of the New Reich.* Hitler's minister of agriculture saw the issue in a way that Pol Pot could have put it: "Neither princes, nor the church, nor the cities have created the German man. Rather, the German man emerged from the German peasantry." Joseph Goebbels, Hitler's propagandist, commissioned at least seven feature films on the topic of "blood and soil." Another antiurban, anti-intellectual semidocumentary, *The Eternal Forest,* idealized the woods. The film depicts a master race represented by the German peasant, whose blood has fertilized the sacred soil for centuries. This view of "blood and soil" has been connected with Nazi anti-Semitism.

Second, the land question is geographic as well as ideological. The decline of the Ottoman Empire from the sixteenth century made fear of further territorial diminution a political preoccupation for the Turks. Ottoman rulers were warned that Europeans would rule over Islamic lands unless defensive action were taken. For the Young Turks the survival of the Ottoman state was the most important issue.

In August 1939 Hitler recited his list of territorial gains—Austria, Czechoslovakia, the Rhineland, Sudetenland—while still proclaiming the threat of Germany's "certain annihilation." German territorial stability was unachievable. Failure to expand meant annihilation. This special perception of the conditions of Germany's survival has a counterpart common among Cambodian nationalists too. The reasons are also similar: a historically recent national territorial formation and the twin peaks, heightened by the proximity of recent gains, of national ambition and national insecurity.

Modern Germany was not the immediate heir to the medieval Holy Roman Empire. A nineteenth-century unification resulted in the establishment of the German Reich in 1871. Anti-Semitism increased and German colonial expansion soon began. Territorial setbacks and defeat in World War I fueled German nationalism and chauvinism.

Medieval Cambodia dominated mainland Southeast Asia, much as medieval Germany had dominated Europe. But modern Cambodian territory was consolidated shortly before World War I, as Germany's had been earlier. The year 1907 saw the "return" to Cambodia (then under French rule) of its entire northwest quadrant, under Thai rule since 1794. In 1914 more territory was restored to Cambodia by the French, in an exchange with another French colony, Vietnam, to the east. A third territorial dispute (with Thailand) was resolved in Cambodia's favor in 1961.

The return of the northwest territories, which included the famous medieval temples of Angkor, had a major impact on Cambodian elite nationalism. When large territories are first regained, especially by a weak colonized state, they raise the stakes in the border conflict, but they also heighten consciousness of further ancestral losses. Cambodian nationalist attention became focused on other, longer lost, Khmer-speaking areas: several provinces of modern Thailand, whose ethnic Khmer majority still call themselves Upper Cambodians, and also Vietnam's Mekong Delta, whose ethnic Khmer minority are known as Lower Cambodians. The territorial gains made between 1907 and 1914 encouraged Cambodia to petition France for the additional transfer of the Mekong Delta from Vietnamese to Cambodian rule for the first time since 1750.

In World War II, with Japanese support, the Thais again seized the northwest of Cambodia (just as Germany had lost territories in World War I). The tide was turned again in 1946, when Thailand had to return the territories. But Khmer vulnerability had been reemphasized in both military defeat and territorial diminution. This became the nationalist nightmare, even though it had been a loss only in post-1907 terms, and only a temporary one. To the Khmer Rouge, like the Nazis, geographical stability was impossible. Cambodia had to recover its long-lost territories at the expense of its neighbors.

Some German historians have emphasized Germany's dilemma as "the country in the middle," unprotected by natural boundaries, and threatened by her great neighbors: Russia on one side, France and Britain on the other. It has been said that Germany has been Europe's No-Man's Land. For its part, Cambodia, with Thailand on one side and Vietnam on the other, has been called "The Land in Between."

Just as Hitler saw Czechoslovakia as "a dagger pointed at the heart of Germany," Pol Pot saw Cambodia's decline as uninterrupted by its twentieth-century territorial gains. His millennial view of the past stressed "2,000 years of exploitation" and rule by national traitors selling off territory. In a major public speech in 1977, Pol Pot urged his people to "prevent the constant loss of Cambodia's territory." This required both "tempering" his country's population and reconquering long-lost territory. The next year, Khmer Rouge radio exhorted its listeners not only to "purify" the "masses of the people" of Cambodia but also to sacrifice "only 2 million troops to crush the 50 million Vietnamese, and we would still have 6 million people left."

See also *Anti-Semitism; Holocaust; Human rights.*

Ben Kiernan

BIBLIOGRAPHY

Andreopoulos, George J., ed. *Genocide: Conceptual and Historical Dimensions.* Philadelphia: University of Pennsylvania Press, 1994.

Browning, Christopher R. *The Path to Genocide: Essays on Launching the Final Solution.* Cambridge: Cambridge University Press, 1992.

Chalk, Frank, and Kurt Jonassohn. *The History and Sociology of Genocide: Analyses and Case Studies.* New Haven: Yale University Press, 1990.

Charny, Israel, ed. *Towards the Understanding and Prevention of Genocide.* Boulder, Colo.: Westview Press, 1984.

Chomsky, Noam, and Edward S. Herman. *The Political Economy of Human Rights.* Vol. 1, *The Washington Connection and Third World Fascism.* Boston: South End Press, 1979.

Fein, Helen. *Genocide: A Sociological Perspective.* Special issue of *Current Sociology* 38 (spring 1990).

Fleming, Gerald. *Hitler and the Final Solution.* Berkeley: University of California Press, 1984.

Kiernan, Ben. *The Pol Pot Regime: Race, Power, and Genocide in Cambodia under the Khmer Rouge, 1975–1979.* New Haven: Yale University Press, 1996.

Kuper, Leo. *Genocide: Its Political Uses in the Twentieth Century.* New Haven: Yale University Press, 1981.

Melson, Robert. *Revolution and Genocide: On the Origins of the Armenian Genocide and the Holocaust.* Chicago: University of Chicago Press, 1992.

Rummel, R. J. *Death by Government.* New Brunswick, N.J.: Transaction Books, 1994.

Totten, Samuel, William S. Parsons, and Israel W. Charny, eds. *Century of Genocide: Critical Essays and Eyewitness Accounts.* New York: Garland Press, 1997.

Turner, Henry A., Jr. *Reappraisals of Fascism.* New York: Franklin Watts, 1975.

Germany

One of the most powerful countries in modern Europe, Germany has been a country religiously divided between Roman Catholicism and Protestantism since the Reformation and Counter Reformation of the sixteenth century.

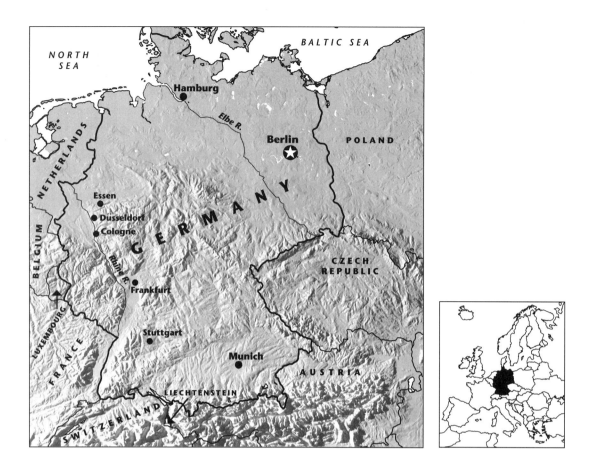

Hence "religion" and "denomination" have been used as synonyms in Germany for centuries. This bitterly fought struggle between the faiths ended in the twentieth century. With the rapid decline of traditional religious life, people increasingly view the two Christian churches largely as not representing their political and social values.

From Religious Schism to the Nazi Period

Unsuccessful attempts by both the Catholics and the Protestants (Lutherans) to achieve ascendancy led to the insight early on that the respective adversary could not be defeated. This acceptance, enshrined in the Peace of Augsburg in 1555, gave the various princes the right to prescribe their subjects' religion. Recognition of religious equality created denominational equilibrium throughout the Holy Roman Empire of the German nation, which henceforth comprised a patchwork of denominationally homogeneous territories. A century later, after exhausting themselves in the Thirty Years' War, the two conflicting denominations reaffirmed this compromise in the Peace of Westphalia in 1648. This

treaty put an end to open hostilities between the denominations until the nineteenth century.

Relations between the denominations worsened after the abolition, in 1806, of the Holy Roman Empire in the course of the Napoleonic Wars—including the disestablishment of its official (Catholic) church. A new European order was created in 1815 at the Congress of Vienna, which ratified the secularization of church territories. The creation of the Second (German) Empire in 1871 upset the equilibrium between the denominations. The exclusion of predominantly Catholic Austria reduced the Catholic population of the new empire to a one-third minority. The Catholics thus perceived in the Protestant majority under Prussian leadership a threat to their religious freedom.

The imperial chancellor, Otto von Bismarck, tried to integrate Catholics into the new empire by force. Ultimately, his *Kulturkampf,* the "struggle for culture" (1871–1878), alienated Catholics, encouraging the formation of Catholic political and social forces that remained aloof from the state. A clearly defined subculture of Catholic organizations and trade unions emerged, represented politically by the Center Party, which, after its founding in 1870, astutely exploited the new opportunities presented by parliamentary representation and mass mobilization. When the National Socialists, or Nazis, came to power in 1933, Catholic society did not initially warm to their ideology, despite the concordat in which the Catholic Church, strongly influenced by the Vatican, made peace with the dictatorship.

German Protestantism never developed institutions comparable to "political Catholicism." As the dominant Christian denomination in Prussian-oriented Germany, and its preeminent cultural marker in the nineteenth century, Lutheranism had no need for organizational unity, protective cohesion, or a denominational political party to represent its ideas and goals. The identification between the Lutheran Church and the authoritarian monarchy culminated in the First World War. After the state (Lutheran) church was disestablished in 1919, German Protestants lacked a political home in the new, constitutionally secular, democratic Weimar Republic, with whose institutions few of them readily identified. Their disregard for democracy is reflected in widespread acceptance of National Socialism.

Only the question of church independence forced prominent Protestants to reconsider their theological position. In response to the blatant politicization of the church by the pro-Nazi "German Christians," they formed a group in 1934 that claimed to be the only legitimate German Evangelical Church. It became known as the *Bekennende Kirche* (Confessing Church). From this came many of those who opposed Hitler and became active in the resistance (such as the theologian Dietrich Bonhoeffer).

Deconfessionalization of Politics in Postwar Germany

The traumatic experience of the two Christian communities under the Third Reich profoundly affected their political attitudes. In 1945, only months after the end of the Second World War, a Christian political party that embraced both denominations was founded, the Christian Democratic Union. The migration of enormous numbers of Germans toward the end of the war and in its aftermath broke up the self-contained denominational regions. The breaking away of overwhelmingly Protestant East Germany to form the German Democratic Republic left a new equilibrium between the denominations in the Federal Republic of Germany. Years of government under Chancellor Konrad Adenauer, a

Catholic, and the mostly Catholic Christian Democratic Union erased Catholics' inferiority complex about politics.

Yet religion in Germany is still a relevant determinant of voting behavior and political orientation, although its influence is difficult to quantify. The dividing line now, however, runs not between Catholics and Protestants but between people with and without close church ties. Practicing Christians of both denominations are more likely to hold traditional values and vote for conservative parties. People who stand aloof from the church tend to vote for left-leaning or liberal parties.

The churches have developed new ways of influencing public opinion. They regularly express their points of view in ecumenical declarations of principle on social and political questions. On occasion these statements have had historical significance, such as the correspondence between the Polish and German Catholic bishops (1965) that fostered reconciliation with Poland and the memorandum on Eastern Europe issued in 1966 by the Evangelical (Protestant) Church in Germany in support of the center-left coalition's policy toward Eastern Europe. In 1991–1992 a profound conflict, which pitted Catholics, in particular, against nonreligious groups, was triggered by proposed changes to the law on abortion. In 1997 the churches' joint declaration on the consequences of flight and migration revived the controversy over the legality of the right of sanctuary that allows the churches to obstruct enforcement of the law in individual cases. Since 1983 approximately 2,500 refugees whose applications for asylum have been rejected by the courts have sought immunity from deportation on church property.

The German churches have a strong institutional position. They are bodies incorporated in public law with constitutionally guaranteed autonomy and special rights. Although the Fundamental Law (the constitution) charges the state of the Federal Republic of Germany to observe neutrality in religious matters, Germany does not practice radical separation of church and state. Rather, the constitution facilitates cooperation between the state and the churches. To cover their financial needs, the churches have powers of taxation; the church tax is collected by state tax offices and employers. State-church cooperation also includes religious instruction in state schools and theological faculties at state universities. Apart from the civil service, the churches are the largest employers in the country and are especially active in health care and social work. They also have substantial economic resources.

Since the mid-1980s the decline in religious conviction and church membership has weakened the churches as institutional and financial forces, and the spread of informal forms of religious expression (the "esoteric" wave) and neo-religious movements (sects) is challenging their representational position. The general attitude toward cults is very critical, however. In 1997 a dispute over Scientology came to a head when the self-proclaimed church, which is controversial in many European countries, alleged that the German government had violated the constitutional guarantee of religious freedom by discrimination against its members. German courts and authorities have defined Scientology as a new form of political extremism on account of its claim to totality and its infiltration of the corporate world and democratic institutions. Accordingly, the constitution protection agencies of most German states are obliged to keep Scientologists' activities under observation.

With unification of the two German states on October 3, 1990, the Protestant Church again became the larger denomination. The approximately 28 million Protestants outnumbered the Catholics by about 1.5 million. When the political system in East Germany collapsed in 1989, the widespread involvement of Protestant clergy in the East German opposition encouraged talk of a "Protestant revolution" in the heartland of the Reformation—until the church's entanglement with the communist powers became apparent. The initial impression of a more Protestant Germany, however, fades on closer analysis. A second shift has been far more spectacular. The former East Germany is one of the most "de-Christianized" regions of Europe: 65 percent of the population do not belong to any church. Whereas only 9 percent of the population in the old Federal Republic were nondenominational, the figure for the new, united Federal Republic is 20 percent. As a result of German unification, a significant segment of the population has dissociated itself from both churches and even from Christian values and traditions per se. This change will doubtless have consequences for Germany's political culture.

Islam is the third largest religious community in Germany, a result of labor migration. Of the 2.7 million Muslims in Germany (most of whom are of the Sunni sect), 1.9 million come from Turkey. As a rule, the Muslim congregations are organized as associations. Because of their organizational fragmentation and diverse political roots, they do not have the status of public bodies enjoyed by the two established Christian churches.

Before the National Socialists came to power, 530,000 Jews lived in Germany, afterward just 30,000. Since 1991 immigration from the former Soviet Union has more than doubled the total membership of Jewish congregations. This shift has caused tension: the congregations' perception of themselves as communities of survivors has been called into question. Many of the immigrants have no religious traditions. Often, their interest in the German congregation lasts only as long as it helps them to adjust to their new surroundings. Only about 20 percent of the immigrants become permanent members of a congregation. This small percentage is unlikely to raise the profile of the Jews in Germany, who, although always a minority, had considerable influence on the country's intellectual, cultural, political, and social life. This has been an irretrievable loss to Germany.

The fundamental cleavage between the two branches of Christianity is also a thing of the past. Much of the emotional vehemence associated with religion was transferred to nationalism—the substitute developed in the nineteenth century by the secularized nation-state. Whereas Protestantism as a pillar of Prussian-ruled Germany had considerable political influence, both the Protestant and the Catholic churches have learned the lesson of the Third Reich and have used their authority in support of the democratic institutions of the Federal Republic of Germany. Although the two churches retain some political influence through established rights and agreements between them and the state, their influence on society is declining rapidly, as is the political activity of their members.

See also *Bonhoeffer, Dietrich; Catholicism, Roman; Christian democracy; Cults; Lutheranism; Sanctuary; Taxation.*

Uwe Berndt

BIBLIOGRAPHY

Conway, John S. *The Nazi Persecution of the Churches, 1933–1945.* London: Weidenfeld and Nicolson, 1968.

Francis, John G. "The Evolving Regulatory Structure of European Church-State Relationships." *Journal of Church and State* 34 (autumn 1992): 775–804.

Nowak, Kurt. *Geschichte des Christentums in Deutschland: Vom Ende der Aufklaerung bis zur Mitte des 20.* Jahrhunderts. Munich: C. H. Beck, 1995.

Rapaport, Lynn. *Jews in Germany after the Holocaust: Memory, Identity, and Jewish-German Relations.* Cambridge: Cambridge University Press, 1997.

Schroeder, Richard. "The Role of the Protestant Church in German Unification." *Daedalus* 123 (winter 1994): 251–261.

Spotts, Frederic. *The Churches and Politics in Germany.* Middletown, Conn.: Wesleyan University Press, 1973.

Ghana

Political life in Ghana, a former British colony in West Africa known as Gold Coast, has been influenced by traditional religion, Islam, and Christianity. In precolonial Ghana various patterns of interaction between political structures and traditional religion prevailed. In what is now Ghana's north, centralized territorial rule (chieftaincy) seems to have developed apart from and later than a primeval Earth guardianship centered on shrines of larger or smaller jurisdiction. These guardians dealt ritually with the Earth as a numinous power that was thought to provide society not only with agricultural fertility but also with its moral base. All the ethnic groups inhabiting this area are ruled internally by elders in one or another clan, but interclan relationships, especially in the so-called stateless societies where there was no central ruler, were often regulated by the guardian of the Earth shrine.

With the stimulus of migration, long-distance trade, and intergroup warfare, centralized territorial rule did arise in some areas of Ghana's north after the sixteenth century. In the colonial era other groups in this territory developed such rule in order to deal with British colonial authorities. In recent years others have sought such recognition of self-rule where tension has developed between large stateless populations and their neighbors with centralized structures of governance.

In the Akan areas of southern Ghana centralized rulership, characterized by ritual veneration of the ruler and his dead ancestors, developed early in many areas. Some traditional myths ascribe the origins of the state as a whole or its leadership to emergence from the Earth. Basically matrilineal in structure, most Akan societies link the male ruler ritually and politically with a queen mother (a royal matrilineal relative, not necessarily the mother of the chief). Akan rulers assume some of the functions associated with the Earth priesthood in northern Ghana, especially mediation between disputing segments of society and placation of the personified Earth when crimes have been committed. Unlike the Earth priest, however, until modern times the Akan ruler traditionally exercised considerable authority in warfare, long-distance commerce, and other areas of executive power.

In the 1690s the rulership in one Akan state, the Ashanti kingdom based in Kumasi, rose to hegemony over many of its neighbors. The Golden Stool, a sacred throne said to have

been brought down from heaven for Osei Tutu and his heirs in the Oyoko clan, has proved to be religiously and politically more significant than the throne of any individual ruler. Placed at the Ashanti ruler's side on the most solemn state occasions, this potent symbol of the Ashanti state and repository of the soul of the people remains a strong focus of religio-political sentiment even in postcolonial Ghana.

In other major ethnic clusters of southern Ghana (the speakers of languages in the Ga-Adangme-Krobo family and the Ewe-speaking population), as well as in many smaller societies scattered throughout these areas (especially the Guan peoples), patrilineal social structures predominate as does centralized, territorial rule with much of the same sort of sacral functions that are associated with Akan rulership, although often over a smaller territory. In some cases centralized rulership in these areas may have arisen in conflict and competition with the Akan states.

More than one-fifth of the population today adhere to forms of traditional religion, and many more are at least partially affected by it. Earth priesthood and centralized territorial rulership continue to influence the politics of land tenure throughout Ghana, as several recent conflicts have demonstrated, most notably the 1994 Konkomba conflict with such centralized neighboring societies as the Dagomba, the Gonja, and the Nanumba. Although every government since Ghana's independence in 1957 has tried to control the outbreak of violence over such matters, it would seem that not only rural populations but also many of their urban relatives still respond to the symbols of chieftaincy or the sacred Earth.

Islam

Islam first made its presence felt in what is now Ghana around the fifteenth century. By the middle of the sixteenth century Islamic influence emanating from a foreign commercial enclave in the Akan forest was felt in what is now the Northern Region and helped to create centralized territorial rule in the Gonja states. Islamic paraphernalia were taken up by Gonja state creators looking for a supra-ethnic system with which they could legitimate their rule over diverse populations. Actual Islamization of Gonja has been slight, but its leaders still bear Muslim names. Islamization of the non-Gonja stateless populations subject to the Gonja is minimal.

Other northern Ghanaian polities attached themselves to the Islamic tradition gradually over the seventeenth and eighteenth centuries, most notably the Wala and Dagomba. For some of these centralized rulerships in northern Ghana, Islamization may have been a byproduct of developing such rule, but the association of Muslim clerics with various royal houses compromised the Islamic character of these clerics and reduced them to the status of amulet manufacturers and diviners for their royal patrons.

Muslims found it more difficult to penetrate the traditional courts of the Akan areas, except as amulet providers and magicians of various sorts, either in symbiosis or competition with traditional providers of such services. The matrilineal structure of most Akan chieftaincies, and especially the Ashanti hegemony, prevented Muslims—encumbered with a revealed patrilineal inheritance system—from acceding to high office. The Akan states have also blocked the access of Muslims to the patrilineal non-Akan states to their south and east, although Muslims play important roles in the commercial dealings of every large town in Ghana, especially when long-distance trade is concerned.

Muslims have, as a community, been much less involved in the politics of postcolonial Ghana than they have in many other West African states. Making up about 16 percent of Ghana's estimated eighteen million people in 1998, they have attached themselves to differing political traditions in the modern state. The one attempt to form a Muslim political party leading up to the independence election proved a disaster for all concerned, with the Nigerian ethnic connec-

tions of some of the Muslim politicians cited as the reason for their deportation.

Ghanaian Ahmadi Muslims, adherents of an Indo-Pakistani Islamic sect deemed heterodox and (since 1974) even non-Muslim in its homeland, have operated Islamic schools since the 1920s in certain parts of Ghana. Their controversies with Sunni Muslims (the majority of Muslims worldwide as well as in Ghana) stem from Ahmadi theological claims for their nineteenth-century Indian founder, Ghulam Ahmad. These religious differences have limited Ahmadi influence on the more general political life of Ghana.

In recent years various Islamic ideological tendencies emanating from the Middle East have been felt in Ghana's Muslim community. Saudi Arabia's control of the pilgrimage to Mecca has given that country much influence in Ghana. In certain urban areas Muslims influenced by the legalistic puritanism of Saudi Arabian Wahhabi thought have come into conflict with Tijani mystics, adherents of a form of fervent piety originating in eighteenth-century North Africa but popularized throughout West Africa in the nineteenth and twentieth centuries by charismatic Senegalese preachers. The Iranian Shi'i government since 1979, aware of Saudi influence on the Wahhabi opponents of Tijani mysticism, has taken up the opposing role of sponsor for this mystical tradition of Sunni Islam.

Christianity

Ghana presents itself today as more Christian than Muslim, with as much as 62 percent of the population at least nominally Christian. Although Christianity first made its influence felt on the Atlantic coast of Ghana from the late fifteenth century, the slave trade and the mortality rate among the Europeans on the coast meant that only a very few coastal people had become Christian by the beginning of the nineteenth century. European Protestants and British Methodists founded Reformed Church and Methodist missions in various parts of southern Ghana after 1828.

The distance between the German-speaking Reformed Church missionaries and the British colonial authorities and the small number of British Methodist missionaries meant that neither of these groups was strongly affected by anti-colonial feeling as it developed among the educated Christian elite from the late nineteenth century. Catholic missions, also conducted by non-British missionaries, began to exercise considerable influence in southern Ghana after 1880 and after 1906 in the north, where the Reformed Church and the Methodists never developed a strong base. The twentieth century also witnessed the introduction of other Christian churches, including fundamentalist and Pentecostal churches of American and British inspiration, as well as the efflorescence of dozens of local spiritual churches, charismatic bodies mainly founded between 1920 and 1960. These churches offer Christian solutions of a somewhat traditional religious orientation (ceremonies of exorcism, healing prayer, the use of blessed ointments and talismans) for problems stemming from such aspects of the worldview of traditional religion as the fear of witchcraft.

Among the most famous of charismatic preachers from whom these spiritual churches take their origin was the Liberian prophet William Wade Harris (d. 1929), who directed his many disciples in the southwestern Gold Coast, which he briefly evangelized in 1914, to the missionary churches, not all of them equally ready to receive these enthusiasts into their communions. The preaching of Harris thus contributed not only to the formation of some of the earliest spiritual churches in this area but also to the formation of nationalist sentiment among some of his Christian hearers at that time.

Even if Reformed Church (after World War I, Presbyterian) piety did not encourage much participation in the process of seeking independence for Ghana, Catholics (albeit estranged ones, like Kwame Nkrumah, Ghana's first president, and military rulers Ignatius Acheampong and Jerry Rawlings) and Methodists (like Prime Minister Kofi Busia) have shaped the political history of Ghana since independence. In the Nkrumah era (1957–1966) the Ghanaians who gradually assumed the leadership of the internationally affiliated ecclesiastical bodies took an independent stance on government policies, especially as Nkrumah developed more authoritarian tendencies.

In subsequent military regimes, especially under Acheampong (1972–1979) and Rawlings (1981–1993), the mainstream Protestant churches and the Catholic Church worked in concert to confront the government on issues of human rights, economic justice, and political freedom. Measures taken by the Rawlings military government (the suppression of the Catholic weekly newspaper, temporary deportation of foreign Mormon missionaries and Jehovah's Witnesses, and an abortive attempt to subject all religious bodies to government registration) led to some silencing of church-inspired opposition in the 1980s. Since the civilianization of the Rawlings regime in 1993, church-state relations have improved somewhat, although the government still remains cool towards the mainstream churches.

The indigenously developed spiritual churches have proved more popular in the south than in the north. These churches, as well as imported fundamentalist and Pentecostal churches, have enjoyed considerable popularity in Ghana in the twentieth century. They have generally avoided involvement in questions of politics, bestowing their blessings where requested on whoever happens to exercise political power at any particular time.

Social, political, and economic chaos afflicted Ghana in the late 1970s and early 1980s, the result of mismanagement of the state by successive military regimes. When the Rawlings regime renounced its earlier socialist rhetoric for reforms mandated by the International Monetary Fund and World Bank in the mid-1980s, many Ghanaians—looking for peace, prosperity, and self-esteem—have preferred the apolitical prosperity gospel of Ghanaian preachers modeling themselves on American televangelists to the social gospel preached at least in some of the mainstream churches.

See also *Africa, Christian; African traditional religions; Islam.*

Patrick J. Ryan

BIBLIOGRAPHY

Apter, David. *Ghana in Transition.* 2d rev. ed. Princeton: Princeton University Press, 1972.

Austin, Dennis. *Politics in Ghana, 1946–1960.* London: Oxford University Press, 1964.

Gifford, Paul. "Ghana's Charismatic Churches." *Journal of Religion in Africa* 24 (1994): 241–265.

Jones, Trevor. *Ghana's First Republic: The Pursuit of the Political Kingdom.* London: Methuen, 1976.

Levtzion, Nehemia. *Muslims and Chiefs in West Africa: A Study of Islam in the Middle Volta Basin in the Pre-Colonial Period.* Oxford: Clarendon Press, 1968.

Pobee, John S. *Kwame Nkrumah and the Church in Ghana, 1949–1966.* Accra: Asempa Publishers, 1988.

———. *Religion and Politics in Ghana.* Accra: Asempa Publishers, 1991.

Ryan, Patrick J. "Ariadne auf Naxos: Islam and Politics in a Religiously Pluralistic African Society." *Journal of Religion in Africa* 26 (1996): 308–329.

Globalization

Globalization refers to the social institutions that emerge as the world increasingly becomes a single society. By the late 1990s the term was most commonly used to refer to the rise of a global market in which financial transactions are instantaneous and worldwide and in which transnational businesses not only sell their products around the world but also locate diverse portions of their operations in various countries. This globalization of the economy is said to lead to less independent national economies and thus to weakened states.

Understanding globalization can begin by distinguishing between the technologies, such as aircraft or telephones, that make the world smaller through rapid worldwide communication and exchange and the social institutions that arise amid such interaction. It is important to distinguish between the ability to travel anywhere in the world in a matter of hours and to understand why people do this, who does it, and what effect it has on people's lives. Globalization concerns primarily the way people live and do business; it affects economies, politics, and culture.

Immanuel Wallerstein, an economic historian, believes that the world-system, as he calls it, is primarily a world capitalist economy. Development of this economy has led to the unequal division of the world into core, peripheral, and semiperipheral regions. Core countries such as the United States and Japan are rich and dominate; peripheral countries like Zaire and Bangladesh are poor and exploited by the core; semiperipheral countries like Brazil and China are in between and act as intermediaries between the core and the periphery. In world-system analysis, states and culture are the tools and expressions of this basic economic reality, and contemporary politics and religion are important expressions of global economic relations. Religion can take the form of political protest—as in the Iranian revolution under the Muslim fundamentalist Ayatollah Ruholla Khomeini in 1979 or in the liberation theology movement in Latin America—or, like Pentecostalism and the Roman Catholic Church, it can help reinforce the capitalist world-system by upholding the status quo.

World-system theory was one of the earliest to define the basic structures of world society. In the past, international relations focused on subglobal state and national societies, not the world as a whole. What was global would then be only the interaction—diplomacy and intergovernmental cooperation, for example—among these principal units. Many scholars now believe that modern states themselves are expressions of a globalized model of what a state looks like and how it acts. For instance, the *world-polity* school, which is associated in particular with Stanford University sociologist

John W. Meyer, has argued that important ideas like development, human rights, citizenship, equality, and freedom have become global standards in terms of which states act and compare themselves with others. Each state also expects to have similar institutions such as a military and school and legal systems. The world-polity with its attendant global culture is the larger context in which states and individuals act and see themselves.

Cultural approaches to globalization focus on several factors, especially social movements such as feminism and environmentalism, mass media like television and film, tourism, popular culture from Sailor Moon to Big Macs, and important cultural models such as ethnicity, individual, nation, and tradition. British sociologist Roland Robertson, probably the first scholar to use the term "globalization" in a technical sense, stresses the degree to which globalization is not simply about a global culture that all the world's people supposedly share but about how people increasingly form local cultures, traditions, and identities in terms of general globalized models. The awareness of the local as particular and unique is possible only by comparison with similar "others." Thus, for instance, the Japanese do not just become more like the Americans, and vice versa; they both become more aware of themselves as either Japanese or American. Globalization means self-aware pluralism.

Religion, like the globalized idea of the nation-state, is both a universal category and a way of identifying differences. There now exists a system of states as the prime political structure of world society. Yet each of these states is deemed to be the instrument of a particular and different national society, whether ethnically based or not. Similarly, we now have the globally spread idea that religions can also be important identifying features of particular cultural groups, with the result that various religious nationalisms arise: Protestant and Roman Catholic in Ireland, Sikh in Punjab, Jewish in Israel, Hindu and Buddhist in Sri Lanka, Protestant fundamentalist in the United States, Muslim in Chechnya, Shi'ite Muslim in Iran. These loyalties can and do contest for state power and the right to determine the identity of national societies. Often, in popular parlance, such religious movements are called *fundamentalisms*.

Religion, however, also has a universalist face. Religions like Islam, Buddhism, and Christianity have always stressed that they are open to all people: individuals can convert to these religions, not just be born into them. In the context of globalization, all religions are increasingly under pressure to see themselves as universal in principle, whether historically they have been or not. They thus become ways of seeing humanity as a single community, a whole that should ultimately be harmonious and not divided in conflict. This ecumenical face of religions makes them resources for criticizing state, economy, and culture for failing to live up to global ideals.

See also *Capitalism*.

Peter Beyer

BIBLIOGRAPHY

Beyer, Peter. *Religion and Globalization*. Thousand Oaks, Calif., and London: Sage Publications, 1994.

Featherstone, Mike. *Global Culture: Nationalism, Globalization and Modernity*. Thousand Oaks, Calif., and London: Sage Publications, 1990.

Luard, Evan. *The Globalization of Politics: The Changed Focus of Political Action in the Modern World*. New York: New York University Press, 1990.

Robertson, Roland. *Globalization: Social Theory and Global Culture*. Thousand Oaks, Calif., and London: Sage Publications, 1992.

Spybey, Tony. *Globalization and World Society*. Cambridge: Polity Press, 1996.

Thomas, George M., John W. Meyer, Francisco O. Ramirez, and John Boli, eds. *Institutional Structure: Constituting State, Society and the Individual*. Thousand Oaks, Calif., and London: Sage Publications, 1987.

Wallerstein, Immanuel. *Geopolitics and Geoculture: Essays on the Changing World-System*. Cambridge and Paris: Cambridge University Press and La Maison des Sciences de l'Homme, 1991.

Waters, Malcolm. *Globalization*. London and New York: Routledge, 1995.

Billy Graham

Graham, Billy

The most famous and successful evangelist of the twentieth century. William Franklin "Billy" Graham Jr. (1918–), born on a farm outside Charlotte, North Carolina, was ordained a Southern Baptist minister in 1939. He preached the Christian gospel in person to more than eighty million people and reached countless other millions by radio, television, films, books, magazines, and newspaper columns. Successful revivals (called "crusades") and international conferences sponsored by his ministry fostered widespread ecumenical cooperation, particularly among evangelical Christians.

Graham's preaching in the early 1950s was filled with political themes—particularly anticommunism and the superiority of the free enterprise system—and he eagerly sought ties with political leaders. President Harry S. Truman rebuffed him, but other politicians saw him as a valuable ally and warmly supported his 1952 crusade in Washington, D.C. Such attention convinced Graham that he wielded considerable political clout, moving him to estimate that he personally could swing at least sixteen million votes to the cause or candidate of his choice.

Graham professed neutrality in the 1952 presidential campaign, but he clearly favored Republican Dwight D. Eisenhower. His transparent support of Eisenhower's campaign and administration led to frequent visits to the White House, unofficial diplomatic errands, and a close friendship with Eisenhower's vice president, Richard M. Nixon, who Graham clearly hoped would succeed Eisenhower to the presidency. When Democratic candidate John F. Kennedy defeated Nixon in 1960, Graham's ties to presidential power were attenuated until Lyndon B. Johnson became president after Kennedy's assassination in 1963.

The evangelist provided valuable support and legitimation for Johnson's causes—the War on Poverty, the Civil Rights Act, the Vietnam War—and drew sharp disapproval from those who felt he had compromised his ability to speak with a prophetic voice. This line of criticism intensified after

Nixon gained the presidency in 1968. An enthusiastic supporter, Graham remained loyal to the beleaguered president until the revelations surrounding the Watergate burglary finally forced some recognition of his old friend's darker side. Deeply stung, Graham drew back from overt political involvement, rarely visiting the White House during the next two administrations. Graham returned to Washington more frequently and more publicly in the 1980s during the presidencies of Ronald Reagan and George Bush, both of whom were longtime friends. His contribution appears to have involved symbolic legitimation of their policies rather than strategic counsel, a course continued by his appearance and prayer at Bill Clinton's inaugurations, in 1992 and 1996.

Graham's political connections and unique stature as a religious leader enabled him to break down formidable barriers, seen most dramatically in a series of successful forays into Eastern Europe and the Soviet Union between 1978 and 1992. These helped widen the scope of religious freedom in the Soviet Union and its satellite nations.

Despite increasing wariness of excessive involvement in politics, Graham encouraged evangelical Christians to assume greater responsibility for social and economic justice, as well as other temporal problems, including most notably nuclear disarmament. In recognition of his achievements and influences, he received, among many accolades and prizes, the Presidential Medal of Freedom (1983) and the Congressional Gold Medal (1996), the highest honors these two branches of government can bestow upon a civilian.

See also *Communication; Evangelicalism; Presidents, American; Revivalism; Vietnam.*

William Martin

BIBLIOGRAPHY

Graham, Billy. *Just As I Am: The Autobiography of Billy Graham.* New York: HarperCollins, 1997.

Martin, William. *A Prophet with Honor: The Billy Graham Story.* New York: Morrow, 1991.

Great Britain

Great Britain, comprising England, Scotland, and Wales, is the "mainland" part of the United Kingdom, a collection of small islands on the northwest fringe of Europe with a population of about 56 million. Generalizations about the country's religion and politics must take account of the variations between the three regions in respect to their histories and cultures. (Northern Ireland, also part of the United Kingdom, is discussed in the article on Ireland.) Many of the variations stem from their individual responses to the Protestant Reformation of the sixteenth century, during which King Henry VIII (and later Queen Elizabeth I) defied the authority of the pope in Rome and asserted the independence of the English church; the Roman Catholic Counter Reformation that followed; and the evangelical revival of the eighteenth century.

In very general terms, two Reformed traditions—Calvinism and Presbyterianism—had the greatest impact on the Lowlands of Scotland and Wales, while Methodism acquired a stronghold in the southeast and southwest of England. Roman Catholicism was confined to isolated pockets of northern England and the Highlands of Scotland after Elizabeth I foiled attempts to retain a Catholic monarch (Mary Queen of Scots) in 1567, but it experienced rapid growth in many industrial towns and cities from the 1830s onward. Meanwhile, the Anglican Church—the Church of England—remained the largest and politically most powerful religious force throughout England.

The Role of Established Churches

The power of Anglicanism was bolstered by sixteenth-century legislation that severely penalized Roman Catholics and Protestants who dissented from the Church of England. In the seventeenth century further legal penalties were imposed on the growing numbers of Protestant dissenters until 1689, when the Act of Toleration granted limited religious liberty to all Protestant sects. Catholics had to wait until 1829 for the beginning of their legal emancipation, and Jews until 1845. Even today, the "established" churches in England and Scotland remain privileged in comparison with other churches and faiths.

Both the Church of England and the Church of Scotland are established in the sense of enjoying privileges and responsibilities that are specified in law. Their status gives them unparalleled access to agencies of the state at national and local levels, although neither of them is aligned with any political parties.

The Church of Scotland, a self-governing Presbyterian

body, is recognized by the British state, but it does not require Parliament's approval for changes in its doctrines or practices. The fact that many of its lay and clerical office-holders are elected to their positions means that the Church of Scotland's official pronouncements are widely regarded as the most authoritative expression of Scottish opinion. Its General Assembly comes close to functioning as an unofficial Scottish parliament when it debates matters of general public concern. The church is also widely regarded as a symbol of Scottish national identity and of Scotland's relative independence from England and the British state.

By comparison, the Church of England's relations with the British state are closer and more complex. The Church of England has never served as a "state church," nor has it ever been a department of state. Yet its position is Erastian—that is, upholding state supremacy in church affairs—in the sense that it is subordinate to Parliament and to the Crown. The British monarch is both head of state and supreme governor of the Church of England. This is why Anglican clerics officiate at most state ceremonies, the twenty-six most senior bishops have seats in the House of Lords, the church's own legal system is recognized as valid, the prime minister is involved in the selection of new bishops and archbishops, and chaplaincy services in prisons and the military are dominated by Anglican priests. Thus, although the state does not finance the church, Parliament monitors its economic activity and retains the right to debate proposed changes in doctrine, worship, and finances.

Establishment can therefore cause problems for both church and state. Problems for the Church of England include the perception that Parliament interferes in the church's internal affairs, that it is not free to select its own leaders, and that the state expects the "national church" to endorse or legitimize government policies. Problems occur for the state when leading Anglicans voice strong criticism of government policies or when representatives of other churches and faiths complain that the Church of England receives excessively privileged treatment from the state.

Neither English nor Scottish law provides for the freedom of religion or for the separation of religion and state. On the contrary, the two established churches enjoy special privileges and responsibilities, whereas members of other religious groups are excluded from certain opportunities. The fact that the United Kingdom is a signatory to the European Convention on Human Rights and the International Cove-

nant on Civil and Political Rights, both of which guarantee the freedom of religion within certain limits, does not in itself override English and Scottish legislation. Until these treaties are incorporated into acts of Parliament, those seeking remedy against perceived restrictions on their religious freedom can only cite the treaties in general support of their cases.

The arrival of large numbers of Jews fleeing from persecution in Central and Eastern Europe in the late nineteenth century introduced a new dimension to the religious and political life of Great Britain. Even more far reaching changes in the religious composition of the country occurred in the 1950s, when migrants from the Caribbean, South Asia, and East Africa began to swell the numbers of Hindus, Muslims, Sikhs, and Christians in black-led churches. The result was that Great Britain became the most religiously diverse country in Europe. Moreover, this diversity was inseparable from ethnic and "racial" diversity.

The size of the communities associated with the major Christian churches and other faith traditions in Great Britain in 1996 was approximately as follows: Christians, 36 million (of whom about 72 percent are Anglicans, 14 percent Catholics, 6 percent Presbyterians, and 3 percent Methodists); Muslims, 1.2 million; Sikhs, 0.5 million; Hindus, 0.4 million; and Jews, 0.3 million. The trend is for the number of active Catholics and members of other faith communities to increase in the foreseeable future and for the mainstream Christian churches' share of the religious "market" to continue declining slowly.

The existence of two established churches, the lack of constitutional guarantees of religious freedom, and the growing strength of non-Christian religious minorities combine to create a highly distinctive nexus of politics and religion in Great Britain. Three aspects of this nexus are particularly important: the absence of strong ties between religious groups and political parties, the lack of ideological polarization based on religion, and the role of education in the country's schools.

Party Politics

No political party in Britain has been exclusively aligned with any particular church or faith, although in the latter half of the nineteenth century and in the first decades of the twentieth century there was a loose affinity between, on the one hand, the Liberal Party and the Nonconformist churches (Baptists, Congregationalists, Methodists, and Presbyterians) and, on the other, between some socialist organizations and Methodism. There is also a tendency for Christian supporters of the Conservative Party to identify themselves more closely with the Church of England than with any other church and for Christians from less advantaged backgrounds to support the Labour Party or the Liberal Democratic Party. But it is rare for religious issues to be expressed in party terms in mainland Britain, if not in Northern Ireland, where Catholics and Protestants tend to be divided along party lines. This is why members of Parliament are often allowed to follow their individual consciences rather than their political parties' instructions when they vote on issues with strongly religious or moral relevance. It is also why the Roman Catholic bishops insisted that the

unquestionably political opinions expressed in their booklet *The Common Good,* published in 1996, were independent of any particular party. *The Common Good* asserts the need for labor to take precedence over capital and the desirability of trade union membership if poverty is to be tackled effectively. The other side of this coin is that, unlike in France, Italy, or Spain, anticlericalism, aggressive atheism, and Christian Democracy have never taken root in Great Britain's politics.

The political sympathies of British Hindus, Muslims, and Sikhs seem to be following the same trajectory as those of Irish Catholics and European Jews who migrated to the United Kingdom much earlier. That is, first-generation settlers tended to support the Labour Party and trade unions, but many members of second and subsequent generations have gravitated toward parties in the center or on the right wing of the political spectrum, especially if they gained economic security or moved up the social ladder. In other words, social class exercises at least as much influence over political views as does religious or ethnic identity. But political friction between faith communities has been politicized in connection with several issues that appear in a multicultural society: the application of zoning laws to the construction of religious buildings, the ritual slaughter of animals for food, the demand that the law against blasphemy be extended to religions other than Christianity, the proposal that unfair discrimination on the grounds of religion be made a legal offense, and the pressure to provide even-handed support from public funds for prison chaplains from all faith communities.

Conservative and Progressive Opinions

There is little evidence that "culture wars" have polarized conservative and progressive opinions about morally controversial issues in Great Britain. Of course, conservative support is strong for imposing harsher penalties on convicted criminals, for encouraging two-parent families, for controlling "adult" publications and video films, and for cutting the cost of social welfare programs. But ideological agreement on these issues has not seriously weakened the bonds of identity and loyalty that bind members of separate churches and other religious organizations together. For example, conservative Methodists are unlikely to leave their church simply to join fellow conservatives in a different church. On the other hand, the swing away from liberal values of social justice and solidarity has been pronounced in many faith communities since the early 1980s, thereby mirroring British public opinion as a whole.

People who attend religious services frequently and who regard themselves as religious tend to hold more conservative political opinions than do people whose relations with religious organizations are more distant or nonexistent. Lay members of the Church of England (but not the clergy), for example, vote in significantly greater numbers for Conservative Party candidates in parliamentary elections than does the rest of the British population. By contrast, Quakers and Catholics are more likely to favor left-of-center parties, often lending support to campaigns for human rights, peace, ecology, justice, and the relief of oppression. Opposition to the radically conservative policies of Prime Minister Margaret Thatcher's governments in the 1980s drew in part on criticisms voiced by the clergy in mainstream churches.

Education

Finally, education in schools has become an arena of intense political concern about religion. The 1944 Education Act, the 1988 Education Reform Act, and numerous other pieces of legislation, administrative directives, and governmental advice have sought to retain and bolster the requirement that every school funded and controlled by a local authority should begin each day with an act of "collective worship" and should include "religious education" in its basic curriculum. Political disputes over the requirement that the daily act of worship should "reflect the broad traditions of Christian belief" and that the syllabus for religious education should "reflect the fact that the religious traditions of Great Britain are in the main Christian while taking account of the teaching and practices of the other principal religions represented in Great Britain" (Education Reform Act 1988, Section 8 [3]) have grown more bitter and more intense in the 1990s.

Conservative thinking tends to blame many of Great Britain's economic and social problems on the failure of schools to inculcate respect for the Christian religion and to resist secular humanist and multifaith ideologies. By contrast, critics of what they see as increasingly intrusive and Christian-oriented policies for collective worship and religious education accuse the government of pandering to nationalistic and even racist interests. Matters are aggravated by the fact that successive governments have refused to contribute toward the funding of separate Muslim and Sikh schools, whereas many Anglican, Roman Catholic, and Jewish schools currently receive partial funding from the state.

Conclusion

There is no separation of religion and state in Great Britain; nor are there any constitutional guarantees of the freedom of religion. Yet many religious organizations are heavily involved in politics, and the growth of Hindu, Muslim, and Sikh communities is generating fresh political and legal challenges for a country whose dissident religious minorities helped to forge basic political rights and freedoms at the dawn of modernity. Reforming the current law on blasphemy, obtaining government funding for non-Christian religious schools, and giving all faiths equal opportunities to participate in publicly funded chaplaincies in prisons and hospitals are among these challenges.

See also *Anglicanism; Europe, Western; Ireland; Religious organization; State churches.*

James A. Beckford

BIBLIOGRAPHY

Beckford, James A. "Politics and Religion in England and Wales." *Daedalus* 120 (summer 1991): 179–201.

Davie, Grace. *Religion in Britain since 1945.* Oxford: Blackwell, 1994.

Hastings, Adrian. *A History of English Christianity, 1920–1985.* London: Collins, 1986.

Medhurst, Ken, and George Moyser. *Church and Politics in a Secular Age.* Oxford: Clarendon Press, 1988.

Modood, Tariq. "Multiculturalism, Establishment and British Citizenship." *Political Quarterly* 65 (1994): 53–73.

Gush Emunim

Established in 1974, Gush Emunim (a Hebrew term meaning "Bloc of the Faithful") is a religio-political movement in Israel whose aim is to extend Jewish sovereignty and presence throughout what it perceives as the Holy Land. Although never formally disbanded, the group gradually ceased to be active as such in the late 1980s.

Gush Emunim became a major political force in Israel amid the political and psychological turmoil that followed the 1967 Six-Day War and the 1973 Yom Kippur War. After the 1967 war in which Israel came to control all western Palestine, including the whole of the city of Jerusalem with its holy places as well as Sinai and the Golan Heights, a euphoric, messianic state of mind prevailed in wide segments of the religious and nationalist population. But after the Yom Kippur War, and in particular the subsequent Israeli withdrawal from Sinai, gloom prevailed.

Although there have been a number of secular leaders in the movement and diverse circles have supported it, the core of its founders and leaders—as well as most of its supporters—have come from the religious Zionist movement, and the nucleus has been disciples or adherents of the messianic, mystical school established by Rabbi Abraham Kook Sr. and led by his son and successor, Rabbi Zvi Yehuda Kook Jr. Based on the notion that the current age signifies the beginning of redemption for the Jews and that the establishment of the state of Israel is a heavenly sign for this new stage, Gush Emunim views itself as the revitalizing force of Zionism. The main tenet of its political theology ordains the sanctity of the entire Land of Israel and prescribes its integrity, which in practical terms envisages the formal annexation of Judea and Samaria (and Gaza) to Israel. From the religious Zionist maxim that unifies the People of Israel, the Torah of Israel, and the Land of Israel, Gush Emunim has made the last of these its foremost responsibility.

Settling Jews on the West Bank and Gaza was Gush Emunim's overriding mission. In its earliest years this was accomplished primarily by extra-legal means, later legalized. After 1977 Gush Emunim worked to speed up mass settlement on the West Bank. A number of subsidiary groups were established that in time became semi-autonomous such as Amana (Covenant), Gush Emunim's official settlement organization, and Moetzet Yesha (the Council of Settlements of Judea, Samaria, and Gaza).

The early 1980s marked Gush Emunim's political apogee, in spite of its failure to stop Israel from withdrawing from Sinai and relinquishing the settlement of Yamit. Within a dozen or so years more than 120,000 settlers took up residence on the West Bank and Gaza, which constituted the core of the Arab population. Only a minority of these settlers actually belonged to the movement, but it is seen as having activated others so that its influence was much wider.

When, in 1979, Gush Emunim decided not to become a political party, its leaders split, with some founding the Tehiya (Renaissance) Party together with secular nationalists. Initially, this party had remarkable electoral success, and it also participated in the government. In the early 1990s, however, it disintegrated and disappeared.

Individuals and groups connected with Gush Emunim have organized self-defense and other vigilante activities on the West Bank and Gaza. The leaders of the small so-called Jewish Underground, active around 1980, were connected to Gush Emunim. They planned to blow up the Dome of the Rock in Jerusalem, a Muslim holy site, to make room for the rebuilding of the (Third) Temple and also attacked the mayors of a couple of Arab West Bank towns. Dr. Baruch Goldstein, who murdered twenty-nine Muslims praying in the Cave of the Patriarchs (Machpela) in Hebron, also had ties to the movement.

Since the beginning of the Arab-Israeli peace process in the early 1990s, the public role of Gush Emunim as pacemaker of the Greater Israel policy has changed. Its successor movements have been in the forefront of opposition to the 1993 Oslo agreement between Israel and the Palestine Liberation Organization. They have renewed expansion of Jewish settlements and staged legal and illegal protests against what is for them a treasonable policy of surrender of holy, indivisible, and inalienable ground.

See also *Israel; Jerusalem; Judaism; Zionism.*

Emanuel Gutmann

BIBLIOGRAPHY

Aran, Gideon. "Jewish Zionist Fundamentalism: The Bloc of the Faithful in Israel." In *Fundamentalism Observed,* edited by Martin E. Marty and R. Scott Appleby. Chicago: University of Chicago Press, 1991.

Don-Yehiya, Eliezer. "The Book and the Sword: The Nationalist Yeshivot and Political Radicalism in Israel." In *Accounting for Fundamentalism,* edited by Martin E. Mary and R. Scott Appleby. Chicago: University of Chicago Press, 1994.

Lustick, Ian S. *For the Land and the Lord: Jewish Fundamentalism in Israel.* New York: Council on Foreign Relations, 1988.

Newman, David, ed. *The Impact of Gush Emunim.* London: Croom Helm, 1985.

Sprinzak, Ehud. *The Ascendance of Israel's Radical Right.* New York: Oxford University Press, 1991.

H

Havel, Václav

Czech playwright, dissident, and president of Czechoslovakia from 1989 to 1992, before being elected first president of the Czech Republic in 1993. Havel (1936–) embodies the struggles of Eastern Europe during the post–World War II period under Soviet domination, both before and after the "Velvet Revolution" of 1989–1990 that brought Soviet rule to an end.

Of Roman Catholic descent, but with a Czech disdain for religious excess born of hard historical experience, Havel owes much of his religious and political inspiration to Tomáš Garrigue Masaryk, president of the first Republic of Czechoslovakia (1918–1938), and to the philosophers Jan Patočka and Emmanuel Levinas. Through Masaryk, he drew upon the examples of the pre-Reformation Czech religious reformer Jan Hus, who was martyred in 1415, and the Czech Brethren.

When his family's assets were nationalized following the Communist revolution of 1949, Havel left private boarding school at fifteen. Denied a university education, he trained (unsuccessfully) as a carpenter, afterward becoming a university laboratory assistant in Prague. Aware of his ability as a writer, he turned to writing plays, in which he explored the irrationality of life under a totalitarian regime. In 1964 he married Olga Spichalova (who died in 1996); his *Letters to Olga* (English translation, 1988) afford insight into the private aspects of their shared struggle.

Havel achieved international prominence with the creation of the civil rights group Charter 77, founded in 1977. This group monitored the implementation of the Helsinki

Václav Havel

Accords, in which the Soviet Union agreed to accept human rights provisions.

Havel's aim is to contribute to a "program for raising the general level of civility" and to a "politics as practical morality." Formulated under conditions of systemic powerlessness, Havel's primary commitment is to grounding the moral personality in an absolute existing beyond individual self-interest. His essay "The Power of the Powerless" is one of the great religio-political tracts of the twentieth century. Although his contemporary reworking of the Hussite battle-cry "Truth shall prevail" has an objective moral clarity, for some of those experiencing rapid economic privatization, his moralistic, indirect, and nonfactional politics are seen as an inadequate check on capitalist excess.

Richard H. Roberts

Health

See *Medicine*

Heresy

Heresy is a belief or doctrine that is at variance with what an orthodoxy, or a dominant belief system, holds to be true. More specifically, heresy signifies adherence to a religious opinion that is contrary to the doctrine of a particular religious faith.

Origins and History

The term *heresy* derives from the Greek word *hairesis*, meaning "a choice." Originally heresy had no pejorative sense but simply referred to any opinion one held. To the extent that heresy was used to refer to a particular phenomenon, it indicated adherence to any of the schools of philosophical thought in late antiquity. This usage is reflected in the Acts of the Apostles (5:17; 15:5; 24:5; 26:5; 28:22) and in the writings of Jewish historian Josephus (A.D. 37–A.D. c. 100) (*Antiquities of the Jews,* 13.5.9 and 18.1.2; *The Jewish War,* 2.8.14). It was later confirmed in the work of Spanish bishop and encyclopedist Isidore of Seville (c. 560–636) (*Etymologies,* 8.3.1).

The pejorative connotation of heresy developed in the late first and early second centuries in response to the theological challenge presented by the influx into Christianity of pagan converts and their diverse heritages and beliefs. This development caused Christians to become increasingly concerned with defining an unambiguous Christian identity, leading them to press for a single exclusive doctrinal orthodoxy.

The conceptual foundations of orthodoxy and heresy were laid in the polemics of the early theologians Justin (A.D. c. 100–c. 165) and Irenaeus (c. 125–c. 202) during the second-century gnostic controversy. The gnostics' claim that "gnosis," or divine knowledge, could be directly accessed without the mediation of those bishops anointed with the power of apostolic succession (the power conferred on the apostles by Christ and passed along to their successors, the bishops) threatened the authority and, therefore, the organizational control of the leaders of the nascent Christian movement.

In response to the challenge of the gnostics, Justin provided a conceptual framework for the demonization of dissent that endures to this day. Drawing from apocalyptic Judaism, Justin associated Christian dissenters with the "false prophets" of Satan whose purpose was to cause the faithful to stray from the truth. In this way, orthodoxy came to be identified with divine truth, while all dissenters, now referred to pejoratively as "heretics," were identified as confederates of the devil.

Irenaeus extended the identity of the heretic from that of an external enemy of orthodoxy to that of an intimate enemy, that is, an insider who purposefully betrayed or distorted the faith. With this formulation any dissenting doctrinal assertion could be discredited as heresy and its advocates branded as heretics and servants of the devil. This broadened meaning of heresy, which came to predominate in Christendom, is reflected in the New Testament evocation of "false prophets" and "false teachers among you who will secretly bring in destructive heresies" (2 Peter 2:1).

Heresy became an enforced category when orthodoxy was intersected with political power upon the emperor Constantine's adoption of Christianity in the fourth century. Constantine and his immediate successors not only convened councils to settle questions of theological orthodoxy but, more importantly, used their civil authority to influence the enforcement of creedal decisions. Christian bishops, previously victimized by the police for promulgating a *religio illicita* (a religion not sanctioned by the state), came to command them. With this development, the definition of heresy became primarily a function of power: it was determined by whoever had the power to enforce what they held to be truth, not by the correctness of a doctrine.

Increasingly, the demonization of dissent into heresy took on more serious and ominous overtones in Christianity, culminating in the Spanish Inquisition in the fifteenth century, in which thousands accused of heresy were excommunicated, tortured, even executed. In the United States the violent clash of extreme formulations of orthodoxy and heresy reached its apogee in the Salem witch hunts of the eighteenth century, in which scores of women and men were hanged or burned alive as heretics.

Heresy in Modern Times

Although the definition of heresy is of Christian origin, the demonization of dissent is not unique to Christianity but is seen in every established religion and belief system. Indeed, heresy was a familiar charge in Iran in the aftermath of its Islamic Revolution in the 1980s.

Despite charges of religious heresy raised by established religions in recent years, it is the phenomenon of "secular" heresy that has garnered most media attention. From paranoid anticapitalism in the era of Joseph Stalin in Russia to paranoid anticommunism in the time of Joseph McCarthy in the United States, secular politicized evocations of orthodoxy and heresy have come to loom large on the political landscape. In the United States a contemporary example of this trend is seen in the Christian religious right, represented by such religio-political groups as the Moral Majority and the Christian Coalition. These groups have attempted to develop a new orthodoxy consisting of both religious and secular elements. Religious elements include legalization of prayer in public educational facilities, opposition to abortion, and censorship of television programs and motion pictures for moral content. The groups' secular concerns include lessening of governmental oversight, lowering of taxes, support of capital punishment, and opposition to affirmative action. Most significantly, these groups, which are generally known by the overarching rubric of "conservatives," seek to advance their agenda by means of well-financed and well-orchestrated lobbies and electoral campaigns. Dissenting opinions are labeled "liberal," which is a pejorative term to conservatives and often meant to be synonymous with heresy.

Despite the differences in their respective spheres of op-

eration, religious and secular conceptions of heresy have one thing in common—both are determined by those in power. See also *Censorship; Inquisition; Witchcraft.*

Obery M. Hendricks Jr.

BIBLIOGRAPHY

Bauer, Walter. *Othodoxy and Heresy in Earliest Christianity.* Translated by the Philadelphia Seminar on Christian Origins and edited by Robert A. Kraft and Gerhard Krodel. Mifflintown, Pa.: Sigler Press, 1996.

Burris, Virginia. *The Making of a Heretic.* Berkeley and Los Angeles: University of California Press, 1995.

Pagels, Elaine. *The Gnostic Gospels.* New York: Random House, 1979.

Simon, Marcel. "From Greek Hairesis to Christian Heresy." In *Early Christian Literature and the Christian Intellectual Tradition: In Honorem: Robert C. Grant,* edited by William Schodel and Robert L. Wilken. Paris: Éditions Beauchesne, 1979.

Herzl, Theodor

Founder of modern political Zionism, the Jewish national movement, and regarded as one of the greatest influences on the creation of the State of Israel. Born in Budapest, Hungary, to well-to-do parents, Herzl (1860–1904) was educated in the spirit of German-Jewish enlightenment, which held that assimilation was the best way to overcome anti-Semitism. He studied law in Vienna, Austria, but became a playwright and journalist. From 1891 until 1895 Herzl served as the Paris correspondent of the *New Free Press,* an influential liberal Viennese daily. While in France, his interest in Jewish problems deepened.

Anti-Semitism made Herzl a conscious Jew: its modern resurgence wounded his dignity. He was particularly stirred by German philosopher Eugen Dühring's anti-Semitic book *The Jewish Question as a Problem of Race, Morals, and Culture,* but it was the trial of Alfred Dreyfus (1894–1895) that shattered Herzl's hopes of assimilation and revealed the deep roots of anti-Semitism in the French Third Republic. Dreyfus was a Jewish officer in the French army accused of espionage. Despite an almost complete lack of evidence against him, he was convicted of selling military secrets to the Germans.

Herzl came to believe that European nations would not be able to cope with their medieval legacy of anti-Semitism, but he also saw that the problem might ultimately prove useful for the Jewish people, forcing them to close ranks. From

Theodor Herzl

world. During his 1898 visit to the Near East, he received Herzl in Constantinople and promised to ask Sultan Abd al-Hamid II to grant a concession to the Jewish Land Company under German protection. When the sultan rejected the suggestion, the kaiser's interest in Zionism waned.

Herzl had also been negotiating directly with the Ottoman Empire since 1896. During his final visit to Constantinople, in July 1902, he received a warm letter from Abd al-Hamid, but on matters of substance his efforts bore no fruit.

At the same time, Herzl was also petitioning the British government for permission to establish a Jewish colony under Britain's protection in the neighborhood of Palestine. British reaction was generally favorable, but a project in the El-Arish area of the northern Sinai proved impracticable. In the spring of 1903 Joseph Chamberlain, the British colonial secretary, offered instead the Guas Ngishu plateau near Nairobi, in East Africa, for Jewish settlement. Herzl thought it politically imprudent to reject this offer because the very fact that a great power was negotiating with him amounted to a de facto recognition of his movement. He considered the British offer primarily in political terms: rather than impeding his ultimate goal, it might bring a Jewish state nearer to realization. For Herzl, consideration of the British plan was merely a ploy to obtain British recognition of the Zionist movement, and of Jews as a people, and to bring Britain gradually to the conclusion that only in Palestine would the Jewish problem be solved. Herzl's strategy eventually was proved to be correct, although it provoked grave suspicions among some Zionists that he had deviated from the main course.

In August 1903 Herzl received a letter from Vyacheslav Plehve, the Russian interior minister. Writing on behalf of the tsarist government, he promised that Russia would intervene with the Ottoman sultan in favor of the Zionists and would assist them in organizing Jewish immigration and settlement in Palestine. Plehve's letter, which became the cornerstone of Herzl's diplomacy, opened doors in the Italian and Austrian capitals. Russia and Austria-Hungary had had a secret Near East agreement since 1897. When Russia endorsed Herzl's ideas, Austria followed the Russian lead. The Austrian foreign minister, Agenor von Goluchowski, told Herzl that the great powers should ask the Ottoman Empire for land and legal rights for five to six million Jews and suggested that England take the initiative.

Had Herzl lived, he would have gone to London to reveal to the Foreign Office Austria's proposal for creating a

then on, he regarded the Jewish question as a national, rather than social or religious, issue that should be solved politically. He believed that only sovereignty over an area to which the Jewish masses could emigrate and form a nation would provide the right resolution. A Jewish state would also ease antagonism between Jew and Gentile.

In 1896 Herzl published his ground-breaking treatise, *The Jewish State*. A diplomat and a man of action as well as a visionary, he endeavored to win over European rulers to his plan. He turned first to Germany, convincing Kaiser Wilhelm II that a Jewish settlement in Palestine would bring prosperity to the Holy Land and help develop and revive Asia Minor, thereby saving Turkey from bankruptcy and making it more difficult for the Allied powers to dismember the Ottoman Empire—a matter of great interest to Germany.

The kaiser was persuaded that Jewish emigration from Europe would weaken anti-Semitism and lessen the danger of revolutionary socialism. He also believed that protecting Herzl's project would earn the gratitude of Jews all over the

Concert of Powers in support of Zionist aspirations. But Herzl died in July 1904, robbing the Zionist movement of a leader of international caliber. Herzl had aroused both admiration and opposition, but nobody could ignore the magnetism of his personality, his intelligence, his sincerity, and his idealism. A shrewd, down-to-earth politician with no illusions about human nature, he was the foremost exponent of Jewish nationalism. Political Zionism became the most dynamic force in modern Jewish history.

Herzl, in his diary, foresaw a Jewish catastrophe in Europe. This prediction was fulfilled under Adolf Hitler as the Nazi Holocaust. Exactly fifty years and eight months after he had recorded his prediction of catastrophe, the State of Israel was proclaimed, in 1948.

See also *Anti-Semitism; Israel; Zionism.*

Isaiah Friedman

BIBLIOGRAPHY

Bein, Alex. *Theodor Herzl: A Biography.* Philadelphia: Jewish Publication Society of America, 1962.

Friedman, Isaiah. *Germany, Turkey, and Zionism, 1897–1918.* Oxford: Oxford University Press, 1977.

Herzl, Theodor. *The Jewish State.* New York: American Zionist Emergency Council, 1946.

Laqueur, Walter. *A History of Zionism.* London: Weidenfeld and Nicholson, 1972.

Vital, David. *Zionism: The Formative Years.* Oxford: Oxford University Press, 1982.

Heschel, Abraham Joshua

Jewish religious philosopher who applied the Hebrew prophets' demands for justice and compassion to social and political situations. The life and works of Abraham Joshua Heschel (1907–1972) exemplify how spiritual sensitivity can incite progressive activism.

As a Jewish thinker, Heschel wrote books and essays on prayer, religious philosophy, the Hebrew prophets, the state of Israel, education, poverty, war, and racial equality. As a teacher, scholar, and expert literary stylist, Heschel explained how ethical positions can be motivated by sensitivity to God's presence, or what he called "depth theology"—an encounter with divine reality that precedes formulations of creed. He believed that the living God of the Hebrew Bible (the "God of pathos") reacts to human actions.

Heschel's vivid writings and speeches combined emotion and incisive analysis as he sought to arouse in readers compassion for afflicted human beings, outrage at injustice, and intuitions of God's presence. His moral and political choices emulated the Hebrew prophets who rejected a politics of expediency and refused to compromise with human callousness and indifference to evil. Heschel supported his judgments with allusions to the Hebrew Bible, Talmud, Midrash (early rabbinical interpretations of the Scriptures), Jewish mysticism, and Hasidic sources.

European Roots

Heschel's social and political activism, first in Europe and then in the United States, grew out of his early life. Born in Warsaw, Poland, in 1907, he was raised in a traditional Hasidic community and imbued from early childhood with daily prayer, study of sacred texts, and ideals of spiritual integrity. Without rejecting his religious faith, he began secular studies in a Yiddish-language gymnasium in Vilnius, Lithuania, and earned a doctorate in philosophy from the University of Berlin.

Heschel's writings in Europe combined loyalty to God with a keen ethical conscience. His 1933 dissertation on the Hebrew prophets provided the foundation of his American theology. That same year he published in Warsaw a book of poetry (in Yiddish) that expressed his unique combination of intense compassion and feelings of closeness with God. In 1935 he published a biography of Moses Maimonides (1135–1204), the medieval rabbi, philosopher, and physician. And from 1936 to 1938 he placed inspirational essays on rabbis of the Talmudic period in German–Jewish community newspapers as Jews were being expelled from Germany.

By the time he emigrated to the United States in March 1940, Heschel had experienced political and ethnic conflicts, widespread Jewish poverty, anti-Semitism, the effects of World War I, the ascent of German dictator Adolf Hitler, and the outbreak of World War II. After arriving in the United States, Heschel taught at Hebrew Union College, a Reform rabbinical seminary in Cincinnati, Ohio. In 1945 he joined the faculty of the Jewish Theological Seminary in New York (representing the Conservative movement), where he held the chair of Jewish ethics and mysticism until his death.

In the 1950s Heschel concentrated on scholarship, writing about the religious experience, and Jewish education. The importance of Heschel's works of religious philosophy—*Man Is Not Alone* (1951) and *God in Search of Man* (1955)—was recognized by Reinhold Niebuhr, the eminent Protestant theologian and political activist.

Heschel's wider public involvement began in 1960 at the

Abraham Joshua Heschel

first White House Conference on Youth and the next year at the White House Conference on Aging. From 1962 on, he consulted at the Second Vatican Council in Rome. There, Heschel worked closely with Cardinal Augustin Bea, head of the Secretariat for Non-Christian Religions, spoke privately with Pope Paul VI, and influenced the declaration on the Jews in *Nostra Aetate* (1965), a document expressing the Catholic Church's positive attitude toward Judaism.

Politics as a Religious Issue

Heschel, who considered politics to be a religious responsibility, a personal problem, was committed to civil rights for all Americans. In 1963 he met the Reverend Martin Luther King Jr. at the first National Conference on Religion and Race. A photograph of Heschel marching with King and Ralph Bunche of the United Nations at the 1965 Selma–Montgomery protest against racial segregation is widely reproduced as an emblem of the black–Jewish alliance of the

period. Also in 1965 Heschel was appointed by the Protestant Union Theological Seminary as Harry Emerson Fosdick visiting professor.

That same year, Heschel, with John Bennett, president of Union Theological Seminary, Father Daniel Berrigan, an activist Jesuit priest, and Richard John Neuhaus, then a Lutheran pastor in Brooklyn, cofounded Clergy (later renamed Clergy and Laity) Concerned about Vietnam, which influenced King to join the antiwar movement. When the United States intervened militarily in Vietnam in the 1960s—an action Heschel forcefully opposed—he repeated phrases from his scholarly book *The Prophets* (1962) to proclaim in his own voice: "In regard to cruelties committed in the name of a free society, some are guilty, while all are responsible." God is involved in history, but human beings have free will and responsibility to redeem the world. Following the biblical dictum that each and every person is an image of the Divine, Heschel sought to educate a radical sense of reverence for humankind. Religious observance should have practical consequences, he wrote, "prayer and prejudice cannot dwell in the same heart." His essays and speeches are collected in *The Insecurity of Freedom* (1966) and *Moral Grandeur and Spiritual Audacity* (1997).

Heschel also confronted painful conflicts between politics and religious integrity in *Israel: An Echo of Eternity* (1969), which explained the centuries' long attachment of the Jewish people to the land of Israel and evoked memories of the Holocaust, the mass destruction of Jews by the Germans under Hitler. His final book, *A Passion for Truth* (1973), denounced the mediocrity of religious institutions, using as models the dissident Protestant thinker Søren Kierkegaard (1813–1855) and the abrasive Hasidic rabbi Menahem Mendel. Heschel reaffirmed his loyalty to God by challenging philosophical absurdity, massive evil, the weak human conscience, and the frailty of society's devotion to truth. He died of a heart attack at age sixty-five on the Sabbath night of December 23, 1972.

See also *Civil rights movement; Judaism.*

Edward K. Kaplan

BIBLIOGRAPHY

Kaplan, Edward K. *Holiness in Words: Abraham Joshua Heschel's Poetics of Piety.* Albany, N.Y.: SUNY Press, 1996.

Kaplan, Edward K., and Samuel H. Dresner. *Abraham Joshua Heschel, Prophetic Witness.* New Haven: Yale University Press, 1998.

Kasimow, Harold, and Byron Sherwin, eds. *No Religion Is an Island.* Maryknoll, N.Y.: Orbis Books, 1991.

Merkle, John C. *The Genesis of Faith.* New York: Macmillan, 1983.

Merkle, John C., ed. *Abraham Joshua Heschel: Exploring His Life and Work.* New York: Macmillan, 1985.

Rothschild, Fritz A., ed. *Heschel, Between God and Man.* Rev. ed. New York: Free Press, 1975.

Hinduism

As the religion of about eight hundred million people, over 90 percent of whom live in South Asia, Hinduism today exists as a world religion in diverse political settings. Some of the linkages between Hinduism and politics have their roots in tradition (for example, the ideal of politics as morality), while others are new (for example, the Indian innovation of the secular state).

The situation is complex. In fact, to write about religion and politics in the context of Hinduism immediately poses several definitional problems. The term *Hinduism* and its equivalents in various European languages derive from nineteenth-century Western discourses about the Orient, which was characterized as exotic, and owe their currency to Christian missionaries, colonial administrators, and Indologists (who study India and its peoples on the basis of classical texts). They have no exact equivalent in classical or modern Indian languages. This being so, is Hinduism purely a con-

struct, or does it have sociocultural and historical substance? The word *Hindu,* originally in Greek and Persian (derived from the Sanskrit *Sindhu,* the name of the major river Indus of Pakistan), had a geographical denotation (peoples living east of the Indus) and was therefore quite unlike such terms as *Christian, Muslim,* or *Sikh.* Hinduism could be, therefore, at best the culture or way of life of the Hindus.

A second problem focuses on the definition of religion. Considering the fact that Hinduism does not have a founder, a set of fundamentals, a core text (comparable to the Bible or the Qur'an), or a church, it surely is not a religion in the sense Judaism, Christianity, and Islam are so. Mutually exclusive Hindu sects, some of which have over time evolved into full-blown religions, do, however, have some of these characteristics.

Nevertheless, it is by now a well-established practice in modern scholarship and contemporary political discourse, whether Indian or other, to regard Hinduism as a religion, although one quite unlike other major world religions. When an Indian has to use an Indian language equivalent for Hinduism, the usual choice is *hindu dharma* or *sanatana dharma,* the Hindu or the universal and eternal norms of life. The normative aspect is of critical importance. Dharma is not how life is lived but how it should be lived, for its absence (*adharma*) means moral normlessness, or chaos.

Dharma as a moral code is comprehensive and encom-

Meenakshi Hindu Temple at Madurai, Tamil Nadu, India

passes every aspect of life. This brings us to the third and last problem. Dharma does not admit of the distinction, fundamental in Western thought, between the sacred and the profane, or the religious and the secular. Within the Hindu religious tradition, legitimate kingship and, in modern times, politics are moral obligations or pursuits and therefore entirely religious in character. Classical Brahmanical formulations (Brahmans, the highest-ranked caste, have traditionally been the ideologues of Hindu society) as well as modern religious thought emphasize that politics outside the domain of religion or dharma is illegitimate.

The Morality of Politics: A Classical View

One of the most widely discussed classical formulations of the relationship of politics and morality is that given in the theory of *purushartha,* or value-oriented action. The highest of value orientations, and also the most comprehensive from which all other values derive, is of course that of dharma, or cosmic moral order. Dharma has a universal component equally applicable to one and all (for example, the requirement of truthfulness) as well as a context-specific component (for example, it is the dharma of the king and of the second-ranked warrior caste generally to engage in warfare, but the Brahman may never shed blood).

This context sensitivity makes room for the second value orientation, namely that of *artha,* or the rational pursuit of political and economic objectives within the framework of dharma. The king rules according to the dictates of dharma, which enjoin him to protect all dharmas, universal as well as specific. Similarly, the merchant trades and the agriculturist cultivates land, but not as purely economic pursuits: the dictates of dharma apply to them also. More significantly, dharma is incomplete unless it incorporates artha.

Finally, there is the third goal of value-oriented action, namely *kama,* or physical pleasure and aesthetic enjoyment generally. Just as artha should not violate dharma, kama may not violate artha and dharma. In other words, dharma embraces artha and kama, which are apparently its contraries, in a hierarchical grammar of values. In a typical Brahmanical twist of the argument, release (*moksha*) from the world of goal-oriented action is provided by a fourth optional value, that of total withdrawal from worldly though moral pursuits through renunciation (*sannyasa*).

Classical texts discuss at length each of the above value orientations. Thus there is a body of literature called *arthashastra,* or the combined science of governance and economics (political economy). One of the most famous of these texts, the *Arthashastra,* attributed to the scholar-statesman Kautilya (ca. 300 B.C.), declares right at the beginning that artha is the supreme value, but the overall spirit of the work suggests that material well-being must be subordinated to spiritual good. Such a view was in fact already a thousand years old. It asserted that secular power was a blind force, not its own principle, but controlled by dharma. After the arthashastra period any ambiguity that one may detect about the relative importance of spiritual authority and temporal power in the texts on statecraft disappears and the priority of dharma is reasserted. Taking an overall view of the Hindu tradition, Robert Lingat concludes in his *Classical Law of India* (1973) that it would be vain to look at the relation between the two powers of the Brahman and the king in terms of the Christian theory of the separation of the domains of God and Caesar. Indeed, if a comparison is made, the Brahmanical doctrine is analogous to the formulation by Pope Gelasius (at the end of the fifth century) that priestly power is much more important than royal power because the priest has to answer for the kings at the divine tribunal.

The Hindu (Brahmanical) and related Buddhist doctrines of the unity of the sacred and the secular predetermined the relationship of religion and politics, acknowledging the supremacy of dharma. In the dramatic imagery of the Buddhist tradition, the world conqueror was indeed also expected to be the world renouncer, and the duty of the king was to be a subject (follower) of dharma. This moral philosophy of power prevailed up to the dawn of the eleventh century, when Muslim rule was established in northern India, offering alternative perspectives on the nature of politics and religion. Although Hindu kingdoms collapsed or retreated one after another, Hindu ideas about the scope and character of kingship did not vanish. Indeed, they survived into modern times, not only in the Hindu princely states that the British tolerated (these states were ultimately integrated into the modern Indian state after independence in 1947), but also as one of the idioms of politics in contemporary India.

The Rise of Modern Hinduism

British rule was established in India in the second half of the eighteenth century, first under the aegis of the East India Company (1757–1857) and then (1858–1947) directly under the British government. The first half-century of expanding British governance in India was marked by the primacy of economic interests and an instrumental view of everything else. Political control was essential to the furtherance of these interests, as was knowledge of the cultural traditions of the land, but cultural and social transformation was not. Noninterference was the watchword, and missionary activity was explicitly forbidden. The ancient Brahmanical Vedic texts (the Vedas date back to at least 1200 B.C.) and later nonreligious, Sanskrit, literary works began to be translated into English and other European languages in the late eighteenth century, and the discipline of Indology was born. Indologists admired the achievements of ancient India in the fields of grammar, belles lettres, and speculative philosophy; they, however, had nothing but contempt for the religions and cultures of contemporary India. In any case, what they called Hinduism was too complex and internally heterogeneous for anybody's comfort. The merchants and the administrators, however, needed information about contemporary society, and thus ethnography too was born, almost a twin of Indology.

In 1813 the British Parliament lifted the ban on proselytization by Christian missionaries in India. Denigration of native cultures and religions became the order of the day. The attacks on Hinduism were generally ill-informed and intemperate. Many British writers considered India to be at the threshold of a new way of life under the combined impact of the new mercantile and administrative dispensations and evangelical Christianity. In their enthusiasm the critics overlooked the inner vitality of Hinduism, which had enabled it to meet many challenges, both internal (the birth of new religions, notably Buddhism and Jainism in the early sixth century B.C.) and external (the advent of Islam early in the eighth century A.D.). The emergence of religious reform and revival movements among the Hindus from the 1820s onward was more in the nature of a creative response to yet another external challenge than an unconsidered rejection of or an unqualified surrender to the many-sided impact of the West. These movements sought not only to rediscover the ancient roots of Hinduism but also to reinterpret it in the light of Christian ethics and liberal politics.

Among the religious and social reform movements of the nineteenth century, those led by Brahmo Sabha (founded in 1828 in Calcutta and renamed Brahmo Samaj, Society of God, in 1843) and Arya Samaj, Society of the Aryas, people of noble descent (founded in 1876 and active in Bombay in western India and in Punjab in northern India) are particularly noteworthy. Both organizations were nonpolitical in character, but their leaders had explicit views about Chris-

tianity and British rule, which were justifiably seen as mutually reinforcing in fact, although not as a matter of explicit policy. Rammohun Roy (1772–1833), the founder of Brahmo Sabha, was deeply appreciative of the ethical character of the New Testament and considered British rule a divine dispensation that all sensible and patriotic Indians should welcome. The founder of Arya Samaj, Dayananda Saraswati (1824–1883), wrote derisively about Christianity, denying it the status of a revealed and true religion. He was critical of the nexus between the missionaries and British officials. In the years to come, members of the Arya Samaj were to be active participants in the national movement.

The program of the Arya Samaj was explicitly revivalist and even fundamentalist in the domain of religion and progressive in regard to social life, disapproving of the inequities of the Brahman-dominated caste system and discrimination against women. In Bengal a reaction set in against the Brahmo Samaj in the last quarter of the nineteenth century and took the form of Hindu revivalism, which was not, however, pure traditionalism inasmuch as it was also innovative. The most outstanding figure in the shaping of modern Hinduism was Vivekananda (1863–1902), a disciple of a prominent religious mystic of Bengal but not excessively inward looking himself. He was sharply critical of Hindu ritualism and of social abuses (caste and gender discrimination). He attacked Christian missionaries but adopted their social activism as his own strategy. He proclaimed that the pluralism of Hinduism (the belief that all religions are true) and its spiritualism, respectively, were superior to proselytizing religions and materialism. He gave the call for making a world religion of Hinduism rooted in Vedanta (the philosophical texts that were the culmination of Vedic religion). Indeed, Vivekananda called Vedanta the mother of all religions, containing in itself the eternal truths of all religions. He took part in the Parliament of Religions at Chicago, an international goodwill conference of religious leaders, in 1896 and was reportedly its most impressive participant. Like Dayananda, Vivekananda was acutely aware of the mutually reinforcing relationship of British imperialism and the church in India, but he refrained from formulating a political agenda. This was done by others, who functioned in an atmosphere that was surcharged with religious revivalism and social reform.

The shaping of a new political consciousness among the Hindu intelligentsia all over India—more radically in some parts of the country (for example, Bengal in the east and the Bombay presidency in the west)—combined the stirrings of nationalist aspirations with religious sentiments and symbolism. This is perhaps best illustrated by the literary and social writings of Bankimchandra Chattopadhyay (1839–1894), one of the outstanding Indian intellectuals of the late nineteenth century.

For Chattopadhyay, political regeneration and cultural and religious reconstruction were two sides of the same coin. He even wrote of a "national religion," the roots of which lay in the Vedas. Added to this emphasis on roots, and on a holistic conception of life in which the social and religious were one and the same reality, was his judgment that the Hindus had been singularly and unfortunately indifferent to power. The subjection of the Hindus to the British for over a century, and before that to the Muslims for more than eight hundred years, was, according to Chattopadhyay, a consequence of this negligence and of apathy to history. It followed that the way to national freedom and honor lay through a positive attitude to power defined in material as well as cultural terms. The first task, then, was Hindu cultural regeneration defined by both patriotism and humanism. Drawing upon Hindu mysticism and the enthusiasm centered on the worship of a supreme mother-goddess, Shakti (literally, "power" or "power embodied"), Chattopadhyay translated this religious idea into the powerful but very Hindu concept of the country as the divine mother, which was, however, anathema to the Muslims. The image of Mother India in chains was for the Hindus, who constituted nearly three-fourths of the population of India, easily the key symbol of political subjugation. It represented spiritual infirmity, material deprivation, and loss of national dignity. The time was thus ripe for the formal shaping of a national movement.

The Birth of the National Movement

By the 1880s the broad-minded and politically liberal among the British rulers of India, and like-minded sections of the public in Britain, had come to recognize that Indians should have a hand in their own governance, at least at the local level. It is not therefore at all surprising that a retired English civil servant should have been prominent among those who founded the Indian National Congress Party in 1885. Religion was still a highly significant aspect of social life in the late nineteenth century everywhere in the world, although it also came under attack in the West. It certainly was important in India, which had long been home or host to nearly all the major world religions. It was thus that, from the very beginning, nationalism here was closely intertwined with religion. Indeed, some of the Hindu intellectuals who joined the national movement maintained that nationalism itself was a religion. It may be added that among the Muslims, too, a widely shared point of view was that political activity could not be separated from religious obligation and that religious identity was the basic principle of social organization in India.

The situation was complex. Part of the complexity was a consequence of the plurality of religions of India, which opened the way for competing religious nationalisms. Part of it flowed from the self-contradictory character of colonial rule. On the one hand, the colonial rulers not only insisted on describing India as a land of disparate religious communities, castes, sects, and tribes but also contributed to the consolidation of such primordial identities through the codification of Hindu and Muslim family laws, compilation of ethnographic notes, and enumeration of "the peoples of India" through the decennial censuses from 1881 onward. These measures contributed to the emergence of religious nationalism, or, as it is called in India, communalism. On the other hand, British rule helped to shape a national secular identity on a subcontinental scale through administrative, judicial, economic, educational, and other policies. The country saw the emergence of a new middle class, which, notwithstanding critical deficiencies owing to its character as a colonial implant, engaged in secular politics based on the concept of equal citizenship rights within the nation-state. The politics of nationalism was thus afflicted by schisms from its birth.

Nobody, not even the secular politicians, denied the importance of religious and cultural differences. The secularists asserted that nationalism would focus on common interests, common benefits, and general reforms (the demand for self-governance and, later, full independence were things of the future) and would recognize the legitimacy of separate community interests within the larger framework. Their opponents, however, expressed deep misgivings about Hindu domination and questioned the applicability of democracy or majority rule in India. The secularists took a hierarchical view of national and community interests, maintaining that the latter should and could be accommodated in the former. Those who disagreed—most notably Sayyid Ahmad Khan (1817–1898), the leader of the Muslims in northern India, and Jotirao Phule (1827–1890), a low-caste social reformer from western India—considered the Indian National Congress Party primarily a high-caste Hindu organization and disagreed with its political plank of self-governance. They saw in the continuance of British rule the best means of protecting the interests of minority communities in India.

The Congress Party derived its membership from all the major religious communities, but the predominance of Hindus was an undeniable fact. The minority communities, particularly the Parsis (Zoroastrians), were prominent in the leadership. The third president of the party was a Muslim, and it was he who tried to negotiate (unsuccessfully) with Sayyid Ahmad Khan and other like-minded Muslim leaders for their support.

With only limited support from the Muslims, the national movement tended to use Hindu cultural symbols and drew upon Hindu perspectives on Indian history to mobilize mass support. A notable instance of this was the successful attempt by a prominent Hindu (of the highest Brahman caste), Bal Gangadhar Tilak (1856–1920), to inject politics into a traditional religious festival and to recruit the Hindu god Ganapati to serve secular goals. He also wrote an interpretation of the religious text *Bhagavad Gita* to promote a vigorous political philosophy of action. The formally adopted objectives of the Congress Party, however, emphasized a fuller development and consolidation of sentiments of national unity. It spoke on behalf of the people of India and not the Hindus alone.

Nevertheless, Muslims became more apprehensive with the passage of time, and in 1906 they established a new political organization called the Indian Muslim League. Those Muslims who had stayed out of the national movement because, they said, they feared Hindu domination (many of them may have simply been reluctant to recognize the end of Muslim control in India, for they continued to recall and insist upon their political preeminence), now had a platform of their own. One of their earliest demands (going back to 1896) was for the institution of separate electorates. Under such a system the Muslims would choose their representatives from among themselves from reserved constituencies demarcated on the basis of community-wise distribution of population. The Muslim leadership considered this the only way Muslim interests could be defended. The British government conceded the demand in 1909. Many historians consider the partition of the subcontinent in 1947 on the basis of religious difference considered alongside of population distribution an inevitable consequence of the grant of separate electorates combined with weightage for Muslims in the Muslim-minority provinces. The Muslims also demanded special treatment because of their historical role as the com-

munity that provided the rulers of India over a period of eight hundred years. This demand was not conceded by the British.

Hindus generally resented the concession of separate electorates, but moderate politicians from within and outside the Congress Party advised their coreligionists to accommodate the Muslim demand. In 1916 the Muslim League and the Congress Party entered into what is referred to as the Lucknow Pact. (Lucknow is a major city in northern India where the two organizations held their parleys.) Under it the Congress Party agreed to both separate electorates and weightage. Moreover, the Hindu leaders who negotiated and advocated it were inspired by Western liberal ideas, despite the rejection of the principle of individual liberty by separatist Muslims. Having joined hands, the two organizations demanded representative government in India but not full independence. The pact was, however, never implemented. A Hindu response to the pact, consciously based on the Hindu preference for religious pluralism combined with some measure of tolerance, had to await the entry of Mohandas Gandhi (1869–1948) into Indian politics.

Gandhi and Religious Tolerance

Few Indians of the twentieth century were more explicit than Gandhi in emphasizing, first, the imperative of morally or religiously informed politics and, second, the philosophy of religious tolerance. He considered it a particular virtue of Hinduism that it had, according to him (and many others), a millennia-old tradition of religious tolerance. In the minds of numerous thoughtful people in India and abroad, it was Gandhi who best exemplified the marriage of tradition and modernity in Hinduism. His admirers came to call him the Mahatma, "great soul." Gandhi was born a Hindu and this fact was for him the very foundation of his life and work. While acknowledging that he had learned some great truths from other religions (notably Christianity), he remained essentially a Hindu because he found Hinduism open to reinterpretation in the light of moral reason and respectful of all religions. Indeed, freedom from dogmatism was, in Gandhi's judgment, the strength of Hinduism.

Gandhi started his political career in South Africa, where he began his experiments with the conduct of political agitations in the light of moral or religious principles, such as insistence upon truth, moral dignity, and nonviolence. He returned to India in 1915 and, after carefully studying the Indian political scene, gradually moved into a position of leadership in the Congress Party. He supported the Lucknow Pact and the policy of accommodation that it advocated. At the end of World War I the issue of the future of the Muslim institution of the caliphate, which was the central locus of political authority in the Muslim world and had long remained vested in the Ottoman emperor, was faced with a crisis, for Turkey was earmarked for dismemberment. The symbolic importance of the caliphate far outweighed its nominal political authority. Among many Muslim national communities that were greatly concerned about the developments were the Indian Muslims. Some of their leaders informed the British government that unless the Turkish sultan was saved, Indian Muslims would have no choice but to engage in a religious war *(jihad)* or to migrate en masse to a Muslim country.

Long mindful of the importance of Hindu-Muslim harmony in both religion and politics, Gandhi lent his unqualified support to the movement for the preservation of the caliphate with all its functions. He asserted that since the issue was of the deepest religious and political significance to the Muslims, it was the moral duty of all Indians, particularly the majority community of Hindus, to make the caliphate their own cause. Gandhi decided to overlook the fact that such support would entail close collaboration with traditional Muslim religious leaders, who tended to be socially conservative and politically reactionary. He made the caliphate a central issue of Indian politics and succeeded in drawing Muslims into the national movement in unprecedented numbers. The experiment failed, however, because the Turkish nationalists who captured power abolished the caliphate in 1924.

Gandhi's support of the caliphate and his involvement with conservative religious leaders seems, in retrospect, to have been one of his major political blunders. It strengthened the separatist tendencies among the Muslims because the conservatives among their leaders tended to be exclusivist in their politics. Consequently, Hindu-Muslim conflicts resurfaced in full force by the mid-1920s. Gandhi's religious tolerance was of little avail in producing harmony between the religious communities. Within the Hindu community itself, the entry of the masses into the national movement, for which Gandhi was largely responsible, resulted in the ascendance of folk forms of religion that were rather remote from the moral reason that he considered crucial for any living religious tradition. Far from being able always to obtain knowing support for the values of truth and nonviolence, he was

recast by his mass following in the image of a holy man and miracle maker. More injuriously, his support of Muslim causes generated a reaction among certain sections of the vast and heterogeneous Hindu community. It was thus that the political ideology of "Hindutva," that is, making India a culturally homogeneous country, was born—a country in which the Hindus would exercise the political dominance that their numbers entitled them to or, at least, made possible.

Hindutva—Making India Hindu

In the development of a politically motivated and culturally hegemonistic Hinduism in the twentieth century, the emergence of the religious and social reform movements of the late nineteenth century, which were at least partly revivalist, played a crucial role. These movements were not overtly political, although their members often had political interests; many of them were in the Congress. A Hindu political party, distinct from the Hindu-dominated secularist Indian National Congress, namely, the Hindu Mahasabha, was established in 1915 (ironically, the very same year in which Gandhi returned to India from South Africa). It began with a modest agenda of the protection of specifically Hindu interests but failed to make much of an impact on the nationalist politics of the day. Demands for its activation were made in the wake of the worsening of Hindu-Muslim relations after the collapse of the caliphate movement. Hindu associations made their appearance in many parts of the country, sounding the alarm that politically assertive Muslims posed a threat to the interests of the Hindu community.

A most significant development was the publication in 1923 of a small book *Hindutva: Who Is a Hindu?* written by a notable Mahasabha leader, Vinayak D. Savarkar, while in prison as a political detainee. The Arya Samaj had put forward a restrictive definition of the true followers of the original Vedic religion, since transformed into Brahmanism and then Hinduism, and named them "Aryas" (the noble people). They were contrasted to degenerate Hindus of the caste system, prisoners of Brahmanic orthodoxy ridden with rituals and social taboos. Savarkar emphatically favored the term *Hindu,* tracing it back to the geographical designation *Sindhu:* Hindus were the people who lived in the lands between the Sindhu (Indus) and the high seas; their original scriptures were the Vedas, as the Arya Samaj had said. For them the country so defined was both their fatherland and their holy land, and they constituted one nation, the Hindu nation. The acknowledgment of a common race, a common culture, and a common nationality constituted, in Savarkar's opinion, the ideology of Hindutva, that is, being a Hindu and, further, making India Hindu.

Savarkar clarified that Hindutva was a complex whole of which Hinduism, the religion, was only a part or derivative. Further, he insisted that the term *Hinduism,* properly used, should denote the religions of all Hindus (including in this category not only all kinds of Hindus but also those of other religions such as Buddhists, Jains, Sikhs, and even the tribal communities). He excluded Christians and Muslims, even descendants of converts from Hinduism, on the ground that, commonalities of descent and culture notwithstanding, their holy places were not all in India. These peoples were in the country but not in the nation; they could be so included if they looked upon India as their premier holy land.

Savarkar's innovative thesis has in recent years acquired the undisputed status of the manifesto of neo-Hindu fundamentalism, which is totalitarian in relation to all those deemed to be Hindus and exclusivist toward those stigmatized as the spiritually alien "others." It is significant that Savarkar diluted the emphasis on true scripture, which was a characteristic of the concerns of the Brahmo Samaj and the Arya Samaj, and replaced it with an overwhelming stress on culture, particularly in its spiritual (rather than material) aspect. Inspired by Savarkar's rhetoric, a member of the Congress Party, Keshav B. Hedgewar (1889–1940), founded an organization for the protection of Hindu culture in 1925, which he named the Rashtriya Swayamsevak Sangh, National Volunteer Association (RSS), two years later. The justification that he provided for the new organization made it quite clear that Hindutva was being defined antagonistically as an identity that was under severe pressure from the Muslims, who had been lately mobilized during the caliphate movement.

The RSS has from the very beginning emphasized character building (through physical culture and ideological instruction) rather than religion. Its principal concern is to save Hindu culture from external influences. To the extent to which religion is an aspect of Hindu culture, Hinduism too is to be saved, but that is not the primary aim. The RSS conceives of culture as encompassing all aspects of life, including religion and politics. Downplaying Hinduism and disavowing any interest in politics are therefore deceptive.

The inclusiveness of culture in the RSS ideology was fully articulated by Hedgewar's successor, M. S. Golwalkar (who assumed leadership of the organization in 1940 on the former's death). He called for the rejuvenation of the ancient Hindu nation, which, according to him, was united by geography, race, culture, religion, and language. In a well-known book (*We or Our Nationhood Defined,* 1938), he called upon the non-Hindu peoples of India to adopt Hindu culture and language, revere Hindu religion, and respect and love the Hindus. In short, he asked them to cease to be foreigners. If they did not do so, they could stay in India only under subordination to the Hindus, deprived of any privileges, even the common rights of citizens. Needless to add, the RSS ideology is, above all, about power. If we recognize the preeminence of the so-called Hindu nation and of its culture and religion, Hindu political domination is ensured ideologically without any elaborate political agenda.

The importance of Hinduism (or religion) in the RSS ideology is unclear. Judging by what the group's ideologues have written, or what the members do organizationally, rituals and theological concerns—particularly the latter—do not receive much attention. Scriptural authority is seldom invoked. The emphasis is consistently on culture (*sanskriti*), which is derived from dharma—a notion that (as we have noted earlier) includes morality as well as religion as commonly understood. It is therefore rather difficult to understand what the RSS ideologues mean when they acknowledge religious pluralism as an element of Hindu culture.

The RSS itself has never adopted a formal political agenda or participated in elections. Some of its leaders, however, formed a political party in 1951 called the Jana Sangh. It has since been renamed the Bharatiya Janata Party, Indian Peoples Party (BJP). Although it derived its support mainly from northern India to begin with, the party has gradually spread its appeal countrywide and is now the largest single party in the national Parliament, although it falls short of a simple majority. It attempted to form a government in the summer of 1996 but failed. It has formed governments in several states in northern and western India or shared power with other parties. In its formal pronouncements of policy, the BJP supports the concept of the secular state based on respect for all religions and universal human rights. Indeed, it accuses other political parties, particularly the Indian National Congress, of being pseudosecularist, given more to the appeasement of religious minorities (notably Muslims) than to the protection of universal human rights. These parties in turn consider the BJP a threat to the ideals of secularism and pluralism and have joined hands to keep it out of power. It is obvious that in any discussion of politics in the context of Hinduism, the issue of secularism occupies a central place.

Hinduism and Secularism

The religious plurality and the numerical preponderance of Hindus, who account for over four-fifths of the population of India (or less than two-thirds if the former polluting or untouchable castes are excluded), pose a challenge in regard to the cultural and political rights of the religious minorities. The largest of these minorities are the nearly 120 million Muslims who are 12 percent of the population, followed by the Christians (2.5 percent), the Sikhs (2 percent), and the others. In the closing years of the nineteenth century, when certain sections of the Muslim leadership sounded the alarm about Hindu political domination, Vivekananda emerged as a charismatic and articulate Hindu religious reformer. He claimed that among all the major world religions Hinduism was both the oldest and the most tolerant. Moreover, he traced Hindu tolerance back to the earliest Veda (c. 1500 B.C.), which declares that the Truth (or the Absolute) is one although the learned describe it variously. Vivekananda's gloss was that the declaration legitimized religious plurality. The importance of this attitude becomes clear by setting it off against the position of Dayananda that the Vedic religion was the only truly revealed and complete religion known to humanity. One of the most radical changes that Dayananda introduced was that of the reclamation—he called it purification—of Hindus who had been converted to other religions (Islam, Christianity, Sikhism) and were desirous of returning to the Hindu fold.

The pluralist perspective of Hinduism found its most eloquent exponent in the twentieth century in Gandhi. Indeed, his pluralism was more genuine than Vivekananda's, for he argued for the complementarity of religions. All religions, according to him, were equally true, but they were also imperfect because of the limitations of human understanding. Gandhi credited Hinduism, however, with being the most pluralist and tolerant of religions.

Religion, understood as a grammar of ultimate values and not as rituals and social taboos and prejudices, was for Gandhi the guiding principle of all activities, including politics. In other words, religion was constitutive of society. He was therefore opposed to the secularization of society, but he insisted that the state should be secular and confined to such activities as the maintenance of law and order. Many Indian social and political thinkers, including the philosopher Sarvepalli Radhakrishnan (India's second president, 1962–1967), who held similar views, put forward the idea that in India, a deeply religious country, secularism could only mean equal respect for all religions or, at least, equal treatment of all citizens, irrespective of their religions, at the hands of the state. Hindu political leaders, including the most liberal and the most conservative, were quick to claim that Hinduism was a secular religion in the foregoing sense of the term and that Hindus would lose their moral vision if they borrowed an atheistic or agnostic secularism from the West.

Many Hindus and other Indians, however, are advocates of science as the temper of society rather than religion and look forward to a gradual decrease in the importance of religion in public life if not to its total elimination from society. The most distinguished exponent of this position among the leaders of the national movement was Jawaharlal Nehru (1889–1964), who was born a Hindu but came under the influence of rational liberal thinkers such as Bertrand Russell and of Marx, Lenin, and the British socialists. From the 1920s onward until 1946, the year before the partition of the subcontinent, Nehru consistently denied the importance of religious antagonisms. He regarded them as a side issue and, at most, a reflection (or mystification) of the clash of economic interests. A little over a year before he finally accepted the demand for the separate country of Pakistan in 1947, he had called it a product of a medieval mode of thinking and simply "fantastic." His emphasis on the material basis of society and on reason and science made him a secularist in the Enlightenment sense of the term.

Nehru was an avid student of history and had written two major historical works, one on world history and the other on Indian history. He was therefore aware of the positive as well as the negative aspects of the historical role of religion generally and of Hinduism in India. In his presentation of it, Hinduism was not to be valued for its mythology, theology, or ritual, but for its metaphysics and speculative thought. After independence, faced with the stupendous task of governing a multicultural country of many religions (the formation of Pakistan reduced the proportion of Muslims in the residual state of India to 10 percent, but in absolute numbers this meant 40 million people), Nehru acknowledged that secularism in India would have to be religious pluralism in the foreseeable future, rather than a narrowing of the role of religion in society. In fact, electoral politics at all levels, ranging from the local to the national, created powerful arenas for the use of religion for the furtherance of secular ends. The formation of new, Hindu-dominated, but in principle not exclusively Hindu, parties, namely, the Jana Sangh and the Bharatiya Janata Party, has already been noted. A third organization, exclusively Hindu, for the promotion of Hinduism and the mobilization of Hindus as a worldwide cultural, religious, and political community, called the Vishva Hindu Parishad, World Hindu Assembly (VHP), also has been established. It represents the aggressive face of Hinduism today.

VHP and the Semitization of Hinduism

Founded in Bombay in 1964 by 150 religious leaders, and invoking a "Universal Hindu Society" of six hundred million people residing in eighty countries, the VHP went beyond the Hindutva concept of a subcontinentally located religion and society. Its half-dozen stated objectives included, first, the consolidation and strengthening of the Hindu society worldwide, second, the promotion of "the Hindu values of life," and third, the rendering of "social service to humanity at large." The behind-the-scenes influence of the RSS leadership in the establishment of the VHP has been asserted and is believable. As stated above, religious concerns (like the political ones) are not prominent in the public profile of the RSS. It is common nowadays to speak of the Sangh family, comprising RSS as the cultural body, BJP as the political party, and VHP as the religious organization. Needless to add, it is the quest for power that is the common element, whether formally acknowledged or not. The VHP's religious concerns, symbolized, for instance, by the holding of ancient fire (sacrificial) rituals and of ceremonies designed to arouse religious consciousness, have different amounts of political content but rarely none. Not only does the VHP present Hinduism as the national religion of India, it also portrays it as a religion beleaguered by Christianity and Islam. To strengthen it, the VHP has devoted considerable attention to missionary work among low-caste Hindus and the non-Hindu tribal peoples. In 1984 the VHP established a youth wing called the Bajrang Dal, invoking the image of a band of warriors, inspired by the monkey hordes of the ancient Rama story contained in the Sanskrit epic *Ramayana*.

It is important to note that when the VHP pursues its objectives, Hinduism is transformed by the expansion of scales (of activities as well as the social spaces) and the inescapable concessions to the very diverse lifestyles of the peoples being mobilized (tribals in India to professionals in the United States). The very existence of an organization like the VHP is a major innovation, for Hinduism traditionally has not had a churchlike body. Other significant changes include the identification of a universally applicable set of values, the selec-

tion of the traditionally calm and benign Rama from the Hindu pantheon of gods as the favorite divinity and the recasting of him as a heroic warrior, and the promotion of particular versions of certain sacred texts (notably the northern Indian, sixteenth-century, version of *Ramayana*). Some observers have seen in these transformations a perhaps subconscious wish to recast Hinduism in the Semitic mold to enable it to face more effectively the perceived challenges of Judaism, Christianity, and Islam.

Demolition of the Babri Mosque

Consolidation means strength, and strength posits the use of force to achieve certain objectives. The demolition of a Muslim mosque in the northern Indian city of Ayodhya on December 6, 1992, was the handiwork of the leaders, members, and followers of the Sangh family. The destruction of the mosque did irreparable damage to the image of Hinduism as a tolerant religion.

The historical background to this act of vandalism takes us back to the middle of the sixteenth century, when Babur invaded northern India and, defeating local Muslim kings, laid the foundations of the Mughal Empire. A mosque named after Babur was built in 1528 in the Hindu temple town of Ayodhya by one of his generals to mark his conquests. It became a source of dispute between Hindus and Muslims after the arrival of the British as the new rulers of the country. The Hindu contention was that the mosque had been constructed after the demolishing of an eleventh-century Hindu temple that commemorated the "birth place" of the god Rama as a human being in mythological time.

The controversy gained further strength after independence in 1947, and the government put the mosque under police protection, denying entry to it to members of both communities. The VHP launched a movement in 1984 for access to the mosque to offer worship to a stone image of Rama, which was placed there surreptitiously in 1949. A magistrate (who happened to be a Hindu) allowed access to the disputed site in 1986, and the performance of Hindu rituals inside the mosque commenced. The Muslims refrained from offering prayers there but staged protests locally and elsewhere.

The next step for the VHP was to ask for the demolition of the mosque so that a "grand" Rama temple could be constructed in its place. The mosque was described as a symbol of Hindu defeat and national shame. The issue became crucial during the general elections of 1989 and saw the Sangh family act jointly in relation to it, although not exactly for the same reasons. Three years later (in 1992) the BJP won the elections in the state of Uttar Pradesh in which Ayodhya is located and formed the government. After benefiting in the elections by using the temple issue, it sought to distance itself from the VHP's aggressive posture of immediate action. The union (federal) government also advocated a negotiated settlement and tried to buy time in the hope that passions on both sides would cool down with the passage of time (the Muslims were represented by an all-India committee set up in 1987 for the protection of the mosque and its restoration to them). This turned out to be a grave miscalculation.

Workers of the VHP and the BJP gathered in Ayodhya on December 5, 1992, for the performance of rituals, some distance away from the mosque, in preparation for the eventual construction of the temple. The BJP government of the state had offered assurances that the mosque would not be harmed. It was reduced to rubble the next day in an obviously preplanned manner with the law-and-order forces of the state looking on. Triumphant bands of Hindu hooligans next resorted to the looting of Muslim properties in Ayodhya and to killings in which more than a dozen lives were lost. There would have been more deaths, but most Muslims had already fled the town. No interreligious riot had ever taken place in Ayodhya before this one. Riots erupted in other parts of the country and also in Pakistan and Bangladesh, where Muslims staged retaliatory action. Thousands of Muslims were killed in the far-off city of Surat in western India. Hindus in similar numbers fled from their homes in Bangladesh to cross into India. A couple of months later Bombay was bombed by Muslim terrorists. Only thereafter was communal peace restored.

Years have passed since the demolition of the Babri Mosque, but the dispute has still not been resolved, although there have been no further violent incidents. The BJP has recognized that the events of December 1992 were unfortunate. The VHP has taken no further steps toward the construction of the temple (the matter is in the hands of the Supreme Court), but it has added two more mosques in northern India to the list of buildings that must be destroyed because temples were demolished in the seventeenth century to raise them. Meanwhile, the Parliament has enacted a law providing protection to all places of worship irrespective of their historical origins. A noteworthy fact is that during the 1996 parliamentary elections, which coincided with elections in some states, including Uttar Pradesh, the mosque-temple issue did not play any significant role. The BJP emerged as the single largest party at the union level and also in Uttar Pradesh, but in the absence of a simple majority it could not form the government.

Hinduism Today

Vivekananda, one of the founding fathers of modern Hinduism, warned that India should not cease to be a religious (spiritual) country. For it to embrace politics and materialism would be not only a break with its prized cultural heritage, he said, but actually suicide. What he failed to realize was that his vision of Hinduism in its Vedantic form as a world religion that is the mother of all religions was hegemonic and political. By contrast, Gandhi emphasized the inseparability of religion and politics in the hope that the latter would be redeemed by the former. As it turns out, Hinduism and, indeed, Islam, Sikhism, and Buddhism have been used in South Asia as markers of ethnic identity and made to serve political goals. When this happens religion becomes, as the French anthropologist Louis Dumont put it in his *Religion, Politics, and History* (1970), its own shadow.

Still, Hinduism as *collective ideology* has not completely displaced Hinduism as *personal faith*. There are millions of Hindus today all over the world for whom Hinduism is a means to spiritual advancement and a way of relating to the Absolute through the path of ritual, knowledge, or devotion to a personal deity—or through a combination of these paths. Given the rate of construction of new neighborhood and larger temples, of attendance at daily rituals, of participation in pilgrimages, and of the emergence of new deities (for example, Santoshi Ma), new sects (for example, the Radhasaomi Satsangh), and new cults (for instance, that around the spiritual guru Sathya Sai Baba), Hinduism as a religion does not seem to be in danger of being swallowed up by politics. For such Hindus, Hinduism is an eternal religion (morality), *sanatan dharma*.

See also *Ahmad Khan, Sir Sayyid; Gandhi, Mohandas Karamchand; India; Pakistan.*

T. N. Madan

BIBLIOGRAPHY

Anderson, Walter K., and Shridhar D. Damle. *The Brotherhood in Saffron: The Rashtriya Swayam Sevak Sangh and Hindu Revivalism.* New Delhi: Vistar, 1987.

Babb, Lawrence A. *Redemptive Encounters: Three Modern Styles in the Hindu Tradition.* Berkeley and Los Angeles: University of California Press, 1986.

Baird, Robert D., ed. *Religion in Modern India.* New Delhi: Manohar, 1995.

Dalmia, Vasudha, and H. von Steitencron, eds. *Representing Hinduism: The Construction of Religious Traditions and National Identity.* Thousand Oaks, Calif.: Sage, 1995.

Jones, Kenneth W. *Socio-religious Reform Movements in British India.* Cambridge: Cambridge University Press, 1989.

Larson, Gerald J. *India's Agony over Religion.* Albany: State University of New York Press, 1995.

Ludden, David, ed. *Making India Hindu: Religion, Community, and the Politics of Democracy in India.* Delhi: Oxford University Press, 1996.

Madan, T. N. *Modern Myths, Locked Minds: Secularism and Fundamentalism in India.* Delhi: Oxford University Press, 1997.

Nandy, Ashis, et al. *Creating a Nationality: The Ramjanam-bhumi Movement and the Fear of Self.* Delhi: Oxford University Press, 1995.

Nehru, Jawaharlal. *The Discovery of India.* Bombay: Asia Publishing House, 1961.

Sontheimer, Gunther D., and Herman Kulke, eds. *Hinduism Reconsidered.* New Delhi: Manohar, 1991.

Van der Veer, Peter. *Religious Nationalism: Hindus and Muslims in India.* Berkeley and Los Angeles: University of California Press, 1994.

Hobbes, Thomas

Prominent (and controversial) English philosopher and political theorist. Hobbes (1588–1679) was active during a period of social and cultural change. In content, his writings on politics and religion reflect the momentous civil conflicts experienced in seventeenth-century England—including the Civil Wars, the execution of Charles I, and the restoration of the monarchy. In method and perspective, his works manifest the influence of the European intellectual revolution of the time, a radical shift from medieval modes of thought to modern forms of science and philosophy.

Hobbes received a traditionally classical education at Oxford University, which he later subjected to withering criticism. After graduation, he entered the employ of the Cavendish family as tutor and companion, a position he held (except for two periods including eleven years of self-imposed exile in Paris) to the end of his life. While serving as tutor, Hobbes spent some years on the continent, especially in Italy and France, during which he interacted with several noted intellectuals (among them, René Descartes, a French philosopher, and Galileo Galilei, an Italian scientist). He became convinced, through his discovery of Euclid's work, that the geometric method of reasoning constituted the most reliable form of scientific and philosophical inquiry.

That conviction, combined with his reaction to civil strife in England, led Hobbes to develop a scientific model of pol-

Thomas Hobbes

itics (centered in a doctrine of sovereignty) and a critical understanding of Christianity (in which the only essential principle of faith is that Jesus is the Christ). In political thought, Hobbes was opposed by both Royalists, who adhered to the doctrine of the divine right of kings, and Parliamentarians, who advocated a form of mixed government, in which the Crown was subordinate to Parliament.

In Hobbes's materialist philosophy, reality is nothing but matter in motion. On a human level, this means that we, in our natural state, live in a condition of constant conflict—a war of all against all—in which we are driven by a ceaseless desire for power yet intimidated by a constant fear of death. But reason (by deducing a set of "laws of nature," which constitute, at the same time, commands of God) provides an alternative: the creation, through covenantal agreement with each other, of a single governing authority—a sovereign or Leviathan—with full power to adopt and enforce a system of laws by which civil order is sustained. Subjects are obliged to obey the sovereign in all things, including religious practice, with one singular exception—when their natural right to self-preservation is seriously threatened.

Religious authority (church) and political authority (state) are thus, within Hobbes's model of social order, merged in the office of the sovereign, at least in a Christian commonwealth. Given this version of Erastianism (the subordination of ecclesiastical to secular power), Hobbes leveled vigorous attacks on Roman Catholicism, Presbyterianism, and Dissenting Protestant churches—all of which, in his judgment, were causes of civil unrest. Hobbes, in turn, was charged with atheism and, in his later years, was banned from publishing his works because of his anticlericalism and materialist philosophy. Hobbes, however, well read in theology, defended his positions, developing modern critical methods in his interpretations of Scripture and Christian doctrine.

Throughout his life Hobbes remained a practicing Anglican, receiving, at his own request, the sacraments on his deathbed.

See also *Anticlericalism; Covenant.*

Douglas Sturm

BIBLIOGRAPHY

Hobbes, Thomas. *Leviathan,* edited by Richard Tuck. Cambridge: Cambridge University Press, 1991.

Martinich, A. P. *The Two Gods of Leviathan: Thomas Hobbes on Religion and Politics.* Cambridge: Cambridge University Press, 1992.

Sommerville, Johann P. *Thomas Hobbes: Political Ideas in Historical Context.* New York: St. Martin's, 1992.

Sorrell, Tom, ed. *The Cambridge Companion to Hobbes.* Cambridge: Cambridge University Press, 1996.

Holidays

Referring most broadly to periods of time free from work, the word *holidays* is derived from the word *holyday* and has come to mean special days of celebration and commemoration. These days can be based on religion, politics, and regional, ethnic, or racial affiliation, and they may or may not be officially recognized by city, state, or national governments.

For instance, in the United States some holidays are widely and popularly celebrated even though they are not recognized by the government or businesses as official holidays. Both Halloween (October 31) and Valentine's Day (February 14) fall into this category. Other American holidays receive official government sponsorship at the local, state, or national level, including Evacuation Day (March 17), in Massachu-

setts's Suffolk County; Juneteenth (June 19), in Texas; and Independence Day (July 4), nationwide.

The British use the word *holidays* to refer to what Americans call vacation. In the following discussion *holidays* will be defined more generally as socially recognized days celebrating an important person or event, such as saints' days or Christmas, or marking a transition of some kind, such as the beginning of the new year or the turning of the season.

Origin of Holidays

Some holidays, such as Halloween and Valentine's Day, have been celebrated in Europe and America for centuries or are related to preexisting, pre-Christian celebrations. Many holidays on the national American calendar, for example, have ancient origins and have been exploited in more recent times by commercial industries, Valentine's Day being a good example. The day is referred to in the medieval writings of Geoffrey Chaucer and, later, in the work of William Shakespeare. Moreover, many holidays, while specific to the United States, are similar to and heavily influenced by preexisting festivals. The American Thanksgiving, for instance, commemorates a feast at Plymouth Colony in 1621 that was most likely inspired by the British harvest home traditions. However, holidays are always being created as social circumstances demand. Thus we see the addition of clergyman and civil rights leader Martin Luther King Jr.'s birthday to the American calendar and the increasingly widespread observance of Kwanza by African Americans.

Controversial Holidays

Despite their celebratory nature, holidays are frequently contested. The establishment of a national day of commemoration for King, for instance, was met with resistance from President Ronald Reagan and the officials of several states, who eventually accepted the holiday only with great reluctance. The ways in which holiday celebrations may reinforce a sense of community for those who participate in them while alienating those who do not are revealed in the controversy surrounding Kwanza.

Kwanza is celebrated from December 26 through January 1. It was invented in the mid-1960s by Dr. Maulana Kerenga, a leading scholar of African and African American studies. He is well known for championing an Afrocentric perspective in the study of culture and society. Sensing that African Americans were alienated from the Eurocentrism and commercialism of Christmas, he adapted African symbols and harvest traditions to construct a festival for African Americans. *Kwanza* is derived from a Swahili word meaning first fruits. The festival is not intended to supplant Christmas so much as to complement it. Many families choose to celebrate both. Kwanza is not a religious holiday but instead speaks to ethnic and racial identity and tradition within the United States. In this sense Kwanza involves the cultural dynamics of identity politics, reflects the growing awareness of pluralism in the United States, and helps create that sense of pluralism as well. When Kerenga invented Kwanza, he provided a ritual for the expression of ethnic and racial identity. In spite of his benevolent intentions, the celebration is sometimes an occasion for racial debate and exclusion.

Similar dynamics can be seen in the increasingly national celebration of Cinco de Mayo, a Mexican celebration of military victory. In the United States it has become something of a pan-Latino holiday, shared by Latino people of many backgrounds, and therefore not without controversy. Any such sharing of one holiday by people representing a variety of national and regional cultures (for example, Puerto Rican, Colombian, Cuban, and so on) does injustice to their real differences. Similarly, traditional occasions such as the Day of the Dead (Día de los Muertos) are growing in popularity in the United States. While these pan-Latino holidays reflect the growth of a culturally diverse population, they can also be seen as a force for standardization. The Day of the Dead traditions taught in schools and presented as authentic in museums and cultural centers are largely based on phenomena found mostly in central and southern Mexico. Like all such traditions, their manner of celebration varies widely from locale to locale; there is no one right way to celebrate them.

The adaptation of the Day of the Dead and other traditional celebrations in the United States demonstrates that celebrations serve different purposes in different circumstances and that meanings change as do personal, social, and cultural contexts. Still, in America, even major holidays such as Independence Day, Thanksgiving, and Christmas are fraught with identity politics and controversy, although this has not always been acknowledged. For instance, in the eighteenth and nineteenth centuries African Americans, both free and slave, held countercelebrations near Independence Day, as an ironic commentary on the celebration of freedom in a land of slaves. More recently Native Americans have declared Thanksgiving a national day of mourning.

Politics and Holidays

Politics and holidays, depending on one's definition of politics, become intertwined whenever a politician marches in a St. Patrick's Day Parade, the public celebrates civil holidays or debates the constitutionality of publicly sponsored nativity scenes, or special interest groups lobby to establish particular days of observance. The American Christmas shows the strain of being both a national, official holiday and a Christian holy day. It is difficult to be an American citizen and not celebrate this major festive occasion, but it is equally difficult to participate if one is not Christian. Moreover, the celebration is complicated by the doctrine of separation of church and state. These contradictions are played out in controversies over the display of crèches, or nativity scenes, on public property such as town squares. Those who object to the presence of nativity scenes, or indeed any Christmas symbolism, on public property maintain that such displays violate the principle of separation of church and state. In contrast, those who support the displays often claim that the United States is essentially a Christian country. Again, these debates reflect people's sense of their own identity as Christians, although the arguments are not usually presented in those terms. Interestingly, a common response to objections to publicly sponsored Christmas decorations is to include other traditions in the public celebration, rather than to ignore Christmas entirely. So along with the national Christmas tree in Washington, D.C., for instance, there is a national menorah representing the Jewish festival of Hanukkah, as well as an Islamic star and crescent.

Holidays have always involved politics in many ways; that association has become overt as holidays increasingly are recognized as public expressions of identity. Thus gay pride days are growing in popularity, Halloween is claimed as a high holy day by neopagans, and Latino people lobby for a day of national recognition for American labor leader Cesar Chavez. Each of these movements is met with organized resistance from other groups within the United States.

Civil Religion

Scholar Robert Bellah has used the term "civil religion" to refer to the use of religious symbols and concepts in the public political discourse of nation states, particularly the United States. The phrases "under God" in the American Pledge of Allegiance and "In God We Trust" on U.S. coins are examples of civil religion. Moreover, Bellah notes the frequency with which politicians invoke God in their speeches, particularly inauguration speeches. Indeed, it is fair to say that most national governmental ceremonial displays in the United States include a religious component such as a prayer or an oath sworn on a Bible.

This blending of the political domain with the religious domain is a means of making sacred the political system itself. If we separate the concept of the sacred from the concept of the religious, we can view politics as having its own sacred realm, beyond that of religion. For instance, the American flag is sacred though not religious. It occupies a special position in public and private spaces, is raised and lowered at certain prescribed times, must be folded in a certain way, and is burned when it has outlived its useful life. However, in spite of its sacred aspect, the flag is subject to civil authority, as the American flag burning controversy has shown. It is the U.S. Congress, after all, that determines whether burning the flag in protest is illegal.

Other examples of sacred symbols in the American political system include the narratives of the pilgrims in Plymouth, those of the War of Independence, and those of the country's Founders, which are analogous to the mythic narratives of many cultures; they, too, are sacred without being specifically religious. Likewise, national texts such as the Constitution and the Declaration of Independence are sacred, almost biblical charters.

Sacred and political symbols often overlap and mimic each other. For example, the monuments to Abraham Lincoln and Thomas Jefferson in Washington, D.C., resemble classical temples. The U.S. Vietnam War Memorial is reminiscent of a gravestone: a slab of granite with the names of the deceased inscribed upon it. It is no wonder that people leave personal memorabilia at this site. Moreover, the sacred-political realm has its holidays, including the American Memorial Day, Flag Day, and especially Independence Day. Interestingly, Labor Day, a celebration of the value of labor and the rights of workers, has been incorporated into this group of sacred-political holidays in the United States, unlike its May Day analogues in Europe.

Until recently the national anthem in Great Britain was sung before theatrical presentations. National anthems are still routinely sung before sporting events throughout the world. In Belfast at the Queen's University, many students have refused for political reasons to participate in singing the British national anthem during commencement exercises.

In the United States professional sporting events are increasingly adapting the devices of festivity, such as the use of fireworks, to extend their appeal. According to its organizers the Super Bowl has become an "unofficial American holiday." It is important to note, however, that the Super Bowl (the championship game of the National Football League) was initiated during the television era and is very much a mediated event. People gather together in small, festive groups to watch it. The cost of commercials is higher than that of any other television advertising, and the commercials themselves are advertised in advance of the broadcast. The Super Bowl celebrates the consumerist, capitalist system of which it is a part. It is made sacred by formal religious invocations and the opening rituals of the game. The graphics promoting the game employ Roman numerals, equating this event with ancient gladiatorial contests, while the winning team receives a congratulatory phone call from the president of the United States. The values and symbols of government, the media, commercial industry, and religion are fused in this one event, justifying and supporting one another.

Commemorating Rites of Passage

Many holidays, both political and religious, commemorate life cycle rites of passage. The Christian church calendar is based on the birth, circumcision, life, death, and resurrection of Jesus, for instance. Holidays also mark the births of great people (at present, exclusively male) such as American president George Washington and Martin Luther King Jr. The assassination of U.S. president John F. Kennedy, in 1963, and his subsequent funeral, was followed by a national ritual of mourning that gripped the entire country for several days.

Similarly, people experience their own rites of passage through the life cycle (and the anniversaries of those events) as personal and family holidays. Birthdays, name days, bat mitzvahs, weddings, jubilees, and even wakes and funerals are occasions for celebration and commemoration.

These personal celebrations occur within families or among groups of friends (associational groups). Large-scale holidays are usually sponsored by church or state and, more recently, by commercial industry. Some holidays are in fact created entirely by self-interested industries. Events such as Secretaries Day and Grandparents Day, which acknowledge relationships, are based on a principle of created guilt: once a day has been set aside to recognize and honor a person occupying a certain social role, such as a secretary or grandmother, it is difficult for people to ignore the day without feeling guilty. Moreover, those who ignore such days, especially those in unequal power relationships, run the risk of being punished for their refusal to participate. If, for instance, a worker overlooks Bosses Day, that worker might invite retaliation.

Imposing and Opposing Ideology

One could argue that the commercialization of holidays is itself a political act. Because the United States is a capitalist, consumerist society, commercializing public celebrations is another way of imposing ideology. In addition to serving the interests of the established political order, holidays are often used to subvert or oppose established political ideas or practices. Opposition groups invert the primary symbols associated with a holiday, as when animal rights groups prepare a vegetarian Thanksgiving dinner and have a live turkey present at the feast, or when a group in Maine holds a Memorial Day antiwar rally. Other examples include the creation of new, oppositional days such as the Native American National Day of Mourning held at Thanksgiving. Scholar David Waldstreicher has noted that slave and free African Americans often held celebrations on or near significant dates such as Independence Day. Also, many groups create days of celebration on which they can display publicly a stigmatized identity, such as Gay Pride Day.

Holidays are developed either from the top down (by the state, the church, or some other overarching institution) or from the bottom up (at the grassroots level, as in the case of a truly popular or folk celebration). Most contemporary holidays include both institutional and popular aspects, such as Halloween, which is clearly promoted by the candy industry but which also involves popular customs such as pranks, street festivals, and masquerades that are often thought to be dangerously uncontrollable by local officials. The arson of Devils Night (October 30) in Detroit is an example of the extent to which holiday celebrations can oppose the established order. Commercialism reigns in the United States, but clearly carnivalesque celebrations such as Halloween and Mardi Gras allow for more popular participation than some other holidays, and that participation is occasionally inversive.

Holidays and celebrations frequently involve conflict. To the extent that a certain group identity is being celebrated, an outgroup is necessarily created. Despite the popular rhetoric, not everybody is Irish on St. Patrick's Day, as the reaction to a group of gay and lesbian Irish Americans at the parades in Boston and New York in the 1990s has demonstrat-

ed. In Northern Ireland, where religion and politics are thought to be the same, ongoing efforts at ending the guerrilla war there have fallen apart on more than one occasion over the issue of parade routes: who gets to parade where on the national commemorations of the Twelfth of July, St. Patrick's Day, and at other times as well.

Ireland was a British colony for centuries before a war that led to a 1921 settlement granting dominion status to twenty-six of the thirty-two counties of Ireland and the partition of the remaining six majority Protestant counties into a political entity called Northern Ireland that would remain British. When Ireland gained full independence, it claimed the six counties as historically Irish. The roughly 60 percent Protestant population of Northern Ireland considers itself British and wishes to preserve the union, while the 40 percent Roman Catholic population would prefer to see unification with the Republic of Ireland. These two groups differ significantly (sometimes violently) over the very definition of Northern Ireland.

Festivals, rituals, and celebrations are ubiquitous in Northern Ireland. There are well over 3,500 parades a year, in a place with a land area roughly equivalent to that of the state of Connecticut and with a population of approximately 2.5 million people. Holidays simultaneously reinforce ingroup identity while constructing and maintaining differential identity as well. The largest celebration of the year is the Twelfth of July, a commemoration of the victory of William of Orange over King James at the Battle of the Boyne. Ulster Protestants believe that the battle captured the British throne for Protestantism and led indirectly to the establishment of Northern Ireland. A major summer festival celebrated with bonfires on the evening of July 11 and parades on July 12, the holiday asks 40 percent of the population to celebrate its own subjugation.

Other calendar celebrations in Northern Ireland are similarly politicized. The Orange Order—a Protestant fraternal organization—marches on Easter Monday, for instance, while Roman Catholics commemorate the Easter Rising against the British government in Dublin in 1916. The Ancient Order of Hibernians parade on St. Patrick's Day, but these parades have traditionally been kept away from major downtown areas, unlike the Orange parades. The period from St. Patrick's Day or Easter until the end of the summer is called the Marching Season because it is marked throughout with small and large parades. Often the routes of these parades are contested by residents who are not of the same political persuasion as those who are parading, and these conflicts often turn violent.

Public celebrations in Northern Ireland also mark the siege of Derry, the establishment of the internment laws, and the anniversary of "Bloody Sunday" in the city of Londonderry (called Derry by Roman Catholics). Throughout Northern Ireland, public displays mark territory, express identity, and profess political positions. Murals are found in both Protestant and Catholic (or Unionist and Nationalist) neighborhoods, and shrines of flowers, notes, and personal memorabilia mark the sites where people have come to an untimely death, often as the result of a bomb or a shooting. Curbstones are painted the colors of either the British Union flag or the Irish Tricolour, depending on the neighborhood. Interestingly, of all the calendar holidays, Halloween is the most nonsectarian, celebrated by all people, regardless of their political allegiances.

Reflecting Society

Holidays are always changing in accordance with society. New holidays replace old ones. Still, among many of our holiday observances there is an air of tradition, a sense of continuity with the past. While the overt and covert ramifications of holiday traditions, especially along race, class, and gender lines, cannot be overlooked or minimized, there is much of great value to be found in holiday celebrations, including the sense of coming together and sharing that we frequently associate with them. Holidays are social and cultural artifacts, and so they reflect the society in which they occur, for better and for worse.

See also *Civil religion; Public theology; Sacred places; Separation of church and state.*

Jack Santino

BIBLIOGRAPHY

Jarman, Neil. *Material Conflicts: Parades and Visual Displays in Northern Ireland.* Oxford and New York: Berg, 1997.

Kertzer, David I. *Ritual, Politics, and Power.* New Haven : Yale University Press, 1988.

Moore, Sally F., and Barbara G. Myerhoff. *Secular Ritual.* Assen, Netherlands: Van Gorcum, 1977.

Santino, Jack. *All Around the Year: Holidays and Celebrations in American Life.* Urbana: University of Illinois Press, 1994.

———. *New Old-Fashioned Ways: Holidays and Popular Culture.* Knoxville: University of Tennessee Press, 1996.

Schmidt, Leigh Eric. *Consumer Rites: The Buying and Selling of American Holidays.* Princeton: Princeton University Press, 1995.

Swanson, Wayne. *The Christ Child Goes to Court.* Philadelphia: Temple University Press, 1990.

Waldstreicher, David. *In the Midst of Perpetual Fetes: The Making of American Nationalism, 1776–1820.* Chapel Hill: University of North Carolina Press, 1997.

Holocaust

A holocaust (from the Greek *holos,* whole, and *kaustos,* burnt) was originally a sacrifice to the Greek gods in which the victim was burned whole, but the word has come to mean slaughter or destruction on a mass scale, especially by fire and nuclear warfare. When written *Holocaust,* now the most frequent use, the term refers to the period (1933–1945) of persecution and extermination of six million Jews and other minorities by Nazi Germany, also known as the Catastrophe, the Sho'ah, the Hurban.

Aftermath of World War I

Any discussion of the Holocaust must begin with World War I, the defeat of Germany, and the punitive measures of the Versailles treaty of 1919. Germany lost one-eighth of her land along the eastern and western borders, her colonies, and her overseas investments. The German army was limited to one hundred thousand men, the navy curtailed, and the German people obligated to pay enormous reparations. The war guilt clause, which blamed the war solely on Germany, infuriated all of German society. The first republican government resigned rather than sign the treaty, and Matthias Erzberger, who signed because Germans were near starvation and the Allies threatened to withhold food shipments until signatures were affixed, was assassinated three years later.

The harshness of the Versailles treaty was compounded by Germany's lack of political experience with democracy and the institutional weaknesses of the newly established Weimar Republic, a coalition government. The Weimar constitution included Article 48, referred to as the suicide clause, which let the president suspend the constitution during emergencies. This left the center parties weak, struggling for survival against political dangers from both the left (communists, Bolsheviks, socialist radicals) and the right (ultra-nationalists).

The German economy after World War I was a disaster. Prices soared when the German government urged workers of the French-occupied Ruhr to strike and the government supported them by printing paper money not backed by gold. The shortage of goods led to an inflation difficult to comprehend in today's world. At the end of the war, for example, $1 equaled 8.4 marks. In 1922 it bought 70,000 marks, and by December 1923 trillions of worthless marks traded for $1. The middle class saw their painstakingly amassed reserves wiped out, with lifetime savings buying only one loaf of bread. Investments were quite literally not worth the paper on which the certificates were printed. Labor unions were nearly destroyed because they could not provide their members with job security and a living wage. But some industrial giants profited mightily as debts melted away, paid off with cheap money. Workers were powerless, and real estate speculators increased their holdings.

All this hardship contributed to increasing political polarization. By 1923 the government controlled runaway inflation by putting the mark on par with the prewar German currency. The medicine was strong, and many already-weak businesses collapsed. The overall standard of living declined as unemployment and low wages demoralized wage earners. But the bitter pill was swallowed and led to partial economic recovery. But by the mid-1920s the German people were reviving, and had this trend continued, Germany might have achieved political stability.

Unfortunately, the Great Depression, especially the Wall Street Crash of 1929 and the failure of the Bank of Austria, caused drastic declines in production, employment, and individual and corporate purchasing power. Banks closed, businesses went bankrupt, and farmers lost farms. In the daily struggle for survival the centrally planned economies that could function without foreign interference or dependence found new supporters.

Industrialists wanted no part of communism, and this fear sent conservative industrial barons searching for alternatives. Into this mood of political hopelessness and economic disintegration entered the Nazi Party, which promised to right the wrongs of the Versailles treaty, offered a scapegoat for political aimlessness, and claimed to know how to decrease restrictions on private property while still managing the nation's business life without foreign meddling.

Hitler and the Rise of the Nazi Party

Born in 1889 in Lower Austria, Adolf Hitler failed the entrance examination for the Vienna Academy of Fine Arts and eked out a living selling picture postcards. He resented groups he saw as non-German who flocked to the heart of the Austro-Hungarian Empire. Hitler came under the influence of Karl Lueger, anti-Semitic mayor of Vienna from 1895 to 1910.

World War I provided Hitler direction, and he was devastated by the armistice. He returned to Munich, where he became the seventh member of the German Worker's party, a small political party made up of penniless ex-soldiers. Hitler quickly reshaped this group of malcontents and discovered his powers as an orator. With an air of absolute assurance in a world he saw as black and white, he offered simple, bold solutions based on his anti-Jewish and antidemocratic convictions, admiration for the outstanding individual, and contempt for the masses, swaying followers with appeals based on emotion, not logic. The party platform of the renamed National Socialist German Workers' Party, or Nazi Party, was highly nationalistic, with membership in the German nation denied to all Jews.

In 1921 Hitler created the Storm Troops, or SA, a semimilitary band of men to protect Nazi Party meetings and harass rivals. These men wore brown shirts (and hence were called Brownshirts) and were mostly unemployed military people. In 1923 Hitler's Nazis attempted a coup in Munich. Known as the Beer Hall Putsch, it collapsed when three thousand SA men ran after being confronted by only one hundred policemen. Hitler was captured and used his trial as a publicity platform. Even though he was found guilty and sentenced to five years in prison, all Germany suddenly knew him. He served less than two years in comfort and wrote his autobiography, the openly anti-Semitic *Mein Kampf* (My Struggle), during that time.

Hitler decided to take power using legitimate means and used the right-wing industrialists' fears of Bolshevism to increase Nazi support in the 1930 Reichstag elections. He challenged Paul von Hindenburg in 1932, when Hindenburg's first term as president ended. Hitler received 30 percent of the vote and forced the aging war hero into a runoff. Hindenburg won, but in the Reichstag elections of 1932, the Nazis held 230 seats and became the largest single party. According to the newly instituted republican constitutional traditions, Hitler should have been appointed chancellor, but Hindenburg resisted, turning instead to Franz von Papen, an aristocrat who thought he could control Hitler.

Hitler was offered the vice chancellorship. He refused, and von Papen called a new election. The Nazis again held the most seats in the Reichstag, despite a thirty-four seat decline. Von Papen then resigned the chancellorship and General Kurt von Schleicher became the last chancellor of Weimar.

Von Schleicher tried to check the Nazis by creating a coalition between the army and the trade unions. When this pairing proved too odd, von Schleicher tried to convince Hindenburg that only a military dictatorship would save Germany. Hindenburg responded that he had sworn to uphold the constitution and would not sign such an order. Although Schleicher resigned, Hitler remembered his attempt to block the Nazi ascent, and during the 1934 Blood Purge six Nazi members murdered von Schleicher in front of his family.

Hindenburg finally was persuaded to ask Hitler to form a government, and Hitler was appointed chancellor on January 30, 1933. Von Papen served as the vice-chancellor, still mistakenly believing his titles and experience would keep Hitler in check. On August 2, 1934, Hindenburg died and on August 3, Hitler declared himself president as well as chancellor; this act was ratified by a 90 percent vote in a referendum on August 18, 1934.

Anti-Semitism and Racism as Law

From the birth of the party in 1920, Nazi racial principles linked citizenship to race, characterizing Jews as subhuman parasites who had infected the German nation and caused all German misfortunes. Only people of "pure" German blood—those the Nazis referred to as Aryans—could be German citizens. Nazi policy was to make Germany and German-controlled areas free of Jews, and the Nazis instituted racial anti-Semitism as a fundamental part of governmental policy soon after they took office.

On April 1, 1933, the Nazis staged a boycott of Jewish shops and businesses. On April 11 they issued a decree defining as non-Aryan anyone with at least one Jewish grandparent or parent. On April 26 the State Secret Police, known as the Gestapo, was created, and in June the Dachau concentration camp was thrown open, with Buchenwald, Sachsenhausen, and Ravensbruck following soon after. On July 14 the Nazi Party was declared the only legal party in Germany. Between September and May 1934 various measures were passed to make life unbearable for Jews, thereby forcing Jews to emigrate—for example, Jews were eliminated from citizenship, public office, the professions, and the intellectual and artistic life of the country. The infamous Nuremberg Laws of September 15, 1935, denied Jews citizenship in the Reich and forbade the "desecration of the race" to protect the purity of German blood by preventing intermarriage.

These laws were followed by a series of anti-Jewish economic measures designed to take away the Jews' economic independence: the "aryanization" of Jewish business concerns and the liquidation of Jewish-owned retail businesses and of industrial enterprises; locally enforced sales of property and business; and the registration and marking of Jewish-owned businesses. Other policies were intended to enforce further personal isolation and ostracism. The first census conducted on a racial basis was on May 17, 1938. Public schools were closed to Jewish children on November 15, 1938, and compulsory identification cards were issued after January 1, 1939.

Physical violence against Jews escalated during the pre–World War II period once the Nazis took power. On May 10, 1933, Jewish books were burned. There were anti-Jewish riots by the SA in Berlin (March 9–10, 1933). Jewish judges and lawyers were chased from the Breslau court on March 13, 1933. The Munich synagogue was destroyed on June 9, 1938, and the Nuremberg synagogue, on August 10, 1938. This was followed by the infamous *Kristallnacht,* the Night of the Broken Glass, on November 9–10, 1938. A massive pogrom, it was so named because thousands of windows were smashed and the shards glistened in the streets like crystal. All 275 of Germany's synagogues were destroyed, and some seventy-five hundred Jewish businesses demolished. Firemen and police did nothing, and most non-Jewish citizens looked the other way. The arrests and the violence continued two days, and some thirty thousand Jewish men were shipped to concentration camp. Most were later released, but eight hundred did not survive their protective custody.

Throughout this period "Jews not wanted" signs were posted on businesses, sports stadiums, and roads leading to towns and resorts, and the names of Jewish dead were erased from war memorials. These policies had their anticipated effect. In 1933 there were 500,000 people in the two-thousand-year-old Jewish community in Germany, including foreign and stateless Jews; by 1939, only 220,000 remained.

These actions against the Jews took place under increasing totalitarianism within Germany, with the German Gestapo essentially above the law after February 10, 1936. The failure of the world to react to these early outrages signaled other countries, especially those in Eastern Europe, that anti-Semitism was an acceptable state policy.

The reaction of the German people during this time ranged from wide-spread Nazi support or apathy to individual acts of humanity. Most Protestant churches accepted the Nazi racial policies, although the dissenting Confessing Church took a strong stand against such racism on March

One of the death trains used by the Nazis to transport Jews and other Holocaust victims to concentration camps at the end of World War II. Allied forces discovered this train after liberating Dachau.

17, 1935, an act that resulted in the arrest of some seven hundred ministers. The Catholic Church took no public stand, although there were registered cases of Catholic protests such as that of the Canon Bernhard Lichtenberg who, after Kristallnacht, used to pray daily and openly for all those persecuted.

It was difficult for Jews themselves to grasp the enormity of what was happening to them. German Jews were highly assimilated and were shocked and bewildered by the slow escalation of so-called legal measures and acts of violence. Many continued to hope they could live in Germany; others argued that expulsion was only a matter of time, and emigration, especially to Palestine, was widely advocated. Some 280,000 Jews did emigrate, despite the legal, financial, and psychological difficulties in doing so. The hard times created by the economic depression made the arrival of poor Jewish immigrants unpopular, and Nazi propaganda made much of this anti-Jewish reaction.

Wartime Acts

After Hitler invaded Poland on September 1, 1939, Nazi policy toward Jews accelerated in its lawlessness, resulting in the mass murder of the Jewish population in any areas occupied or influenced by the Nazis. This violence culminated in the extermination of millions by shooting and gassing from 1941 to 1945 and was accompanied by the starvation, forced labor, and death marches of many other Jews. Most of these atrocities were carried out under the code name the Final Solution. The Wannsee conference of January 20, 1942, coordinated the mass murder and moved the Holocaust beyond mass shootings (such as the SS [Elite Guard] murder of 33,771 Jews at Babi Yar near Kiev, Russia, in September 1941) and killings in mobile gas vans to more technologically sophisticated, bureaucratized mass murder in concentration camps such as Auschwitz and, as the war was ending, death marches designed to cover Nazi crimes by destroying all traces of victims.

Range of the Holocaust

Although Nazi treatment of many subject peoples (Slavs, homosexuals, and gypsies) was inhumane and cruel, the Jews seemed particularly singled out for mistreatment. Decisions on the ultimate fate of many of the other subject groups within the Reich, for example, were postponed until Hitler's anticipated victory, but the destruction of the Jews was carried out immediately, even taking precedence over Nazi wartime aims.

As the Nazis captured more territory, the geographic areas affected by anti-Jewish measures expanded. Nazi policies extended into Poland after September 1, 1939; to Denmark and Norway after April 9, 1940; and to the Netherlands, Belgium, Luxembourg, and France (including French Africa and the French Levant) after May 10, 1940. The Germans occupied part of Italy as of September 8, 1943, and Yugoslavia and Greece after April 16, 1941. From June 22, 1941, anti-Jewish measures were imposed on the occupied parts of the Soviet Union and, once the United States had entered the war against Japan, these policies were applied to the Jews living in Japanese-controlled parts of Asia, such as Shanghai.

Jews living in geographic areas occupied by the Italians were more fortunate because the Italians were much more humane in their treatment of them. But other German satellites were just as cruel toward the Jews as were the Nazis. The extent of this mistreatment remains the subject of controversy to this day.

Religion and the Churches

Religion played an integral part in the Holocaust. Christian churches from the time of Constantine in the fourth century had wanted to convert Jews, and medieval Christian churches throughout Europe engaged in varying degrees of anti-Semitic persecution because they felt it was the Jews who had crucified Christ. This belief formed the basic foundation for anti-Semitism and was never contradicted, or even addressed directly, by any religious groups throughout this period. The Nazi assault on the Jews thus took place in a climate of opinion conditioned by centuries of anti-Semitism that existed throughout the Christian world. Indeed, various canonical laws from 306 to 1434 bear striking similarity to Nazi laws against the Jews.

The extent to which religion and cultural differences lay at the core of the Holocaust is clearly seen in the Nazi genocidal psychology, which requires the intentional identification of a particular group for destruction. For the Nazis, religion, and the cultural and ethnic differences that flowed from religious differences, became the foundation for discrimination and destruction. Nazis claimed—and appeared to believe in many cases—that Jews as non-Christians represented a threat to the majority German population. An individual German could not be Jewish, the Nazis argued, and still share the same desires for Germany non-Jewish Germans did. Allegiances and goals were believed to be ascriptive, flowing inevitably from birth into a particular group. This belief sets genocide apart from other conflicts in which allegiances can shift and opponents can be converted and means that victims are killed not for their individual acts or beliefs but rather because of their membership in a particular group.

The specific reaction to various aspects of the Holocaust among religious groups was mixed. In general the Roman Catholic church under Pope Pius XII was one of studied neutrality. The response of Protestant churches varied greatly by country, with protest found more often among churches in occupied countries in Western Europe, as part of patriotic resistance to the Nazis. National differences also affected church willingness to protest Nazi policies, with churchmen in Western Europe, especially Holland, Belgium, France, and Italy, taking much stronger stands in support of Jews than did Christians in Eastern Europe, where anti-Semitism had far deeper roots.

Pope Pius XI, who held office when the Nazis began their persecution of the Jews, limited his public concern to Catholic non-Aryans. His encyclical of March 1937 rejected the myth of race and blood as being contrary to Christian truth but did not mention anti-Semitism itself. During a reception for Catholic pilgrims from Belgium on September 7, 1938, Pius XI supposedly condemned Christian participation in anti-Semitic movements, noting that Christians were spiritual descendants of Abraham and therefore spiritually Semites, but this statement was not published in the accounts of the Italian papers.

After Pius XII succeeded Pius XI in the spring of 1939, official papal comments became even more circumscribed. Although the Vatican had been informed about the murder of Jews in concentration camps as of 1942, Pius XII's public comments were limited to carefully crafted expressions of sympathy for victims of injustice in general and to calls for more humane conduct of wartime hostilities. (In his Christmas message of 1942, for example, Pius XII expressed concern for those innocent people who had been killed merely because of nationality or descent.)

The Vatican policy of neutrality was more difficult to maintain once the Nazis began rounding up the eight thousand Jews of Rome late in 1943. German authorities had feared Pius XII might speak out and were relieved when he was silent as, on October 18, 1943, more than one thousand Roman Jews, mostly women and children, were transported to Auschwitz. Some seven thousand Roman Jews went into hiding, with four thousand of these given refuge in the many houses of religious orders in Rome, apparently with the pope's knowledge and approval. A few dozen were hidden in the Vatican itself, and the rest were concealed by ordinary Italians, who had never liked the Fascists' anti-Jewish policy.

Pius XII's failure to speak publicly against Nazi atrocities, especially after the arrests of the Italian Jews, drew criticism from many, who pointed out that the Vatican's silence endangered its moral prestige. Wladislaw Raczkiewica, president of the Polish government in exile, called on the pope to denounce Nazi violence unequivocally, arguing that this would strengthen the willingness of Poles to help Jews. The chief rabbi of Palestine, Isaac Herzog, and Bishop Preysing of Berlin were other prominent officials who urged the pope to speak out. They argued that the pope could have threatened the Germans with an interdict or with the excommunication of Hitler, Nazi propagandist Joseph Goebbels, and other leading Catholic Nazis. Furthermore, the critics continued, even though the pope could not have halted the machinery of destruction itself, just a public papal statement would have saved many lives, if only by encouraging Catholics living under Nazi rule to resist anti-Jewish policies. These critics pointed to the effective public protest led by the German episcopate against the euthanasia program. And finally, the critics argued, a public broadcast over the Vatican radio would have made clear to all what awaited the Jews in the East, thereby encouraging more Jews to attempt escape and more Christians to shelter them.

Would a papal decree of excommunication against Hitler have had any effect? What were the pope's private views on Nazi policies? Did his inaction reflect lack of concern or a more statesmanlike fear of pushing too far? The pope's defenders argue that a strong stand by the pope on the Jewish question would have led to mass desertion from the church, but no one knows the answers to these questions. Whatever his motive, the pope would not take such action, arguing that doing so would risk the allegiance of the German Catholics, whom he felt were largely indifferent to the fate of the Jews. Beyond this, the pope saw the Nazis as aiding the fight against communism, and he considered Bolshevism more dangerous than German National Socialism.

The failure of the pope to take part in public protest contrasts sharply with activities of several papal nuncios. Nuncios in Slovakia, Romania, Turkey, and Hungary saved many thousands of Jewish lives. (The nuncio in Istanbul, Monsignor Roncalli, who saved thousands of Jews, later became Pope John XXIII.) It seems doubtful, but by no means clear, that these individuals acted on orders from Rome. In general Rome's attitude seems to have followed the political winds, with Pius XII becoming more willing to speak out publicly only after it was evident that Germany was losing the war.

The church and state had long ties in Germany and the official Lutheran Church did little to protest Nazi policies, even excluding Christians of Jewish origins from membership in the church. This attitude reflected centuries of Protestant anti-Semitism as embodied by Luther's ugly depiction of the Jews as vermin who craved world domination.

The Confessing Church took a more courageous stand; it defended the rights of its members who had Jewish origins but did not publicly oppose persecution of such Jews outside the church. The Confessing Church did send a memorandum to Hitler on May 1936, arguing that even when anti-Semitism was forced on the Christian by National Socialist ideology, the Christian nonetheless has a divine commandment to love his neighbor. Many ministers of the Confessing Church refused to cooperate with anti-Jewish directives and were sent to concentration camps as a result.

Protestant churches in occupied countries spoke out more aggressively against Nazi policies. The Lutheran Churches in Denmark and Norway protested publicly when the Nazis began deportations from their countries, and both Protestant and Catholic Churches in Holland sent similar protests. Some of these protests were read from the pulpits, as was a letter from the Reverend Marc Boegner, president of the Protestant Federation, addressed to the French chief rabbi and to important French political leaders.

Orthodox Church leaders stood up for the Jews. In Greece the archbishop of Athens sent a strong protest against Jewish deportations to the prime minister of the German puppet regime, and the bishop of Salonika intervened to help Jews. But many of the Orthodox were persecuted, and many of these protests appear to have been based mainly on national, rather than religious, considerations.

Given the extent of Nazi control and the deeply embedded anti-Semitism in Eastern Europe, it is perhaps noteworthy how many church leaders did speak out publicly for Jews. The Lutheran Church in Slovakia protested in November 1939 and again in May 1942. Patriarch Nicodemus of Romania personally—and successfully—intervened with the Romanian government on behalf of Jews. In Bulgaria the metropolitan of Sofia and the metropolitan of Plovdiv intervened with King Boris, and the Holy Synod of the Bulgarian Orthodox Church repeatedly sent strong written protests to the government. This resulted in the rescue of many Bulgarian Jews. The Hungarian situation was more mixed, with the Lutheran bishops voting for the first and second anti-Jewish laws of 1938 and 1939; when the bishops did finally draft a statement against the deportations in 1944, they caved in to government pressure and never read the statement publicly.

Protestant church leaders in Britain, France, Sweden, Switzerland, and the United States had protested the first anti-Semitic measures in Germany, the promulgation of the Nuremberg Laws, and Kristallnacht in 1938. The Church of Sweden protested publicly against the deportation of Norwegian Jews. And protest by the Protestant churches of Switzerland helped change the Swiss government's policy of returning illegal Jewish refugees to their countries of origin. Church leaders in both Britain and the United States protested against their governments' policies of turning away Jewish refugees but had little effect on actual policy. The churches did collect aid money for refugees and sent parcels to Jews in concentration camps.

What Caused the Holocaust?

Did Hitler's rhetoric seduce an otherwise civilized people? How much of the Holocaust resulted from fear and forceful intimidation by a small group of marginal thugs? How widespread was support for the Nazis? Why did the Holocaust happen in Germany and not elsewhere?

As early as 1946 British historian A. J. P. Taylor traced the roots of Nazism back to Luther and suggested the German tendency toward authoritarianism and brutality was a fact established long before Hitler. The view that there is a special path of German history that led to Hitler was expanded on by many scholars and became known as the Sonderweg theory, which stressed the idiosyncrasy of German history that lay at the heart of the Nazis' power and that set Germany apart from France or Britain. Original proponents emphasized the structural factors of German history, such as the Thirty Years' War (1618–1648), which gave Germans a fear of

being encircled. Other historians rejected the Sonderweg theory, with Marxist scholars viewing the Holocaust as a result of Fascism, itself a part of a dying capitalism. German-born American political scientist Hannah Arendt argued that the Holocaust was an inherent part of totalitarianism, but others treated the Holocaust as part of Europe's tradition of anti-Semitism, which dated back to the Middle Ages and which was enhanced by the turn-of-the-century pseudoscience of eugenics and social Darwinism, movements that appeared in other countries, too.

Most historians conclude that Hitler's role was central but far from predetermined. One debate focuses on the extent to which the Holocaust was a calculated attempt to solve the population problem in newly conquered lands or a policy carried out in spite of its economic irrationality. The intentionalists make Hitler central, claiming that he had always intended to kill all the Jews and that the timing of the Final Solution merely reflected Hitler's waiting for the most appropriate moment. They stress Hitler's ideology, explaining the Jewish policy as determined primarily by Hitler himself, whose efforts were calculated or intended to realize the goals of an ideologically derived plan that Hitler had always advanced with fanatical consistency. Functionalists, however, emphasize the structure and institutions of the Third Reich, arguing that the Holocaust was unplanned, more the result of the chaotic decision making of an ideologically focused regime. These historians stress the extent to which the different bureaucracies within the Nazi system competed for Hitler's attention by developing solutions that became increasingly more extreme, arguing that the development of the Final Solution came only after much indecision and trying other policies (for example, expulsion).

Why Germany? Was there something unique in Germany that made the Holocaust more likely there, or was it merely chance? Most experts point to several factors that led to the Holocaust's occurring in Germany. Unstable political conditions after World War I threatened the social order. The First World War and the harsh terms of the Versailles treaty brought great geographic and psychological dislocations and gave the German people a grievance and a feeling that they had been wronged. A weak Weimar government attempted to establish a democratic government in a political culture that had little democratic roots. Unlike other countries of Western Europe, Germany had no liberal democratic tradition on which to build. The forces of moderation were essentially drowned out by extremists during the Weimar period. The economic chaos of the depression was made worse in Germany because of the harsh terms of the Versailles treaty, especially the reparations.

All of these factors prepared the Germans psychologically to look for a scapegoat, which Hitler supplied them through both the Jews and the democratically elected politicians who supposedly betrayed Germany at Versailles. Hitler exploited the ancient stereotype of Jews as cosmopolitan elites who feel no loyalty to the homeland. This view prevailed throughout much of Europe, and Nazi propaganda fanned this fear shamelessly. And the Holocaust was carried out secretly, under conditions that discouraged intervention by the outside world. The tight control of information by the totalitarian Nazi regime greatly facilitated the massacre of the Jews. And there was a widespread desire—among Germans and non-Germans alike—not to know too much. It was difficult to face facts too horrible to comprehend, yet alone believe, a phenomenon that affected both Jews and non-Jews as they slowly learned more details of the Holocaust.

It would be comforting to attribute the Holocaust to backward people, crippled by lack of education and socioeconomic poverty. But the links among biology, prejudice, and genocide existed among even the most respected academic, political, and social circles in the nineteenth and early twentieth centuries. (Indeed, the British delegation to the first international eugenics conference, called to improve the race through the science of eugenics, was led by Winston Churchill.) In Germany the bizarre Nazi double-think existed at all levels of society, and support for the Holocaust extended into the well-educated classes, including respected scholars such as Nobel Prize winner Konrad Lorenz and Paul de Lagarde, a prominent professor of Asian studies.

But how widespread was public support for the Holocaust? Was support greater in Germany than in other countries? How much cooperation resulted from fear and force? Most psychosociological explanations look to the identification of Jews and other minorities as outsiders, internal strife, territorial ambitions, propaganda, organized destruction, and the failure of social control. Analysts groping for explanations for the worst aspects of the Holocaust point to factors ranging from the geographic origin or social background of the perpetrators to party membership and ideology, virulent eliminationist anti-Semitism, and the suggestion that personality characteristics of certain individuals lie dormant until particular conditions awaken them. Such explanations build on the idea that most people are capable of great cruelty and

simply fall into the roles society assigns them. Ironically, these explanations return to the kind of authoritarian explanation originally offered in the postwar period, suggesting that it is the rare individual who resists such assignment and follows personal ethics instead. They echo Theodore W. Adorno's early arguments on authoritarianism and Stanley Milgram's work on obedience to authority, not obedience out of fear of immediate reprisals but rather obedience at a more general level of deference and arising out of long-term socialization.

General works on genocide all suggest a psychological connection to a victim affects perpetrators' willingness to participate in inhumane behavior toward members of the persecuted group. This connection was clearly evident during the Holocaust. In a process replicated in other genocides, the Nazis changed the way people looked at the Jews. Extensive ideological indoctrination, stressing the importance of keeping the Aryan blood pure, and a tightly controlled press that sanctified the German people and blood community were critical. The German people were depicted as facing a constant struggle for survival, ordained by nature, against the weaker peoples who would contaminate them with their impure blood.

Arendt explained the Holocaust's mass psychology as one of banality, in which killing becomes mechanized and impersonalized, thus removing the individual from moral responsibility. This concept of impersonal and bureaucraticized murder has been challenged in recent work focusing on the killing units in Eastern Europe. Arendt's explanation of impersonal, bureaucratic murder cannot apply to these men, who killed face to face. This does not discount the general value of her explanation, since the reserve order policemen found it vastly easier to put Jews on transports and send them to their death that way than to physically murder the Jews themselves, but it does suggest that segmentation and routinization, the depersonalizing aspects of bureaucratized killing, are not sufficient to explain much of the ugly brutality and sadism directed against the Jews.

Typically in genocides, both a scapegoat and a victim are needed to explain the disintegration of the old economic, political, and social order and to justify the beginning of the new. The stereotype of the wealthy, cosmopolitan Jews provided a handy scapegoat; the good German people filled the role of victims. Both elite and masses responded to threats to their economic situation, political power, and way of life. The political elite may have done so in a more cynical and calculating way, but the followers, the ones who actually performed the genocidal acts, were moved out of their own personal frustration and hostility as much as in response to orders.

The psychological effect of this deluge of racist and anti-Semitic propaganda, when combined with the reprisals for helping Jews—the Nazis killed the families of those found guilty of rescuing Jews—made it easier for people to conform to the norms of their immediate community. The years of anti-Semitism were accentuated by the polarizing effects of war. The dichotomy of racially superior Germans and racially inferior Jews, central to Nazi ideology, easily merged with the image of a beleaguered Germany surrounded by warring enemies.

Ironically, the Nazi genocide seems related to the German search for national identity and power. Because it is state-sanctioned, if not state-induced, genocide requires a legitimizing principle or ideology to justify the scale of human destruction. Anti-Semitism and the myth of Aryan superiority filled this need. The doctrine of biological determinism served as further facilitating justification for the Holocaust, and the massacres of the Jews became identified with a holy crusade to free the German body politic of diseased tissue. Thus the Holocaust was defended as a scientifically necessary response to prevent contamination by agents of racial pollution who were viewed as parasites and bacteria causing sickness, deterioration, and death in the host peoples. The mass murder of the Jews was justified through a twisted logic in which it becomes necessary to prevent the members of a biologically degenerate group from destroying a biologically superior group.

See also *Anti-Semitism; Fascism; Genocide; Germany; Prejudice; Zionism.*

Kristen Renwick Monroe

BIBLIOGRAPHY

Adorno, Theodor W., et al. *The Authoritarian Personality.* New York: Harper, 1950.
Arendt, Hannah. *The Origins of Totalitarianism.* New York: Harcourt Brace, 1958.
Bauman, Zygmunt. *Modernity and the Holocaust.* Ithaca, N.Y.: Cornell University Press, 1989.
Browning, Christopher. *Ordinary Men: Reserve Police Battalion 101 and the Final Solution in Poland.* New York: Aaron Asher, HarperCollins, 1992.
———. *The Path to Genocide: Essays on Launching the Final Solution.* New York: Cambridge University Press, 1993.
Burleigh, Michael, and Wolfgang Wippermann. *The Racial State: Germany 1933–1945.* New York: Cambridge University Press, 1991.
Goldhagen, D. J. *Hitler's Willing Executioners.* New York: Knopf, 1996.
Hilberg, Raul. *The Destruction of the European Jews.* Vol. 1–3. New York: Holmes and Meier, 1985.
Martin, Gilbert. *Atlas of the Holocaust.* New York: DaCapo Press, 1982.
Milgram, Stanley. *Obedience to Authority: An Experimental View.* New York: Harper and Row, 1974.
Monroe, Kristen R. "The Psychology of Genocide: A Review of the Literature." *Ethics and International Affairs* 9 (February 1995): 215–239.
Steiner, John M. "The SS Yesterday and Today: A Sociopsychological View." In *Survivors, Victims, and Perpetrators: Essays on the Nazi Holocaust,* edited by Joel E. Dimsdale. Washington, D.C.: Hemisphere Publications, 1980.
Taylor, A. J. P. *The Course of German History.* New York: Capricorn Books, 1946.

Holy See

See *Vatican*

Homosexuality

German scientists coined the term *homosexual* in the nineteenth century to describe both same-sex erotic behavior and persons attracted to others of the same sex. The use of the word as an adjective describing behavior and as a noun categorizing people creates confusion about its meaning. Throughout history labels have existed for same-sex erotic behavior, some loosely synonymous with the adjective, but *homosexual* as a noun is a recent invention. Homosexuality became politicized in the latter part of the twentieth century. Activists of the 1950s called their cause the homophile movement, which became known as gay liberation. Increasingly, the word *queer* is being reclaimed as a positive designation encompassing non-heterosexual orientations. The evolving labels indicate how quickly our understanding of homosexuality may change.

Scholars disagree on whether self-identified homosexuals lived in various times and cultures. "Essentialists" believe that homosexuals, keenly aware of their sexual orientation, existed in many societies including those described in the Bible. "Constructionists" hold that gay, lesbian, or queer self-perception is a modern creation, reasoning that in agrarian societies, where the biological family was the main economic unit, people lacked the leisure time to build a sexually based self-identity. Constructionists do not dispute that homosexuals can be found throughout history but argue that these individuals lived in urban settings such as the city-states of ancient Greece and Rome or of the Renaissance. City life allowed leisure time for erotic pursuits and community with others who shared the same sexuality. Industrialization undermined the family as an economic unit and brought leisure time to the masses, thus enabling the rise of modern queer communities.

The Biblical Record

Because *homosexual* is a recent addition to the vocabulary, biblical inferences about it are complicated. The word *homosexual* does not appear in the Bible, and no known writings in Hebrew or ancient Greek contain a synonym for it. The belief that homosexual behavior is immoral is rooted in several biblical passages. The most well known is probably the story of the destruction of Sodom in Genesis 19. Although *sodomy* eventually became vaguely synonymous with homosexuality, most biblical scholars now posit that the city was destroyed because its residents were inhospitable to visitors sent by God. Chapters 18 and 20 of Leviticus contain statements condemning male same-sex behavior. The theme of these chapters is the distinctiveness or purity of the Jews contrasted with the habits of other peoples. These passages describe acts considered unclean, such as eating pork, rather than inherently evil, like theft. Therefore, one interpretation of Leviticus is that it condemns same-sex behavior but only as a practice of non-Jews, or Gentiles. The distinction between these two types of wrongdoing may have been obscured as early as the third century B.C.E., when Leviticus was translated from Hebrew into Greek.

Three of Paul's New Testament writings are thought to deal with homosexuality: I Corinthians 6:9; I Timothy 1:10; and Romans I:26–7. These passages denounce lust and unrestrained sexual behavior, not specifically homosexuality. Paul's letters implored believers to stay on the path they had chosen and eschew worldly pleasures. In Christian antiquity the idealized life was sexual abstinence. This view contrasted with Jewish beliefs that embodied an obligation to multiply. Historian John Boswell amassed much empirical evidence to support the controversial proposition that throughout the first millennium the Christian Church often was accepting of same-sex friendship in which eroticism played a central role. By the thirteenth century, however, the church had grown hierarchical and became hostile to sexuality in general. For example, until that time priests had been allowed to marry.

Thereafter, Christianity served as the cornerstone of Western reproach toward homosexuality. Religious opposition to homosexuality undoubtedly influenced its late-nineteenth-century medical construction as illness. (Only in 1973 did psychiatry drop the classification of homosexuality as a mental illness.) Many religions are silent on the question of same-sex relations. Islam is mildly negative. Christianity, however, continues to be a formidable source of opposition for gays and lesbians.

Changing Attitudes

The status of gays and lesbians in secular and religious institutions is remarkably similar. After the end of World War II, in 1945, homosexual communities emerged in most large U.S. cities. They first organized around issues touching their personal lives, notably police entrapment and harassment. Local governments, which regulate public safety, were the objects of the first protests by homosexuals. Then, with safety more assured, lesbians and gays sought protection from discrimination. They also took these demands to local governments. More than one hundred municipalities in the United States ban discrimination based on sexual orientation, but by 1990 only one state, Wisconsin, had a similar law. In the 1990s several other states, including California and all of New England, quickly passed antidiscrimination laws.

The post–World War II gay and lesbian movements in most developed nations have been urban centered. The extent to which U.S. activists pursued their agenda in local government is unusual. It is probably due to the dispersion of power in the U.S. federal system. In many other democracies, especially in countries with unitary forms of government, gay and lesbian advocates took their cause more directly to central policy makers.

When lesbians and gays first enter any political arena, their claims to legitimacy tend to be debated in terms of morality. As they become familiar to policy makers, they establish themselves as an interest group to be accommodated in a pluralist society. The issues mature from morality to rights.

Acceptance of gays and lesbians in religious institutions followed a parallel track. Religious opinion on same-sex eroticism spreads across the board. To some, homosexuality is another gift from God. To others, it is a mortal sin. The gay and lesbian rights movement brought homosexuality to the attention of religious leaders. In many denominations this generated profound changes in teachings about sexuality. Quakers were the first major U.S. religious organization to reevaluate their position on homosexuality. They debated the morality question but before settling it moved on to accept homosexuals in their congregations. Unitarians also pioneered in welcoming gays and lesbians. Both composed ceremonies for the union of same-sex couples. Other liberal religious organizations including the United Church of Christ and Reformed Jews began to acknowledge a place for homosexuals in their denominations and ordain them into the clergy. They viewed the biblical injunctions against homosexuality as focusing on condemning pagan religions and unbridled lust. Gay Christians organized the Universal Fellowship of the Metropolitan Community Church in 1968. It takes as an article of faith that humans are sexual beings and has a primarily gay and lesbian membership with nearly three hundred congregations across the United States. These groups have all voiced their support for the civil rights of gays and lesbians when they have been a political issue.

Continuing Opposition

At the other end of the spectrum are fundamentalist Christians who maintain that homosexual behavior is sinful and immoral. Their congregations have few if any openly gay or lesbian members, but even within some of these denominations formal organizations have been established as support groups for gays and lesbians. These include the National Gay Pentecostal Alliance, Evangelicals Concerned, and Dignity (which was organized among Roman Catholics).

Although many religious organizations are hostile to lesbians and gay men, studies of urban politics have found three distinct groups to be the most active in mobilizing opposition in secular matters. First are white evangelicals, represented by denominations such as Assemblies of God and Seventh-day Adventists. The Southern Baptist Convention, the largest of the numerous Baptist denominations in the United States, steadfastly opposes the civil rights of lesbians and gays. Most but not all Baptist organizations share this position. Second, black evangelicals are concentrated in many Baptist denominations. It is the strength and political activism of the evangelicals that likely causes efforts to ensure the civil rights of lesbian and gay citizens to be met with much fiercer opposition in the United States than in other Western democracies. Third, Catholic Church leaders have maintained a firm position against legal protection for ho-

mosexuals whose behavior they regard as sinful. The position of the Catholic Church is more complex than that of the evangelicals. Although it labels homosexual behavior immoral, it views same-sex erotic orientation as a disorder but not wrong in and of itself. Gay male Catholics who vow to remain celibate may enter the priesthood.

In this regard the teachings of modern Catholicism are similar to those of most mainline white Protestant denominations, all of which have at least one gay or lesbian organization formed by members. The Episcopal Church, the Evangelical Lutheran Church in America, the United Methodist Church, and the Presbyterian Church (U.S.A.) all prohibit sexually active gays and lesbians from serving as clergy. Nevertheless, all of these denominations are on record as opposing discrimination against lesbians and gays in civil society and confirm that gays and lesbians are welcome in their congregations. The numerous black Methodist denominations are also seen as generally supportive of gay and lesbian rights.

At the middle of the twentieth century, no U.S. religious organization welcomed homosexual members, much less considered their ordination as clergy. Conditions changed rapidly. This process of change is far from over, especially among the mainline Protestant denominations. Within their ranks are members who accept the interpretations of the Bible that are supposed to refer to homosexuality as describing Jewish distinctiveness and condemning wanton sexual behavior in general. Others cling to the belief that the Bible intends a strict prohibition on same-sex erotic behavior. As time passes, predominant tenets will shift too. The fact that virtually all major religious organizations have gay and lesbian members who have formed their own associations guarantees that discussion of homosexuality will continue even among the most conservative of the fundamentalist Protestant denominations. The dialogue may work itself out along the lines of earlier religious conflicts over issues perceived in terms of morality, such as divorce.

See also *Feminism; Human rights; Sexuality.*

Steven H. Haeberle

BIBLIOGRAPHY

Boswell, John. *Christianity, Social Tolerance, and Homosexuality: Gay People in Western Europe from the Beginning of the Christian Era to the Fourteenth Century.* Chicago: University of Chicago Press, 1980.
Button, James W., Barbara A. Rienzo, and Kenneth D. Wald. *Private Lives, Public Conflicts: Battles over Gay Rights in American Communities.* Washington, D.C.: CQ Press, 1997.
Haeberle, Steven H. "The Role of Religious Organizations in the Gay

and Lesbian Rights Movement." In *The Role of Religious Organizations in Social Movements,* edited by Barbara M. Yarnold. New York: Praeger, 1991.

Haider-Markel, Donald P., and Kenneth J. Meier. "The Politics of Gay and Lesbian Rights: Expanding the Scope of the Conflict." *Journal of Politics* 58 (May 1996): 332–349.

Hartman, Keith. *Congregations in Conflict: The Battle over Homosexuality.* New Brunswick, N.J.: Rutgers University Press, 1996.

Human rights

The notion of human rights, that all human beings have inherent rights that cannot be abridged or denied, has evolved historically from a traditional religious emphasis on collective entitlements, earned by having performed certain obligations, to a modern recognition of individual rights, grounded in the humanity of the individual person. Today, as a result of parallel and, sometimes, intersecting political and religious endeavors, the concept of human rights includes civil, political, social, economic, developmental, and spiritual rights, that is, an aggregate of freedoms that reflect a broad contemporary commitment to social justice and the right of conscience.

Religious Notions of Rights

Since recorded history, the theological interpretation of an individual's rights were inextricably tied to one's collective and personal obligations to God, to one's neighbors, and to the community. Among the world's religions, responsibilities to the group overshadowed the importance of individual rights and freedoms. In Judaism, for example, collective obligations were emphasized and represented the defining element of being one of God's Chosen People. Faith in a divine mandate to maintain a separate and revealed path to holiness thus led to the development of a legalistic approach to rights within Judaism. Societal prohibitions and duties were codified and enumerated in the biblical books of Leviticus and Deuteronomy. These, as well as the divine precepts handed down in the Ten Commandments, became the basis of Hebraic law. Interpreted through the centuries by rabbis, these rules have reflected a legalistic, and implied, collective approach to rights, in which individual entitlements have emerged as an unintended result.

Islam, too, has stressed the religious obligation to submit to God's will. To ensure the maintenance of monotheism and a public order based on justice and mercy, Islam has based its concept of rights on divinely promulgated moral principles and collective legal regulations as codified in the Qur'an, the Islamic holy book, and the *shari'a,* the religious law. Serving as the supreme law and legal framework of the state, these holy regulations have emphasized the public responsibilities, contractual obligations, and social rules that would make it possible for an individual, as a member of the community, to surrender to "the One." These rules were regarded as so sacred that the state was expected to extend the law by *jihad,* or holy war, if necessary.

Hinduism as well has understood group rights in the context of obligations. Based on polytheism, mysticism, asceticism, and the teaching tradition of the ancient texts known as the Vedas, the Hindu belief system assumes order. The maintenance of the cosmic design in the social order, then, is determined by the distribution of responsibilities among the various groups in society. One's position in this life is determined by one's actions in a prior life. The notion of reincarnation, therefore, carries with it obligations that are identified in the Upanishads, the teachings of the high tradition. They spell out the *dharma,* the meaning of righteousness, religion, and law—in short, all that is morally binding on human beings according to their birth. Equally important is the belief that all beings are seeking unity with the spiritual force that sustains the universe. Such beliefs have been used historically to maintain the social order, and they have served as a justification for the caste system, which establishes a system of rights based on birth and responsibilities within one's social position.

Shintoism has traditionally based a notion of "rights" within a three-dimensional universe, one in which humans are part of the middle domain. It is believed that this position is maintained through the clan system and a series of obligations that individuals must carry out to serve their ancestors. Again, in this religious framework, ritual purifications, offerings, supplications, and feasts place the major stress on duty rather than on the rights of the individual.

Christianity, in contrast to other religions, emphasizes both a legalistic and a relational approach to rights. This is the result of its seminal theological belief: the notion that individuals are created in the image and likeness of God, that they possess a spiritual nature embodied in the immortal soul, and that they are destined to seek their own salvation. Christianity has, therefore, understood that humans have certain natural, collective obligations to God and others but that they also have certain personal obligations and rights because they possess a soul. This belief has generated the justification and pursuit of those rights necessary within the state or temporal world to achieve one's salvation. Thus secular law and institutions have always been understood to be subservient to one's conscience. They were to be served in the context of God's revealed, codified law of the Old Testament as well as the new teachings of Jesus. The New Testament does not set down specific laws that define the relationship between individuals, the community, and God. Instead, it calls on Christians to obey the spirit as well as the letter of the law and to respect the rights of others in their quest for salvation. The Beatitudes and the commandment to love one's neighbor as oneself contain the essence of this teaching.

Thus, for much of history, institutionalized religions emphasized and enforced the collective obligations of their adherents over personal freedoms. Consequently, the traditional relationship between religion and the state revolved around the necessity of religions to maintain their autonomy so that they could carry out their divine missions. In the past, and still in many parts of the world, religious groups have demanded a privileged status within various states to complete their spiritual tasks. Historically, some pursued a fusion of church and state or even established theocracies. Many have acted with fanaticism and zeal, a phenomenon that can be seen in the Crusades and the Inquisition, *jihads*, witch hunts, writing of concordats, establishment of caste systems, and ancestor, as well as emperor, worship.

Political Notions of Rights

By the seventeenth century political philosophers began to question traditional religious teachings and to argue for a new understanding of individual rights. They sought to merge natural law, which was based on reason and nature, universal applicability, and immutability with new notions of natural rights, ones that recognized that all persons are born equal and with rights, among them life, liberty, property, happiness, and the right to consent to being governed. The English had established the earliest political document institutionalizing rights with the writing of the Magna Carta in 1215, but this granted certain civil rights only to the nobility.

In 1625, however, Hugo Grotius, a Dutch legal scholar, wrote *De jure belli ac pacis* (concerning the law of war and peace), the first codified jurisprudence that regulated the relations between sovereign states. Based on the natural law,

Grotius' international legal system was founded on prudence and rationality, attributes that maintained an orderly state, protected property, and promoted general agreement about the conduct of society. In 1651 Thomas Hobbes, an English philosopher, translated Grotius' natural law theory into individualistic terms in the *Leviathan*. Consumed with the need for self-preservation, Hobbes reasoned that individuals had a "right" to protect themselves and to establish a corporate body, or state, headed by a sovereign whose duty it would be to maintain societal order and stability and, in turn, the individual's right to existence.

Thirty years later, John Locke, another Englishman, advanced the theory of inalienable rights in *The Second Treatise of Government*. Moving traditional political thinking about rights from collective obligations to individual entitlement based on humanity, Locke maintained that each individual, because he or she was human, had certain inherent claims against society. These included the rights to life, liberty, and property as well as the right to consent to government by means of a social contract. Locke's notions were embodied in the English Bill of Rights, in 1689, and translated politically into guarantees: the right to petition the governing authority, protection against illegal detainment or imprisonment *(habeas corpus)*, taxation based on representation, free elections, the appointment of jurors, free speech and debate in Parliament, and protection from excessive bail as well as from cruel and unusual punishment.

The notion of inalienable rights became the basis for the American democratic experiment and was reflected in the principles advanced by Thomas Jefferson in the Declaration of Independence (1776). Honed and refined, these ideas took the form of civil and political rights in the United States; were enumerated in the Bill of Rights of its Constitution, and for the first time in history, expressed the right to the free exercise of religion and the prohibition of a state religion within a founding political document.

Renewed and Redefined Notions of Rights

A global insistence on the definition and protection of religious freedom and other human rights emerged after World War II. The reasons for a renewed interest in rights, and religious freedom in particular, can be traced to a broad confluence of political events. First, the horror of the Holocaust under Adolf Hitler brought world attention to genocide based on religious, as well as ethnic, discrimination against Jews. Second, the spread of communism after the war was predicated on the enforcement of atheism in Eastern Europe, China, and various developing countries in Africa. Third, the rise of repression in autocratic states led to an exaggerated role of the state and the persecution of clerics, particularly in Latin America. Fourth, the establishment of the United Nations in 1945 provided a forum for the discussion and implementation of human rights in a global context.

The human rights movement initially was impelled forward as part of the mandate of the United Nations. In the 1950s the United Nations fostered international agreements to create a common standard of achievement among its member nations, particularly through the adoption of the Universal Declaration of Human Rights (1948) and a series of covenants on genocide, fundamental freedoms, civil and political rights, economic, social, and cultural rights, and racial discrimination. Together, these documents reaffirmed the inherent dignity and equality of all people, stressing their inalienable rights to freedom, justice, and peace. The pursuit of human rights by the United Nations reawakened a political interest and commitment to human rights, particularly as emergent nations began to cast off their colonial yokes and seek their own nationalistic identities and interpretations of freedom and social justice.

The most significant religious group to move in a parallel direction with the United Nations to advance human rights was the Roman Catholic Church. In 1962 it held a General Council, known as Vatican II, to renew its mission and reappraise its relationship to the world. As a result, Vatican II promulgated sixteen major decrees, among them the Declaration on Religious Freedom *(Dignitatis Humanae),* the Declaration on the Dogmatic Constitution of the Church *(Lumen Gentium),* the Decree on the Bishops' Pastoral Office in the Church *(Christus Dominus),* and the Decree on Ecumenism *(Unitatis Reintegratio).*

These documents changed the religious and political course of the Catholic Church. For example, as a result of the Declaration on Religious Freedom, the hierarchy accepted the notion that theology is evolutionary, that conscience is formed in different ways, and that each individual has the right to the freedom of his or her own beliefs. In the Declaration on the Constitution of the Church, the hierarchy rejected the privileged political status of Catholicism in the world and committed itself to support those organizations and governments that would work toward the advancement of human rights. In the Decree on the Bishops' Pastoral Office in the Church, the bishops supported the es-

tablishment of regional organizations to work on matters of social justice; and in the Decree on Ecumenism, the council accepted the notion of interfaith cooperation to further a combined religious-political agenda for human rights and social justice.

In 1967 Pope Paul VI gave impetus to this institutional commitment by establishing the Pontifical Commission for Justice and Peace within the Vatican infrastructure. Charged with the defense and advancement of international human rights, the work of the commission was further supplemented by the pope's landmark encyclical *Populorum Progressio* in the same year and his subsequent apostolic letter *Octagesima Adveniens* (1971). Reaching a worldwide audience, both papal writings called for the integral development of individuals and nations in society and the community of nations.

With the accession of Pope John Paul II to the papacy in 1978, the Vatican moved the international human rights agenda even further along the political continuum. Visiting almost every nation in the world, the pope spoke "truth to power," evangelizing against unjust leaders, structures, and practices; challenging autocracy; raising consciousness about the persecution of indigenous peoples; challenging racial and ethic discrimination; and questioning the policies of dictatorial regimes. Many believe that the pope played a major role in the downfall of communism in Eastern Europe and the rest of the world.

While the pope's journeys have served as a world forum to address political and religious leaders personally, John Paul has also used encyclicals to engender a greater concern for social justice. His most important documents include *Sollicitudo Rei Socialis* and *Centesimus Annus,* both of which call for a reappraisal of international economic rights, a recognition of the gulf between technologically developed and developing countries, and the implementation of an authentic democracy. In 1980 he also wrote to selected heads of state to remind them that all human beings have reason and free will and that, as a result, individuals are impelled to seek the truth, especially religious truth, and to be bound by it. Clearly, the Catholic notion of individual "rights" had changed radically within the twentieth century.

In conjunction with the Vatican's efforts to advance human rights and social justice, regional and international meetings of the Catholic hierarchy were also held in the 1960s and 1970s. Simultaneously, the bishops also made breakthroughs, declaring that social justice is a "constitutive dimension" of the work of the church, that evangelization and liberation are inextricably intertwined with its mission, and that the church should give a preferential option to the poor in its mission to transform society.

Thus, by the end of the 1970s, the Catholic Church began to shift away from many of its former expedient relationships, such as those in Latin America where the church had provided credibility to repressive regimes in return for its own autonomy and privileged status. In contrast, it established Christian-based communities, spurred on and often challenged by lay and clerical activists, many of whom espoused a movement known as liberation theology. As a result, the church began to work, at all levels to transform the social infrastructure in the Southern Hemisphere into one based on democracy and a communitarian economic system.

From the Vatican down to the grass roots, the Catholic Church had firmly established itself as a force for human rights and social justice in the Western Hemisphere. Creating a structural revolution, the church worked to bring an end to the human rights abuses embodied in the various coups of the 1970s known collectively as the "dirty war" in Argentina; to challenge the secret, repressive activities of the military forces known as the *mano blanco* in Guatemala; to bring about an end to the Sandinista dictatorship in Nicaragua, the tyranny of the right in El Salvador, and the successive, abusive military regimes in Brazil and Chile.

By the 1980s the Catholic Church had enlarged its areas of social justice concerns and become involved on behalf of human rights and social justice in other parts of the world. The Vatican's outreach to Eastern Europe and countries of the developing world to create a moral vanguard against atheistic communism has been credited with the ousting of Ferdinand Marcos's regime in the Philippines and Gen. Wojciech Jaruzelski's government in Poland. By the end of the decade the Catholic Church had become the chief religious activist for human rights in the world.

Other Christian denominations had also been playing various roles around the world. In Germany, the *Evangelishe Kirche,* that is, a combination of Lutheran and Reformed Churches, led major protests and played a critical part in the transition of the former German Democratic Republic to democracy. South Africa's Council of Churches had challenged the government's policy of apartheid, and with the Nobel Prize–winning Anglican archbishop Desmond Tutu, is credited with the demise of institutionalized racial discrimination. The Presbyterians took on the task of providing sanctuary for political exiles in the United States. The Quakers have served as conciliators in the Nigerian civil war and in the transition of colonial Rhodesia into independent Zimbabwe.

Christian religious institutions, because of their basic belief in the value of the human being as a creature created in the image and likeness of God, have played the most significant roles in the advancement of human rights in the world. Intersecting with various governments, they have worked to monitor repression, to educate governments and the media about human rights violations and social injustice, to lobby and bring pressure to bear on social and public institutions, and to use their resources to transform society.

Other religious groups, however, have not moved to this point in either their theology or their politics. The rise of global Islamic fundamentalism, for example, reflects a worldwide reactionary religious movement embodied in political activity that denies equal rights to women, freedom of conscience, and other basic civil, social, and economic rights. Often, institutionalized religions, such as those in Asia, view human rights in the context of Western, colonial, or "first world" values, arguing against human rights and the establishment of elements of social justice that might bring radical change to their thousand-year-old cultures. They oppose human rights as a Western notion, charging that its interpretations do not apply to them. Others, such as Judaism, interpret personal rights in terms of national survival, thus finding it possible, or even necessary, to deny basic human rights to other ethnic groups within their own sphere of influence.

Yet, in the future, religious groups will not be able to assume such positions; indeed, they will be needed to play even larger roles in creating a new world order in a post–cold war world. In the twentieth-first century, they will be called on to help recreate the world, mediate conflicts, oppose oppression, open lines of communication and reconcile enemies, reduce suspicions and act as peacemakers, provide sanctuary, resources, and support for the least free, help reorder values, serve as information gatherers, promote moral discussion and ensure disciplined listening, promote solidarity and witness, and continue objective truth telling. If progress is to occur, religion and politics will need to work together as the world becomes more complex and interdependent in order to advance human rights and social justice.

See also *Justice, Social; Liberation theology; Vatican Council, Second.*

Jo Renee Formicola

BIBLIOGRAPHY

Abbott, Walter M., ed. *The Documents of Vatican II.* New York: Herder and Herder, 1966.

Donnelly, Jack. *International Human Rights.* San Francisco: Westview Press, 1995.

Formicola, Jo Renee. *The Catholic Church and Human Rights.* New York: Garland, 1988.

Huntington, Samuel. *The Third Wave.* Norman: University of Oklahoma Press, 1995.

John Paul II. *Sollicitudo Rei Socialis* (On Social Concerns). Washington, D.C.: United States Catholic Conference, 1987.

———. *Centesimus Annus* (One Hundred Years). Washington, D.C.: United States Catholic Conference, 1991.

Johnston, Douglas, and Cynthia Sampson, eds. *Religion, The Missing Dimension in Statecraft.* New York: Oxford University Press, 1994.

Laquer, Walter, and Barry Rubin, eds. *The Human Rights Reader.* New York: Meridian Books, 1990.

Tutu, Desmond. *Hope and Suffering.* Grand Rapids, Mich.: Eerdmans, 1986.

Witte, John, Jr., and Johan D. Vander Vyver, eds. *Religious Human Rights in Global Perspective.* Netherlands: Martinus Nijhoff, 1996.

Humanitarianism

Humanitarianism refers to theologies of moral agency focusing on the transformation of spiritual life through active commitments to changing social, political, and economic conditions. The movement represents both a specific doctrinal strand in the evolution of American religion and a broad theme involving the commitment of many religious groups to charitable, philanthropic, and reformist endeavors.

As a specific body of doctrine, humanitarianism was a component of seventeenth-century liberal Anglican and Calvinist theology which, evolving out of Arianism and Arminianism, emphasized the role of good works as a dimension of spiritual development and, in particular, stressed the integration of spiritual and worldly concerns. The theological rationale for humanitarianism, like its institutional expressions, developed as part of a transatlantic culture of religious and social reform.

In the eighteenth century the Enlightenment gave rise to contradictory—but ultimately complementary—religious impulses. On the one hand, it nurtured a spirit of rationalism that de-emphasized the emotional and mystical aspects of religion, humanized Christ, and portrayed the natural order as an expression of divine reason. For some, it led to the deism of American statesmen Benjamin Franklin and Thomas Jefferson. On the other hand, the Enlightenment also influ-

enced the revivalists. Jonathan Edwards (1703–1758), an American who was the intellectual leader of the Great Awakening (the revivalist movement that swept through the American colonies from 1740 to 1750), drew on the philosophy of Englishman John Locke both to conceptualize the psychology of religious experience and to promote a voluntaristic approach to religious institutions. However profound their differences, both strands of Protestantism came to share a common belief in the importance of institutions in shaping religious experience and in the capacity of individuals to change the world through reforming institutions.

Unitarian Humanitarianism

Although late eighteenth-century religious rationalism took many forms in the United States, among its most influential spokesmen were the Congregationalist clergy of eastern Massachusetts. In the 1780s they began to question openly the divinity of Christ, to argue for the possibility of universal salvation, and to advocate strict congregational independence. By the 1820s a clearly defined body of Unitarian doctrine had emerged and, along with it, an infrastructure of charitable and cultural institutions (among them, the Boston Athenaeum and Massachusetts General Hospital) anchored by Harvard University and supported by new mercantile and industrial wealth.

Typifying Unitarianism and its humanitarian concerns was William Ellery Channing (1780–1842), a Boston clergyman who, in the first decades of the nineteenth century, emerged as an influential commentator on social and political issues. His 1816 sermon on war led to the organization of the Massachusetts Peace Society. In 1822, influenced by the efforts of the Reverend Thomas Chalmers among Edinburgh's poor, Channing organized the Beneficent Association whose goals reflected an ambitious agenda for social reform.

The association became a platform for launching an assortment of reform efforts, the most notable of which was a mission to Boston's growing population of impoverished citizens. One of Channing's colleagues, the Reverend Joseph Tuckerman (1778–1840), gave the effort national visibility through his essays on the condition of the poor. Although grounded in a social and theological conservatism that viewed poverty as a product of spiritual deficiency, the work of Tuckerman and his successors, in calling attention to the importance of social and economic factors, gave rise to a host of institutional efforts to relieve and prevent poverty.

By the 1830s, Channing, who also visited the West Indies, had become an outspoken opponent of slavery. Although he died before antislavery agitation reached its height, his forcefully expressed concerns led the way for a younger generation of Unitarian activists such as Theodore Parker (1810–1860) and Thomas Wentworth Higginson (1823–1911), who became leaders of the movement on the eve of the Civil War.

Despite their role as pioneers in the use of voluntary associations, many Unitarians, such as Channing's colleague Ralph Waldo Emerson (1803–1882), rejected all forms, traditions, and institutions that stood in the way of spiritual self-discovery. Emerson's protégé, Henry David Thoreau (1817–1862), took this anti-institutionalism to an extreme by withdrawing from society and building a hermitage at Walden Pond in Massachusetts. (This physical withdrawal was not in any sense an intellectual disengagement, however. It was during his sojourn in the woods that Thoreau wrote "Civil Disobedience"—an essay that later would have a profound impact on humanitarian reformers such as India's Mahatma Gandhi and America's Martin Luther King Jr.—as well as trenchant criticisms of capitalist society.) Others in the Unitarian tradition pursued reform by organizing alternative communities such as Brook Farm in Massachusetts, where from 1841 to 1847 a group of writers and scholars experimented in cooperative living.

Trinitarian Humanitarianism

For Trinitarians (believers in the doctrine of the Trinity, unlike Unitarians), resolving the tension between their Calvinist belief in the omnipotence of God and the efficacy of human action was no easy task. The influence of Enlightenment psychology led Jonathan Edwards to explore the theological implications of the link between the emotions and the intellect. His psychology of conversion clarified the role of human agency by suggesting that believers did not have to wait passively for God to act. A variety of activities—the reform of individual behavior, family worship, "social religion," and evangelical preaching—could "awaken" and prepare them for "evidences of God's saving mercy." Thus Edwards both revitalized Calvinism and legitimated assertive lay piety.

The efforts to shift the center of spiritual gravity from the clergy to the congregation and legitimate religious voluntarism would have a dramatic political impact. Because the church was a public institution, debate over the fundamen-

tals of spiritual sovereignty and ecclesiastical polity inevitably involved the newly "awakened" laity. As time went on, then, the debate moved from a theological to a political focus, encouraging a shift in the nature of public discourse. That shift, in turn, helped to fuel the struggle for American independence from Britain which began in 1763 and the emergence of political voluntarism based on abstract principles and harnessed to tactics of popular mobilization and electoral and legislative strategizing.

Through the 1780s political rather than social reform framed the Trinitarians' agenda, and it was politics rather than theology that ultimately moved them into the forefront of social movement activity. Led by Timothy Dwight (1752–1817)—preacher, poet, politician, and president of Yale University from 1795 to 1817—Trinitarians began to create entirely new kinds of voluntary organizations in the hope of stemming the rising tide of religious dissent and irreligion in Connecticut and in the nation at large.

Though maintaining the central tenets of Calvinism, Dwight and his protégés—Nathaniel W. Taylor (1786–1858), Lyman Beecher (1775–1863), and Leonard Bacon (1802–1881)—built Edwards's ideas about the importance of human agency in advancing God's purposes into a theological justification of the role of institutions in social and political reform.

Taylor, Yale's first professor of divinity, emphasized the role of man's free, moral, rational, creative nature in the process of salvation and, in doing so, highlighted the role of churches in nurturing those capacities. This theological innovation enabled Taylor and his followers to replace conceptions of humankind as passive instruments of divine will with a more activist vision.

Beecher, a brilliantly persuasive preacher, pioneered a pragmatic and profoundly influential activist response to the new religious marketplace. Dismayed by the political and economic disorder that characterized the presidency of Andrew Jackson (1829–1837), Beecher became convinced that the churches—not as direct political actors but as forces for the political empowerment of their members—could play a central role in the redemption of society. To this end he encouraged believers to create voluntary associations to act in every domain of public life. These associations became vehicles for a broad range of social reform efforts, including antislavery, Bible, debating, library, mechanics, and temperance societies; schools and colleges; and a national network of lyceums, which provided forums for Americans to discuss public issues and hear the ideas of leading philosophers, scientists, and literary figures.

Leonard Bacon, pastor of New Haven's Center Church and professor of divinity at Yale, focused his theological energies on organizational issues, writing pioneering essays on stewardship and the governance of associations. He engineered the emergence of Congregationalism as the nation's first denominational body, as well as played a leading role in antislavery agitations.

If Beecher and Bacon mapped the forward integration of Edwardsian logic from the church to the world, Horace Bushnell (1802–1876), another avatar of the "New Haven theology," integrated backward from church to family life by redefining religious conversion as a developmental process involving child-rearing, schooling, and family life. This step necessarily extended spiritual citizenship to women and children and, in doing so, constructed a theological rationale for intensive religious investment in innovative educational and youth-serving activities.

Conservative Dissent

In the year leading up to the Civil War the rising power of the Trinitarians' voluntary enterprises alarmed some Americans. Theological conservatives such as Francis Wayland (1796–1865), the leading political economist and Baptist intellectual of the period, challenged the Trinitarians' notion that individuals could delegate moral responsibility to associations. They feared that Trinitarians would lead people to believe that benevolence consisted only of giving money, thereby excusing the giver from "personal service and self-denial in the cause of charity." Despite Wayland's qualms, Baptist and Methodist institutions were springing up all over the country by the mid-nineteenth century. Unlike the Congregationalist enterprises, which sought to serve the general public and a broad variety of humanitarian purposes, the conservatives' institutions primarily served their core-religionists and tended to be local rather than national in focus.

The Congregationalists' increasing focus on humanitarian concerns led ultimately to a basis for accommodation with rival denominations and to alliances among theological liberals in support of national reform initiatives. The most important of these was the U.S. Sanitary Commission, a private group that provided public health services for the Union Army. A national enterprise modeled on the Trinitarians' antebellum "benevolent empire," the commission eventually

aroused the opposition of theological conservatives, who argued that its professionalized, bureaucratic institutionalization of relief efforts and emphasis on quantifiable efficiency and effectiveness drained these activities of the essential attributes of Christian charity, particularly the spiritual bond between giver and receiver. Such struggles, replayed with greater intensity after the Civil War, nearly wrecked the effort to "reconstruct" the defeated Confederacy.

Religion and Social Reform: 1870–1930

In the late 1860s religious humanitarians turned their attention to the problems of poverty, dependency, and public order resulting from industrialization and urban growth. In doing so, they took the lead in organizing state boards of charities which sought to centralize, rationalize, and professionalize relief for the poor. By the mid-1870s a more ambitious agenda had emerged. It sought not merely to ameliorate poverty but also to prevent it through "scientific" fact-gathering and cooperation between public and private agencies. These efforts laid the groundwork for a national organization—the National Conference of Charities and Corrections—which helped to launch a national charities reform movement.

By the late 1880s many Christians—liberal and conservative alike—were becoming uncomfortable with approaches to poverty and dependency whose calculated punitiveness was plainly at odds with scriptural conceptions of charity. The response, like so many aspects of American humanitarianism, drew on the transatlantic culture of charity, particularly initiatives such as London's pioneering settlement house, Toynbee Hall, which opened its doors in 1884. Within two years American clergy and religiously committed laity were experimenting with workingmen's clubs, neighborhood guilds, and settlement houses. By 1910 more than four hundred settlement houses were operating in the United States.

Jane Addams (1860–1935), the movement's most articulate and influential advocate, gave voice to a uniquely American combination of pragmatism and spirituality, calling for the extension of "democracy beyond its political expression," bringing "the accumulation of civilization to those portions of the race which have little," and promoting a revival of Christianity's "early humanitarian aspects." Viewed as particularly important was the capacity of the movement to address the spiritual impoverishment of the upper classes; the settlement house offered a setting in which one could combine spirituality with the practical tasks of political education and organizing.

The settlement houses played a key role in the development of the social sciences and social work. Pursuing social, educational, health, housing, and economic initiatives, settlement workers were transformed from well-intentioned amateurs into social service professionals. Close ties to universities ensured that the work of these community-based enterprises was both guided by and served to enrich broader, more systematic forms of knowledge building and to inform the creation of social policy. Ultimately, however, the conditions for successful settlement house work—political pragmatism, the cultivation of expertise, professionalism, and nonsectarianism—undermined the movement's religious commitment.

Though certainly the most influential manifestation of Social Gospel humanitarianism, the progressively oriented settlement houses were only one of many humanitarian responses to the urban crisis. Challenging the comfortable assumptions of middle-class parishioners, Kansas Congregationalist minister Charles M. Sheldon sought in his best-selling novel *In His Steps* (1896) to promote social activism by pointing out the ways in which social ills resulted from the failure of Christians to carry their professed beliefs into their public and private lives. Baptist Walter Rauschenbusch, who spent the 1890s preaching to a working-class congregation in New York's Hell's Kitchen, articulated an encompassing rationale for the affirmative role of religion in public life in his 1907 bestseller, *Christianity and the Social Crisis.* His delineation of the stake of the church in the social movement not merely as an instrument for shaping the consciences of individuals but also as a centrally important social institution in its own right did much to define the role of religion in American public life for the rest of the twentieth century.

Although at the beginning of the century interest in the social implications of the Gospel was limited to a small group of social reformers and theological students, as the Progressive Movement gained momentum all the leading Protestant, Catholic, and Jewish denominations embraced the Social Gospel. By the late 1920s the churches' social mission had begun to include international affairs, social justice, racial problems, the family, education—indeed, almost every phase in the development of the individual and society. Through the 1920s denominational bodies, congregations, and interdenominational organizations made significant commitments to various forms of service provision, particularly youth-serving activities. Churches also became active promoters of secular philanthropy, particularly the Community Chest and community foundation movement.

If religious and other private charitable initiatives were eclipsed by the depression of the 1930s and the Second World War, the challenges of the postwar years—particularly America's emergence as the preeminent leader of the free world—did much to rekindle activist humanitarian commitment. America's donning of the mantle of global leadership set in motion a process of national self-examination that focused not only on broad issues of public values but also on the nation's failure to live up to its own ideals, particularly racial equality and religious tolerance. Often working through denominations and ecumenical bodies such as the Federal Council of Churches and the National Council of Churches, clergy and laity led efforts to right long-standing wrongs. In the fifties and sixties, churches would stand in the forefront of the civil rights, antipoverty, and anti–Vietnam War movements—even though the clergy and denominational executives often positioned themselves considerably in advance (and to the left) of the attitudes of the faithful.

The Rise of Conservative Humanitarianism

In the postwar years liberal elements in Protestantism, Catholicism, and Judaism had forged a humanitarian consensus that sought relevance by de-emphasizing spirituality in favor of "civil religion" and liberal reformism that promoted internationalism, religious tolerance, women's rights, and racial and economic equality. But in doing so, liberals opened the way for a resurgence of religious conservatism embraced by Catholics disenchanted with the edicts of the Second Vatican Council; ultra-Orthodox Jews rooted in mystical traditions and Zionists for whom the national interests of the state of Israel eclipsed social democratic pluralist ideals; Southern Baptists, Methodists, Presbyterians, and a variety of fundamentalist and evangelical groups resisting the civil rights movement; and groups within every faith tradition for whom "relevance" and authenticity were spiritual rather than political issues.

The theological anti-institutionalism of conservative Christians was affirmed by the increasing secularism of American culture after World War I. But political events after World War II pushed conservative groups toward activism and into unlikely partnerships over issues such as government support for religious institutions, race, women's rights (including reproductive freedom), and patriotism. Legislation and court decisions on race, reproductive rights, and religious freedom alarmed believers disenchanted with the liberal tilt of the mainstream denominations and helped to transform conservative Christians into activist Christian conservatives.

By 1990 Christian conservatives had moved from being a reactive voting bloc that reluctantly chose between the lesser of evils to a tightly organized, proactive political force that not only played a major role in the national nominating process but also began to articulate its own political program. The key actor in this process was Marvin Olasky, a young Yale-educated journalist, whose book *The Tragedy of American Compassion* (1992) offered not only a harsh critique of the liberal welfare state but also a thorough reinterpretation of the history of American social welfare and its religious roots. Rejecting mainline religion's perfectionist humanitarianism (the evolution of which paralleled and justified the growth of the liberal state), Olasky offered a radical anti-institutionalist approach to charity which stressed the importance of one-to-one relationships between those who give and those who receive. Offering a common meeting ground for secular and religious conservatives, Olasky's religiously grounded rationale for a fundamental reordering of social welfare policy served as the intellectual road map for the "Republican revolution" that began to unfold in 1994 with the midterm congressional elections.

Olasky's significance went well beyond politics. In surprising ways he gave voice to ideas that had become increasingly important to countercultural elements in the liberal community, particularly those involved with disabilities rights and the provision of human services. When the states, forced by the federal courts to release the mentally disabled from institutional care, sought help in establishing community-based treatment mechanisms, the federations of Jewish, Catholic, and Protestant charities proclaimed themselves unequipped to deal with the problems of the profoundly disabled who made up the bulk of the population of state institutions. Much greater enthusiasm was found among less traditional groups: minority social services organizations spawned by President Lyndon B. Johnson's War on Poverty, new groups created by members of Catholic religious orders newly empowered by the Second Vatican Council, and radical social workers disenchanted with the traditional institutional methods of social provision. Between the mid-1970s and mid-1980s state governments placed the majority of institutionalized mentally disabled clients in nonprofit group homes, many of them operated by conservative religious individuals and groups.

Developing incrementally over two decades, deinstitutionalization and privatization became components of the devolutionary policies of the Republican revolutionaries for whom Olasky's work had supplied a coherent, if contested, rationale. While these ideas and practices present a compelling alternative to the agendas of liberal religion and the liberal state, the question remains as to whether such individualized and spiritualized approaches to helping others constitute *humanitarianism* as the term is commonly understood. Olasky's most recent work—summarized in *Renewing American Compassion* (1996)—suggests that, framed by government policy and phrased in reformist rhetoric, such efforts to transform society from the inside out and the bottom up might be, for all of their emphasis on individuals, no less socially and institutionally perfectionist and, as such, might appropriately be viewed as a new variant of humanitarianism.

See also *Civil society; Enlightenment; Philanthropy; Social gospel; Unitarians.*

Peter Dobkin Hall

BIBLIOGRAPHY

Davis, Allen F. *Spearheads for Reform: The Social Settlements and the Progressive Movement, 1890–1914.* New York: Oxford University Press, 1967.

Foster, Charles I. *An Errand of Mercy: The Evangelical United Front, 1790–1837.* Chapel Hill: University of North Carolina Press, 1960.

Frederickson, George M. *The Inner Civil War: Northern Intellectuals and the Crisis of the Union.* New York: Harper and Row, 1965.

Griffen, Clifford S. *Moral Stewardship in the United States, 1800–1865.* New Brunswick, N.J.: Rutgers University Press, 1960.

Hall, Peter Dobkin. *The Organization of American Culture, 1700–1900: Institutions, Elites, and the Origins of American Nationality.* New York: New York University Press, 1982.

Hodgson, Godfrey. *The World Turned Right Side Up: A History of the Conservative Ascendancy in America.* Boston: Houghton Mifflin, 1996.

Katz, Michael B. *In the Shadow of the Poorhouse: A Social History of Welfare in America.* New York: Basic Books, 1986.

Olasky, Marvin. *The Tragedy of American Compassion.* Washington, D.C.: Regnery, 1992.

Wright, Conrad Edick. *The Transformation of Charity in Postrevolutionary New England.* Boston: Northeastern University Press, 1992.

Wuthnow, Robert, ed. *Faith and Philanthropy in America.* San Francisco: Jossey-Bass, 1990.

Hungary

A partly Catholic, partly Protestant country in central Europe, Hungary between the ninth and early twentieth century included contemporary Slovakia, Croatia, and parts of Ukraine, Romania, Serbia, and Austria. Four historical features characterize the relation of religion and politics in Hungary.

Hungary is a buffer between the East and the West. For centuries wars were fought against non-Christians attacking from Asia. Acting as a "fortress of Christianity" and "defender of the Christian faith" created a strong feeling among Hungarians of having been chosen for a historical mission, and this became a key notion of the national identity.

The second feature is plurality. Post-Reformation religious wars in Western Europe (1618–1648) ended with the geographical separation of the denominations. The European past is mostly a history of monoreligion empires, such as Catholic France and the Habsburg Empire, Lutheran Sweden and Scandinavia, Orthodox Russia, and the Ottoman Empire. But this is not the case in Hungary: the Hungarian Principality of Transylvania declared very early the principle of religious freedom (1568). Hungary has ever since remained multidenominational.

The third feature of religion in Hungarian political development is a result of the divergence of Eastern and West-

ern Christianity. Orthodox Christianity, which prevailed to the east of Hungary, did not experience the Renaissance, the Reformation, the Age of Enlightenment, secularization, or the emergence of autonomous spheres of politics, science, and economy as separate from reli-

gion. Orthodox countries preserved state churches and homogeneous cultures that intrinsically resisted pluralization. Differing capacities of Eastern and Western Christianity for promoting social differentiation and pluralism helped maintain the division between the respective geopolitical regions. The invisible cultural border in the middle of Europe is also the eastern border of the ethnic Hungarian region. Samuel P. Huntington calls it the border of Western civilization *(The Clash of Civilizations.* New York: Simon and Schuster, 1996). Political identification with Western Europe shaped religious orientation in Hungary.

The fourth feature is the economic, cultural, and political role that the churches played in the past. Wars, foreign domination, and the geographic distance to areas of economic expansion hindered modernization in central Europe, which therefore remained a backward region as compared with its western neighbors. Neither the relatively weak state nor the underdeveloped middle classes, but rather the churches, provided institutions such as hospitals and social service and educational organizations. These institutions were public in the sense that they were open to all. The economic basis of these activities was the real property of the churches, which gained public and political influence both by their wealth and services as well as by the power of their bureaucracies and their institutional networks. In a cultural as in an institutional sense, religion and the churches were the backbone of the social organization and of the political system prior to World War II in Hungary.

Totalitarianism Opposing Religion

Communist leaders, imposed by the Soviet Union following World War II, tried to replace historical determination and the indigenous social system with their own ideology and order. They started a forced modernization of society in all its manifestations—economic, social, political, religious—under totalitarian conditions. Political parties, civil organizations, even informal clubs were forbidden. The network of religious associations was prohibited as were all other associations. The state attempted to destroy the public presence and influence of religion. Still, the churches remained the only public bodies not entirely controlled by the state. They became the refuge of the disinherited, the persecuted, all those people who were not willing to accept totalitarianism. In Western secularization, the position of the churches was relativized by the differentiation of the social organization, that is to say, by the growing autonomy of politics, economy, the sciences, and civil society from religion. Totalitarian practice hindered differentiation. The contraposition of church and state perpetuated the oppositional function of the churches in a bipolar political structure. The previously latent political quality of religion and church became explicit—both on a macrosocial, organizational level and on a microsocial and individual one.

The communist rulers openly declared war on the dominant churches. Their organizations were destroyed, their property was confiscated, and thousands of priests, ministers, and members of religious orders were imprisoned, deported, or exiled. Show trials against church dignitaries were used to weaken the social prestige of church leaders. Prelates and church activists were placed under surveillance by the police or by the agents of the Communist Party. The homes and offices of church officials were bugged. Communication and organized cooperation among religious figures were rendered impossible. The conventional social organizations of the churches, as established in their respective constitutions and traditions, became facades.

Still, the destruction or paralysis of these organizations did not eliminate the faithful or their religious needs. Lay persons soon began to fulfill the religious duties by themselves. The churches started to live from their social roots, in parishes and in newly emerging religious circles, often unknown even to the church authorities. Totalitarian legislation labeled underground church groups, similarly to all other autonomous groups, as "organizations against the state." Activists and members in such "illegal" groups and communities became a central target of persecution. Nonreligious social cells could be destroyed relatively quickly. In their continuous regeneration, religious communities relied on the religious socialization in the family. Religious mobilization from below proved its social and political dynamic. It broke the monopoly of communism by organizing society and shaping its culture. Religious communities maintained cultural and social positions that contradicted the official expectations and ideology as espoused in the schools and the media. These groups consciously cultivated their faith and culture by educating their members. Their mutual support created a visible social alternative to the totalitarian system, before and independently from the political opposition movements of the 1970s and 1980s. The mere existence of groups of committed religious persons inside a system of state atheism demonstrated the inefficiency of the latter and relativized the absolutness of totalitarianism. In the late 1970s, for example, religious youth festivals started. The more such groups became visible, the more they contributed to the public delegitimation of the communist system and to its rejection. By this role the underground churches exercised a political function even if they did not issue political declarations in explicit opposition to the communist system.

Social Discrimination of the Believers

The most basic and enduring dimension of the confrontation between religion and politics in Hungary during the communist era was the attempt by the regime to form a new society without ties to the old system and culture. This goal coincided with the antireligious Marxist ideology. The denial of religion became a formal requirement for party members. Believers were discriminated against in the admission to higher education. Practicing Christians could not become (or remain) teachers, journalists, police or army officers, or high-ranking administrators. They could not reach leading positions at all since the precondition for these was party membership. Discrimination in evaluations and promotions reduced incomes and living standards, and it led to less access to information and fewer chances of sociopolitical participation. Curriculum content and propaganda furthered the same antireligious re-education. Openly confessed belief resulted in formal social discrimination for four decades. Communism did not create a new society, but rather a nonreligious upper class.

Official policy was to appoint only those who were avowed secularists and atheists as heads and chief executives in the state-owned economy and the entire public domain. Believers who were in the lower ranks of the social hierarchy had to hide their religious convictions if they wanted to keep white-collar jobs. Communism succeeded in implanting the impression that nonreligiosity was a normal requirement for an academic career, for higher appointments, and for occupations in education and the media. After some decades of communism, these formal proscriptions received tacit acceptance by the ruling strata. Educated in a totalitarian and secularist spirit, many people were prejudiced against any faith and against believers who "obviously cannot be converted to modernity." By the 1970s the communist state felt it could liberalize its official stance as the social expectations of the ruling class guaranteed the continuation of discrimination against believers. The institutionalization of the second-rate status of religious citizens thus became independent from the state and its political structure. It also became a social fact that survived the political changes of 1989 and the disintegration of the communist system.

The strong association between nonreligion and upward mobility under communism divided the Hungarian population both culturally and structurally. This pattern dominates the present political field, religion being the most powerful factor in party preferences. This religious identification is strange considering the lack of religious references in most party programs. The party landscape of Hungary is split into three main camps. The two larger camps, each with about two-fifths of the votes, are the Socialists (the follow-up party of the former Communist Party) and the conservatives (uniting several smaller parties). The third group is the liberals, representing about one-fifth of the voters. The liberal camp is composed mainly of intellectuals and strata that gained their social position under communism but became opponents of Marxism and of the one-party system in the 1980s. Socialists represent a historically stabilized ideological

opposition to religion and church. Conservatives receive most religious votes (the Christian Democrat People's Party is regarded as Catholic, and the Smallholder Party has a Calvinist constituency). The leading liberal party, the Association of Free Democrats, is an ideologically interesting mixture. A dynamic evangelical sect, the Congregation of Faith, contributed decisively to the party's establishment. This religious community has been well represented in the leadership of the party since then. Actually, the Association of Free Democrats aims at a clear-cut technocracy and opposes any social presence of major denominations.

Finally, certain denominational differences carry a political implication as well. Communism established equality between smaller and stronger religions by demolishing the organizations and institutions of the larger ones. Capabilities that resulted from networks and multifunctional activities were cut. In contrast, the face-to-face religious practices of smaller sects could not be effectively impaired by the state. These sects would include the small religious communities that appeared in Hungary at the end of the nineteenth century or later and have a membership of at most a few thousand people, like the Seventh-day Adventists, the Pentecostal community, the Nazarene Congregation, Jehovah's Witnesses, and the Methodist Church—but not the Baptist Church. Notwithstanding the general persecution of religion, these sects welcomed the religious policy after World War II since it disrupted the hegemony of the historical churches and introduced a style in communal life where the size of membership became almost irrelevant. This arrangement came to an end with the collapse of communism.

Prior to the consolidation of communist rule (1948), Hungary's population was 70.5 percent Catholic, 21.9 percent Calvinist, 5.2 percent Lutheran, 1.5 percent Jewish, 0.8 percent other, and 0.1 percent claiming no affiliation. Cultural identification did not change much thereafter. Church membership declined, however, to less then half of the population in the late 1970s but has been increasing since. The denominational distribution in 1997 was 54.1 percent Catholic, 14.7 per cent Calvinist, 4.5 percent Lutheran, 0.4 percent Jewish, 1.0 percent other, 0.7 percent unknown, and 24.6 percent nonaffiliated.

The renewal of the big churches in postcommunist Hungary includes the restoration of their institutional framework. The law on restitution of church property excludes real estate and other church possessions but guarantees the restitution of former denominational institutions under the condition that they continue or restart their previous activities. More than eighty Catholic religious orders reemerged. Prior to the communist era, 60 percent of elementary schools and almost 50 percent of higher schools were Catholic, Protestant, or Jewish. Even the present proportion of 4 percent denominational schools is an important step to plurality. Similarly, churches gained broadcasting time in public media. Charity institutions of the churches grew to become an important supplement to public social services. These developments heighten the churches'—especially the big churches'—functionality inside and outside their own organization. On the other hand, small religions consider these political developments as a threat and try to prevent them. Their efforts to exclude religion from public life and to define it as a purely private matter is a position very close to that of the communists or to the ideology of technocracy of the liberal Association of Free Democrats. Interests and principles instantly create political identifications. Summing up,

it may be said that small churches and sects support socialist and liberal parties, while the membership of the traditional, big churches leans toward the conservative parties.

Miklós Tomka

BIBLIOGRAPHY

Andràs, Emeric, and Julius Morel. *Hungarian Catholicism: A Handbook.* Vienna: Hungarian Institute for Sociology of Religion. Toronto: St. Elizabeth of Hungary Parish, 1983.

Beeson, Trevor. *Discretion and Valour. Religious Conditions in Russia and Eastern Europe.* Rev. ed. London: Fount Paperbacks; Philadelphia: Fortress Press, 1982.

———. "Church and Religion in a Communist State, 1945–1990." *New Hungarian Quarterly* (spring 1991): 59–69.

———. "Religion in Eastern and Central Europe." *Social Compass* 1 (1995): 17–26.

Tomka, Miklós. "Stages of Religious Change in Hungary." In *World Catholicism in Transition,* ed. Thomas M. Gannon. New York: Macmillan; London: Collier, 1988.

I

Ibn Khaldun

Distinguished Muslim historian, sociologist, and philosopher. Abd al-Rahman Ibn Khaldun (1332–1406) wrote *Muqaddimah,* the acclaimed first volume of his world history, *Kitab al-Ibar. Muqaddimah* described his philosophy of human culture and civilization, and, in particular, the reasons for the rise and fall of civilizations.

Life and Work

Born in Tunis to an influential family who served a succession of Muslim dynasties in Spain and then in Tunis, Ibn Khaldun pursued an education that followed the traditional Islamic model. At age twenty he entered public life as secretary to the sultan of Fez, Morocco, but the political turmoil that ensued after the collapse of the Almohad dynasty in North Africa spurred his departure in 1362 for Spain, where he entered the service of the king of Granada.

It turned out to be a brief interlude, however, for shortly Ibn Khaldun left Spain for reasons of political prudence and returned to North Africa where he served as prime minister in the court of the sultan of Bourgie, Algeria. Over the next several years Ibn Khaldun's life was entangled in a complex web of political and diplomatic intrigue and military skirmish.

In 1375, weary of this turbulent life, he retired to a castle near Oran, Algeria, to begin work on *Muqaddimah.* In 1382, en route to Mecca, Ibn Khaldun arrived in Cairo, which appealed to his cosmopolitan political interests. Not surprisingly, when the Mameluke sultan offered him the post of chief justice, Ibn Khaldun needed little persuading, putting off his pilgrimage plans.

As chief justice, Ibn Khaldun swept away the political corruption that had clogged up the city and suffocated the courts, leading his enemies, in revenge, to instigate a commission of inquiry into his tenure. Although no charges leveled against him were upheld, the inquiry affected his usefulness for the patronage-minded rulers. When the sultan requested his resignation, Ibn Khaldun, having recently lost his family in a shipwreck between Tunis and Egypt, resumed his interrupted pilgrimage to Mecca in 1387 and then returned to Egypt, intending to lead a quiet life.

But it was not to be. In 1400 the sultan took him and a group of leading jurists and scholars to Damascus to undertake urgent negotiations with the Tartar conqueror Tamerlane. The Tartar reputedly was impressed enough with Ibn Khaldun's abilities to offer him a court position, which Ibn Khaldun declined. But he took advantage of the offer to collect valuable historical information on Mongol and Tartar history and to rehearse with Tamerlane some Maghrebi history. Later he was able to escape the Tartar sacking of Damascus, rescuing in the process many of the city's important nobles before returning to Egypt. There, as a reward for his services, he was reappointed chief justice. Shortly thereafter, in 1406, he died at age seventy-four.

On Politics and Religion

In *Muqaddimah* Ibn Khaldun was able to draw on his vast practical experience of public life and on his meticulous scholarly investigations to delineate the relationship between political affairs and religious life. He was ambivalent, however, about where to place religion in society, whether as an established value at the center or as a secondary source of influence. For him religion had two senses: it was either a social ornament or a ruling ideology, useful or necessary.

Ibn Khaldun looked at the secular roots of political institutions, convinced that the theocratic view of history was too simplistic and lacking in empirical realism. He argued that political society is founded on group cohesion, or solidarity (*asabiyah*). Aware of other traditions that have the prophet Muhammad abolishing kinship, Ibn Khaldun preempted criticism by turning to the same source to find the Prophet intending his followers to understand how kinship is useful only when blood ties lead kin to cooperate and help one another in the face of danger. Indeed, Ibn Khaldun defended kinship by asserting that the Prophet did not intend to neglect group solidarity, but merely to emphasize its relative merit as a worldly arrangement vis-à-vis the higher obedience centered in revelation. In all this, Ibn Khaldun was seeking to discern the sociological laws in collective historical institutions and hierarchies while distancing himself from dogma. According to him, rulership as such was not divine but was the outgrowth of social development because rulership evolved naturally from social solidarity. Indeed, the establishment and the effectiveness of laws, religions, and institutions depended on the underlying social solidarity.

In his writings, Ibn Khaldun gave preeminence to such solidarity, calling it identical with the spiritual community. No religious movement can succeed unless it is based on solidarity, he concluded. Solidarity is the backbone of religion as it is of the state. Such views also have implications for political legitimacy, Ibn Khaldun noted. He was at pains to point out that effective leadership is a matter not of revealed truth but of pragmatic competence. Good leaders are determined by the quality of their rule as seen by their subjects rather than by the purity of the ideals to which they subscribe. Governments, then, are the just deserts of the societies in which they are found: "If such rulership is good and beneficial, it will serve the interests of the subjects. If it is bad and unfair, it will be harmful to them and cause their destruction" (*Muqaddimah*). Ibn Khaldun, writing here as a scholar, was not primarily concerned with spelling out the practical institutional arrangements by which harm may be determined and remedied. Rather, his insights would be compatible with modern notions of democratic political liberalism, constitutional accountability, and participation.

Ibn Khaldun's views on the relation of politics and religion continued to be ambivalent. He seemed in one move to lean toward the centrality of politics only to revert to religion in the next. One must note, however, that Ibn Khaldun's theory of history received its most cogent and explicit development from the preponderance of fact and practice, thereby implying he downgraded religious speculation in favor of empirical observation. In his methodology, he was a pragmatist first and a moralist last. Thus it is still a valid question about where religion stands after the dust has settled.

See also *Islam*.

Lamin Sanneh

BIBLIOGRAPHY

Gibb, H. A. R. "The Islamic Background of Ibn Khaldun's Political Theory." In *Studies on the Civilization of Islam, Collected Essays,* edited by Stanford J. Shaw and William R. Polk. London: Routledge and Kegan Paul, 1962.

Issawi, Charles. *An Arab Philosophy of History.* London: John Murray, 1963.

Weber, Max. *The Sociology of Religion.* Translated by Ephraim Fischoff. Boston: Beacon Press, 1963.

Ibn Taimiyya

Islamic theologian and scholar. Ibn Taimiyya (1263–1328) is perhaps the most important medieval theologian inspiring the thought and actions of modern Muslim fundamentalists. Born in northeastern Syria, at age six he and his family moved to Damascus, fleeing advancing Mongol armies. The rest of his life was spent in the Mamluk realms of Syria and Egypt. His was a family of scholars, and he followed that tradition, later succeeding his father as professor of Hanbali law in Damascus. His temperament and the times, however, worked against a quiet life of scholarship. Ever inclined to act on his theological principles, Ibn Taimiyya was often jailed or placed under house arrest. His death came while he was imprisoned, yet again, in the Damascus citadel. Even so, at other times he was often favored by the Mamluk rulers and more than once was appointed to exhort the faithful to *jihad* (holy war).

Ibn Taimiyya was a strict scripturalist. He insisted on the supremacy of the Qur'an, the Islamic holy book, and the *hadith,* narratives of the sayings and actions of the prophet Muhammad, in their literal sense to such an extent that his theological rivals accused him of anthropomorphism. His stern literalist stance pitted him against the more esoteric interpretations advanced by the Sufi mystics.

He was uncompromising in his approach to both non-Muslims and to non-Sunni Muslims. He was first jailed for agitating for summary punishment against a Christian alleged to have insulted the Prophet. His strictures on the Shiʿi Alawis were as harsh. They were, he maintained, more infidel than Jews or Christians, and fighting them was obedience to God. Such fulminations from past centuries resonate with today's Muslim Brethren in Syria in their resistance to the rule of Hafiz al-Asad's Alawi-dominated government. Ibn Taimiyya even questioned the more accommodationist positions of the mainstream Sunni theologians.

To Ibn Taimiyya, religion and the state were necessarily linked. Without the coercive power of the state, religion would be in danger, but without the comprehensive body of Islamic law (the shariʿa) government would become tyranny. His most famous work, *Al-Siyasa al-Shariʿiyyah,* might be loosely translated as Shariʿah Politics or, perhaps more accurately, Shariʿah Public Policy.

In modern times the ideas of Muhammad ibn Abd al-Wahhab (1703–1787) build in large measure on the doctrines of Ibn Taimiyya, whose influence continues in present-day Saudi Arabia. Certain of Ibn Taimiyya's ideas were picked up by the more meliorist and modernist stance of Egyptian theologian Muhammad Abduh (1849–1905) and his followers, especially the emphasis on individual intellectual effort to establish religious doctrine *(ijtihad)* and resistance to the consensus of the conservative orthodox *ulama* (legal scholars).

The fit between the ideas of Ibn Taimiyya and those of today's radical Islamists is striking. The strict scripturalism and the belief that any pious Muslim can understand and thus live according to Qurʾanic injunctions has roots in Ibn Taimiyya's thought. The same holds for the idea that government is necessary to protect and preserve religion but that the only legitimate government is one that carries out the *shariʿa.* Ibn Taimiyya offers a dramatic example of confronting the establishment *ulama,* just as do modern Islamists.

Moreover, the sharpest break with conventional Muslim political thought advanced by contemporary Islamists is the notion that Muslim rulers who do not adhere to the strict canons of the faith have become like infidels. They have lapsed into *jahilivya.* A *jihad* is, accordingly, proper against such rulers. This idea too comes from Ibn Taimiyya. The

Mongols, by Ibn Taimiyya's time, had become at least nominal Muslims, but they remained no less a threat to Mamluk rule. The Mamluks sought a legal opinion *(fatwa)* justifying a *jihad* against the Mongols, and Ibn Taimiyya obliged them. To him, their laws remained tainted with infidel sources. The Mongols, he maintained, should be combated until they complied with the laws of God.

A prolific scholar, Ibn Taimiyya wrote on many subjects. His many legal opinions, for example, fill thirty-five volumes. Virtually all of his works are available in modern Arabic editions, and many have been translated into other languages.

See also *Islam; Jihad; Sufism.*

L. Carl Brown

BIBLIOGRAPHY

Ibn Taimiyya. *Ibn Taimiyya on Public and Private Law, or Public Policy in Islamic Jurisprudence* (Translation of *Al-Siyasa al-Shariʿiyyah*). Translated by Omar A. Farrukh. Beirut: Khayat's, 1966.

Laoust, Henri. *Essai sur le doctrines sociales et politiques d'Ibn Taymiyya.* Cairo: Imprimerie de l'Institut Français d'Archéologie Orientale, 1939.

Sivan, Emmanuel. *Radical Islam: Medieval Theology and Modern Politics.* New Haven: Yale University Press, 1985.

India

The largest and most populous of the countries of South Asia, India, with 900 million people, is home to many faiths, including world religions such as Hinduism (80 percent of the population), Islam (12 percent), Christianity (3 percent), and Sikhism (2.5 percent). The notion of separate sacred and secular domains of society, which is characteristic of the Christian (Roman Catholic) tradition and of social science literature, must be abandoned when speaking of India in the context of religion and politics. One must instead focus on the relationship of two kinds of power, namely, the sacred and the secular, which may be derived from dynastic succession or popular election.

In the early Indian religious traditions (Buddhism, Hinduism, and Jainism) the sacred and the secular are united; the secular is only relatively autonomous and ultimately encompassed by the sacred. The ethical principle that guides the wielders of secular power is an aspect of the overarching

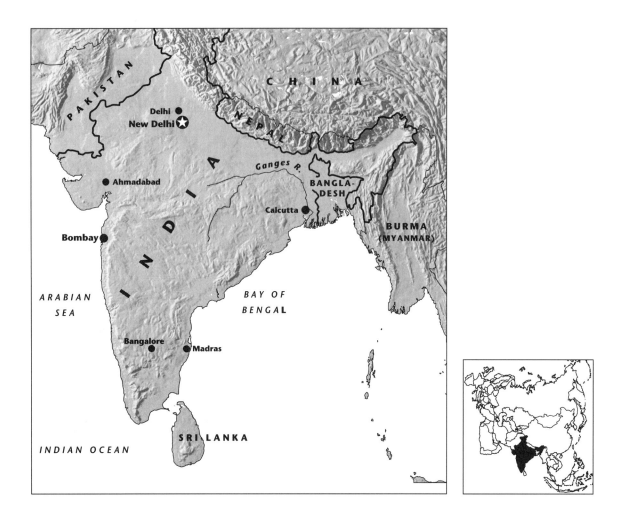

moral principle, *dharma,* that sustains not only human society but the entire cosmos. The Sikhs hail the sword as a symbol of the divinity, but it is placed at a lower level than the holy scripture in the temples. In Islam the nondifferentiation of the secular from the sacred is even more emphatically stated through a repudiation of the secular. The Islamic holy book, the Qur'an, teaches that whatever is apparently secular is sacred in its very roots.

The Nineteenth Century

Classical formulations of the relationship of religion and politics provide the background, but they do not anticipate the complexities of contemporary times. An appropriate time from which to begin discussion is the early nineteenth century, when the ruling British Parliament allowed evangelical efforts by Christian missionaries to begin in India. Religious differences in India ultimately became politicized in the late nineteenth century, following the introduction of administrative reforms, which included local self-government.

Many Indian intellectuals were deeply impressed by the moral tone of the New Testament. While some of them embraced Christianity, others endeavored to combine what they considered the best elements of Hinduism and Christianity. One notable effort was by Rammohun Roy in Bengal, who founded the Brahmo Samaj (Society of God) in 1828 as a new religious way of life. Such experiments produced a reaction within a generation, and Hindu revivalism emerged as a significant phenomenon. Bengal witnessed the emergence of an ecstatic form of Hinduism, centered on the worship of a supreme mother-goddess. Politically sensitive intellectuals translated this religious idea into the mystical concept of the country as divinity, Bharat Mata (Mother India). Her liberation from foreign rule thus emerged as a sacred duty, and nationalism was conceived of almost as a religion.

A rejuvenated Hinduism was different from the religious combinations in that its appeal was to an exclusive though reinterpreted past. The need for reinterpretation was seen to arise from the corruption of the original (Vedic) religion over the millennia, accompanied by social degeneration. Many late-nineteenth-century religious reform movements, among the Hindus and among the Sikhs, had a dual agenda: the restoration of the purity of religious belief and ritual and the eradication of undesirable social practices, including gender- and caste-based discrimination.

The most successful movement among the Hindus was led by Dayananda Sarasvati, who founded the Arya Samaj (Society of Noble People) in Bombay in 1875. It was in the north, however, that the Arya Samaj achieved its most notable success, and the reason for this was political. Not only had Punjab been under Muslim domination longer than other parts of India, during which time it had acquired a considerable Muslim population through immigration and conversion, but it had also become the site of Christian missionary activity after the British annexed the province in the middle of the nineteenth century. A crusade against Islam and Christianity was, according to Dayananda, essential to Hindu rejuvenation and, indeed, to patriotism.

Regional socioreligious reform movements were active in the last quarter of the nineteenth century among Hindus, Sikhs, and Muslims alike. These movements had implicit political significance if not explicit political agendas too. A national political party, the Indian National Congress, was established in 1885 by a group of urban elites drawn mostly from the Hindu community but including Muslims and Parsis. (The Parsis were a religious community descended from refugees who fled from Persia in the eighth century to escape persecution by Muslim conquerors.) The representative character of the Congress Party, however, was questioned from the very beginning because many Muslim leaders refused to join it. Among those who refused to join was one of the most prominent among them, Sayyid Ahmad Khan. Muslim separatism from then on was a significant issue in Indian politics; it eventually led to the partition of the subcontinent in 1947 and the creation of Pakistan.

A thousand years of Muslim rule in India ended in 1857 with the banishment of the Mogul emperor Bahadur Shah from Delhi, the imperial capital, for his support of a soldiers' mutiny directed against British rule. The period of decline had lasted a century and a half, and when the so-called Sepoy Mutiny erupted that year, the old shah could be its head

only symbolically. The Muslim community came under suspicion, or so its leaders believed, of being disloyal to the British rulers. They reacted in two ways, both of which focused on the need for education. Sayyid Ahmad Khan chose the path of modern education and of cooperation with the British, from whom he sought protection against future domination by a resurgent Hindu community. A college he established at Aligarh in northern India sought to reconcile the basic teachings of a reinterpreted Islam with the ideals of the European Enlightenment. Other, more conservative leaders, opted for religious and cultural revival through traditional forms of education and abstention from politics. They established a seminary at Deoband, not far from Aligarh, and trained teachers who would communicate the Islamic principles of everyday life to the common people through the widely understood Urdu language. Thousands of decrees and opinions issued from Deoband, providing guidance in the Muslim way of life.

The Early Twentieth Century

Gradually the Deoband *ulama* (religious scholars) cultivated political interests and sided with the avowedly secular politics of the Congress Party. They believed that the Muslim way of life would be safe if politics were religiously neutral. The Aligarh modernists too joined the struggle for self-rule but on the basis of the notion that Sayyid Ahmad Khan had first put forward and which had been taken up by the Muslim League, founded in 1906—that of two nations, the Hindus and the Muslims. One of the first demands of the Muslim League was for the institution of separate electorates in local elections, which were the only elections then held in India. The Muslims would choose their own representatives (obviously Muslim), and the other religious communities would choose theirs. The ideology of religious nationalism—or communalism as it is generally called in India—according to which nationhood is defined primarily in religiously exclusive terms and only secondarily in territorial ones was thus introduced into Indian politics.

The basic premise of communalism was (and is) that the political interests of a religious community are unaffected by ethnic, linguistic, class, or any other such divisions within the community. These interests were defined antagonistically in relation to other, similarly conceived religious communities. Religiously neutral, or secular, nationalists regarded themselves as engaged in a struggle to end colonial domination and considered religious, linguistic, ethnic, and similar differences to be of secondary importance, if not illusory. Secular nationalism and communalism thus emerged as rival ideologies of political emancipation. Communalists, who were religious nationalists in their own eyes, maintained that the fight against colonialism could not be joined unless the postindependence political and economic rights of the religious minorities were first guaranteed.

In the rhetoric of religious nationalism, religion appears as a collective ideology of renewal rather than a personal faith of redemption. When faith becomes political, as it does under communalism, ultimate values recede from view, and religion becomes a sign of political differentiation. It has been said that the religious element that enters into the composition of communalism is but the shadow, if not a mockery, of religion.

Secular nationalism generated its own problems because it was defined in terms of religious pluralism rather than as a religious rationalism or agnosticism. The Indian National Congress recognized the plurality of interest groups but considered subnationalisms as the enemy of secular nationalism unless they were included in it. It was thus at the very beginning of his political career in India that Mohandas K. Gandhi espoused the cause of the distant Ottoman sultan, who claimed the status of caliph, the religious leader of Muslims worldwide. Gandhi had returned in triumph to India in 1915 from South Africa (where he had organized and led people of Indian origin in their struggle for political rights). He made the sultan's cause part of the noncooperation movement against British rule in India because Indian Muslims were deeply concerned about the fate of the ancient Muslim institution of the caliphate. His mixing of religion and politics produced serious misgivings among secularists. At first Gandhi seemed to have worked a miracle as Muslim participation in the national movement led by the Congress Party reached unprecedented heights. But the abolition of the caliphate in 1924 by secular Turkish nationalists brought the Hindu-Muslim collaboration to a quick end, never to be revived again.

In fact, Hindu-Muslim hostility resurfaced with greater intensity. The political stance of accommodation by the Congress Party leadership, particularly Gandhi, toward the Muslims was deeply resented by right-wing Hindu leaders. The currently popular communal ideology of Hindutva, or "Hindu identity," was put forward in 1924. An apparently nonpolitical cultural organization, the Rashtriya Swayamsevak Sangh (RSS), was established soon afterward. Hindutva promulgated a restrictive definition of Indian identity by merging the notions of "native land" and "holy land." This meant in effect that those Indians whose most holy lands were outside India—namely, Christians, Jews, and Muslims—were likely to be treated as foreigners, and even denied citizenship rights, unless they assimilated with the Hindu cultural mainstream. A concept of "national culture" was put forward, denying the religious pluralism that had been built up by the Congress Party as the distinctive character of Indian nationalism, rooted in Indian history and arguably in the Hindu religious tradition itself.

Although secularism as religious pluralism was the dominant mode of thinking within the Congress Party, some leaders like Jawaharlal Nehru, its president for many years and the first prime minister of India after the nation achieved independence in 1947, were secularists in the Western sense of the term. Nehru had been greatly influenced by British socialist thinkers and by Marxist-Leninist thought. From the 1920s to the eve of the partition of India, he consistently denied that nationalism had any legitimate connection within religious identities. He considered national independence a prerequisite to the reordering of socioeconomic relations in society. Once such a reconstruction was achieved, Nehru was convinced, religious differences would retreat into the privacy of individual lives. As things turned out, Nehru's faith in the primacy of an economic approach to nationalism remained a minority, though strongly articulated, viewpoint within the nationalist movement. It had a severe setback when the country was partitioned in 1947.

Partition and Afterward

The partition of India on the basis of religio-cultural difference was far from a satisfactory solution to the clash of multiple identities and subnationalisms. The Muslim majority areas of the northeast and northwest were constituted into Muslim homelands (East and West Pakistan) and, potentially, an Islamic state. In the months after partition several million Muslims left their homes in India to migrate to Pakistan, just as Hindus and Sikhs moved in the other direction. About 40 percent of the 100 million Muslims of the subcontinent remained in India, scattered over most parts of the country.

These Muslims decided out of conviction or necessity to dissociate themselves from the ideology of religious nationalism. For the limited purpose of the preferred form of government, they supported the concept of a secular state, but many among them did not embrace the broader ideology of secularism as a worldview. In the years following partition, the ideology of communalism seemed to wane in India. Religion as the principal marker of collective identities was replaced by others, notably language and ethnicity.

The respite turned out to be temporary, however. As the shock of partition abated, the economic improvements that the secularists had hoped would end communal hostility reinforced it in some places, while in others the older forms of communal politics and competition for scarce resources resurfaced. A major irritant has been the unresolved dispute between India and Pakistan over whether the State of Jammu and Kashmir should belong with India, of which it is a constituent state by virtue of constitutional status, or with Pakistan in view of its Muslim majority. Since the mid-1980s a Muslim fundamentalist movement, which is pro-Pakistan, and a cultural-nationalist, or ethnic, movement, which is pro-independence (secessionist), have emerged in the state. There has been much bloodshed and destruction. A craving for normalcy enabled the Indian government to hold elections in Jammu and Kashmir in 1996, and a popular government was installed after more than six years of federal rule backed by the police and the military.

A similar situation had earlier developed in Punjab. Economic grievances of the Sikhs, combined with political skulduggery by right-wing Hindus and the federal and state governments, strengthened an earlier demand for independence put forward by a sector of the Sikh political leadership. In June 1984, in a misconceived and ill-executed military action code-named "Bluestar," the government attempted to arrest a charismatic fundamentalist preacher. He, along with heavily armed followers, had taken sanctuary inside a major Sikh temple in Amritsar called the Akal Takht. There were heavy casualties on both sides. The preacher was killed, and the temple was severely damaged. Fundamentalism and terrorism swept Punjab, and Prime Minister Indira Gandhi was assassinated by her Sikh bodyguards. It took ten years to bring militancy under control and restore normal politics in the state.

In the years since Operation Bluestar there has been an eruption of Hindu fundamentalism in protest against the alleged partiality of the government toward Muslims, who are, among other things, exempt from government-sponsored reform of personal (family) laws. Hindu communal organizations called for the demolition of a Muslim mosque at Ayodhya in northern India. It was asserted that the mosque had been erected in the mid-sixteenth century as a symbol of Muslim power at the site of a sacred Hindu temple that had been destroyed. The Hindu fundamentalists proposed building a new, grand temple on the site. While the federal government dithered, the state government, run by the right-wing Hindu Bharatiya Janata Party (Indian People's Party, or BJP), provided covert assistance to the agitators, and the mosque was razed in a matter of hours in December 1992. Widespread killings of Muslims followed, bringing about violent Muslim retaliation, mainly in Bombay.

The mixing of religion and politics in India reached a bloody high in 1992–1993, generating serious misgivings about the future of secularism. The Ayodhya incident seems to have been a watershed. The BJP suffered reverses in state elections in 1993, but since then it has also had some successes. Although it failed to capture the federal government, it emerged from the 1996 parliamentary elections as the single largest party. The BJP is generally considered a cover for the RSS, which hopes ultimately to capture power. The dangers of culturally intolerant and politically reactionary Hindu domination, denying religious minorities their constitutional rights, are real. The secular parties cutting across ideological boundaries have come together to form a multiparty coalition union government and have isolated the BJP. More significantly, perhaps, India has witnessed intercommunal peace and harmony since 1993. It is too early to say that India is destined to become a Hindu state or to assert that the country has reaffirmed its commitment to secularism and religious pluralism. Religious divisions may well remain and continue to shape Indian politics.

See also *Gandhi, Mohandas Karamchand; Hinduism; Islam; Pakistan.*

T. N. Madan

BIBLIOGRAPHY

Brass, Paul. *The Politics of India since Independence.* Cambridge: Cambridge University Press, 1990.

Gopal, Servepalli, ed. *Anatomy of a Confrontation: The Babri Masjid-Ram Janambhumi Issue.* New York: Viking Penguin, 1991.

Jones, Kenneth. *Socio-religious Reform Movements in British India.* Cambridge: Cambridge University Press, 1989.

Madan, Triloki Nath. *Modern Myths, Locked Minds: Secularism and Fundamentalism in India.* New York: Oxford University Press, 1997.

Nehru, Jawaharlal. *The Discovery of India.* New York: New American Library, 1946.

Pandey, Gyanendra. *The Construction of Communalism in Colonial North India.* New York: Oxford University Press, 1990.

Van der Veer, Peter. *Religious Nationalism: Hindus and Muslims in India.* Berkeley: University of California Press, 1994.

Individualism

Individualism is a political, religious, and social theory and set of associated institutions that hold that each individual is intrinsically dignified and that his or her autonomous moral choices and religious conceptions must be given the highest level of respect and protection. Max Weber, one of the most celebrated sociologists of the twentieth century, wrote in 1905 that individualism includes the most heterogeneous things imaginable and that individuality and individualism can mean very different things. Although some disagreement remains over the meaning of individualism (and individuality), during the twentieth century scholars have moved close to a consensus on its meaning at least in political and religious matters.

At the center of this consensus is the belief that every human being is a unique, rights-bearing moral entity and the final arbiter of the moral and religious truths that he or she believes and chooses to put into practice. Furthermore, this classical understanding requires that the political system be designed to protect, at the minimum, each fully rational adult from inappropriate public or private intrusion into his or her protected sphere of choice, especially in matters of religious or moral conscience. And in a more aggressive romantic stance, individualism finds that the well-being of each decision-making individual is the most important social goal, with the meaning of well-being defined by each individual. Individualism thus is most importantly about knowing religious and moral truth—how and what one knows—and envisioning how the political system should protect and help realize individual religious-like choices in a wide range of social spheres.

This understanding of the individual and his or her appropriate relationship to larger authoritative structures was not one traditionally embraced by Western and non-Western cultures. Indeed, for nearly all of recorded human history, most elites viewed critical elements of what has come to be individualism as a form of selfishness and godlessness that was to be strictly controlled. In fact, not until the nineteenth century was the concept *individualism* defined in a recognizable form. But the roots of individualism go back far deeper into the history of the West, and the history of individualism provides a panoramic backdrop against which to view the development, after 1650, of modern thought and practices. This history is essentially one of the changing understanding in Western thought of internal standards of moral and reli-

gious truth. These matters of conscience that had once been viewed as reflecting an innate, divine, and wholly objective moral compass, so aptly described in the moral teachings of Roman Catholic natural law, over time would become increasingly subjectivized and, depending on the preferred school of thought—Enlightenment or Romantic, drawn from either the individual's own reason or sentiments.

The Elements of Individualism

Because individualism is central to almost every major modern intellectual, social, and artistic movement, either in support of or in opposition to it, it is essential to understand the meaning of individualism. Indeed, individualism does much to divide the modern world of ideas: capitalism, liberalism, existentialism, progressive religiosity, rationalism, libertarianism, and anarchism lie on the liberating side of this divide; conservatism, corporatism, collectivism, communitarianism, and fascism lie on the other, restrictive side; and Romanticism and Marxism draw from both. Steven Lukes, an Oxford University political philosopher, has already done much of the work of cataloguing the major elements and varieties of individualism.

Individualism first insists that each human being enjoy an inherent dignity and intrinsic value (traditionally uniquely awarded to humans and denied to other species, though this discrimination has become philosophically more difficult to maintain). Individualism also holds that each individual must be morally autonomous, that is, rationally self-directing and free from coercive and intrusive governmental direction in all moral and religious matters of conscience. And an idea readily associated with liberalism is that each individual is protected within a cocoon of privacy in which his or her most essential life concerns are to be explored and pursued free from intrusive public intervention. Put in popular vernacular, these last two traits treat as a hallowed right individuals' doing their own thing as long as the similar capacity of others is respected. Romanticism captures another attribute of individualism—its emphasis on self-development or the fullest development of each person's inherent abilities.

Less a particular goal and more a way of understanding or viewing individuals, abstract individualism holds that hypothetical individuals logically and historically precede an existing social or political setting whose principal goal is to meet the needs of such abstract individuals. Although associated with such celebrated thinkers as Thomas Hobbes and John Locke, the seventeenth-century English philosophers of the social contract, and John Rawls, the late-twentieth-century American political philosopher, this attribute of individualism, from the moment it was articulated in the mid-seventeenth century, has been subject to attack from both political philosophers and incipient sociologists. They have found this thesis incapable of describing or explaining how such individuals are created without being first constituted by the cultures that they are claimed to have preceded.

Individualism manifests itself in all of the most significant cultural realms of modern life. Certain of these manifestations of individualism have developed their own particular forms and have been given separate names. Among them is political individualism, which describes a form of politics in which the state reflects the aggregate interests and protects the inherent rights of abstract individuals who, through their representatives, give individual consent to the actions of the state. Following Locke, the goals of the state are to be limited to those that are consistent with the autonomous choices of individuals. This precludes the state from pursuing moral ends that are corporate or that interfere with individual self-direction or matters of conscience.

In the economic domain, individualism insists on the freedom of individuals who are self-possessing of themselves and their labor to pursue their own interest in buying and selling, owning private property, and employing human labor in a largely unregulated market. The hoped-for goal of this form of individualism, again envisioned by Locke at the end of the seventeenth century, is that wealth will be created for individuals and the society at large, thus fully satisfying, through a generally self-regulating system, the needs of both.

Religious individualism and moral (or ethical) individualism hold in common the equal sanctity of the individual and the inviolate nature of his or her moral conscience. In each instance, an individual's spiritual well-being depends on his or her religious and moral commitments being unmediated and uncoerced by government. From this perspective, the only life that is worth living is one in which individuals closely examine their religious and moral choices and follow a pathway their consciences demarcate. Accordingly, in both cases, the individual carries a heavy burden, to some impossibly so, and thus must be afforded considerable latitude in choosing a life of religious or moral excellence. The difference between these two forms of individualism turns on the religious form being necessarily tied to objective standards that have been handed down by a superior divinity, but ethical individualism need not be committed to objective or universal standards. Indeed, many forms of contemporary moral philosophy that are kinds of ethical individualism, such as existentialism and emotivism, deny in a godless world the existence of anything resembling objective moral principles. Yet, Immanuel Kant, a late-eighteenth-century German philosopher and one of the most famous proponents of what we are describing as ethical individualism, held that true moral standards must be objective and universal.

Two forms of individualism are primarily philosophical and are readily associated with Hobbes: one wishes to explain the individualist nature of knowledge—epistemological individualism—and the other argues that all social phenomena are, in truth, reducible to the action of individuals following their particular ends—methodological individualism. Each tends to dismiss as fictitious transindividual phenomena, be it deductive metaphysics or social organicism. Although distinct from other individualisms, these two are necessitated by the collective insistence of other forms on the primacy and inviolability of individual experience and self-consciousness. These two philosophical perspectives, though, like the idea of the abstract individual, are subject to the critiques of sociologists, anthropologists, and political theorists who question the accuracy of placing individuals before or outside a defining formative culture.

The Individual and the Group

Individualism stands in stark contrast to two terms, collectivism (or holism) and communalism, ideas that themselves are often confused with one another. Collectivism, most recently defended in the early twentieth century in an absolute form by the German National Socialists (Nazis) and Italian Fascists, describes a political, religious, and social vision that views individuals as incomplete elements of the whole who flourish only through their complete subordination to the corporate good (of the religious group, people, nation, state, or class). It is not dissimilar to the relationship between a finger and a hand in which it makes little sense to talk of the finger (the individual) having an end or good distinct from that of the hand (the collective whole).

Different from both collectivism and individualism is communalism. Like individualism, communalism holds that the highest moral end is the flourishing of individuals as individuals, but it contends that this prosperity is not best achieved through an individual's autonomous self-direction. Instead, communalism, the most traditional of moral teachings, which stretches back to the ancient Greek philosopher

Aristotle and beyond, argues that individual human advancement is best pursued through familial and communal shaping of individual character through the active inculcation of corporately agreed-on virtues. Furthermore, this sanctioned formation of individual character by intermediate social and political institutions is guided by an underlying moral, invariably religious, definition of a well-lived human life. This template further necessitates a common morality, universal and absolute, that is commonly judged intrusive by the standards of individualism. In effect, the quest after personal virtue is not a fully private nor even wholly familial project but rather a corporate and public one that involves political, social, and usually theological elements. But for communalism, as with individualism and unlike collectivism, the highest end remains individual human development.

Individualism is essentially distinct from but related to individuality. Each concept anchors contrasting visions of liberalism, a political philosophy with at least two significant varieties: in its classical form, liberalism leaves to individuals the direction and implementation of their personal development and overlaps with individualism, but in its more intrusive and ambitious romantic form, it shows great affinity with individuality. Individuality, though, is not wholly distinct from individualism; it describes an all-powerful commitment to two features of individualism, self-development and absolute autonomy. And compared with most proponents of individualism, the mostly Romantic (and often French or German) defenders of individuality settle for nothing less than a total dedication to the fullest development of the absolutely free individual.

Not surprisingly, such an inherently elitist concept shows little regard for human equality or even the social consequences of heroic action. The truly individuated individual, as celebrated by the nineteenth-century American essayists Henry David Thoreau and Ralph Waldo Emerson, must be capable of standing against the tide of common perceptions and norms and resolutely going his or her own way. Yet the influential nineteenth-century English philosopher John Stuart Mill defended individuality not only on individualist grounds but more emphatically by arguing that geniuses were essential to a society's overall welfare. For Mill, social utility and human progress depended on the thought of extraordinary men and women cutting through old nostrums and their freedom to experiment in novel lifestyles.

Individualism is both a set of normative principles and a set of institutional arrangements. But what frequently goes unquestioned is whether the institutions, in truth, facilitate the end goal defended by individualism as a normative principle, the creation of fully flourishing individuals. A world in which each individual is systematically, in the memorable language of Kant, treated as a moral end rather than only as a means may prove to be an impediment to the development of those noble characteristics associated with true individuality. The creation of egalitarian political and social institutions, with no appropriate social obstacles to oppose, may create only soft and intellectually flabby individuals without any heroic features. For the defenders of individuality, the true individual's development requires struggle and the overcoming of powerful opposition, quite often that of the majority. This is a dilemma without an immediate resolution, but it should raise concern over the desirability of individualist political and social institutions among those most attracted to the elevated goals of individuality.

Although romantic liberals may be little concerned with the absence of widespread individual well-being, they should be troubled by the possibility that individualist political and social institutions might have debilitating effects on even those few with heroic potential. As the disturbing nineteenth-century German philosopher Friedrich Nietzsche predicted, what we have come to call individualism would produce what he described as a race of last men, pathetic creatures incapable of nobility of spirit or soul, rather than great men and women.

There is also an important distinction between individualism and familism. Because it is small compared with other social groupings, the autonomous nuclear family is likely to be conflated or confused with the self-directing individual. Yet the subordination in traditional families of the individual to the values and demands of the larger family is surely distinct from individualism. Thus contemporary critics often contend that the traditional or patriarchal family is an institution guilty of suppressing the individual freedoms of subordinate women and children. They rightly hold that it is only when liberated from the bonds of the family that all individuals can achieve full independence from each other, though not equally so from the state and its professional providers of economic and therapeutic assistance. And as contemporary feminists have shown, a doctrine that subordinates a woman's individual interests to a corporate body, even a small one such as the family, cannot be equated with the tenets or goals of authentic individualism. The strength of familism has consistently limited the power of individualism, be it religious or political, because of the often encountered solidarity of the nuclear family unit. But the combined effects of feminist-inspired individualism and the continuing emphasis on the quest for personal happiness and its achievement through romantic love, independent of all familial and communal ties and duties, seems finally to be taking its toll on the strength of the family. Possibly, then, with the continual decline in the nuclear family's social and economic importance, this distinction will become less salient in the near future.

Origins of Individualism in the West

The roots of individualism as a moral goal and a set of institutional arrangements are neither short nor simple. Pericles, leader of Athens during the Peloponnesian War in the fifth century B.C., had boasted that each Athenian citizen was the rightful lord and owner of his own person. Clearly, then, critical elements of individualism have been long present in Western thought. Still more striking is the degree to which the Hellenistic philosophies of Cynicism and Stoicism and, in particular, the legalism, voluntarism, atomism, and hedonism of Epicureanism anticipated the inward turn of modern individualism. But these philosophies mostly defended an elevated spiritual realm and elite, and the everyday features, and universal and egalitarian nature of modern individualism, would have to find another way to reach maturity in modern European thought.

It would be in Christianity, and its insistence on the sanctity of the individual conscience and a morality or right intentions versus pleasing results, that many of the central elements of individualism would find a vehicle to carry them to maturity in the early years of the nineteenth century. This is not to say that other religions, for example Judaism, lack individualist tendencies. For in the teachings of the major prophets, Judaism gives voice to powerful individuals who opposed the people, their leaders, and their national norms. Ezekiel is especially insistent in defending individual accountability in which each will suffer for his or her own sins, clearly an early instance of the triumph of the individual conscience over that of the collective. Yet, Judaism remained a religion primarily of law in which God's covenant was with a nation. It was not, as is Christianity, wholly concerned with belief and the inner conscience of each individual, where God's covenant (of grace) is made with individuals rather than a people. Indeed, Christianity defined itself through its emphasis on the authentic belief and moral and religious intentions of its adherents and through its rejection of the legalism of Judaism and its consequentialist emphasis on an individual's correct actions.

It is with Christianity and its claim of God's generous and loving sacrifice of his son for fallen humanity that the idea of each individual's infinite worth, regardless of earned merit, develops. This belief demanded that morality focus on the individual's right intention rather than the consequences of his or her actions, with a resulting emphasis on the sanctity of individual religious conscience. Yet the distance between these authentic seedlings in early Christianity and their powerful presence in Roman law and what would become individualism is so great that it would take some eighteen centuries for them to blossom fully. What had to be overcome before modern individualism could emerge from historic Christianity was its adherents' widespread belief in objective moral truths, their dependence on Christ, their acceptance of corporate intrusiveness, and their depressing (to modern sensibilities) confidence in human original sin. And overcoming these not so negligible obstacles did much to form the substance of Western intellectual history.

Across the eighteen centuries after Christianity's introduction, major elements of what would become individualism continued to mature. But as to when individualism stepped forth fully grown on the world stage, there remains considerable disagreement. Some scholars have argued that its coming of age was during the Italian Renaissance; some hold that it was with the rise of Protestantism; others find its take-off point to be the rapid growth of market forces in seventeenth-century England; and yet others associate it with nineteenth-century Romanticism. But there is little controversy over the first use of the term itself.

It was in the 1820s that Joseph de Maistre, a French opponent of a then-emerging understanding of the individual as an absolute moral center, coined the term *individualism*. For him and other French reactionaries, individualism designated the disintegration of society and the spread of egoism, which they believed had resulted from the dissemination during the French Revolution of the doctrine of individual natural rights. But in the early nineteenth century, the reactionaries were not alone in their condemnation of individualism. Other European thinkers and political figures, even progressive ones, initially rejected the new word as a form of abuse or employed it themselves as a pejorative label.

The first use of *individualism* in English would also be derogatory and would come with the translation of the work of one of two French authors who had used the new term to criticize early-nineteenth-century American social and political life. Henry Reeve, in his 1840 translation of French man-of-letters Alexis de Tocqueville's second volume of *Democracy in America,* noted that he adopted the term from the French because he knew of no English equivalent to the expression. And if not then, individualism had made its first appearance in English a year earlier in 1839 in the translation of Michel Chevalier's *Society, Manners, and Politics in the United States.* But from then on, individualism gradually began to assume a more favorable sense in the English-speaking world, particularly in Great Britain. Indeed, by the second half of the nineteenth century, all manner of English liberals had begun to use the term *individualism* and to embrace it; individualism had in truth become almost synonymous for them with liberalism.

But in embracing individualism, Anglo-American elites had stood on its head the traditional Western condemnation of idiosyncratic inwardness. Individualism's defense of the particularity of each individual occurred as an older Christian consensus, and the more recent rationalist one, specifying the objective nature of religious and moral claims, began to unravel among progressive thinkers. With a loss of confidence in the objective character of the moral cosmos, the uniqueness and particularity of the self became less objectionable; indeed, with modernity, it came to be the source and standard of moral value.

Modernity and the Rise of Individualism

How did a culture like the West, recognized as Christendom for more than a millennium, become one in which God was replaced by each individual as the source and arbiter of religious and moral truth? No simple explanation, ideal or material, can be given. But any attempt at answering this question, ironically, must begin with the nature of Christianity itself and its development over two millennia. What is immediately obvious is that the history of individualism and Christianity are inextricably linked. Quite possibly, the central elements of no other concept have moved as promiscuously from the spiritual and religious realm of thought and practice to that of the temporal and secular, and back again, as have those of individualism.

Over a two-thousand-year history, central elements of what would become individualism in the nineteenth century, most importantly the scientifically impossible-to-defend claims of equal human dignity and the structural benefi-

cence of the cosmos, moved from one sphere to the other, only later to be reflected back, though slightly altered, into intellectual and lived provinces from which it had migrated. Such transference from one sphere to another has not occurred in a fully clear or defensible manner and, not surprisingly, the foundation that made individualist tenets reasonable in one realm has proved incapable of following them and providing the needed foundation in another. Thus Western elites now find themselves confronting a range of widely shared moral and social values, such as equal moral dignity, the inviolability of individual conscience, and universal benevolence for which they are unable to provide adequate philosophical or theological foundations. Significantly, this reiterative process continues even today as liberal political theory, originally derived from important elements in Catholic and Protestant theology and moral thought, reshapes progressive Christianity in its own image.

Still left unidentified, though, are those features of Christianity that facilitated the West's transformation from a God-centered to an individual-centered elite culture. In partial explanation, Tocqueville noted in the early nineteenth century that society had distanced itself more from Christian theology than from Christian philosophy. This shift is of critical importance, because when one turns away from Christian theology to philosophy, one must also turn away from the Protestantism of the sixteenth-century Reformers. Those scholars who hold Protestantism singularly responsible for this transformation, while overlooking Catholicism's rich and long development of a Christian humanism, have missed Catholicism's essential contribution to the development of individual-centered religiosity and politics. In particular, the dignity and almost sacred character awarded to the natural reason of each individual and his or her unredeemed conscience in Catholic thought, especially as envisioned by St. Thomas Aquinas, the thirteenth-century Italian theologian, and his influential followers, is entirely absent in the thought of the Protestant Reformers. Instead, the Reformers argued that the natural reason found in fallen humanity elevated human beings only marginally above that of God's other creatures. John Calvin, one of the most influential of sixteenth-century Christian Reformers, goes so far as to argue that man's likeness to God had been eviscerated with the Fall.

In a manner too often overlooked, only Catholicism, then, is able to teach that the unredeemed individual, through his or her intact reason, is largely able to know the moral good and to will it. The Reformers, in their insistence on the total depravity of humans, reject the idea that the individual can significantly know the full nature of the good and, more emphatically, they are confident that fallen humanity is incapable of willing it. This failure leaves the individual, then, in a dependent relationship—on Christ, on the Holy Spirit, on family, and on a gathered community of witnessing fellow-Christians. Accordingly, the elevated status, self-direction, and self-centeredness that modern thought accords the free individual is difficult to envision flowing out of the Reformers' theology of total human depravity and irresistible grace.

The hugely disruptive effects of the Reformation on the unity of Western Christendom and society and the thought of the Protestant Reformers were also enormously important in fostering modern individualism, but it was less direct than many have suggested and resulted from consequences wholly unintended by the Reformers. Protestantism's valuation of the unregenerate individual was anything but elevated; indeed, quite the opposite. But beyond the rupture created by the Reformation itself, what the Reformers critically added to the mix of ideas that culminated in modern individualism was their distrust of human-made hierarchies, particularly ecclesiastic; their sacralization of everyday life, of work, and of family; and their tactical but shared insistence with Catholicism on the importance of religious conscience and right intention rather than primarily right action. These aspects produced a theology in which the divisions present in Catholicism between Christian professionals, that is those who profess (priests, nuns, and monastics), and lay persons and between heavenly demands and those of daily life were rejected, and the recalcitrant individual and his or her tender conscience were given a new more elevated standing.

The Protestant Reformers and their followers, though, demanded that all true Christians, regardless of occupation or wayward conscience, give themselves entirely to Christ and that ordinary life be dedicated to glorifying God. There was no other acceptable choice; there was only one right answer. When removed from their theological moorings and transformed by emerging secularism, however, such teachings supported a form of egalitarianism in which each man (later, woman) enjoyed equal human dignity, each moral conscience—right or wrong as viewed against external objective standards—was inviolate, and each person became the final arbiter of all values. But again, the Protestantism of the Reformers is able to help create these effects only when the centrality to the human experience of original sin, God, and

a community of brothers and sisters joined in Christ that closely follows and disciplines the actions of its member sinners is denied.

In the modern and contemporary periods, the West moved with seventeenth-century French philosopher René Descartes, rationalism, and Kant, from the individual's inner self or conscience as the conduit to objective truth to the Romantic sense of the individual's feelings as the sole standard of truth, and finally, in the contemporary period, to an existentialist and postmodern denial of truth as such and the apotheosis of the radically free and self-determining individual. Yet this modern reverence for the individual is founded on a mixture of an empirically indefensible secular faith in human goodness and irremediable epistemic uncertainty about the particular ends humans are to pursue—a seemingly unstable combination of ideas.

And by the early years of the twentieth century, in spite of having triumphed across a wide array of cultural areas, individualism did come under withering attack from various sides in an inflamed cultural war. Indeed, for much of the early twentieth century it must have seemed certain that individualism had passed its zenith and would be eclipsed by one or more prevalent collectivist political alternatives, of both the right and the left. Quite likely what prevented individualism from waning, however, was the physical defeat in World War II of certain of these collectivist perspectives and the horrific and uninspiring nature of others. This defeat helped produce the relative intellectual cautiousness or quietism of the post–World War II era, which is unlikely to continue indefinitely.

Among late-twentieth-century intellectuals it once again became fashionable to attack individualism—in particular, what is described as the ideal of the abstract individual and the associated concept of methodological individualism. Yet those doing so—communitarians, feminists, and postmoderns—are caught in a curious bind. They are free to attack the putative flaws and excesses of individualism but only if they decline to challenge the sacrosanct claims of individualism: individual dignity, autonomy, privacy, and self-development. To do so, they must realize, would relegate their writings to obscurity. Still, one must wonder how much longer Nietzsche's challenge to confront the disparities between the West's individualist values and its lack of a credible and coherent foundation can be delayed. How much longer can the magical table of values, without legs, continue to stand? The answer might be, unexpectedly, for a good long while. For individualism, in the various guises described above, in spite of Nietzsche's insights, works. That is, individualism has contributed greatly to improving human life, particularly in reducing all manner of physical suffering and increasing material abundance, across a wide range of activities and arenas. Quite possibly, then, as long as the Western economies remain robust, individualism will continue to be the central organizing principle of Western religiosity, politics, economics, ethics, and art and literature.

See also *Calvinism; Catholicism, Roman; Communitarianism; Conservatism; Enlightenment; Fascism; Feminism; Hobbes, Thomas; Liberalism; Natural law; Protestantism; Reformation; Secular humanism; Secularization; Tocqueville, Alexis de.*

Barry Alan Shain

BIBLIOGRAPHY

Arieli, Yehoshua. *Individualism and Nationalism in American Ideology.* Baltimore, Md.: Penguin, 1966.

Coleman, Janet, ed. *The Individual in Political Theory and Practice.* Oxford: Clarendon Press, 1996.

Curry, Richard O., and Lawrence B. Goodheart, eds. *American Chameleon: Individualism in Trans-National Context.* Kent, Ohio: Kent State University Press, 1991.

Dumont, Louis. *Essays on Individualism: Modern Ideology in Anthropological Perspective.* Chicago: University of Chicago Press, 1992.

Lukes, Steven. *Individualism.* Oxford: Blackwell, 1973.

Macpherson, C. B. *The Political Theory of Possessive Individualism: Hobbes to Locke.* New York: Oxford University Press, 1962.

Morris, Colin. *The Discovery of the Individual, 1050–1200.* Toronto: University of Toronto Press, 1995.

Shanahan, Daniel. *Toward a Genealogy of Individualism.* Amherst: University of Massachusetts Press, 1992.

Taylor, Charles. *Sources of the Self: The Making of the Modern Identity.* Cambridge: Harvard University Press, 1989.

Indonesia

A Southeast Asian nation made up of 12,000 islands and 300 ethnic groups, Indonesia is the fourth most populous nation and the largest majority-Muslim country in the world, with 88 percent of its 200 million citizens professing Islam. Although in the fourteenth century the Hindu Javanese kingdom of Majapahit controlled much of the archipelago, it was Dutch colonialism that carved out the nation's present-day expanse. Building on the missionizing efforts of the Portuguese (who in the sixteenth century had converted natives on several islands in eastern Indonesia to Christiani-

ty), the Dutch also introduced Christianity into the few tribal and pagan territories that had escaped the great wave of Islamic conversion that swept the archipelago from the fifteenth to the eighteenth centuries. Unlike the Spanish in the Philippines, however, Dutch officials remained half-hearted promoters of Christianity, prohibiting mission activity outright in Muslim strongholds.

Opposition to Colonialism

In the late nineteenth century European colonialism penetrated into remote corners of the Indonesian archipelago. Muslim sultanates in northern Sumatra put up fierce resistance, but in most regions native aristocrats were overwhelmed by the superior firepower and military organization of the Europeans. Anticolonial resistance continued among the peasantry, especially on the island of Java, where Dutch economic programs had their most intrusive impact.

The trade and communications fostered by colonialism also facilitated the spread of non-European ideas. Although Islamic reformers, influenced by Arabia's Wahhabis (Muslim reformists who conquered Islam's Arabian holy lands in the nineteenth century), had appeared in central Sumatra in the early 1800s, steamboat travel to the Middle East later in the century facilitated an unprecedented diffusion of Muslim reformist ideas. Reformist Muslims, promoting piety and opposition to European colonialism, were also among the first to take advantage of the new technologies of the printing press and European paper.

Not all people who identified as Muslims agreed with reformist ideas. Traditionalist Muslims supportive of Islamic jurists (*ulama*) and Muslim schools of law took exception to the reformists' rejection of traditionalist legal scholarship. Muslims of a mystical or nominal Islamic persuasion rejected what they regarded as the reformists' stridency and intolerance.

Despite these disagreements, Islam provided the symbols around which the first mass organization against colonialism took shape in the early twentieth century. Founded in 1912, the Islamic Association (Sarikat Islam, the first nationalist political party) used Islam to appeal to the country's diverse populations. From the beginning, however, there was another, more secularist wing in the emerging nationalist movement. Some of these secular nationalists came from Indonesia's small Hindu or, more important, Christian community. Under Dutch colonialism, Christians (who today constitute about 9 percent of Indonesia's population but in the early

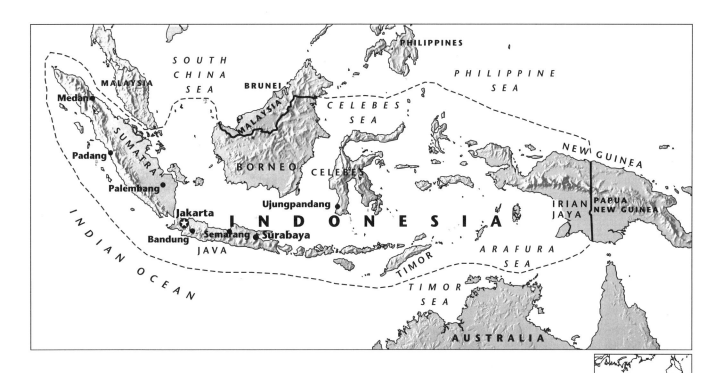

twentieth century were half that number) enjoyed educational and economic advantages over other natives and were thus well prepared to play a leading role in the nationalist leadership. Also prominent in that leadership, however, were Javanese of a nominally Islamic, or *abangan* ("red," "of the earth," connoting "peasant"), persuasion. Almost half of Indonesia's polyglot population is ethnic Javanese, and the majority profess an Islam of a localized, Javanese cast. This "Javanist" Islam emphasizes religious mysticism rather than Islamic legalism and stresses the essential unity of all religions. Javanist Muslims also were—and today still are—strongly opposed to the establishment of an Islamic state.

Tensions between Islamic nationalists and the Christians, Hindus, and Javanist Muslims, who tended to support nondenominational nationalism, marked Indonesian politics for most of the twentieth century. Building on the dissatisfaction of the poor, the Islamic Association grew rapidly in the second decade of the twentieth century, developing a leftist, increasingly secular nationalist wing among Javanist Muslims as its mass base grew. In 1921 the Muslim League split in two, as orthodox Muslims expelled from the organization those members who had embraced Marxism. During preparations for independence in mid-1945, tensions between Islamic nationalists and the secular nationalist community grew. Muslim demands for an Islamic state were again opposed by Hindus, Christians, and Javanist Muslims. In the end, the nondenominational nationalists prevailed, as a result of inter-vention by the nationalist leaders Sukarno and Mohammad Hatta.

After Independence

At the end of the war for independence in 1949, tension between supporters of an Islamic state and those favoring a secular state exploded again, this time in the form of fierce struggles between political parties organized along religious lines. This rivalry polarized the countryside and, aggravated by the nation's economic decline, degenerated into violence. In September 1965 a failed left-wing army officers' coup was blamed on the Communist Party, and Muslims joined with military forces to wipe out communist cadres. The violence killed a quarter-million people and destroyed what had been the largest communist party in the noncommunist world. It also led some two million Muslims, mostly victims of the violence, to convert from Islam to Christianity and Hinduism—the largest mass conversion from Islam in modern times.

The "New Order" government that began ruling Indonesia in 1965 placed strict limits on mass politics and social freedoms, but its economic programs catapulted Indonesia from the ranks of the world's poorest societies to one of Asia's emerging, if corruption-plagued, industrial giants. Having marginalized Muslim organizations during its first two decades, in the 1980s the New Order government awoke to find the country in the midst of an Islamic revival. The government responded by adopting policies conciliatory to cultural Islam. It committed resources to Muslim social and educational programs but suppressed political organizations advocating an Islamic state. The government's efforts have been assisted by many Muslim leaders who themselves have promoted ambitious programs of Islamic "renewal" *(pembaruan),* emphasizing the compatibility of Islam with democracy, pluralism, and human rights. Insisting that Islam itself does not require an Islamic state, most Muslim leaders now accept the official doctrine of the "five principles" (Panca Sila) as the ideological basis of the state.

Among the Panca Sila's distinctive features is its rejection of a formal separation of religion and state. The Panca Sila affirms that religion is a public good (an idea reinforced by the campaign against the communists in the 1960s), and the state is enjoined to promote religious life. Religious education is mandatory in all schools. Rather than establishing one national religion, however, the state accords equal rights to each of the five nationally recognized religions: Islam, Protestantism, Roman Catholicism, Hinduism, and Buddhism. In response to the Islamic revival, however, the government elevated its support for Islam in the 1990s, leading non-Muslims to wonder whether the nation's multidenominational heritage was in jeopardy. A political force in its own right, the armed forces remains strongly committed to religious pluralism, fearing that favoritism toward any one religious community might threaten national unity.

See also *Colonialism; Islam, Southeast Asian.*

Robert W. Hefner

BIBLIOGRAPHY

Bresnan, John. *Managing Indonesia: The Modern Political Economy.* New York: Columbia University Press, 1993.

Cribb, Robert. *The Indonesian Killings, 1965–1966: Studies from Java and Bali.* Clayton, Victoria, Australia: Centre of Southeast Asian Studies, Monash University, 1990.

Hefner, Robert W. "Of Faith and Commitment: Christian Conversion in Muslim Java." In *Conversion to Christianity: Historical and Anthropological Perspectives on a Great Transformation,* edited by Robert W. Hefner. Berkeley: University of California Press, 1993.

Ramage, Douglas E. *Politics in Indonesia: Democracy, Islam, and the Ideology of Tolerance.* New York: Routledge, 1995.

Reid, Anthony. "A Religious Revolution." In *Southeast Asia in the Age of Commerce, 1450–1680.* Vol. 2, *Expansion and Crisis.* New Haven: Yale University Press, 1993.

Ricklefs, M. C. *A History of Modern Indonesia since c. 1300.* Stanford: Stanford University Press, 1993.

Inquisition

A system of inquiry *(inquisitio)* in the Roman Catholic Church dating from the thirteenth century and associated principally with the countries of southern Europe, the inquisition was originally a normal part of the judicial process. It was taken over by the church in order to inquire into a particular offense—heresy—that began to be identified and persecuted with special vigor during the later Middle Ages. The accused came principally from sectarian movements, such as the Cathars (twelfth century), that questioned the political power of secular princes, who consequently gave their full support to persecution and backed the establishment of inquisitions.

The Inquisition as an institution did not exist in medieval times: the term was a generic description for the various commissions issued by the papacy for inquiries into heresy. These inquisitions were created by papal bull and then supported by the laws of the local prince. They came into existence from the 1230s in France and Aragon and above all in the Holy Roman Empire, where the emperor, Frederick II (1272–1337), gave them his firm support and extended them into his Italian dominions, including Sicily. As a result, the machinery of inquisitions could be found in most states from the Mediterranean to the North Sea but not in Castile, England, and Scandinavia. A papal decree for the Inquisition was first issued by Gregory IX (1143?–1241) in 1233, and administration of the commissions was put into the hands of the Dominican and Franciscan orders. The first full-scale Inquisition, directed against the Cathars, was set up in Languedoc in 1233–1234, and jurisdiction over heresy was put in the hands of the new tribunals and taken out of the hands of bishops.

Pope Innocent IV (d. 1254) in his bull *Ad Extirpanda* (1252) laid down a detailed constitution for the prosecution of heresy. In most countries the close alliance of state and papacy created an Inquisition that was subject directly to the pope and allowed to override local laws when necessary. In late-fourteenth-century Germany the papal inquisitors were influential in the persecution of Waldensians, members of a Protestant religious sect, and Beghards, religious associations of men.

The most famous of the Inquisitions was that in Spain. Social pressure against converts of Jewish origin *(conversos),* who were suspected of embracing Catholicism publicly but continuing to practice Judaism privately, led the Spanish rulers Ferdinand (1452–1516) and Isabella (1451–1504) to ask the papacy to sanction the establishment of a tribunal in Castile to inquire into their orthodoxy. The bull for an Inquisition was issued in 1478, and the new tribunal began functioning in 1480. Three years later the tribunal was also established in Aragon, where it replaced the medieval tribunal. In time local tribunals were set up all over the peninsula and also (from 1571) in the American colonies of Spain.

There were important differences between the medieval and the Spanish Inquisition. In Spain, for example, the Inquisition was in practice dependent wholly on the state and extended its functions beyond the mere pursuit of heresy. Most of its activity also involved persecution of cultural minorities not found in other countries: the *conversos* and later the Moriscos (descendants of the forcibly converted Muslim population of Spain). The tribunal was famous for the *auto de fe,* a normally public ceremony at which sentences were decreed; executions were later carried out in a different location. Though notoriously savage in its treatment of the *conversos,* the Inquisition executed fewer people than is generally believed. Deaths in its first fifty years, when most prosecutions occurred, are unlikely to have exceeded two thousand.

In the sixteenth century three important new Inquisitions were set up. In the Netherlands a papal Inquisition was founded in 1522 and acted vigorously against the new heresies of the Protestant Reformation. In Italy Pope Paul III (1468–1549) in 1542 set up a central tribunal, the Sacred Congregation of the Holy Office, which received further powers in 1588. Though busy in Naples and Milan, its main sphere of activity was the Papal States. Among its more lasting acts was the creation of an Index of Prohibited Books. The Spanish Inquisition was the model for the new Portuguese Inquisition, initially established in 1536 and then fully set up in 1547 by papal bull. The new tribunal was also exported to the colonies (in Goa in Portuguese India from 1560).

In the eighteenth century, when in most of Europe heresy had ceased to be a secular offense, the Inquisitions were restricted largely to a political role and were usually inactive. In Spain a few dissidents were prosecuted, but the activity of the tribunal was limited mainly to censorship and blocking the entry of Enlightenment ideas. In the second half of the century only four people were burnt at the stake. The Spanish Inquisition was suppressed by the French when they invaded Spain in 1808 but was afterwards restored by Ferdinand VII (1784–1833). It was not finally abolished until 1834. The Roman Inquisition survived into the twentieth century, but the Congregation of the Holy Office, which had administered the Inquisition, no longer carries out that role and was merged into the Congregation de Propaganda Fide in line with the reforms of the Second Vatican Council (1962–1965), the twenty-first ecumenical council recognized by the Roman Catholic Church, which became the symbol of the church's openness to the modern world.

See also *Enlightenment; Heresy; Protestantism; Reformation; Spain; Vatican Council, Second.*

Henry Kamen

BIBLIOGRAPHY

Bethencourt, Francisco. *L'Inquisition á l'époque moderne: Espagne, Portugal, Italie, XVe–XIX siècle.* Paris: Fayard, 1995.

Kamen, Henry. *The Spanish Inquisition: An Historical Revision.* New Haven: Yale University Press, 1998.

Lea, Henry Charles. *A History of the Inquisition of Spain.* New York: Macmillan, 1906–1908.

van der Vekene, Emil. *Bibliotheca Bibliographica Historiae Sanctae Inquisitionis.* 2 vols. Vaduz: Topos Verlag, 1982–1983.

Iqbal, Muhammad

Indian poet and philosopher. Sir Muhammad Iqbal (1877–1938), a Muslim in British-ruled India, was influential in the movement for a separate state for India's Muslims and accordingly is regarded as the spiritual father of Pakistan. Born on the Kashmir border, between what is now India and Pakistan, Iqbal was early exposed to the modernist ideas of Sayyid Ahmad Khan and the Aligarh movement, which advocated that Indian Muslims adapt European scientific knowledge to their own cultural situation.

After studying in Lahore, Iqbal went to London to study law and then took a Ph.D. in philosophy from the University of Munich. His poetry in Urdu and Persian addressed the issues of modernity as framed by European thinkers while retaining classical Islamic idioms and references. Iqbal was knighted by the British Crown in 1924 for his literary achievements. His English lectures on *The Reconstruction of Religious Thought in Islam* (1930) argued the need to incorpo-

Muhammad Iqbal

rate an awareness of modern European philosophy and science into Islamic theology.

Politically, Iqbal was impressed by the Russian Revolution of 1917, though the dilemmas of colonialism and social justice also preoccupied him. His most important political legacy was his recommendation to the Muslim League (the principal political party representing the interests of Indian Muslims) in 1930 to form a Muslim state of the provinces of northwestern India. He believed a state that was separate from Hindu India was necessary for the self-determination of Indian Muslims. His formulation of the two-nation theory of India and Pakistan was adopted by Muhammad Ali Jinnah, who in 1947 with the creation of Pakistan became the new nation's first head of government .

In religious terms, Iqbal was highly critical of certain aspects of Sufism, a branch of Islam that he regarded as passive, fatalistic, and excessive in claiming union with God. The complexity of his religious and political thought is exhibited best by poems like *The Book of Eternity,* a Dante-inspired journey through the heavens (led by the thirteenth-century Persian mystic poet Rumi), which includes encounters with many Eastern and Western politicians, philosophers, and religious figures.

See also *Pakistan; Sufism.*

Carl W. Ernst

Iran

Iran, officially the Islamic Republic of Iran, is located in southwestern Asia between Iraq and Afghanistan and is the world's first theocratic republic. About 93 percent of its population belong to the Twelver Shi'ite branch of Islam, and some 6 percent to the Sunni (mainstream) branch. Bahais and Armenian Christians constitute the larger religious minorities, and there are smaller religious communities of Nestorian Christians, Jews, and Zoroastrians.

Religion and Revolutionary Change in Iranian History

Iran is the birthplace of Zoroastrianism, the oldest millenarian world religion, whose fundamental dualism of the eternal struggle between good and evil has served as powerful imagery for numerous religio-political movements in several religious traditions. The only Muslim country where Shi'ism, which also has a strong millenarian component, has been the state religion for centuries, Iran has been a fertile land for the growth of religious hierarchies, or hierocracies, as in the Catholic Church. The Zoroastrian hierocracy, with extensive control over the social life, grew during the Sassanian dynasty in the fourth and fifth centuries C.E. Since the sixteenth century, Iran has witnessed the continuous growth of a Shi'ite hierocracy. This hierocracy survived the modernization of the Iranian state through the first three-quarters of the twentieth century, overthrowing the secularizing state in 1979 and declaring Iran a Shi'ite theocratic republic under a supreme religious leader.

Four revolutions in which religion played a major role can be found in Iran's long history: those accompanying the rise of the Sassanian dynasty in the third century and the Safavid dynasty at the beginning of the sixteenth century, the constitutional revolution of 1906–1911, and the Islamic revolution of 1979. Furthermore, Iran was critically important in the revolution in which the Abbasid dynasty overthrew the Umayyad caliphs in the eighth century, Islam's first social revolution. In that revolution, too, religion played a major role.

The rise of the Sassanian dynasty in the third decade of the third century can be considered a revolution because it unified a large number of feudal petty kingdoms to make an empire. There was no organized Zoroastrian clergy when Ardashir (d. 240), the founder of the Sassanian dynasty, posed as the restorer of Zoroastrian religion. The gradual growth of a Zoroastrian hierocracy, which became enormously powerful by the end of the fourth century, was the long-term consequence of the central role given to the restoration of religion in the nationalist ideology of the Sassanian revolution.

The foundation of the Sassanian empire was shaken by the massive religious rebellion of Mazdak, who preached an early form of communism at the end of the fifth century. The empire was overthrown by the conquering Muslims in the second quarter of the seventh century. The conversion of Iran to Islam was slow, however, and occurred on a large scale only after the Abbasid revolution in the mid-eighth century. The proselytizing Islamic movements, which proposed equality between Arabs and the non-Arab converts, played a critical role in the Abbasid revolution, as did the long-settled Arab Muslims of Khurasan in the northeast. The Abbasid revolution thus opened the way for the full integration of Iranians into Islamic society and brought about the conversion of the majority of the Iranian population to Islam.

Until the end of the Middle Ages, the majority of the Iranians were Sunni Muslims. In the fourteenth and fifteenth centuries, however, a number of Shi'ite millenarian movements appeared in Iran, usually in connection with Sufism (popular, mystical Islam). The last of these, the Safavid movement, culminated in what may be considered the first successful Shi'ite revolution. The leader of the Safavid movement, Shah Isma'il I (1486–1524), was considered the mahdi (Islam's messianic restorer and rightly guided leader of the end of time) and the incarnation of God by his Turkoman followers. His millenarian movement turned the Turkoman tribesmen into a zealous fighting force for the conquest of Iran and its subsequent conversion to Shi'ism. Once in power, the Safavid rulers modified their millenarian claims, saying that their reign would continue until the mahdi appeared. The Twelver Shi'ism that was spread in Iran under the patronage of the Safavid rulers by Shi'ite *ulama* (religious leaders), who often came from Lebanon and Arab Iraq, was more doctrinally systematic than the extremist faith of the conquering Turkomans. These *ulama* also founded a Shi'ite hierocracy, which became increasingly powerful and began to assert itself against the Safavid monarchs in the latter part of the seventeenth century.

After the collapse of the Safavid dynasty in the eighteenth century, the Shi'ite religious authorities were forced to subsist on their own without state support. They developed the

doctrinal basis of their juristic authority during the civil wars of that century and emerged as a powerful hierocracy at the end of it. The hierocracy remained independent of the state and consolidated its power throughout the nineteenth century. Its highest ranking members assumed the title of Ayatollah (sign of God) by the beginning of the twentieth. State and *ulama* were drawn together in the face of the common threat from the Babi millenarian movement, which initiated the Bahai religion, in the middle of the nineteenth century. The incipient modernization of the autocratic state and the accompanying subservience to imperialist powers, however, drew them increasingly apart thereafter.

The Shi'ite religious authorities appeared in the forefront of the massive popular protests that forced the shah to grant Iran a constitution in 1906, in what was Asia's first modern political revolution. As the secularizing implications of parliamentary legislation became clear, and especially as secularization of the judiciary could be seen as loss of clerical power, some religious leaders distanced themselves from the constitutionalists, while others actively opposed them. The Shi'ite hierocracy generally withdrew from politics in disillusionment at the end of the revolutionary period.

The modernization of the state under Reza Shah Pahlavi (1877–1944) in the 1920s and 1930s resulted in a drastic diminution of the institutional prerogatives and social power of the hierocracy. However, it did not impair the legitimacy of the exclusive hierocratic authority of the *ulama*. Consequently, the hierocracy not only survived but also withstood the modern state's challenge to its virtually exclusive control over religious learning and over the authoritative interpretation of Shi'ite Islam.

The Islamic Revolution

The establishment of an Islamic theocracy ruled by the Shi'ite *ulama* can be regarded as the last stage of the evolution of clerical authority in Shi'ite Islam. After the Shi'ite hierocracy had freed itself from the tutelage of political authority characteristic of the Safavid era, the next logical possibility was to assert the superiority of the hierocracy over the state by extending clerical authority to the political sphere. This logical possibility was actualized when Ayatollah Ruholla Khomeini (1900–1989) transformed a sizable section of the Shi'ite hierocracy into a revolutionary political party. The projected final stage of the growth of Shi'ite clerical authority then became the blueprint for the militant clerics who overthrew the shah in 1979.

Khomeini and his followers drew on the cult of martyrdom and on the millenarian elements in the Shi'ite tradition to mobilize the Iranian masses for the revolution that was to realize the Shi'ite clerical rule. With the emergence of an Islamic revolutionary movement in the late 1960s, for instance, the lay Islamic ideologue Ali Shari'ati interpreted the belief in the coming of the mahdi as an allegory of the imminent revolution of the oppressed masses of the developing countries.

As massive demonstrations and strikes paralyzed the government, all political groups who formed the revolutionary coalition against the shah, Mohammad Reza Pahlavi, accepted the leadership of Khomeini, who was a Grand Ayatollah. After the overthrow of the monarchy in 1979, Khomeini appointed Mehdi Bazargan, the leading member of the liberal and nationalist elements in the revolutionary coalition, as the prime minister of a provisional government. Nevertheless, a clerically dominated Assembly of Experts, elected in place of a constituent assembly, bypassed a draft constitution submitted by the provisional government and proposed a theocratic government based on the Mandate of the Jurist, as advocated by Khomeini, with an elected parliament (Majlis) and president. This was approved by a referendum in December 1979, shortly after the occupation of the American embassy and the taking of its staff as hostages resulted in the toppling of the provisional government of Bazargan. Although another moderate, Abol-Hasan Bani-Sadr, was elected president in

January 1980, the Majlis, which was controlled by the clerical party, impeached him in June 1981. The revolutionary power struggle moved into the streets and entered its most violent phase. The new president and prime minister and some seventy organizers of the clericalist Islamic Republican Party died in explosions, while many important members of the clerical elite were assassinated by suicide attackers belonging to the *mujahedin,* the Islamic radical group that had supported Bani-Sadr. The revolutionary terror did not abate until early 1983, after thousands of men and women belonging to the *mujahedin* and other rival revolutionary groups had been executed or killed in street fights.

With the ending of the revolutionary power struggle and elimination of nonclericalist partners in the revolutionary coalition of 1978, Khomeini's clericalist theory of government on the basis of the Mandate of the Jurist was implemented. Iran became the first theocratic republic in the world. The constitution of the Islamic Republic of Iran gives its *rahbar,* the head of state and supreme religious jurist, extensive religious and secular powers, including appointment of the commanders of the armed forces and the head of the judiciary and confirmation of the elected president. The position was held by Khomeini until his death in 1989. Ayatollah Sayyid Ali Khamanei succeeded him. Although the 270 representatives in the Majlis are elected, all Majlis legislation must conform with Islam as determined by six clerical jurists of the Council of Guardians. This council automatically reviews all enactments. The constitution was amended in 1989 to strengthen the presidency by eliminating the position of the prime minister. The amendment also clarified the authority of the clerical Assembly of Experts in electing and dismissing the *rahbar.* The Council for the Determination of the Interest of the Islamic Republic, which had been set up by Khomeini to arbitrate in cases of deadlock between the Majlis and the Council of Guardians, was given the additional function of acting as an advisory body to the *rahbar.*

See also *Bahai; Islam; Khomeini, Ruholla Musavi; Mahdi; Revolutions; Sufism; Theocracy.*

Said Amir Arjomand

BIBLIOGRAPHY

Akhavi, Sharengh. *Religion and Politics in Contemporary Iran.* Albany: State University of New York Press, 1980.

Amanat, Abbas. *Resurrection and Renewal: The Making of the Babi Movement in Iran, 1844–1850.* Ithaca: Cornell University Press, 1989.

Arjomand, S. A. *The Shadow of God and the Hidden Imam: Religion, Political Order, and Societal Change in Shi'ite Iran from the Beginning to 1890.* Chicago: University of Chicago Press, 1984.

———. *The Turban for the Crown: The Islamic Revolution in Iran.* New York: Oxford University Press, 1988.

Bakhash, Shaul. *The Reign of the Ayatollahs.* New York: Basic Books, 1984.

Brown, E. G. *The Persian Revolution, 1905–1909.* Cambridge: Cambridge University Press, 1910.

Hairi, A. H. *Shi'ism and Constitutionalism in Iran.* Leiden: E. J. Brill, 1977.

Keddie, Nikki R. *Religion and Rebellion in Iran: The Tobacco Protests of 1891–92.* London: Frank Cass, 1966.

Iraq

A republic in Southwest Asia, Iraq is a multisectarian, multiethnic country with a mixed history of cohabitation among different religious communities. Some 97 percent of the population are Muslim; 3 percent are Christian, divided among various denominations. A tiny community of a few hundred Jews still exists. Jews and Christians have migrated abroad since the end of the Second World War. In the early 1950s, after the establishment of the Israeli state, tensions between the Iraqi government and the Jewish community involving some local hostilities increased, resulting in an exodus of Jews to Israel. Christians, fleeing political instability, have also migrated in large numbers in the past three decades.

Since the founding of the state in 1920, Iraqi governments have sought to create a secular, unified government, relegating religion mainly to the private domain. This principle has sometimes been challenged. In 1933 the Assyrians, seeking autonomy for their community in northern Iraq, rebelled against the central government. The Iraqi army put the rebellion down swiftly and brutally.

Shi'i-Sunni Tensions

The most important religious division in Iraq is that between the Muslim Sunni and Shi'i sects. The Shi'ah compose about 55 percent to 60 percent of the population and are increasingly demanding more power in political decision making. The Arab Shi'i population lives in the south of Iraq; the Arab Sunnis and Kurds (mainly Sunni) live in the north. In the capital, Baghdad, Shi'ah and Sunni live together.

Until recently sectarian violence between Shi'ah and Sunnis has been rare. The Shi'i tribes in central and southern

Iraq took part in the famous 1920 revolt against the British occupation of Iraq. But since the creation of the state in 1920, political power has rested largely in Arab Sunni hands, a fact increasingly resented by Shi'ah. During four centuries of Ottoman rule over Iraq (1524–1918), the Shi'ah were excluded from military service and important public positions. Under a British mandate (1920–1932) the Sunnis inherited political power and continued to maintain their dominance, especially in the military.

Under the monarchy (1921–1958) some Shi'ah were admitted into the army and held public office. A few Shi'i statesmen such as Fadhil al-Jamali, Muhammad al-Sadr, and Salih Jabr became prime ministers, but their numbers were few compared with those of their Sunni counterparts. Dissatisfied with this situation and increasingly alienated from government, some Shi'i youth joined underground, extremist political parties, mainly the Iraq Communist Party. To combat this trend Shi'i clerics at the Shi'i shrine cities of Najaf and Karbala began forming religio-political movements, such as al-Da'wah (the Call).

Religious Politics under the Ba'th Regime

The Ba'th Arab Socialist Party came into power in Iraq after a military coup in July 1968. The party advocated a secular, socialist state and opened its ranks to Sunni and Shi'ah, Christians, and even Kurds. But power soon gravitated into the hands of Saddam Husayn, who increasingly relied on Sunni support, based not on religion but on Sunni clan and family ties from the town of Tikrit in central Iraq. Although non-Tikritis, Shi'i and Sunni, have reached the top of the Ba'th Party and the Revolutionary Command Council, the nation's supreme authority since 1968, their real power remains marginal.

When the Iran-Iraq war started in 1980, Iraq had a strong secular orientation. In fact, Iraq entered the war to prevent the Shi'i revolution in Iran from penetrating the Shi'i community in Iraq. Ayatollah Ruholla Khomeini, the spiritual leader of Iran, had called on the Iraqi Shi'ah to rise up and overthrow the Ba'thist regime in Iraq, but Iraqi Shi'ah, for the most part, fought the Iranians, proving that they would choose defending their country and their Arabic identity over following Iranian Shi'i leaders.

Although the war ended with no real winners, it affected the Iraqi regime as a whole. During and after the war the regime began to adopt some religious symbols and terminology. The flag was modified to include the religious slogan "Allahu Akbar" (God is Great), and in photos distributed all over the country, President Husayn was seen praying. He declared his intention to build the largest mosque in the world.

Today, religious opposition to the regime is strictly underground. The Sunni opposition, mainly the Muslim Brotherhood, is negligible and too weak to constitute a threat. But Shi'i religious groups, although a minority, are active both inside and outside Iraq in attempting to destabilize the regime. The main political group, al-Da'wah, has called for an Islamic regime in Iraq. The regime severely repressed the Da'wah, which originated in the 1960s. In the 1970s a number of its members were executed after a series of bomb explosions and acts of violence against the regime, but the group gained impetus again after the Iranian revolution of 1979. The Iraqi government arrested and executed Ayatollah Muhammad Baqr al-Sadr, a noted Shi'i cleric, who had led the formation of the party and the Shi'i political movement.

After Iraq's defeat in the Persian Gulf War the Shi'ah of the south revolted against the regime in the winter of 1991, but the regime brutally crushed the rebellion. Today, the Supreme Council for the Islamic Revolution in Iraq, an umbrella organization that includes many Shi'i opposition factions, is based in Tehran and is headed by Baqr al-Hakim, a well-known Iraqi Shi'i religious authority.

See also *Iran; Islam; Khomeini, Ruholla Musavi.*

Louay Y. Bahry

BIBLIOGRAPHY

Batatu, Hanna. *The Old Social Classes and the Revolutionary Movements in Iraq.* 2d ed. Princeton: Princeton University Press, 1982.

Mallat, Chibli. "Iraq." In *The Politics of Islamic Revivalism,* edited by Shireen Hunter. Bloomington: University of Indiana Press, 1988.

Marr, Phebe. *The Modern History of Iraq.* Boulder, Colo.: Westview Press, 1985.

Nakash, Yitzhak. *The Shi'is of Iraq.* Princeton: Princeton University Press, 1994.

Ireland

An island to the west of Britain, Ireland is politically divided into Northern Ireland, part of the United Kingdom of Great Britain and Northern Ireland, and the Republic of Ireland, since 1922 a sovereign state. Northern Ireland has one and a half million people. Roughly 60 percent are Protestant and unionist (pro–United Kingdom), and the remainder are Roman Catholic and nationalist (pro–united Ireland). The Republic of Ireland has three and a half million people, 95 percent of whom are Catholic. The historical origins of division go back four centuries to English colonialism, when English and Scottish Protestants settled in Catholic Ireland.

Division and Partition

Over time, three religious groups developed and can be ranked hierarchically in terms of power. The rulers were "the Ascendancy," or landowning elite, whose origin was English. They formed the leadership of the Protestant (Anglican) Church of Ireland, set up after the English Reformation of the sixteenth and seventeenth centuries, and favored those farmers and servants who were its members. Their church membership came to make up more than 10 percent of the Irish population. The Presbyterians and related smaller churches were next, also at about 10 percent. Mainly from Scotland, they settled largely in the northern province of Ulster and had few rights until the late eighteenth century. Third were the majority Catholic Irish, who preceded by centuries the Scottish and English settlers. They were pauperized by the elite until the late eighteenth century, when they began their slow ascent to political power. This was achieved through the steady democratization of British politics and their own self-motivated fight for the right to land and self-government.

As the Catholic Irish began to achieve their aims, Presbyterians and the Church of Ireland in the north combined to form a political alliance against them (1886–1912) in the form of the Unionist Party. In 1912 their pact was sealed with the mass signing of a "Solemn League and Covenant" committed to removing Ulster from any future united Ireland. The partition of the island came in 1921, after a period of rebellion from the Irish Catholics seeking an independent republic and reprisals against British troops. The new structure was a compromise between three centers of power, the Protestants of Ulster, the Catholic nationalists throughout Ireland but weak in Ulster, and the British government in London. The partition meant that the newly constituted Northern Ireland would include half a million Catholic nationalists who would suffer economic and political discrimination for the foreseeable future. The British government turned a blind eye as Northern Ireland became dominated by Protestants. Catholic nationalists found it difficult to get jobs or decent housing, and the Northern Irish parliament (set up in 1921) tinkered with the voting system and electoral boundaries to the detriment of Catholic representation. The police were given draconian powers of arrest and detention, using them mainly against Catholics. Only with the development of the civil rights movement in the 1960s did unrest grow and threaten Protestant unionist supremacy. Public order collapsed in 1968 as riots broke out. In 1971 local minorities were forcibly cleared from their homes, and terrorist paramilitaries from both sides, including the Irish Republican Army, began campaigns of bombing and assassination. The violence has continued, leaving some 3,500 people dead. By 1972 the British government felt compelled to act decisively. The British abolished the provincial parliament and introduced direct rule from London.

Until 1997 the British government in effect backed the unionist cause by maintaining the status quo. Then the new Labour government restarted talks about a political solution. The negotiators recognized that the continuation of civil disturbance and demonstrations was encouraged by the lack of a form of government in the province that was acceptable to both unionists and nationalists. The result was an agree-

ment signed April 10, 1998, known as the Good Friday peace accord, which was designed to bring peace to Northern Ireland. Voters in the Republic of Ireland amended their constitution, abandoning claims to the north. And by voting for a new assembly that would fairly represent Catholics and Protes-

tants alike, a strife-weary majority in the north rejected the sectarian violence that had plagued the province for so long. Elections for the assembly were held in June. Only time will tell if democracy prevails over the traditional centers of sectarian power.

Protestantism and Northern Ireland

The Protestant coalition is due to the need for unity to sustain the separate status of Northern Ireland. Protestantism is strong, with half its population attending church on a regular basis, with youth, young adults, and the urban working class the least likely among them to attend. The Presbyterians and the Church of Ireland remain the largest denominations, but there are also some twenty smaller ones, including the Free Presbyterians, a breakaway church founded by the Reverend Ian Paisley. Paisley, a militant unionist, has led demonstrations aimed at preventing any compromise between Protestants and Catholics. The predominant characteristic shared by Protestant churches and sects in Northern Ireland is Calvinism. This sometimes appears in the form of Sabbatarian politics, with efforts to keep alcohol, sports centers, and places of entertainment inaccessible on Sundays (the Sabbath, the biblical day of rest).

Although Protestants from various churches are frequently kept apart by differences over biblical interpretation and matters of church order, they are bound together by biblical preaching and common opposition to a united Ireland dominated by Catholic, nationalist, and republican traditions. There is even some direct element of anti-Catholicism. Rhetoric is frequently derived from the Reformation period, with the papacy and the Catholic Mass particular targets. Powerful stereotypes of Irish Catholics as drunks, with large families, who are ruled by priests, bishops, and pope, are still part of populist imagery. Large numbers of the working- and middle-class populations are involved in religious-political societies dedicated to the defense of "a Protestant state for a Protestant people." The most important of these are the Orange Order, the Apprentice Boys of Londonderry, and the Black Preceptory (a small society made up of the Protestant elite). These societies help bind political activists on a local basis from their diverse church affiliations. As well as being part of these organizations as chaplains, a number of Protestant clergy are involved directly in formal party politics. The unionists are split between moderate, British-oriented politics and more obstinate, Ulster-oriented politics. The latter, who describe themselves as loyalists, are made up of a largely unchurched, proviolence wing and a religious fundamentalist wing. Roy Wallis and Steve Bruce argue that the exclusivity of some forms of Calvinism, particularly the stress on being chosen, reinforces ethnic ideas of Protestant superiority over Catholics and strengthens the sense of being a people apart. This argument seems supported by the Protestant fundamentalists' affirmation that their religious freedom is under threat from the tyranny of a Catholic state, which the Republic of Ireland is purported to be. They see the British government as unfaithful to them and likely to betray their cause.

Catholicism and the Republic

Fundamentalist anti-Catholic rhetoric in Northern Ire-

land is fostered by the presence of Catholic themes in the formal and informal cultures of the Republic of Ireland. Since the independent state was established in 1921–1922, there has been an increase in both anti-unionist rhetoric and the explicit influence of Catholicism. The political party that originated the southern state, Sinn Fein ("We Ourselves"), split internally over Britain's treaty demands to retain the British Crown as head of the new state. Although most of Sinn Fein's leadership was republican, the majority still voted reluctantly to accept the king. The dissenting minority, led by Eamon De Valera, split away and fought a civil war (1922–1923), which it soon lost. The bitter division set the pattern for politics in the southern state for sixty years, with continuing confrontation between protreaty and antitreaty parties; until the 1980s the antitreaty republicans usually won. A major republican victory was the replacement of the British-imposed constitution of 1922 with the republican constitution of 1937.

Within the new state, the leadership of the Catholic Church controlled significant aspects of moral culture. This type of religious politics, termed "monopoly Catholicism" by David Martin, was characteristic of the church's approach to state rulers (kings, dictators, democratic governments) in the predominantly Catholic countries of Austria, Spain, Portugal, Italy, and Poland as well as Ireland. The church encouraged loyalty and law and order in return for control over the people's beliefs and moral values. It was often successful in developing and running school systems funded by the state and in obtaining legislation to preserve family morality, such as banning birth control and censoring publications. In the case of independent Ireland, where today 85 percent of the population attend church regularly, the republican constitution of 1937 was infused with Catholic themes. The preamble identifies the "fathers" of the people of Ireland as the oppressed Catholic community of the past. Articles 41–44 embody papal social teaching grounded in natural law theory: the state plays a subsidiary role to the family, which in turn is seen as the basic unit of society. Divorce is banned; private property is protected, as is religious ownership of schools and other institutions. The Catholic Church even had a special position "as the guardian of the faith professed by the great majority of the citizens," until a referendum in 1971 removed this phrase from the constitution.

The church influenced decisions on ordinary legislation. Bishops advised on various acts, including those concerning censorship of films (1923) and publications (1929), vocational education (1929), and public health (1945). They successfully and secretly opposed the introduction of health and welfare measures for mothers and their children in the 1947–1951 period, though this was to be the high point of their power. Since then there has been a steady erosion of their influence, and a successful referendum in 1995 introduced a measure of divorce against the bishops' wishes. This peaking of monopoly Catholicism has been partnered by a diminution in the power of republicanism and a new mood of realism within the nationalist alliance. The growing acceptance of the rights of the Protestant unionist minority and the need for compromise over the Northern Ireland question led to the Good Friday peace agreement.

See also *Anglicanism; Calvinism; Catholicism, Roman; Great Britain; Nationalism; Natural law; Papacy; Presbyterians; Protestantism; Reformation; State churches.*

John Fulton

BIBLIOGRAPHY

Bruce, Steve. *The Edge of the Union: The Ulster Loyalist Political Vision.* Oxford: Oxford University Press, 1994.

Fulton, John. *The Tragedy of Belief: Division, Politics, and Religion in Ireland.* Oxford: Clarendon Press, 1991.

Harkness, David W. *Ireland in the Twentieth Century: Divided Ireland.* London: Macmillan, 1996.

Inglis, Tom. *Moral Monopoly: The Catholic Church in Modern Irish Society.* Dublin: Gill and Macmillan, 1987.

Martin, David. *A General Theory of Secularization.* Oxford: Blackwell, 1978.

O'Halloran, Clare. *Partition and the Limits of Irish Nationalism: An Ideology under Stress.* Dublin: Gill and Macmillan, 1987.

Todd, Jennifer. "Two Traditions within Ulster Unionism." *Irish Political Studies* 2 (1987): 1–26.

Wallis, Roy, and Steve Bruce. *Sociological Theory, Religion, and Collective Action.* Belfast: Queen's University Press, 1986.

Whyte, John H. *Church and State in Modern Ireland, 1923–1979.* 2d ed. Dublin: Gill and Macmillan, 1980.

Islam

Beginning as the faith of a small community of believers in Arabia in the seventh century, Islam rapidly became one of the major world religions. The core of this faith is the belief that Muhammad (c. 570–632), a respected businessman in Mecca, a commercial and religious center in western Arabia, received revelations from God that have been preserved in the Qur'an. The heart of this revealed message is the affirmation that "there is no god but Allah (The God), and

Muhammad is the messenger of God." The term *islam* comes from the Arabic word-root *s-l-m,* which has a general reference to peace and submission. Specifically, Islam means submission to the will of God, and a Muslim is one who makes that submission.

This submission or act of Islam means living a life of faith and practice as defined in the Qur'an and participating in the life of the community of believers. The core of this Islamic life is usually said to be the Five Pillars of Islam: publicly bearing witness to the basic affirmation of faith; saying prescribed prayers five times a day; fasting during the month of Ramadan; giving a tithe or alms for support of the poor; and making a pilgrimage to Mecca at least once during the believer's lifetime, if this is possible.

Muslims believe that Islam is the basic monotheistic faith proclaimed by prophets throughout history. The Qur'an is not seen as presenting a new revelation but rather as providing a complete, accurate, and therefore final record of the message that had already been given to Abraham, Jesus, and other earlier prophets. As the basis for a historical community and tradition of faith, however, Islam begins in Mecca with the life and work of Muhammad in the early seventh century.

The Early Community

Muhammad's life as a preacher and leader of a community of believers has two major phases. He proclaimed his message in a city in which the majority did not accept his teachings. Mecca was a major pilgrimage center and sanctuary in the existing polytheism of Arabia, and the proclamation of monotheism threatened this whole system. The message presented in the Meccan period emphasizes the general themes of affirmation of monotheism and warnings of the Day of Judgment. Muhammad did not set out to establish a separate political organization, but the nature of the message represented a major challenge to the basic power structures of Mecca.

The second phase of Muhammad's career and the early life of the Muslim community began when Muhammad accepted an invitation from the people in Yathrib, an oasis north of Mecca, to serve as their arbiter and judge. In 622 Muhammad and his followers moved to Yathrib, and this emigration, or *hijrah,* is of such significance that Muslims use this date as the beginning of the Islamic calendar. The oasis became known as the City of the Prophet, or simply al-Medina (the city).

Muslims believe that the Ka'ba, within the Grand Mosque in Mecca, Saudi Arabia, was an altar built by Abraham and is the holiest place on earth. Followers of Islam face the cubic, black-draped stone structure during their prayers and walk around it during the hajj, *the pilgrimage that Muslims try to make at least once in their lifetime.*

In Muslim tradition the sociopolitical community that was created in Medina provides the model for what a truly Islamic state and society should be. In contrast to tribal groups, the new community, or *ummah,* was open to anyone who made the basic affirmation of faith, and loyalty to the ummah was to supersede any other loyalty, whether to clan, family, or commercial partnership. The political structure of the new community was informal. Although Muhammad had great authority as the messenger of God, he could not assume a position as a sovereign monarch because he was only human and only a messenger. The emphasis on the sole sovereignty of God provides an important foundation for Islamic political thinking throughout the centuries, challenging both theories of monarchy and absolutism, as well as later theories of popular sovereignty.

In this early era the characteristically Islamic sense of the ummah or the community of believers, rather than a concept of church or state, was firmly established as the central institutional identification for Muslims. In this way Islam is frequently described as a way of life rather than as a religion separate from politics or other dimensions of society. In Medina Muhammad provided leadership in all matters of life, but Muslims carefully distinguish the teachings that are the record of revelation and recorded in the Qur'an from the guidance Muhammad provided as a person. Because of his role as the messenger of God, Muhammad's own personal actions and words have special prestige. In addition to the Qur'an, the accounts of these, called *hadith,* provide the basis

for a second source of guidance for believers, the Sunnah (customary practice) of the Prophet.

By the time of Muhammad's death in 632, the new Muslim community was successfully established. Mecca had been defeated and incorporated into the ummah in important ways. The Ka'ba, a shrine in Mecca that had been the center of the polytheistic pilgrimage, was recognized as an altar built by Abraham, and Mecca became both the center of pilgrimage for the new community and the place toward which Muslims faced when they performed their prayers.

Sunni and Shi'i

When Muhammad died, Muslims faced the challenge of creating institutions to preserve the community. Muslims believe that the revelation was completed with the work of Muhammad, who is described as the seal of the prophets. The leaders after Muhammad were described only as *khalifahs* (caliphs), or successors to the Prophet, and not as prophets themselves. The first four caliphs were companions of the Prophet and their period of rule (632–661) is described by the majority of Muslims as the age of the Rightly Guided Caliphate. This was an era of expansion during which Muslims conquered the Sasanid (Persian) Empire and took control of the North African and Syrian territories of the Byzantine (Eastern Roman) Empire. The Muslim community was transformed from a small city-state controlling much of the Arabian Peninsula into a major world empire extending from northwest Africa to central Asia.

This era ended with the first civil war (656–661), in which specific conflicts between particular interest groups provided the foundation for the broader political and theological divisions in the community and the Islamic tradition. The first two caliphs, Abu Bakr and Umar, had been successful in maintaining a sense of communal unity. But tensions within the community surfaced during the era of the third caliph, Uthman, who was from the Umayyad clan. Uthman was murdered in 656 by troops who mutinied over matters of pay and privileges, but the murder was the beginning of a major civil war.

The mutinous troops and others in Medina declared the new caliph to be Ali, a cousin of Muhammad who was an early convert and also the husband of Muhammad's daughter Fatimah (and, therefore, the father of Muhammad's only grandsons, Hasan and Husayn). According to Shi'i Muslim tradition, there were many people who believed that Muhammad had designated Ali as his successor. An Arabic term for faction or party is shi'ah, and the party or shi'ah of Ali emerged clearly during this first civil war. Ali's leadership was first challenged by a group including Aisha, the Prophet's most prominent wife and a daughter of the first caliph, Abu Bakr. Although Ali defeated this group militarily, it represented the tradition that became part of the mainstream majority, or Sunni, tradition in Islam, recognizing that all four of the first four caliphs were rightly guided and legitimate.

Ali faced a major military threat from the Umayyad clan, who demanded revenge for the murder of their kinsman, Uthman. The leader of the Umayyads was Muawiya, the governor of Syria. In a battle between the Umayyad army and the forces of Ali at Siffin in 657, Ali agreed to arbitration. As a result, a group of anti-Umayyad extremists withdrew from Ali's forces and became known as the Kharijites, or seceders, who demanded sinlessness as a quality of their leader and would recognize any pious Muslim as eligible to be the caliph. When Ali was murdered by a Kharijite in 661, most Muslims accepted Muawiya as caliph as a way of bringing an end to the intracommunal violence.

Many later divisions within the Muslim community were to be expressed in terms first articulated during this civil war. The mainstream, or Sunni, tradition reflects a combination of an emphasis on the consensus and piety of the community of the Prophet's companions, as reflected in the views of Aisha and her supporters, and the pragmatism of the Umayyad imperial administrators. The Sunni tradition always reflects the tension between the needs of state stability and the aspirations of a more egalitarian and pietistic religious vision. Shi'i Islam has its beginnings in the party of Ali and the argument that God always provides a special guide, or imam, for humans and that this guide has special characteristics, including being a descendant of the Prophet and having special divine guidance. Leadership and authority rest with this imamate and are not subject to human consensus or pragmatic reasons of state.

The Kharijites represent an extreme pietism that expects sinlessness from its leaders and asserts the right of the pious believer to declare others to be unbelievers. Over the centuries, explicitly Kharijite movements have declined in importance within the Muslim world, and by the late twentieth century were represented by small communities in the Arabian Peninsula and North Africa. The spirit of puritanical anarchism, however, although always a minority position within the Muslim community, has continued to provide a marginal but significant critique of existing conditions. Activist, sometimes militant, movements of puritanical renewal that exist throughout Islamic history are sometimes accused of being Kharijite in method if not in theology.

Another major period of civil conflict followed the death in 680 of the first Umayyad caliph, Muawiya. The Umayyad victory by 692 affirmed the pragmatic, consensus-oriented approach of the rising Sunni mainstream. Umayyad military power and the emerging pious elite's fear of anarchy resulted in the majoritarian compromise that is fundamental to Sunni views of society, community, and state. There is a tension between the pragmatic needs of soldiers and politicians and the moral aspirations of religious teachers. The Sunni majority usually accepted the necessary compromises, legitimized by the authority of the consensus of the community.

The main opposition to the structures of the new imperial community came from developing Shi'i traditions. Husayn, Ali's son, and a small group of his supporters were killed by an Umayyad army at Karbala in 680, and Husayn became a symbol of pious martyrdom in the path of God.

When the Umayyads were overthrown in the civil war of 744–750, the core of the revolutionary movement was Shi'ah. Piety-minded scholars, who were increasingly opposed to the worldly materialism of the Umayyads, joined the opposition. The organizers of the revolution were supporters of the Abbasids, the family of Abbas, an uncle of the Prophet, and when an Abbasid was proclaimed caliph following the defeat of the Umayyads, the supporters of the line of Ali remained in opposition. The new Abbasid caliphs reestablished the pragmatic compromise with the pious mainstream, and the Abbasid state succeeded as the new version of the Sunni caliphate.

Caliphs, Sultans, and the New Community

The world of Islam continued to expand, even during periods of civil war. By the mid-eighth century, Muslim conquests extended from the Iberian Peninsula to the inner Asian frontiers of China. The new Muslim state was, in many ways, the successor to the imperial systems of Persia and Rome, but the caliphates were clearly identified with Islam. The boundaries of the state and the Muslim community were basically the same, and the rulers, even when they were not known for piety, were still viewed by the majority as the successors to the Prophet.

It was the people of knowledge, or *ulama,* of the mainstream and not the caliphs who defined Islamic doctrine. Although there were state-appointed judges, Islamic jurisprudence *(fiqh)* was defined by independent ulama. The Sunni majority came to accept four schools of legal thought—the Hanafi, Maliki, Shafi'i, and Hanbali—as legitimate. By the eleventh century the ulama had also compiled authoritative collections of hadith, providing a standard for understanding the Sunnah of the Prophet. In this way, the Sunni tradition developed within the caliphal state but was not identical to it.

By the middle of the tenth century, the effective political and military power of the Abbasid caliphs had been greatly reduced. Power shifted to the military commanders who frequently took the title of sultan, meaning authority or power. The Abbasid caliphs continued to reside in Baghdad and provided formal recognition to sultans. Increasingly, military leadership was Turkish. Turks had come to the Middle East from Central Asia as slaves and mercenaries, but by the eleventh century there was a significant migration of Turkish peoples into the region. In 1055 Turks, under the leadership of the Seljuqs, took control of Baghdad and established a major sultanate in cooperation with the Abbasid caliphs. The new Seljuq sultanate represented a reorganization of Muslim institutions with great patronage for the ulama and establishment of the sultanate as the legitimate political system. This caliph-based sultanate system came to an end when the Mongols invaded the Middle East and conquered Baghdad in 1258.

In the era of the decline of the Sunni caliphate, Shi'i influence increased. During the eighth century Ja'far al-Sadiq,

the sixth imam in the line of succession from Ali, provided the first fully comprehensive statement of Shi'i beliefs that became the basis for subsequent Shi'i mainstream groups. He provided opposition-ideology to the Sunni definition of the community but did not advocate revolution or virulent opposition to the Abbasids. The role of the imam was emphasized, and by the middle of the tenth century the moderate Shi'i mainstream accepted the imamate as spiritual and eschatological guide. This view defined a succession of twelve imams, the last of whom would enter a state of occultation and return as a messiah, or *mahdi,* in the future. The willingness to postpone expectations of a truly Islamic society until that return is an important part of Twelve-Imam (*ithna ashari*) Shi'ism. A minority maintained a more radical opposition, calling for messianic revolt, and identified with Ismail, a son of Sadiq who was not recognized by the Shi'i majority as being in the succession of imams. Ismaili Shi'ism provided the basis for the Fatimid movement in North Africa, which conquered Egypt in the tenth century and established a powerful Shi'i caliphate that lasted for more than two hundred years.

The fall of Baghdad to the Mongols did not mean the end of the sultanates. The military commanders continued to rule as sultans, even in the absence of caliphs, working with ulama and popular societal associations. This system of rule by military commanders without caliphs but identified as defenders and supporters of Islam became common in many parts of the Muslim world. The Mongol advance had been stopped by the Mamluk commanders of Egypt. Mamluks were legally slaves, and in the crisis of the thirteenth century, the commanders simply took control of the state and created a distinctive, self-perpetuating slave elite that ruled Egypt and much of Syria until the early sixteenth century.

In northern India Turkish slave-soldiers established the Delhi Sultanate, and in Anatolia remnants of the Seljuq state provided a basis for a number of Turkish military states, including the Ottomans, who gradually came to dominate the region. Even the Mongol commanders in the Middle East and Central Asia, often with the title of khan rather than sultan, converted to Islam and ruled sultanate-style states. In North Africa caliphal authority had been supplanted in the eleventh and twelfth centuries by first the Almoravids (Murabitun) and then the Almohads (Muwahhidun). Successor states in Morocco, Algeria, and Tunisia were more in the sultanate model.

Although the Muslim world was no longer politically unified, the era of the sultanates was a time of creativity and dynamism when the classical formulations of many aspects of Islamic faith and community were fully articulated. The schools of Islamic law were consolidated and supported by the rulers, and standard texts came to be used throughout the Muslim world.

The traditions of mystic piety, called Sufism in the Islamic world, were formulated in works of people like Abu Hamid al-Ghazali (1058–1111), who promoted acceptance of inner spirituality as an important part of Islamic life, and Muhyi al-Din Ibn al-Arabi (1165–1240), who extended Sufism with a more pantheistic outlook that became the heart of subsequent presentations of Muslim mysticism. More puritanical renewalism received a classic articulation in the works of Ahmad Ibn Taimiyya (1263–1328), who argued that rulers who did not strictly rule in accord with Islamic law should be considered infidels and opposed by jihad if necessary. He defined this position in opposition to the newly converted Mongol rulers of the early fourteenth century, but his works have been an inspiration to many later activist movements.

Spread of Islam

From the end of the effective power of the caliphs in the tenth century to the beginning of the sixteenth, the size of the Muslim world almost doubled. The vehicles for expansion were not conquering armies so much as traveling merchants and itinerant teachers. In Saharan and sub-Saharan Africa, in Central Asia, and in the many different societies in the Indian Ocean basin, a growing number of people came to be included within the world community of Islam.

Islamization usually involved an increasing familiarity with the basic texts and teachings of Islam and an awareness of being part of a larger community of believers. In contrast to early expansion in the Middle East, where monotheistic faiths like Christianity, Judaism, and Zoroastrianism were well established, much of this later growth was in areas where faith traditions were polytheistic or naturalistic. As Muslim teachers and merchants interacted with local rulers, they helped transform political systems that had been based on divine rule or rulers with special naturalistic powers and obligations. In the courts of Java and West Africa, as well as among the shamans of Central Asia, the coming of Islam changed both political structures and popular faith. Often this involved incorporating local beliefs and customs that

created distinctive local Muslim communities within the intercontinental community of believers.

Devotional teachers were also important in the world of the sultanates. The spiritual life associated with Sufism came to be institutionalized in organizations identified by the devotional paths, or *tariqahs,* of famous Sufis. One of the earliest of these was the Qadiriyya Tariqah, tracing itself back to Abd al-Qadir al-Jilani in twelfth-century Baghdad. Because they were tied to popular piety, tariqahs often served to meld local practices with Islamic ideas, and the brotherhoods were a major force in the gradual Islamization of many societies.

By the end of the fifteenth century the Muslim world was very different from what it had been at the height of Abbasid power. No single state could be identified, even in theory, with the whole community of believers. Although the society and culture of the early caliphates were primarily Middle Eastern, the Islamic world of the fifteenth century brought together peoples from different civilizations and nonurban societies. Islam was no longer a faith identified with a particular world region; it had become more universal and cosmopolitan in its articulation and in the nature of the community of believers.

Early Modern Expansion and Transformation

The Muslim world continued to expand in the early modern era. A broad belt of societies undergoing Islamization stretched across the Eastern Hemisphere. More than seven centuries of Muslim rule in the Iberian Peninsula came to an end in 1492 with the completion of the Spanish Christian reconquest. Elsewhere, however, new states and social institutions consolidated the gains of previous centuries and initiated a new wave of growth. Eventually, interaction with the rising states of Europe brought conflict on a global scale, with European military victory but continued conversion of peoples and societies to Islam.

A number of major Islamic states emerged during the sixteenth century. The largest was the Ottoman Empire, which had been expanding from its original base as a Turkish warrior state in western Anatolia. Ottoman forces conquered Constantinople in 1453 and Syria and Egypt in 1516–1517. Under the rule of Sultan Sulayman the Magnificent, virtually all of the Balkan Peninsula became part of the empire in the sixteenth century. In South Asia, Babur, a Central Asian military adventurer, used gunpowder to defeat the Delhi Sultanate and establish the foundations for the Mughal empire. By the end of the reign of Babur's grandson, Akbar, in 1605, the Mughals ruled virtually all of India.

Small military states in Iran were conquered by a new movement, the Safavids. Under Ismail al-Safavi, who proclaimed himself Shah in 1501, the movement was transformed from a Sufi-style organization to a dynastic state. Twelver Shi'ism was proclaimed the official religion and, although most Iranians had been Sunni, Shi'ism soon became the religion of the general population as well.

The empires of Mali and Songhay in West Africa, the merchant city-states of East Africa, the expansion of the Uzbek state under Shaybanid leadership, and the sultanates of the peninsulas and islands of Southeast Asia all reflect the political and social influence of Islamization by the sixteenth century.

By the seventeenth century this picture started to change as empires began to weaken in the face of war and internal strife. Ottoman expansion ceased in the seventeenth century, and the empire lost wars and territories to expanding European states. The Safavids' empire came to an end when Nadir, a military commander, assumed the title of shah. Nadir Shah was militarily successful, but his state collapsed after his death in 1747. The Mughals faced similar internal conflicts, revolts by non-Muslims, and ultimately, conquest by the British. Elsewhere, smaller Muslim states also suffered from civil wars and conquests by outside forces.

During the next two centuries, most of the Muslim world came under direct or indirect European control, and cultural life was increasingly shaped by European influences, although there were important movements of Islamic renewal that also had long-term significance.

European expansion in Muslim areas was relatively limited during the eighteenth century. The Ottoman Empire lost territories, but the continued existence of the empire itself was never in question. In the Indian Ocean basin Islamization continued alongside European expansion. The rise of the Muslim states in Southeast Asia had stopped Portuguese expansion. The Dutch and British often worked with local rulers, and the network of Malay sultanates was preserved by imperial rule. Mughal sultans still ruled even as they lost much effective power to local princes and the British East India Company. Muslim societies in Central Asia were gradually being conquered by the neighboring Russian and Chinese empires in a sequence completed by the end of the nineteenth century. Large Muslim states in West Africa collapsed primarily as a result of internal developments.

Movements of self-conscious reform developed during this transition. Within the Ottoman Empire, leaders like the grand viziers from the Kuprulu family tried to restore administrative and military effectiveness through reform. Some local Ottoman governors also worked to create more efficient and relatively autonomous administrations. In these efforts Islam provided only the background for the political system as a whole. But throughout the Muslim world, there were also movements of reform with explicitly Islamic programs of renewal.

Movements of renewal have been a long-standing part of Islamic history. By the eighteenth century there was a broad repertoire of traditions that Islamically based reform efforts could draw on. In some areas, as Islamization continued, syncretist adaptations would be rejected as non-Islamic by scholars more familiar with the more universal forms of Islam. Scholars who had been on pilgrimage often would oppose local customs on their return. Sometimes this would lead to open conflict with authorities whose position reflected the syncretism of earlier stages of Islamization.

In West Africa a tradition of renewalist jihad developed during the eighteenth century, reaching a climax with the efforts of Uthman Dan Fodio (1754–1817), whose holy war of reform resulted in the establishment of the caliphate of Sokoto in northern Nigeria and a network of related renewalist principalities. One of the last of these jihads was proclaimed by al-Hajj Umar in 1852. Although it began as a more traditional renewalist movement, it soon became a part of the new, nineteenth-century pattern of conflict with European imperialism. Similar movements of reformist jihad, often associated with tariqahs, were established in western China and Southeast Asia.

Scholars interpreted the message of Islamic reform in ways significant even through the twentieth century. In the Arabian Peninsula Muhammad Ibn Abd al-Wahhab (1703–1792) presented an absolutist vision of reform based on a strict interpretation of the Qur'an in the tradition of Ibn Taimiyya. He was supported by a local prince, Muhammad Ibn Saud, laying the foundations for the Saudi state in Arabia and the Wahhabi style of reformism. In south Asia Shah Wali Allah of Delhi attempted a broad synthesis of traditional Muslim legal thought and hadith scholarship. His vision of socio-moral reconstruction inspired generations of south Asia scholars, and his influence is still visible in twentieth-century Muslim intellectual movements. Ahmad Ibn Idris (d. 1837), a North African scholar in Mecca, emphasized the importance of Sufi spiritual piety and organization. His students established a number of tariqahs, like the Sanusiyyah and the Khatmiyyah, that gave birth to organizations of social cohesion, resistance to European imperial expansion, and twentieth-century political parties.

Imperialism and Reform

During the nineteenth century European expansion became an increasingly important force in Muslim societies. Many observers identify the ease with which Napoleon conquered Egypt in 1798 as a symbol of the new era. The major states that remained independent undertook a wide range of reforms, although these were not generally defined in explicitly Islamic terms. Ottoman state reforms began with attempts by Selim III to institute a *Nizam-i cedid,* or "New System," of military and bureaucratic organization. Although he was overthrown in 1807, his successor, Mahmud II, significantly changed both military and administrative institutions. At his death in 1839 Mahmud's successor Abdall-Majid issued an imperial proclamation that enhanced the secular and more liberal aspects of reform as a part of the Tanzimat (reorganization), which led to promulgation of the Ottoman Constitution of 1876. Although advocates of these reforms at times tried to show that they were not contrary to Islam, the programs were not presented as Islamic reform.

In Egypt, Muhammad Ali, the Ottoman governor after French withdrawal, initiated similar reforms, and by the second half of the century, Egypt was virtually independent and undergoing major sociopolitical transformations. Iran was reunified by the conquests of the Qajar dynasty in the 1790s. Qajar Iran remained independent, but the leadership did not initiate significant systematic reforms. Reform did not prevent continued military losses to European powers. Britain occupied Egypt in 1882, the Ottomans lost other territories in the Balkans and North Africa, and Iran was politically and economically dominated by European powers by the end of the century.

The most effective direct resistance to European expansion came from Islamic organizations, although they were also unsuccessful. In West Africa the jihad tradition became an important part of resistance to European expansion, as can be seen in the wars of al-Hajj Umar and his Tijaniyyah forces. In Algeria it was the Amir Abd al-Qadir, with his Qadiriyya organization, that led the strongest opposition to the French invasion in 1830.

In the Caucasus opposition to Russian expansion was strongest from the Naqshbandiyyah, led by the imam Shamil, and at the end of the century, the most visible war against imperialists was the jihad of Muhammad ibn Abdallah in Somalia. The Mahdi in Sudan led a holy war that successfully drove out the modernized Egyptian army, defeated British-led forces, and established a state that lasted from 1884 to 1898, when it was reconquered by Anglo-Egyptian forces. This tradition of resistance continued into the twentieth century, when the Sanusiyyah provided the only effective resistance to the Italian invasion of Libya.

The old-style resistance of the brotherhoods did not create an effective alternative to European expansion in either military or intellectual terms. Intellectual and ideological responses developed during the second half of the nineteenth century. Some of these were Western in style and represented the beginnings of nationalism, but others were more explicitly Islamic. The ideal of pan-Islamic unity was expressed by a number of people, most importantly in the work of Jamal al-Din al-Afghani (1838 or 1839–1897) and, in official terms, by the policies of the Ottoman sultan at the end of the century, Abd al-Hamid II.

The major new development was the emergence of Islamic modernism, in which people in a number of areas worked to create an effective synthesis of Islam and modernity. Muhammad Abduh in Egypt argued that faith and reason were compatible and that Islam was a reason-based faith. He and his student, Rashid Rida, published *al-Manar,* a journal that helped to inspire modernist groups from Morocco to Indonesia. In India Sayyid Ahmad Khan led another major modernist trend, which emphasized the compatibility of scientific understandings of nature with Islam and established a college in Aligarh which combined Islamic and modern Western studies.

The Jadid movement developed in the Russian Empire under the inspiration of Ismail Gasprinskii, whose periodical *Tarjuman* was widely read. The Jadid curriculum for schools combined Russian and Muslim traditions. Islamic modernists tended to accept the realities of European military domination, working to reform Muslim societies from within and create a synthesis that could be both effectively modern and authentically Islamic.

Muslims in the Twentieth Century

World War I was the beginning of a new era in the history of Islam. The last of the older Muslim political systems came to an end in the aftermath of the war. The Ottoman

Empire, which had been allied with Germany, was defeated and occupied, and the sultanate was formally abolished as a part of the reforms of the new Turkish nationalism led by Mustafa Kemal Atatürk. The Qajar dynasty in Iran was overthrown and, although the monarchy was retained, Reza Shah, the new leader, worked to create a new state system.

Both Kemal Atatürk and Reza Shah were secularists who worked to limit the influence of Islamic institutions. In most of the rest of the Muslim world, similar Westernizing reform and the development of more secularist nationalism dominated. In this, Islam was not rejected but it did not define the central concerns of emerging Arab nationalism in the Fertile Crescent or of Egyptian nationalism under Sa'd Zaghloul.

In the period between the two world wars, some explicitly Islamic movements emerged, but they usually developed in the context of more secular radicalism or nationalism. Islamic perspectives ranged from those of the Communist intellectual, Mir Said Sultangaliev, whose efforts to create a national communism for Muslims within the revolutionary movement ended when he was purged by Soviet leader Joseph Stalin, to the *Manar*-influenced Association of Algerian Ulama, which protested the growth of a French-inspired intellectual elite in North Africa and sought to affirm the Islamic base of Algerian culture.

Indian Muslims began to define their communal identity in terms of Indian nationalism. Some like Abu al-Kalam Azad worked closely with the Indian National Congress Party and advocated Hindu-Muslim nationalist cooperation. At the end of World War I Azad and others mobilized Muslim opinion through the Khalifat movement supporting the preservation of the Ottoman caliphate and working with the National Congress in opposition to British imperial policy. Other Indian Muslims began to define themselves as a separate community, which ultimately led to the partition of India when it achieved independence in 1947 and the creation of the Muslim state of Pakistan. A leader in this movement was Muhammad Iqbal, who was also important in the continuing development of Islamic modernist thought, further synthesizing Western philosophy and Islamic thought.

In a few isolated areas states maintained older Islamic traditions of rule in the 1920s–1930s. In southern Arabia Zaydi Shi'i imams ruled with the support of conservative mountain peoples in Yemen, and the Kharijite state of the sultans of Oman continued. In central Arabia the Wahhabi religious and political tradition was revived under the leadership of Abd al-Aziz Ibn Saud (c. 1888–1953), whose conquests in the

first three decades of the century created the basis for the Kingdom of Saudi Arabia. Neither nationalist nor modernist, the new Saudi state was a distinctive attempt to carry out a strict interpretation of traditional Islamic law.

New movements advocating a more direct adoption of Islam in modern society also developed. Their followers came from the modern educated elements in society, and their leadership was not explicitly ulama in background. Among the most important of these movements were the Muslim Brotherhood, established in Egypt in 1928 by Hasan al-Banna (1906–1949), and the Jama'at-i Islami (Islamic Society), founded in India in 1941 under the leadership of Mawlana Abu al-Ala Mawdudi (1903–1979). These groups, and others like them, opposed the more traditional, popular Islamic practices and conservative ulama, as well as criticized the secularism of the Westernizers. They argued that Islam defined a whole way of life and should be applied in economics and politics as well as in individual religious life.

In the second half of the twentieth century Muslim societies became politically independent as the era of European imperialism came to an end. A final step in this process was the end of the Soviet Union and the emergence of new states in Muslim-majority areas of the old Russian Empire in the 1990s. Nationalism and the rise of Western-style radicalism were the most visible political dynamics in the first three decades after World War II as states in the Middle East and South and Southeast Asia gained their independence. In the already independent states of Turkey, Iran, and Saudi Arabia, political patterns established in the interwar era continued, with Turkey committed to upholding a democratic Kemalism, Iran to continuing Reza Shah's Westernizing reforms under the leadership of his son, Muhammad Reza Shah, and Saudi Arabia to maintaining its strict Islamist approach in the new context of great wealth from the sale of oil.

In some of the newly independent states, socially conservative interpretations of Islam legitimized monarchies. In Morocco, Jordan, Oman, and Malaysia, these monarchies continued through the end of the century, although monarchies were overthrown by more secular and radical movements in Egypt (1952), Tunisia (1957), Iraq (1958), Yemen (1962), and Afghanistan (1973). In Iran the monarchy was overthrown in 1979 by an Islamic revolution, a major indication of the resurgence of political Islam in the late twentieth century. In other areas older elites were also overthrown or displaced by newer and frequently more ideologically radical groups. By the 1960s Western-style radicalism was the most dynamic element in the politics of the newly independent Muslim world. The most visible leaders were people like Sekou Toure in Guinea, Gamal Abdel Nasser in Egypt, and Sukarno in Indonesia and parties like the National Liberation Front, which spearheaded the war for Algerian independence, and the Ba'th (Arab Socialist) Party in Syria and Iraq.

This new radicalism did not directly reject Islam. It often attempted to include Islamic images in its platforms, sometimes talking about Islamic socialism, but the creation of Islamic societies or implementation of Qur'anic rules was not a prominent feature of ideologies or programs.

Rise of Islamist Movements

Movements with primarily Islamic identification existed, but with less political influence. Pakistan, as an explicitly Islamic state, was unable to develop a clear constitutional self-definition. Internal divisions led to a civil war in 1971 and the secession of Bengal as independent Bangladesh. The Jama'at-i Islami continued to advocate its Islamist program and was respected but had limited political influence.

The Muslim Brotherhood in Egypt cooperated briefly with the new military revolutionaries led by Nasser, but they were suppressed in 1954. In the 1960s the Brotherhood message was reshaped into more radical terms by Sayyid Qutb, who condemned Westernized societies as being ruled by sinful ignorance (*jahiliyyah*) and called for jihad against existing states in Muslim societies. Qutb was executed in 1966, but his writings laid the foundation for a new generation of underground Muslim revolutionaries. During the 1970s movements like Islamic Jihad and Takfir wal-Hijrah in Egypt may have differed in doctrinal specifics from Qutb, but they followed his mode of analysis. In many areas of the Muslim world, Qutb helped to define Islamic revolution.

There were other Muslim movements of revolutionary opposition to the establishment of the nationalist and sometimes socialist states. The Darul Islam movement in Indonesia fought a jihad against the new state from 1948 until its founder's execution in 1962. In Iran the Fida'iyan-i Islam was created in 1945, advocating a strict application of Islamic law and engaging in a series of terrorist assassinations. The organization ended with the execution of its founder in 1956, but former members were a part of later militant antigovernment groups.

Other Islamic organizations opposed to the increasing secularism and Westernization of Muslim societies adopted methods of education and mission to transform and Islamize societies. One of the largest Muslim associations in the world is the Tablighi Jama'at (in Urdu, "Party which Propagates"), which began as a devotional and educational organization in northern India in the 1920s. After World War II the movement spread rapidly throughout the world among Muslims in Western Europe and North America, as well as in Muslim societies. Many of the established Sufi orders have also adapted themselves to the conditions of modern society and quietly grew to be large devotional associations in virtually every Muslim community. In the United States a major movement developed among African Americans that was self-identified as Muslim, but this Nation of Islam association created by Elijah Muhammad (1897–1975) was not recognized as Islamic by most Muslims because of its distinctive doctrines of black separatism. But Malcolm X, a major figure in the movement, broke with its leaders in the mid-1960s and espoused a more mainstream Islamic perspective. When Elijah Muhammad died in 1975, he was succeeded by his son, Imam Warith Deen Muhammad, who transformed the movement into a clearly Sunni Muslim one. A smaller organization led by Louis Farrakhan continued to advocate the older black nationalist and separatist beliefs.

The Islamic Resurgence

A new Islamic spirit of renewal gained increasing visibility in the final quarter of the twentieth century. The most dramatic manifestation of this was the Islamic revolution in Iran. Secular and Islamic opposition to the autocratic rule of the shah increased in intensity during the 1970s. Leftist definitions of resistance had little appeal, and opponents increasingly mobilized around Islamic aspirations. Ali Shariati, who died under suspicious circumstances in 1977, presented a call for a rejection of state Shi'ism, advocating an egalitarian program of social justice that some saw as an Islamic form of Marxism.

The central figure of the revolution and the republic it created was Ayatollah Ruholla Khomeini. He declared the possibility of an authentically Islamic state, even in the absence of the imam, if it represented the rule of the Islamic legal scholars (*wilayat al-faqih*). The constitution of the new republic created a system that survived a series of major political crises, including a long and costly war with Iraq in the 1980s and the death of Khomeini in 1989. Political life was strictly controlled, and minorities and opposition groups were suppressed. But within the limitations of the constitution, there was a remarkable degree of debate and disagreement over policy, which was confirmed in the presidential elections of 1997, when an advocate of a more open but still Islamically committed line of policy decisively defeated a more hard-line candidate supported by the more conservative clergy.

As leftist ideologies and nationalist state policies proved ineffective in coping with the social, economic, and political transformations of the late twentieth century, there was a significant shift to more Islamically oriented approaches throughout the Muslim world. This frequently was centered in movements of modern-educated professionals and students that neither advocated Qutb-style jihad nor accepted conservative ulama leadership. They viewed Islam as providing a comprehensive program for society but generally worked for the gradual Islamization of state and society rather than a revolutionary overthrow of existing institutions.

A variety of Islamic groups developed in Egypt that were separate from the Muslim Brotherhood although similar in aspirations. Former student militants became leaders of professional syndicates in the mid-1980s and helped to direct official policy and general public opinion in a more openly Islamic direction. In Malaysia the Islamic student movement ABIM was an important force on campuses, and in the 1980s its leader, Anwar Ibrahim, became a major political figure in the leading political coalition. The Islamic Tendency Movement in Tunisia gained political influence during the 1980s under the leadership of Rashid al-Ghanoushi. Although it was suppressed and its leadership jailed or exiled, in its reorganized form as the Nahda Party in the late 1980s and 1990s, al-Ghanoushi and most of the movement continued to advocate democratic participation rather than violent revolution.

In Algeria the emergence of political Islam as a major force took place quite rapidly when the National Liberation Front, facing demands for greater political participation, agreed to hold competitive elections. The Islamic Salvation Front won municipal elections in 1990 and was on the verge of gaining control of the national parliament when a military coup suspended the election in 1992. Throughout the 1990s open conflict between government and Islamist forces caused more than sixty thousand deaths.

Among Palestinian activists an Islamist movement, Hamas, developed alongside the long-established Palestine Liberation Organization led by Yasir Arafat (1929–) and won significant support among those who mistrusted Arafat for his willingness to negotiate with Israel. Even in Turkey, where religion-based political parties are illegal, the Welfare Party, which advocated a greater formal Islamization of Turkish life, won more than 20 percent of the vote in national elections in 1996, and, in a highly divided electorate, its leader, Nejmettim Erbakan, served as prime minister in a coalition government until pressure from the Kemalist Turkish military forced him to resign in 1997.

The only country outside of Iran in which an Islamist movement came to power was Sudan. The Sudanese Muslim Brotherhood had been organized in the early 1950s and had participated actively in the politics of the parliamentary periods in 1956–1958 and 1964–1969 but had never had much electoral success. As an active political party in the third era of multiparty politics (1985–1989), the Brotherhood, reorganized as the National Islamic Front, was an important but minority force, winning about 20 percent of the votes. The military coup in 1989 was led by Islamically oriented officers who soon became closely identified with the front and its leader, Hasan al-Turabi. Turabi had an international reputation as an imaginative advocate of renewal and rethinking the foundations of Islamic law. He helped the regime establish a system of elective consultative councils and application of Islamic law, but the suppression of minorities and opposition in a brutal civil war raised doubts about the long-term Islamic significance of the Sudanese experience.

The New Islamists

In the 1980s and 1990s, the position of Islamic activist movements and advocates of greater Islamization of public and private life changed dramatically. In the heyday of radical socialism in the 1960s, such groups were marginal. In the 1970s they came to be viewed in many areas as a dangerous militant minority that could disrupt society through terrorism. But by the 1980s, political Islam had become an important part of the mainstream of politics in the Muslim world. The threat of groups like Nahda in Tunisia and the Islamic Salvation Front in Algeria was that they might be able, through democratic processes, to win the support of a majority and gain control of governments.

At the end of the twentieth century the Muslim world continued to change under the influence of a new generation of Islamically active intellectuals. In the new thinking there was still an emphasis on the importance of the Islamic message for all aspects of life, but this did not mean an adherence to older, comprehensive political programs or a demand for uniformity in acceptance of Islamic ideals. Muslim intellectuals accepted pluralism in a global context, not just as a practical necessity but as a positive aspect of life, and were open to historical, critical analysis of the foundations of the faith and the Islamic tradition.

In Iran Abd al-Karim Soroush, who supported the Islamic revolution and republic, argued that Islam should provide values and norms for all of life but should not be turned into a political ideology. A Syrian intellectual, Shahrur, wrote a widely read and influential analysis of the sources of Islamic law in terms of their historical context and evolution. Some older scholars whose work received little attention became more visible. Mohammed Arkoun, an Algerian living in Paris, criticized both the tyranny of old-style reason and the rigidity of religious fundamentalism. Egyptian philosopher Hasan Hanafi had been working since the 1960s to define an Islamic theology of liberation, and his critical methodological approach received increasing attention by the 1990s. Sudanese thinker Mahmoud Muhammad Taha presented a dramatic reinterpretation of the Islamic experience, distinguishing between the general principles presented in the revelation, which are universally applicable, and the specific rules that in his view were meant to be applied only in particular circumstances. After his execution for apostasy by Jafar Numayri in 1985, a growing number of Muslims have been influenced by at least some aspects of his thought.

Some of the new thinkers come from Muslim minority communities whose works can now be read by Muslims throughout the world. For example, the writings of Farid Esack, a South African Muslim who was active in the African National Congress's struggle against apartheid, are gaining visibility.

The Islamic experience over the centuries provides a rich repertoire out of which social institutions and political systems can be created, and Muslim societies in the modern era vary in their interpretations of that repertoire. Even specific movements like Islamist renewals are not monolithic or identical. But despite these differences, all Muslims continued to affirm the basic core of the faith in monotheism as defined by the revelation to Muhammad and preserved in the Qur'an.

See also *al-Afghani, Jamal al-Din; Ahmad Khan, Sir Sayyid; Algeria; Atatürk, Kemal; Banna, Hasan al-; Crusades; Egypt; Ibn Taimiyya; India; Indonesia; Iqbal, Muhammad; Iran; Jihad; Khomeini, Ruholla Musavi; Mahdi; Malaysia; Mawdudi; Mecca;* *Morocco; Muhammad; Muslim encounters with the West; Nasser, Gamal Abdel; Nation of Islam; Pakistan; Qutb, Sayyid; Sudan; Sufism; Sukarno, Achmad; Syria; Turkey.*

John O. Voll

BIBLIOGRAPHY

Abu-Rabi, Ibrahim M. *Intellectual Origins of Islamic Resurgence in the Modern Arab World.* Albany: State University of New York Press, 1995.

Ahmed, Akbar S. *Discovering Islam: Making Sense of Muslim History and Society.* London: Routledge, 1988.

Esposito, John L. *Islam, The Straight Path.* New York: Oxford University Press, 1991.

———, ed. *The Oxford Encyclopedia of the Modern Islamic World.* New York: Oxford University Press, 1995.

Hodgson, Marshall G. S. *The Venture of Islam.* Chicago: University of Chicago Press, 1974.

Hourani, Albert. *Arabic Thought in the Liberal Age, 1798–1939.* New York: Cambridge University Press, 1983.

Keddie, Nikki R. *Roots of Revolution: An Interpretive History of Modern Iran.* New Haven: Yale University Press, 1981.

Lapidus, Ira. *A History of Islamic Societies.* New York: Cambridge University Press, 1990.

Lee, Robert D. *Overcoming Tradition and Modernity: The Search for Islamic Authenticity.* Boulder, Colo.: Westview Press, 1997.

Lewis, Bernard. *Islam and the West.* New York: Oxford University Press, 1993.

Rahnema, Ali, ed. *Pioneers of Islamic Revival.* London: Zed, 1994.

Voll, John Obert. *Islam, Continuity, and Change in the Modern World.* 2d ed. Syracuse, N.Y.: Syracuse University Press, 1994.

Islam, Nation of

See *Nation of Islam*

Islam, Southeast Asian

Far from the Middle Eastern terrains conventionally identified with Islam, Southeast Asia is home to the largest majority-Muslim country in the world (Indonesia) and contains an aggregate Muslim population in excess of that of the Arab Middle East. Stretching across Indonesia, Malaysia, Brunei, Singapore, southern Thailand, and the southern Philippines, the Muslim population of this region is made up of hundreds of ethnic groups, most of whom live alongside representatives of other world religions.

Southeast Asia's pluralism has left its mark on the local

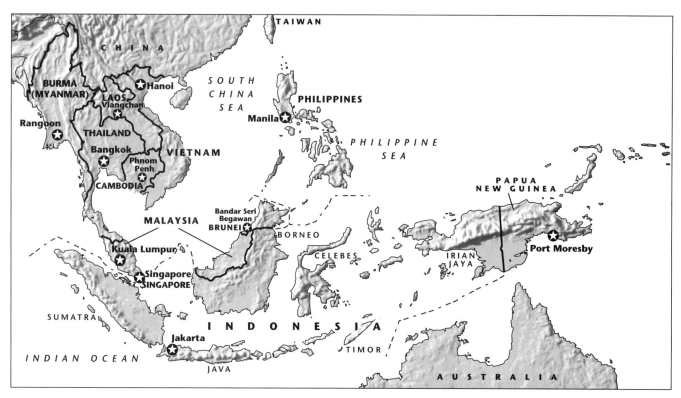

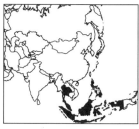

practice of Islam. This is a region where Islam has long been characterized by a high measure of social tolerance, an eclectic attitude toward Islamic law, and the elevated status of women. Since the late 1970s, this same region has experienced an Islamic resurgence of unprecedented proportions. The revival has raised new questions about the proper relationship of religion and state, and it has set in motion a religious reformation with profound implications for the Muslim world as a whole.

Premodern Precedents

For many years Western scholars believed that the most distinctive quality of Islam in Southeast Asia was the strength of "pre-Islamic" survivals in ritual, belief, and the arts. By comparison with Persia and the Arab heartland, it is true that Islam became a civilizational force in Southeast Asia late in the region's history, long after most of its kingdoms had assimilated a rich assortment of Hindu-Buddhist influences. These non-Islamic influences are still apparent in the classical arts, as well as in some folk rituals and beliefs.

Although Islam had distinctive characteristics in Southeast Asia, comparable influences from other religions were

also found in many other parts of the Islamic world. The more distinctive feature of Southeast Asian Islam is not the presence of pre-Islamic survivals but the region's intellectual and organizational pluralism. Southeast Asian Islam has long been characterized by varied modes of piety and politics. The historical origins of this pluralism lay in the fact that, unlike in much of the Middle East, Islam was not introduced to the region by world-conquering potentates but through trade and a network of city-states dispersed across the region. This multicentric pattern of political organization was reinforced during the colonial era, when European authorities limited the influence of Islam in government. Elements of this pluralistic pattern have survived to this day, in a manner that has helped to make Southeast Asian Islam among the most theologically liberal in the world.

The first Islamic settlement in Southeast Asia was established in the late thirteenth century in a port in northern Sumatra known for its role in the trade with Arabia and Muslim India. In the fifteenth and sixteenth centuries the new religion spread east, first to trading towns along Java's north coast, and then to the Malay Peninsula and present-day southern Thailand. By the late seventeenth century Islam had completed its eastward journey, becoming the predominant religion in coastal principalities across eastern Indonesia and the southern Philippines. The primary impetus for conversion was the Muslim role in the trade linking India, Southeast Asia, and China. Interior portions of the islands of Southeast Asia and agrarian states on the mainland were less directly involved in this pan-Asian trade and experienced a dramatically lower incidence of Muslim conversion.

The diffusion of Islam to Southeast Asia occurred at a time when Sufism exercised great influence in Persia, the Arabian peninsula, and northern India, areas to which Southeast Asian traders regularly traveled. Sufism is a generic term for a variety of Islamic mystical traditions, the unifying characteristics of which are believers' concern for personal awareness of divinity and a less stringent emphasis on Islamic law (shari'a). Sufi literature and ritual were among the first items appropriated into popular Islam in Southeast Asia. The ease with which this transfer occurred was related to the fact that Sufism shared certain qualities with the region's earlier Hindu-Buddhist traditions, including the belief that, rather than standing apart from the world, divinity infuses it. In the works of such learned mystics as Hamzah Fansuri and Abd al-Rauf, Southeast Asian Muslims developed a literary variant of Islamic mysticism among the richest in the world. Although reformists in the twentieth century have challenged many Sufi traditions, mystical beliefs figure in popular Islam to this day.

The impact of Sufi ideas was not limited to spiritual matters. Local kings involved in the Asian trade were among the first converts. As was the case in Persia and northern India, court-based variants of Islam emphasized that the ruler, rather than religious jurists (ulama), was the central authority in religious matters. The sultan, or raja, was identified as the defender of the faithful, the "shadow of Allah on earth," and, consistent with Sufi traditions, a mystically wondrous "perfect man." The ruler also decided which elements of Islamic law were to be implemented in society. Although a few applied it strictly, most rulers were highly selective in their application of Islamic law. The courts' flexibility on legal matters was conducive to the proliferation of diverse mystical groups and folk-Islamic traditions. Indeed, in general there were a variety of practices of Islam, and no single authority imposed its will on the Muslim community as a whole.

Unlike many Middle Eastern countries, this pluralistic pattern was reinforced rather than diminished in the colonial era. In the Dutch East Indies, in particular (a territory that is today the nation of Indonesia), the colonial government enforced a strict separation of religion and state, and in

so doing pushed Muslim institutions away from the state and out into society. In the nineteenth century a network of Qur'anic schools spread across Java and other parts of Indonesia, exposing many ordinary Muslims to orthodox learning for the first time. This vast educational network was managed independently of the colonial state. A similar pattern of civic independence characterized Islamic institutional development in southern Thailand and the Philippines. The pattern was less pronounced in colonial Malaya. Building on their experience with Muslims in India, the British in Malaya sought to depoliticize Islam but nonetheless encouraged rulers to play a central role in the management of religious institutions.

Reform and Resurgence

In the first decades of the twentieth century, Southeast Asia witnessed new movements of Islamic reform demanding far-reaching changes in religion and public ethics. Influenced by new trends emanating from the Middle East, the reformists emphasized the self-sufficiency of scripture and decried what they regarded as unacceptable "innovations" in matters of worship. They were especially critical of folk and courtly traditions, which, they felt, sanctioned polytheistic deviations from Islam. They also criticized what they saw as the elitist conservatism of traditional religious jurists, insisting that all Muslims must study the Qur'an and abide by its strictures. Welcoming such Western innovations as modern science and mass education, the reformists were determined to create a modern and progressive Muslim community.

After the Second World War, which ended in 1945, the reform groups made great headway in reshaping public institutions, especially in Malaysia and Indonesia. By the early 1970s they had succeeded in abolishing numerous indigenous traditions they believed were contrary to Islam. In the 1980s (and benefiting from considerable government support in Malaysia and Indonesia), they helped to bring about an Islamic revival of historically unprecedented proportions. Mosques were erected in towns and villages across insular Southeast Asia; religious schools and devotional programs expanded; a vast market in Islamic books, magazines, and newspapers developed; and, very important, a well-educated Muslim middle class began to raise questions about a host of characteristically modern concerns, including the status of women, the challenge of pluralism, and the role of morality in market economies.

The resurgence has complicated but not done away with

the intellectual and organizational pluralism of the Muslim community. The resurgence ushered in a new style of religious activism that challenged the traditionalist jurists and sought to open religious discussions to a wider public and a broader range of social concerns. In place of esoteric doctrine, these "new Muslim intellectuals," as they are known, see Islam as a source of practical and systematic knowledge, relevant to the challenges of the modern age.

Although in some parts of the world the new Islamic movements have sought the establishment of a unitary Islamic state, their most striking feature in Southeast Asia has been the diversity of their adherents' political views. Inspired by Middle Eastern Islamic brotherhoods and Iran's Islamic revolution (1978–1979) that toppled the monarchy, a small minority among the new Muslim intellectuals have demanded the establishment of an Islamic state. For these purists, Islam is a "total way of life" and allows no separation of religion from government. These activists see the multicentered pluralism of Southeast Asian Islam as a source of political weakness, rather than a precedent for modern civility. In their eyes, too, concepts of civil society and pluralist democracy have a decidedly Christian air, amounting to an abnegation of what they believe is most essential among Islam's ideals: that religion should serve as the groundwork for the total reformation of society.

Among most Southeast Asian Muslims, however, this totalizing view of Islamic politics remains a decidedly minority view. In Indonesia the 1970s and 1980s saw the emergence of a theologically liberal movement for Islamic revitalization known as the "renewal" group. The renewalists deny that Islam requires the establishment of an Islamic state and advocate a system of government based on religious tolerance, constitutional protections, and civil freedoms. The religious precedents for such ideals, the renewalists insist, go back to the Medina Charter, worked out among Muslims and Jews in the city of Medina during the rule of the prophet Muhammad. The renewalists also criticize the leaders of Indonesia's Islamic parties, who in the 1950s and early 1960s were locked in a bitter struggle with the Indonesian Communist Party. By the late 1950s the communists had established themselves as the largest of Indonesia's political parties, and the largest communist party in the noncommunist world. In response, many Islamic leaders renounced their earlier commitment to a nonconfessional state and demanded the establishment of an Islamic state.

In renewalists' eyes, this politicization of Islam distracted Indonesian Muslims from their proper spiritual and social goals. Worse yet, it created an environment in which nominal Muslims of secular and socialist persuasion came to see Islam as their enemy. The resulting religious tensions, the renewalists insist, contributed to the breakdown of Indonesian society during 1965–1966. At that time, in the aftermath of a failed military coup by left-wing officers, Muslim militants and anticommunist officers in the armed forces joined in a campaign against the Indonesian Communist Party, slaughtering as many as a half-million people. The aftermath of the killings saw some two million nominal Muslims repudiate Islam for Christianity and Hinduism, effecting the largest mass conversion from Islam in modern history. In the face of these and other developments, Indonesia's Muslim liberals in the 1970s and 1980s emphasized that Islam must not be profaned through too direct association with political intrigues. One of the most famous of the renewalists, Nurcholish Madjid, went further, insisting that Islam is consistent with the desacralization or "secularization" of the state and political parties. Other Indonesian Muslim leaders have shown similar boldness. In recent years, one of the most outspoken critics of the military government has been Abdurrahman Wahid, the leader of Indonesia's largest Muslim organization, the Nahdatul Ulama. In addition to calling for greater democracy and the rule of law, Wahid has been an ardent defender of religious minorities and a tireless critic of Muslim radicals.

Historically, Muslim leaders in Malaysia have been less daring than their Indonesian counterparts, but in recent years they too have introduced many bold innovations. Unlike in Indonesia, the Islamic resurgence that swept Malaysia in the 1970s and 1980s at first had an explicitly anti-Chinese emphasis. Making up a third of the entire population, Chinese dominate the economy, and violence between Chinese and Malays has broken out several times since the Second World War. However, as the ranks of the Muslim middle class have grown, ethnic tensions have diminished, and the Muslim leadership has shown a new confidence in the viability of Malaysia's multireligious federation and in a pluralist understanding of Islam.

In the Philippines and southern Thailand, the relationship between Muslims and the nation-state has been more complex. In both regions, Muslims have attempted to defend their social dominance in areas of their historic settlement. In recent years (especially in the Philippines) this dominance has been threatened by an influx of non-Muslims from other parts of the country. Muslims in both countries have also sought to diminish their marginalization in national institutions controlled by non-Muslim majorities. Some militants have responded to this marginalization by demanding the establishment of an independent Islamic state. Most, however, have sought greater political protections within the framework of a multireligious state.

From Pluralism to Civil Tolerance

Southeast Asian Islam reminds us that, contrary to some recent claims, there is no single, "civilizational" pattern to Islamic politics. Southeast Asian Muslims are varied in their political views and include in their ranks many ardent democrats and social liberals. A few Southeast Asian Muslims lament the Muslim community's pluralism, seeing it as a hindrance in their efforts to promote a unitary Islamic state. But a larger number believe that this pluralism may well be a blessing in disguise, one that allows them to renounce the myth of the Islamic state in favor of pluralism, tolerance, and civil values. Of course, even theological liberals reject the Western secularist argument that there must be a high wall between religion and state and that religion should remain a "private" matter. On this point, however, their views are consistent with many religious Westerners, who also insist that there should be no establishment of religion in state but that religion can and should play a role in public life.

Whether, in the long run, Islamic liberalism predominates in Southeast Asia will depend on more than the force of religious ideas alone. Southeast Asia has other political precedents that owe little to Islam, some of which are hostile to civic independence and pluralism. Attempts by the Indonesian government from 1996 to 1998 to split secular democrats from Muslim activists in the pro-democracy movement provide one illustration of this problem. The prominent role of democratic Muslims in overthrowing Suharto in May 1998, however, shows that those forces are not insurmountable. These and other events indicate that Islamic politics in Southeast Asia owes less to the timeless precedents of "civilizational identities," as claimed by some Western observers, than to contemporary reconfigurations of religious aspirations.

See also *Civil society; Islam; Pluralism;* specific countries.

Robert W. Hefner

BIBLIOGRAPHY

Che Man, W. K. *Muslim Separatism: The Moros of Southern Philippines and the Malays of Southern Thailand.* New York: Oxford University Press, 1990.

Geertz, Clifford. *The Religion of Java.* New York: Free Press, 1960.
Hefner, Robert W., and Patricia Horvatich, eds. *Islam in an Era of Nation-States: Politics and Religious Renewal in Muslim Southeast Asia.* Honolulu: University of Hawaii Press, 1997.
Hooker, M. B., ed. *Islam in South-East Asia.* Leiden: E. J. Brill, 1983.
Ibrahim, Ahmad, Sharon Siddique, and Yasmin Hussain, eds. *Readings on Islam in Southeast Asia.* Singapore: Institute of Southeast Asian Studies, 1985.
Mutalib, Hussin. *Islam and Ethnicity in Malay Politics.* New York: Oxford University Press, 1990.
Nagata, Judith. *The Reflowering of Malaysian Islam: Modern Religious Radicals and Their Roots.* Vancouver: University of British Columbia Press, 1984.
Reid, Anthony. *Southeast Asia in the Age of Commerce, 1450–1680.* Vol. 2, *Expansion and Crisis.* New Haven: Yale University Press, 1993.

Israel

Established as a state in 1948, the product of Zionism, the Jewish nationalist movement, Israel is bounded on the north by Lebanon, northeast by Syria, east by Jordan, southwest by Egypt, and west by the Mediterranean Sea. About 82 percent of the approximately 5.4 million Israelis are Jews; the rest are Muslim, with smaller Christian and Druze communities.

The area of Israel before the June 1967 war against Egypt, Jordan, and Syria (aided by Iraq, Kuwait, Saudi Arabia, Sudan, and Algeria) was about 21,000 square kilometers. Acquired after the war were territories comprising about 7,500 square kilometers. These territories have caused intense conflict between Israel and its neighbors, and among Israelis. Many Israelis who want to retain the territories view them as the God-given patrimony of the patriarchs and kings of biblical Israel: Jewish settlement is a fulfillment of God's will and a prerequisite for the coming of the messianic age. Thus religion is central to the most important political questions facing Israel today, but it has always played a role in Israeli politics.

Background to the State

In the pre-state Jewish community of Palestine there were two major religious parties, which differed in their orientation toward Zionism. Mizrahi, founded in 1902 in eastern Europe, supported the Zionist enterprise in Palestine because its adherents saw in the resettlement of the land—even if by secularists acting unawares—the hand of the divine. Agudat Israel, founded in Germany in 1912, interpreted the

Zionist enterprise as a usurpation of God's own messianic (and unknowable) timetable.

After World War I the League of Nations formally approved, in 1922, the terms of a British mandate over Palestine. These terms recognized "the historical connection of the Jewish people with Palestine" and called on mandate authorities to help "secure the establishment of a Jewish National Home." To this end, the Jewish Agency instituted by the World Zionist Organization undertook formal representation of the Palestinian Jewish community to the mandatory power. It also coordinated efforts within the sometimes fractious Jewish community itself. Mainly, it helped to establish an extensive infrastructure in the Jewish sector of Palestine—quite separate from the Arab sector—that included an elected assembly and national executive council, a Hebrew school system (including universities and technical colleges), a confederation of labor, banks, a social welfare system, and a Jewish defense force (the Haganah) that became the core of Israel's army after independence.

During the mandate, as the Jewish population increased through immigration, tensions began to mount between Arabs and Jews. There were riots in 1929 and much more serious violence—called "disturbances" by Jews and "the revolt" by Arabs—beginning in 1936.

The State of Israel

By the end of the mandate, many of the institutions of a sovereign state were already in place. An elected assembly presaged the Knesset (parliament), the Jewish Agency had executive functions, and various militia formed the basis of the Israeli army. There were also many political parties, from religious to secular and leftist-socialist to rightist-capitalist. The political system of the new state was designed to be inclusive, excluding only those parties that rejected the Zionist premise of the polity: the ultra-Orthodox, Arabs, and communists. As the extent of the European Holocaust became known after World War II, the anti-Zionist Agudat Israel softened its anti-Zionism in return for concessions from the new state. These concessions, gained in 1947 from the Jewish Agency, became known as the "status quo agreement." They formed the basis for the institutionalization of Judaism in postindependence Israel.

According to this agreement, the Jewish Shabbat would be the official day of rest for Jews, and the observation of dietary laws (*kashrut*) would be maintained in governmental institutions, especially the army. The existing Mizrahi religious school system would remain separate from secular schools but, as part of the national education system, would receive funding from the state; ultra-Orthodox (including Agudat Israel) schools would also remain separate and outside the national system, retaining their autonomy entirely. Ultra-Orthodox youth would be exempt from army service, and rabbinical courts would decide on matters of personal status (such as marriage, divorce, or inheritance) concerning Jews.

Under this agreement, other religious institutions such as the joint Chief Rabbinate and rabbinical council originally established in 1921 became organs of the state, along with a new Ministry of Religious Affairs. Although mainly concerned with the Jewish community, this ministry also supervises local religious councils and religious courts of the non-Jewish communities in Israel, including all Muslim religious endowments. Among Christians, Greek Catholic, Greek Orthodox, Latin, Maronite, and Arab Anglican communities operate their own courts, with jurisdiction over matters of their respective religious laws and personal status. Since 1962 separate Druze courts have also operated in Israel.

The religious parties saw the status quo agreement as a baseline and sought to extend its reach whenever they could. Although between two-thirds and three-quarters of Jewish Israelis are not religiously observant and do not vote for the religious parties, the Orthodox minority has been able to exercise disproportionate power because the electoral system by which members of the Knesset (and prime minister until 1996, when direct election was instituted) are chosen is a proportional list system. The Knesset, a unicameral legislative body of 120 members serving four-year terms, is voted on by Israelis constituting a single constituency. The parties put forth lists of candidates, and Knesset members are selected from them in proportion to the votes the party as a whole received. The threshold for election is very low—1.5 percent of the vote. Originally, the party with the largest proportion of votes was asked by the president (elected by the Knesset for a five-year term) to form a government; now the elected prime minister does so. Because no party has ever received an absolute majority in national elections, the "winning" party has always had to form a coalition government with other parties. In negotiating coalition agreements, smaller parties extract promises and resources in return for their support. The religious parties have pushed especially for stricter (Orthodox) definitions of "who is a Jew," leading to conflict and calls for electoral reform by secular Israelis.

The Rise of Political Judaism

The connection between religion and politics runs deeper than do electoral mechanisms. For example, many of the symbols of Judaism pervade public life, and political leaders use aspects of Judaism selectively in the service of nationalism or social integration. But, since the late 1970s, a much greater range of traditional Jewish symbols have come into Israeli political discourse. Groups such as Gush Emunim (Bloc of the Faithful) oppose the return of the territories occupied since the 1967 war for religious reasons rather than primarily for strategic or security reasons. For them, the return to Israel's control of the biblical heartland of ancient Israel—Judaea, Samaria, and Zion (Jerusalem)—marked the beginning of a divinely inspired messianic era. To relinquish the territories is thus to risk the wrath of God. Many of the Jewish settlers in the territories are there for religious reasons and will not be easily persuaded to leave.

Moreover, some rabbis have publicly questioned the legitimacy of any Israeli government that orders the relinquishment of the territories. Some have extended this anathema to political leaders. Prime Minister Yitzhak Rabin was labeled a traitor in terms derived from rabbinical law. Such traitors are liable to capital punishment, and the label proved fatal: Rabin was assassinated by a religious Jewish law student in November 1995.

As Judaism's influence has intensified in Israeli politics, it has become the basis for reformulated Zionism and nationalism. Since the late 1970s Israeli Judaism has emerged as a political religion with profound implications for the future of a democratic Israeli polity.

See also *Druze; Fundamentalism; Gush Emunim; Jerusalem; Judaism; Zionism.*

Kevin Avruch

BIBLIOGRAPHY

Abramov, S. Z. *Perpetual Dilemma: Jewish Religion in the Jewish State.* Rutherford, N.J.: Fairleigh Dickinson University Press, 1976.

Aronoff, Myron J. *Israeli Visions and Divisions: Cultural Change and Political Conflict.* New Brunswick, N.J.: Transaction, 1989.

Beilin, Yossi. *Israel: A Concise Political History.* New York: St. Martin's, 1992.

Horowitz, Dan, and Moshe Lissak. *The Origins of the Israeli Polity: Palestine under the Mandate.* Chicago: University of Chicago Press, 1978.

Liebman, Charles, and Eliezer Don-Yehiya. *Religion and Politics in Israel.* Bloomington: Indiana University Press, 1984.

Lustick, Ian. *For the Land and the Lord: Jewish Fundamentalism in Israel.* New York: Council on Foreign Relations, 1988.

Medding, Peter. *The Founding of Israeli Democracy, 1948–1967.* New York: Oxford University Press, 1990.

Sprinzak, Ehud, and Larry Diamond, eds. *Israeli Democracy under Stress.* Boulder, Colo.: Lynne Rienner, 1993.

Italy

A country in southern Europe, bordered by the Mediterranean Sea on three sides and by the Alps to the north, Italy achieved political union only between 1860 and 1870. Before then the Italian peninsula was divided among a number of small states, some self-governing, some dominated by other European powers, and one ruled directly by the pope as a sovereign prince. The story of politics and religion in Italy during the nineteenth and twentieth centuries is in large part the story of the pope's gradual reconciliation to his loss of temporal power and his equally gradual acceptance of the reality and legitimacy of the Italian state. The attitude of the Holy See to a unified Italy progressed from bitter opposition, through denial and passive hostility, to acceptance, recognition, and finally cooperation. It was only late in this process, in 1913, that the pope even permitted obedient Catholics to take part in the political life of their country.

The attitude of the Roman Catholic Church toward the new Italian state was supremely important because its citi-

zens were almost exclusively of Catholic background. Many Italians, though nominally Catholic, had no use for the clergy. But a significant number felt some duty to obey a pope who believed he had a right to lay down the law on political as well as religious matters. Immediately before Italy's final unification there had been serious thought of turning the peninsula into a federal, democratic union of states, presided over by the pope. But Pius IX (reigned 1846–1878) would not compromise what he felt was his divine right to rule over state as well as church, and the idea came to nothing.

The Roman Question

The Kingdom of Italy, which was basically established by 1860, comprised all of the peninsula except a small area, including Rome, which the pope ruled directly. It was not un-

til September 1870 that the new Italian government decided to take over Rome and establish it as the kingdom's capital. A final—almost symbolic—assault deprived the pope of his personal residence at the Quirinal and made him a "prisoner in the Vatican," as he termed himself. After a thousand years of temporal power, the papacy had to deal with a completely new situation.

The decision of the First Vatican Council, in July 1870, to recognize the primacy of the pope and his infallibility when he spoke on faith and moral matters "from the throne" (Latin *ex cathedra*) was made for religious reasons, but it had some political side effects. Among other things it tended to increase hostility between the Vatican and some national governments. The Prussian chancellor, Otto von Bismarck, for example, declared that his state would refuse to talk with the Prussian bishops because only the pope could make decisions. Bismarck's declaration led to an official explanation of the council's position by Pius IX, making clear the unchanged responsibility of local bishops. In Italy nothing of this kind ever happened.

The intractable problem of the pope's status, known as the "Roman Question," caused a global rejection of any relationship between the Vatican, supported by bishops naturally beholden to the pope, and the new Italian state. By an act of an anticlerical Parliament the Italian government protected some of the church's properties and its right to operate, but this act received no thanks from the pope. The sincere Catholic was discouraged (in the papal statement known by its opening Latin words *Non Expedit*—"It is not appropriate") from taking any active part in political life. But the strictest prohibitions often had little force in the country as a whole. Catholic movements such as cooperative associations, savings banks, and trade unions were alive and well, even if the pope formally prohibited more than this level of political activity.

It is hard to overestimate the importance of the Roman Question in shaping Catholic participation in and exclusion from political life in the late nineteenth century. On the side of the state, the political establishment was vigorously anticlerical, and those voices urging a more open attitude toward the church were silenced as dangerous, naive, or both. On the church's side, a battle was raging by the end of Leo XIII's pontificate (1878–1903) between those opposed to modern society (and specifically opposed to any political compromise with the state) and those who looked for a point of contact between liberal positions and Catholic doctrine. However, any attempt to organize a political party free and committed to developing "Christian democracy" was not only stopped but condemned as political modernism. Pius X (1903–1914) used the term "modernism" as an accusation with which to persecute the spirit of free inquiry on religious matters. Even some of the leading branches of the Catholic social movement were singled out and destroyed. Prominent leaders, priests as well as layman, were denounced and deprived of chairs in seminaries and schools, denied responsibility, and even made to lose basic acceptance by other Catholics.

Socialism and World War I

By the turn of the century a new scare had arisen to distort the relations between religion and politics in Italy—namely, the spirit of socialism. The efforts of a generation of Italian Catholics to fight socialism on its own ground, by the side of the workers, were wasted. After a general strike in 1904 the pope permitted Catholic politicians in local government to take an active role as conservative support to the liberal order. But bishops who expressed their personal views about social problems were immediately suspected of not being loyal to the pope.

Italian Catholics became officially and directly involved in electoral politics in 1913, when for the first time the vote was extended to almost all male citizens. Catholic voters were urged to help nonsocialist candidates at the polls, even those not affiliated with the church. The electoral strength of Catholic voters was thus directed toward helping conservative candidates.

World War I (1914–1918) showed that Italian Catholics felt themselves to be Italians not only by geography but also by citizenship. Movements of troops (often accompanied by priests in uniform) to the northeast front from all over the country made the war and ultimate victory the first event in which all Italians could feel a sense of unity and participation—even if papal consent was lacking.

In 1919 the pope nullified the prohibition on participation in national elections. At about the same time a Sicilian priest, Luigi Sturzo, founded the Italian Popular Party, which aimed to bring Catholics, "free and strong," into the political arena, not as representatives of the church but as autonomous citizens. Suspected of excessive independence by the church hierarchy, the Popular Party was nonetheless a success in elections, and the first hundred Catholic representatives entered Parliament, in Rome. The Popular Party, however, was unable to foresee that the immediate danger to the liberal state was not so much from socialist and communist strikes but from a silent alliance that linked northern agrarian interests, industrialists, and middle-class people—often deriving from a Catholic culture of authority and order—with a new political force, the Fascist Party of Benito Mussolini.

Mussolini's Regime and World War II

Mussolini came to power in stages. At the beginning his regime appeared only authoritarian, but even the revelation of his tyrannical goals did not arouse serious opposition in the Vatican. Many church leaders were pleased that Mussolini supported them in matters in which they were interested (for instance, the rescue of the Bank of Rome, where Vatican money was heavily invested), and they accepted the exile of Sturzo from Italy as a favor to the Vatican: had not Mussolini stopped the communist danger?

Mussolini achieved his greatest success in solidifying Catholic support for his regime in February 1929, when he signed, with the papal secretary of state, a set of agreements between Italy and the Vatican. The Lateran Treaty, by which pope and state recognized each other's existence, "gave back the pope to Italy, and Italy to the pope." The papal enclave at the Vatican was recognized as a tiny independent state, and Roman Catholicism became the official religion of Italy, with a special status recognized for priests and seminarians. The act was greeted as something more that the overdue resolution of a problem that belonged to the past; indeed, it was hailed as the fruit of a divine plan, accomplished by "the man of Divine Providence," as the pope called Mussolini.

Some small opposition to fascism did exist among Catholics, but it took a long time to become visible. Between 1931 and 1933 there were confrontations in several towns between Catholic Action, a church organization, and corresponding Fascist organizations. These confrontations showed how unrealistic was the idea of "Christianizing" fascism. At Easter 1937 three papal documents were issued, condemning Nazism, communism, and the Mexican revolution (with some difference of severity). Although nothing was said about Mussolini, it was a symptom of a growing papal willingness to be critical. When, in October 1938, Mussolini applied racist and anti-Jewish laws to Italy, Catholics were split in their attitude. Many were indifferent, and a few actively supported Mussolini's action, but some priests and lay people offered their help to persecuted Jews. When he died in 1939, Pius XI had not finished working out a policy of appropriate reaction, and war was on its way. The new pope, Eugenio Pacelli, elected as Pius XII, had been the papal secretary of state.

The beginning of the Second World War gave the Catholic hierarchy problems of interpretation. The old justification for war—that it comes as a punishment for sin—was advanced again, but it was no longer convincing. The Vatican diplomat (and future pope) Giovanni Battista Montini; some lay members of Catholic Action, such as the future prime minister Aldo Moro; and some young professors of the Catholic University saw beyond the war the need to reconstruct a non-Fascist Italy, where Catholics could find their place.

The tragedy of the war and the destruction caused by fascism climaxed when Mussolini's regime collapsed in July 1943. There followed rapidly an armistice with the Allies, the occupation of much of Italy by the Germans, and finally the installation of Mussolini as dictator of northern Italy in a short-lived, Nazi-supported Italian Social Republic. These events were paralleled by a growing resistance from young people, from such diverse backgrounds as the Communist Party, from liberal circles, and even from Catholic parishes. A new generation of Catholics discovered democracy in practice as a way to rebuild the nation. The radio broadcasts of Pius XII, especially his Christmas broadcasts between 1942 and 1944, gave greater impulse to this new commitment.

Early Postwar Politics

A new generation of Catholics entered politics after the war, but the Italian religious situation had not really changed. There was no national church organization—not even a national conference of Catholic bishops, which would have been considered an offense to the privilege of having the pope "among us." But although there was no national identity for the church, there was a national Catholic party. The Christian Democrats took over from the old Popular Party the role of representing Catholic interests in Italian democracy. During the working out of the new constitution, where Catholic and Communist leaders reached significant agreements, the Christian Democratic members represented both the hopes of a new generation and the interests of the Holy See: preservation of the concordat, freedom for Catholic schools, and a constitutional prohibition of divorce. There was, on the ecclesiastical side, no further interest in the nature or form of Italian democracy. The only aim was to repel the communist threat and to ensure Catholic control over society, even if this meant an undeclared attitude of tolerance for illegal organizations like the Sicilian Mafia.

The final version of the constitution was decided upon in 1947, after the Marxist parties had been ejected from the cabinet, in accordance with an agreement between the prime minister, Alcide De Gasperi, and the United States. The first democratic elections in April 1948, which saw a large victory by the Christian Democrats over the Socialist and Communist alliance, confirmed the exclusion of leftist parties from the government. Although the Christian Democrats won, it was the end of the dream of a young generation of Catholic politicians, who hoped to direct Catholic politics toward a more equal society, with all classes participating in the democratic process. The leadership of De Gasperi and his young aides gave to the Catholic political presence a moderate, even conservative stamp. This conservatism was strengthened in 1949, when the church excommunicated Communists and their supporters.

Vatican II

The election, in 1958, of a new pope, John XXIII, marked a watershed in politics and in religion. The elderly cardinal Roncalli had been elected as a transitional pope, his papacy to be a moment of rest after the turbulent theological controversies in the last years of Pius XII. However, his summoning of the Second Vatican Council (1962–1965), which was intended to reconsider the position of the church in the modern world, had profound repercussions. With the new attitude of reform and diversity that came from Vatican II, Christian Democratic leaders in Italy were enabled to involve the Socialist Party in the country's government and proceed with far-reaching economic reforms, through the nationalization of energy and heavy industry.

The effects of this mutual accommodation between a Catholic and Vatican orientation, on the one hand, and the political choices of the ordinary citizen, on the other, were impressive. Within the church the responsibility for political affairs was shifted from the office of the "substitute" (a sort of vice secretary of state) to the newly created national conference of Catholic bishops. The person to order this change was Pope Paul VI, himself a former substitute, who succeeded John XXIII in 1963 and continued the reforms of Vatican II. For the first time Italian bishops did not regard themselves simply as the "life jacket" of the Roman papacy. They began to feel a sense of responsibility toward their country.

Most Italian bishops, even after Vatican II, shared the opinion that "Catholic political unity" was necessary. The acceptance of a Socialist presence in the government did not prevent the bishops from urging all Catholics to vote for Christian Democratic candidates. Thoughtful Catholic voters often had to make political choices in conflict with their bishops. Political pluralism (which meant votes for the Communist Party) had long been a general practice, but it became a controversial issue at the end of the 1960s. Instead of being the voice of order, priests were urging the young to

refuse military service in the army in the name of Christian pacifism.

Terrorist Campaigns

Three events jolted the relations between church and state during the 1970s. Two national laws, permitting divorce and abortion, were approved by Parliament. In both cases the reaction of the church was one of discomfort, even shock. Instead of accepting that the times were demanding radical changes, the bishops and some Christian Democratic leaders tried to abolish the laws through the constitutional procedure of referendum. Only a minority of voters were for abolition, and even many Catholics supported the laws. The defeat of the bishops' challenge was seen in many circles as a symptom of a crisis, but fears were even greater when hundreds of young people, coming both from the ranks of the Communist Party and from Catholic families, started a terrorist campaign.

Increasingly, after 1973, these terrorists described democratic institutions as a masquerade for capitalist power. Brutal murders and attacks were used as a means to force the government to abandon what the terrorists believed was a sham democracy, and by revealing its true face to bring the masses to revolution. Both Christian Democrats and Communists—now coming together in a common government of "national solidarity"—were favorite targets. Among hundreds of other crimes, the Red Brigades in 1978 kidnapped Aldo Moro, the former prime minister and president of the Christian Democrats, who was a personal friend of Paul VI. Political leaders refused to consider negotiations to save Moro, and even the Vatican accepted this strategic choice. Moro was killed by the Red Brigades in August 1978, a few months before the end of Paul VI's pontificate. The first pope with leanings to the Christian Democrats ended his life in the realization that the support offered by the church to one political party was having an effect on the church and its choices.

Change and Rebuilding

The election of a Polish cardinal to the papacy in 1978 increased the independence of Catholics in political life, but Italian politics was still dominated by an international situation that was beyond Italy's power to alter. There had been no fundamental changes since World War II—during the cold war no change was possible—and the effects on the morality of the political establishment had been disastrous. It was with the end of European communism and the disintegration of the Soviet Union in 1991 that this crisis came to the surface. Many political parties simply disappeared after their leaders were put on trial for corruption.

Between 1992 and 1995 the Christian Democratic Party splintered into several minor political groups and signed alliances with parties that were proving more stable in the new political atmosphere. Some Catholic voters went to a conservative alliance, strengthened by the support of the extreme right movement (formerly neofascist, now converted to democratic methods). Others, resurrecting the name of the Popular Party, went to the left and allied with the parties that inherited the electoral weight of the old Communist Party, now renamed the Democratic Party of the Left.

The first election after these big changes, in 1994, was won by the conservative groups led by a media businessman, Silvio Berlusconi. Only during the next general election, in 1996, did the Conference of Catholic Bishops release a statement recognizing the complete freedom of each Catholic voter. Although this freedom had existed in practice since the beginning of the republic, the statement marked the end of an era that brought political and religious issues to an equilibrium very different from that of the beginnings of Italy as a nation.

See also *Anticlericalism; Christian democracy; Papacy; Vatican; Vatican Council, Second.*

Alberto Melloni

BIBLIOGRAPHY

Gentile, Emilio. *The Sacralization of Politics in Fascist Italy.* Translated by Keith Botsford. Cambridge: Harvard University Press, 1996.
Giammanco, Rosanna Mulazzi. *The Catholic-Communist Dialogue in Italy: 1944 to the Present.* New York: Praeger, 1989.
Ginsborg, Paul. *A History of Contemporary Italy: Society and Politics, 1943–1988.* London and New York: Penguin, 1990.
History of Vatican II. Edited by Giuseppe Alberig. English version edited by Joseph A. Komonchak. Maryknoll, N.Y.: Orbis Books, 1995.
Kertzer, David I. *Comrades and Christians: Religion and Political Struggle in Communist Italy.* Cambridge and New York: Cambridge University Press, 1980.
Leonardi, Robert, and Douglas A. Wertman. *Italian Christian Democracy: The Politics of Dominance.* New York: St. Martin's, 1989.
Mack Smith, Denis. *Modern Italy: A Political History.* New Haven: Yale University Press, 1997.
McCarthy, Patrick. *The Crisis of the Italian State: From the Origins of the Cold War to the Fall of Berlusconi.* New York: St. Martin's, 1995.
Miller, James Edward. *From Elite to Mass Politics: Italian Socialism in the Giolittian Era, 1900–1914.* Kent, Ohio: Kent State University Press, 1990.
Tarrow, Sidney G. *Democracy and Disorder: Protest and Politics in Italy, 1965–1975.* Oxford and New York: Clarendon Press, 1989.

Ivory Coast

A former French colony situated along the Atlantic coast of West Africa, Ivory Coast, or Côte d'Ivoire, is a country of great cultural, linguistic, and religious diversity for its small size. Indeed, no religious community can claim a majority. Roman Catholics and Protestants of various denominations are concentrated in the more prosperous southern half of the country, home to large plantations growing coffee and cacao—the major export commodities—and thus most of the country's cities and towns.

Although Muslims predominate in the north, large communities of Muslims also arc found in the south, where people from the north have migrated in search of better opportunities. In addition, Ivory Coast's prosperity has attracted large numbers of immigrants from neighboring countries, many of them Muslim. Thus Islam has expanded rapidly and Muslims now constitute the country's largest religious community.

The Precolonial Period

Ivory Coast is bisected into different climactic zones identified by the tropical rain forest that covers most of the southern half of the country and the grasslands, or savannas, that cover the north. In the years before 1893, when Ivory Coast became a French colony, the frontier between the rain forest and the grasslands was the locus for exchange of commodities as well as ideas. Kola nuts from the forest were traded for rock salt mined in the Sahara. Northbound trade was controlled by Muslims, many of whom settled along trade routes throughout the savannas. The larger trading towns, such as Kong and Bondoukou, also served as major centers of Muslim learning. Although the Muslim traders lived as minorities and were the subjects of non-Muslim rulers, it generally was in the interest of both the chiefs and their Muslim subjects to maintain close relationships. Around 1700 the Muslim leader Sekou Wattara seized power in the kingdom of Kong. The coup d'état, however, was not in any sense a jihad—an attempt to construct an explicitly Muslim

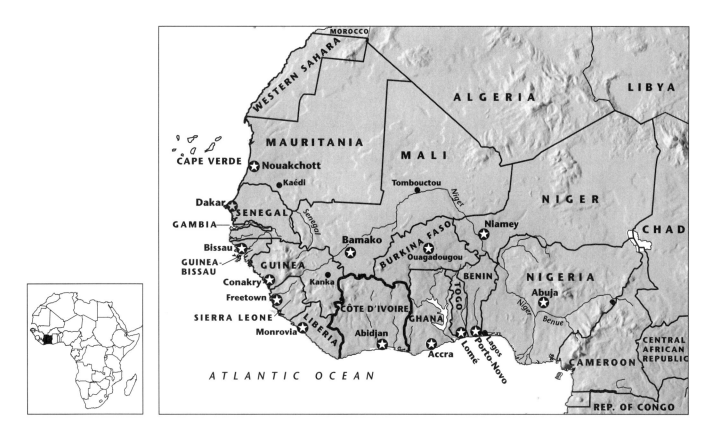

state. All in all, then, Islam as practiced in northern Ivory Coast was not of a militant variety.

The rain forest region in the south was more oriented toward the coast and to overseas trade with Europe. In 1637 five Capuchin missionaries landed at Assinie, along the coast, but their mission was a total failure. Fifty years later, the French established a fort there, but it too was soon abandoned. The European powers took little interest in Ivory Coast until the nineteenth century, when it began producing palm oil for export to Europe. Despite this European presence, Christianity made no significant inroads in Ivory Coast, unlike Islam in the north.

The Colonial Period

In 1893, when Ivory Coast became a French colony, the territory was relatively peripheral, both economically and strategically. The French already had established a series of outposts along the coast which were linked, by the creation of the colony, to French territories along the Niger River. The major obstacle to these French projects of expansion was Samori Toure, a Muslim warlord who controlled much of northern Ivory Coast in the 1890s. Nonetheless, the French were not entirely hostile toward Islam during the early years of rule when the colony was under military leadership. Most of the French colonial troops were Africans from the colonies of Senegal and Sudan (now Mali), many of whom were Muslims themselves. Military officers and Louis-Gustave Binger (the first governor of the colony and one of the first explorers of its interior), convinced that Muslims were more "evolved" than African "fetishists," were not at all averse to the spread of Islam. At the same time, Binger called for the establishment of Catholic missions in the new colony. Initially, these missions were restricted to the coastal regions, which were the most accessible to Europeans.

Meanwhile, the outcome of the Dreyfus affair in France was to have profound repercussions for colonial policy on religion. In the affair a French military officer of Jewish descent, Capt. Alfred Dreyfus (1859–1935), was accused and convicted of treason and sentenced in 1894 to life imprisonment. Pardoned in 1906 when it became clear that the military had suppressed evidence of his innocence, Dreyfus became a symbol of injustice for liberal intellectuals who bitterly opposed right-wing reactionary forces such as the military and church.

By 1906 the official policy of the French government was

strict separation of church and state. The army, which until then had enjoyed relatively free rein in France's African colonies, was particularly suspect, along with the Catholic Church and organized religion in general. Any official collaboration between Catholic missionaries and the colonial government of Ivory Coast was categorically ruled out. Unlike in many British colonies where education was largely left in the hands of missionaries, the colonial government of Ivory Coast was committed in principle to the establishment of a secular school system. But Catholic missions were permitted to establish their own schools, and they pursued proselytization in the southern half of the country. This separation of church and state, however, dictated that the colony be open to Protestant missionaries as well as Catholic.

This openness had its limits, however. In 1913 William Wade Harris (c. 1860–1928), a native of Liberia, crossed the border into Ivory Coast, baptizing people and announcing his prophetic mission. He urged Ivorians to burn their masks and statues, to renounce their gods, and to practice Christianity. Harris was apprehended and jailed but quickly released. He continued to proselytize, making his way along the coast and ultimately into the Gold Coast (modern Ghana). There British authorities sent him back to Ivory Coast, where he continued to preach. The outbreak of the First World War in 1914 fueled French suspicions of outsiders, especially anyone like Harris who could mobilize masses of people; Harris was expelled back to Liberia. Nevertheless, the Harrist church, among the oldest independent African churches in West Africa, continued to flourish in Ivory Coast.

The colonial government was equally suspicious of Muslims, fearing that pan-Islamism would constitute a threat to colonial domination. Such suspicions escalated with the outbreak of World War I, when France was at war with Turkey, the world's leading independent Muslim power. During the war the French actively solicited declarations of support from notable *ulama,* or Muslim clerics. Throughout the colonial period the French kept very close watch on all *ulama,* even though they never posed a serious threat. More generally, French authorities tried to "contain" Islam, hoping both to discourage followers of traditional religions from converting to Islam and to foster varieties of Islam that they identified as more "African" and less orthodox. It is one of the paradoxes of colonial rule that the same authorities who welcomed "African" Islam were highly suspicious of "African" Christian movements such as Harrism.

French efforts to insulate Muslims in Ivory Coast from global currents in Islam were doomed to failure. After World War II ended in 1945 young Africans returning from the pilgrimage to Mecca or from study in the Middle East (notably Cairo) began to challenge local Islamic practices. Bouaké, in central Ivory Coast, was one of the leading centers of these Wahhabis, as the French called them. Many local African Muslims were even more hostile to the Wahhabis than the French, with the result that violence erupted in the 1950s in Ivory Coast between supporters and opponents of the new movement. The violence produced no fatalities, however, as it did in nearby Mali.

After Independence

Félix Houphouët-Boigny (1905–1993), president of Ivory Coast from its independence in 1960 until his death in 1993, was able to remain in relatively firm control of a country as diverse as Ivory Coast only through a pattern of strategic alliances with representatives of all sectors of the population. In religious terms these alliances entailed the distribution of money and services to different religious communities and organizations; the construction of churches and mosques; the organization of national religious youth conferences; and the attribution of air time on public radio and television. Traditional religions were excluded from this process for several reasons. Because they were associated with specific localities and ethnic groups, any government sponsorship risked being construed as illegitimate favoritism. In any case, such religions lacked the formal organizations, both local and national, that might have lobbied for patronage or acted as conduits for resources.

As Houphouët-Boigny's tenure lengthened, Protestants and especially Muslims began to realize that he was favoring his own religion, Catholicism. Their concerns peaked with the construction of a sumptuous basilica, inaugurated in 1990 by Pope John Paul II in person, in Yamoussoukro, the president's home town. The president's claim that he was funding the construction entirely out of his personal fortune did little to allay such jealousies.

The competition for government resources, not only between different religions but also among different organizations and individuals in each religion claiming to represent the religious community as a whole, continues with Houphouët-Boigny's successor, Henri Konan-Bédié. But now that Ivory Coast is effectively a multiparty democracy, Bédié no longer can afford to appear to favor any particular religion. Most recently he has attempted to appease the Muslim community by constructing a grand mosque in the heart of Abidjan, the country's principal city.

In religious matters, as in its economy, Ivory Coast has been relatively open to outside money and influence. Although the government has prevented interference by Muslim countries identified as "radical," such as Iran and Libya, it has allowed politically conservative countries, notably Saudi Arabia, to fund schools, mosques, and religious organizations. At the same time, Protestant evangelical groups, supported by funds from the United States and Europe, have been aggressively proselytizing Ivorians. The liberalization of the mass media, as well as the growing proliferation of video and audio cassettes, is accelerating the competition for converts as well as for government patronage while privileging religious groups with access to foreign funds and technical expertise.

See also *Africa, Christian; Africa, West: The Mande World; African independent churches; African traditional religions; Colonialism; France; Islam; Separation of church and state.*

Robert G. Launay

BIBLIOGRAPHY

Haliburton, Gordon Mackay. *The Prophet Harris.* New York: Oxford University Press, 1973.

Harrison, Christopher. *France and Islam in West Africa, 1860–1960.* Cambridge: Cambridge University Press, 1988.

Kaba, Lansine. *The Wahhabiyya: Islamic Reform and Politics in French West Africa.* Evanston, Ill.: Northwestern University Press, 1974.

Launay, Robert. *Beyond the Stream: Islam and Society in a West African Town.* Berkeley and Los Angeles: University of California Press, 1992.

Walker, Sheila. *The Religious Revolution in Ivory Coast: The Prophet Harris and the Harrist Church.* Chapel Hill: University of North Carolina Press, 1983.

J

James, William

American philosopher and psychologist. James (1842–1910), the son of an iconoclastic religious thinker and brother of the novelist Henry James, was educated in Europe. After receiving a medical degree in 1869, he taught at Harvard University.

Broadly conceived, both politics and religion played a lifelong role in his writings and thought. His father, Henry James Sr., combined a deep interest in the religious impulses of human beings apart from formal, organized religion with a profound respect for communal life apart from political institutions. James absorbed from him a suspicion of institutions, a refusal to accept authoritarian boundaries in intellectual matters, and a sympathy for the human urge toward religious belief.

Perhaps James's most important contribution to American philosophy was his development of the doctrine of pragmatism, which in essence was a call for philosophical contemplation to culminate in action. In attempting to resolve a metaphysical or moral problem, the pragmatist tries to trace the respective practical consequences of a question. If no practical differences can be traced, the question is rejected as an idle one. Pragmatism thus offers a model for meaningful and courageous action in the world.

James's interest in the possibilities of human heroism was developed in his essays in popular philosophy. Like many thinkers in the post–Civil War era, he reacted strongly to the glorification of military heroism prevalent at the time. On the one hand, he believed in the value of heroic action; on the other, he considered it distasteful to conquer those

William James

weaker than himself. For James, heroism lay in the struggle rather than in the triumph. He devoted himself to developing a portrait of heroism apart from the horrors of modern technological warfare, one that would emphasize the best of the human spirit free of the worst excesses of human evil. In "The Moral Equivalent of War," one of his most famous essays, James acknowledged that the urge to do battle is an important part of the human psyche and argued that the heroic impulses and virtues that are brought out in times of war must somehow be preserved in a different context; in other words, a "moral equivalent of war" must be found. For James, religion arguably was one important such moral equivalent.

James believed that all people have the capacity to reach heroic levels of experience because all possess a subliminal consciousness that operates according to laws unknown by the waking consciousness. To face the profound challenges of the subliminal realm squarely, to grapple with what can never be fully understood, was the ultimate act of heroism. His *Varieties of Religious Experience: A Study in Human Nature* (1902) was a testimony to the most extraordinary levels of human experience. This popular work was James's ultimate expression of his father's distrust of institutional religion and his own desire to preserve the possibility of deep experience and meaningful action in the world.

Heather L. Nadelman

BIBLIOGRAPHY
Cotkin, George. *William James, Public Philosopher.* Baltimore: Johns Hopkins University Press, 1990.
James, William. *The Varieties of Religious Experience: A Study in Human Nature.* Penguin, 1982.
Levinson, Henry Samuel. *The Religious Investigations of William James.* Chapel Hill: University of North Carolina Press, 1981.

Japan

Religion and politics have been closely allied in Japan, a series of islands in the Pacific Ocean off the east coast of Asia, since the beginning of its history. This relationship has assumed a variety of forms in different eras and with respect to Japan's major religious traditions—Shinto, Buddhism, Christianity—and, since the beginning of the nineteenth century, numerous "new religions," independent religious organizations exhibiting a great variety of doctrines. Significant connections between religion and state exist in the contemporary period (since 1945), even under a national constitution upholding principles of religious freedom and separation of religion and state.

Prehistory and Ancient Japan

The Japanese archipelago was originally inhabited by peoples from East and Southeast Asia. Based on this mixture of peoples, ancient Japanese society and culture were highly diverse. Social organization was based on clans. The Yamato clan extended its rule from a base in central Japan north to the Kanto Plain (around present-day Tokyo) and south to Kyushu (southernmost of the four main islands) by the beginning of the fourth century C.E. The Yamato clan's hegemony marks the beginning of the ancient Japanese state.

The *Kojiki* (712) and the *Nihonshoki* (720) are collections of the oral literature of the ancient period compiled into a continuous historical narrative for the purpose of establishing the legitimacy of Yamato rule. The main narrative, into which a variety of myths from other clans are woven, identifies the Yamato clan as descended from the sun goddess Amaterasu. The early chapters explain the origin of the islands themselves, as discovered or created by two primal deities (called *kami*) named Izanagi and Izanami. They produce Amaterasu and her brother Susanoo, the founding ancestor of the Izumo clan, the Yamato's main rival. After overcoming the opposition of Susanoo and his allies, Amaterasu sends her grandson Ninigi from the High Fields of Heaven, to the Land of the Heavenly Reed Plains (the Japanese islands), to rule as the first emperor of Japan.

The mythic narrative established the divine origins of the Yamato clan, implying that usurpation of rule by any other clan would be a violation of divine plan. Other ideas significant for the relation between religion and state were also set out in these mythic texts. For example, directly descended from the *kami,* the sovereign is a sacred being and rules in accord with divine will; indirectly, all the Japanese people share these divine origins; and the Japanese land itself was divinely created. These ideas were given concrete expression by the construction of monumental *kofun* (tumuli, or mounds over a grave) for each deceased sovereign. Also, the ancestral gods of the Yamato clan began to be venerated at Ise (in what is now Mie Prefecture) in the third century, eventually resulting in a great complex of shrines known as the Ise Shrines. Concurrent with Yamato construction of tumuli and shrines, other important clans built their own shrines and their own tumuli.

Introduction of Buddhism

A great many advisers, technicians, and artisans from China and Korea came into Japan beginning in the late fourth century. Many of these new immigrants practiced Buddhism. The concentration of immigrant clans under the wing of the Yamato clan tended to weaken the old system of

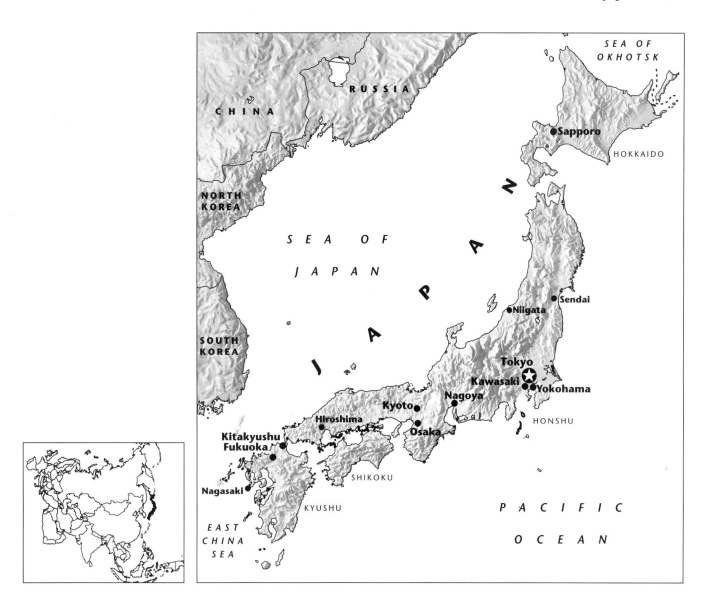

rule by clan federation and to aid the Yamato in establishing a bureaucratic state as an alternative. Both Buddhism and Chinese statecraft provided invaluable aids to the Yamato in transforming a clan-based system of rule into a bureaucratic state on a Chinese model. Buddhism provided a symbolic representation of national unity under Yamato rule, supplanting the myths of various clans.

In 538 or 552 the king of Paekche, on the Korean peninsula, who hoped for Japanese military assistance in a war against his neighboring states, presented a gold and copper image of the Buddha Shakyamuni and some scriptures to the Yamato court. The powerful clans around the Yamato throne quarreled as to whether these gifts should be accepted. The Soga argued that Buddhism should be accepted because all the neighboring countries had accepted it, and Japan should not be left behind. The Mononobe and Nakatomi violently opposed the Soga position. The decision for Japan, in the eyes of all the political players, was about which type of *kami*, the foreign or the indigenous, was likely to most benefit the people and be the most helpful to the political regime. The theological subtleties distinguishing the *kami* from the Buddhas were not yet apparent. Eventually, the pro-Buddhist faction prevailed.

A religious system emerged in which Buddhism and Shinto, or, more accurately, Buddhism in the form it took under state patronage, and the cults of *kami* in the analogous form, were all called upon to provide an essential part of political rule. The term used for the rule of the state was *mat-*

surigoto, a term that does not distinguish between religious ritual (*matsuri*) and affairs of state. The role of the emperor in this state was being constructed along the lines of a cosmic ruler who, because of his divine descent, is in some sense in touch with or inspired by the *kami*. If he performs rites for his divine ancestral spirits regularly, sincerely, and correctly, he can be assured that his rule will go smoothly and the country will be free of famine, disease, and natural disaster. Conversely, if he fails, or if his officials fail in ritual performance, those misfortunes will be visited upon the people. He must then make a ritual atonement for those offenses in order to reinstate a smooth rule and to be assured of the beneficence of the *kami*.

At the same time, emperors were understood to represent the ideal Buddhist monarch, the *cakravartin,* or "Wheel-Turning King," who protects and promotes Buddhism as the religion of the land on the model of the Indian king Asoka. To sponsor the growth of Buddhism was, among other things, to sponsor a single standard of faith, ethics, and allegiance among the people that would undercut primordial ties based on kinship or territory. But in order to use Buddhism in this way, it was also crucial to be able to control the religion, so that it would not develop in a way that went against the direction the state was trying to take.

In 740 an imperial edict ordered the establishment in each province of a pair of temples (called *kokubunsoji* and *kokubunniji,* "monks' temple" and "nuns' temple"). At the apex of this network of temples stood the mammoth Todaij temple built at Nara by Emperor Shomu to house the Great Buddha and to serve as "head temple" to the provincial temples.

The monks and nuns of the provincial temples were expected to study Buddhist teachings, copy scriptures, and perform rites on a set schedule. Many of these rites—praying for rain, or apologizing for errors by the emperor, which might be responsible for crop failures, eclipses, and natural disasters—were supposed to protect the state. At least 136 provincial temples were constructed throughout the country, as pairs on the same site. They were given special grants of land, and the clerics were excused from the duties of taxation, corvée labor, and military service.

Once the state became involved in the performance of large-scale Buddhist rites, it was necessary to guarantee that a certain number of nuns and monks would be ordained annually. If anything, however, the supply exceeded the demand, not least because of the provision freeing clerics from the duties of taxes and corvée labor. Thus the concern of the state turned more to regulating the conduct of clerics than to ensuring an adequate number. The conduct of clerics was minutely regulated in the twenty-seven-article set of regulations for monks and nuns (*Soniryo*), instituted in 701 and reissued several times, based on earlier Chinese texts.

Limits on Buddhism's influence at court were established by the Dokyo affair (764–770), in which a monk of the Hosso sect, named Dokyo, exerted extraordinary influence as adviser to Empress Koken, a post he achieved after supposedly curing the empress of an illness. Over the next few years, Dokyo enjoyed a meteoric rise and was appointed to a new post almost equal to the empress herself. As his political influence soared, he attempted to be made emperor, but with the death of the empress, he was punished with banishment, and women were thereafter barred from ascending the throne.

Heian and Kamakura Periods (794–1600)

Dokyo's banishment did not expel the power of Buddhism from the political arena; because of the incorporation of monks into the civil service of the day (through state-supported ordination), their influence was great. So great, in fact, that the capital was moved from Nara to Kyoto precisely to get away from the power of great temples and Buddhist sects. This is not to say, however, that the state sought to sever all connection, by any means. The understanding that Buddhism functions to "protect the state" persisted, and temples continued to be much occupied with ritual for that purpose. During the Heian period (794–1185), great monastic centers for the Tendai and Shingon sects were founded with state support, and state-sponsored ordination continued. The court sent noted monks to China to study and to retrieve new scriptures and commentaries. Toward the end of the period, the bureaucratic state based on the Chinese model broke down and was replaced by a semifeudal system of local military warlords.

During the Kamakura period (1185–1600), and corresponding to the growing independence of Buddhist institutions, the former rhetoric of religion existing in service to the state was supplanted by the idea that Buddhist law and imperial law were complementary and functioned together to sustain the realm. The older understanding of religion's function to protect the state was not entirely swept away, but other developments resulted in new relations between religion and state. The era saw the founding of new varieties of Buddhism based on personal faith and preaching universal salvation, rather than the bureaucratic, aristocratic, ritualistic, and state-centered orientation of earlier times. Established in the twelfth century, the Pure Land, True Pure Land, Nichiren, and Zen sects did not immediately find mass popular followings, but increasingly by the end of the period all but Zen had done so. The founders of the first three of these sects all came into conflict with the state and suffered banishment and other punishments. While the specific charges varied, the root of the problem lay in the ability of the new groups to assemble a popular following, thus presenting the possibility of independent power bases outside the sphere of state control. The efforts of these sects to proselytize nationwide resulted in their gradually founding networks of temples, although the sects did not do so at a uniform rate or with equal geographical coverage. The clerics of these sects were ordained outside the former framework of state ordination and patronage and hence had primary loyalty to the sect.

The period of political disunity in the fifteenth and sixteenth centuries paralleled the spread through the countryside of temples of all the new Kamakura sects, as well as branches of the major shrines. As before, the cults of *kami* and Buddhas continued to coexist, sometimes within a single temple-shrine complex, but religious institutions increasingly became caught up in protracted warfare. The warlord Oda Nobunaga (1534–1582) burned the monastery called Enryakuji in 1571 after it gave shelter to Nobunaga's fleeing enemies. But a much longer campaign was needed to defeat the Honganji, the primary temple of the True Pure Land sect, which by this time had adherents throughout central Japan. They fought Nobunaga from 1570 to 1580, and he was able to defeat them only by slaughtering great numbers of both lay people and monks.

Christianity

For a period of about a century, Roman Catholic missionaries were active in medieval Japan, beginning with Francis Xavier, who arrived in Japan in 1549. Missionaries accompanied Portuguese (and later, Spanish) traders, who introduced the warlords to many aspects of European culture and technology, especially firearms. As the dominant local warlords (*daimyo*) entered alliances with the traders, they gave missionaries free rein in large areas of Kyushu and also around Kyoto. Whole domains were converted by fiat, and by 1579, it is estimated that there were 100,000 Christians in Japan. The so-called Christian *daimyo* were largely defeated

during sixteenth-century warfare, however, and the existence of Christianity was increasingly viewed as a threat by Japan's new rulers. As they saw it, Japanese Christians worshiped a foreign deity and owed allegiance not to themselves, but to the pope, whom they perceived to be a close ally of European traders in the matériel of advanced warfare. The potential for Christianity to become a fifth column and a source of domestic rebellion posed so significant a threat as to warrant the religion's complete extermination. Spectacular mass, public crucifixions of missionaries and their followers began in earnest in the 1580s, to accompany prohibitions of the religion. In 1637 a group of peasant Christians fought to the last man, woman, and child in the Shimabara Rebellion. After this, all remaining Christian stalwarts practiced in secret. A surprising number managed to perpetuate their religion in secret, finally to reemerge in the 1870s. Meanwhile, much of the Edo period's framework of religious control was constructed to enforce the ban on Christianity.

Edo Period (1600–1868)

Originating with the policies of several domains that demanded certification of suspected Christians' renunciation of their faith in favor of Buddhism, a universal requirement was established by the state that all subjects become parishioners of a Buddhist temple. Temples then were authorized to issue certificates authenticating each person as a Buddhist. Without these, a person could be suspected as a Christian, interrogated, arrested, executed, and the entire family subjected to the same treatment. In that sense, the Buddhist clergy had great power over the population. In turn, parishioners were required to support the temples and priests economically. The temple records of this policy came to function like census data, and the Buddhist priesthood began to be perceived as similar to village officials. The Buddhists amassed great wealth through this state-sponsored system of temple registration, and as a result Buddhism penetrated the religious lives of individuals and communities with a new intensity.

It was in this period that the practice of Buddhist funerals and ancestral ritual was virtually universalized, each step accompanied by hefty payment to a temple for grave sites, grave markers, ritual performance, and the like. Buddhist scholarship and learning advanced greatly when formal seminary training was established. Decrees from the shogun, or military governor, set out a model for the priesthood as learned moral exemplars and teachers of virtue, especially the virtue of social conformity, in dual support of "kingly law" and Buddhist law. Simultaneously, the state initiated intensified control of Buddhism, limiting the construction of new temples and requiring existing temples to accept supervision by a pyramidal chain of head and branch temples in each sect. This system of head and branch temples intensified the sectarian character of Japanese Buddhism and greatly concentrated the power of the head temples of each sect over the branch temples.

This massive system of state control inevitably provoked resistance from those who perceived a contradiction between the state's ideal of Buddhism as an extension of its other measures for social control and the religion's own aspirations for personal salvation through faith, religious discipline, and vigorous proselytization. "World renouncers" appeared as early as the late seventeenth century, charging that the seminaries had degenerated to mere credentialing factories, their graduates shallow careerists lacking religious conviction or any intention to set an example of virtue for their parishioners. These reformers were accompanied by a diverse assortment of the self- or quasi-ordained who preached and worked "miracles" among the growing urban population. Popular preaching developed into a form of entertainment and gave rise to a sophisticated verbal art form in which the preacher was indistinguishable from a storyteller. The temples and the secular intelligentsia thundered against these unauthorized upstarts, but the crowd called out for more. Reformers went on nationwide tours of proselytization, and as roads and other facilities expanded and the currency-based economy grew, the populace also became able to travel on pilgrimage to distant temples and shrines.

By the beginning of the nineteenth century, the impulse for religious reform and escape from state structures of religious control began to be expressed not only by those in religious orders but also by the laity. Many "new religions" were founded by those seeking a new religious path and an ideal of salvation unencumbered by state-imposed restraints. Not all the seekers were Buddhist. For example, Kurozumi Munetada was a Shinto priest in service to the Okayama domain whose intense experience of revelation from the sun goddess in 1814 led him to elaborate a path of personal perfection based on daily worship of the rising sun. In the process he developed religious healing and collected followers on an egalitarian basis. Offering healing to all, he came into conflict with professional religious healers affiliated with Buddhism, and his egalitarianism presented a strong

contrast with the parishes of most Buddhist temples and Shinto shrines, whose organizational hierarchies closely mirrored the local communal status order. In 1838 Nakayama Miki experienced intense revelation from a previously unknown god eventually named the Parent Deity. She began to minister to women seeking safe childbirth, and on this basis Nakayama developed an extensive theology now known as Tenrikyo. A devout Buddhist before her religious experience, her new religion, a completely novel doctrine, broke out of the mold of both Buddhism and Shinto. Her ministry showed the same egalitarianism as Kurozumi's. Both of them denied prevalent Buddhist ideas proclaiming the pollution of women, women's spiritual inferiority, and the impossibility of women's salvation. New religious movements such as these have continued to be founded down to the present day.

Modern Japan (1868 to present)

Japan's modern period was initiated with the Meiji Restoration of 1868. One faction of Restoration leaders was devoted to Shinto nativism, called National Learning (*kokugaku*). This philosophy laid many of Japan's problems at Buddhism's door in an expression of the Shinto priesthood's long-pent-up bitterness at the state patronage Buddhism had enjoyed during the preceding era. Briefly, it set the Shinto priesthood loose for random (but extensive) sacking, plundering, and destruction of Buddhist temples in an attempt to destroy Buddhism. When the pillage subsided, the state initiated a longer-lasting move to separate the two religions. As a result, the character of the relation between the worship of Buddhist figures and the *kami* was greatly changed. Previously it had been standard practice for Buddhist temples (with the sole exception of the True Pure Land sect) to enshrine *kami* alongside Buddhas and bodhisattvas, and for Shinto shrine altars to house Buddhist objects of worship alongside symbols or pictorial representations of the *kami*. This practice rested on the long-accepted idea that the *kami* are the earthly protectors and phenomenal manifestations (*suijaku*) of the Buddhas, who are the "original" supernaturals (*honji*). Overnight, temple-shrine complexes were transformed, usually to Shinto shrines shorn of Buddhist paraphernalia; many Buddhist priests were forcibly returned to the status of lay people; and hundreds of Buddhist temples were closed.

Simultaneously, the state attempted to consolidate and legitimate its rule purely with Shinto ritual, symbolism, and proselytization. Shinto enjoyed extensive state patronage, flourished, and extended its control over the populace, stimulating criticisms of formalism and excessive (slavish) dependence on the state, to the detriment of purely religious pursuits.

Contemporary relations between religion and state have centered on litigation to test and interpret the 1947 constitution's provisions of religious freedom (Article 20) and the prohibition on state support of religion (Article 89). The judiciary and the Ministry of Justice are so closely connected that significant rulings more closely resemble bureaucratic decisions of expediency than the exertion of independent judicial interpretation.

The issue of state support for the Yasukumi Shrine was repeatedly taken up by the Liberal Democratic Party until 1988, apparently as a sop to nationalists and hard-line conservatives hoping to roll back postwar political and social reforms across the board. These legislative attempts have consistently resulted in refusal of state support, but the associated political maneuvering has allowed ultraconservatives significant opportunity to perpetuate their retrogressive perspective.

Court suits have repeatedly sought to prohibit public expenditure by local administrations on Shinto ground-breaking rites for public buildings, or on the installation of memorials for the war dead. The result of these suits has been mixed. Shinto ground-breaking ritual was eventually declared "customary" rather than religious in nature (thus allowing expenditure of public funds), while publicly constructed war memorials have frequently been disallowed.

The largest of Japan's new religions, the Buddhist group Soka Gakkai, with twelve million members, formed a political party in 1964. It acts as a swing party capable of determining the outcome in issues pitting (usually) the Liberal Democratic Party against the Socialist Party. Its tight-knit organization has allowed it to be extremely effective, especially in prefectural elections. It is a party of the center that favors the expansion of social welfare and restriction of the defense budget.

Another strand of contemporary religion-state relations concerns legislation on ethical issues. As has been the case in many industrialized nations (with the exception of the United States), legislation permitting abortion has mostly been uncontroversial, with only one new religion, Seicho no Ie (founded in 1930), intermittently protesting it. Far more uncertainty has been expressed about legislation proposing to recognize brain death as defining the death of an individual. Religious organizations have not spoken out on this issue nearly so frequently, however, as diverse patients' rights organizations, which generally see the proposed legislation as tacit permission to physicians to expand organ transplant surgery without fear of prosecution.

The poison gas attack on the Tokyo subway in March 1995 by the religious group Aum Shinrikyo has given rise to widespread questioning of the postwar relation between religion and state. Religions are allowed to incorporate in order to be free of taxation on donations and revenues from ritual performance, and currently some 184,000 organizations, large and small, including many ordinary temples, shrines, and Christian churches, are incorporated. Until 1995 police and prosecutors tended not to become involved in complaints about fraudulent advertisement of miracle cures and the like, nor did they frequently assist former believers claiming to have been bilked by religions. Although a handful of religions that had ceased to function had lost their corporate registration, no religion before Aum had been the subject of a criminal investigation or stripped of its corporate registration as a result. Indeed, the interpretation of this move in Aum's case has been highly controversial, pitting those who see great danger in allowing the religion to continue to proselytize against those who see a violation of religious freedom in any attempt to muzzle the group or restrict its rebuilding.

The Aum Shinrikyo incident seems likely to stimulate the state to strengthen its oversight of religious organizations. Shorn of the prerogative to patronize particular religions extensively, however, the state is unlikely under the current constitution to resume its former pattern of sponsorship leading to religious reform and eventually a reintroduction of state control. Nevertheless, public calls for greater control may embolden administrative efforts in the future.

See also *Buddha; Christianity in Asia; Shinto.*

Helen Hardacre

BIBLIOGRAPHY

Ebersole, Gary L. *Ritual Poetry and the Politics of Death in Early Japan.* Princeton: Princeton University Press, 1989.

Fridell, Wilbur M. *Japanese Shrine Mergers, 1906–12: State Shinto Moves to the Grassroots.* Tokyo: Sophia University, 1973.

Gluck, Carol. *Japan's Modern Myths: Ideology in the Late Meiji Period.* Princeton: Princeton University Press, 1985.

Holtom, Daniel Clarence. *The Japanese Enthronement Ceremonies.* London: Kegan Paul International, 1996.

————. *The National Faith of Japan: A Study in Modern Shinto.* London: Kegan Paul International, 1995; distributed in the United States by Columbia University Press.

Ketelaar, James Edward. *Of Heretics and Martyrs in Meiji Japan: Buddhism and Its Persecution.* Princeton: Princeton University Press, 1990.

Kitagawa, Joseph Mitsuo. *Religion in Japanese History.* New York: Columbia University Press, 1966.

Lokowandt, Ernst. *Die rechtliche Entwicklung des Staats-Shinto in der ersten Halfte der Meiji-Zeit (1868–1890).* Wiesbaden: Harrassowitz, 1978.

McMullin, Neil. *Buddhism and the State in Sixteenth-Century Japan.* Princeton: Princeton University Press, 1984.

O'Brien, David M., with Ohkoshi, Yasuo. *To Dream of Dreams: Religious Freedom and Constitutional Politics in Postwar Japan.* Honolulu: University of Hawaii Press, 1996.

Jefferson, Thomas

Author of the Declaration of Independence, the third president of the United States, and an advocate for civil rights and religious freedom. Arguably more than any other Founder, Jefferson (1743–1826) set the tone of the debate over the relationship between politics and religion in America. His views on religion and its role in the new nation are complex—so much so that Jefferson has been quoted by partisans on opposing sides of church-state issues ever since.

Jefferson himself remained a lifelong member of the Anglican (Episcopal) Church into which he was born, and he often contributed to religious causes and churches. Yet for most of his life he worked to define and limit the relationship between government and religion. Furthermore, he compiled his own version of the Bible (known as the Jefferson Bible), which removed all mention of miracle and revelation and instead focused on the moral teachings of Jesus and the early church.

After writing the Declaration of Independence, which was adopted in July 1776, Jefferson returned to Virginia to take a seat in the state assembly, where he labored to make Virginia's laws more appropriate for a republican nation. Jefferson worked to end what he had long believed was an offense to the natural freedoms of citizens—the preferred position of the Anglican Church. He wrote and unsuccessfully advanced a bill for religious freedom, clearly outlining the case that religious freedom cannot be separated from the political liberty for which the American Revolution had been fought. According to Jefferson, a citizen's civil

Thomas Jefferson

rights and religious opinions have no bearing on each other.

It was not until 1779, when Jefferson was governor of Virginia, that state laws impinging on religious liberty were amended or repealed and Virginia's state support of Anglican clergy was phased out completely. In the mid-1780s the Virginia Assembly again debated whether Protestant Christianity was the official religion of the state and should be taught in all schools and whether approved denominations should receive state financial support.

By 1786, when Jefferson was serving in Paris as minister

to France, his bill was finally approved. Shepherded through the assembly in 1786 by Jefferson's close friend and ally James Madison (later to be fourth president of the United States) and actively supported by Jefferson from France, this statute altered the course of discussion about the role of religion in public life by making religious privilege antithetical to individual freedom. Thereafter, state-supported religion remained on the defensive, gradually losing nearly all previous privileges. Although still in Paris, Jefferson pushed for the addition of a Bill of Rights as a requirement for the adoption of the new U.S. Constitution, especially the First Amendment prohibition on the government establishment of religion.

A lifelong advocate of the need for universal free public education as the foundation of a democratic society, Jefferson was willing to include in the curriculum those moral teachings that the major religions agreed on. But he argued persuasively that the details of dogma and doctrinal differences should be left out of the public schools.

Many Americans assume that one of Jefferson's most quoted writings—that the First Amendment erects "a wall of separation between Church and State"—is a part of the Constitution. Jefferson actually articulated this position in a letter in 1802 responding to a convention of Connecticut Baptists who urged him to declare a day of fasting to help heal the political wounds of the nation; Jefferson consistently refused to do so because he considered it an inappropriate mixing of religion and politics. The phrase has been at the center of church-state controversies ever since and was, in fact, quoted by the Supreme Court in the 1948 case banning religious instruction in public school buildings (*Illinois ex rel. McCollum v. Board of Education*).

See also *Civil religion; Constitution, U.S.; Education; Freedom of religion; Madison, James; Presidents, American; Separation of church and state; State churches.*

William B. Rogers

BIBLIOGRAPHY

Adams, Dickinson W., ed. *Jefferson's Extracts from the Gospels.* Princeton: Princeton University Press, 1983.

Gaustad, Edwin S. *Sworn on the Altar of God: A Religious Biography of Thomas Jefferson.* Grand Rapids, Mich.: Eerdmans, 1996.

Healey, Robert M. *Jefferson on Religion in Public Education.* New Haven: Yale University Press, 1962.

Peterson, Merrill D. *Thomas Jefferson and the New Nation: A Biography.* New York: Oxford University Press, 1970.

———, ed. *Thomas Jefferson: Writings.* New York: Library of America, 1984.

Jehovah's Witnesses

A Christian movement of American origin, Jehovah's Witnesses combine a commitment to the separation of church and state with a strong premillennial outlook, both of which have often placed it in conflict with civil and religious authorities around the world. The core tenet of Jehovah's Witnesses is the apostle Paul's triumphant hope at 1 Corinthians 15:52: "In a moment, in the twinkling of an eye, at the last trump, the trumpet shall sound and the dead shall be raised incorruptible, and we shall be changed."

Origins and Beliefs

Sometime during the mid-1870s, Charles Taze Russell (1852–1916), a successful businessman from Pittsburgh, Pennsylvania, concluded from intensive Bible study that Paul's prophecies would be realized in his lifetime—and furthermore that rational computation from Scripture would yield the date. Through dynamic preaching, effective pastoring, and prolific writing (notably, articles in *The Watchtower* magazine, which he created, and his six-volume *Studies in the Scriptures*), Russell gathered a group of people who at first called themselves "Bible Students" (but were also known as Russellites and Millennial Dawnites). After various false starts, they committed themselves to 1914 as the year in which they expected to witness Armageddon and, thereafter, the establishment on earth of Christ's millennial kingdom, paradise on earth. Because the coming destruction would spare only a faithful remnant, they had not only a duty but also a deadline to speed the good news everywhere and to expose false teaching.

For more than a century, Jehovah's Witnesses have not mitigated their sharply premillennial accent on that Christian rejection of "the world" that has periodically discomfited religious establishments. As a result, Witnesses have often courted discrimination, mob violence, and prosecution, under virtually every kind of sacred and secular regime. Their world-rejecting outlook has entailed disinterest in such improvements to this world as schools, hospitals, and charities but has nonetheless contributed to reform. In the United States and Canada, Jehovah's Witnesses have brought or participated in many legal cases that have redefined religious and press freedom, separation of church and state, and conscientious objection.

For Christians in Russell's milieu, the world rumbled with discontent with the social inequities and economic dis-

Charles Taze Russell

locations of large-scale capitalism, rampant in the Gilded Age at the turn of the century, and with the religious dislocation of the Bible as a result of modern intellectual trends, epitomized by "higher criticism" and Darwin's theory of evolution. Contemporary answers included socialism, social Darwinism, sociology, the Social Gospel, and, not least, literal and metaphorical prophesying that the end was at hand. Apart from his adoption of the Seventh-day Adventists' original interest in date setting, Russell's own premillennialist answers flowed with the conservative Protestant mainstream— when he taught that human beings had neither the duty nor the capacity to reform the world's evil, for example, and when he anathematized greedy capitalists and apostate churches. Populism and fundamentalism were compatible.

Even Russell's preaching against worldly political allegiances remained a commonplace, until World War I, when militants thundered out on street corners against military service and against those clergy who abetted recruitment. Less commonplace, however, but widely resented and resisted from the start, were his teaching against the Trinity, hell, the immortality of the soul, and the Roman Catholic Church virtually in toto. Probably most resented, however, was his own, his followers', and their successors' disruptive enthusiasm for converting and rebaptizing Christians. Witnesses' characteristic door-to-door proselytizing and distribution of literature evolved from the religious countdown of Russell's soldierly generation toward the final struggle of Armageddon.

Expansion Overseas

The deployment of the Witnesses abroad was rapid and early. Russell authorized missions to Canada and Britain in the early 1880s and in 1884 incorporated the Zion's Watch Tower Tract Society, the first of several legal entities that govern Witnesses worldwide. By the outbreak of World War I, the Bible Students had expanded into Australia, New Zealand, and South Africa (black and white), as well as into nearly a dozen countries of eastern and western Europe. That expansion surged when the war came on schedule, ebbed temporarily through defection and schism when Armageddon did not, but gained its old élan and a new date, 1925. British West African colonies received missionaries in the early 1920s. From the South African base established in 1902, African labor migrants carried *The Watchtower* and their (often heterodox) interpretations of it back to their homes in colonized Malawi, Mozambique, Zaire, Zambia, and Zimbabwe, there to lay politico-religious explosives under missions and sometimes regimes. The German Bible Students, established in 1897, grew rapidly after World War I, firing at and fired upon by churches and later by Hitler's Gestapo.

The name "Jehovah's Witnesses" was adopted in 1931, during the presidency of Russell's successor, Joseph F. Rutherford, an attorney. In that era, Russell's talk of a satanic alliance between capital and churches led fascists and democrats to identify Witnesses as socialists and even communists. In 1935, when striking colonial Central African miners took inspiration from Jehovah's Witnesses, local police looked for ties to the Third International, an association of national Communist parties, and an Anglican prelate styled the doctrines against hell and the immortality of souls as "ecclesiastical bolshevism."

Beginning in 1917, from the society's headquarters in Brooklyn, New York, Rutherford established in outline the centralized hierarchical structure and highly disciplined "theocratic" organization that has enabled Witnesses to function worldwide even amid repression. Their activities are treated as subversive wherever a majority faith binds society to a political organization, for example, in colonial Mozambique, when it was under the domination of fascist Portugal. At times, they have operated like the resourceful underground organizations in Allied and Axis countries during World War II and in the Soviet bloc thereafter. More recently, especially under conditions of mass mobilization, the stand Witnesses have made against political allegiance has made them obnoxious—for example, to the builders of postindependence, one-party states in Malawi, Mozambique, and Zambia. Even so, in the mid-1970s Zambia was reputed to have the highest per capita concentration of Witnesses in the world. As 1975 approached (another marked year), the Watchtower Bible and Tract Society claimed to be growing more rapidly than any other Christian body. Although apparently later outstripped by others, in 1996 it was publishing in 100 languages and claimed some 5 million adherents in 233 countries, with especially vigorous growth in countries of the former Soviet Union.

See also *Anabaptists; Fascism; Fundamentalism; Millennialism; Seventh-day Adventists; Social Gospel.*

Karen E. Fields

BIBLIOGRAPHY

Cole, Marley. *Jehovah's Witnesses: The New World Society.* New York: Vantage, 1955.

Fields, Karen E. *Revival and Rebellion in Colonial Central Africa.* New York: Heinemann's, 1985; reprinted 1997.

Franz, Fred W. "Jehovah's Witnesses" and "Charles Taze Russell." *Encyclopedia Americana.* Danbury, Conn.: Grolier, Inc., 1992.

Harrison, Barbara Grizzuti. *Visions of Glory: A History and a Memory of Jehovah's Witnesses.* New York: Simon and Schuster, 1978.

Penton, M. James. *Apocalypse Delayed: The Story of Jehovah's Witnesses.* Toronto: University of Toronto Press, 1985.

Watchtower Bible and Tract Society of Pennsylvania. *1997 Yearbook of Jehovah's Witnesses.* Brooklyn, N.Y.: Watchtower Bible and Tract Society of Pennsylvania.

Jerusalem

With a 4,000-year recorded, almost uninterrupted, checkered history, Jerusalem is one of the oldest cities in the world. It is the only city venerated as holy by all three major

The Dome of the Rock (Qubbat al-Sakhra), an Islamic monument in Jerusalem. Muslims believe that the monument, completed in 691–692, marks the spot from which the prophet Muhammad ascended to heaven.

monotheistic religions—Christianity, Islam, and Judaism. Through the millennia Jerusalem has had many names in several languages and been inhabited by many peoples, ruled by many rulers, conquered more than thirty times by many armies. It has been a city-state; head city of a tribal domain; capital of a fiefdom, of a kingdom, and of a modern republic; seat of a provincial governor; remote county-borough of an empire—and most of these more than once. Jerusalem's municipal boundaries and population have varied enormously, its area ranging from the 0.06 square kilometers of the biblical City of David to its present-day 123 square kilometers, of which the walled Old City occupies 0.85 square kilometers.

Jerusalem was for four hundred years (1517–1917) the chief city of a minor subprovince of the Ottoman Empire and then for about thirty years the seat of the colonial government of British-administered Palestine (1917–1948). A proposal to make Jerusalem and its vicinity, including Bethlehem with its Church of the Nativity, an internationally administererd area (a *Corpus Separatum)* was part of the United Nations resolution on the partitioning of Palestine (1947), but this proposal was never carried out. The international community was unable to devise a viable solution to the major component of what had become the Arab-Jewish national conflict, and the Christian world was keen to prevent Muslim or Jewish control of Christian holy places.

In 1948, on Israel's independence and with the Arab military onslaught on it, Jerusalem was divided by the Israeli-Jordanian armistice line into the western (Israeli) part and the eastern (Jordanian) part. The Old City and, within and around it, the major holy places of all three religions are located in the eastern part. In 1959 Jordanian Jerusalem was formally designated the second capital of Jordan and granted a status equal to that of Amman.

Since 1949 Jerusalem has been the capital city of Israel—at first within what was then the prevailing border line running right through the city and, since the 1967 Six-Day War between Israel and Arabs, encompassing a much enlarged municipal area on both sides of the previous dividing line. In the mid-1990s about 70 percent of Jerusalem's almost 600,000 inhabitants were Jews, and most of the rest Arabs, of whom some 90 percent were Muslims and 10 percent Christians.

But neither the Arab world, including the Palestinian authorities who regard Jerusalem as the political and cultural center of Palestine and as its capital, nor most of the international community has become reconciled to Israel's rule over eastern Jerusalem. Most states, although treating Jerusalem as the seat of Israel's government, have refrained from formally recognizing it as its capital. In the 1994 Israel-Jordan peace agreement, Israel respects the present role of the Hashimite Kingdom of Jordan in the Muslim holy places in Jerusalem.

Jewish, Christian, and Muslim Connections

In Jewish lore Jerusalem, synonymous with Zion, is the reputed location of Mount Moriah, scene of Abraham's temptation to sacrifice his son Isaac; the capital of David's kingdom and that of his successors' Kingdom of Judah; the site of Solomon's temple and that of the Second Temple. After the destruction of the first temple and since the destruc-

tion of the second nearly 2,000 years ago, Jerusalem has been, in turn and concurrently, the object of lamentation and messianic aspirations for the return to the Holy City, the resurrection there of all the dead, and the rebuilding of the temple. Whenever permitted, Jews took up residence in the city, and since the middle of the nineteenth century they have constituted a majority of the population. A handful of them are even today pursuing preparations for the restoration of the temple services of old. The Western (or Wailing) Wall, archeological remnants of the outer perimeter of the Second Temple, together with the Temple Mount, have become major Jewish holy places. Modern Zionism, whose very name evokes the pivotal importance of Jerusalem, has politicized and partially secularized these sentiments into aspirations for the restoration of Jewish sovereignty and the renaissance of Jewish culture.

Jerusalem became holy to Christians because it was the site of the life, crucifixion, and resurrection of Jesus; because the city was sacred to him; and because for Christians it is the City of Christ, the City of God. Their attachment to it takes many forms, not the least of which are the pilgrimages or devotional visits to the sites identified with the Passion of Christ.

During the Middle Ages the crusaders set out to liberate these sites from the Saracen infidels. Some Christians chose even to regard British field marshal Edmund Allenby's entry into Jerusalem (1917) to capture it from the Turks in the same light as a modern crusade. For others, the spiritual vision of Jerusalem became ever more remote from its physical presence and was even transplanted to other landscapes—thus John Winthrop, governor of the Massachusetts Bay Colony, envisaged the foundation of a city on a Hill, God's new Israel, in seventeenth-century Massachusetts, and English poet William Blake committed himself to a spiritual quest to "build Jerusalem in England's green and pleasant land."

The most important Christian holy place inside Jerusalem is the Basilica of the Holy Sepulcher, situated according to Christian tradition on the rock of Golgotha, or Calvary, which is really an edifice housing a number of churches and sanctuaries of different Christian denominations. For centuries disputes, at times violent, have erupted among these denominations over the demarcation between their respective shares of the space and the control of shrines and relics. Governments have had to intervene, and their adjudications became the source of the so-called Status Quo of the Holy Places, which regulates rights, first extended to include the Church of the Nativity and later all the major holy places of the three religions. The Stations of the Cross, which together make up the Via Dolorosa and lead toward the Holy Sepulcher, are also located within the Old City.

Jerusalem's place in Islam originated with Muhammad's miraculous nocturnal journey, reported in the Qur'an, to Al-Masjid al-Aqsa (the Farthest Mosque) and his ascension from there to heaven and return to Medina. Al-Aqsa is traditionally identified with Jerusalem, which during the first Arab period (638–1099) was called Bayt al-Maqdis (from the Hebrew *beit hamiqdash,* which means temple), and from the tenth-century al-Quds al-Sharif (the Noble Holy City), usually shortened to al-Quds. Under Muslim rule Jerusalem's significance was mainly religious, and the administrative capital of the province was the town of Ramleh, thirty miles away. Jerusalem also was, albeit only for a few years, the original *qibla* (direction of prayer) for Muslims. The al-Aqsa mosque together with Qubbat al-Sakhra (Dome of the Rock) and lesser shrines located on al-Haram al-Sharif (the Noble Sanctuary, also called the Temple Mount) have made Jerusalem the third holiest site of Islam. The crusader Latin Kingdom took over Jerusalem, and a literary genre of anthologies called *fada'il al-Quds* (Praises of Jerusalem) expressed Muslim longings for the city. Almost 1,200 years of continuous Muslim rule, interrupted only by the Latin Kingdom, have marked the culture of Jerusalem and its importance for the Muslim world.

Religion and Nationalism

Jerusalem's worldwide prominence stems primarily from its religious significance, more specifically from the sacredness each of the three religions and their respective denominations and sects attribute to locations and shrines within the city and around it and to the city as a whole. In the twentieth century, however, Jerusalem has become the epicenter of the Arab-Jewish conflict. The blending of geographical, politico-national, and religious elements has made the city the seemingly intractable problem it has become. The holy places are cases in point: in addition to their predominantly religious role, they also serve as emblems of national identity for both Arabs (Muslim perhaps more so than Christian) and Jews. The conflict is even more exacerbated when more than one religion claims holy places, such as the Temple Mount or Abraham's tomb in Hebron.

A new trend in Arab nationalist historiography claims an uninterrupted Arab presence in Palestine and Jerusalem, with Arab roots going back 5,000 years to the time when the mythical Arab city Yabous (Jebus) was founded. Together with the holiness of the city, this is ostensibly the basis for the insistent call not to obliterate what had been the predominant character of the city.

Jerusalem Below and Jerusalem Above

Jerusalem's history and its present plight are the consequence of a unique, uncanny tension between reality and metaphysics—between Jerusalem Below, the terrestrial of the here and now and its mundane conflicts, and Jerusalem Above, the mythological, the epiphanic, and of the apocalyptic quest for peace and redemption in a New Jerusalem. Despite the putative elation created by such spirituality, or perhaps because of it, this tension has, on balance, stirred interfaith rivalries and almost obliterated interethnic comity. It is the coupling of the religious with the national, such as the linking of the problem of the free access and control of the holy places with those of borders of and the sovereignty over Jerusalem, that reinforces the intractability of the situation.

No final or lasting Israeli-Palestinian accommodation is feasible without an agreement on Jerusalem, and the obverse is also the case. But an accommodation is not feasible without far-reaching mutual concessions that will necessarily entail distinguishing between what is strictly sacred and what is not and detaching arrangements for the holy places from other political and territorial issues. A 1993 agreement between the Vatican and Israel indicates that the Christian world would not oppose an Israeli-Palestinian accommodation for Jerusalem. One thing is certain: whatever solutions are adopted, they will resonate far and wide throughout the Muslim, Jewish, and Christian worlds.

See also *Christianity; Crusades; Islam; Israel; Jordan; Judaism; Muhammad; Nationalism; Sacred places; Zionism.*

Emanuel Gutmann

BIBLIOGRAPHY

Armstrong, Karen. *A History of Jerusalem: One City, Three Faiths.* London: HarperCollins, 1996.

Bovis, H. Eugene. *The Jerusalem Question, 1917–1968.* Stanford: Hoover Institution Press, 1971.

Dumper, Michael. *The Politics of Jerusalem since 1967.* New York: Columbia University Press, 1997.

Friedland, Roger, and Richard Hecht. *To Rule Jerusalem.* Cambridge: Cambridge University Press, 1996.

Gilbert, Martin. *Jerusalem in the Twentieth Century.* London: Chatto and Windus, 1996.

Rosovsky, Nitza, ed. *City of the Great King.* Cambridge: Harvard University Press, 1996.

Sharkansky, Ira. *Governing Jerusalem.* Detroit: Wayne State University Press, 1996.

Tibawi, A. L. *Jerusalem: Its Place in Islamic and Arabic History.* Beirut: Institute for Palestine Studies, 1969.

Jesuits

Founded in 1540 by Ignatius of Loyola, a former courtier and soldier from the Basque country of northern Spain, the Society of Jesus (or Jesuits) is the largest, one of the most influential, and certainly the most controversial male religious order in Roman Catholicism. The Jesuits became the prototype for active religious congregations engaged in a variety of enterprises, surpassing older monastic communities. The outgoing worldliness often noted in Jesuits can be traced to Ignatius's injunction to "find God in all things." From the beginning, with their focus on education and foreign missions, Jesuits have referred to themselves as "contemplatives in action."

On the one hand, the "black robes," as they were called by the Iroquois nations of upper New York and Canada, among whom they ministered in the seventeenth century, were primary agents in the Counter Reformation of the sixteenth and seventeenth centuries, which attempted to reverse the advances made by the Protestant Reformation. On the other hand, in their commitment to learning and the cultivation of human resources, Jesuits have been allied with the forces of enlightenment germinating in the Renaissance of early modern Europe. This tension between tradition and creativity runs through the tumultuous history of the society.

Historical Development

The story of the Jesuits can be divided into three acts. The first ended abruptly in 1773, when the pope issued an edict to suppress the society. The Jesuits, celebrated not only for their schools but for their far-flung missionary work and their activities as court advisers, had aroused the hostility of European monarchs with ambitions to retain absolutist authority as well as the enmity of rivals within the church. Except in Russia, whose rulers declined to receive the papal edict, the Jesuits were disbanded and their property confis-

cated. Many became secular priests, and the superior general died in a papal prison in Rome.

After a forty-year hiatus, a papacy alarmed by political upheavals attendant on the French Revolution restored the Society of Jesus. The period from 1814 until the Second Vatican Council in the 1960s constitutes the second act in the adventures of the Jesuits. Once again growing rapidly, the restored society was associated with conservative, anti-democratic positions through much of the nineteenth and the first part of the twentieth centuries in Europe. Jesuits were identified with "ultramontanism," a movement backing the universal supremacy of the pope, that culminated in the decree of papal infallibility at the First Vatican Council (1869–1870).

Generally defending the prerevolutionary norms of the Old Regime, European Jesuits contributed to the social teaching of the church that, in its early stages, was a compound of precapitalist paternalism and aversion to socialism. A German Jesuit wrote the encyclical *Quadragesimo Anno* (Fortieth Anniversary), issued in 1931, on reconstructing the social order to protect workers. This encyclical outlined the Catholic version of corporatism, an attempt to formulate a third way between capitalism and communism. Its most durable legacy is the notion of subsidiarity: decisions that can be taken at a lower level, the argument went, should not be referred to higher levels of a political system. This principle of decentralization, originally designed to protect the autonomy of a church threatened by totalitarian governments in Italy, Germany, and the Soviet Union during the years between the First and Second World Wars, has since become a watchword to guard the sovereignty of member states of the evolving European Community.

Jesuits in the United States, though growing rapidly, had a lower political profile than their counterparts in Europe. Georgetown University, the country's oldest Catholic institution of higher learning, was inaugurated in 1789 under the auspices of Bishop John Carroll, a former Jesuit who had become a secular priest with the suppression of his colleagues. American Jesuits catered to a burgeoning clientele of Catholic immigrants and their offspring. More than Jesuits elsewhere, the American branch deployed its manpower throughout a network of high schools, colleges, and universities. The high schools especially became a major source of recruits. By the end of the 1930s the Society of Jesus in the United States had overtaken Spanish Jesuits to form the largest regional grouping in the worldwide order.

In the years following World War II the energy of the

American Jesuits was expressed not only in their colleges and universities, expanding exponentially under the stimulus of the G.I. bill, which paid for college educations for returning soldiers, but in the emergence of scholars. Most conspicuous of these was the theologian and political theorist John Courtney Murray, who pushed the boundaries of Catholic orthodoxy. In the late 1950s Murray's advocacy of religious toleration and political pluralism earned him the opprobrium of reactionaries in the Vatican, and his superiors were compelled to silence him.

The Second Vatican Council and Afterward

The Second Vatican Council (1962–1965), called by Pope John XXIII, touched off the third act of Jesuit history, one whose scenario has yet to be completed. The promulgation of Vatican II's decree on religious freedom, drafted by Murray, vindicated his views. At the same time, Pedro Arrupe, the first Basque to head the order since its founding, was elected superior general and undertook an energetic program in line with the reform-minded shift in Catholicism. The training of Jesuits became less regimented, and greater priority was placed on social justice. By 1965, when the council drew to a close, the Jesuits were at their numeric peak, with more than 35,000 men across the globe, about 8,500 of whom were Americans.

Even then, however, signs of trouble were evident. As early as the mid-1950s the number of entrants had begun to stagnate and then drift downward. In the wake of Vatican II, which left the identity and the role of the priesthood unclear, the volume of recruits shrank. Jesuits left in droves. Thirty years after the council, global membership had fallen to the low-20,000 mark. Concurrently, with the drop in young entrants, the average age of Jesuits climbed. The decline in membership was especially precipitous in advanced industrial societies. In 1997 the number of American Jesuits fell below 4,000, and they were overtaken as the biggest regional bloc by the Jesuits of India.

The shrinking and graying of the society have prompted a transition to greater collaboration with lay people in educational and other operations. By the mid-1980s there were more than a million alumni of Jesuit colleges and universities in the United States, and the scale of these operations surpassed the capacity of Jesuits to control them. Conscious of the secularization of universities like Harvard, Princeton, and Yale, whose origins were bound up with Protestant denominations, Jesuits and their colleagues struggled to clarify the mission of the institutions of higher education affiliated with the order in the United States. The process is not unlike decolonization, with Jesuits withdrawing from positions of leadership while leaving signs of a distinctive ethos in place.

With the ascent to the papacy of Karol Wojtyla as John Paul II in 1978, the power of the Jesuits waned. The experimentalism and ecumenicism of many Jesuits did not sit well with the militant centralism of the new pope. In 1981, when Arrupe was immobilized by a stroke, the pope bypassed the usual rules of the society and appointed an elderly Jesuit as caretaker. Jesuits, some of whom referred to this event as a mini-suppression, were enjoined to get their house in order. In 1983, at a general congregation of the society in Rome, the Dutch Jesuit Peter-Hans Kolvenbach was elected superior general of the Society of Jesus.

Despite these changes, Jesuits have continued to get caught up in politics. During the 1970s and 1980s a number of Jesuits were instrumental in the liberation theology movement in Central America. In El Salvador in 1989 six members of the order were assassinated by the military for their criticism of the regime. Individual Jesuits, like the peace activist Daniel Berrigan in the United States, occasionally make political statements and engage in social advocacy. In 1997 a Jesuit was slain in India because of his work with untouchables, and Jesuits have fallen victim to internecine warfare in Africa. The society is a collective presence in a few areas bearing on public policy, most notably in private education. But the greater part of the politics involving Jesuits touches on relations with the ecclesiastical hierarchy and on sensitive issues such as the role of women in the church.

Future Directions

Several mixed features characterize the situation of the Society of Jesus as Christianity enters its third millennium. Although the Jesuits' commitment to social justice continues to receive rhetorical support, practical means for delivering on this commitment are still being thrashed out. The process is complicated by their obligations, especially in the schools, and by the ambiguities inherent in education. Some of the schools serve relatively well off constituencies, while others care for poor people, many of them non-Catholic, in inner cities.

The task of redirecting priorities is aggravated by manpower shortages. Only in India does Jesuit membership appear to be growing steadily, and even there the forecast is for a flattening out and eventual decline as the country modernizes. The Society of Jesus is an understaffed conglomerate, and the diversity of its activities makes the corporate direction of the order uncertain.

Finally, there is a serious question about the survival not only of the Jesuits themselves but of all celibate religious orders—at least in advanced industrial societies. Though ideologically more conservative than the Jesuits, the Opus Dei, founded in the 1920s, is a less exclusively clerical organization than the Jesuit order. Other groups—notably the Ignatian Associates, an organization of lay people with ties to the Society of Jesus—have a centrist or progressive tenor. Variations on these formats may point the way as Catholicism becomes more lay centered. What forms of religious life may emerge in Catholicism remains an open question.

See also *Catholicism, Roman; Education; Justice, Social; Liberation theology; Missionaries; Reformation; Vatican; Vatican Council, Second.*

Peter McDonough

BIBLIOGRAPHY

Hooper, J. Leon, and Todd David Whitmore, eds. *John Courtney Murray and the Growth of Tradition.* Kansas City, Mo.: Sheed and Ward, 1996.

McDonough, Peter. *Men Astutely Trained: A History of the Jesuits in the American Century.* New York: Free Press, 1992.

O'Malley, John W. *The First Jesuits.* Cambridge: Harvard University Press, 1993.

Padberg, John W. *Together as a Companionship: A History of the Thirty-First, Thirty-Second, and Thirty-Third General Congregation of the Society of Jesus.* St. Louis, Mo.: Institute of Jesuit Sources, 1994.

Polner, Murray, and Jim O'Grady. *Disarmed and Dangerous: The Radical Life and Times of Daniel and Phillip Berrigan.* New York: Basic Books, 1997.

Reese, Thomas J. *Inside the Vatican: The Politics and Organization of the Catholic Church.* Cambridge: Harvard University Press, 1996.

Whitfield, Teresa. *Paying the Price: Ignacio Ellacuría and the Murdered Jesuits of El Salvador.* Philadelphia: Temple University Press, 1994.

Wittberg, Patricia. *The Rise and Fall of Catholic Religious Orders.* Albany: State University of New York Press, 1994.

Jesus

Jewish teacher and prophet whom Christians regard as the Messiah. A Galilean Jew, Jesus was born about 4 B.C.E. and died about 30 C.E. His last two years were spent in a mission of preaching, miraculous activity, and the gathering of a group of disciples, which took him back and forth between

A mural of Jesus overlooks Revolution Square, in Havana, Cuba. The mural anticipated the January 1998 visit of Pope John Paul II, whom Roman Catholics regard as a successor of Peter, an apostle of Jesus.

Galilee and Jerusalem. His teaching, given with great authoritativeness, was radical moral instruction, stressing forgiveness and generosity and relaxing the severity of the ritual and Sabbath law, combined with an emphasis on the imminent coming of God's kingdom. It threatened the authority of the Jewish priesthood and could appear subversive to Roman rule, although Jesus' teaching was both pacifist and unpolitical. Arrested on a visit to Jerusalem, in which he had led a triumphal procession and caused a disturbance in the Temple, he was crucified by order of Pilate, the Roman governor.

His followers, however, did not disperse. Convinced that he had risen from the dead and was both Son of God and the Messiah, or "Christ," God's anointed one, whom many Jews were expecting, they began to spread the good news ("gospel") of salvation. They preached first to Jews and then to all non-Jews (the Gentiles) as well, focusing on the life and death of Jesus. Within a few years the community ("church") of believers in Jesus Christ, as he was now regularly described, was to be found in towns around the Mediterranean.

The earliest surviving Christian writings are the first letters of Paul, a dynamic missionary theologian, written to believers in Thessalonica, Corinth, and elsewhere about twenty years after Jesus' death. The four Gospels, accounts of Jesus' life and death, three of which (Matthew, Mark, and Luke, the so-called synoptic Gospels) have much overlapping material, were written some twenty years later still. Jesus wrote nothing himself. It is essential to remember that what we know of him was written a generation after his death, based on memory, earlier shorter writings, or the evolving needs of the young church. Paul's letters, the four Gospels, and other writings were eventually put together to form the Christian New Testament, a collection of twenty-seven short works by some ten different writers. All are centered on the figure of Jesus Christ, though from a variety of angles. For all of them this socially unimportant Galilean teacher who ended his life as an executed criminal represented the definitive expression of the wisdom and power of God.

See also *Christianity*.

Adrian Hastings

BIBLIOGRAPHY

Sanders, E. P. *Jesus and Judaism*. Philadelphia: Trinity Press International, 1985.
Theissen, Gerd, and Annette Merz. *The Historical Jesus: A Comprehensive Guide*. London: SCM Press, 1998.
Vermes, Geza. *Jesus the Jew*. London: Collins, 1973.

Jihad

The Islamic idea of *jihad,* which is derived from the Arabic root meaning "to strive" or "to make an effort," connotes a wide range of meanings, from an inward spiritual struggle to attain perfect faith to an outward material struggle to promote justice and the Islamic social system. The former meaning was emphasized by Sufis (Muslim mystics), who popularized a tradition describing the inner jihad as greater than the outer jihad. When used in the latter sense, jihad is closely identified with the injunction in the Qur'an, the revelation of God to the prophet Muhammad, to the Muslim community to "command the right and forbid the wrong" (3:104, 110). The close connection of jihad with the struggle for justice is reinforced in the *hadith,* the sayings and actions attributed to Muhammad. One of the best known states that a Muslim must strive to avert injustice first by actions, and if that is not possible, by words, and if that is not possible, at least by intentions.

During the period of Qur'anic revelation while Muhammad was in Mecca (610–622), jihad meant essentially a nonviolent struggle to spread Islam. Following his move from Mecca to Medina in 622, and the establishment of an Islamic state, fighting in self-defense was sanctioned by the Qur'an (22:39). The Qur'an began referring increasingly to *qital* (fighting or warfare) as one form of jihad. Two of the last verses on this topic (9:5, 29) suggest a war of conquest or conversion against all unbelievers.

The Medieval Doctrine

In medieval legal sources (compiled roughly between the eighth and eleventh centuries), jihad generally referred to a divinely sanctioned struggle to establish Muslim hegemony over non-Muslims as a prelude to the propagation of the Islamic faith. Islamic legal scholars divided the world into two spheres: *Dar al-Islam* (land of Islam), where Islamic law applied, and *Dar al-Harb* (land of war), where the absence of Islamic law presumably fostered anarchy and immorality. The Islamic state's duty was to reduce *Dar al-Harb*—through peaceful means if possible, through war if necessary—until it had been incorporated into *Dar al-Islam*. Jurists differed on the possibility and duration of peace between the two spheres. The majority held that jihad could be suspended if the Muslim commander deemed it in the interest of the Islamic state, but usually not for more than ten years. The Qur'anic verses that suggest peaceful accommodation or coexistence with unbelievers (especially 2:193, 8:61) were declared abrogated by the later, more belligerent ones.

The medieval theory included elaborate rules on the right conduct of jihad. No war was a jihad unless authorized and led by the *imam,* the leader of the Islamic state. Enemies were to be given fair warning, and, should they choose not to accept Islam or to fight, they were to be offered protected *(dhimmi)* status, which allowed them to retain communal autonomy within the Islamic state in return for tax payments. This provision initially applied to Christians and Jews but later was broadened to include other religious communities living under Muslim rule. Noncombatants were not to be killed, nor was enemy property to be destroyed unnecessarily.

In addition to the expansionist jihad, medieval scholars also dealt with internal conflicts against rebels within Islam. In this form of jihad, stricter rules of engagement and greater protection for the lives and property of the enemy applied than in the case of non-Muslims. The aim of this type of jihad was to rehabilitate the rebels as quickly as possible into the Muslim body politic.

Modern Interpretations

Three broad approaches to the modern reinterpretation of jihad may be discerned. First, the apologetic arose in the late nineteenth century in response to Western criticism that jihad meant "holy war" and that Islam was spread through force. Muslim apologists argued that the Qur'an and Prophetic traditions allow war only for self-defense against persecution and aggression. Some Muslim writers, particularly those in British India, restricted even further the legitimate scope of jihad by arguing that so long as no direct threat to Islamic worship was posed by European imperialists Muslims should not challenge colonial rule. The medieval theorists who had defined jihad as expansionist war were, according to this view, simply misguided.

The second approach, the modernist, also diminishes jihad's military aspects and emphasizes its broader ethical dimensions within Islamic faith and practice. Like the apologists, the modernists dismiss the medieval theory as a distortion of Qur'anic ethics, pointing out, for example, that the division of the world into Dar al-Islam and Dar al-Harb is found nowhere in the Qur'an or Prophetic traditions. A war is jihad, therefore, only if it is fought in defense of Muslim lives, property, and honor. Unlike the apologists, however, the modernists are motivated less by Western criticisms of jihad than by the desire to interpret this concept in a way compatible with modern international norms. Jihad in the modernist view is the Islamic equivalent of the Western idea of just war, a war fought to repel aggression with limited goals and by restricted means.

The third approach, the revivalist, arose in response to the apologist and modernist writings. By limiting jihad to self-defense, the revivalists claim, the apologists and modernists have debased the dynamic qualities of jihad. In the final years of the Prophet's life, the revivalists argue, jihad clearly meant the struggle to propagate the Islamic order worldwide. The goal of jihad today ought not to be to coerce people to accept Islam, because the Qur'an clearly encourages freedom of worship (especially 2:256); rather, it ought to be to overthrow un-Islamic regimes that corrupt their societies and divert people from service to God.

For revivalist writers, un-Islamic regimes include those ruling in most Muslim countries. The immediate goal of the revivalist jihad is to replace hypocritical leaders with true Muslims. Only when this long and painstaking internal struggle has succeeded in reestablishing an authentically Islamic base can the external jihad resume. Thus jihad is today largely synonymous with Islamic revolution in the works of most Muslim activists.

See also Crusades; Islam; Muhammad; Sufism; Violence; War.

Sohail H. Hashmi

BIBLIOGRAPHY

Hamidullah, Muhammad. *Muslim Conduct of State.* 7th ed. Lahore: Shaykh Muhammad Ashraf, 1961.

Johnson, James Turner, and John Kelsay, eds. *Cross, Crescent, and Sword: The Justification and Limitation of War in Western and Islamic Tradition.* New York: Greenwood Press, 1990.

Kelsay, John, and James Turner Johnson, eds. *Just War and Jihad: Historical and Theoretical Perspectives on War and Peace in Western and Islamic Tradition.* New York: Greenwood Press, 1991.

Khadduri, Majid. *War and Peace in the Law of Islam.* Baltimore: Johns Hopkins University Press, 1955.

Morabia, Alfred. *Le Gihad dans l'Islam médiéval: Le "Combat sacré" des origines au XIIe siècle.* Paris: Albin Michel, 1993.

Peters, Rudolph. *Islam and Colonialism: The Doctrine of Jihad in Modern History.* The Hague: Mouton, 1979.

———. *Jihad in Classical and Modern Islam.* Princeton: Markus Wiener, 1996.

Jinnah, Muhammad Ali

Indian politician, leader of the Indian Muslim League, and founder of Pakistan. Jinnah (1876–1948) served as Pakistan's first governor general (1947–1948).

He was born in Karachi, then part of British India, and would be buried in Karachi, Pakistan. He spent most of his professional life in Bombay, however, where he practiced law. Although Jinnah was not religious in the traditional practicant sense, he was born into a Shi'ite Muslim family. He remained a secular, liberal modernist.

Jinnah was elected to the Indian National Congress Party

Muhammad Ali Jinnah

1930, and articulated the two-nation theory, which stipulated establishing separate Muslim states within or outside the British empire.

Iqbal's position was not acceptable to Jinnah until the period of 1938–1940, when Hindu leaders had refused to form a coalition government with the Muslim League and Britain had entered World War II without guaranteeing India's independence. Jinnah finally presided at a meeting of the Muslim League in 1940 in Lahore, where a resolution was adopted demanding two Muslim states. These states did not emerge as Bangladesh and Pakistan until the 1970s, although India was partitioned into India and Pakistan in 1947.

By 1940 Jinnah had become so popular among Muslims that they began calling him the *Quaid-i-Azam*, the Great Leader.

See also *India; Iqbal, Muhammad; Islam; Pakistan.*

Hafeez Malik

BIBLIOGRAPHY

Khairi, Saad R. *Jinnah Reinterpreted: A Journey from Indian Nationalism to Muslim Statehood.* Karachi and New York: Oxford University Press, 1995.

Malik, Hafeez. *Moslem Nationalism in India and Pakistan.* Washington, D.C.: Public Affairs Press, 1963.

Wolpert, Stanley. *Jinnah of Pakistan.* New York: Oxford University Press, 1984.

in 1906. Early in his political career he supported a united India in which Muslims would attain guaranteed rights of representation in the government, but by 1940 he had become a champion for the cause of a separate Muslim state.

To satisfy Muslims' determination to have guaranteed rights in the future political system of India and to maintain territorial unity of the Indian state, by 1929 Jinnah produced the formula known as the Fourteen Points of Mr. Jinnah. The Fourteen Points included separate electorates for Muslims in the provinces of India, parity of electoral representation in the Punjab and Bengal, and electoral considerations for Muslims in those provinces in which they were a minority, although they would retain clear majority in the Northwest Frontier Province, Baluchistan, and Sind.

By this time, however, the Muslim League had split into two factions, one led by Jinnah, and the other one in the Punjab, led by Mian Mohammed Shafi. Muhammad Iqbal (1877–1938), who later came to be known as the Poet-Philosopher of Pakistan, delivered a presidential address at the annual session of the Muslim League on December 29,

Jordan

The Hashimite Kingdom of Jordan is a small state bordered by Syria on the north, Israel and the Palestinian territories on the west, and Saudi Arabia and Iraq to the east. It gained full independence from Britain after World War II. About half of Jordan's population of some 4.2 million is of Palestinian origin; 90–95 percent of the population is Muslim, with the remainder indigenous Christians.

Jordan's monarch since 1953, Husayn bin Talal al-Hashimi (hence the name of the kingdom), claims descent from the prophet Muhammad. For generations Husayn's forebears governed Mecca and were known by the title *sharif*, which implies descent from the Prophet. This tie to Muhammad and to the responsibility for the holy cities of Mecca and Medina (as well as Jerusalem, which was part of Husayn's realm until the Israeli occupation of the eastern part of the

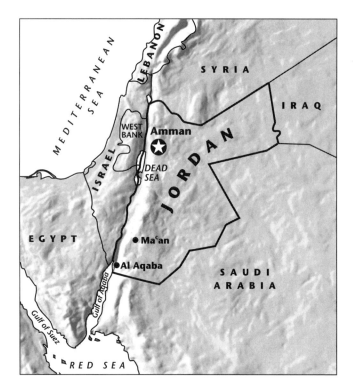

city in 1967) is periodically featured in royal discourse. The regime carefully distinguishes between what the Hashimites call their "moderate Islam" and the Islam of other regimes—certainly that practiced in Iran after the Islamic revolution but also that of the stricter Wahhabi Islam of the House of Sa'ud, whose founder drove Husayn's great-grandfather from the Hashimites' home region in the Hijaz (which subsequently became Saudi Arabia). As a result, the Hashimite-Sa'udi rivalry has at times been an important element in inter-Arab politics, especially in issues related to responsibility for the Islamic holy sites in Jerusalem.

Influence of the Muslim Brethren

In 1957, in response to domestic political challenges, Husayn outlawed political parties and imposed martial law. Exempted from the ban was the Muslim Brethren, a transnational politico-religious organization originally founded in Egypt in the 1930s, which was allowed to continue its organizing under the rubric of a social institution. In this way, Husayn was perhaps the first Arab leader to use a strategy of encouraging the development of the religious right to

counter the power and appeal of Arab nationalist or Marxist political parties. As a result, as other political groups faced repeated arrests and harassment, the Brethren was able gradually to expand its influence. At the same time, despite creating the impression of a relatively Westernized or forward-looking society, domestic social policy in the kingdom remained conservative: personal status law (concerned with such issues as marriage, divorce, and inheritance) was drawn from a combination of Islamic law (shari'a) and traditional (village or tribal) law. Women did not receive the vote until 1974, and their participation in the labor force outside the home remained limited.

The Brethren's thirty years of relative freedom of activity led to a stunning electoral success, in 1989, in the first free elections in the kingdom since 1956. Members of the Brethren along with other, independent Islamists took thirty-four of the eighty seats in the lower house of the National Assembly. Their campaign slogans had been simple. "Islam is the solution" was a convincing argument to a largely conservative population that had been increasingly disillusioned by the corruption of the previous government. The regime was surprised and concerned by the strength of the Islamists but soon found that they were willing to work within the system. Members of the Brethren were included in the 1990–1991 drafting of the National Charter, a document that supplements the constitution and stresses, among other values, political pluralism. The Islamic Action Front, the political party that emerged from the Brethren, accepted the terms of the National Charter as a precondition for being licensed as a political party in 1992, when the ban on political parties was lifted. As the political system opened up from 1989 to 1993, Islamists increasingly won leadership positions in professional and student organizations as well as on municipal councils.

Foreign and Domestic Clashes

Islamists in the National Assembly made several attempts to change legislation related to alcohol (which is forbidden under Islamic law), mixing of the sexes in schools, and inheritance, but their initiatives avoided opposing programs to which the king was committed, such as the kingdom's agreement with the International Monetary Fund. Not until the king decided that Jordan would participate in the Middle East peace conference in Madrid, Spain, in October 1991, did the Islamists find themselves on a collision course with the government and Husayn himself. The Madrid conference brought Israeli and Arab state representatives together for the first time in a formal setting to discuss ways to achieve an end to the Arab-Israeli conflict. Opposition became more vocal after the Palestine Liberation Organization signed a peace agreement with Israel in September 1993, followed the next summer by Jordan's first peace accord with the Jewish state.

In anticipation of and to undercut this opposition, the prime minister introduced amendments to the electoral law while the National Assembly was out of session in August 1993. The modifications had the desired effect: the number of Islamist deputies elected in November 1993 was half the 1989 figure. In response, many members of the Brethren and other independents joined with leftists and traditional Arab nationalists to protest against normalization of relations with Israel. They subsequently have complained bitterly of harassment and arrests of their members, all during a time when the regime continued to claim a commitment to democracy.

Confrontation over foreign affairs has not led to a battle over domestic policy, however. Although the regime has made several important improvements in women's rights and status, the most critical issues continue to be governed by the personal status law, an area that is too sensitive to attempt serious amendment. And, despite a commitment to educational reform, the Ministry of Education remains a bastion of Brethren influence, apparently a part of a continuing policy of concessions to conservatism on domestic social issues, regardless of the modernizing rhetoric of the leadership.

See also *Islam; Jerusalem; Mecca; Saudi Arabia.*

Laurie A. Brand

BIBLIOGRAPHY

Brand, Laurie. "'In the Beginning Was the State . . . ': The Quest for Civil Society in Jordan." In *Civil Society in the Middle East,* edited by R. Augustus Norton. Leiden: Brill, 1995.

Cohen, Amnon. *Political Parties in the West Bank under the Jordanian Regime, 1949–1967.* Ithaca, N.Y.: Cornell University Press, 1982.

Hourani, Hani, et al. *Islamic Action Front Party.* Amman: Al-Urdun al-Jadid Research Center, 1993. [In English and in Arabic.]

al-Kaylani, Musa Zayd. *Al-Harakah al-Islamiyyah f-il-Urdunn [The Islamic Movement in Jordan].* Amman: Dar al-Bashir, 1990.

Kraemer, Gudrun. "The Integration of the Integrists: a Comparative Study of Egypt, Jordan, and Tunisia." In *Democracy without Democrats: The Renewal of Politics in the Muslim World,* edited by Ghassan Salame. New York: I. B. Taurus, 1994.

Judaism

Judaism is the culture of the Jews and one of the world's oldest religious traditions. The Jewish people and Judaism are theo-political phenomena in both theory and practice. The combination of *theo* and *political* expresses the comprehensive character of Judaism as a way of life and of the Jews as both a people and a faith community. Understanding the synthesis of the theological and the political is vital for understanding Jewish existence and survival.

There are two ways to view Judaism and politics, medieval or modern. One is by looking at the Jewish writing on political thought produced by the thinkers of the time and the other is by examining the political behavior, or what was written at the time about the political behavior, of Jewish communities and their members. When most scholars have considered politics in the study of Judaism, they have studied the thinkers, apparently assuming that the theoretical ideas represented the reality of Jewish political life at the time, especially in the Middle Ages. That is roughly equivalent to assuming that Plato's *Republic* described a real polity in ancient Greece.

Only in the twentieth century have necessary historical and legal data become available to begin to understand medieval Jewish political life and how it was informed by the Judaism of medieval Jews. That information had been available in the responsa literature—the formal questions and answers of rabbinical judges of the period—but it had never been examined systematically for what it could teach about Jewish political life. The responsa represent at least 1,500 years of cases and case law from Jewish communities throughout the world.

There are tens of thousands of such responsa available, and today many thousands are computer accessible. Such discoveries as the Cairo Geniza, an archive of ancient Jewish manuscripts, give detailed documentary evidence of almost every aspect of political life derived from Judaism. In looking at the modern epoch, scholars have studies of Jewish political behavior using all of the methods and tools of contemporary social science disciplines to analyze Jewish political phenomena.

Unity and Autonomy

During the Middle Ages, the period from the fall of the Western Roman Empire in the fifth century through the fifteenth century, the Jewish people had substantial autonomy and self-government wherever they were to be found; they were understood to be a separate nation living in their own communities with their own religion and laws. These were religious laws in the sense that there was no formal separation between religious and civil law any more than there was a formal separation between public and private law. In many places their communities even had criminal jurisdiction over them, and they invariably controlled their self-organization. Judaism therefore was applied most directly to the concerns of the Jews as Jews.

The Jewish Middle Ages began with the Islamization of the Arabs and their seventh- and eighth-century conquest of first the Middle East, two-thirds of the Mediterranean world (the entire south shore across into the Iberian peninsula to the Pyrenees), and the East well into central, south, and southeast Asia, ultimately as far as China and the Philippines. The vast territory conquered by the Muslims meant that more than 95 percent of world Jewry lived within the Islamic caliphate, which had its capital in Baghdad. Only a handful of Jews in the Balkans and Italy, and perhaps a few farther to the north, remained outside the Muslim world.

Politically, this was an auspicious situation for the Jewish people: for the first time since the destruction of the northern kingdom of Israel in 722 B.C., virtually all Jews lived within one political jurisdiction and, with the autonomy granted them by their Islamic rulers, they were able to live under their own laws and rulers in a single, if very extended, polity. This situation prevailed for the next three centuries, allowing Jewish institutions and processes to develop under a common Jewish law.

The Three Domains

In the years following the disastrous revolt led by Simon Bar Kokhba against the Romans in Judea (132–135), the religious and civil system of government by which the Jews would live had developed in Babylonia. Some parts of the system were ancient, and all were based on classical models of Jewish government dating back to the earliest years of the Jewish people—the domains of prophet, king, and priest. They included a political and legal system resting on the Torah, or teachings of Judaism as constitution, as modified and elaborated in the Talmud, the commentaries on the Torah.

Both general rules and specific rules for community organization were sufficiently well developed for application,

resting on a three-fold division of power that took into consideration the religious, legal, and civic dimensions of the Jewish polity. Authority and powers were divided among the *keter* Torah (the domain of scriptural interpretation, literally "crown of Torah"), whose bearers had the task of communicating and interpreting God's teachings to the community; the *keter malkhut* (the domain of civil rule, literally, "kingship"), whose bearers had the task of handling the day-to-day civil governance of the community; and the *keter kehunah* (the domain of priesthood), whose bearers were charged with the responsibility of communicating the people's needs to God. Thus the three-fold division continued to function as it had in biblical times, only with different institutions from the classic biblical prophets, kings, and priests.

After the destruction of the second Temple by the Romans in 70, the *keter kehunah* had undergone a vast transformation that removed it from all but a few symbolic acts of governance and confined its tasks to matters of public worship and family ritual. Many of the former ritual tasks of hereditary priesthood were assigned to *hazzanim* (the term *hazzan* originally meant governors of the synagogue; only later did they become prayer leaders) and other such functionaries.

Interpretation of scripture and laws also had changed over the years, beginning with the restoration of the Jews to Judea in the fifth century B.C. Its tasks were taken from prophets who received divine communication directly and placed in the hands of those learned in Torah texts, beginning with the Anshe Knesset Hagedolah (Men of the Great Assembly), which convened in Jerusalem in the fifth century B.C. as the governing parliament of the Jewish people.

An important Jewish community had lived in Babylonia since the sixth century B.C., and by the Middle Ages, interpretation was vested in the *yeshivot* (bodies charged with legal interpretations of the Torah that also served as advanced academies for Talmudic study) at Sura and Pumbeditha, which had acquired worldwide responsibilities. The Babylonian *yeshivot* received queries on Jewish law from every part of the medieval Jewish world, and their answers—responsa—became part of standard religious practice. Local *yeshivot* retained regional, countrywide, and local responsibilities. Unlike the *yeshivot* known in modern times, these schools were not only academies for Torah study but also assemblies for adjudication and governance by those most learned in Torah. They had ultimate authority for interpreting the Torah and as such performed the functions of adjudication and legislation for the community. Decisions in each case were reached through interpretation of the Torah and the Talmud in light of the specific circumstances of time and place.

Perhaps least changed of all was the *keter malkhut* (ruling class), this despite the fact of Jewish exile and dispersion in the Diaspora. The bearer of authority through that *keter* was the *resh galuta* (exilarch) based in Baghdad, whose family was deemed to be descended from King David, the biblically legitimated king of Israel, from the female line. The exilarch was recognized by the non-Jewish authorities as the legitimate civil ruler because of that lineage.

Halakhah: Ritual and Rule

For legitimate governing to take place, there had to be sufficient coordination between the exilarch and the *yeshivot,* something not always easily attained. Only from the eighth century onward did they reach accommodation, and that only after fierce conflicts between the exilarchs and the *gaonim,* the heads of the *yeshivot* movement. The *yeshivot* also maintained a network of connections with Jews throughout the world through responsa and emissaries.

Those responsa dealt with the full range of life's issues, not merely with ritual matters, as the comprehensive character of Jewish law required. It has been estimated that over the years from the closing of the Talmud in the sixth century until modern times, 80 percent of the responsa that have survived were devoted to civil and public matters, with only 20 percent given over to ritual and what are today defined as religious matters. But as Jews entered modernity in the nineteenth century, the ratio shifted to 80 percent to 20 percent in the other direction. Nothing could more clearly demonstrate the way in which Judaism is a theo-political phenomenon, whereby the life and behavior of the community has more to say about its religious character than theological positions or speculations.

The exilarch also had empirewide authority that he often shared with his *negidim* (commissioners), who represented the *keter malkhut* in particular countries or provinces within the Muslim caliphate. As the regional and provincial Muslim rulers grew stronger within the empire, the power of the exilarch declined in favor of the commissioners in each area. The breakup of the empire affected the power of the *yeshivot* as well, not because the local Jewish population was unwill-

ing to continue in its loyalty to national authorities but because the local, non-Jewish rulers did not want to see "their" Jews subordinate to the caliphate in Babylonia.

Indeed, transmission of many of the ancient religious materials of the Jewish people to the newer areas of Jewish settlement came about because the *yeshivot* saw the necessity for equipping Jewish communities in the provinces with the knowledge and methodology required to enable them to function independently. Thus the *siddur tefillah,* the Jewish prayer book, reached Europe in response to an appeal from the Jewish community in Barcelona, Spain, to the Babylonian *yeshivot* for its precise delineation. The Barcelona community wanted to maintain their prayer services according to tradition, and it was becoming too difficult and dangerous for them to turn to the Babylonian authorities.

From Union to Fragmentation

After 1042 there was no longer even a nominal worldwide Jewish authority. Separate rulers had assumed power in the various Muslim countries, and the empirewide Jewish institutions were closed down. From then until the late nineteenth century, there was not even a pretense of a worldwide Jewish organization that claimed to encompass all Jews. The only institution of the Jewish nation that held Jews together was the system of responsa, the case law correspondence that remained worldwide or close to it, throughout the millennium. Still, the fact that adjudicators of Jewish law and disputes arising under it were always in communication worldwide, and had some higher authority beyond their localities or regions to whom to turn, served to hold the Jewish people together by ensuring that Jewish law would not only remain intact but would also be held in common to a remarkable degree. The law was viewed and accepted as religious law, even when dealing with the most secular matters, and was preserved with the faithfulness with which people conserve a religious tradition, especially one based on sacred texts and the legal system that flows from them.

The one great theoretical work to emerge during this early period is the tenth-century *Book of Beliefs and Opinions* of R. Saadia Gaon. Saadia set down the principles of Jewish piety and polity in the traditional manner, combining the theological and the political. Indeed, by making the point that Jews are Jews by virtue of the Torah as their constitution, his work is not separable into religious and civil sections. In that sense, Saadia laid down the principle of the

Torah-as-constitution that remained at the heart of medieval Jewish thought until Moses Mendelssohn, a Jewish Enlightenment philosopher, found a way both to affirm and to destroy it as part of the modernization of the Jews of Europe in the eighteenth century.

Late Middle Ages

After the mid-eleventh century, political life in medieval Jewry took a new turn. Jewish political organization followed one of two patterns. In West Asia and North Africa, Jewish communities were organized countrywide, with the *nagid* (commissioner) occupying the chief position in the *keter malkhut* and a *yeshiva* or, as in the case of Egypt, *yeshivot* representing both the Babylonian and the Land of Israel traditions, designating the *keter* Torah. These communities tended to be relatively centralized in the manner of the Babylonian. In Europe, however, each local community was separate and self-governing, or in some cases a larger community in a region would have a number of satellite communities linked to it.

In the Iberian peninsula, some countrywide organization continued to exist in those territories under Muslim rule, which tended to disappear as the Christians reconquered the peninsula. The Christian kingdoms periodically attempted to bring their local Jewish communities together to develop some kind of territorywide organization. In the fourteenth-century kingdom of Aragon, for example, the Jewish communities of Aragon, Catalonia, and Valencia attempted to confederate, and in fifteenth-century Castile, the government of Castile brought representatives of the Castillian Jewish communities together at Valladolid for a synod that led to the composition and adoption of the Takhanot (ordinances) of Valladolid. These ordinances became the classic statement of the self-government of the Jewish communities in the Sephardic world (those in the Iberian peninsula) and were used by communities established by those exiled from Spain in 1492 and by their descendants.

The Ashkenazic world (Jewish communities in Germanic lands) also was based on autonomous local communities. From time to time these local communities came together to meet in regional synods or to establish nationwide federations, usually at the behest or encouragement of the country's non-Jewish rulers. Examples of these could be found in Bohemia and Moravia, Lithuania and Poland. The Polish community had the most extensive, comprehensive, and famous. It was known as the *Va'ad Arbah Aretzot* (Council of the Four Lands), which functioned from the mid-sixteenth to the mid-eighteenth century.

A Constitutional Revolution

For these communities to be constituted and become autonomous, Jewish law had to undergo a constitutional revolution of great magnitude from the eleventh century to the Black Death in the middle of the fourteenth century, particularly between the mid-twelfth and the mid-thirteenth centuries.

Functioning within the guidelines of *halakhah* alone, the great constitutional architects of the Jewish people of that time—led by Spanish Jewish scholar R. Shlomo ben Aderet (commonly known as Rashba), German Talmudic scholar R. Ashi (commonly known as Rosh), and Ashi's teacher R. Meir of Rothenberg—fashioned an analog to modern popular sovereignty doctrines that enabled Jews to establish their local communities and endow them with the formal powers of *halakhic* courts, thereby enabling them to enact the requisite ordinances of local self-government within Torah law.

As a consequence of this revolution, there was a revival of the classically Jewish theo-political principle of covenant. Originally a pact between God and humans based on their shared moral commitment to certain common principles and the laws that enforce them, the idea of covenant, so prominent in the Bible, was transformed in the Talmud into an emphasis on the Torah as covenant and covenant law, which led to an eclipse of the covenant idea itself. The necessity to restore the idea of consenting individuals forming partnerships and communities made it necessary for the Jews to go back to first principles and to rediscover, as it were, their covenantal foundations. This flowering of covenantal constitutionalism produced a whole body of consent theory within the *halakhic* tradition. It has been compared to the revolution in political thought of seventeenth-century England, with considerable justification.

Political Thought

Jewish systematic theo-political thought of the eleventh through fifteenth centuries in general reflected elements of this constitutional revolution. Jewish thinkers of the period such as Judah Halevi, Moses Maimonides, Joseph Albo, Nachmanides, Gersonides, R. Nissim of Gerona, Hasdai, Crescas, and Don Isaac Abravanel all have dimensions of covenant built into their political thought.

Halevi and Maimonides both draw their exemplary figures from covenantal tradition. In Halevi's *Kusari,* the *chaver,* a covenantal term that can be roughly translated as "partner," is the one who brings the message of Judaism to the King of the Khazars. For Maimonides it is the *navi* (prophet) who is the highest expression of political leadership, his equivalent of Plato's philosopher-king. Albo, Nachmanides, Gersonides, and Crescas emphasize covenantal relationships in their thought. Abravanel is one of the few Jewish political theorists before modern times who discusses the structure of the ideal polity, not merely ideal political relationships.

In his responsa, R. Nissim of Gerona discusses governmental structures, processes, and relationships from a covenantal perspective. For all of these figures it is well nigh impossible to separate their religious and political thought, so intertwined are the two.

This covenantal model lasted until Jewish communal autonomy ended in the eighteenth century. Especially in their early years, Jewish communities were commonwealths in the sense that they were the property of their citizens who participated fully or substantially in their governance and were designed to serve public purposes under conditions in which there were common norms.

In the high Middle Ages most Jewish communities had fewer than one hundred families. A thousand Jews was considered a substantial community. Thus the heads of all families could participate in the community's general assembly as Jewish law prescribed. The entire community comprised one congregation, and because all were required to remain faithful to religious tradition and practice, all the men met together daily and took part in all decisions, especially after customs developed such as the one that allowed aggrieved parties to stop the public reading of the Torah on Sabbaths, Mondays, and Thursdays, thereby holding up the service until their grievance was attended to. The close connection between Judaism the religion and the politics of Jewish life gave that politics a special religious sanction and sacral character even in its most ordinary dimensions.

As the generations passed, many communities became oligarchies, with the rich and the rabbis holding a severely restricted franchise and power to the exclusion of the rest of the Jewish population. Certain families acquired inordinate power, especially as communities grew larger. Not surprisingly, common medieval class-based divisions were introduced to change the relationship and decision-making patterns in the larger communities.

Judaism in the Modern World

The breakdown of the autonomous Jewish community in the modern epoch was the result of a number of factors. The rise of the modern state required the elimination of the multitude of medieval institutions sharing political power within its territory, including autonomous Jewish communities. As modern secularization made its inroads into the Jewish community and Jews' religious loyalties declined, their needs or desires for Jewish political attachment also waned. Modern statism in its democratic form began to encourage the idea of one citizenship for all within the national territory. In Europe, the modern states at first took away Jewish autonomy without granting Jews national citizenship, leading Jews to see citizenship as extremely important if they were to be emancipated from their otherwise restricted lives. The decoupling of Jewish communal governance and politics from Judaism became a reality in Western Europe in the eighteenth century. In the New World, Jewish communities never had political autonomy.

To survive as Jews in the modern world, Jews came to emphasize their synagogues not as houses of assembly, the meaning of *beit knesset,* the Hebrew name for synagogue, but as places for religious observance. This decoupling could be done in the Old World only through some formal means that recognized the theo-political character of the existing Jewish constitution. A good example of this was the Sanhedrin that Napoleon convened in France in 1806, in which the Jewish notables in territories under French rule had to repudiate the political dimension of Judaism and reformulate Judaism in strictly religious terms so that being Jewish would not be incompatible with being French citizens.

Earlier, Moses Mendelssohn's argument in his major work, *Jerusalem* (1783), had been that the Torah is indeed the constitution of the Jewish people, covering both theological and political matters, but that, for purposes of integration into European society, the political dimension of the Torah is to be deferred until Messianic times. The separation between Judaism the religion and politics seemed to move on inexorably. In the latter part of the eighteenth and early nineteenth centuries, a number of minor Jewish political theorists wrote about forms of government in a Jewish state, but the acknowledged major figures in Jewish thought are those who pressed for even sharper separation, insisting that Jews who wanted to become part of the modern world had to abandon a separate Jewish politics as the price of admission and to recast Judaism in strictly religious terms. Depolitization went so far that even Rabbi Samson Raphael Hirsch, a noted German Orthodox leader, took great pains to eliminate the political dimension from the reinvigorated Orthodoxy he was propounding in the nineteenth century, insisting that German Jews were good Germans in their political loyalties and did not need to be anything else.

Even as the Jews ceased to be considered a separate nation, the continuing realities of the political dimensions of Jewish life were such that the term *coreligionists* was coined to describe the Jewish interconnections that continued to reassert themselves. Only occasionally were dissenting voices heard. Some were philosophically unsophisticated communal leaders in the New World who persisted in speaking of a Jewish nation. Others were biblical commentators of the old school such as Meyer Leibush Malbim, who lived in Romania, where Jews were not emancipated.

The Jews of each Western European state tried to follow the wishes of their governments and to separate themselves at least formally from Jews in other countries, but the pressure of the Jewish problems of emancipation, equal citizenship, and anti-Semitism were not state-bound but international. From the time of the Congress of Vienna (1815), the European conference called to reestablish the territorial divisions of Europe after the defeat of Napoleon, onward, "the Jewish problem" was considered in every nineteenth-century international forum. The accepted view was that the Jews were a religious group but there was at least a tacit recognition that they were more than that—a race, a community, a tribe, or the like. Jewish leaders were forced to recapture a collective identity in different form to speak for the Jewish people in these international forums and also to intervene to protect Jewish interests in the unemancipated east. Violence against Jews in Russia, Syria, North Africa—and even in 1858 in Italy—all overtly had to do with issues of religious ritual but covertly reflected strong anti-Jewish feelings.

At first individual Jews who had distinguished themselves in the politics of their countries of origin and developed informal cooperation together dealt with Jewish issues that went beyond their countries' boundaries. When these issues demanded the attention of more than a handful of notables, they tried to form elite organizations to extend the scope of their work. Those organizations were prevented from uniting across state borders by their respective governments and European power rivalries, but they were able to cooperate informally.

By the end of the nineteenth century these elite organizations began to be displaced by new worldwide, mass-based Jewish organizations reflecting revolutionary ideas of Jewish nationalism, the first two of which were the World Zionist Organization and the Jewish Socialist Workers Bund, both founded in 1897. They completed the formal separation of religious and political expression for modern Jews. The elite organizations could and did function under the cover of religious identification in order to serve their coreligionists, but both the Zionists and the Bund were avowedly secular.

Jewish communities underwent similar separations. Synagogues became strictly houses of prayer, and new organizations secular in character were established to unite communities and speak in their name. Only where state law insisted on defining Jews strictly as a religious group was there a need to organize Jewish communities on formally religious lines, such as the Consistoire in France and the United Synagogue in Britain. In such cases, Jews were allowed to practice Judaism, but Jewish communities were essentially forbidden to organize themselves as political communities.

Reuniting Judaism and Politics

The (at least partial) reunification of Judaism and politics is a twentieth-century phenomenon. Intellectually, it began with the writings of the founders of religious Zionism and was deepened and widened by Jewish philosopher and Zionist leader Martin Buber (1878–1965) and Jewish Reconstructionist founder Mordecai Kaplan (1881–1983). The 1912 founding of Agudat Israel, a world movement of Orthodox Jews, gave it its first institutional expression. Agudat Israel was unabashedly structured on closely linking Judaism and politics to enable followers of traditional Jewish religion to function in the contemporary world. Its political leadership was explicitly subordinated to its Council of Torah Greats.

Agudat Israel did openly what less traditional Jewish communities found that they were doing inadvertently because of the nature of Judaism. In the synagogues themselves, congregational boards assumed the mantle of *keter malkhut,* and congregational rabbis assumed the powers of the *keter kehunah,* modeled after the Christian ministry. In larger communities some combination of community relations organizations and communal welfare organizations took the powers of the *keter malkhut,* congregations became expressions of the *keter kehunah,* and traditional Torah scholars or their non-Orthodox equivalents in rabbinical seminaries assumed the powers of the *keter* Torah.

In the 1920s when the *yishuv* (Jewish community) in

Palestine acquired autonomy under the British mandate, it did so by establishing a Jewish Agency and a national assembly, both secular bodies albeit with religious parties represented in them that effectively spoke in the name of the *keter malkhut*. The chief rabbinate, along with the great *yeshivot* in the country, had assumed the mantle of *keter* Torah, and local religious councils fulfilled the function of the *keter kehuna*. This pattern, with one transformation by which the government of Israel became the supreme civil body, continued after 1948 and the restoration of Jewish statehood. Thus, even in the formally secular state of Israel, a product of the formally secular Zionist enterprise, traditional Jewish practice provided the basis for shaping its political organization, albeit imperfectly because of the lack of consensus about the role of Judaism within either the Zionist movement or the state.

From the beginning of the Zionist movement, religious Zionist theorists attempted to develop a proper religious theoretical framework within which to build the new state. Those who rejected such a religious framework obviously did not find such theories either acceptable or satisfying, and divisions within the religious community meant that no single theory was acceptable even to those within it. The issue remains in the matter of debate, at times serious, at times quiescent, between religious and non-religious Jews, and within the religious camp.

In the meantime, Buber and Kaplan developed religious philosophies in the West that reintegrated Judaism and politics in a modern way. Although their thought had relatively little effect on the Zionist movement or in Israel, it had considerable influence in the diaspora, especially in religious ways. Each presented the idea that for Jews politics had to be grounded in Judaism.

Thus, by the end of the nineteenth century, Judaism and politics had been reunited in Jewish communities around the world. The matter had become a critical issue in Israel, where Judaism and democratic politics were perceived by many non-religious Israelis as being antithetical, something denied by religious Zionists, and in the United States and the Jewish communities influenced by the United States as being in harmony with a liberal humanitarian Judaism informing the moral content of Jewish politics.

Judaism and U.S. Politics

All communities that survived the mass migrations of the Jews, the Nazi Holocaust and World War II, and the exodus from the former Soviet Union in the early 1990s discovered that they somehow had to define their involvement in the politics of the states in which they were now citizens in terms of their Judaism. This process was fully developed in the United States, the first modern nation and the first to provide not only equal citizenship to Jews as individuals but also to define Judaism strictly as a matter of individual choice. Even in the United States there were some issues of Jewish self-interest that demanded political involvement of Jews, such as the fight against anti-Semitism, the battle for fully equal opportunities, and the search for American governmental assistance in the struggle to protect the rights and interests of Jews outside American boundaries.

American Jews also felt the need to develop a politics based on the moral demands of Judaism, in part to justify their pursuit of their own self-interest but which they extended far beyond that. Thus the struggle against anti-Semitism and for equal opportunity was extended to become a Jewish struggle on behalf of all minorities, especially minorities of color. Moreover, the Jews have consistently been liberals in the United States, at least since the American Revolution. They have supported those positions that they saw as just and humanitarian according to their understanding of Judaism, which was frequently adapted from their understanding of what liberal politics determine to be just and humanitarian.

This definition has its difficulties—Jewish support for social welfare measures could be understood as derived directly from the Jewish reading of the Bible. But the strong support the American Jewish community has given to the right of women to abortion involves a serious reinterpretation of Judaism in light of liberalism. In other countries, where Jews have been far smaller minorities and far more limited in their political involvement by local custom, they also have tended to be of the left. But they have not been as active in promoting their ideas as Jews in public life. This is true even in France, the European home of Jewish emancipation from the time of the French Revolution.

Traditionalist Movements in Judaism

The medieval theory of autonomous Jewish communities survives in a variant attracting a small group of fervently Orthodox Jews such as the Hasidim and those Jews who gathered around the modern *yeshiva* world. In this variant the Jews were to retain their separate corporate status insofar as possible and seek to live at peace with their non-Jewish

Members of the Bratslav Hasidic movement gather for prayer in Uman, Ukraine, in October 1997. Hasidic Jews have been critical of what they view as Judaism's increasingly secular character and have called for a return to traditional Jewish beliefs and practices.

neighbors but in their own civilization. Both groups and their ideologies were actually products of modernity, necessitated by the dissolution of the medieval Jewish community.

Hasidism arose in eighteenth-century Europe at approximately the same time that Methodism developed in England and North America. It was a pietistic movement designed to respiritualize Jewish life so that ordinary people could be more involved with Judaism and could find a better place for it in their lives, something that increasingly had been denied them as oligarchy closed in on late medieval Jewish life.

Like many populist movements, as it fostered populism the movement also generated authoritarian forms of leadership in the form of the Hasidic rebbes who, in the words of the spokesman of Chabad Hasidism in the later years of the late Chabad rebbe, Menachem Mendel Schneerson, claimed for the rebbe all three *ketarim,* or domains. The Hasidim of a particular rebbe subordinated themselves to that rebbe not only as their spiritual guide but also as their guide in secular matters as well. Hasidic rebbes of New York, for example, are thus able to deliver large blocs of votes to the candidates of their choice at election time.

The modern *yeshiva* world took form at the end of the eighteenth century in opposition to Hasidism, but over time it has acquired many of the characteristics of Hasidism, including intense loyalty to the rabbinical heads of the *yeshivot.* The proliferation of Hasidic "courts" and *yeshivot* has meant that whatever the loyalties of their individual adherent, even for fervently Orthodox Judaism authority and power have had to be shared along the Agudat Israel model.

See also *Anti-Semitism; Covenant; Enlightenment; Gush Emunim; Herzl, Theodor; Heschel, Abraham Joshua; Holocaust; Islam; Jerusalem; Liberalism; Millennialism; Nationalism; Theocracy; Traditionalism; Zionism.*

Daniel J. Elazar

BIBLIOGRAPHY

Birnbaum, Pierre, and Ira Katznelson, eds. *Paths of Emancipation: Jews, States, and Citizenship.* Princeton: Princeton University Press, 1995.

Elazar, Daniel J. *Community and Polity: The Organizational Dynamics of American Jewry.* Rev. and updated ed. Philadelphia: Jewish Publication Society.

———. *People and Polity: The Organizational Dynamics of World Jewry.* Detroit: Wayne State University Press, 1989.

Elazar, Daniel J., and Stuart A. Cohen. *The Jewish Polity: Jewish Political Organization from Biblical Times to the Present.* Bloomington: Indiana University Press, 1985.

Frankel, Jonathan, and Steven J. Zipperstein, eds. *Assimilation and Community: The Jews in Nineteenth-century Europe.* Cambridge and New York: Cambridge University Press, 1992.

Mendelsohn, Ezra. *On Modern Jewish Politics.* New York: Oxford University Press, 1993.

Mittleman, Alan. *The Politics of Torah: The Jewish Political Tradition and the Founding of Agudat Israel.* Albany: State University of New York Press, 1996.

Polish, David. *Give Us a King: Legal-Religious Sources of Jewish Sovereignty.* Hoboken, N.J.: Ktav, 1989.

Schweid, Eliezer. *Democracy and Halakhah.* Lanham, Md.: University Press of America, 1994.

Just war

See *War*

Justice, Social

Social justice is an approach to ethics in which religious beliefs and practices provide a direct or indirect basis for evaluating societal, institutional, and cultural relations in pursuit of justice as a social ideal. Social justice is generally identified with religious and philosophical views on the nature of human beings, a good society, and responsibility defined in relation to compassion, individual worth, community, interdependence, equality, and fairness. Approaches entail deductive and inductive justifications variously based on ideal and regulative principles, natural and moral law, and relationships and responsiveness. Social justice is associated historically with issues of human rights, the organization and distribution of resources, and evaluations of power.

Formation of Ideas of Social Justice

Contemporary religious notions of social justice emerge from several sources in the nineteenth and early twentieth centuries. The Social Gospel movements of American and British Protestant Christianity advocated the belief that the fundamental goodness of humans makes social-moral progress a historical possibility; as part of this process, they attempted to apply biblical teachings to problems associated with industrialization. Prompted by inequities such as harsh working conditions, the movements claimed that Jesus' teachings are an indictment of the injustices of society and a mandate for institutional redress. This argument for religiously defined social activism on behalf of those most disadvantaged emerged in critical response to the Marxist view that religion legitimates bourgeois power, as well as to the Victorian Christian view that the church should limit its role to the care and salvation of individual souls. African American religious leaders developed regional and national groups at the turn of the century to address the racism often ignored by white reform and radical religious thinkers; some leaders and movements addressed capitalist exploitation and worker organization in conjunction with racism.

In 1891 Pope Leo XIII issued *Rerum Novarum* (on the condition of labor), which revived Catholicism's historical mission to the poor as the heart of its concern for society. In 1920 a committee of U.S. bishops issued as guidance the "Program of Social Reconstruction" in which several U.S. priests addressed a number of labor issues within the larger claim that the peace following World War I must be a just peace.

Religious and secular Jewish movements, particularly in Europe, sought justice to protect Jewish people from ongoing persecution and the threats of European modernization and nationalism. These threats included the failure of modern assimilation policies to extend political equality to Jews and the assault on Jewish religious traditions and communities by claims for nationalist loyalties. Their most concrete strategy entailed different plans for settlements in what was then called Palestine, some of which emphasized the shared Jewish and socialist or nationalist values and some of which emphasized the preservation of Jewish religious traditions.

Muslim reformers of the nineteenth and early twentieth centuries argued that original Islamic teachings complemented a liberal or socialist society. Of particular concern were rights for women and minority groups, economic and educational equity, and an end to colonial rule in Islamic societies.

In the 1980s and 1990s some Buddhists have made the case for a socially responsive Buddhism and Buddhist social ethic that is critical of society and not confined to teachings and practices of individual enlightenment.

Religion and Society

Those espousing religious involvement in questions of justice see the relationship between religion and society as one in which actions and beliefs join, and as one that requires justifying varying degrees and kinds of action given religious prohibitions about the limits of human power. Nowhere has this concern been more visible in the twentieth century than with disagreements over the justifiable use of violence. Christian pacifist and just war doctrines gained renewed attention in debates about the Vietnam War and about nuclear armament during the cold war. Roman Catholic liberation theologians differed over sanctions of revolutionary violence, but others in the Catholic Church, including the pope, argued against violent and nonviolent involvement in Latin American worker and peasant movements.

In Latin America and in the struggle against apartheid and its legacies in South Africa, the question of violence has been expanded by the argument that societal institutions can be so unjust that they are violent. Movements of nonviolent protest in India against colonialism and in the United States against racism have emphasized peaceful noncooperation with injustice and the willingness not to retaliate in the face of violence. The problem of violence against women has extended the historical focus of social justice from the public into the private sphere, and arguments for the legalization of abortion have emphasized the social justice of the private right to choice.

Ideas about social justice develop continuously as religious bodies shape their positions and activities around particular questions, which have come to include class, race, gender, the environment, sexual orientations, and mental and physical disabilities. Increased understanding of prejudice makes evident the complex and not necessarily symmetrical relations between institutional and individual attitudes and practices, belying simple divisions and connections between individual and societal justice. In the 1990s it is more accurate to consider that, even when consensus prevails, there are a variety of ideas of social justice bearing family resemblance rather than a single conception of justice within any one religious tradition. And differences may be so distinct in conception or application that resemblance breaks down within traditions as groups disagree markedly in their ideals of social justice. Nonetheless, religious notions of social justice share the capacity to sustain activity and hope in long-term struggles and address new social questions flexibly.

Religious Basis for Social Justice

The religious basis for notions of social justice varies with and within the tradition and the specific injustice being addressed. Several patterns prevail, all of which indicate that religious understandings of social justice are larger in application and ultimate significance than are strictly political understandings of justice. One major pattern identifies the religious mandate for social justice with prophetic judgment against injustice; this understanding undergirds the Jewish tradition that social justice and its moral codes are radically critical of societal convention. Christians have often borrowed from Jewish prophetic texts when making justice claims, as did American civil rights leader Martin Luther King Jr. Prophetic criticism has been particularly important when traditional legal and political mechanisms were ineffective.

A second approach associates the original religious tradition with justice, in contrast to the later corrupted, unjust tradition. For example, Muslim women argue that Muhammad's teachings place women and men on the same religious plane, in contrast to the lesser respect for women found in holdover pre-Islamic practices and post-Qur'anic corruptions. A third pattern identifies social justice with what is interpreted to be the essential claim of the tradition, evident in Gandhi's argument that Krishna's love for all beings requires abolition of the caste system in India and Christian arguments that justice is a consequence of love of God and neighbor. A fourth trend borrows across traditions to help create new religious expressions in the belief that religious traditions as they stand are themselves too unjust to be reformed. Examples include ecological and feminist movements that have drawn from native peoples, Buddhism, Hinduism, and matristic traditions to articulate the interrelations of all beings, the sacred qualities of nature, and nonhierarchical notions of divinity.

Over the nineteenth and twentieth centuries, religions in industrial societies have increasingly emphasized the religious significance of this world instead of a dualism separating the political world of human affairs from the religious world of divine affairs. From an older perspective, this shift, with its focus on earthly justice, would have been identified as the secularization of religion. Both religious and political elements remain identifiable in this shift, however, and it seems appropriate to consider instead that religions develop in new ways as they engage in public debate and involvement.

Ethical Considerations

Although some traditions draw their notions of justice exclusively from canonical texts, others develop further analyses and theories of social justice. In these theories, the idea most consistently used in tandem with justice is that of love or compassion. Arguments about the bearing of different notions of love on justice have been central to Christianity. In a conflict earlier in the twentieth century, Christian realist Reinhold Niebuhr (1892–1971) defines justice in tension with love in his argument against the Social Gospel view of justice as a direct outgrowth of love. Niebuhr's position that the exercise of power and self-interest are entailed in justice emphasizes the political aspects of justice in contrast to disinterested love. Although the Social Gospel view stresses critical socio-historical analysis, it pays less attention to the power relations of justice and instead emphasizes the complementary connections of love and justice necessary to developing the ideal community.

In the late twentieth century, all dichotomies of justice and love have been criticized on the grounds that they disguise power relations that politics and religion share—for example their oppression of women and denigration of women's bodies. African American womanists and North

American Christian feminists have developed arguments from their different communities of experience in which justice is a form of love and in which both love and justice address care for the body, identity, and community.

Some Buddhists have reexamined the ideal of compassion for all beings or extended the practice of right relations as a basis for justice in contrast to the individual, internal, non-political emphases of the monastic ideal. By linking issues of justice such as human rights and ecology, Buddhists have challenged individualistic and anthropocentric models of social justice. They understand all living beings to exist in relations with each other, not as autonomous beings who come together in aggregates.

At the end of the twentieth century, notions of love and justice from Buddhists, womanists (who give primacy to African American women's experience), feminists, and ecologists provide new orientations. Justice and love expand in conjunction with third concepts such as reciprocity, caring, and mutual support that are often tied to historical experience and that indicate the relational orientation of ethical judgments.

We have yet to see how differing notions of interdependence will develop as their criticisms or reconstructions of justice become more refined. To what extent can notions of mutual support or care absorb the category of social justice? To what extent can justice be redefined beyond political traditions of individual rights? African theorists, for example, criticize Western individualized notions of human rights for their neglect of human rights within communities or tribes. Discussion of such differences has broadened the sociocultural experience considered relevant to ideas of social justice and expanded the lexicon of social justice theory.

Redefining Injustice

The new orientation has also allowed for broader considerations of the relation of justice to suffering by emphasizing differing kinds of vulnerability and oppression as a basis from which to understand justice in contrast to strictly political categories of equality and right. In this context, as much attention has been given to notions of injustice as to notions of justice in analyses of oppressions, for example, economic class and poverty. The question persists within and across religious traditions of how to characterize and reconcile affronts and limits to justice, variously explained by sinfulness, historical conditions, or ignorance and illusion. No single idea of good or evil prevails as an account of the kinds

and scopes of injustice that many have experienced in events of the past two centuries—the enslavement of Africans in the Americas, the Holocaust of the Jews, or the oppression of the Maya in Guatemala.

In developing their ethical claims, theorists of social justice have drawn on the social sciences, especially in critical analyses of economic life, as with the earlier Social Gospel and more recently with the U.S. Catholic bishops' pastoral letter of 1984. In this letter the bishops document the extremes of affluence and poverty in the United States and argue for just participation in economic life within a larger code of moral solidarity in keeping with democratic ideals. Theologians and philosophers are concerned with the conditions under which people communicate, formulate, and criticize notions of justice. This discussion includes debates between formal, universal, and objective models of justice and models rooted within the narratives and practices of particular communities. Challenges to both kinds of models come from those arguing for conceptions of justice that do not assume an essential self or a unitary system of beliefs but instead assume that the postmodern conceptions of the knowing subject and of democracy entail recognition of differing and shifting standpoints and identities, with the consequence that justice is understood to be a fluid notion open to continuous individual-societal renegotiation. Renegotiation is, however, generally guided by reference to historical practices of freedom, held to be evident in the malleability of all forms of communication, including ritual and myth.

Diversity and Social Justice

The debate about the formulations of social justice has been closely tied to debate about the limitations of liberal society, some arguing for a strengthening of liberal commitments to just institutions, and others arguing that liberalism is unable to sustain such moral commitment because it values individualism to the exclusion of societal, communal, and familial ties.

Earlier assumptions that justice is governed by impartiality and disinterestedness have also been criticized in this debate, with some arguing that such claims are completely untenable given the social-historical quality of human beings, and others arguing that objectivity may exist but only in relative ways, dependent on context and the position or positions people and groups hold within that context. According to these ways of thinking, objectivity may be impossible or there may be many, culturally specific objective positions.

Questions of diversity and plurality also bear on the relation between religious claims and ideas about social justice. The question may be posed in terms of what kind of agreement is required for the understanding and pursuit of justice: agreement in religious or theological belief as a precondition of moral agreement; agreement in ethical ideals about justice without requiring religious or theological consensus, in which case nonreligious views also could be included; or agreement in activism and strategy without requiring assent in religion or ethics. These questions may be negotiated in actual decision making about a particular issue, but they are also negotiated in the theory and institutional structure through which religious thinkers and organizations consider questions of social justice. The choice of position bears on the kinds of decisions religious people make not only about what is just but also about what justice is.

Political and theoretical articulations of social justice have been a primary way in which religions have developed their native, public reasoning and contributed to symbolic elaborations of public life. Current religious discussions of social justice encompass issues such as health care and the rights of children, migration and immigration, anti-Semitism and racism. Criticisms of the inequalities of capitalism have long been part of many religious notions of social justice, some from liberal reform and others from social democratic or socialist perspectives. How these critics will respond to new economic formations remains to be seen. There is renewed interest in justice as part of a critical theory of democracy, for example, among liberation theologians who reject a simple connection between belief and action as they shift from a focus on crisis to one on democracy building.

Some theorists are interested in establishing a minimal, unified universal definition, but here, too, there is disagreement and divergence in approaches. Questions of human rights, for example, are being developed along at least three lines: one emphasizing notions of inherent individual rights and duties; another stressing society as the basic unit of obligation for human needs and well-being; and a third underscoring the relations of societies, individuals, and the rest of nature.

However notions of social justice evolve in differing cultural and political contexts, social justice continues to work on behalf of those people and other life forms most endangered by contemporary society and to be motivated by religious claims of love and peace. Whether or not religious groups will agree on ideas of social justice within their own traditions, they increasingly find themselves engaged with and influenced by movements and traditions other than their own.

See also *Buddhism, Theravada; Buddhism, Tibetan; Capitalism; Civil rights movement; Environmentalism; Feminism; Gender; Holocaust; Human rights; Humanitarianism; Individualism; Islam; King, Martin Luther, Jr.; Liberation theology; Niebuhr, Reinhold; Pacifism; Prejudice; Social Gospel; Utopianism; Violence; War.*

Ruth L. Smith

BIBLIOGRAPHY

An-Na'im, Abdullahi Admed. *Toward an Islamic Reformation: Civil Liberties, Human Rights, and International Law.* Syracuse: Syracuse University Press, 1990.

Craig, Robert H. *Religion and Radical Politics: An Alternative Christian Tradition in the United States.* Philadelphia: Temple University Press, 1992.

Eppsteiner, Fred, ed. *The Path of Compassion: Writings on Socially Engaged Buddhism.* Berkeley: Parallax Press and the Buddhist Peace Fellowship, 1988.

Garcia, Ismael. *Justice in Latin American Theology of Liberation.* Atlanta: John Knox Press, 1987.

Gottlieb, Roger, ed. *The Sacred Earth: Religion, Nature, Environment.* New York: Routledge, 1995.

Nolan, Hugh J., ed. *Pastoral Letters of the United States Catholic Bishops.* 4 volumes. Washington, D.C.: U.S. Catholic Conference, 1984.

O'Brien, David J., and Thomas A. Shannon, eds. *Catholic Social Thought: The Documentary Heritage.* Maryknoll: Orbis, 1997.

Index